Practical Financial Statement Analysis

PRACTICAL FINANCIAL STATEMENT ANALYSIS

ROY A. FOULKE

*Vice-president, Dun and Bradstreet, Inc.; Author of
Commercial Paper Market, Behind the Scenes of Business
Sinews of American Commerce, Practical Bank Credit (coauthor)*

FIFTH EDITION

McGRAW-HILL BOOK COMPANY, INC.

New York   Toronto   London

1961

PRACTICAL FINANCIAL STATEMENT ANALYSIS

II

THE MAPLE PRESS COMPANY, YORK, PA.

Preface

A volume which is concerned with any segment of the operation and analysis of American business contains both in the text and in the footnotes references to many current pertinent facts and figures of our economy. All such references, numerous as they are, have been brought up to date in this fifth revised edition. The most recent available ratio figures used in Chapters VI to XV, XIX, XXI, and XXII, and in the Appendix have been incorporated. These tables, with the exception of Schedule 66 in Chapter XIX, include the yearly median and the 5-year average ratios based on yearly compilations from many thousands of actual financial statements of industrial and commercial business concerns located in all sections of the United States for the years of 1955 to 1959.

All references to Regulation S-X of the Securities and Exchange Commission, which is concerned with the form and content of financial statements, have been brought up to date from the latest edition of this basic material. All references to *Accounting Trends and Techniques in Published Corporate Annual Reports*, prepared annually by the American Institute of Certified Public Accountants, also have been brought up to date from the latest edition of this extensive research work.

Applicable material in the Accounting Research Bulletins of the American Institute of Certified Public Accountants issued since the fourth edition of this volume was published in 1957 has been included in proper chapters. Accounting terminology and phraseology, which is in constant evolution, has been brought up to the minute. The guide to the classification of balance sheet items in Chapter IV has been materially expanded.

The entire volume has been studied and examined word by word, chapter by chapter, and every change, no matter how incidental, of wording, new facts, or up-to-date material, has been carefully made in text and footnotes so that the volume will be of the widest possible practical help to business executives, industrial engineers, bank credit executives, bank examiners, investment analysts, and mercantile credit managers in their everyday work and to the steadily increasing number of students of the analysis of American business enterprises at universities, colleges, and business schools.

Roy A. Foulke

Contents

PART I

BACKGROUND OF ANALYSIS

PART II

ANALYSIS OF SMALL BUSINESS ENTERPRISES

PART III

INTERNAL ANALYSES OF BALANCE SHEETS

PART VII

SYNTHESIS

Schedules

Chapter XIV

Chapter XV

Chapter XVI

Chapter XVII

Chapter XIX

Chapter XX

Chapter XXI

Chapter XXII

Forms

Chapter I

Chapter IV

CHAPTER VI

CHAPTER XVIII

CHAPTER XX

PART I

Background of Analysis

PART I *of this volume, consisting of four chapters, gives the historical and the credit background leading up to the analyses of financial statements. In colonial days, financial statements were rarely made available to outsiders for any purpose. The practical need of balance sheets for the use of creditors arose with the change in the basis for granting bank loans from endorsed notes receivable and accommodation paper to single-name paper, and with the trend from the proprietorship and partnership forms of business organization to the corporate form. Then followed the rise of public accountancy standards, of accounting associations, and the creation of the Securities and Exchange Commission. The analyses of financial statements by different individuals or groups, if thorough, are fundamentally the same, but different interpretations develop from the same analyses, depending upon a particular interest in a situation. A mercantile creditor, a commercial banker, a stockholder, or a member of the management staff will probably interpret identical information somewhat differently. In fact, the interpretation of any one of these interested sources may vary according to the degree of his interest. Moreover, one's interpretation of the bare figures may depend upon his knowledge of supplementary information such as antecedent records of the principals in the business, investigational facts covering the details of bank and trade relations, knowledge as to whether the figures are individual, consolidated, or partly consolidated, and information regarding particular items in the financial statement.*

CHAPTER I

Importance of Arabic Figures in the Business World

For the successful operation of commercial and industrial business enterprises, the fundamental, clear, definite understanding of three sets of figures is essential. This does not mean that a business executive, a commercial or an investment banker, an investor, a speculator, a business counselor, a mercantile credit man, or a financial analyst must know how to prepare these three financial statements; trained accountants are available in every city in the United States for that purpose. But the unchallenged ability to interpret these three sets of figures intelligently and accurately is essential to an understanding of the operations of business enterprises in a highly competitive profit and "loss" economy. These three financial statements are the *balance sheet,* the *income statement,* and the *reconciliation of surplus.*

When gross profits and net profits are decreasing, or when black figures have turned into red figures without professional legerdemain, the active management of the typical business enterprise generally follows two policies simultaneously; sales are pushed just as hard as the aggressiveness, the energy, and the ingenuity of the organization will permit; and the amount and the percentage of each expense item in the income statement are compared with the amount and the percentage of the corresponding item for the previous fiscal period to ascertain where expenses may be reduced materially. The emphasis is primarily on increased sales and on decreased expense. It is a natural and logical emphasis.

Over a period of years, the author has found that the typical business executive knows his income statement forward and backward. He can always find some place where expenses may be cut, perhaps the advertising budget, perhaps salesmen's expenses, salaries, wages, telephone, or postage. Probably not more than one business executive out of ten gives the slightest particle of intelligent thought or analysis to the balance sheet of his business. If he recognized the implications in the relationships between items in the balance sheet as clearly as he sees the implications of the relative size of individual items in comparative income statements, he would realize the effect that operating policies which anticipate profits and losses have upon the future financial condition. With this understanding, he would be more careful in making policy decisions which so often result in anxiety, sleepless nights, and the necessity for the subsequent study of the income and expense figures.

Here are examples. If receivables are heavy and include a large number of past-due or questionable accounts, a charge-off for bad debts that is greater than usual will make inroads upon subsequent profits; if the inventory is top-heavy and prices should happen to fall, nothing can stop a write-down, generally to that well-known accounting convention of "cost or market, whichever is lower," which will reduce or possibly wipe out net profits; if fixed assets are excessive, the annual depreciation charges will represent an overbalance charge to expense; if a large funded debt exists, the interest will eat into net profits. These conditions become evident from an analysis of the balance sheet. Skilled managements realize the intimate effects of these unbalanced conditions upon a future income statement, and therefore determine and follow financial policies that prevent such unsound conditions from arising in the first place. To do so, however, the individual must know what represents sound and unsound relationships in a balance sheet.

Therefore, the fundamental importance of understanding the delicate shades in meaning of balance sheet proportions must be emphasized. If a balance sheet is out of line in any important respect, intelligent operation and consistent, sound financial policy are essential to bring affairs into healthy condition over the years. No balance sheet will recover its health by itself; the management staff must guide the business consciously. Too many business enterprises are constantly adrift, blown by the variable winds of the season, and the conditions of their balance sheets are the unfortunate results of extraneous influences instead of conscious managerial direction. *Every managerial policy, or absence of managerial policy, is reflected somewhere in the figures—in the balance sheet, in the income statement, or in the reconciliation of surplus.* The extension of credit to customers in excess of their reasonable needs will be shown in excessive receivables and a heavy collection period; the purchase of merchandise in excess of reasonable requirements, because an executive officer "is sure" that prices are going up, will be shown in a larger inventory and a slower turnover; and expansion in plant facilities, home offices, or retail stores will be reflected in a larger proportionate investment in fixed assets. The payment for an insurance policy will appear in the expense account, the return of merchandise will be evident in the income statement, and the payment of dividends in the surplus account.

EARLY SCARCITY OF FINANCIAL STATEMENTS

The extension of mercantile credit to commercial and industrial business enterprises, the lending operations of commercial banking institu-

~ competitive

tions, the underwriting activities of investment bankers, and the investment policies of endowed institutions and of individuals did not always depend upon this understanding and ability to analyze financial statements which are now so essential in our existing economy. The current importance of finanical statements has its roots in the transition period when the proprietorship and partnership forms of organization began to be succeeded by the corporation, a process that provided greater opportunities for investment at a "profit" or a "loss." This expansion in the significance of the Arabic figure began to take place in the fourth quarter of the last century; it developed more rapidly when the accounting profession assumed a place of key importance in the American business world, around the turn of the twentieth century.

During the entire period of our colonial history and the early years of our national life up to the economic, social, and political crisis of the Civil War, two practices were customarily followed to place credit information in the hands of actual or potential mercantile creditors. By one practice, the buyer would forward with his order for merchandise letters of reference and recommendation that he had obtained from friends, from his local minister, from a neighboring lawyer, or from locally established fellow merchants. By the other practice, the importer-wholesaler or the wholesaler-distributor, as the case might be, would write to customers or to friends located in the neighborhood of the potential buyer, requesting information and personal opinions regarding the honesty and the local reputation of the applicant for credit. Both techniques were widely used. They were used in domestic trade by wholesale distributors of merchandise in the important trading centers along the Atlantic seacoast—New York, Boston, Philadelphia, Baltimore, and Charleston; inland at the great distributing center of Cincinnati; and in foreign commerce by English factors, exporters, and merchant-bankers, who carried on extensive business relationships with American importers over all these years.[1]

Credit References and Recommendations

The practice of offering credit references and recommendations to potential creditors served its purpose in a world of domestic and foreign commerce at a time when commercial and industrial activity was carried on almost entirely by proprietorships and partnerships. Over these many decades capital accumulation was rather modest, transportation was relatively slow, the market was widely scattered, and mercantile credits were for long periods ranging from 8 months to several years in the

[1] Typical examples of both practices will be found in *The Sinews of American Commerce* by Roy A. Foulke (Dun & Bradstreet, Inc., New York, 1941). For credit information for domestic colonial merchants, see pp. 66–68; for foreign merchants during the colonial period, pp. 74–75, 358–359; and for domestic and foreign merchants during the early days of our national life, pp. 105–107.

colonial era, and from 6 to 12 months in our early national life. Under the proprietorship and partnership forms of organization, the outside means of the owner or owners of a business enterprise, which often were known by general reputation to be substantial, were at the risk of creditors.

Rarely did the creditor obtain any exact information regarding the financial responsibility of the potential buyer from references, from letters of recommendation, or by correspondence with customers or friends located in the vicinity of the buyer. He obtained more often general information and neighborly opinions regarding the reliability, the honesty, the trustworthiness, and the local reputation of an individual than exact financial information such as balance sheets and income statements, which creditors expect and are so accustomed to obtain today.

In the early years of the nineteenth century, letters of reference and of recommendation that potential country debtors presented to wholesale merchants in the Eastern cities occasionally contained misleading favorable information regarding the country trader's locally known character. This subterfuge was used as a means of obtaining merchandise on credit, after which the debtor would silently, but none the less completely, vanish from the scene of action. Here was a basic reason for the need and the immediate success of the early specialized credit organizations such as The Mercantile Agency, organized in 1841 in New York City, and The Bradstreet Company, organized in 1849 in Cincinnati.[2] Both of these organizations proceeded to make independent credit investigations that gradually superseded the earlier general reliance on letters of reference and recommendation.

Early Bank Credit without Financial Statements

The first commercial banking institution to be organized in America was the Bank of North America, Philadelphia, in 1781; the second was the Bank of New York, New York City, in 1784; and the third was the Massachusetts Bank, Boston, which also obtained its charter in 1784. The early procedure of these banks in granting loans took little or no consideration of balance sheets or income statements. Potential borrowers were individuals or partnership business enterprises, and the outside means of the individual, or of the owners of partnerships, supported the bank borrowings along with such collateral as might be requested by the banker and furnished by the borrower.

The place of the modern corporation in everyday business life was not to be evolved for many decades. During the entire colonial period only

---

[2] On Mar. 1, 1933, The Mercantile Agency, then known as R. G. Dun & Co., acquired the busines of The Bradstreet Company. Since that time The Mercantile Agency has operated under the corporate style of Dun & Bradstreet, Inc.

7 American business charters for corporations had been granted; only 11 were issued in the United States between 1781 and 1785, of which 5 were banks; 22 were issued between 1786 and 1790, and 114 between 1791 and 1795.[3] Of the members of the New York City Chamber of Commerce in 1775, 61 carried on their businesses in association with others (that is, partnerships and associations), and 43 were independent (that is, proprietorships).[4] Not one was associated with that rarity, a corporation, which was to make so great a change in business operations in the future.

A loan might be granted by the Massachusetts Bank "upon a single name if secured by deposited collateral, either in the form of merchandise or securities; or it might be made upon personal credits of two persons of 'ample property.' If the former, the loan might run for sixty days; if the latter, only for thirty days."[5] Loans were granted similarly by the Bank of North America and the Bank of New York. In these original practices loans were based, not on financial statements, but on an individual's reputation for trustworthiness and a general—often a very general—idea of his outside affluence.

Accommodation and Trade Paper. Seth B. Hunt was employed as a clerk by Arthur Tappan & Co., one of the larger wholesale and retail dealers in dry goods in New York City, for slightly over 5 years, from June, 1830, to December, 1835. Late in 1835, when Hunt had failed to come to mutually satisfactory arrangements with Arthur Tappan regarding his 1836 salary, he decided to start his own business.

In later years, writing of certain episodes in this early part of his business career, Hunt went on to narrate quaintly: "What was my surprise, one day, soon after my leaving him [Arthur Tappan], when he stood at my desk, looking earnestly at me, and said, 'I thought you might need a bank endorser, and I came to say that we would go on your paper for twenty-five thousand dollars.' Before I recovered from my surprise or had time to thank him, he was half way out of the store. The custom then was for merchants to exchange papers to use in banks."[6] This method of borrowing, on what subsequently came to be known as *accommodation paper*, was one of the general practices for obtaining credit from banking institutions over a period of many decades beginning early in the nineteenth century.

---

[3] DAVIS, JOSEPH STANCLIFFE, *Essays in the Earlier History of American Corporations*, Vol. II, p. 26 (Harvard University Press, Cambridge, Mass., 1917).

[4] HARRINGTON, VIRGINIA D., *The New York Merchant on the Eve of the Revolution*, p. 50 (Columbia University Press, New York, 1935).

[5] *1784–1934, The First National Bank of Boston*, p. 25 (privately printed, Boston, 1934); this is a brief history of its 150 years of continuous existence with emphasis on the early days of its first forebear, the Massachusetts Bank, organized in 1784.

[6] TAPPAN, LEWIS, *Life of Arthur Tappan*, p. 287 (Hurd & Houghton, New York, 1870).

In addition to extending credit on accommodation paper, banking institutions also granted credit against a variety of securities, such as Federal and state bonds, unimproved government land immediately prior to the panic of 1837, merchandise, and on endorsed notes receivable and trade acceptances covering actual commercial transactions, which were known as *trade paper*. Audited financial statements were unknown at this stage of our economic life, and statements signed by an owner or a partner in a concern were virtually unknown. Credit was widely and generally extended during these years on the assumed financial strength of the maker and the endorser of notes and trade acceptances, which too often was as mythical as Aesop's fables. In the country districts, where money was invested largely in fixed property, farm land, houses, farming equipment, improvements, and cattle, bank credit was extended more extensively on endorsed accommodation paper than in the cities, which were providing the headquarters for growing industrial and commercial establishments. In the cities, notes receivable and trade acceptances covering actual commercial transactions were often available as a basis for bank credit.

Several decades later, James B. Forgan, while chairman of the board of directors of the First National Bank of Chicago, succinctly described how one banker made loans on accommodation paper. "In a town where I was learning the business a generation ago," he wrote, "it was told of a bank president that during a long banking career he had never but once been known to refuse positively any loan applied for. His sole requirement was a satisfactory endorser and if the borrower offering his note for discount did not comply with that condition, his uniform answer was, 'My friend, you will have to find another endorser.' The exception was in the case of an applicant for a loan who presented his note ten or twelve times, having each time complied with the request that he get another endorser until the back of the note was well-nigh covered with endorsements. Finally he secured an endorser whose name induced the president to depart from his usual formula and to say, 'My good man, you had better start another note, the last name you have got on this one would damn anything.'"

Subsequently, Forgan described the typically involved financial conditions which were created in another town, where he had obtained additional banking experience, as a result of the extensive use of accommodation endorsements. "There were three banks in the town," he explained, "and practically all their loans were made on notes having two endorsers. A great depression occurred in the principal industry of the locality and a very considerable liquidation of bank credits became necessary. The banks soon found, however, that the money they had thus loaned had been largely invested in fixed property and that their notes were of anything but a liquid character. The banks in many cases refused to renew the notes and they lay past due. They began to bring pressure on the makers and endorsers alike but soon awoke to the fact that all their borrowing customers were so involved as endorsers for each other that they resembled a row of bricks standing on end so that if one were knocked down it would fall on another until all were laid low."[7]

Figures in Early Credit Reports

The practice of extending mercantile credit during the early days of our national life on the reputation of individuals among their neighbors and business associates for honesty, reliability, and business acumen, and on a very general idea regarding the wealth of an individual or a firm, is exemplified by the extensive reports which Thomas Wren Ward rendered to Baring Brothers & Company, the great English firm of merchant bankers from 1829 to 1853, and by the credit reports of two of the early credit reporters for American business, Sheldon P. Church and Washington Hite. The confidential credit reports which Thomas Wren Ward[8] rendered to Baring Brothers & Company contained here and there, among other pertinent information, a definite assertion—mostly estimated—of the financial means, the worth, of individuals and firms. Israel Trask of Gloucester, for example, "is represented to be a careful, smug, discreet, punctilious man with $40,000 property or more. . . . " Charles A. Harper Co., Philadelphia, is "worth 60,000 to 80,000 dollars. . . . " William Goddard, shipowner, of Boston, "Safe and handsome property. Say $60,000 upwards. . . . " Henry Porter of Medford is " . . . economical and prudent—worth $30,000."[9] No balance sheets were ever obtained.

The credit reports of Sheldon P. Church contained more gossip than those of Thomas W. Ward and probably somewhat fewer estimates of worth. Church represented quite a group of New York merchandise distributors, not just a single client, and to serve his clients proceeded to print many of his reports. Occasionally he wrote that an individual or a

---

[7] FORGAN, JAMES B., "Evolution in Banking Thought during the Past Generation," *Bulletin of the National Association of Credit Men,* Vol. XIX, No. 10, pp. 935–936, October, 1917.

[8] HIDY, RALPH W., "The Organization and Functions of Anglo-American Merchant Bankers, 1815–1860," *The Tasks of Economic History,* pp. 53–66, December, 1941, a supplemental issue of the *Journal of Economic History.* See also *House of Baring in American Trade and Finance; English Merchant Banker at Work, 1736–1861* by Ralph W. Hidy (Harvard University Press, Cambridge, Mass., 1949), and Foulke, *op. cit.,* pp. 329–332, 360–366.

[9] These reports are from pen-and-ink correspondence between Thomas Wren Ward and Baring Brothers & Company on file in the Office of the Public Archives of Canada, Ottawa, Canada. The correspondence containing these particular reports bears dates during the years 1833 to 1835.

firm had means, such as William Stettinius of Petersburg, Va., " . . . is said to have $8,000 or $10,000 capital. . . . "; J. H. Stanwood of Woodville, Miss., " . . . is worth say $20,000. . . . "; A. A. Wootten of Griffen, Ga., " . . . is thought to be worth $3,000. . . . "; and John I. Stockard of Brockville, Miss., " . . . is worth $6,000 or $7,000. . . . "[10] In these reports likewise, no balance sheets were ever quoted. The practice simply did not exist of obtaining comprehensive financial information in our present-day meaning of the term.

Washington Hite's reports were more condensed and less often had similar round number estimates of means. No balance sheets were quoted. Round figures or general estimates served the purpose of commerce in a day when outside means were at the risk of creditors.[11]

With the development of more systematized credit reporting by the organization in 1841, and the subsequent development of The Mercantile Agency, came the practice on the part of businessmen of making available to actual and potential creditors additional financial information, but not detailed financial statements. The amounts represented by specific asset items, such as cash, receivables, "stock" (that is, merchandise), and the extent of liabilities were quoted rather frequently in credit reports by the 1850's. Because of the long terms of sale, light liabilities were the exception and not the rule. Credit continued to be extended largely on the reputation for probity and general financial responsibility. No attempt seems to have been made to measure the amount of liabilities against the investment in a business.

Although balance sheets were not made available directly or indirectly to actual or potential creditors over these years, that policy does not mean that balance sheets were not drawn up. The record books of colonial merchants, and of those who operated in the first half of the nineteenth century, in many cases do contain balance sheets. These financial statements were prepared by the owners of business enterprises for their own information and were considered absolutely confidential. They were also prepared whenever a partnership dissolved; it was quite customary to divide among the partners not only the assets but also the liabilities.

The credit agencies were well up in the van of the practical developments in the business world. In the 1870's The Mercantile Agency prepared and distributed its first blank soliciting a statement of assets and liabilities to be used in credit reports. This financial statement form was a very simple but practical one, containing five items in the assets and five in the liabilities. It seems to have been made up primarily for partnerships as the blank requested the *Full Names of Partners*. The explanation that

<hr/>

[10] These reports are contained in a volume giving credit information on merchants in the West, the South, and the Southwest, 1844–1847.

[11] HITE, WASHINGTON, *Credit Reference Book* (Bardstown, Ky., 1846).

accompanied this initial request for a balance sheet clearly epitomized the evolution that had been going on in business circles:

In responding to the inquiries made by our numerous subscribers as to the responsibility of parties with whom they have business transactions, we experience frequent perplexity from an inability to give *definite* information as to pecuniary

---

Statement of ———————— *of* ————————

County of ————————— *State* —————————

on the —————————— *day of* ——————————— *187*——

ASSETS:

Merchandise on hand (at actual present value)..............................$

Amount Outstanding...

Real Estate, consisting of...

Personal Property, consisting of...

Cash on hand and in Bank..

                                                   $

LIABILITIES:

Owing for Merchandise..$

Owing Creditors at Home, including Depositors, Bank Indebtedness, Borrowed Money, &c..............................

Owing on Real Estate...

Owing for any other cause, or to any other person whatsoever.

      Net worth...$

Insured on Stock, $...........................

Full Names of Partners.

FORM 1. Earliest known financial statement blank used by The Mercantile Agency (now Dun & Bradstreet, Inc.) in the 1870's.

resources and indebtedness. It is true, we can give, and do give, the *impressions* prevailing upon these points, but the want of something beyond this very generally necessitates a request for statements from the parties themselves. In fact, so nearly universal has this practice become, that many dispensers of credit regard a refusal to comply with it as an unfavorable indication, except in the cases of houses of undoubted wealth. We are well aware that it is a delicate matter to ask such an exposé of private affairs, except as a safeguard in business transactions; but our disinterested position between buyer and seller, and the knowledge that we have no purpose in asking such statements, except to enable us to answer the inquiries that are necessarily presented to us in the course of our business understandingly and intelligently, and also the fact that our responses are confined to those who have a legitimate and justifiable object in making such inquiries, will remove any objection arising from this view of the matter. The object of THE MERCANTILE AGENCY is not only to enable its patrons to avoid the hazardous and unsafe, but to strengthen their confidence where confidence is deserved—in other words, to *promote* as well as to *protect* trade. A statement made by a person of respectability and probity carries with it much weight, and we are induced by these considerations to ask, from all who are disposed to give them, statements of their liabilities and assets, as an important aid to us in our business, and that these statements may be made of real use to us, we suggest the annexed form as one containing the essential features required.

EVOLUTION OF UNSECURED BANK LOANS

The typical nineteenth-century practice of commercial banking institutions of extending credit primarily against two-name accommodation and trade paper, invariably without financial statements, continued up to the decade beginning with 1870. During this decade, as a matter of sound banking and business policy, loans were first made on single-name paper based upon the analysis of current balance sheets and income statements of the borrower.

This striking evolution arose from one of the fundamental economic consequences of the Civil War, the depreciation of our currency. The United States went through no such stirring currency inflation as did Greece and China following the Second World War, France, Italy, or Germany following the First World War, or as did the original thirteen colonies during the Revolutionary War, when "a wagonload of money would scarcely purchase a wagonload of provisions." From 1862, however, until 1879, when specie payment was finally resumed, wholesale and retail transactions, the purchase of raw materials by manufacturing plants, the payment of wages, rents, insurance premiums, and insurance policies were made in a unit of fluctuating monetary value.

Changes in Mercantile Terms of Sale

At one time during the Civil War, the value of paper money dropped to 35 cents on the gold dollar. The constant fluctuations in the unit of everyday currency naturally made the extension of credit by banks and mercantile houses precarious. The daily fluctuating value of greenbacks in terms of gold, in the years following the Civil War, reversed the almost universal example of depreciation, and in 1879 a paper dollar again was exchangeable for a gold dollar. While greenbacks were fluctuating below par in terms of gold during and for several years after the Civil War, wholesale merchants were naturally unwilling to sell a bill of goods on the customary 4 to 6 months' terms, because of fear that the greenbacks with which they would be paid at maturity would be worth materially less than at the time of the sale.[12] The same situation had existed during the Revolutionary War. Uncertainty and apprehension have never been conducive to the use of long terms for credit.

Under these conditions, Eastern wholesale merchants proceeded to shorten their terms of sale to 30 days on open account, and in some cases to 10 days. This evolution in mercantile terms of sale was assisted by the rise of a sellers' market with the demand for merchandise greater than the supply, so that creditors were in an ideal position to select strong customers who could meet their obligations on the new shorter terms. In addition, merchants began to offer a premium in the form of a cash discount for early payment, instead of requiring payment by note or trade acceptance as had been the practice from the earliest of colonial days. This shift in an established business practice was facilitated by the growth in the means of communication and transportation. Buyers could now come to market several times each year and order by mail or from samples carried by salesmen, instead of ordering their merchandise requirements once or twice each year as previously. Simultaneously, the banking system developed to keep pace with the expanding needs of local businesses. In 1860 there were 1,492 incorporated commercial banks; in 1875, 1,937; and in 1880, 2,726.

Rise of Single-name Paper

This simple but expedient shortening in mercantile terms of sale brought about an equally revolutionary change in banking practice. It was under these circumstances that James Buell, president of the Importers and Traders National Bank of New York City, proceeded in the 1870's to show his depositors the distinct advantages of borrowing funds upon their own credit standing and using these funds to pay for merchandise purchases on discount terms. This revolution in lending technique was predi-

[12] A typical situation, showing how the fluctuation in the gold value of paper money was taken into consideration by a businessman, is exemplified in a letter dated Jan. 20, 1864, written to the Hon. J. Dixon Roman of the Hagerstown Bank, Hagerstown, Md. This letter read as follows: "Dear Sir, I was called upon to-day by Mr. Thos. Dixon, who informed me that you desired a bid based on paper currency instead of gold as has already been offered by me for the new Marble Front and Portico for the Hagerstown Bank. In considering the length of time it will take to complete the work as contemplated, and also the uncertainty of paper currency, I deem my bid as based on gold the safest for both parties, and therefore most respectfully decline contracting for the work based entirely upon what is requested, viz; Paper Currency. I have the honor to remain, Yours Truly, Alex C. Pacten, Stonecutter." [Baltimore, Md.] (This letter is in the archives of Dun & Bradstreet, Inc., New York.)

(C.)

STANDARD FORM.

NEW YORK STATE BANKERS' ASSOCIATION.

To ....
(Insert here the name of the loaning Bank.)

For the purpose of procuring and establishing credit from time to time with the above Bank for claims and demands against the undersigned, the undersigned furnish the following as being a true and correct statement of his or their financial statement of his or their condition on the .... day of .... 189......, and agree that in case any change occurs that materially reduces his or their ability to pay all claims and demands against him or them, the undersigned will notify the said Bank without delay.

In consideration of granting any credit by said Bank, the undersigned agree that in case of failure or insolvency on the part of the undersigned, or in the event of it appearing at any time that any of the following representations are untrue, or in case of the occurrence of such change as aforesaid or of failure to notify such change as above agreed, all or any of the claims or demands against the undersigned held by said Bank shall, at the option thereof, immediately become due and payable.

Further, that the exercise of or omission to exercise such option in any instance shall not waive or affect any other or subsequent right to exercise the same.

ASSETS.			LIABILITIES.	
Cash in.................... Bank....................			Bills Payable for Merchandise....................	
Cash on hand			Bills Payable to Own Banks....................	
Bills Receivable, Good			Bills Payable for Paper Sold....................	
Accounts Receivable, Good....................			Open Accounts....................	
Bills or Accounts Receivable, due from Officers			Bonded Debt (When due....................)	
Merchandise, finished (How Valued....................)			Interest on Bonded Debt....................	
Merchandise, unfinished (How Valued....................)			Mortgages or Liens on Real Estate....................	
Raw Material (How Valued....................)			Chattel Mortgages....................	
Real Estate....................			Deposits of Moneys with us....................	
Machinery and Fixtures....................				
Total....................			Total Liabilities....................	
			Capital....................	
			Surplus, including undivided profits....................	
Total....................			Total....................	

Contingent Liability. { Accommodation Endorsements..
{ Endorsed Bills Receivable Outstanding ....

Specify any of above assets or liabilities pledged as or secured by collateral, and state collateral.

....
....
....
....
....
....

FORM 2. Statement blank for corporations used by members of the New York State Bankers' Association in 1896.

cated upon giving to the banker a current balance sheet and such other financial information as the banker felt he needed to analyze the condition of the borrower. Here was the most radical change in banking practice since the organization of the Bank of North America in 1781. Nothing could have been more simple, more logical, or more eventful.

Bankers generally, however, were reluctant to follow Buell's example. They lacked the credit experience, the background in gathering essential credit data, the ability to draw independent logical deductions on credit risks, and the vision of what this change would mean to banking and to business. To these bankers it appeared safer to continue to extend credit on two-name accommodation paper or trade paper, even though little or no exact information was available regarding the actual financial responsibility of either name. Finally, on February 9, 1895, the executive council of the New York State Bankers' Association set an example for the banking profession of the country by recommending to its members "that they request borrowers of money from their respective institutions to give them written statements over their signatures, of their assets and liabilities, in such form as the Committee on Uniform Statements of the various groups recommend." This was the first occasion on which the subject of a "property" statement blank had been brought before a bankers' convention.[13]

New York State was divided into nine sections geographically, and before July 11, 1895, when the second annual state convention was held at Saratoga, the bankers in all sections had adopted uniform statement blanks. At this convention, it was explained that although an increasing number of bankers in all parts of the state were now requesting financial statements from borrowers, others, through fear of offending their customers or because of severe competition, were refraining from making requests for financial statements from borrowing accounts.[14]

The Pennsylvania Bankers' Association, at its annual convention held at Pittsburgh on December 16, 1896, adopted three statement forms, a long and a short form for proprietorships and partnerships, and a slightly different form for corporations, all of which had been originated during the previous year and had been put into use by the bankers in Section 9 of New York State.[15]

At the twenty-fifth annual convention of the American Bankers' Association held in Cleveland, Ohio, in September, 1899, a resolution was adopted providing "that the Secretary of this Association be and hereby is requested to confer with the Vice-Presidents from the various States, and prepare a uniform property statement blank which can lawfully be used in each State of the Union by the members of this Association, the

[13] CANNON, JAMES G., vice-president of the Fourth National Bank, New York, "Uniform Statement Blanks and Credit Department Methods," *Proceedings of the Twenty-fifth Annual Convention of the American Bankers' Association*, held at Cleveland, Ohio, Sept. 5–7, 1899, p. 175 (American Bankers' Association, New York, 1899).

[14] CANNON, JAMES G., "Losses from Bad Debts," an address delivered before the convention of the New York State Bankers' Association, Saratoga, N.Y., July 11, 1895.

[15] *Proceedings of the Second Annual Convention of the Pennsylvania Bankers' Association*, pp. 76–81 (Pennsylvania Bankers' Association, Philadelphia, 1897).

STANDARD FORM

AMERICAN BANKERS' ASSOCIATION

To The _____ Bank of _____

The undersigned, for the purpose of procuring credit from time to time from you for the negotiable paper of the undersigned or otherwise, furnish you with the following statement, which fully and truly sets forth the financial condition of the undersigned on the _____ day of _____ I _____, which statement you can consider as continuing to be full and accurate unless notice of change is given you. The undersigned agree to notify you promptly of any change that materially reduces the pecuniary responsibility of the undersigned.

In consideration of the granting of such credit, the undersigned agree that if the undersigned at any time fail or become insolvent, or commit an Act of Bankruptcy, or if any of the representations made below prove to be untrue, or if the undersigned fail to notify you of any material change as before agreed; then and in either such case all obligations of the undersigned held by you shall immediately become due and payable without demand or notice, and the same may be charged against the balance of any deposit account of the undersigned with you, the undersigned hereby giving a continuing lien upon such balance of deposit account from time to time existing to secure all obligations of the undersigned held by you.

ASSETS			LIABILITIES		
Cash on hand			Bills Payable for Merchandise		
Cash in _____ Bank			Bills Payable to own Banks		
Bills Receivable, good, owing by Customers			Bills Payable for Paper Sold		
Bills Receivable, owing by Partners			Open Accounts		
Accounts Receivable, good, owing by Customers			Deposits of Moneys with us		
Accounts Receivable, owing by Partners			Mortgages or Liens on Real Estate		
Merchandise (How Valued					
Real Estate belonging to Firm					
Machinery and Fixtures					
			Total Liabilities		
			Net Worth		
Total			Total		

Contingent Liability. { Accommodation Endorsements _____
{ Endorsed Bills Receivable Outstanding _____

Specify any of above assets or liabilities pledged as, or secured by, collateral, and state collateral

_____

_____

_____

_____

_____

_____

_____

FORM 3. Statement blank for partnerships presented by James G. Cannon at the annual convention of the American Bankers' Association, held at Cleveland, Ohio, Sept. 5-7, 1899.

same to be designated as the Standard Form of the American Bankers' Association. . . . " It was brought out at this same convention that the National Association of Credit Men, "a large and powerful organization of 2,700 members, after a year's investigation of this subject,[16] has also adopted uniform property statement blanks," and they were then being used.[17] By April, 1900, D. Cary Keith of the Geo. E. Keith Company, Campello, Mass., was able to write William N. Fitzgerald, chairman of the Boot and Shoe Conference at the Milwaukee convention of the National Association of Credit Men, that he was using the statement forms devised and endorsed by the association. "I have found," he explained, "that by insisting on this plan of getting statements from our customers, we have been able to weed out many who are slow, and thereby have brought our losses down to a comparatively small amount, during the last two years. . . . "[18]

The leader in this movement of commercial bankers to investigate credit risks more adequately and to base the extension of credit upon exact information instead of upon generalities or assumed financial strength was James G. Cannon, who at the time was vice-president of the Fourth National Bank, New York. In many of his enlightening addresses, which were subsequently printed in small pamphlets,[19] he stressed over and over again the basic importance of obtaining and studying the exact financial statements of the potential borrower. "An itemized statement, provided it is correct, is to a banker what a map is to a traveler; it points out and

[16] "For some time past the National Association of Credit Men have had under consideration the forms of standard property statement blanks adapted to different classes of business. An exhaustive comparison has been made of blanks in use by different trades and leading houses throughout the country. The forms suggested for approval have been extensively discussed by the different local associations and by leading credit men in every part of the land. As a result of this work, standard forms have been prepared which have been generally approved by all interests, and these have been formally adopted and endorsed by the Board of Administration of the National Association of Credit Men. Uniformity in matters of this kind is extremely desirable, and the credit men are to be congratulated upon having devised forms which are so generally approved as to indicate that they will come into almost universal use."—*Business Topics*, p. 3, June, 1898, compiled and issued monthly by the Business Literature Committee of the National Association of Credit Men, New York.

[17] *Proceedings of the Twenty-fifth Annual Convention of the American Bankers' Association*, pp. 23, 176–177.

[18] *Business Topics*, p. 3, May, 1900.

[19] In addition to addresses of James G. Cannon listed elsewhere in other footnotes in this chapter, the more important ones in which bank credit was the primary subject were: "Profit or Loss on Bank Accounts," delivered before the American Bankers' Association, Baltimore, Md., 1894; "Uniform Statements," delivered before the New York State Bankers' Association, 1896; "Credit, Credit Man, Creditor," delivered before the National Association of Credit Managers, Toledo, Ohio, 1896; and "Individual Credits," delivered before the National Association of Credit Men, Kansas City, Mo., 1897.

PROPERTY STATEMENT BLANK
Recommended and endorsed by the National Association of Credit Men

"Large assets are not always necessary to the creation of credit; what is most desirable is, that credit be in relative proportion to the actual assets. The giver of credit is a contributor of capital, and becomes, in a certain sense, a partner of the debtor, and, as such, has a perfect right to complete information of the debtor's condition at all times."

DATE.................................. 190.......

For the purpose of obtaining credit now and hereafter for goods purchased, I or we herewith submit to you the following statement of my or our resources and liabilities, and I or we will immediately notify you of any material change in my or our financial condition.

In consideration of your granting credit to the undersigned I or we agree that in case of my or our failure or insolvency, or in case I or we shall make any assignment for the benefit of creditors, bill of sale, mortgage or other transfer of my or our property, or shall have my or our stock attached, receiver appointed, or should any judgment be entered against me or us, then all and every of the claims which you may have against me or us shall at your option become immediately due and payable, even though the term of credit has not expired. All goods hereafter purchased from you shall be taken to be purchased subject to the foregoing conditions as a part of the terms of sale.

ACTIVE BUSINESS ASSETS.	Dollars	Cents
Present cash value of merchandise on hand...........................		
Notes and accounts, cash value........................		
Cash in hand.................................		
Cash in bank.................................		
Fixtures, machinery, horses and wagons..........		
Total Active Business Assets...............		

BUSINESS LIABILITIES.	Dollars	Cents
Owe for merchandise, open acct.,		
of which $.................is past due		
Owe for notes for merchandise........		
Owe bank.............................		
Owe others for borrowed money		
Owe taxes and rent....................		
Mortgages on fixtures, machinery, horses and wagons.		
Total Business Liabilities..............		
Net worth in Business		

OUTSIDE ASSETS.

Total real estate, assessed valuation, $ ....

Total encumbrances on real estate, $ ....

Equity.....................

Personal property.........................

Other assets.........................

Grand Total net worth in and out of Business...................

Full given and surname of each partner	Age?	Married?	Possible liability of each member of firm as endorser, bondsman, etc.

What portion of Real Estate described is homestead ?..........................

Have you any other debts than herein mentioned ?..........................

What kind of business do you conduct ?.....

Insurance on Stock..........................

On Fixtures, Machinery, Horses and Wagons ?..........................

On Real Estate ?..........................

Amount of sales last year ? ....

Amount of expenses last year ?..................

What proportion of your sales is on credit ?

How often do you take an inventory of stock?

Date of last inventory ? ....

If you have borrowed money in the business, state what amount is secured and in what way ?..........................

Are any merchandise creditors secured in any way ? ....

Have you any judgments, judgment notes, chattel mortgages, or other liens against you, recorded or unrecorded ? If so, describe ....

Suits pending, and of what nature ? ....

Keep bank account with ....

What books of account do you keep ?..........

REMARKS.—Give details and explanations of questions not fully answered above........

_The above statement, both printed and written, has been carefully read by the undersigned, and is a full and correct statement of my or our financial condition as of...190......

Firm Signature..........................

Town....................................State............................   By.......................... a member of the firm.

FORM 4. "Property" statement blank recommended for the use of mercantile creditors by the National Association of Credit Men in 1906.

makes clear things and conditions that would otherwise be obscure and mysterious."[20] He prophesied that "banks will be obliged to loan more and more upon single name paper, which is a simple promise to pay, and in making loans of this character, they should certainly know what the

[20] CANNON, JAMES G., "Losses from Bad Debts."

promise to pay represents, or has behind it,"[21] implying the essential need of detailed financial statements. He explained how, with the use of balance sheets, he had discovered that certain concerns had several borrowing accounts when he had been under the assumption they had had only one, his own bank. Such information was readily available by comparing the amount of cash on hand and outstanding loans in a balance sheet with the borrower's deposits at his bank and outstanding credit on the books of his bank on the statement date. Financial statements were becoming a medium of obtaining exact information, but at this early stage there was little thought of any analysis consisting in a study of the relationship of items.

This radical change in the lending technique of commercial banks involved a gradual evolution in perspective and outlook, in banking forms, and in knowledge. Skepticism of a new principle is followed by toleration, and toleration by the extension of the practice. In this case, the change during the last quarter of the nineteenth century, so clearly indicated by the spread in the adoption of uniform statement blanks, brought about appreciation of the value of balance sheets and income statements, and led to the training of bankers to interpret these financial statements. By the turn of the century, the extension of loans on single-name paper had become a recognized practice of American commercial banking institutions.

The Federal Reserve Act, which became law on December 23, 1913, provided for the establishment of the 12 Federal Reserve banks, and since November 16, 1914, they have been in active operation. In describing typical operations, the original act provided that member banks might rediscount with the Federal Reserve banks "notes, drafts, and bills of exchange arising out of actual commercial transactions; . . . the Federal Reserve Board to have the right to determine or define the character of the paper thus eligible for discount." The Board now proceeded to emphasize the fundamental importance of financial statements to member banks in carrying on banking operations by requiring that "after January 15, 1915, no paper shall be discounted or purchased by Federal Reserve Banks that does not bear on its face evidence that it is eligible for rediscount . . . and that the seller of the paper has given a statement to the member bank."[22] This basic interest of the Federal Reserve Board was shortly to blossom out in 1917 in a study entitled *Uniform Accounts*,[23] which was to be the forerunner of successively enlarged studies to be made by the American Institute of Certified Public Accountants setting forth the

[21] CANNON, JAMES G., "Bank Credits," an address delivered at the Drexel Institute, Philadelphia, Pa., Nov. 17, 1892.

[22] WILLIS, H. P., *The Federal Reserve System*, pp. 903–934 (The Ronald Press Company, New York, 1923).

[23] *Federal Reserve Bulletin*, Vol. III, No. 4, April, 1917.

minimum requirements for the verifications of assets and liabilities by an accountant and providing for more uniform thoroughness in setting up financial statements.

ASSETS.

Cash:
1a. Cash on hand—currency and coin.......
1b. Cash in bank.............................

Notes and accounts receivable:
3. Notes receivable of customers on hand (not past due).......................
5. Notes receivable discounted or sold with indorsement or guaranty............
7. Accounts receivable, customers (not past due)................................
9. Notes receivable, customers, past due (cash value, $)..........................
11. Accounts receivable, customers, past due (cash value, $....).
Less:
13. Provisions for bad debts..
15. Provisions for discounts, freights, allowances, etc.

Inventories:
17. Raw material on hand..:
19. Goods in process............
21. Uncompleted contracts........
Less payments on account thereof...............
23. Finished goods on hand...........

Other quick assets (describe fully):
....

Total quick assets (excluding all investments)..

Securities:
25. Securities readily marketable and salable without impairing the business.......
27. Notes given by officers, stockholders, or employees....................
29. Accounts due from officers, stockholders, or employees.....................

Total current assets................

Fixed assets:
31. Land used for plant.................
33. Buildings used for plant.............
35. Machinery........................
37. Tools and plant equipment.............
39. Patterns and drawings..............
41. Office furniture and fixtures.........
43. Other fixed assets, if any (describe fully)..

Less:
45. Reserves for depreciation............

Total fixed assets...............

Deferred charges:
47. Prepaid expenses, interest, insurance, taxes, etc.
Other assets (49)..........................

Total assets................

LIABILITIES.

Bills, notes, and accounts payable:
Unsecured bills and notes—
2. Acceptances made for merchandise or raw material purchased........
4. Notes given for merchandise or raw material purchased...............
6. Notes given to banks for money borrowed.......................
8. Notes sold through brokers.........
10. Notes given for machinery, additions to plant, etc...................
12. Notes due to stockholders, officers, or employees.....................

Unsecured accounts—
14. Accounts payable for purchase (not yet due)....................
16. Accounts payable for purchases (past due)...................
18. Accounts payable to stockholders, officers, or employees.............

Secured liabilities—
20a. Notes receivable discounted or sold with indorsement or guaranty (contra)....................
20b. Customers' accounts discounted or assigned (contra)..............
20c. Obligations secured by liens on inventories....................
20d. Obligations secured by securities deposited as collateral..........

22. Accrued liabilities (interest, taxes, wages etc).................
Other current liabilities (describe fully):
....

Total current liabilities..............
Fixed liabilities:
24. Mortgage on plant (due date ....)..
26. Mortgage on other real estate (due date ....)...........
28. Chattel mortgage on machinery or equipment (due date ....)........
30. Bonded debt (due date ....).......

32. Other fixed liabilities (describe fully):
....

Total liabilities...............

Net worth:
34. If a corporation—
(a) Preferred stock (less stock in treasury)....................
(b) Common stock (less stock in treasury).................
(c) Surplus and undivided profits..

Less—
(d) Book value of good will...............
(e) Deficit............

36. If an individual or partnership—
(a) Capital...............
(b) Undistributed profits or deficit..

Total................

FORM 5. Balance sheet form suggested by the Federal Reserve Board in 1917.

On July 15, 1915, the Federal Reserve Bank of New York addressed a letter to the cashiers of all member banks in the Second Federal Reserve Region enclosing four financial statements forms, one for corporations, one for firms, one for farmers or livestock dealers, and one for merchants, manufacturers, or other individuals. "These forms," continued the letter, "are designed to assist member banks to assemble and maintain credit files relating to borrowers. Statements made on these forms will show clearly the relation of quick assets to current liabilities. Only such supplementary information is called for as seems essential to a full understanding of a borrower's position. On the back of each form, space is provided for additional questions or records. . . . Member banks may prefer to use their own or other forms of statements but those banks which wish to use the Federal Reserve bank forms are requested to advise the number of each required." The creation and distribution of these financial forms in the most concentrated business and banking part of our country provided one more urge toward a wider use of detailed financial statements.

Early Days of Accountancy

In the years following the example set by James Buell in granting credit on the financial statement of a borrower, it was difficult to obtain exact financial information, even when a depositor was willing to cooperate by turning over his books to the banker for careful perusal. Few commercial or industrial business enterprises in the third and fourth quarters of the nineteenth century had reliable figures, even for the use of their own operating managements. The principal exceptions were railroads, several of which were keeping quite complete, accurate records. American accountancy was in its early stages of development and was just beginning to make some feeble effort toward becoming recognized as an actual profession. If a banker had requested a businessman in the latter years of the nineteenth century to have his books audited by an accountant, the typical businessman would innocently and naïvely have asked, "What is an accountant?"

When President Buell of the Importers and Traders National Bank was showing the partners of mercantile houses in New York City the desirability and profitableness of borrowing funds on their own financial responsibility to earn discounts on trade bills, strange as it may seem, there was not a single firm of public accountants in the United States to assist this eventful development. The earliest use of a firm name in accountancy in the United States seems to have been Nelson, Shepard & Cooke of Cincinnati in 1876, a concern that apparently was in existence only a year or so and that operated as a "real-estate and collection agency" as well as accountants. The second firm was Candor & Carnes, listed in Cincinnati in 1881 as "expert accountants."[24]   In 1873 Price, Waterhouse & Co. of

[24] As early as 1786, individuals who practiced law advertised in city directories that they also acted as accountants. In fact this early public practice, which consisted in little more than making the opening entries in books of account and explaining bookkeeping practices from theory rather than from experience, seems to have been considered a minor but integral department of the legal profession. In the early part of the nineteenth century, teachers and authors on the subject of bookkeeping occa-

London had sent employees to the United States on special auditing assignments.[25]

In 1883, Edwin Guthrie, a receiver for a bankrupt English financial organization, visited the United States to ascertain the value of certain assets which the bankrupt enterprise owned here. On arrival, Guthrie was unable to find a public accounting firm to assist him in his investigations. He became acquainted with John Wylie Barrow, an actuary employed by the New York branches of certain British fire insurance companies, and out of this acquaintanceship grew the third known accounting firm, the first one of importance on this side of the Atlantic ocean. It was not until 1896 that the accounting profession was first legally recognized, when New York State conferred the power upon the Regents of the University of the State of New York to grant certificates of qualification. Pennsylvania followed three years later in 1899, Maryland in 1900,[26] and California in 1901. Similar recognition was not extended by the District of Columbia until 1923.

During the early years of accountancy, the profession had no specialized field of activity. What little business came its way, and it was very little, generally consisted in opening and balancing sets of books, in "straightening out" books that had become charmingly "mixed up" because of the inexperience of amateur bookkeepers. Some managements considered the early accountant "an experienced bookkeeper and no more, others looked upon him as a man whose business it was to detect fraud, embezzlement, and stealing, and that his employment was of value only in this direction, while quite a few had a vague idea that he was merely a man of figures, a rapid and unerring calculator who could add up two or three columns of figures at a time, could tell you immediately the square or cube root of any given number, or say off-hand, for example, what one dollar put out at six per cent compound interest per annum at the time Columbus discovered America would amount to today."[27]

It was often feared that the employment of public accountants would be looked upon as evidence of "suspected fraud or irregularity, losses, and

---

sionally sought outside engagements. See Norman E. Webster, "Public Accountancy in the United States," *The American Institute of Accountants, Fiftieth Anniversary Celebration Volume*, 1937, pp. 104–108 (American Institute of Certified Public Accountants, New York, 1938), and A. C. Littleton, "Directory of Early American Public Accountants," *University of Illinois Bulletin*, Vol. 40, No. 8, Oct. 13, 1942.

[25] DeMond, C. W., *Price, Waterhouse & Co. in America*, p. 5. (Price, Waterhouse & Co., New York, 1951).

[26] In 1900 there were only 243 certified public accountants in the United States. See T. A. Wise, "The Auditors Have Arrived," *Fortune*, Vol. XLII, No. 5, p. 152, November, 1960.

[27] Anyon, James T., *Recollections of the Early Days of American Accountancy*, p. 41 (privately printed, 1925).

doubt regarding financial strength." As late as 1907 investigations by public accountants were at times made secretly, often at night and on Sunday.[28]

The field of making audits and of verifying financial statements was to be developed as commercial banking institutions, and later mercantile creditors, began to insist upon receiving exact financial statements as the basis for the extension of credit, as investment bankers needed the verification of earnings from a qualified source outside the management as a basis for pricing and selling securities to the avid public, and as the sixteenth amendment to the Federal Constitution became effective in 1913 and Congress was empowered "to lay and collect taxes on income, from whatever source derived." Officers of corporations who had never before realized the necessity for having a correct system of accounting now found themselves compelled to prepare statements of income and expenditures. The passage of the Revenue Act of March 3, 1917, containing the first excess-profits tax, finally heightened this emphasis as nothing else could possibly have done.

EXPANSION IN USE OF FINANCIAL STATEMENTS

In 1870 there were 427,000 active manufacturing, assembling, converting, jobbing, wholesaling, importing, exporting, and retailing business enterprises in the United States. With present-day air transportation, color television, photoelectric cells, and atomic energy, we are ages away from the year when the fifteenth amendment to the Federal Constitution, extending the franchise to Negroes, became the law of the land. With the exception of four brief periods, the number of active commercial and industrial business enterprises listed in the Reference Books[29] of The Mercantile Agency climbed ~~quite steadily~~ upward from 427,000 in 1870 to 2,708,000 in 1960, and dropped to 2,527,000 in 1965.

[28] MONTGOMERY, ROBERT H., "What Have We Done, and How?" an address delivered before the 1937 convention of the American Institute of Accountants; *The American Institute of Accountants, Fiftieth Anniversary Celebration Volume*, 1937, p. 80 (American Institute of Certified Public Accountants, New York, 1938). C. W. DeMond reported that Edwin Waterhouse wrote in his diary that visits to certain private banking firms in London, England, in 1889 were made in secret "with the work done occasionally after office hours, since the clients feared damage might be caused their firm's reputation if it became known that an auditor was in the bank premises."— *Price, Waterhouse & Co. in America*, p. 9.

[29] The Reference Book, published every 2 months by Dun & Bradstreet, Inc., is a volume of approximately 4,000 pages, containing the names of active commercial and industrial business enterprises in every city, town, village, and hamlet in the United States, together with various symbols, indicating the line of business activity, estimated financial strength, and general credit worthiness.

for continental United States,

Growth in Number of Business Enterprises

As a result of the depression that started in 1893, the first brief relapse occurred and the number of business concerns listed in the July Reference Book dropped from 1,193,000 to 1,114,000 in 1894, reacted moderately to 1,209,000 in 1895, and then dropped again in both 1896 and 1897 to 1,059,000. For a period of 33 years, with the exception of the one year of 1918, no shrinkage occurred in the aggregate number of active commercial and industrial concerns.

The First World War brought a drop from 1,733,000 to 1,708,000 concerns in 1918, a moderate decrease of 25,000, or 1.4 per cent. In 1919, the number expanded nominally to 1,711,000 and in 1920 to 1,821,000, the greatest increase in any one year up to that time.

By 1929 there were 2,213,000 concerns listed in the Reference Book of The Mercantile Agency, more than twice the number in active operation in 1894. Then came the cyclone. The toll of inventory losses, heavy short- and long-term liabilities, losses from bad debts, top-heavy fixed assets, shrinking sales, and poor management brought about a long and sustained drop in the number of active commercial and industrial enterprises. From 1930 to 1933, inclusive, the number dropped successively each year, reaching 1,961,000 in 1933, an aggregate decrease of 11.3 per cent in 4 years. In 1934, when the outlook for business success and profits had begun to allow some rays of sunshine to penetrate the murky atmosphere, notwithstanding the vast army of unemployed, the number started to expand and by 1941 had reached 2,172,000, not quite the peak of 1929.

Between July, 1941, and July, 1944, the number of active commercial and industrial business enterprises dropped 317,000, from 2,172,000 to 1,855,000. Then the trend reversed itself, the number of listings increasing steadily, year by year, to an all-time high record of 2,667,000 in 1953, with a nominal decrease to 2,632,000 in 1954. Since then listings have expanded every year.

This record is the most impressive surge in the growth of active business enterprises in all history. During these years, millions of European immigrants settled in the towns, in the cities, and on virgin farming land, and a vast expansion took place in the number of people who became vitally interested in making a living or a fortune through the medium of the business enterprise. The infinite variety in the ways of earning a modern livelihood is in spectacular contrast to the pursuits of colonial days when agriculture, fur trading, shipbuilding, small retail stores, hostelries, and foreign commerce encompassed the principal economic activities of the individual.

In 1870 there was one active commercial and industrial concern for every 91 people in the United States; in 1900 one for every 65 people; and in 1960, still one for approximately every 65 people.

It is rather surprising that accountancy had not become established sooner in the United States, in view of the earlier development of the profession in England and Scotland and the importance of business activity in a rapidly expanding economy. Possibly the tardiness was due to the fact that prior to 1883 few corporations except the railroads, the larger banking institutions, the express companies, and some cotton mills had public distribution of their securities in the United States. Business enterprises were still closely controlled and operated. Not until 1886 did the courts decide that a corporation was a person in the meaning of the "due process" clause of the Federal Constitution. This decision brought an element of unprecedented security to the existence of the larger corporation, or, as Thomas W. Lawson phrased it, the corporation became " . . . a separate entity which could do all the things the individual might, and yet exist apart from the individual and independent of his personal dealings and comings and goings."[30]

This picture of the expansion in the nation's commercial and industrial life during the past 85 years indicates the growing importance of the institution of the business enterprise in economic life and shows as clearly as possible that accountancy from 1883 onward assumed a place of increasing distinction in the world of business affairs. As an increasing percentage of business enterprises took the corporate form of existence in contrast to the early proprietorship and partnership forms, accountancy made headway.[31]

Influence of the New York Stock Exchange

In 1880, 219 stocks of 183 corporations were listed on the New York Stock Exchange. These corporations consisted of 64 New York City banks, 81 railroads and street railway companies, 10 public utilities—gas and telegraph companies—and 28 industrials, mostly coal-mining companies and metal-mining enterprises. These were the corporations whose securities were the most widely held by the American public. Naturally there existed an implied obligation on the part of the operating managements of these corporations to inform security holders of their financial condition by issuing some sort of yearly report containing a measure of financial information.[32] In 1900, 377 stocks of 278 corporations were listed on the Big Board; in 1910, 426 stocks of 304 corporations.

[30] LAWSON, THOMAS W., *Frenzied Finance*, p. 211 (The Ridgway-Thayer Company, New York, 1905).

[31] The growing numerical importance of corporations in American business life is discussed in *Are You a Stockholder?* by Alden Winthrop, pp. 253–255 (Covici, Friede, Inc., New York, 1937).

[32] At times the implied obligations carried no weight with the management. On Mar. 22, 1866, for example, G. L. Gerrard, chairman of the Committee on Securities of the New York Stock Exchange, wrote a letter to the secretary of the Delaware, Lackawanna & Western Railroad Co. for copies of any reports and documents it had

Between 1910 and 1920 the number of listed industrial issues gradually exceeded the railroad stocks, assuming the place of prime importance. By 1920 stocks were listed on the New York Stock Exchange for 268 industrial corporations, 131 railroads, 34 New York City banks, and 23 public utilities, for a total of 691 separate issues of stocks. Stockholders who had furnished the funds to develop and to expand these enterprises became increasingly desirous, and naturally so, of having a disinterested and qualified accounting of funds, particularly as the inside activities of notorious financial speculators such as Commodore Cornelius Vanderbilt, Jim Fiske, Daniel Drew, and Jay Gould became more widely known to the public.

The early reports to stockholders of corporations whose securities were listed on the New York Stock Exchange contained unaudited financial statements. As the number of listings on the New York Stock Exchange increased, the Exchange became vitally interested in seeing that an increasing amount of reliable information was given to stockholders and to the public. This development took a practical form in the following early rulings of the Exchange;

1. In 1897, the Kansas City Gas Company, in its application to list $3,750,000 first mortgage five per cent bonds, agreed to the suggestion of the New York Stock Exchange that the company would, "from time to time, make publication of its net profits, not less than twice in each year."

2. In 1898, the Glucose Sugar Refining Co., in its application to list its preferred and common stocks, agreed that "a detailed statement would be made public" in time for its annual meeting of stockholders.

Both of the above rulings were important moves in the popularization of pertinent financial information. The securities exchanges in admitting securities for trading on their floors now felt an increasing obligation to provide investors with certain safeguards in the form of more comprehensive historical and financial information, which would be available to the general public. Some measure of control over the corporations whose securities were listed was assumed by securities exchanges through their right to prescribe regulations for the listing of securities.

No figures are available showing the number of corporations whose securities have been widely distributed among the public. On March 31, 1961, however, 1,117 United States corporations had stocks listed on the

---

issued during the years immediately preceding. The reply, signed by A. C. Odell, treasurer of the railroad, contained but one brief sentence, "The Delaware, Lackawanna & Western R.R. Co. make no reports and publish no statements—and have not done anything of the kind for the last five years."—SHULTZ, BIRL E., *Stock Exchange Procedure*, pp. 11–12 (New York Stock Exchange Institute, 1956). It was to be many years before the issuance of yearly reports to stockholders would become a recognized practice among listed corporations.

New York Stock Exchange, represented by 69 railroads and manufacturers of railroad equipment, 117 utilities, 47 financial companies, 42 mining corporations, and 842 industrial enterprises operating in a wide variety of fields. The listed stocks of these 1,117 corporations on that date had a market value of $342,093,000,000; the market value of the 842 industrials was $245,112,000,000, or 71.7 per cent of the total, indicating the importance which industrials, that is, manufacturing, wholesale, retail, amusement enterprises, and service corporations, had assumed in the scheme of American life.

In 1930, J. M. B. Hoxsey, the technical assistant to the Committee on Stock List of the New York Stock Exchange, asked that the American Institute of Certified Public Accountants appoint a committee to advise the Exchange with respect to problems of accounting and corporate reports. The committee that was subsequently appointed worked closely with the Stock Exchange. In 1933, the correspondence between the two groups was published, together with a standard form of auditor's report or certificate which the Institute's committee had suggested and which the Exchange had approved. Five broad fundamental principles of accounting, on which the Institute's committee and the Exchange agreed, were also included in the correspondence, clearly stating the nature of accounts and the purpose and limitations of independent audits. All this material, published in a pamphlet entitled *Audits of Corporate Accounts*, constitutes a historic document that had a profound effect on financial and accounting practice in the United States.[33] These principles are outlined and discussed in Chap. XXIV.

Securities and Exchange Commission

The Securities Act of 1933 and the Securities Exchange Act of 1934 created the Securities and Exchange Commission and gave it the power to obtain such information in such detail as the Commission might by rules and regulations require from registrants under these two acts, as necessary and appropriate in the public interest or for the protection of investors. These acts were supplemented by the Public Utility Holding Company Act of 1935 and the Investment Company Act of 1940. Prestige was added to the accounting profession by regulations of the Commission to the effect that substantially every corporation except railroads,[34] common and contract carriers by motor vehicle, and commercial banking institutions, with securities listed on a national security exchange, and

---

[33] *The American Institute of Accountants, Fiftieth Anniversary Celebration Volume,* 1937, p. 19 (American Institute of Certified Public Accountants, New York, 1938).

[34] Title I, Sec. 3(a), (6) of the Securities Act of 1933 provides that the act shall not apply to "any security issued by a common or contract carrier the issuance of which is subject to the provisions of 20a of the Interstate Commerce Act, as amended."

The number of decisions and releases covering accounting principles and practices has been relatively limited, reflecting the view of the Commission that it would not be in the public interest for an agency of the Government to accounting rule making in an extensive manner to undertake[39]

substantially every corporation, with the exception of the lines noted, offering to the public an issue of securities in excess of $300,000[35] must file certified financial statements[36] with the Commission.

Under the law, the Securities and Exchange Commission has power to require balance sheets, income statements, surplus accounts, and supporting details, in any form, from all corporations whose affairs come under its scrutiny. Of equally fundamental importance, the Commission also was given power "to define technical, trade, and accounting terms," a privilege that offers untold possibilities in setting standards in the future.

For many several years the Commission made no attempt to utilize this its power except in the delineation of the exact manner in which its various financial forms had to be filled and in the review of financial information filed under the various acts. In January, 1937, however, the chief accountant issued the first of a series of releases, which has been continued up to this time, giving interpretations and tending to set standards of accountancy practice.[37] Most of these opinions have suggested standards in a particular situation, rather than determining fixed broad standards for the profession, but the gradual accumulation of interpretations in individual situations has tended to result in the creation of broad standards.

The extensive information obtained by the Commission unfortunately does not necessarily carry through to the stockholder, the investor, or the speculator, except on the occasion of an underwriting of securities. The Commission may insist that in a report made to it certain items be charged to expense in the income statement and not to surplus. The management of that particular corporation, however, in its annual report to stockholders may present the information according to some other accounting policy and in such a condensed form that the interpretation may be materially different. The Securities and Exchange Commission, moreover, has no direct or indirect contact with the majority of corporations whose securities are not held by the public, the only exceptions being subsidiaries or affiliates of corporations whose securities are substantially held by the public.

[35] The Securities Act of 1933 originally imposed a maximum limit of $100,000 upon the amount of a security offering which the SEC was empowered to exempt from registration. By amendment of the statute effective May 15, 1945 (see Regulation A, Rule 217(a) of the Securities and Exchange Commission), this limit was raised to $300,000. Financial statements of corporations offering new issues not in excess of $300,000 "need not be certified by independent or certified public accountants."

[36] Article 2, entitled "Certification," in Regulation S-X of the Securities and Exchange Commission, dated Aug. 20, 1958, gives the detailed qualifications of accountants who may certify to these financial statements, and the requirements, representations, opinions, and exceptions to be covered in the certificate.

[37] This series of accounting releases of the Securities and Exchange Commission is discussed in Chap. XXIV.

[38] Grady, Paul, Inventory of Generally Accepted Accounting Principles for Business Enterprises, p. 8, (American Institute of Certified Public Accountants, Inc., New York, 1965)

Oct. 15, 1964

Rule 254: "Amounts" "Aggregate offering price of all of the following securities (i) the issuer (a) the issuer (b) its predecessors and (c) all affiliates which have been incorporated within the past two years, or become affiliates of the issuer within the past two years, shall not exceed $300,000."

On December 20, 1934, the Securities and Exchange Commission published Instruction Book for Form 10 to assist officials of business enterprises in preparing forms for the correct registration of securities. This instruction book was amended eighteen times, the last amendment having been announced on February 2, 1939. That part of the material in this instruction book which pertained to the form and content of financial statements was superseded by the more elaborate Regulation S-X on February 21, 1940.[38] The current pamphlet of ~~72~~ 80 pages outlines the minimum data to be covered in preparing balance sheets, income statements, and supporting schedules of registrants under the Securities Act of 1933, the Securities Exchange Act of 1934, the Public Utility Holding Company Act of 1935, and the Investment Company Act of 1940.

Unaudited Financial Statements

All financial statements that come under the scrutiny of the Securities and Exchange Commission and a considerable proportion of those given to commercial banking institutions are audited. The thousands of practicing certified public accountants handle their work with varying degrees of thoroughness and independence. Even the larger nationally known firms of accountants that pride themselves on the uniformly high character of their work have had in their employ, at times, men whose ability or standards in emergencies have not always proved quite equal to some situations.[39] However, notwithstanding unusual situations and individuals, an analyst invariably, and quite naturally so, has a greater feeling of confidence and reassurance when studying financial statements that bear the imprint of an independent certified public accountant.

The greater proportion of all financial statements made available for mercantile credit are unaudited, and many of these statements are estimated. This condition is a natural one because of the fact that smaller business enterprises lack the means to utilize the services of certified public accountants and about 82 per cent of all active commercial and industrial business enterprises have a tangible net worth of $35,000 or less. Unaudited financial statements range from ultraconservative to highly exaggerated, overoptimistic valuations, from highly condensed to very detailed figures. There are balance sheets and balance sheets, but one and all come under the eye of some analyst at some time.

PHILOSOPHY OF NUMBERS

Accounting is the language of finance. It is the means of recording through Arabic numerals the forces and values that represent everyday

---

[38] The most recent copy of Regulation S-X ~~was published Aug. 20, 1958.~~

[39] Several of these ~~interesting~~ situations are discussed in footnotes in Chap. XXIV.

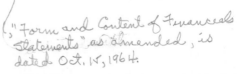

"Form and Content of Financial Statements" as Amended, is dated Oct. 15, 1964.

business transactions.[40] By its very nature, accounting adapts itself to business procedure and to business policy, not business procedure or policy to accounting. No decision concerning operating policies of a commercial or industrial business enterprise can be made and carried out that will not be reflected in figures. That is why we live in a world of mathematics, why Arabic figures have become so tremendously important in a business civilization based upon competition, the profit economy, and perhaps some growing degree of national capitalism. The figures of a business enterprise are the reflection of management operating policies or lack of operating policies. Here is the resurrection of the philosophy of Pythagoras, which applies more to the business civilization of today than it did 500 years before Christ when Pythagoras flourished on the shores of the Mediterranean Sea.

John Dewey phrased it in more philosophic terms. "Development of the systems of unit," he wrote, "by which to measure sensible objects (or form ideas of them) has come along with discovery of the ways in which the greatest amount of free movement from one conception to another is possible."[41]

THEORY AND PROBLEMS

1. Describe, with supporting reasons, the importance or the lack of importance of financial statements (a) in the extension of mercantile credit during the colonial period, (b) in the extension of mercantile credit and bank credit during the early years of the United States, and (c) in the early credit reports.

2. Why did mercantile terms of sales change radically during the Civil War?

3. How did the changes in terms of sales bring about a subsequent evolution in the form of bank credit instruments and the need for financial statements?

4. Explain why and how the rise and expansion of the corporate form of business organization affected the public use of financial statements.

5. The bankers of what state were the first to recommend the use of a financial statement, then known as a "property" statement blank, as a basis for the extension of credit? When?

---

[40] "I never see an executive engaged in what is termed figure study without being reminded of the orphan lad in one of the stories of Charles Dickens who after going through the agonies of learning the alphabet remarked that he never thought it would be possible to go through so much to get so little! . . . One day, and for this, I will ever revere his memory, I was hired as his controller by a man, the late William L. Ward, who taught me that figure study could have a purpose well worthy of any intelligent being, and that my job was to use figures so that he, his corporation, and incidentally, myself, could make more money. Today, not that I am particularly crazy about making money but because I know that profit-making is a constructive and worth-while undertaking, I find figures the most fascinating thing in the world."—HARRISON, G. CHARTER, *The Profit Pattern Road Map of the Manufacturer*, p. 5 (G. Charter Harrison, Madison, Wis., 1947).

[41] DEWEY, JOHN, *The Quest for Certainty*, pp. 134–135 (Minton, Balch & Co., New York, 1929).

6. Who was the leader in this bank movement to base the extension of bank credit on actual financial knowledge and not on generalities?

7. Describe the early difficulties in the establishment cf the accounting profession.

8. In 1870 there were 427,000 business concerns listed in the Reference Book of The Mercantile Agency, and in 1960, 2,708,000. In 1880 there were 183 U.S. corporations which had stocks listed on the New York Stock Exchange, and in 1961, 1,117. What effect, if any, did the expansion reflected by the increase in these figures have upon the development in accountancy?

9. Why should (a) the New York Stock Exchange and (b) the Securities and Exchange Commission be interested in standards of accountancy?

10. Why are unaudited as well as audited financial statements important?

CHAPTER II

Viewpoints toward Analyses

Strange coincidences take place every day in the world of business, just as naturally as in the novels of Balzac and Dickens, Kenneth Roberts and John Steinbeck. Recently, four persons interested in an analysis of the annual figures of the Folding Carton Corporation discussed them with the author, each from a different viewpoint, and all within the short period of a month.

The Folding Carton Corporation is an established enterprise, with substantial capital, engaged in producing and marketing a widely used, patented folding carton. The four individuals were a mercantile credit manager, a commercial banker, a stockholder, and a member of the operating staff, the treasurer. What did each of these individuals consciously see and understand when he studied the financial statements of this corporation? What did one see that the others failed to recognize? Were their viewpoints divergent or were their analyses, although inherently qualified by experience and knowledge, fundamentally the same? How competent was each one to analyze these figures? Let us see.

ANALYSIS OF THE MERCANTILE CREDIT MANAGER

The first of the four to present this interesting business situation was the credit manager of a creditor corporation engaged in producing kraft paperboard that was sold extensively to manufacturers of cartons and containers. The Folding Carton Corporation had been an active buyer of this particular kraft paper for the past 8 years. Kraft paper is customarily sold on terms of 1 per cent discount in 10 days, net 30 days. Payments made by the Folding Carton Corporation for its purchases from this concern over the 8 years had run from strictly prompt to 60 days slow. The discount of 1 per cent had rarely been taken. At the time, payments were running about 20 days slow. The credit manager had set a line of $100,000 for the account; in view of the current slowness he was anxious to discuss his interpretation of the case with someone outside his own industry. Was credit of $100,000 too high, should it be reduced moderately or substantially, or should the line of credit be completely eliminated? There was no question of extending greater credit!

Basis of Line of Credit

It was early in March when the credit manager of the kraft-paperboard manufacturer dropped in to review the "case." The annual report to the stockholders of the Folding Carton Corporation as of the preceding December 31 had arrived that very morning. The financial statements in that corporate report were also new to the credit man, as he had not seen the report.

The existing credit line of $100,000 had been in force approximately 3 years. It had been confirmed each successive year, based partly upon the favorable experience with the account even though payments had been more than occasionally slow, and partly upon a yearly review of the financial statements. The last balance sheet that the credit manager had studied was now 14½ months old. These figures appear in the column marked B in the comparative tabulation shown in Schedule 1 on page 38.

At the end of year B, the corporation had a tangible net worth of $1,643,453, of which $1,523,720 was represented by the investments in real estate, plants, machinery, and equipment, net after accumulated depreciation. The concern was certainly a representative business enterprise. The current assets totaled $769,603 and the current liabilities $560,063, leaving a net working capital of $209,540. In addition to the current liabilities, there was outstanding $732,670 of 5 per cent debentures, due 12 years in the future. A loss of $161,446 had been assumed on operations for the year. All in all, the financial picture was not exactly bright. As will be shown in later chapters, the investment in fixed assets was obviously top-heavy, the net working capital was light, and the funded debt was excessive for sound operations. However, in view of the fact that the account had been a profitable and a steady customer of the kraft-paperboard manufacturer for a number of years, the credit manager had decided to continue the established line of credit.

Review of Current Figures

Here was the current corporate report to stockholders containing the recent fiscal figures. What did they show? What changes had taken place in the financial picture during the intervening 12 months? So that the changes in the various items in the assets and liabilities from one year to another could be readily observed, the current figures were posted in column A on the comparative statement blank, beside the figures for the two preceding years.

It was now clearly evident from a casual glance at these comparative figures that a material improvement in the financial condition of the corporation had taken place during the preceding year. Net profits after all taxes had amounted to $200,614 and had been kept entirely in the business. No dividends had been declared or paid. The current assets had increased from $769,603 to $852,960, and the current liabilities had been reduced from $560,063 to $390,891, providing a splendid increase in the net working capital to $462,069. The outstanding 5 per cent debentures showed a nominal decrease.

After this very brief and incomplete review of the comparative figures, the mercantile credit manager felt quite reassured. If the corporation had been entitled to a credit line of $100,000 on the figures that were now 14½ months old, the business was surely entitled to at least the same line of credit on the basis of the improvement made during the past year and on the change from an operating loss of $161,446 to a net profit of $200,614 between the 2 years. The credit manager was, of course, assuming that his decision of a year ago had been sound, which might or might not have been the case. This brief study of the figures strengthened his confidence in his earlier judgment, and he went on his way with a light heart, completely reassured.

Desirability of Supplementary Information

Any thorough analysis of the fiscal figures for year A would certainly have involved an attempt to obtain additional essential information. The interpretation of the credit manager, as far as it went, was superficially reasonable; it certainly skimmed the surface. He had made no attempt to apply the X ray and get beneath the surface. No blood count had been made. No blood pressure had been taken. A great deal of vital information was needed for a basic understanding of the financial condition of this enterprise; that information, if obtained, would then need to be carefully studied and analyzed. For example, in spite of the top-heavy investment in land, plants, machinery, and equipment, additional funds had been invested in these assets during the past year. Normally during the year the valuation would have declined to the extent of the depreciation charges less capital funds spent for nominal improvements. The net depreciated value of these fixed assets, however, had actually expanded from $1,523,720 to $1,654,880. What policy had motivated this change? Such information might well have a vital bearing upon the analysis of the figures.

Did the plans of the operating management include any additional expansion in fixed assets during the current year? If not, that was fine. If such expansion was planned, why was it contemplated in the light of the still strained financial condition, and could it be postponed? If it could not be postponed, how large an expenditure would be involved in carrying out the unfinished expansion program? This information was vital for a sound analysis of this corporation.

Miscellaneous receivables, which had been carried at $219,708 in year *C* and at $190,430 in year *B*, had been reduced during the last fiscal year to $23,629. What did this item represent on each of these balance sheets, and what was the explanation of this very desirable and expedient decrease? Were any substantial loans contemplated which might again increase the miscellaneous receivables unduly? Could any additional portion of the receivables due from officers and directors, carried at the not very insignificant figure of $395,889 in year *A*, be collected during the current year? Here were fundamental questions to be answered as a basis for any sound interpretation of the figures.

The careful analysis of balance sheets often involves a clear knowledge and understanding of the financial policies of the operating management, as these policies may result in rapid and radical changes in the financial condition of a business enterprise. These matters were of little interest to the credit manager. If he had considered them of sufficient importance, he would have requested explanations from the treasurer of the debtor corporation. In some cases the information would have been freely given. In other cases it would not have been made available. If the information had not been given, that very policy would then have had to be evaluated by itself as a favorable or an unfavorable piece of information. What reason could a management have not to answer such reasonable questions fully, especially to a large creditor? Absolutely none.

ANALYSIS BY THE COMMERCIAL BANKER

This manufacturer of patented folding cartons maintained depository accounts and obtained credit from three commercial banking institutions. The respective lines of credit granted by these three banks ranged from $200,000 to $300,000. The experienced lending officer of a commercial banking institution operates in a somewhat different manner from the credit manager of a commercial or industrial concern. He handles a much smaller number of accounts. The importance of these accounts, the fact that the banker is rarely very pressed for time, and the fact that he invariably insists upon obtaining more complete information over the years have resulted in a technique whereby he generally secures comprehensive information to assist him in analyzing his accounts. This effective policy on the part of bankers has evolved over the years since James G. Cannon in 1895 remarked that a large number of bankers "through fear of offending their customers, or because of severe competition, . . . have refrained from requesting the information, when they were clearly entitled to receive it."[1] Such days of the mauve decade have long since passed.

Two weeks after the interesting visit from the credit manager of the kraft-paperboard manufacturer, a vice-president of one of the three depository banks met with the author to examine the financial condition of the Folding Carton Corporation from the viewpoint of the lending banker. His viewpoint was somewhat more fundamental than that of the mercantile credit manager. Instead of the rather concise annual corporate report to stockholders, which had contained only the balance sheet and a very condensed income statement, the banker had obtained the complete audit, a report about $\frac{1}{2}$ inch thick consisting of 46 pages, with full supporting information for every item in the balance sheet, a detailed income statement, and a full reconciliation of surplus. The questions outlined in the preceding paragraphs, which had appeared to be casual, or of only passing interest to the credit manager in analyzing the figures, had been of such considerable importance to the banker that he had already discussed them fully with the treasurer of the corporation. This is what he had learned:

Analysis in the Light of Supplementary Information

The increase during the year from $1,523,720 to $1,654,880 in the net depreciated value of the real estate, plants, and equipment had resulted from extensive expenditures to bring the plants to a state of reasonable competitive efficiency. That program was only partially completed. Approximately $200,000 more would be expended during the current year to finish this program. From a long-term viewpoint, the plans were undoubtedly logical but such expenditures would certainly result in an added financial strain for several years. The management had fallen down in the years immediately preceding by not keeping the plants up to operating par by moderate expenditures each year. This growing problem had passed unnoticed until operating costs higher than competitors' had brought the sudden realization of basic past errors.

The decrease in the miscellaneous receivables from $190,430 to $23,629 during the year had resulted primarily from the anticipation of the receipt of $150,000 from a corporation to which a Pacific coast plant had been sold 6 years earlier. According to the original terms of sale, the purchase price of this plant was to have been liquidated by annual payments of $10,000 each year for 9 years, and the balance of $125,000 at the end of the tenth year, with interest at the rate of 4 per cent per annum on the unpaid balance. The entire unpaid balance of $150,000 had been liqui-

---

[1] CANNON, JAMES G., "Losses from Bad Debts," an address delivered before the convention of the New York State Bankers' Association, Saratoga, N.Y., July 11, 1895.

dated during the past year, when a reduction of $5,000 had been offered for an immediate settlement.

The substantial receivables due from officers and directors represented friendly loans that should never have been made. Of the $395,889 outstanding at the end of year A, $350,000 had been borrowed by the four executive officers 8 years earlier to purchase control of a neighboring concern engaged in manufacturing electrical specialties such as fans, motors, and switches. This corporation had become bankrupt 4 years ago and in the interim had been operated by a receiver. To all intents and purposes, the $350,000 had "gone with the wind." When, if ever, and how it would be repaid was a deep mystery. This item, the banker was informed by the treasurer of the corporation, would not be increased under any circumstances during the current fiscal year, and would be decreased only nominally, if at all.

The fixed assets and the miscellaneous receivables were the two items in the comparative balance sheets that had changed substantially during the last fiscal year. With full information at his disposal as a result of these pertinent explanations, the banker was in a quandary. He had been following all developments in the business closely, as any involved program that reduced the net working capital could metamorphose into a serious situation with all bank loans frozen. Such a condition could materialize from operating losses or from relatively heavy expenditures for fixed assets. No chance could be taken on any decrease in net working capital. Here was a basic possibility that apparently had not occurred to the mercantile credit manager.

Bank loans had been granted for several years on the note of the corporation guaranteed by the four officers and the six other directors. This guaranty added moral but no material financial responsibility. In view of the added financial strain that would result in the further expenditure of $200,000 to fulfill the renovation plan, the banker had begun to feel from his analysis that, if he was going to support the management during the very crucial period of the next few years, he should be additionally protected by any available security. If profits were earned to cover the cost of the renovation program while the program was being carried out, the first hurdle would be passed. If losses were assumed, the story would be very different.

The existing bank loans could not possibly be liquidated, even during the low point of seasonal operations, and some moderate increase in the loans might be needed during the peak season of the current year. In the light of this discussion, the banker now decided that it would be necessary for him to obtain and to study monthly budgeted figures, including monthly balance sheets forecast through each month of the current fiscal year, to ascertain the progressive changed conditions which would result

[Schedule 1]   FOLDING CARTON CORPORATION
Comparative Figures for Years Ended December 31, 19—

	(C) Three Years Ago	(B) Two Years Ago	(A) One Year Ago
ASSETS			
Cash........................ $	53,558	$ 141,224	$ 158,596
Notes Receivable..............	32,587	28,642	43,601
Accounts Receivable...........	239,957	193,293	227,604
Inventory.....................:	610,810	406,444	423,159
Current Assets................ $	936,912	$ 769,603	$ 852,960
Plants and Equipment, Net.....	1,609,200	1,523,720	1,654,880
Miscellaneous Receivables.......	219,708	190,430	23,629
Due from Officers and Directors.	446,374	429,289	395,889
Prepaid Expenses..............	24,466	23,144	25,302
Treasury Stock................	9,400	9,400	19,400
Good Will.....................	1	1	1
TOTAL....................	$3,246,061	$2,945,587	$2,972,061
LIABILITIES			
Due to Banks................. $	370,000	$ 275,000	$ 120,000
Accounts Payable..............	197,610	133,938	105,214
Accruals......................	41,559	74,994	63,096
Reserve for Taxes.............	22,792	23,111	49,861
Interest Accrued..............	45,400	43,020	42,720
Cur. Maturity 5% Debentures..	10,000	10,000	10,000
Current Liabilities.............. $	687,361	$ 560,063	$ 390,891
5% Debentures................	744,400	732,670	727,302
Total Liabilities................	$1,431,761	$1,292,733	$1,118,193
5% Cumulative Preferred Stock.	372,300	372,300	372,700
Common Stock................	614,900	614,900	614,900
Earned Surplus................	827,100	665,654	866,268
TOTAL....................	$3,246,061	$2,945,587	$2,972,061
Net Working Capital........... $	249,551	$ 209,540	$ 462,069
Current Ratio..................	1.36	1.37	2.18
Tangible Net Worth............	$1,804,899	$1,643,453	$1,834,467
Net Sales.....................	$3,212,164	$2,846,978	$3,177,128
Net Profits...................	(L)136,562	(L)161,446	200,614
Dividends....................	None	None	None

from the contemplated program and the possible need for greater bank support. If aggregate bank loans in excess of $600,000 would be required during the year, probably a field warehousing arrangement should be set up and the warehouse receipts pledged as additional security to the banks. The banker would know better after he had obtained and studied the budgeted figures.

ANALYSIS BY THE STOCKHOLDER

Two days later, while commuting on the train in the evening, a neighbor of the author sat down beside him. After glancing hastily at the headlines of his newspaper, he put it aside and took an annual corporate report from his pocket. That report had been issued by the same manufacturer of patented folding cartons; it was the same corporate report that had been studied a few days earlier with the mercantile credit manager. The neighbor explained that he owned 200 shares of common stock in the corporation, which he had purchased 6 years ago at $18 per share and which was now selling at $10 per share. When he had purchased the stock, quarterly dividends of 25 cents per share were being paid, but during the last 4 years no dividends whatsoever had been disbursed. Dividend arrears were even accruing on the moderate amount of outstanding 5 per cent cumulative preferred stock. As a stockholder, and a not very experienced financial analyst, he had been studying the figures in the report to determine whether he should continue to hold or sell the stock.

Interest Concentrated on Earnings

In the rather hurried manner so typical of the commuting stockholder he scarcely glanced at the pages containing the balance sheet and the message to stockholders signed by the president, concentrating his attention on the study of the final figure in the income statement, the amount of the net profit for the year. This financial statement disclosed a final net profit, after all charges including taxes, of $200,614, or $1.47 per share after deducting the dividend requirements on the outstanding 5 per cent cumulative preferred stock. This showing was quite impressive, especially when compared with the loss of $1.46 per share of common stock that had been sustained in year B, and the loss of $1.25 per share for year C. My friend now asked if it wouldn't be worth while to hold such a stock, as the trend from a loss of $1.46 per share to a net profit of $1.47 per share was certainly in the right direction. "Moreover," he added, "the stock is now selling at less than eight times earnings," in a voice as though that fact confirmed his assertion. Then, in a more open-minded manner, he asked, "Have you ever heard of the Folding Carton Corporation?"

I am no E. H. Harriman, William Rockefeller, or Mike Meehan! What a security will bring in the market at some time in the future is a mystery that has defied the analysis and intelligence of all except a few insiders, since the days when the agreement that organized the New York Stock Exchange was signed beneath the buttonwood tree in 1792. Fortunately, although there was no categorical answer to the query, the important changes that had taken place in the balance sheet during the preceding fiscal year could be described; he could be told that the financial condition, although somewhat improved, was still noticeably unbalanced, that the program for bringing all plants to competitive efficiency would strain the financial condition more during the present year but improve the possibilities of earning larger profits sometime in the future. All this, however, was on the assumption that the corporation would not become financially involved in the meantime. From this brief but pointed description of what was going on, my investing neighbor would have to draw his own conclusions. The problem of analysis was a considerably more complicated matter than a superficial comparison of net earnings or losses from one year to another.[2]

Absence of Analysis of Financial Statements

Too many stockholders, investors, and speculators unfortunately analyze figures in this rapid and rather irrelevant manner. If they own or contemplate the purchase of bonds or debentures, they are primarily, and

[2] Net profits of business enterprises from one year to another are not the absolute figures which the layman is prone to consider them. George O. May explained the relativity of this net profit figure that appears in audited reports in a lecture "The Accountant and the Investor," given at Northwestern University, Chicago, on Jan. 11, 1932: "In the case of the annual report the primary responsibility for the financial statements submitted to shareholders rests with the officers and directors, and the function of the accountant is to advise the shareholders whether, in his opinion, the statements so submitted fairly present the position of the company and the results of its operations. The investor has the right to assume that the figures, let us say, of earnings, presented by an accountant in a prospectus represent the accountant's own best judgment of the results for the period which they cover. In the case of similar figures appearing in the annual report of a corporation, not quite the same assumption can properly be made. In this case, the figures should represent the best judgment of the officers and the directors—a judgment, however, which the auditor either concurs in or regards as being within the reasonable limits of a legitimate difference of opinion, unless the contrary is indicated by his certificate. . . . Often, perhaps usually, the accounts presented in an annual report are the results of discussion between the officers or directors of the corporation and its independent auditors, and represent their combined judgment. But the representatives of the corporation, on the one hand, and the accountant, on the other, may not entirely agree, and in such a case the accountant can properly accept the judgment of the corporation's representatives if he is satisfied that it is honestly formed and inherently reasonable. Suppose, for instance, the question to be what provision for depreciation is required; and suppose that the directors, if left to themselves, would consider a provision of $50,000 as adequate, while the auditor would favor the provision of from $80,000 to $100,000. The directors may agree to provide $70,000 if thereby they can secure the auditor's unqualified certificate to the accounts. For the purposes of an annual report, the auditor would be quite justified in accepting this solution, perhaps saying in his certificate that the provision made is reasonable. But if he was preparing figures for a prospectus, the sole responsibility for which would be his, he would be bound to give expression to his own final judgment, though in reaching that judgment he would naturally give full consideration to the views of the company's representatives."—MAY, GEORGE O., *Twenty-five Years of Accounting Responsibility, 1911–1936*, Vol. I, pp. 6–7 (American Institute Publishing Co., Inc., New York, 1936).

often solely, interested in ascertaining how many times the interest requirement is earned; if they own or contemplate the purchase of stocks, they are substantially interested in learning what the earnings are per share on the various issues of outstanding stock. Whether the financial condition of the corporation is healthy, unhealthy, or affected by a touch of jaundice—a situation which the mercantile credit manager and the banker investigate in various manners and in widely different degrees of individual thoroughness—is too rarely of real interest. Occasionally corporations, even though their figures show yearly earnings, simultaneously are headed downhill for the crash of bankruptcy. This fact is often recognized by a little more fundamental analysis of the relationship between strategic items in comparative yearly balance sheets.

It is the unusual annual report to stockholders that contains sufficient information for a comprehensive financial analysis. That is why wide-awake creditors require more basic supplementary information. The thoroughgoing technique of the banker in obtaining this information particularly exemplifies the care used in a complete analysis. The need for this essential information never entered the head of the stockholder. He was too inexperienced, too much an amateur in the game of utilizing figures to the greatest possible advantage, to understand their limitations and their inadequacies.

ANALYSIS BY THE TREASURER

Finally, to make this coincidence complete, after a week had passed the treasurer of the Folding Carton Corporation came in. He had no idea that the author was familiar with his business. He came in to discuss the practicability of his long-term financial program for placing the corporation in a gradually but steadily improving financial condition. Here was a person who was in a position different from that of any of the other three men who had explored the affairs of this enterprise, each in his individual way; the treasurer had the maximum amount of operating, financial, and supplementary information.

The credit manager, who should have sought more facts, had very limited information; the lending banker had obtained full details on those particular points that had seemed essential to him when analyzing the figures; the stockholder had failed to take advantage of even the limited amount of available information and had given not even a passing thought to obtaining the additional facts necessary to draw reasonable conclusions from the available figures. The treasurer, with the full information, was making a basic analysis to determine financial policies. Was the business in satisfactory financial shape? If not, why not, and what should be done about it? If the business was in satisfactory financial shape, what policies should be set in motion that would improve even that condition? His interest was from the long-term viewpoint of obtaining the maximum of net profits over the years, not the maximum of immediate profits, the shortsighted policy that has been the ruin of untold thousands of business enterprises.

The treasurer was forty-six years of age, sincere, hard-working, conscientious, and capable. His entire business career had been spent with this corporation. He had entered its employ when he had graduated from college 24 years ago and here he had remained, gradually receiving increased responsibilities as he had grown with the business. For 6 years he had held his present office. Although the treasurer was most conscientious, this background of many years of experience had not of necessity trained him to meet all the problems with which he might be confronted. He was faced with decisions on problems that he had never had occasion to study.

By now the financial background of this particular corporation was quite familiar to the author, who listened while the treasurer outlined what was on his mind. The analysis in this case was not difficult, but sometimes it is hard to present the basic conclusions of an analysis to a businessman, even to a treasurer, who often has preconceived ideas based upon rarefied generalities rather than on experience or genuine knowledge. To crystallize the situation, the visitor was asked what proportion of the tangible net worth of a manufacturer of paper cartons should normally be invested in fixed assets, that is, in the net depreciated value of real estate, buildings, machinery, and equipment. After a moment or two of cogitation he pointed to the item of $1,654,880 in the balance sheet of year A and explained that the management had plans to spend $200,000 more, together with earned depreciation, to bring the plants to top efficiency during the current year; that would make a total of approximately $1,850,000, which he believed was necessary for proper operations. That was not a direct answer. The question called for a normative answer; the reply was nothing but a statement of the existing and the contemplated conditions in this particular enterprise.

Fixed Assets Heavy

The last fiscal balance sheet showed a tangible net worth of $1,834,467. This figure represented the sum of the outstanding 5 per cent cumulative preferred stock carried at $372,700, the common stock of $614,900, and the earned surplus of $866,268, less the two intangible items in the assets, treasury stock carried at $19,400 and good will at $1. When the reconditioning program was completed the corporation, if operations in the meantime had been conducted on a break-even basis, would have slightly more than its entire tangible net worth invested in fixed assets. That was certainly an excessive proportion, as the typical concern in this field has approximately 54 per cent of its tangible net worth invested in fixed assets, and in many cases the proportion is below $33\frac{1}{3}$ per cent. Here was the basic trouble with this corporation. The center of gravity was too high. The plant investment to allow a normally healthy financial condition for a corporation of this size should have been in the neighborhood of $990,000. The actual investment in fixed assets was top-heavy and, according to plans which were being carried out, the investment in these assets was going higher.

Funded Debt Heavy

A mistaken policy of expansion had been pursued 8 or 10 years ago when the last plant had been erected. Sufficient funds had not been invested in the corporation at that time to support such an expansion program; as a result, the business had been continuously cramped for net working capital. In fact, there would have been no net working capital over the years if there had not happened to be outstanding an issue of 5 per cent debentures, amounting to $727,302 on the last fiscal balance sheet. As will be shown later, the financial condition of commercial and industrial concerns is extended when the net working capital is less than the amount of any outstanding funded debt. At the end of year A, the net working capital at $462,069 was 36.5 per cent less than the amount of the outstanding 5 per cent debentures.

Net Working Capital Light

Under the existing program of expansion, an increased volume of business would need to be obtained to keep the machinery in full operation. An increased volume of sales would necessitate the carrying of a larger raw-material inventory and larger receivables which, in turn, would mean more borrowings, if possible, from depository banks. In the meantime the net working capital would shrink to the difference between the additional $200,000 to be put into fixed assets and any net profits earned during the year plus depreciation. In other words, the financial condition was going to become more strained during the next year or two under the contemplated program, rather than less strained.

Alternative Policies for the Management

The management was gambling on the future. If net profits were earned the funds would need to be kept in the business for many years to improve the condition gradually; no dividends could be declared to stockholders under a sound financial policy. Net profits, however, were not assured, as the income account would be overburdened from a competitive viewpoint with depreciation charges on the top-heavy investment in plants and equipment, and with the interest charges on the outstanding debentures. In other words, most competitors would be operating with smaller depreciation charges and with no interest costs on funded debt. If little or no profits were earned to reduce the bank debt, the bankers might feel that it would be necessary to take hold, that is, to put new management in the enterprise for the express purpose of liquidating the bank debt in any and every possible manner. Moreover there was a distinct possibility that with increasing loans necessary during the current season, the banks might insist on additional collateral to protect their loans. The outlook was quite clouded.

As these matters were considered step by step, the treasurer clearly understood the reasoning in this analysis. The receivables were in good shape, the inventory had been kept down to the lowest possible level, and the current liabilities fluctuated primarily with the amount of bank borrowings. The fundamental problems of this business could be traced to the single decision of overexpansion with insufficient capital funds, which had occurred 8 years or so ago.

It now became a matter of deciding upon the policy for the immediate future. What could be done, if anything, to ease the situation? Four different policies could be followed. First, an attempt might be made to raise at least $400,000 additional capital from the stockholders to be invested in the business and be represented by some type of prior preferred stock. Second, an attempt might be made to sell one of the plants, and any cash funds obtained in this manner could be used to increase the net working capital. Third, the present policy of renovation, involving the additional expenditure of $200,000, could be immediately discontinued. Fourth, the present management policy of bringing the plants up to the minute could be carried out with the full knowledge that such a policy was gambling on the future and that the business might become bankrupt if a high level of sales was not obtained at a profit during this period.

RECAPITULATION

This problem illustrates how four men in possession of varying amounts of information analyzed the annual financial statements of the same business enterprise, each from a somewhat different viewpoint, and each with a different background of financial knowledge and experience. The treasurer, with complete information at his disposal, was trying to make the most fundamental analysis. Many men in similar positions have lacked adequate knowledge and qualified experience to arrive at sound conclusions based upon the logical analysis of figures. This particular treasurer was interested in determining the policies that would improve, if possible, the financial condition of his corporation in the long run. The banker, in his analysis, was interested in ascertaining whether his extension of short-term credit was fundamentally sound, whether it was adequately secured, and whether any changes might take place in the condition of the business during the current year that might jeopardize the soundness of his loan. The mercantile credit manager, who in this particular case was somewhat less thorough, was interested in continuing his line of credit, but with no undue risk of loss. The stockholder, with no information at his disposal except the annual corporate report to stockholders, lacked the background to make any real analysis. If his interest had been substantial, a condition that occurs whenever control of a business enterprise is purchased, the analysis would have been made on the basis that the investment would be a continuing one for a number of years. Such a viewpoint would have been similar to that of the treasurer who was concerned with both earnings and financial strength.

A fundamental analysis of the financial statements from the viewpoint of the treasurer would have served the banker, the mercantile credit manager, and the stockholder, but rarely do these individuals have the complete information at their disposal to make such a thorough, independent analysis. Moreover, the credit manager, who handles from 100 to 5,000 accounts, often lacks the time to study his accounts in an intensive manner, except those few to which large lines of credit have been accorded and those that give clear evidence of weakness. On the other hand, the lending officers of commercial banking institutions and mercantile credit managers are often more experienced in the interpretation of figures than the treasurers of business corporations, as it is a part of their everyday livelihood to be able to analyze financial statements conclusively.

The interpretation of financial statements, no matter from what point of view, is the same provided the analyst has obtained full essential information, provided he is qualified to make the analysis, and provided the analysis is basic and thorough. Whether the analyst is a business executive, a commercial or investment banker, an investor, a speculator, a business counselor, a mercantile credit manager, or a layman makes no material difference. After the basic analysis is made, then individuals in different positions will act upon the conclusions of that analysis in different ways.

An analysis might indicate that a particular enterprise is carrying an excessive inventory. On the basis of this conclusion a business executive might decide the risk is worth while because a shortage of certain raw materials is indicated, in his judgment, by the market. The commercial banker on the same analysis might decide that the business executive was overoptimistic, that there probably would be no shortage, and that prices might fall. In this situation, he would demand additional security to protect his loan. The investor or the speculator might take either viewpoint, or he might decide that prices would probably remain stable, and as long as the excess inventory was worked off during the next 10 or 12 months, it would make no material difference one way or the other. The business counselor might agree with the banker that a business enterprise should never carry excessive inventory and would advise that it be reduced to a reasonable level as rapidly as possible without disturbing normal operations. The mercantile credit manager, who is passing on the credit for the sale of that merchandise on 30- or 60-day terms, probably would decide that he was taking no risk for such a short term, but that he might well look the account over carefully in 6 months or so. The fact that the inventory was heavy should have been recognized by each analyst, but after that recognition was established, conclusions drawn from the same fact would vary.

In this volume balance sheets and income statements will be analyzed in cases where no supplementary information, supporting data, or segregation of important items is available. In other cases, the help and light thrown on situations by pertinent supplementary information and explanations of changes in balance sheet proportions between successive years will be utilized.

THEORY AND PROBLEMS

1. If a thorough, comprehensive analysis of comparative figures were made by several different individuals, would there be appreciable differences in the analyses? Explain your answer. Would there be differences in their respective viewpoints? Explain your answer.

2. In what two ways are analyses by different individuals fundamentally qualified?

3. Describe the viewpoint of a mercantile creditor toward an account where his extension of credit is (a) relatively small, (b) relatively large.

4. Is a commercial banker likely to analyze a risk more or less thoroughly than a mercantile creditor? Explain.

5. What financial information interests the typical stockholder in analysis? Is such an interest fundamental? If you were a stockholder would you make a more thorough analysis?

6. Who is likely to have the most comprehensive information, including supplementary facts, up-to-date knowledge of operations, and policies? Should such an individual be able to make the most logical analysis? Is he generally able to do so? Why?

7. Compare briefly the viewpoints toward the same business concern of (a) a mercantile creditor, (b) a commercial banker, (c) a stockholder, and (d) a financial executive of the business.

8. Commercial bankers extend credit to commercial and industrial business concerns on many different bases: unsecured, against trust receipts, warehouse receipts, assigned accounts receivable, discounted notes receivable, the pledge of life insurance policies, and the pledge of securities or properties. Should the fact that a banker may grant credit in these different ways affect his analysis of the financial condition of a prospective borrower?

9. In this chapter analyses of the affairs of the Folding Carton Corporation were made by a mercantile credit manager, a commercial banker, a stockholder, and the treasurer of the company. State briefly the high lights of each analysis.

CHAPTER III

Desirability of Supplementary Information

The aggregate of credit information obtained regarding any business enterprise falls into three divisions. These divisions of information, even if logical, are somewhat arbitrary. This classification applies as well to a business concern where the owner is carefully laying a basis for a fraudulent failure as to a business enterprise that is legitimate according to all recognized standards; to a general country store selling merchandise on Tobacco Road and to a $100,000,000 corporation engaged in the manufacture of automobiles, trucks, refrigerators, and electric-light systems through a galaxy of subsidiary organizations, and then the distribution of these products in every state in the Union and in foreign countries throughout the world. These three helpful, if absolute, divisions of credit information are (1) antecedent information, (2) investigational facts, and (3) financial information. What is the exact field of each of these divisions of credit information and why do they tie in with the analysis of financial statements?

Antecedent information covers the complete business record of each of the men who comprise the operating management of a business, and of the owners if they are not included in the active management in the case of all except large corporations, their age, whether they are married or unmarried, and, if they have children, the number, sex, and age of the children. It also includes information as to whether each of these individuals had previously been employed by others, if so by whom and in what capacity; whether they had previously been in business on their own account and where; the lines of business activity in which they had formerly been employed or had operated; the department that each is now handling of the particular business under scrutiny; his particular experience in that division of business activity; and a detailed historical record of the business enterprise itself. If the record of any of these individuals involved fires or failures, full information regarding the surrounding circumstances is absolutely essential; and if any have been involved in failures, how much on the dollar was paid to unsecured creditors in each case. Accurate, comprehensive information on all these points is essential background for practical credit analysis. There is no system that will provide this information automatically; it is obtained by bankers, mercantile credit men, and the trained reporters of mercantile credit agencies, all of whom realize the deep significance of comprehensive antecedent information, by digging deeply, by being ever alert, and by searching inquiringly.

Investigational facts cover the relative information obtained from depository banking institutions, from lending agencies of the Federal government, from finance companies and factors, occasionally from insurance companies that have granted term loans, and from mercantile trade circles.

From banking quarters there would be developed the approximate size of the average balances that had been maintained during recent months, whether checks had been drawn on uncollected funds, whether checks had been returned because of insufficient funds; whether the concern was or was not borrowing at the moment, if so, how much, and whether on a secured or on an unsecured basis. If borrowings were on a secured basis, then it would be extremely pertinent to ascertain whether this security consisted of real estate mortgages, stock exchange collateral, cash surrender value of life insurance, warehouse receipts, trust receipts, assigned receivables, discounted notes receivable, assignment of claims under a government contract, or some other form of security. It would also include the candid regard, based upon his direct relationship, that the banker who handled the account had for the management of the particular business enterprise under consideration. From lending agencies of the Federal government, from finance companies and factors, there would be developed the size and fluctuations in borrowings and the nature of security pledged to secure the loan; in case of a term loan, the yearly installment payments to maturity would also be ascertained.

The trade investigation would cover the multitude of facts that are obtained from merchandise suppliers such as recent high credit, amount owing, amount past due, if any; whether payments are discounted, prompt, or slow, and if slow, how many days slow; whether notes are given to close out past-due accounts, whether unearned discounts are ever taken, whether, in the parlance of the market, the management is likely to welch on orders or contracts in a falling market. While this information might just as well be written in Sanskrit for the uninitiated, it is vital information to the skilled credit analyst.

Financial information would cover all available financial facts. These facts might consist in an extreme case merely of a rumor that a concern had an investment of a certain amount of money, $5,000, $10,000, or $100,000. At the other extreme, a $100,000,000 corporation with 103 active subsidiaries might readily furnish detailed annual audits with individual and consolidated balance sheets of the parent company and all subsidiaries, income statements, reconciliation of surplus in all instances, explanations of all unusual items, breakdowns of merchandise and receivables, explanations of changes in proportions between items, and full explanations of all intercompany loans and merchandise transactions.

In other words, financial information comprises only a part of all the data that are utilized, studied, and analyzed in the determination of the soundness of the credit risk of a commercial or industrial business enterprise. Analyses of financial statements can be made without supplementary information, but the most thorough interpretation of financial information often can be made only when a considerable amount of these pertinent supplementary data have been obtained. The appreciation of the full significance of antecedent information, investigational facts, explanations of unusual balance sheet items, and changes in proportions between items in comparative financial statements is far more widespread in commercial banking credit and mercantile credit circles than in investment banking and investment circles.[1] The pertinent supplementary information may be summarized very succinctly as follows:

1. Antecedent information and investigational facts which tend to give a viewpoint toward the analyses of financial statements; that is, which tend to indicate whether a particular financial statement is:
    a. An incorrect representation dishonestly made.
    b. An honest representation incorrectly made.
    c. An adequate representation, according to accepted accounting principles and practices, honestly made.
2. Explanations regarding all items in a financial statement which are not clear per se and then further explanations regarding the reasons for the increases or the decreases in important items at least during the period over which the figures are being analyzed.

Examples of an incorrect representation dishonestly made and an honest representation incorrectly made will be found in the following pages of this chapter. Many examples of adequate representations, according to accepted accounting principles and practices, honestly made, which are characteristic of most financial statements, will be found in succeeding chapters. Many examples showing the need of explanatory infor-

---

[1] "The conference revealed further that, while the New York Stock Exchange was accepting these qualified and unrevealing balance sheets, credit men generally realized their danger and have insisted for a considerable period on balance sheets that were not qualified as to 'collusive fraud.' The credit men inform us that they have been extraordinarily successful in this regard. It appears, therefore, that credit men are less gullible and trusting than the investment group in that they demand information more completely verified for their employers than do the investment bankers for their clients."—From the *Report on Conference on Accounting Practice and Procedure,* dated Jan. 17, 1939, called pursuant to the order of John J. Bennett Jr., attorney general of the State of New York, as a result of the fraud perpetrated by the management of McKesson & Robbins, Inc.

mation of specific items in financial statements and changes in these items from year to year will appear in Part III of this volume.

ANTECEDENT INFORMATION

The balance sheet of a retail business enterprise that had been in existence 18 months disclosed a tangible net worth of $35,230. The president of the corporation, over a period of 16 active and interesting years prior to the organization of this particular enterprise, had been associated with a variety of concerns that had had five fires and four failures. After one of the fires, this commercial adventurer had been convicted of arson and sentenced to 4 years' confinement behind massive stone walls; in three of the failures, creditors had received less than 20 cents on the dollar.

Many businessmen are unconsciously prone to overstate their assets and to understate their liabilities, particularly if they are operating small or moderate-sized concerns. It is so simple to value a piece of merchandise just a trifle higher than it should be valued, to purchase a secondhand printing press or a used showcase and then give the asset a value on the books that is somewhat higher because "it was purchased low and is actually worth more than it cost." This viewpoint has been fostered in a refined way by appraisal companies,[2] so it would be very unnatural if small enterprises did not follow the same policy to some modest extent.

An individual with a record of five fires and four failures would be quite prone to exaggerate, not unconsciously but consciously, and probably to a very marked degree. No one with a practical knowledge of credits would attempt to analyze the figures of a business concern under such irresponsible management on the same basis as he would analyze the figures of a business enterprise that had had a successful operating record of 12 years under the leadership of one individual who had had no fires or failures, and who bore a widespread reputation for probity. The confidence with which figures are studied and analyzed depends, in the first place, upon the confidence with which the active management of a business enterprise is generally regarded. That is axiomatic in the credit world. It is not quite so axiomatic in the investment world.

Typical Situation with Unfavorable Antecedent Information

A successful manufacturer of cotton thread recently stated that he had been having difficulty in collecting a particular past-due account, and described the following situation: Credit for $1,100 had been extended to a wholesaler of textile specialties, such as thread, buttons, pins, and

[2] See Chap. VII, "What Re-appraisals Mean to the Stockholders," in *Are You a Stockholder?* by Alden Winthrop (Covici, Friede, Inc., New York, 1937).

needles, located in Chicago. When the account had been 4 months past due and the creditor had been unable to obtain even a partial payment on account, a representative had visited the wholesaler to ascertain, if possible, the reason for the continued delinquency. The manufacturer then went on to explain, "When our representative arrived at their quarters, he found that the concern had moved about 90 per cent of its merchandise next door where it was on the premises of a neighbor; the shelves in the place of business, when carefully examined, were found to be stacked with empty boxes."

That credit of $1,100 had been extended on an analysis of a comparatively recent balance sheet that showed an excellent financial condition. Anyone with a superficial knowledge of everyday practical credit technique would have known, however, that the figures were absolutely worthless in view of the impaired records of the two partners in that business. The balance sheet on which that credit had been so freely and innocently granted showed current assets of $28,156.20, a current debt of $7.15, and a tangible net worth of $26,774.05.[3] On a casual examination, if the concern owed only $7.15 it was probably entitled to reasonable credit, but hardly to credit of $1,100.

One partner in that concern, an individual who was only thirty-six years of age, had had four failures in which creditors had received 20, 24, 22, and 28 cents on the dollar. Those failures had been eminently successful! The other partner was thirty-eight years of age, and, in the course of his unique and checkered career, had been involved in one fire and in three failures. On the bare record of these two individuals, it was evident that the figures were just about as reliable as Cook's reported discovery of the North Pole, and should have been given no passing consideration whatsoever, except as a running study in the current technique of perpetrating one more mercantile fraud.[4]

---

[3] For legal recourse of a defrauded creditor who has extended credit on the basis of a signed fraudulent financial statement, see Arthur E. Fixel, *False Financial Statements: Remedies of Defrauded Creditors*, 2d ed. (Matthew Bender & Co. Inc., Albany, N.Y., 1934). See also *Credit Manual of Commercial Laws*, published annually by the National Association of Credit Management.

[4] The laws of France which were made under the watchful eyes of Colbert (1619–1683) were particularly stringent regarding fraudulent bankruptcy. Colbert, who used every means in his power to foster French industry and commerce, had no consideration whatsoever for the fraud. The Code of Commerce of March, 1673, based upon years of painstaking investigation, provided the death penalty for a fraudulent bankruptcy. Apparently the penalty was not immediately carried out, as a description has come down of the punishment meted out to two such offenders, Jean Francois Le Mercier and Jean-Baptiste Desues on May 30, 1673. "Condemned to make the *amende honorable*, the two offenders, clad only in shirts, a cord around the neck of each, a placard proclaiming his crimes, fastened to each, and each grasping a lighted torch weighing two pounds, were led to the steps of the Palais de Justice. There they were made to ask pardon for their sins of God, of the king, and of justice. Then, conducted by an executioner, they were led along the rue Saint-Honoré and the rue

The inevitable finally happened, and without much loss in time. Within 2 weeks after the visit from the representative of the thread manufacturer, the partners closed the premises and never again appeared on the scene of that action. In military science that would have been termed a successful strategic retreat. When the premises were examined the following morning, absolutely nothing of value was found. The maximum of possible credit had been incurred; when things began to get too hot, the partners had double-locked the front door and had disappeared. Trade obligations were not confined to $7.15; they were actually in excess of $18,400, several of the items having been placed in the hands of attorneys for collection. Even the landlord was a creditor to the extent of $190. Losses to creditors were 100 per cent, no more, no less! Here was an evident case of an incorrect representation dishonestly made.

Antecedent Information Important in Large Corporations

The fundamental importance of having comprehensive information regarding the records of those who comprise the management staff and, wherever possible, qualified opinions regarding their ability and conscientiousness as well as their integrity is just as essential with large corporations as with small business enterprises. Lightning may not strike quite so often on large corporations but when it does, financial statements are wrecked beyond all recognition.

If any creditor, stockholder, or investor in McKesson & Robbins, Inc., had had the slightest inkling in 1938 that Frank Donald Coster, for 12 years the president of the corporation, was actually one Philip M. Musica who, many years previously, had been convicted of notorious commercial frauds, the annual financial statements over the years would never have been accepted with such complete confidence, even though the audits bore the signature of an outstanding, nationally recognized firm of public accountants. In carrying out this particular calculated fraud, Coster had been assisted by his three brothers: George E. Dietrich, assistant treasurer of the corporation, who in reality was George Musica; Robert J. Dietrich, head of the shipping, receiving, and warehousing department at the home

---

Saint-Denis to the Croix du Tiroir, where they asked pardon again. Then they were led through the rue des Prouaries to the public pillory. There they asked pardon for the third time. Later they were attached to the pillory for two hours on each of three market days. Finally they were made to pay heavy fines and were sent to the galleys for nine years. Savory reports that everyone 'agreed that the punishment of death would not have been so cruel.' "—COLE, CHARLES W., *Colbert and a Century of French Mercantilism*, Vol. 1, pp. 360, 368 (Columbia University Press, New York, 1939). The laws of Catalonia (now the eastmost part of Spain) "punished by death the moneychanger who was unable to pay his creditors; an unfortunate changer was beheaded in front of his *taula* (bank) as late as 1360."—*The Cambridge Economic History of Europe*, Vol. II, p. 347 (Cambridge University Press, New York, 1952).

, and of Allied Crude Vegetable Oil Refining Corporation
under the ~~dual~~ management of Anthony D² Angelis ✓.

offices, a strategic department in the perpetration of this fraud, who in
reality was Robert Musica; and George Vernard, who managed the
offices, mailing addresses, bank accounts, and other activities of the
dummy concerns with which McKesson & Robbins, Inc., supposedly conducted business, and who in reality was Arthur Musica.

Of greater importance financially and internationally were the even
wider ramifications of the International Match Corporation under the
mysterious and enlightened touch of Ivar Kreuger. The loss to stockholders of McKesson & Robbins, Inc., was approximately $21,000,000,
while the losses to the stockholders and to the creditors of Ivar Kreuger's
fantastic creations went into the hundreds of millions of dollars. Cagliostro
was a babe in arms compared with these practical fertile minds.

These cases illustrate the great importance of correlating adequate
antecedent information with financial information.[5] In banking and mercantile credit circles the basic importance of antecedent information is
quite uniformly realized.[6] Outside these circles, antecedent information
is more infrequently used, for two reasons: first, such information is rarely
available in other quarters; and second, there is little realization of the
distinct importance of this type of supplementary information. In this
volume the financial statements of commercial and industrial business
enterprises, both small and large, will be analyzed without any antecedent
information. The assumption will be made, however, that if available, the
antecedent information would be of a uniformly favorable nature.

INVESTIGATIONAL INFORMATION

Information that is developed in banking and in mercantile trade quarters occasionally provides a helpful bearing toward the analysis of a particular financial statement. This information is not so spectacular as the
varied escapades of a confirmed business marauder, but it is often just as
useful.

Bank Investigation

Now and then it is learned, for example, that a depository bank is extending credit to a commercial or industrial business enterprise only on a

✓ This story is told in great detail in The Great Salad Oil Swindle by Norman C. Miller
(Coward McCann, Inc., New York, 1965).

[5] Breakdown in the moral hazard plays a prominent part in fraudulent fires as well
as in planned failures. See Chap. VII in *Behind the Scenes of Business*, pp. 105–131,
by Roy A. Foulke (Dun & Bradstreet, Inc., New York, 1953).

[6] The mercantile credit agencies, large and small, general and specialized, are the
great sources of antecedent information. The Better Business Bureaus, operating
in ~~January, 1961~~, in ~~the 102~~ principal cities in the United States, ~~12~~ in Canada, ~~and~~
1 in Mexico, are also valuable sources of information regarding the escapades of
questionable characters.

July, 1965

120

, in Venezuela, and 1 in Israel,   , 1 in Porto Rico)

secured basis, while other concerns in the same line of business activity and of about the same size are granted credit freely on their own unsecured promissory notes. Such a situation immediately raises the questions "Why is security sought from this enterprise? Why must one concern pledge assets for a 3 or 6 months' loan while others in the same approximate category are not required to do so?" A background of some business routine, knowledge, and experience is needed to answer these questions.

Once in a great while, a business enterprise in healthy financial shape will pledge stocks and bonds as collateral to a loan, not because it is necessary to pledge these assets to obtain the loan, but because a lower rate of interest may be charged by the banker in extending credit on an adequately secured basis than on an unsecured basis. This situation, however, is one which only rarely comes to light.

A second situation occasionally arises when a business enterprise owns government securities that have been in the custody of a depository bank for safekeeping and for servicing over many years. At some time over these intervening years when the financial condition of the concern was slightly extended, cash was needed; instead of selling the securities, the management pledged them to the bank for a loan. At the time, no loan could have been obtained from the depository bank without the pledge of these securities. The financial condition has since improved, but the earlier outdated arrangement has continued automatically in force. If the treasurer of the corporation should discuss this situation with his banker, the security would most certainly be released and current loans would be granted on unsecured promissory notes.

A third set of circumstances exists in cases where it is customary in certain lines of business activity to pledge security to a bank for a loan, as in the importation of foreign merchandise under letters of credit, in day loans to an investment banker, and in secured loans to stock exchange brokers. These situations are all more or less normal and carry no suspicious implications when financial statements are under analysis. The unfavorable situations are of more interest, as they indicate a financial condition that appears weak to the commercial banker who is in intimate touch with the account, and who feels that, in order to protect the interest of the bank, he must obtain adequate security. The mere fact that borrowings are secured in such cases should confirm the views of the analyst, or make him pause if, in his opinion, the figures seemed to represent a satisfactory financial condition.

Implication of Secured Bank Loan. Wood Turning Company, Inc., has been in existence 18 years as manufacturers of an extensive line of wooden products such as pillboxes, handles, spindles, spools, dowels, buttons, moulds, and shooks. The last fiscal balance sheet disclosed what seemed to be an apparently satisfactory financial condition with current assets of

$128,790, current liabilities of $60,025, and a tangible net worth of $105,602. The current assets were slightly more than twice as large as the current liabilities and the current debt, in turn, represented a satisfactory relationship with the tangible net worth. The annual net sales amounted to $315,621, indicating what we shall learn later are attractive turnover relationships.

The current liabilities, however, contained an item of $24,568 due a depository bank. This item immediately drew attention as it ended in an exact number "568." All bank loans, except where some unusual situation exists, are made in round numbers. In this case the amount due to the bank would normally have been $24,500 or $25,000. An explanation was sought. That explanation centered around the fact that the bank loan was secured. Instead of granting the loan on the customary unsecured promissory note basis, the banker has extended credit on assigned accounts receivable. What was the reason? Why did the banker not consider the account a safe loan on the typical unsecured basis? Why did he insist upon some kind of security?

A friendly interview gave the answer. Of the current assets, $73,212 represented inventory. An inventory of this size without additional information was a little large. The banker explained that of this inventory, $36,000 represented one order for wooden handles of a very specialized design that had been manufactured during the preceding year for a concern that had become bankrupt just prior to the time the order was completed and ready for delivery. No prospective purchaser had since been found for these handles. If a purchaser could be located during the next few months, probably the handles could be sold at only a moderate loss or possibly with a moderate profit. If a purchaser could not be located shortly, the handles would have to be disposed of as secondhand merchandise and a very substantial loss would be assumed. The banker was anxious to see how this situation turned out before granting unsecured credit.

In a situation such as this, the analysis is thus tied up with intimate knowledge of the exact operations of the business enterprise. Information of this confidential nature is at times known to the analyst; at other times it is not available. The skillful analyst would probably have elicited the information from the management, if he had not visited the banker, by seeking an explanation as to why the inventory was somewhat heavy.

Trade Investigation

Time and time again, a casual study of a balance sheet has seemed to disclose a fairly satisfactory condition, but a review of the results of a current trade investigation has shown that a substantial portion of payments was running slow. Here is a danger signal never to be overlooked. If the figures were actually as sound as they seemed to be, there could have been no slow payments unless the bookkeeper had gone to sleep on his job. Sometimes the fiscal figures have been 10 or 11 months old and the financial condition has changed substantially in the interim. At other times the fundamental condition has not changed, but the exact situation is not evident without a deep-probing, basic analysis. The contradiction between slow trade payments and an apparently satisfactory financial condition always necessitates study. The facts must correlate.

Sometimes a business enterprise will be "in season" and the financial condition with heavy merchandise, substantial receivables, and heavy liabilities will be so different from the fiscal figures that the fiscal figures are absolutely useless for a current analysis. Only an up-to-the-minute trial balance or balance sheet would indicate the exact financial condition. The concern may actually be overextended because of its seasonal operations. This condition develops with concerns in many lines of activity, such as canners of fruit and vegetables and manufacturers of ladies' coats, suits, dresses, silk underwear, men's suits, and bathrobes.

The fiscal figures in other cases may be fundamentally unsound, and the weakness may be discovered only by a most careful analysis. Any one or all of five situations may exist: (1) part of the cash may be tied up or blocked; (2) the accounts and notes receivable may include a substantial amount of past-due accounts, or a large sum due from officers, employees, subsidiaries, or affiliated concerns; (3) the inventory may be heavy with items long out of style, or overvalued with secondhand items or with returns, or arbitrarily inflated at a figure higher than cost or market, whichever is lower; (4) the current liabilities may have been understated, consciously or unconsciously; and (5) a particular asset in the balance sheet may be carried at an equity figure and consequently fail to disclose a substantial offsetting liability.

Pertinent information that will give a more exact approximation of each of these five items, which at times are over- or undervalued, should always be sought from the operating management. The management staff knows, or should know, how the amount of each item is determined, and if they are frank and open in their discussions regarding the figures, the analyst could not misunderstand them. The analyst, however, often has no opportunity to discuss these problems verbally with the management. The lack of net sales figures may also present a problem, as net sales figures, if available and properly used in an analysis, may indicate that the receivables are heavy, for which an explanation should then be obtained, or that the inventory is excessive for the sound operation of the business.

Implication of Slow Trade Payments. Two or more of these unusual situations occasionally come to light in the study of a particular account. A hosiery manufacturer, for example, was running from 10 to 30 days slow in the payment of its yarn accounts. The business had been in existence about 8 years, producing fine-wearing hosiery. In recent years, net profits had increased steadily. A fiscal balance sheet that was about 3 months old gave no evident reason for the trade slowness. These figures disclosed current assets of $422,434 and a current indebtedness of $201,866. The current assets were well distributed among cash, receivables, and merchandise, although the receivables appeared to be somewhat heavy.

As the mill was located in the South, further investigation was postponed until the treasurer's next visit to New York, when he furnished explanations regarding certain items in the fiscal balance sheet. Two items in particular provided all the answers to the temporary mystery. The first was receivables of $170,788. Questioned whether this entire amount was due from customers for the sale of hosiery, or whether it included some miscellaneous receivables due from officers, employees, stockholders, or others, he admitted that through some "oversight" there had been included $60,000 of loans made to officers and directors during the preceding year. By no stretch of the imagination, or according to any sound accounting theory, should such an item have been included with regular trade receivables and have been considered a current asset. To say the least, it was a unique "oversight"!

Second, the merchandise had been included in the balance sheet under the most unusual caption of *Equity in Merchandise*. He was asked what the "equity" meant. Actually, the concern had an inventory of $304,532! One-half this inventory, that is, $152,266, had been pledged to a local bank for a loan of $100,000; this equity of $52,266 plus the unpledged inventory had been carried in the balance sheet at $204,532. The inventory, should, of course, have been carried at $304,532 and an additional $100,000 should have been included in the current liabilities. With the adjustments in the receivables, the inventory, and the current liabilities, the balance sheet disclosed current assets of $462,434 and current liabilities of $301,866. Instead of the net working capital being $230,568, it was really $170,568. Perhaps this case was an honest representation incorrectly made!

FINANCIAL INFORMATION

A substantial percentage of all balance sheets is made up of 15 items or less. Such concerns generally have a tangible net worth of no more than $35,000. As approximately 82 per cent of all active commercial and industrial business enterprises have a tangible net worth no greater than this amount, the tremendous extent of this field may easily be realized. The larger concerns are of more importance because of their very size. Their purchases are heavy, their bank borrowings are substantial, their employees are numbered by the thousands, their tangible net worth by the hundreds of millions of dollars, their security holders by the hundreds of thousands; their economic and social influence and power are immense.[7]

Corporate Structure

A substantial proportion of large corporations, as well as a reasonable percentage of smaller corporations, have subsidiaries and affiliated companies. As a chain is no stronger than its weakest link, it is important in such cases to ascertain the names of all subsidiaries and affiliates with information regarding the percentage of control owned in each subsidiary, and the nature of the relations which create the affiliate. Weaknesses have often been concealed by loading unprofitable business on weak subsidiaries, by offsetting gains against losses in consolidated financial statements, and by draining profits from subsidiaries by charging higher than normal prices, higher than normal interest rates, and management fees. American businessmen have taken unstinted pride in the creation of groups of subsidiaries of various degrees and relationships. In recent years, there has existed a moderate tendency to simplify many of these highly complicated corporate business structures.

Consolidated Financial Statements. "A consolidated balance sheet is one which sets forth the combined assets and liabilities of a parent company and some or all of its subsidiary companies as if the enterprise were a single entity."[8] It is the financial statement of no "single corporation but an amalgamated statement giving accounting data of two or more separate corporations." The final justification of the device "rests on the reality of the group as a single economic and administrative enterprise despite the existence of separate legal entities." The need for consolidated financial statements is found in the failure of the legal financial statements of a corporation, or of a group of corporations, to convey in a readily understandable manner adequate information regarding "the commit-

[7] This is amply brought out by Harry W. Laidler in *Concentration in American Industry* (The Thomas Y. Crowell Company, New York, 1931); Adolf A. Berle and Gardiner C. Means in *The Modern Corporation and Private Property* (The Macmillan Company, New York, 1933); in Monograph No. 21, *Competition and Monopoly in American Industry*, pp. 117–118, Investigation of Concentration of Economic Power by the Temporary National Economic Committee, 1940; *Economic Concentration in World War II*, a report of the Smaller War Plants Corporation to the Special Committee to Study Problems of American Small Business, U.S. Senate, 1946 (79th Cong., 2d Sess., Senate Committee Print No. 6); and *Changes in Concentration in Manufacturing 1933 to 1947 and 1950*, a report of the Federal Trade Commission, 1954.
[8] LENHART, NORMAN J., and PHILIP L. DEFLIESE, *Montgomery's Auditing*, 8th ed., p. 471 (The Ronald Press Company, New York, 1957).

ments of a single group of investors—investors in a corporation which itself owns and controls other corporations."

On the books of a parent company, the interest in a subsidiary is represented by the investment in the securities of the subsidiary and by any advances made to it. The accounts of the parent company contain no record information concerning the assets and the liabilities of the subsidiary, nor do they record the revenues and expenses of the subsidiary. Such information, however, is necessary in any analysis of financial condition and progress of the parent company.

The consolidated financial statement is the best medium that has yet been devised for presenting a bird's-eye view of such a group of corporations operated as a single enterprise. Nevertheless, so long as the parent-subsidiary relationship exists, the subsidiary retains its separate corporate status; it continues to own its assets and consequently has all the responsibilities and may exercise all the privileges that such ownership confers. Its profits may become legal income of the parent company only through the formality of the declaration and payment of dividends. It is because of this very situation that parent corporations filing reports with the Securities and Exchange Commission, as explained on page 62, must file individual as well as consolidated financial statements.

If a financial statement carries the heading *General Motors Corporation, Condensed Consolidated Balance Sheet* or *National Steel Corporation and Subsidiaries, Consolidated Balance Sheet*, then the corporation obviously has subsidiaries. The words *consolidated balance sheet*[9] mean that and nothing else. Whenever possible in this situation, the names, addresses, nature of business operations of the subsidiaries, percentage of capital stock owned by the parent corporation in each subsidiary, the amount and reasons for intercompany loans, the nature and the terms of intercompany merchandise sales should be obtained. Whether there are 3 subsidiaries, or 103, this information should be obtained wherever possible.

If a corporation has 103 subsidiaries, possibly the assets and the liabilities of only 50 have been consolidated, the interests of the parent company in the other 53 corporations being carried in the assets under an item of *investments*. In this event, the list of subsidiaries and accompanying information should be obtained in two groups, the first group containing the names of subsidiaries with supplementary information that have been consolidated, and the second group, those that have not been consolidated. Even when the heading of a financial statement does not contain the

[9] In a sweeping and historic decision, the New Jersey Court of Errors and Appeals upheld a decision of a lower court in the suit of *Oscar B. Clintas v. the American Car and Foundry Company*, that a consolidated balance sheet "is nothing more than an imaginative figment for there is actually no individual business having the assets and liabilities depicted by it." Well-known accountants testified on both sides of this important and fascinating case.—*The New York Times*, Oct. 18, 1942.

words *consolidated balance sheet*, the corporation may still have subsidiaries. In this case the heading is not self-explanatory. The assets and the liabilities of none of the subsidiaries may have been consolidated, the interests in these subsidiaries being carried in the assets of the parent corporation as an item of *investments*. If a financial statement does not contain in its heading the word *consolidated*, and if the assets do not contain an item of *investments*, then one may feel quite assured that the corporation has none of these modern appendages which, at times, make the analyses of some financial situations quite difficult. If there is an item of *investments*, the analyst must dig deeper, as outlined on pages 89–91.

Rules of the Securities and Exchange Commission provide that corporations which come under its scrutiny "shall follow in the consolidated statements principles of inclusion or exclusion which will clearly exhibit the financial condition and results of operations of the registrant and its subsidiaries: *Provided, however*, that (a) the registrant shall not consolidate any subsidiary which is not a majority-owned subsidiary."[10] The Securities and Exchange Commission handles this problem as follows:

For majority-owned subsidiaries not consolidated with the registrant there may be filed statements in which such subsidiaries are consolidated or combined in one or more groups pursuant to principles of inclusion or exclusion which will clearly exhibit the financial condition and results of operations of the group or groups. If it is essential to a properly summarized presentation of the facts, such consolidated or combined statement shall be filed.[11]

The principle adopted in determining the inclusion and exclusion of subsidiaries in each consolidated balance sheet and in each group balance sheet of unconsolidated subsidiaries shall be stated in a note to the respective balance sheet.[12]

As to each consolidated statement and as to each group statement of unconsolidated subsidiaries, a statement shall be made as to whether there have been included or excluded any persons [concerns] not similarly treated in the corresponding statement for the preceding fiscal period filed with the Commission. If the answer to the foregoing is in the affirmative, the names of such persons [concerns] shall be given.[13]

These rules allow considerable leeway to the managements of corporations that must file financial statements with the Securities and Exchange Commission, for the inclusion or exclusion of subsidiary companies in consolidated or grouped statements. Which corporations are included, excluded, consolidated, or grouped must be explained in the detailed re-

---

[10] Regulation S-X, Rule 4-02, p. 7, Aug. 20, 1958.
[11] *Ibid.*, Rule 4-03.
[12] *Ibid.*, Paragraph (a), Rule 4-04.
[13] *Ibid.*, Paragraph (b), Rule 4-04.

ports to the Securities and Exchange Commission, information that is freely available for consultation by any interested individual or analyst. This information, however, is rarely included in the annual reports of corporations to stockholders, and in few secondary sources of information. While often helpful, this information is never as valuable or enlightening as the individual financial statements of each subsidiary along with a consolidated financial statement of the entire family of corporations, and with full explanations of all intercompany relations of each kind and character.

Individual Financial Statements. When the list of subsidiaries is obtained, every effort should be made to secure their individual financial statements, which are as essential for a complete analysis as the consolidated figures. In complex corporate systems, the direct subsidiaries in turn may have subsidiaries—children, grandchildren and great-grandchildren, first cousins, and second cousins. When the corporate relationship is complicated, a chart often helps in ferreting out essential connections.

Individual figures of the parent corporation and of each subsidiary as well as the consolidated balance sheet are essential in examining thoroughly the financial condition of any enterprise in a hierarchy. Individual financial statements showing tie-ups in stock interest, and amounts due to and from each other for loans or merchandise sales, are contained in the complete audits of accounting firms. This comprehensive information is generally made available to depository commercial banks but rarely to anyone else outside the organization. The analyst must keep constantly in mind that creditors of subsidiary corporations enjoy a preferred position to the extent of the amount and quality of the assets of the obligated concern.

Since the passage of the Securities Act of 1933, the names of all underlying subsidiary units have been made available, with rare exceptions in the case of minor units, in registration statements filed with the Securities and Exchange Commission, and by the Commission to the public on practically every corporation that has offered its securities to the public. The same information is filed with the Securities and Exchange Commission by every corporation (except railroads, common and contract carriers by motor vehicles, and commercial banks) whose securities are listed on a national security exchange and is available for public perusal at the office of the Commission or the Exchange on which the security is listed. Only the names of subsidiaries, however, are generally available, not their individual financial statements, their addresses, or the extent, nature, and terms of intercompany loans and merchandise indebtedness.

The Securities and Exchange Commission does, however, obtain an individual balance sheet on all corporations coming under its supervision which are also holding companies and which issue consolidated financial statements. As of June 30, 1960, there were 2,307[14] issuers having securities listed and registered on national security exchanges, in contrast to 2,192 as of June 30, 1951.

According to Section 15d of the Securities Exchange Act of 1934, registration statements filed pursuant to the Securities Act of 1933 as amended, that is, by corporations that are distributing securities with a market value of $300,000 or over, to the public, must contain an undertaking by the issuer to keep up to date by the supplementary and periodic filing of financial and other data pertinent to the company if "the aggregate offering price of such issue of securities, plus the aggregate value of all other securities of such issuer of the same class outstanding, computed upon the basis of such offering price, amounts to $2,000,000 or more," and provided such information has not already been required by the fact that the security is listed on a national security exchange. Under this section of the act, a total of 1,543 issuers (not including 275 investment companies) were required as of June 30, 1960, to file annual reports with the Securities and Exchange Commission. The necessity for filing "supplementary and periodic information" is suspended where "the aggregate value of all outstanding securities of the class to which such issue belongs is reduced to less than $1,000,000, computed upon the basis of the offering price of the last issue of securities of such class offered to the public."

THEORY AND PROBLEMS

1. Name the three broad divisions of credit information and describe briefly each division.

2. Would the antecedent records of the principals of a business enterprise be of any interest to you if you were analyzing the figures of that concern? Why?

3. What would be your point of view regarding the desirability of antecedent information if the business enterprise was (a) a proprietorship with a tangible net worth of $8,621, (b) a corporation with a tangible net worth of $26,610,000?

4. Would information regarding bank borrowings and depository bank relationships have any bearing toward an analysis of financial statements? Explain.

5. What are the implications of secured bank loans from the viewpoint of the analyst?

6. If you learned that trade payments of a particular concern whose figures you were analyzing were running slow, would that knowledge help you or hinder you in your analysis? Why?

7. Define a consolidated balance sheet.

8. How can you tell from a balance sheet if a corporation probably has no subsidiaries?

[14] *Twenty-sixth Annual Report of the Securities and Exchange Commission, Fiscal Year Ended June 30, 1960*, p. 67.

9. It has been said that a consolidated balance sheet is a "legal fiction." What is meant by that expression?

10. Suppose you are analyzing the figures of a corporation that has a large number of subsidiaries. Into what two groups should you separate these subsidiaries? Why? List five points of information you would like to obtain regarding each subsidiary.

11. You are analyzing a consolidated balance sheet. Would you be interested (*a*) in learning the names, addresses, and method of operation of each subsidiary whose assets and liabilities are also consolidated, (*b*) in obtaining individual balance sheets of each subsidiary? Explain your answer.

12. You are analyzing the affairs of 1 of 10 subsidiaries of the *A* corporation. For your purpose, would you prefer to have the individual financial statements of that subsidiary or the consolidated financial statements of the parent company and the 10 subsidiaries? Would you like to have both sets of financial statements? Explain your answer.

CHAPTER IV

Classification of Balance Sheet Items

In a study characterized by delightful originality entitled "An Histori-cal Defense of Bookkeeping,"[1] Henry Rand Hatfield goes back to the very beginning of that amazing awakening in Italy, later to become known as the Renaissance, and to the venerable year 1494, for the origin of the refined and noble art of keeping systematic double-entry bookkeeping records.[2] This art arose to meet three very definite commercial needs: to describe transactions arising from commerce, industry, and government, to place responsibility, and to prevent fraud.

As expanding commerce became more and more important in Genoa, in Florence, and in Venice, careful records of sales and of income and expenses became necessary to indicate the degree of profitableness. Trade

---

[1] HATFIELD, HENRY RAND, "An Historical Defense of Bookkeeping," a paper read before the American Association of University Instructors in Accounting, Dec. 29, 1923, and published in *The Journal of Accountancy*, Vol. XXXVII, No. 4, pp. 241–253, April, 1924.

[2] Edward Peragallo, in the *Origin and Evolution of Double Entry Bookkeeping*, p. 16 (American Institute Publishing Company, Inc., New York, 1938), traces double-entry bookkeeping back more than 150 years earlier. He wrote, "It is now clear that double-entry bookkeeping was fully developed at Genoa in 1340, and it is also clear that its origin must have been of a considerably earlier date. It is inconceivable that a system such as double entry should come into being suddenly in the mature form shown in the Massari ledgers; it could only have evolved gradually over a long period of time. The double-entry system used by the Commune of Genoa dates back probably no further than 1327, when the government decreed that its accounts were to be kept in the same way as banks kept their accounts." In a study "Greek and Roman Account-ing" by F. E. M. de Ste. Croix, included in *Studies in the History of Accounting*, pp. 62–63, by A. C. Littleton and B. S. Yamey (Richard D. Irwin, Inc., Homewood, Ill., 1956), the author throws additional light on this subject. "Recently two Italian scholars," he wrote, "the philologist Castellani and the historian of accounting Melis, have traced the origin of double entry still further back. Both Melis and Castel-lani believe that the system can be found in the accounts of the Florentine merchant Rinieri Fini and his brothers, whose books relating to dealings at the fairs of Cham-pagne survive for the years 1296 to 1305; and Melis (who also believes that the books of other Florentine merchants, from the year 1299 onwards, are in double entry) is a strong advocate of the view that double entry actually originated in the towns of Tuscany. However that may be, we shall be safe in concluding that bookkeeping by double entry had established itself in the towns of northern Italy by the very end of the thirteenth century or the first half of the fourteenth century at the latest."

expanded to relatively large proportions during the sixteenth and seventeenth centuries. The origin of the art of bookkeeping in this environment of expanding commerce attracted the attention and challenged the ingenuity of men of unquestioned intellectual attainment. "We look upon the Franciscan monk Paciolo," Hatfield wrote, "as the father of modern accounting, as his *Summa*,[3] published in 1494, which is the first printed work[4] dealing with algebra, also contained the first text on bookkeeping, a slender tractate entitled *De Computis et Scripturis*."[5]

DEVELOPMENT OF THE BALANCE SHEET

A balance sheet, from an analyst's point of view, is a written representation of the resources and liabilities of an individual, a partnership, an association, or a corporation.[6] When it is a correct representation honestly

[3] A *Summa* was a kind of early encyclopedia. It was written by a learned man and touched on all known fields of knowledge. A *Summa* often contained a few chapters on the merchants' art of keeping books.

[4] Peragallo, *op. cit.*, p. 54, writes that Benedetto Cotruglio, a native of Dalmatia, was really the first writer on double-entry bookkeeping. Cotruglio finished his book in 1458 but "it lay unpublished at Ragusa for more than a century, until a certain Giovanni Guiseppe had a copy made and brought it to Venice, where it was published in 1573."

[5] Little is known of Paciolo, aside from his writings, but from these works it would appear that he was a learned individual. He was an important if not a great mathematician. After he had made an enviable reputation for himself at the University of Perugia where he was wont to describe himself as "a humble professor of sacred theology," he was called in 1496 to Milan by the reigning duke, Ludovico Sforza, called il Moro, whose court was a center of light and learning. To be established here was a signal honor. "At Milan, Paciolo was brought into contact with many eminent persons, the most significant being Leonardo da Vinci, perhaps the most eminent man of his day. Between the two there grew up an intimate friendship. Da Vinci himself tells that he hastened to buy a copy of Paciolo's *Summa* as it came off the press, and he collaborated with Paciolo on a later book, the *Divina Proportione*, for which Paciolo furnished the text and Da Vinci the illustrations. . . . " It is seldom the case that the first book on a subject so dominates its literature as did Paciolo's *De Computis et Scripturis*. "It is nearly true," Hatfield (*op. cit.*) continued to explain, "to say that for a hundred years the texts appearing in England, France, Germany, Italy, and the Low Countries were 'at best, revisions of Paciolo, at the worst, servile transcriptions without even the courtesy of referring to the original author.' But, further than that, many little matters of bookkeeping technique were followed for at least four centuries, merely because they were inculcated by Paciolo, persisting like buttons on our coat sleeves, long after their significance had disappeared. . . . " The first presentation of double-entry bookkeeping made by Paciolo so many centuries ago was neither crude nor immature. It contained the essentials of bookkeeping as it is known today.

[6] W. A. Paton and A. C. Littleton, in *An Introduction to Corporate Accounting Standards*, pp. 66–67 (American Accounting Association, Chicago, 1940), emphasize a contrasting viewpoint. In their synthesis of accounting theory the balance sheet serves the fundamental purpose of carrying forward costs that will gradually be used up in operations. "A cost is initially an acquisition price and only finally a deduction from revenue. . . . The fundamental problem of accounting, therefore, is the division of the stream of costs incurred between the present and the future in the process of measuring periodic income. The technical instruments used in reporting this division

made, it portrays the financial condition of a concern, an organization, or a business enterprise at a given date.[7] Paciolo advised the use of a separate set of books for each voyage or trading journey; only after several hundred years was the continuous system finally evolved to the point where accountants found it essential to emphasize that the yearly closing based on an "accounting convention" was one of the reasons why modern accountancy is an art.

During the fourteenth and fifteenth centuries, ledgers usually were not balanced at any regular fiscal period. They covered any period from one to several years,[8] and many ledgers were balanced only when completely filled and the open accounts were to be transferred to a new ledger. The Datini ledgers of the Avignon branch were notable exceptions, as they were regularly balanced at the end of every year and financial statements were prepared. Peragallo quotes one for the fiscal year 1367–1368. Because the very early writers on bookkeeping referred only to the procedure for closing accounts in a ledger and opening them in a new one, there is a general belief that financial statements were nonexistent at this early period. However, the early family partnerships of Florence had developed financial contracts to a high degree of perfection, entailing an equal development of partnership accounting. Financial statements were necessary to show the partners' interests.[9]

---

are the income statement and the balance sheet. Both are necessary. The income statement reports the assignment to the current period; the balance sheet exhibits the costs incurred which are reasonably applicable to the years to come. The balance sheet thus serves as a means of carrying forward unamortized acquisition prices, the not yet deducted costs; it stands as a connecting link joining successive income statements into a composite picture of the income stream." This point of view is one which creates problems for the analyst as he must learn the current values of asset items, which are often materially different from "unamortized costs." As William J. Vatter has also pointed out, "The definition of an asset in terms of unamortized cost is weak in that it does not include all the things that are commonly regarded as assets. . . . Financial claims (cash, bank deposits, and receivables) are certainly assets—at least they are so regarded in practice—but they are not *costs*. . . . Financial claims cannot as such be fitted into the pattern of amortization which is suggested by the definition of assets; they are not 'charges awaiting future revenue' or 'charges against present revenue.' The trouble with the definition is that the operations specified are not broadly enough conceived to encompass all the activities in which assets are involved, so as to include in a homogeneous pattern all the items that are brought together in the definition."—*The Fund Theory of Accounting and Its Implications for Financial Reports*, p. 15 (The University of Chicago Press, Chicago, 1947).

[7] In Chap. XXIV, "Recent Evolution in Accountancy Theory and Practice," it will be shown that this assertion is not strictly true as a balance sheet generally does not reflect current economic values. Financial statements actually represent a "combination of recorded facts, accounting conventions, and personal judgments; and the judgments and conventions applied affect them materially."

[8] Article 16 of the "charter" of the French East India Company, organized in 1664, provided that "the company was to have a thorough general accounting every six years."—COLE, CHARLES W., *Colbert and a Century of French Mercantilism*, Vol. I, p. 479 (Columbia University Press, New York, 1939).

[9] *Origin and Evolution of Double Entry Bookkeeping*, pp. 27–29.

In a study of the development of financial statements, Littleton also quotes several simple, fascinating balance sheets made up from the year 1545 onward. The first of these balance sheets consisted of three asset items and three liability items and appeared in the text of one Gotlieb, a German author, in 1546. The second was quoted from Angelo Pietra's text of 1586 and is much longer.[10]

Colonial Business Records

Record books of colonial American proprietorships and partnerships[11] contained balance sheets prepared at periodic or irregular intervals, so that the owners would have clear pictures of their assets and their liabilities. These detailed figures were rarely, if ever, made available to outsiders. Enterprising colonial businessmen learned the elements of bookkeeping from one of the few published volumes on the subject. They did their own bookkeeping in their own individual handwriting. When Jonathan Jackson organized the importing and exporting firm of Jackson & Bromfield at Newburyport in the Massachusetts Bay Colony in 1765, he wrote to a friend, "I have undertaken the care of the Books intirely myself, but find myself a little bewildered how to begin the C? acc^ts—which Mair allows the most difficult part of Bookkeeping."[12] John Mair, to whom Jackson referred, was the well-known author of *Bookkeeping Methodiz'd*, published in Edinburgh in 1752.

The problems of accounting in the eighteenth century were simple and uncomplicated compared with the problems of today. At that time there were no large manufacturing establishments where the accounting procedure called for depreciation on a vast number of different types of assets, where the production process involving long periods of time and expenses had to be cut off at a fixed date, where heavy expenditures such as advertising were made in one period to show increased profits in another period, where the valuation of finished merchandise and work in process played such a great part in the size of net profits, not only in the year being closed, but also in the following year. Business was almost entirely private, and the business unit was the proprietorship or the firm. There were no investment bankers to underwrite issues of securities. There were no stock

[10] LITTLETON, A. C., *Accounting Evolution to 1900*, pp. 128–129 (American Institute Publishing Company, Inc., New York, 1933).

[11] Many libraries and historical societies in recent years have made collections of these fascinating and economically valuable original business records of our colonial days. Among these institutions are the New York Public Library, the New York Historical Society, the Massachusetts Historical Society, the Connecticut Historical Society, the Historical Society of Pennsylvania, and the Baker Library of the Harvard Graduate School of Business Administration.

[12] PORTER, KENNETH WIGGINS, *The Jacksons and the Lees*, Vol. I, p. 162 (Harvard University Press, Cambridge, Mass., 1937).

exchanges. There were no commercial banks or trust companies. Business activity was largely trade, that is, importing, exporting, commission selling, wholesaling, and retailing.

In the second and third quarters of the nineteenth century, the corporation, with its restricted liability, became a more prominent vehicle of industrial and commercial business activity. The Supreme Court decision in 1886 that a corporation was a person in the meaning of the due process clause of the Federal Constitution brought increased demands from creditors for detailed balance sheets and gave a marked impetus to the creation of corporations with distributed stock interests.

Divisions of the Balance Sheet

As outlined in Chap. I, the number of active commercial and industrial business enterprises in the United States expanded quite steadily from 1870 to 1960, with the exception of four brief periods. As this expansion took place, more and more balance sheets were made available to different groups of interested individuals. This evolution was the result of (1) the change in bank lending operations from utilizing two-name paper to single-name paper, (2) the operations of mercantile credit agencies that realized the need of obtaining exact financial information as a trained intermediary for creditors, (3) the direct demands of mercantile creditors for more exact financial information, (4) the growth in the number of corporations that sold securities to the public and the development of the practice of issuing annual corporate reports to stockholders, (5) the rules of the New York Stock Exchange which insisted that more and more comprehensive financial information be filed prior to the listing of a security, (6) the passage of income-tax laws by Congress, and finally (7) the activities of the Securities and Exchange Commission.

Balance sheets are drawn up and presented in the same manner whether the figures are round-number estimates made by the proprietor of a small retail hardware store with an investment of $12,000, or are apparently exact figures carried out to two decimal places and carefully prepared by a certified public accountant on a nationally known corporation with a tangible net worth of $40,000,000. One balance sheet might contain 9 items and the other 99, but fundamentally they are similar financial schedules.

Whether it is a financial statement of a proprietorship, a partnership, a corporation, or a common-law trust, whether individual, consolidated, or combined, the balance sheet is divided in accounting practice into three parts: the *assets*, the *liabilities*, and the *proprietary interest* (also termed *capital*, *net worth*, or *proprietorship*). In this volume the proprietary interest will be termed *net worth*. The great majority of balance sheets published in the everyday practical business world, however, refer to only two groups of accounts, assets and liabilities, the liability group covering general liabilities and proprietary interest.

The assets are divided into four groups and the liabilities into three groups. The four groups of assets are: (1) current assets, (2) fixed assets, (3) miscellaneous assets, and (4) intangible assets. The three groups of liabilities are: (1) current liabilities, (2) deferred liabilities, and (3) net worth. A fundamental understanding of these various classifications of items is absolutely essential for any sound analysis of financial statements, especially as no uniform system of classification has been developed up to the present time.

ASSETS

The assets of a small business enterprise such as a corner drugstore, a meat market, or a retail candy store might consist of only four or five small items, whereas the assets of a large steel corporation, a paper mill with extensive timber holdings, or a manufacturer of heavy chemicals might consist of 20 to 30 items. If a business is a proprietorship or a partnership, the assets might or might not include the outside means of the proprietor or of the partners that are subject to the claims of creditors, with certain exceptions such as homesteads and personal property in several states.[13] If the outside means are not included, the financial strength of the business from the viewpoint of creditors might be stronger than is apparent from the balance sheet. If the outside means are included the analyst should be aware of that fact.

It is in the classification of the various items in the assets that the judgment and the experience of the analyst first come into play. He must be absolutely independent, follow his own judgment or some separate standard, and not follow in the footsteps of accountants, who often differ from each other and who arrive at classifications for "accounting purposes," not for credit, investment, or business purposes. In no other way will he have a uniform system of classifying items in the analysis of comparative balance sheets. This initial problem of the classification of balance sheet items will be discussed in the latter part of this chapter.

Current Assets

The man who best defined current assets was neither a banker, an accountant, nor a businessman. He was a gentleman named Adam Smith.

---

[13] The laws of the several states which allow exceptions from the claims of creditors are kept up to date in the *Credit Manual of Commercial Laws*, published annually by the National Association of Credit Management (New York).

In his volume which revolutionized political economy, *The Wealth of Nations*, published in 1776, Adam Smith explained, "The goods of the merchant yield him no revenue or profit till he sells them for money, and the money yields him as little till it is again exchanged for goods. His capital is continuously going from him in one shape, and returning to him in another, and it is only by means of such circulation, or successive exchanges, that it can yield him any profit. Such capital, therefore, may very properly be called circulating capital." What we call *current assets*, Smith called *circulating capital*.[14] The investment always must be kept there, but it keeps running through. The classification of current assets is undoubtedly the most important classification in a balance sheet, as current assets largely determine the going solvency of a business concern.

"Current assets," according to one of the outstanding students of statement analysis, "are such assets as in the orderly and natural course of business move onward, through the various processes of production, distribution, and payment for goods, until they become cash or its equivalent, by which debts may be readily and immediately paid."[15] The current assets are cash, temporary investments which are readily convertible into cash, receivables created by the sale of merchandise, merchandise, and advances on merchandise.[16] All these items, with the exception of tempo-

[14] SMITH, ADAM, *The Wealth of Nations*, pp. 262–263 (Modern Library, Inc., New York, 1937).

[15] WALL, ALEXANDER, *How to Evaluate Financial Statements*, p. 11 (Harper & Brothers, New York, 1936).

[16] *Restatement and Revision of Accounting Research Bulletins*, *Accounting Research Bulletin No. 43*, p. 20 (American Institute of Certified Public Accountants, New York, 1953), contains a definition of current assets. This definition as indicated by its first three words is not for credit purposes, management purposes, or analysis purposes; it is solely "for accounting purposes." The definition reads as follows: "*For accounting purposes*, the term current assets is used to designate cash and other assets or resources commonly identified as those which are reasonably expected to be realized in cash or sold or consumed during the normal operating cycle of the business." Then the following explanation appears: "Thus the term comprehends in general such resources as (*a*) cash available for current operations and items which are the equivalent of cash, (*b*) inventories of merchandise, raw materials, goods in process, finished goods, operating supplies, and ordinary maintenance material and parts, (*c*) trade accounts, notes, and acceptances receivable, (*d*) receivables from officers, employees, affiliates, and others, if collectible in the ordinary course of business within a year, (*e*) installment or deferred accounts and notes receivable if they conform generally to normal trade practices and terms within the business, (*f*) marketable securities representing the investment of cash available for current operations, and (*g*) prepaid expenses such as insurance, interest, rents, taxes, unused royalties, current paid advertising service not yet received, and operating supplies. Prepaid expenses are not current assets in the sense that they will be converted into cash but in the sense that, if not paid in advance, they would require the use of current assets during the operating cycle." Later in this bulletin there appears a list of items to be excluded from current assets "for accounting purposes." Among them are "depreciable assets." This comprehensive explanation of what does and does not comprise current assets would seem to contain some hidden discrepancies. In the first place, the definition includes "other assets or resources commonly identified as those . . . consumed during the normal operating cycle of

rary investments in readily marketable securities, which are the "equivalent" of cash, are convertible into cash by successive steps in the normal operations of a business. This classification does not include the cash surrender value of life insurance, as such an item is more in the nature of a semipermanent investment. It is not used in the normal operation of a business; it does not represent working capital; and it rarely is used as a basis for a loan except when all other sources of credit have been used or are unavailable. Cash, securities of the United States government (when negotiable) such as bonds, Treasury notes, and certificates of indebtedness, securities of Federal agencies, most securities of states and municipalities, receivables for the sale of merchandise, and readily marketable (generally listed) stocks and bonds when not valued in excess of market, as explained in Chap. VI, are also termed *liquid* or *quick* assets. Current assets consist of any one, any combination, or all of the following eight items:

1. Cash on hand and in a bank or banks
2. United States government (when negotiable), Federal agencies, state, and municipal securities
3. Accounts receivable for the sale of merchandise
4. Notes receivable for the sale of merchandise
5. Trade acceptances for the sale of merchandise
6. Merchandise—finished, in process, and raw material
7. Advances on merchandise
8. Marketable securities

It is from these items that funds are provided, day in and day out, to meet maturing obligations whether for wages, the payment of merchandise, insurance, rent, taxes, or interest, to meet a current installment on a note given in payment of a recently acquired piece of machinery, or any other business purpose. These assets provide the current funds that keep a business enterprise running from week to week and from month to month.

---

the business." All so-called fixed assets except land are so "consumed during the normal operating cycle of the business" but no one so far has suggested that fixed assets or any part thereof be considered a current asset. In the second place, the explanation includes "operating supplies and ordinary maintenance material and parts" as current assets. "Depreciable assets" are excluded, but still, ordinary maintenance material and parts are often depreciable assets! In the third place, the explanation includes prepaid expenses, and several items are specifically mentioned as current assets. Very few credit analysts would include prepaid items as current assets. Moreover, there is a wide difference of opinion among accountants regarding the classification of prepaid expenses, "for accounting purposes," and many accountants do not include such items among the current assets. In this volume, operating supplies and ordinary maintenance material and parts, receivables from officers and employees, no matter how they arose, and prepaid expenses are excluded from current assets.

1. *Cash on Hand or in a Bank or Banks.* In the daily operation of a business enterprise, cash is increased by the sale of assets for immediate payment and by the collection of receivables, by obtaining a loan from any source, and simultaneously decreased by the withdrawal of funds to meet obligations. When it is evident to the operating management that cash will be too low to meet obligations on time in the near future, cash is replenished temporarily if the concern is able to obtain a short-term loan from its bank or banks, from some other financial institution, from officers, directors, friends, or from others on an unsecured or on a secured basis. If the management is unable to borrow the funds, payments of maturing obligations are deferred until funds are available or until a settlement is made under a compromise agreement or under bankruptcy.

At times it is important for the analyst to know how much cash is actually on hand, that is, how much is held by the concern itself, and how much by each of its depository banking institutions. Many of the balance sheet blanks used by commercial banking institutions call for this segregation, for the reason that cash in banks, and particularly if there is only one depository bank, is more easily verified than cash on hand. Any situation where the amount of cash in a bank or banks as shown on the balance sheet is greater than the sum actually on deposit calls for an immediate explanation; every so often this discrepancy is the basis for detecting a fraudulent financial statement. Cash on hand is more easily misrepresented, particularly in the unaudited balance sheets of small concerns, by including "temporary" loans to officers, advances to salesmen, demand notes, and outright exaggeration without any basis. When the amount of cash on hand is relatively large, an explanation or investigation should always be made as many of these unusual situations are found to be the result of deliberate action rather than oversight.

In addition to these peculiarities against which the analyst must ever be on his guard, there are four unique situations regarding cash which appear not infrequently over the signature of independent public accountants and which, when discovered, throw an entirely different light on balance sheet figures:

A. Occasionally, cash which should have been set aside under a separate caption in the balance sheet as funds earmarked for a specific purpose, such as retiring some portion of a funded debt or preferred stock, is included with the unrestricted cash. The entire amount of cash as shown in the balance sheet is always assumed to be at the disposal of the enterprise for general purposes,[17] a situation which the management in this

---

[17] An important lawsuit which covered this situation was brought in 1934 by a stockholder of the defunct G. L. Miller & Co., Inc., against a firm of public accountants that certified a financial statement in which the cash item included $1,377,000 of restricted funds, with no enlightenment or explanation.

instance knows to be quite contrary to existing facts. The financial statement forms used by some commercial banks have been prepared with this situation in mind by including the brief explanation that the item of cash should represent "Cash on hand, and unrestricted in banks."

B. If a concern does business in one or several foreign countries, it is always expedient to obtain a breakdown of cash, showing the amount in the United States and the amounts in the various foreign countries. In times of peace, the value of such cash varies from day to day with fluctuations in the rates of foreign exchange; in abnormal times the restrictions on the withdrawal of funds from foreign countries vary from minor requirements to absolute prohibition, from the temporary freezing to the possible total loss of funds.

C. In the case of a consolidated balance sheet where one or more of the subsidiaries whose assets and liabilities are consolidated operate in foreign countries, it is often expedient for the analyst to obtain a breakdown of the cash showing the amount in the names of the parent company and of each subsidiary in each foreign country. Unusual situations have occurred where consolidated balance sheets disclosed an apparently satisfactory condition until these details were obtained. Then it was immediately apparent that the parent company was short on cash, that the bulk of the cash shown in the consolidated figures was in the name of one or more subsidiaries, and that a high percentage of that cash was in foreign countries and not readily available.

D. Cash in closed banks should always be carried as a separate item and never as a current asset, as such cash is not available for the general daily use of a business.

Where any one of the above four situations is discovered, the balance sheet figures must be adjusted before an analysis is made. Any and all amounts included in cash that are not strictly cash, such as loans, advances, and notes, and any amount not currently available for the unrestricted general use of the business must be deducted from the cash shown in the original balance sheet, and such amounts included under a proper caption among the miscellaneous assets. These amounts by no stretch of the imagination are current assets.

Commercial banks and trust companies, particularly those in large cities, commonly require a borrowing account to maintain cash balances on deposit that bear some fairly definite relationship to the line of credit or to average yearly borrowings. In most banks, the deposit requirement is between 10 and 20 per cent. In other words, if a borrower has an established confirmed line of credit of $100,000, the bank balance should normally average between $10,000 and $20,000. These percentages are not hard and fast, but as a rule a depositor that maintains an average balance of $1,000 would hardly be eligible for a loan of $100,000. Other things being equal, a depositor that maintains an average balance of $10,000 is not entitled to the same credit as a depositor with average balances of $100,000.

This rule of compensating balances varies somewhat under different circumstances. If the banking system of the country has a large amount of excess reserves, and if little demand exists for commercial loans, bankers will not be quite so strict in the application of the requirement for adequate balances. In a period when demands for loans are great, there is a natural tendency to hold more closely to the general policy of compensating balances. Proportionate balances play no part in analysis when a business is obtaining its current financing from a factor, a discount finance company, a sales finance company, the officers, the directors, or friends or relatives of the owners.

In addition to this general but practical relationship between the amount of unrestricted cash and lines of bank credit, it is also expedient that actual cash be sufficiently large to cover all operating expenses exclusive of merchandise invoices, for a minimum period of at least 1 month. There should always be sufficient funds for salaries, wages, rent, taxes, light, heat, telephone, and other essential services. Any excess over this absolute minimum, as a general thing, places a concern in an improved financial condition. In Chap. V, it will be shown how important this absolute minimum requirement is for smaller business enterprises that have no lines of bank credit. In the case of concerns that do have lines of credit, funds are generally borrowed for seasonal operations so that cash, after excluding the necessary bank balance, does not fall below this practical minimum proportion.

2. *United States Government, Federal Agencies, State, and Municipal Securities.* Investment obligations of the Federal government of one kind or another appear in the balance sheets of many industrial and commercial businesses: Treasury bonds with short and long maturities, Treasury notes, certificates of indebtedness, and short-term bills.

Over the years, funds have also been sought from the investing public by numerous agencies of the Federal government. One of these agencies, namely, the Federal Housing Administration, sells its securities guaranteed by the Federal government. In years gone by, the Reconstruction Finance Corporation, the Commodity Credit Corporation, and the Home Owners' Loan Corporation also used the guaranty of the Federal government. Others, such as the Bank for Cooperatives, the Federal Land banks, the Federal Home Loan banks, and the Federal National Mortgage Association, sell securities on their own responsibility and without the guaranty of the Federal government to the public.

Second in standing only to the securities issued or guaranteed by the Federal government are the securities of states[18] and municipalities. In the not too distant past, quite a few municipalities have defaulted in paying interest and in meeting maturities. Bond issues of municipalities in default[19] are not current assets; they are miscellaneous assets until such

[18] Eleven states either have no general obligation bonds in the hands of the public or have only a negligible amount. They are Arizona, Colorado, Florida, Georgia, Indiana, Kansas, Nebraska, South Dakota, Utah, Wisconsin, and Wyoming. Georgia's general obligation bonds are fully offset by sinking funds. Each of the 50 states has some long-term debt, however, including, in addition to general obligation bonds, limited obligation securities and nonguaranteed or revenue bonds of state agencies. Limited obligation and nonguaranteed debt have their commonest usage for state institutions, particularly institutions of higher education, and for highways, while revenue bonds have come into widespread use in the postwar period for financing toll highways, usually through a semiautonomous state commission or authority. The gross long-term debt of the states on June 30, 1959, including both full faith and credit and nonguaranteed debt, was $16,421,154,000, according to the Division of Governments of the Bureau of the Census, and net long-term debt was $14,180,344,000. The gross long-term state and local debt combined, as of June 30, 1959, was $61,127,-000,000, a new high.

[19] The number of local government units in default reached its peak of 3,252 on Aug. 1, 1935, and in the 1950's had dropped to approximately 150. Even at the high point in the depression of the 1930's, the number was negligible compared with the totality of local units. In recent years the defaulters have been mainly small places, about one-half cities and towns, one-third school districts, and the remainder counties and special districts. While, in the acute period of the depression of the 1930's, one state, Arkansas, and several prominent local units, including such places as Akron, Atlantic City, Detroit, Miami, Toledo, and Cook County, Ill., did default on their bonds, these defaults were of relatively short duration and were cured by refunding operations, most of which involved little or no scaling down of principal or interest. Recent defaults have been mainly in overpromoted resort or suburban areas and submarginal agricultural territory whose debts were entirely out of proportion to resources for payment, but also included the revenue bonds of the West Virginia Turnpike Commission in 1958. At all times the number of units in default has been relatively small. In 1942, according to the Bureau of the Census, there were approximately 155,000 political subdivisions, and in 1957 about 102,328, the reduction reflecting mainly school district consolidations. The number of school districts declined from 108,600 in 1942 to 70,400 in 1951 and 50,446 in 1957. Municipalities numbered 17,183 in 1957, little more than in earlier enumerations. The number of counties has held relatively constant, with 3,047 in 1957, but special districts have shown marked increases, from 8,300 in 1942 to 11,900 in 1951 and about 14,405 in 1957. Townships numbered 17,198 in 1957.

There have been enough defaults to show that by no means all municipal securities are entitled to be classified as current assets, and that some are quite vulnerable to changing conditions. It would be unwise to judge a bond to be sound merely because it was a municipal, without having some knowledge of the resources of the community, its taxing power, its debt load, its current financial position, and its management. The term *municipal* is used, moreover, to cover an increasingly wide variety of obligations, differing as to the nature of the security for their payment and often as to the quality of the security. Among the important types are: general obligation bonds supported by legally unlimited taxing power; general obligation bonds supported by legally limited taxes; general obligation bonds supported both by the taxing power and by the pledge of the earnings of a public service enterprise; bonds, notes, and warrants secured only by some one or more limited sources of tax revenue; revenue bonds payable solely from the earnings of a public service enterprise,

time as the financial condition of the particular municipality is revamped. Securities of the Federal government, of agencies of the Federal government, of states and municipalities normally do not fluctuate greatly in market value. The market values of even the best securities do, however, fluctuate in keeping with interest rates. With this fact in mind, these securities should be carried in balance sheets at values not in excess of market. If carried at cost, and cost is greater than market on the statement date, the figures should be adjusted when posting, by deducting an amount to bring the value of the securities to market, and by deducting a similar amount from the surplus account.

Some accountants set up United States Treasury tax-anticipation notes as a deduction from accrued Federal taxes and show only the excess of such taxes over the amount of the notes at a so-called "net" figure. Purchase of these tax notes does not reduce the tax liability but is an indication of the steps that have been taken toward meeting Federal taxes. The tax liability is not discharged until the tax notes have been turned over to the Collector of Internal Revenue in payment of taxes. It is the considered opinion of the author that the full tax liability is a current liability until paid, and that the tax-anticipation notes should unequivocally be shown as a current asset.[20] Moreover, the negotiable value of these notes

---

such as a water system, electric plant, toll bridge, toll road, or housing project; special assessment bonds payable primarily from assessments levied on property benefited by a local improvement but contingently a responsibility of the municipality; and special assessment bonds payable solely from such assessments. Defaults on this last type, not included in the totals shown above, have been extensive over the years, and investor losses have been large. This summary by no means covers all the types and subtypes of municipal securities, but it does indicate the necessity for discrimination in the appraisal of obligations listed under this general title.

[20] While this undoubtedly is the preferable practice, *Restatement and Revision of Accounting Research Bulletins, Accounting Research Bulletin* No. 43, pp. 25–26 (American Institute of Certified Public Accountants, New York, 1953), states: " . . . It was considered acceptable, and in accordance with good accounting practice to show the notes in the current liability section of the balance sheet as a deduction from federal taxes . . . ." In partial explanation of an attempt to make this decision jibe with other accounting theory, the *Bulletin* contains the following fascinating sophistry: "It is a general principle of accounting that the offsetting of assets against liabilities in the balance sheet is improper except where a right to offset exists." In other words, there must be no relaxing or modifying of this general rule of accounting while breaking that rule! By the same theory, excess cash may be used as an offset against any one of several liability items. If the offset is not noticed by the analyst, the relationship of the current assets to the current liabilities and the current liabilities to the tangible net worth will be determined incorrectly; that, of course, is the basic purpose for offsetting. No one questions the fact that the full tax liability exists on the balance sheet date regardless of whether tax notes have been accumulated or not. William A. Paton has analyzed the statement as follows: "This development is somewhat alarming, not because it represents anything particularly harmful in itself but because it constitutes a violation, or near violation, of a fundamental rule of reporting, and thus may be the entering wedge to more seriously objectionable practices. The movement to deduct tax notes from liabilities seems to have originated in the desire in certain

is not confined to the payment of taxes alone as they may be redeemed for cash at par.

3. *Accounts Receivable for the Sale of Merchandise.* Accounts receivable are classified as a current asset only when they represent amounts due for merchandise sales in the normal course of everyday operations. A reserve for doubtful accounts should be set up against slow and doubtful items, but too often this practice is not followed, especially in the case of unaudited figures. If any unreasonable proportion of this item is past due and questionable, this fact can generally be discovered by an analysis of the receivables as described in Chap. XIII. If any of the receivables have been pledged or assigned as collateral for a loan to a commercial bank, to a sales or discount finance company, or to any other institution, that information should appear in the balance sheet, as such receivables are subject to the prior claims of the secured creditor. At times it does not so appear.[21]

Accounts receivable due for the sale of a plant, for the sale of used machinery, or from officers, directors, salesmen, or other employees are not current assets; they are miscellaneous assets. If the accounts receivable are known to include such amounts, the figures must be adjusted by making these deductions so that the accounts in the current assets represent only sales of merchandise in the normal course of business.

Accounts receivable due from subsidiary or affiliated concerns should likewise be segregated and carried separately in the balance sheet. In every case, these items should be carefully studied and investigated. Such an item may represent normal sales made on regular terms that are met

cases to maintain an apparent current ratio equal to the conventional minimum, or equal to some required minimum as expressed in a trust indenture or other underlying agreement. With tax liabilities at a phenomenal level it has sometimes been difficult, even in the case of a strong company, to maintain a conventional or specified relationship between the component elements of working capital if the tax liability was included in the liability total in the full amount accrued. As a means of meeting this difficulty the proposal to improve the ratio artificially, by the simple expedient of offsetting, has emerged . . . deducting tax notes owned from an accrued liability is no more warranted than would be the practice of deducting other government securities or even cash from such liability. The excuse for this departure from the rule, moreover, hardly seems adequate. Actual working capital position is, of course, not strengthened by the offsetting procedure. . . ."—"Balance Sheet," Chap. 2, p. 16, in *Contemporary Accounting, a Refresher Course for Public Accountants*, edited by Thomas W. Leland (American Institute of Certified Public Accountants, New York, 1945).

[21] The accounts receivable of a corporation in two successive years dropped from $800,000 to $300,000. In investigating the circumstances, it was discovered that the corporation during the year had organized a subsidiary corporation to which it had transferred $500,000 of its receivables. These receivables had then been assigned by the subsidiary to a commercial bank as security for a loan. This fact failed to show up in the balance sheet of the parent company as the management refused to issue consolidated figures; the individual figures of the parent company merely showed its stock investment in the borrowing subsidiary.

promptly on those terms. On the other hand, the subsidiary or affiliate to which the sales were made may be in an extended financial condition and the particular receivables may be running several months past due. In view of the community of interest it may be difficult or impossible to press for payment and the receivables may represent at best a temporarily frozen asset. Moreover, particularly in unaudited statements, the accounts receivable from a subsidiary or an affiliate may represent, not merchandise sales, but direct loans for working capital, which may be repaid shortly or which may represent a fairly permanent loan. Because of these varieties of circumstances, it is always desirable to have receivables due from a subsidiary or an affiliate separate from other receivables; if in the investigation any slight indication is found that the receivables are not due for normal merchandise sales or that they are not or will not be paid on regular terms, or that the receivable is really a loan, the item should be taken out of the current assets and carried as a miscellaneous slow asset. In studying such an item, it is generally necessary not only to obtain an explanation from the management of the occasion and circumstance for the origin of the item, but also to obtain and to analyze the financial statement of the subsidiary or the affiliate. At times, the item may represent funds due not from one but from several subsidiaries and affiliates.

The subject of accounts receivable due from subsidiary and affiliated concerns is treated in a particularly thorough manner in the long financial statement form suggested for use by the Federal Reserve Bank of New York. Three different figures are requested. First is the regular item of accounts receivable but carrying the explanation, "*current and collectible from customers, excl. subsidiaries and affiliates.*" Second is the item "Due from subsidiaries and affiliates, *current and collectible, for sale of goods on regular terms.*" Third is the interesting segregation discussed in the preceding paragraph, "Due from subsidiaries and affiliates, *loans, advances, and other receivables.*" In our classifications, the first two items are current assets, while the third item is a slow miscellaneous asset.

As a result of the open account practice of handling merchandise transactions, there has developed a bewildering number of wholly different terms of sale.[22] Every industry has its own customs, and in practically every industry the recognized terms of sale are constantly being modified by particular concerns[23] so that a process of evolution is always going on. In some instances substantial inducements in the form of cash discounts

[22] STEINER, W. H., *The Mechanism of Commercial Credit* (Appleton-Century-Crofts, Inc., New York, 1922). See also BECKMAN, THEODORE N., and ROBERT BARTELS, *Credits and Collections in Theory and Practice*, 6th ed., pp. 591–596 (McGraw-Hill Book Company, Inc., New York, 1955); and *Terms of Sale* folder, published by Dun & Bradstreet, Inc., New York, 1956.

[23] FOULKE, ROY A., *Current Trends in Terms of Sale* (Dun & Bradstreet, Inc., New York, 1959).

are offered for early payment; in other cases obligations are normally permitted to run on open account for several months. Accounts receivable arising from the sale of merchandise are generally unsecured, and normally are very liquid.

4. *Notes Receivable for the Sale of Merchandise.* The widespread use of open account terms of sale in American commerce resulted from the great changes that came about in the methods of transacting everyday business on a fluctuating paper currency during the Civil War and subsequently from the practice, beginning in the 1870's, on the part of banking institutions of granting credit to business enterprises on an unsecured basis. Immediately prior to the Civil War, most manufacturers and wholesalers sold merchandise on credit terms that were met by notes receivable and trade acceptances running from 6 to 8 months.

Today there are very few lines of business in which it is customary to settle trade obligations by giving promissory notes. The practice, however, continues to be current in some divisions of the jewelry and fur industries.[24] Promissory notes are also given at times by distributors of automobile tires to the manufacturers of tires,[25] although customary settlement in this trade is made on open book account terms. Manufacturers of numerous types of heavy equipment, including air conditioning, construction and road machinery, laundry equipment, bakery equipment and supplies, printing machinery, heavy restaurant equipment, store fixtures, and machine tools, frequently sell on long-term arrangements under which the buyer makes some down payment and gives a series of installment notes ranging up to 36 months, the seller holding a protective lien such as a chattel mortgage or conditional sales contract until the final installment is paid.

In practically all other lines of commercial and industrial activity, the practice of settling merchandise obligations by notes, being unusual, is a general indication that the buyer is not as strong financially as competitors

[24] Jewelry manufacturers that purchase precious stones generally pay on cash terms but, at times, give notes running 3 and 4 months. Jewelry retailers generally make their purchases on terms of 2 per cent discount in 10 days, net 30 days, but some retailers pay by notes running 4 to 6 months, representing seasonal terms. In the fur trade, the fur dealer selling to the manufacturing furrier sells on notes which have an average maturity of 4 months. Raw furs are sold at auction for cash to dealers, but from that point through the various processing and manufacturing stages, up to and including the final sewing of the fur garments and fur trimmings and the subsequent sale to retail outlets, notes and trade acceptances are used extensively.

[25] In the sale of automobile tires the customary terms used by the manufacturer selling to wholesalers are 10th prox. However, during the winter months of November, December, January, and February, when sales to wholesalers are usually at a low level, manufacturers give season's dating. On shipments made in November and December, terms often call for equal payments in March, April, and May. No down payment is required. On shipments made in January and February, terms often call for equal payments in April, May, and June. Some sales are made on open account terms, and some are paid with promissory notes falling due on the above terms.

that purchase their merchandise on regular open account terms. Under these circumstances, notes receivable generally arise in three ways: (1) when a buyer desires extra terms which are longer than those customary in the particular division of trade, the seller might be more inclined to grant the longer terms if acknowledgment of the debt is immediately made by a promissory note; (2) if a buyer is weak financially, a note is often taken as a written evidence of the obligation; and (3) to close out a past-due account on the theory that the obligation is thus acknowledged. In case of suit, the sum might thereby be more easily collected than if evidenced only by an open book account. With the exception of the specific lines of business mentioned, typical promissory notes that comprise the item of notes receivable in the balance sheet are generally given by the less desirable accounts.

Any amount due from a subsidiary or affiliate that is found to be included in notes receivable should be segregated, studied, investigated, and handled in the same manner as accounts receivable due from a subsidiary or affiliate. Likewise, any amounts due for sales other than merchandise in the normal course of business, such as the sale of used machinery, sums due from officers, directors, salesmen, or other employees, should be deducted and included as slow miscellaneous assets and not as current assets.

It is not unusual to run across a balance sheet with a footnote showing contingent liabilities for notes receivable discounted with a commercial banking institution or a finance company. In this situation, the analyst should adjust the balance sheet by adding the amount of the discounted notes receivable to the item of notes receivable in the current assets, and then add a corresponding sum to the amount due to a bank or banks, or a finance company, in the current liabilities. If this practice is not followed, the balance sheet will not have been set up on a comparative basis so that an intelligent comparison may be made between respective items from year to year. This practice is absolutely essential for sound analytical deductions.

5. *Trade Acceptances for the Sale of Merchandise.* In the years following the First World War, an effort was made by a group of American businessmen to resurrect the use of trade acceptances, which had been an extensive medium for settling merchandise obligations from the days of the early colonial settlements down to the Civil War. The American Acceptance Council[26] was organized to distribute publicity showing the distinct advantage of selling on trade acceptance terms.

Notwithstanding this intensified crusade, the typical American businessmen continued to favor the established practice of settling by check after examining invoices or monthly statements. In addition, banking

[26] The American Acceptance Council went out of existence in 1937.

institutions showed no particular inclination to favor the change. In lines of business where a cash discount was allowed for early payments, the financially strong buyers naturally persisted in buying on those terms and in taking the discount so essential to proper modern business operation. At the present time trade acceptances are only occasionally and sporadically used. They are invariably classified and carried by auditors and accountants as part of the notes receivable.

6. *Merchandise—Finished, in Process, and Raw Material.* Merchandise is the largest and the most important item in many balance sheets, of both large and small concerns. Unlike accounts and notes receivable, merchandise does not represent definite claims to dollars. Merchandise must first pass through the sales process before it reaches the stage of representing an absolute monetary claim. The number of opportunities for misrepresenting its value are practically limitless. The general practice of the more responsible business enterprise is to value inventory at cost or market, whichever is lower, but the very methods of determining exactly what is "cost or market, whichever is lower" are so varied and give such different results in the aggregate amount that they are discussed in considerable detail in Chap. XI.

Until recent years, all well-managed concerns took a physical inventory, that is, actually counted and valued each item of merchandise on hand, as of approximately the statement date. Then along came the retail method of valuing inventory.[27] By this method a physical inventory is taken at least once a year in each department of the store and the inventory records adjusted to this actual count. As the retail method came into widespread use, concerns in many lines of industry and commerce developed more and more accurate statistics showing a continuous record of incoming and outgoing stocks. These perpetual-inventory records have, in many large corporations, become so accurate that the book inventory varies only nominally from the physical inventory when taken. The inventory of less responsible and smaller concerns is often an estimated figure and is generally so recognized by the round numbers with which the item appears on the balance sheet.

The more comprehensive financial statement forms of commercial banking institutions, Dun & Bradstreet, Inc., and larger mercantile concerns invariably call for a breakdown of the inventory of manufacturers into three parts, *raw materials, in process,* and *finished merchandise.*

The long financial statement forms of the Federal Reserve Bank of New York also request a segregation of *supplies* under inventory, a segregation which, as subsequently explained, is generally carried as a slow miscellaneous asset in a conservative analysis. The size of each of these divisions of the inventory depends upon the statement date. If the natural business

[27] See Chap. XI, pp. 308.

year[28] is used, raw materials, in process, and finished merchandise will generally be at their low point; if the date is early in the season, raw material will be relatively heavy; a little later, merchandise in process will be relatively substantial; and then, as manufacturing gets well under way, the finished merchandise will be heavy.

Raw materials naturally have a wider market than the finished merchandise, and in case of need, generally can be sold readily. Seasoned lumber can be sold more readily than furniture, woolen and worsted cloth more readily than men's or women's suits, grey goods more readily than printed cotton cloth, and high-carbon-steel bars more readily than machinery. The analyst must keep in mind at all times when he is studying financial statements that he is really analyzing the business, and that the condition reflected by financial statements on his desk has changed while those very figures were being prepared. Perhaps 2 or 3 or 4 months have passed since the statement date, and the raw material on hand has increased or decreased. Whether it is more or less can be reasoned from a knowledge of the seasonal operations of the concern, but confirmation of a most exact and reliable nature may be obtained by requesting that the figure of the inventory be broken down into these three divisions as of the first of the current month as shown by the perpetual-inventory records, when such records are kept.

Merchandise in process generally represents the value of raw material to which has been added labor and a proper proportion of the indirect expenses of production such as light, heat, power, depreciation on machinery, and burden. Where highly coordinated cost systems have been properly instituted and carried out, it is possible to value this part of the inventory with real accuracy. To smaller manufacturers the costs of carrying on such systems are prohibitive. "However crude the accounting system, no concern of any size is without some sort of cost records," explains Montgomery from the viewpoint of the auditor. "It may be difficult to get access to them, because many so-called practical superintendents are strangely uncommunicative about their determinations of cost. They contend, with much vigor, that modern cost systems are complicated and not good. These superintendents believe that they can calculate their costs accurately without so much detail; but they rarely consent, voluntarily, to open up their records. Yet there is nearly always somebody who prepares cost figures. . . ."[29]

The inventory of retail and wholesale enterprises is finished merchandise purchase from others. That portion of the inventory of a manufacturer which is finished merchandise has been produced on the premises,

[28] See Chap. VII, pp. 210–217.

[29] MONTGOMERY, ROBERT H., *Auditing Theory and Practice*, 6th ed., p. 146 (The Ronald Press Company, New York, 1940).

and the value, as we have seen, is a computed cost. There is always the necessity of making a sale to convert the finished merchandise, part by part, into receivables or, in the case of cash retail stores, into cash. At times, merchandise that is partly or wholly worthless from a market point of view, because of age and general deterioration, or because of changes in demand, style, and fashion, is included. In such cases the inventory is correspondingly inflated and heavy, and it is the job of the analyst to interpret that condition from his study of the figures.

In many audited and unaudited balance sheets, the item of *supplies* is carried in the inventory. Supplies might consist of coal at a mill, wrapping paper and twine in a retail store, boxes in an apple orchard, stationery and office supplies in any good-sized concern. In analyzing balance sheets, any item of supplies carried in the inventory should be deducted and carried among the slow miscellaneous assets. Even though the supplies may be valuable and will gradually be utilized, the fact remains that such an item is no part of the inventory; it should always be segregated; and it is rarely, if ever, a current asset.

7. *Advances on Merchandise.* An advance on merchandise is a slower asset than merchandise, as the initial step of obtaining possession of the merchandise must be made before the merchandise may then be converted into accounts or notes receivable. This item is an important one in case of canners of fruits and vegetables that advance seed and fertilizer, or make loans to farmers to finance the growing of the crops needed for canning. It is important to manufacturers which obtain parts for an assembly line from outside concerns that are in weak financial condition and that require the advance of funds to carry on their operations.

8. *Marketable Securities.* An item of marketable securities, to be carried as a current asset, must represent invested surplus cash which has been put into stocks or bonds which are known to be readily marketable and which may be liquidated at a moment's notice when the cash is needed in the business. Such securities generally are listed on a national security exchange, although in occasional instances they may represent stocks in banks, trust companies, insurance companies, or well-known industrials, public utilities, or railroads which are known to have an active over-the-counter market and are quoted daily. These securities should be valued at cost or market, except when cost is greater than market.

If there is any doubt whatsoever as to whether a particular security has an active market, it should be eliminated from the current assets. If any securities are included which obviously are owned for the purpose of controlling a substantial interest in one or more corporations, and not as a short-term investment, the values of these securities should be transferred from the current assets to miscellaneous assets.

Marketable securities are constantly fluctuating in quoted value. Many operating managements, however, continue to carry the investments at cost. Obviously, securities which have cost $25,000 and have dropped to $18,000 in market value should not be carried in the current assets at $25,000. The fact that the investment, at times, is carried at the cost of $25,000 is one of the conventions of the accounting profession. These assets are currently worth no more than the market quotation, no matter what the cost might have been. In fact, if the securities consist of a large block of stocks or bonds, and there is little support to the market at the time, even the market quotation may not be realized in full liquidation. In this predicament it is advisable for the analyst to adjust the value of the securities to market, reduce the surplus the same amount, and then carry the item in the current assets. Such an adjustment is necessary to obtain a clear picture of the financial condition of the business enterprise. Rules of the Securities and Exchange Commission define marketable securities when carried as a current asset as follows:

Include only securities having a ready market. Securities of affiliates shall not be included here. State the basis of determining the amount at which carried. The aggregate cost, and aggregate amount on the basis of current market quotations, shall be stated parenthetically or otherwise.[30]

Simultaneously, a registrant must file a schedule with the Securities and Exchange Commission giving the name of each issuer of a marketable security which is owned with the title of the issue, the number of shares or the principal amount of bonds and notes owned, the value at which each security is carried in the balance sheet of the registrant, and the value based on current market quotations at the balance sheet date. Each issue must be stated separately, except "that reasonable groupings, without enumeration, may be made with respect to (1) securities issued or guaranteed by the United States government and (2) investments as to which the aggregate amount" carried in the balance sheet "is not more than two per cent of total assets."[31]

Fixed Assets

Adam Smith defined fixed assets just as soundly as he defined current assets. "Some part of the capital of every master artificer or manufacturer must be fixed in the instruments of his trade," he carefully wrote many years ago. "This part, however, is very small in some, and very great in others. A master tailor requires no other instruments of trade but a parcel of needles. Those of the master shoemaker are a little, though but a very little, more expensive. Those of the weaver rise a good deal above those of

---

[30] Regulation S-X, Rule 5-02-2 p. 9, Aug. 20, 1958.
[31] *Ibid.*, Rule 12-02, p. 45.

the shoemaker. The far greater part of the capital of all such master artific-
ers, however, is circulated either in the wages of their workmen, or in
the prices of their materials, and repaid with the profit by the price of the
work. In other works, a much greater fixed capital is required. In a great
ironwork, for example, the furnace for melting the ore, the forge, the slit
mill, are instruments of trade which cannot be erected without a very
great expense. In coal works, and mines of every kind, the machinery
necessary both for drawing out the water and for other purposes, is frequently still more expensive."[32]

Fixed assets are items not readily convertible into cash in the normal
operations of a commercial or industrial business enterprise. These items,
unlike inventory, are not subject to periodic purchase and sale. They are
fairly permanent and although of the utmost importance to a going business enterprise, they are not liquidated in the orderly operations of a business except as depreciation is added to the cost of goods sold. As Paton and
Littleton explain in their synthesis, "A unit of plant is a 'store' of service-
capacity, and the service is rendered in terms of the entire active history
of the unit. . . . These 'assets' are in fact 'revenue charges in suspense'
awaiting some future matching with revenue as costs or expenses."[33] In a
small concern they generally consist of one item, namely, fixed assets; in a
large corporation they may consist of several or all the following six
items:

1. Land
2. Buildings
3. Machinery, tools, and equipment
4. Furniture and fixtures
5. Trucks and automobiles
6. Leasehold improvements

Few businesses with a tangible net worth of less than $25,000 own
land for business purposes, although the balance sheets of unaudited
proprietorships and partnerships often contain such an item, representing
outside means of the principal or principals. Manufacturing concerns are
the only ones that have such items as machinery, tools, and equipment on
their books, and generally only the larger retail stores or chain organizations carry an item such as leasehold improvements. The figures at which
any of these items are carried in the balance sheet may be the original
cost, less accumulated depreciation; it may be a figure based on reappraisal; it may represent an estimate based upon the probable reproduction cost, or upon some other valuation, particularly in smaller concerns.

[32] *The Wealth of Nations*, p. 263.
[33] PATON, W. A., and A. C. LITTLETON, *An Introduction to Corporate Accounting
Standards*, pp. 25, 82 (American Accounting Association, Chicago, 1940).

Land should, as a general rule, be shown separately in a balance sheet as it is not ordinarily subject to depreciation.[34] There, it should be excluded from the other depreciable assets so as to reveal the valuation against which the reserve for depreciation is properly applicable.

A piece of land, a building, or a plant that 10 years ago cost $100,000 may have a current economic value of only $25,000. If the asset was land, it would generally be carried on the books at the cost of $100,000. If the asset was a building or a plant it would generally be carried at cost plus improvements, less accumulated depreciation. The fact that such an asset had fallen materially in market value might have been due to a depression, to the fact that the asset was purchased at an inflated figure, or to the fact that the neighborhood had changed and values had accordingly fallen. That an asset would be carried in a balance sheet at cost, considerably in excess of its actual economic value, is another so-called "convention" of the accounting profession. It was such fixed assets of which George O. May apparently was thinking when he explained, "Writers of textbooks on accounting speak of the purpose of the balance sheet as being to reflect the values of the assets and the liabilities on a particular date. They explain the fact that in many balance sheets certain assets are stated at figures which are obviously far above or far below true values by saying that the amounts at which such assets are stated represent 'conventional' valuations. Such statements seem to involve a misconception of the nature of a balance sheet."[35] According to this school of thought a balance sheet is not supposed to reflect economic values, but merely values that have not been used up in business operations.

It was this very point to which MacNeal took violent exception. For him, a balance sheet would be more nearly correct if fixed assets that had market values were carried at market—this might well involve annual appraisals—and nonmarketable reproducible assets at replacement cost less depreciation. For him appraisals, no matter how vast or complicated, would give values in balance sheets more representative of actual values than carrying at $100,000 a plant which was generally and widely known to be worth less than $25,000.[36]

An elaborate schedule of property, plant, and equipment must be filed by registrants with the Securities and Exchange Commission. This schedule must give the major classifications, if practical, such as land, buildings,

[34] LENHART, NORMAN J., and PHILIP L. DEFLIESE, *Montgomery's Auditing*, 8th ed., p. 263 (The Ronald Press, New York, 1957).

[35] MAY, GEORGE O., *Audits of Corporate Accounts.* Correspondence between the Special Committee on Cooperation with Stock Exchanges of the American Institute of Accountants and the Committee on Stock List of the New York Stock Exchange, 1932–1934.

[36] MACNEAL, KENNETH, *Truth in Accounting* (University of Pennsylvania Press, Philadelphia, 1939).

equipment, and leaseholds, the value at the beginning of the period, amount of additions at cost, amount of retirements or sales, other changes —debit or credit—and the amount at the close of the period. Simultaneously the registrant is requested to "comment briefly on any significant and unusual additions, abandonments, or retirements, or any significant and unusual changes in the general character and location of principal plants and other important units, which may have occurred within the period."[37]

Miscellaneous Assets

Miscellaneous assets are those not included in the preceding two groups (that is, current assets and fixed assets) which are not of an intangible nature. They are like the odd pieces of furniture that go to furnish a home, not absolutely essential so far as livability is concerned but necessary to round out the comfort. Miscellaneous assets consist of a variety of items, the more common of which are the following:

1. Cash surrender value of life insurance
2. Due from officers, directors, and employees
3. Investments
4. Investments in and advances to subsidiaries and affiliates
5. Deferred charges and prepaid expenses

1. *Cash Surrender Value of Life Insurance.* Insurance is taken out, from time to time, on the lives of officers, partners, or executives of a business enterprise and the premiums paid by the business. At death the proceeds of the insurance policies are paid to the concern. Part of the premiums paid on life insurance of this nature generally accumulate and have a cash surrender value which is carried as an asset in the balance sheet.

An occasional accountant sets up the cash surrender value of life insurance as a current asset; most accountants now treat the item as a miscellaneous asset, keeping in mind, however, that it is an asset generally worth the stated amount. Occasionally the writer has run across situations where, upon inquiry, it was learned that a particular item was not the cash surrender value but the aggregate of all premiums paid, an amount somewhat greater than the cash surrender value and so inflated from the viewpoint of actual value. Such a practice would seem to have little justification. Those who consider the cash surrender value of life insurance as a current asset do so on the theory that current assets represent the sum of cash and all items that are readily convertible into cash. Almost every asset in the balance sheet, however, may readily be turned into cash if the price is sufficiently low.

[37] Regulation S-X, Rule 12-06, p. 47, Aug. 20, 1958.

56, Oct. 15, 1964

The cash surrender value of life insurance is in the nature of a fairly permanent growing investment. Rarely is it turned into cash. The item grows from year to year as additional premiums are paid, up to the time that the business enterprise obtains a windfall at the death of the insured, or until the concern goes out of business. When cash is needed in an emergency, the cash surrender value of life insurance is often pledged as security for a loan from the underwriting life insurance company or from a commercial banking institution. The item then is out of temporary reach of general creditors or investors. It is evident from this explanation that in no sense of the word does the cash surrender value of life insurance create working capital, nor can it be used to meet current liabilities in the normal course of business operations.

2. *Due from Officers, Directors, and Employees.* Under unusual circumstances, comparative figures may indicate that an increasing amount of funds is being loaned to one or more officers, directors, and employees. Diligent inquiry might develop the fact that one or several officers are living beyond their means and that funds are being borrowed from the business for vacation or other expenses, a policy which, in time, has wrecked many enterprises when the borrowed amount had reached large proportions and could not be repaid. On the other hand, amounts due from officers, directors, and employees may be decreasing as monthly payments are received on account.

Amounts due from one or more officers, directors, and employees for advances are occasionally lumped with receivables for the sale of merchandise. This fact, if the amount is relatively large, may generally be discovered by the analysis of the receivables as described in Chap. XIII. If the exact amount may then be learned from the management, the balance sheet must be adjusted by decreasing the receivables by the amounts due from officers, directors, and employees and carrying this item as a miscellaneous asset.

A separate schedule of this item is requested from registrants by the Securities and Exchange Commission. This schedule must show the name of each debtor, the amount of receivables at the beginning of the accounting period, additions if any, amounts written off as uncollectible from each debtor, collections from each debtor, and the balance receivable at the end of the accounting period divided into two parts, current and noncurrent.[38]

3. *Investments.* Investment is a mystery item and a full explanation should always be obtained, with a detailed breakdown showing how each part is valued. Never should an item of investments be passed by or overlooked. It is a most uncertain and frequently a most misleading item. Under this head there may be included securities of the Federal govern-

[38] *Ibid.*, Rule 12-03, p. 45.

ment, securities or an investment of a speculative nature, listed and unlisted, or securities which are absolutely worthless. The investment may be in some other operation or corporations, or in a property that has nothing to do with the conduct of the main enterprise. This item often has a distinct bearing upon a clear understanding of the financial condition of a business enterprise.

Here, for example, is a simple item of investments carried at $100,000 in a balance sheet. What does the item represent? The balance sheet could be studied indefinitely and under existing accounting conventions no analyst would be one whit the wiser: he would never discover whether the item was a current asset or a slow asset. Let us see what such a simple item could mean, what it could actually represent.

In the first place, the entire $100,000 might represent the value of listed securities, stocks, and bonds purchased for investment with surplus funds. But even here some additional explanation is necessary to determine whether the $100,000 represents the cost of the securities, or their market value on the date of the statement; or even cost or market, whichever is lower, for each of the securities that make up the total. This information, according to present-day accounting practice, should be included in the balance sheet.[39] Often it is not. The interpretation of this item in any analysis would be very different if the cost were $100,000 and the market value on the statement date only $40,000, than if the item represented cost of $100,000 and the market value were $140,000.[40]

In the second place, the item might represent not listed stocks and bonds purchased for temporary investment, but controlling stock interest in one or several subsidiaries that the corporation had organized to carry on certain specific operations. Even then the analyst would have very limited information. At this point, if there were several subsidiaries, he would need a detailed breakdown giving the name of each subsidiary and the amount at which the investment in each is carried in this item. He would need additional information of an intimate character as to whether the stock interest in each of the subsidiaries was carried at cost, at book value, or possibly at some arbitrary figure. If detailed individual balance

[39] "The balance sheet description should indicate the basis on which the amount [marketable securities] is stated, whether cost, current market, or other. If the balance sheet amount is substantially different from the currently quoted values, then the amount of the latter should also be stated."—SANDERS, THOMAS HENRY, HENRY RAND HATFIELD, and UNDERHILL MOORE, A Statement of Accounting Principles, p. 72 (American Institute of Certified Public Accountants, New York, 1938). Regulation S-X, Rule 5-02-2, of the Securities and Exchange Commission, p. 9, Aug. 20, 1953, about marketable securities, reads as follows: "Include only securities having a ready market. Securities of affiliates shall not be included here. State the basis of determining the amount at which carried. The aggregate cost, and aggregate amount on the basis of current market quotations, shall be stated parenthetically or otherwise."

[40] In accounting theory, readily marketable or listed securities should be carried as Marketable Securities and not under a caption of Investments.

regarding the treatment of readily marketable securities has been quoted on p. 8 √.

sheets could be obtained showing the financial condition of each of the subsidiaries, it would be evident at a glance whether the investment in each subsidiary was carried at its respective book value in the individual balance sheet of the parent company, or on some other basis. Then a separate analysis would need to be made of the balance sheets of each of the subsidiaries to determine whether they were in sound financial condition, or, as occasionally happens, whether one or several were on the verge of bankruptcy.

In the third place, the item might represent a conglomeration of stock interests, each moderate in amount, in a large number of business enterprises. Some of these investments might have been made over the years to assist officers and directors in outside ventures or to assist friends in personal ventures; some might represent stock investments made in accordance with business policies to hold or to build up sales, as when an institutional wholesale grocer purchases an interest in a successful restaurant; and still others might represent securities accepted in reorganizations where the concern was a creditor.

To obtain the exact information in any individual case, it is absolutely necessary to secure a detailed segregation of the amount of the investment carried in the balance sheet, with verbal explanations regarding each item in that breakdown from someone in the operating management. Further explanations would then be needed to ascertain whether one, or several, or all the items were valued at cost, market, book value, or some arbitrary amount. Not only could an investment item represent any one of these three types of assets but it could also represent the entire three types together. What chance would any analyst have of utilizing such an item in an intelligent study of the figures without the quite comprehensive information outlined in the preceding paragraphs? An item of investments is always important because the actual value might be appreciably above or below that shown on the balance sheet.

4. *Investments in and Advances to Subsidiaries and Affiliates.* An all-inclusive item of investments in and advances to subsidiaries and affiliates also has characteristics of a far-reaching nature which always need explanation. Such an item with its complexity and almost infinite ramifications has arisen from the development of big business and of the corporation as the basic unit of modern business. In order to evaluate its significance, supplementary information must be obtained from some member of the operating management or from the accountant.

Let us consider this item by steps. First of all, the item must be broken down into its component parts showing the respective amounts carried as investments in each subsidiary[41] and each affiliate,[42] and the respective

[41] A subsidiary is a corporation, the majorities of the voting stocks (generally the common stock) of which are owned by another corporation. The owning concern is

individual amounts carried as advances to each subsidiary and each affiliate. Second, an explanation must be obtained concerning the exact basis on which the investment is carried in each particular subsidiary or affiliate, at cost, at market if there is a ready market for the stock, at book value, or at some arbitrary figure. Third, individual balance sheets should be obtained on each subsidiary or affiliate. From these balance sheets and with prior information regarding the per cent of interest owned in each concern, the analyst may then determine whether the investment in each enterprise is carried at cost, above, or below book value. If a 60 per cent interest in a subsidiary is carried at cost of $80,000 and the individual figures of the subsidiary show only a tangible net worth of $30,000 and a loss on operations for the year, it is evident that the balance sheet under analysis is inflated by this one item to the extent of $62,000, the difference between 60 per cent of $30,000, or $18,000, and $80,000.

Fourth, after the advances are segregated to show the amount due from each subsidiary and affiliate, an explanation is needed to understand how each advance arose. Does a particular advance represent a loan, or does it represent an amount due for the sale of merchandise? If the advance was made as a loan, has it been running for several years or several months? Is it a long-term loan that was made to keep the enterprise alive or is it a short-term loan merely to cover a seasonal peak? From a study of the individual figures of the debtor corporation, the analyst at this point should determine whether the loan, in his judgment, is likely to be repaid in the near future or has already become frozen. If the item arose from the sale of merchandise, was the sale made on regular or on special terms? If made on regular terms, have similar obligations in the recent past been paid on those terms? If made on special terms, what are those terms, why

---

called the parent corporation. An enterprise may be a subsidiary of one corporation and the parent of another corporation. A subsidiary is wholly owned when the entire outstanding capital stock is owned by the parent corporation. A subsidiary is partly owned when only part, but controlling interest in the voting stock, is owned by the parent corporation. In the evolution of big business in the United States, an almost infinite number of complicated family arrangements have been created with successive layers of wholly and partly owned subsidiaries. In such situations it is often necessary to make a chart of the family connections in order to understand the relationships clearly. The Securities and Exchange Commission defines a "significant subsidiary" as a subsidiary that meets any one of the following conditions: "(a) The assets of the subsidiary, or the investments in and advances to the subsidiary by its parent and the parent's other subsidiaries, if any, exceed 15 per cent of the assets of the parent and its subsidiaries on a consolidated basis, (b) the sales and operating revenues of the subsidiary exceed 15 per cent of the sales and operating revenues of its parent and the parent's subsidiaries on a consolidated basis, (c) the subsidiary is the parent of one or more subsidiaries and together with such subsidiaries would, if considered in the aggregate, constitute a significant subsidiary."—Regulation S-X, p. 2, Aug. 20, 1958.

[42] An affiliate is a corporation in which a part interest is owned by another corporation, or by a member or members of the operating management of another corporation. A subsidiary is an affiliate, but an affiliate is not necessarily a subsidiary.

were they extended, and, from the analysis of the figures, is the obligation likely to be repaid at maturity?

Rules of the Securities and Exchange Commission require a registrant to file a schedule with extensive information regarding any investment in the securities of subsidiaries or affiliates. This schedule includes the name of each such subsidiary or affiliate with the title of the security owned in each case, the number of shares or principal amount of bonds or notes and the value in dollars at the beginning of the period, the amount of increase in units and dollars for each security, and the balance at the end of the period in units and dollars. The securities are required to be "grouped separately for (1) subsidiaries consolidated; (2) subsidiaries not consolidated; and (3) other affiliates, showing shares and bonds separately in each case."[43]

Registrants, as a general policy, must file individual figures with the Securities and Exchange Commission, as well as consolidated or partly consolidated figures including the assets and liabilities of all or some of the subsidiaries. In these individual figures, the rules of the Commission require that securities of subsidiaries and affiliates must be stated separately for amounts which in the related consolidated balance sheet are (1) eliminated and (2) not eliminated. Likewise, the indebtedness of subsidiaries and affiliates to the registrant, which for any reason is not considered a current liability, must be stated separately in the individual balance sheet of the registrant for that indebtedness which in the related consolidated balance sheet had been (1) eliminated and (2) not eliminated.[44]

5. *Deferred Charges and Prepaid Expenses.* The two items of deferred charges and prepaid expenses "are generally considered to represent the balance of amounts paid for services not yet received from the payee, such as insurance premiums for which the insurance company still must provide coverage. Deferred charges on the other hand usually represent the balance of amounts paid for goods or services which have been received and for which the payee has no further obligation. Thus the pro rata amount of rent paid applicable to the unexpired portion of a lease is a prepaid expense, while the cost of experimental work that may reasonably be expected to produce income in the future is a deferred charge."[45] This technical distinction is not always followed.

The item might appear in balance sheets under varied captions: deferred (or prepaid) assets, deferred (or prepaid) items, deferred (or prepaid) expenses. For industrial and commercial concerns such an item usually covers prepaid rent, insurance, interest, and commissions. These expenses generally are paid in advance, and to the extent that the services

---

[43] Regulation S-X, Rule 12-04, p. 46, Aug. 20, 1958.
[44] *Ibid.*, Rules 5-01-09 and 5-01-10, p. 9.
[45] LENHART AND DEFLIESE, *op. cit.*, p. 307.

have not been wholly used or consumed, they are carried in a balance sheet and are applicable to a later period. They are of varying importance, although it is an exceptional situation when the item is relatively large. In occasional balance sheets the item is broken down into component parts.

Intangible Assets

Intangible assets are not available for the payment of the debts of a going business. They depreciate greatly in case of liquidation. Rarely are they found in the balance sheets of small concerns. The principal intangible items are:

1. Bond or debenture discount
2. Brands
3. Catalogues
4. Contracts
5. Copyrights
6. Designs
7. Development expense
8. Drawings
9. Formulas
10. Franchises
11. Good will
12. Leaseholds
13. Licenses
14. Magazine titles
15. Mailing lists
16. Models
17. Organization expense
18. Patents
19. Patterns
20. Processes
21. Subscription lists
22. Tracings
23. Trademarks
24. Trade names
25. Treasury stock, when carried as an asset

Thirty years ago, items of an intangible nature were far more common in balance sheets than they are today. Since the introduction and the spread in the use of no-par stocks, it has been unnecessary to use such items for legal fiction.[46] Managements of many corporations that have

[46] "One of the principal reasons for the creation of no-par stock has been the elimination of fictitious intangible values recorded in the books and approved by the directors

good will of real value, indicated by a high rate of sustained earnings, now refuse to set up such an item in their balance sheets. This situation comes to light in cases of mergers and consolidations where the capital stock of one corporation receives much greater relative weight because of the larger sustained net earnings.

Of the intangible items listed above, treasury stock is now the most common. This item arises from the practice of a corporation in repurchasing shares of its own stock. While it is the consensus of ~~writers on~~ accountancy that treasury stock should be treated as a deduction from capital stock, the item is carried quite commonly in the assets at the purchase price until retired or resold. As the corporate form of organization has become more prominent, treasury stock has appeared with greater frequency. Of the other items, those which the analyst is likely to come across more or less frequently are patents, copyrights, good will, organization expenses, development expenses, patterns, leaseholds, trademarks, and trade names.

In determining the tangible net worth of a concern, the value at which any of these intangible items is carried in the balance sheet is deducted from the net worth (that is, the proprietary interest) in proprietorships or partnerships, and from the sum of the capital stocks and surpluses in corporations. A business enterprise with $50,000 of outstanding 5 per cent cumulative preferred stock, $100,000 of common stock, and an earned surplus of $42,976 would have a net worth of $192,976. If, in the assets of the balance sheet, there were an item of development expenses carried at $10,362 and an item of treasury stock carried at $6,942, or total intangible items of $17,304, then this total would be deducted from the net worth of $192,976 to give a *tangible net worth* of $175,672.

LIABILITIES

The liabilities of a small business enterprise such as a newsstand, a stationery store, or a cigar store might consist of only two items, accounts payable for merchandise and net worth. Large corporations such as manufacturers of automobiles, wholesale hardware dealers, and installment furniture stores might have 15 or 20 items including accounts payable, notes payable for merchandise, bank loans, provisions for taxes, due to officers and directors, accruals, funded debts payable over the years, and various classes of outstanding capital stock. The classification of these

in the case of par-value stock in order that the amount of the assets might be made to equal the amount of the liabilities and capital stock. . . . The trend of public opinion seems to be in this direction, and it is becoming more and more common to eliminate intangible values altogether or to carry them at a nominal value only."—BRUNDAGE, PERCIVAL F., "Treatment of No-par-value Stock in New York, New Jersey, and Massachusetts," "*The Journal of Accountancy*," Vol. XLI, No. 4, p. 246, April, 1926.

items is not as difficult as the classifications of items in the assets, but they do need considered attention.

All items on the liability side of balance sheets of commercial and industrial concerns fall into three broad groups: current liabilities, deferred liabilities, and, in accordance with the term used in this volume, net worth.

Current Liabilities

Current liabilities, from the viewpoint of an analyst, are all short-term obligations generally due and payable within one year.[47] They are usually incurred in the normal course of business and must be paid on fairly definite dates. A debt may be for a short-term bank loan running from 3 to 6 months, for the purchase of merchandise, for the premium on an insurance policy, for rent, or for accrued interest on a mortgage. In every case the liability is a definite one. Quite often values on the asset side shrink; obligations never shrink, and it is not unusual for the liability side to increase when debts are discovered which apparently were casually overlooked. Current liabilities generally consist of one or several of the following items:

1. Notes payable to banks
2. Notes payable and trade acceptances for merchandise, machinery, or equipment
3. Accounts payable
4. Loans payable
5. Accruals
6. Deposits
7. Advance payments
8. Reserves for taxes
9. Dividends declared but not paid
10. Reserves for contingencies against possible losses
11. Current maturity of a funded debt

[47] "The term *current liabilities* is used principally to identify and designate obligations whose liquidation is reasonably expected to require the use of existing resources properly classified as current assets, or the creation of other current liabilities. As a balance sheet category, the classification is intended to include obligations for items which have entered into the operating cycle, such as payables incurred in the acquisition of materials and supplies to be used in the production of goods or in providing services to be offered for sale, collections received in advance of the delivery of goods or performance of services, and debts which arise from operations directly related to the operating cycle, such as accruals for wages, salaries, commissions, rentals or royalties, and income and other taxes. Other liabilities whose regular and ordinary liquidation is expected to occur within a relatively short period of time, usually twelve months, are also intended for inclusion, such as short-term obligations, amounts required to be expended within one year under sinking fund provisions, and agency obligations arising from the collection or acceptance of cash or other assets for the account of third persons."—*Restatement and Revision of Accounting Research Bulletins, Accounting Research Bulletin No. 43*, pp. 21–22 (American Institute of Certified Public Accountants, New York, 1953).

In the study of the individual items that make up the current assets, it was shown how easily each of these various items could be inflated purposely or by oversight, and how important it was for the analyst to adjust the figures by making deductions for such excesses which really belonged in the miscellaneous group of slow assets. In the study of current liabilities, the problem is just the opposite; the auditor or the bookkeeper who prepares the balance sheet occasionally omits from the current liabilities items which the analyst must include. A bank overdraft is at times placed in the current assets in red ink indicating a deduction; actually the item is a debt and should be carried as a current liability. A reserve for Federal income taxes at times is omitted, more particularly on interim balance sheets; unless the analyst notices the omission and computes and adds the approximate amount of the tax, his analysis will be unsound. With existing high tax rates, the amount involved may be very substantial.

In case of financial difficulty and subsequent liquidation of a business, all creditors, except those that have received priority under the law, expect to share in the assets in proportion to their just claims. If a loss is involved, the unsecured creditors share the loss pro rata. When certain assets such as discounted notes receivable, the assignment of accounts receivable, warehouse receipts covering merchandise, factor's lien on merchandise, cash surrender value of life insurance, or marketable securities are pledged to secure some one or a limited number of creditors, then the risk of all other creditors is greatly increased. As a result it is extremely important that a balance sheet clearly disclose the amount of liabilities which are secured claims, and the assets which are specially pledged to secure these claims. Without this information, the balance sheet cannot be intelligently analyzed, and new creditors will have no idea that they are junior to certain other creditors.

Concerns in healthy financial condition have no occasion to pledge assets to banks or other creditors for short-term credit. So, whenever certain assets are so pledged, that very fact is an indication that some creditor, who has presumably made a more or less intimate study of the financial condition of the business, is dissatisfied and has insisted upon the pledge of some type of security to protect his claim. At times, a wise or knowing creditor will insist upon the guaranty of an obligation by the principal stockholder in a corporation or a parent corporation for added protection; this information is often difficult for the analyst to obtain except through a most thorough and painstaking outside investigation. These situations represent tacit admissions of weakness that should never be overlooked.

1. *Notes Payable to Banks.* It is good accounting practice to show the various note obligations separately in a balance sheet: notes payable to banks, notes payable and trade acceptances for merchandise, notes pay-

Form CR 9		
Statement Form Suggested By	**FINANCIAL STATEMENT**	**PARTNERSHIP**
FEDERAL RESERVE BANK OF NEW YORK	As of 19	(SHORT FORM)

NAME ....

BUSINESS ....DATE ESTABLISHED...

ADDRESS ....

We make the following statement of all the assets and liabilities of this partnership at the close of business on the date indicated above

to ....

(Name and Location of Financial Institution)

and give other material information for the purpose of obtaining advances on notes and bills bearing our signature, endorsement, or guaranty, and for obtaining credit generally upon present and future applications.

BALANCE SHEET

ASSETS		LIABILITIES and NET WORTH	
Cash on Hand	$	Notes Payable to Banks — Unsecured	$
		Direct borrowings only	
Cash in Banks		Notes Payable to Banks — Secured	
		Direct borrowings only	
Notes Receivable — Current & Collectible		Notes Payable to Trade Suppliers	
From customers, excluding affiliates		Excluding affiliates	
Accounts Receivable — Current & Collectible		Notes Payable for Machinery & Equipment	
From customers, excluding affiliates		Due within one year	
Due from Affiliates — Current & Collectible		Accounts Payable to Trade Suppliers	
For sale of goods on regular terms		Excluding affiliates	
Inventory		Advances & Deposits from Customers	
Life Insurance — Cash Surrender Value		Loans against Life Insurance	
(Do not deduct loans)			
Securities — Readily Marketable		Due to Affiliates	
U. S. Government & listed on Stock Exchanges			
		Due to Partners	
Total Current Assets	$	Due to Relatives & Friends	
		For loans, advances & other payables	
Securities — Not Readily Marketable		Real Estate Mortgages Payable	
Unlisted stocks & bonds		Mortgages & installments due within one year	
Investments in Affiliates		Accrued Liabilities	
		For taxes, wages, interest, etc.	
Due from Affiliates			
Loans, advances & other receivables			
Mortgages Owned			
		Total Current Liabilities	$
Land & Buildings		Notes Payable for Machinery & Equipment	
(Do not deduct mortgages or depreciation reserve)		Due after one year	
Leasehold Improvements		Real Estate Mortgages Payable	
(Do not deduct amortization reserve)		Due after one year	
Machinery, Equipment, Furniture & Fixtures		Other Deferred Liabilities	
(Do not deduct mortgages or depreciation reserve)		Due after one year	
Notes & Accounts Receivable			
Past due, slow or doubtful of collection			
Due from Partners			
Loans, advances & other receivables		Total Liabilities	$
Due from Employees, Relatives & Friends		Depreciation & Amortization Reserves	
Loans, advances & other receivables			
Prepaid Expenses		Other Reserves	
Taxes, insurance, interest, rent, etc.			
Goodwill, Patents, Trademarks, etc.			
		Net Worth — General Partners' Account	
		— Special Partners' Account	
TOTAL ASSETS	$	TOTAL LIABILITIES & NET WORTH	$

O P E R A T I N G   S T A T E M E N T — For the .... month period ended .... 19 ....

Gross Sales	$_____	Administrative, General & Selling Expenses (Incl. depreciation & amortization $_____)	
Less Discounts, Returns & Allowances	_____	Net Operating Profit	$_____
Net Sales	$_____	Other Income	
Cost of Sales (Including depreciation & amortization $_____)	_____	Other Expense (Incl. bad debts $_____)	
Gross Profit	$_____	Net Profit for the Period	$_____
Opening Inventory $................. ; Closing Inventory $................. ; Basis of Inventory Valuation:_____			

R E C O N C I L I A T I O N   O F   N E T   W O R T H — For the .... month period ended .... 19 ....

Net Worth—Beginning of Period	$_____	Carried Forward	$_____
Additions to Net Worth:		**Deductions from Net Worth:**	
Net Profit for the Period	$_____	Partners' Salaries and	
Partners' Capital Contributions		Other Withdrawals	$_____
Forward.............	$_____	Net Worth—End of Period	$_____

(Continued on Reverse Side)

NOTE: The use of Form CR 109 is suggested for a more detailed presentation of the financial condition of a partnership.

(CR 9-9M-4-50)

FORM 6. Short form of financial statement blank for firms suggested by Federal Reserve Bank of New York (front).

SUPPLEMENTARY INFORMATION

NOTE: The following data should be furnished as of the same date as this Financial Statement. Fill in all spaces; insert "NONE" where appropriate.

Notes Receivable — Customers — Original Notes $....................;
Renewed Notes $....................; Past Due Notes $....................; Reserve for Doubtful Notes $....................

Accounts Receivable — Customers — Not Due $....................; Past Due — less than 3 months $...................., 3 to 6 months $...................., more than 6 months $....................; Reserve for Doubtful Accounts $....................

Regular Selling Terms — ....

Inventory — Raw Materials $....................; In Process $....................; Finished Goods $....................; Supplies, etc. $...................., Slow Moving or Obsolete $....................; Pledged $....................; On Consignment to Others $..................... Goods on Consignment from Others $....................

Securities— Describe each investment and indicate basis of valuation shown: ....

....

....

Registered owner of securities: ....

Life Insurance — On Partners for Benefit of Partnership: Face Amount $....................; Persons Insured: ....

Notes & Accounts Payable — Renewed Notes $....................; Past Due Notes $....................; Past Due Accounts $....................

Regular Purchasing Terms — ....

Current Liabilities — High & Low Points — Latest full fiscal year:
High Point $..................... on .... 19..........
Low Point $..................... on .... 19..........

Contingent Liabilities — As of the date of this financial statement, the partnership had no contingent liabilities, except as follows: Notes Receivable Discounted or Sold $....................; Accounts Receivable Assigned or Sold $....................; Accommodation Endorser, Guarantor or Surety $....................; Mortgage Bonds $....................; Leases $....................; Purchase Commitments for Merchandise $....................; Contracts for Building Construction, Improvements or Equipment $....................; Claims for Taxes $....................; Other (describe): ....

....

....

....

NOTE: If space is insufficient, separate schedules, which should be clearly identified as being part of this statement, may be attached hereto. Such schedules should be dated and signed in the same manner as this statement.

Land & Buildings — Location and Description	Cost with Improvements	Assessed Value	Market Value	Book Value	Mortgages Payable	Mortgage Payments Due Within one Year	Taxes, Assessments, Mortgage Interest Due & Unpaid
	$	$	$	$	$	$	$

The title to all of the above described properties is solely in the name of this partnership, except as follows: ....

Pledged, Assigned or Hypothecated Assets — Describe all assets not noted elsewhere in this statement as having been pledged, assigned or hypothecated and indicate the liabilities which they secure: ....

As of the date of this financial statement, this partnership had not pledged, assigned, hypothecated or transferred the title to any of its assets, except as noted on this form or on a supporting schedule, nor has any such action been taken since that date, except as follows (give details): ....

Legal Actions — No lawsuits, claims, judgments or other legal actions are outstanding or pending against the partnership or any partner and, to the best of our knowledge, no legal actions are to be started against the partnership or any partner, except as follows (give details): ....

Insurance Coverage — Fire Insurance: Inventory $...................., Buildings $...................., Machinery & Equipment $...................., Furniture & Fixtures $....................; Indicate if policies have extended coverage endorsement: ....; Use & Occupancy Insurance $....................; Liability Insurance: Autos & Trucks $...................., General Public $....................; Burglary Insurance $....................; Fidelity Bonds $....................; Other Insurance (describe): ....

Date of latest independent analysis of insurance: ....; Indicate adequacy of coverage: ....

Ownership — List all General and Special Partners:

Name (Designate General Partner "G. P." and Special Partner "S. P.")	Age	Capital Contribution	Current Annual Compensation from Partnership	Partners' Personal Financial Data			
				Date	Outside Net Worth	Direct Outside Debts, Including Mortgages	Liability as Co-maker, Guarantor, Endorser, etc.
		$	$		$	$	$

Our.................... Partnership Agreement went into effect on.................... and expires on.................... The responsibility
(Written or Oral)   (Date)   (Date)
of the Special Partners for the partnership's debts is limited to.................... until....................

Affiliated Companies & Interests — Give names, extent of interest, and nature of interrelations: ....

....

Accounting Data — Name of Independent Accountant....................; Indicate if Certified Public Accountant....................; Frequency of Independent Audits....................; Date of Latest Independent Audit....................; Date of Fiscal Year End....................; Date of Latest Physical Inventory....................

Certification — This is to certify that the foregoing figures were taken from the books and records of this partnership and that they and all other statements on this form and on any supporting schedules are true and give a correct showing of the financial condition of the partnership as of the date indicated. IN THE EVENT OF ANY MATERIAL ADVERSE CHANGE IN THE FINANCIAL CONDITION OF THIS PARTNERSHIP, WE AGREE TO NOTIFY THE FINANCIAL INSTITUTION NAMED HEREIN IMMEDIATELY IN WRITING.

Signed this.................... day of...................., 19..........
.... (Partnership Name)
NOTE: When there is no written partnership   By...................., General Partner
agreement, all the partners should sign.   (Signature)

IMPORTANT: If an audit was made as of the date of this statement, a copy of the accountant's report should be submitted herewith.

FORM 6. Short form of financial statement blank for firms suggested by Federal Reserve Bank of New York (reverse).

able for equipment, and notes payable to officers or others. It is important and desirable that these different sources of credit, when in use, be distinguished one from the other, as the amount of the liability and the source of the credit throw light on the facts behind the figures. A different interpretation is placed upon an item of notes payable of $30,000 representing a loan from a bank, and an item of notes payable of the same amount given in settlement of merchandise obligations because no bank credit is available. Notes payable to banks often bear the endorsement or guaranty of officers and directors of a corporation, a practice that gives additional security to the bank loan. It is highly desirable, as indicated in the preceding paragraph, to learn whether bank borrowings are on the straight paper of the borrower, whether they bear the endorsement or guaranty of officers, directors, or a parent corporation, or whether such loans are secured by the pledge of certain assets.

The fact that a banking institution is extending credit to a business enterprise on an unsecured basis, while favorable, is not an absolute indication that the business is basically sound, as bankers make their full share of errors in incomplete investigations, unsound analyses, and extension of credit. In such a situation, however, the analyst does know that all creditors are on the same basis and that certain assets have not been cornered. In a well-managed, sound business, notes payable to banks are relatively large and accounts payable relatively small, as funds are borrowed from banking institutions to discount merchandise purchases.

2. *Notes Payable and Trade Acceptances for Merchandise or Equipment.* Notes payable for merchandise as outlined on page 80 do not appear as a trade custom outside the jewelry, fur, leaf tobacco, automobile tire, and various durable goods lines of business. Sales in these fields are quite customarily made on promissory note terms, but in other lines of industry, notes would appear generally when extra time was required by the purchaser, or when a past-due account was being closed out by the creditor who desired an acknowledgment of the debt. Machinery and equipment are often purchased on installment terms calling for 12 or more equal monthly payments. As previously explained in this chapter, trade acceptances are little used in the United States today. The appearance of notes payable or trade acceptances for merchandise in a balance sheet thus tends to indicate some degree of financial weakness.

Notes payable for machinery and equipment are often secured by a chattel mortgage or conditional sales contract until the liability is completely liquidated. In good accounting practice any such asset pledged to secure a particular liability should be so earmarked and the two items related, so that the analyst will have a clear picture of any asset or assets not available to general creditors. Unfortunately, this practice is not always followed.

3. *Accounts Payable.* Accounts payable are incurred by the purchase of merchandise. When merchandise is purchased on terms that provide a discount in 10 days and the purchaser discounts all invoices, the item is relatively small. In some lines of business activity, longer terms are customary. Purchases of rayons and other synthetic piece goods by cutters, for example, are made on net 60 day terms; of woolen and worsted piece goods for men's wear on terms of net 60 days with 60 days extra with interest at the rate of 6 per cent per annum on any extra days; of fur garments on 4 months' terms; of rugs on terms of 5 per cent discount in 10 days, net EOM, or 4 per cent discount EOM with 60 days extra (*i.e.,* 4 per cent discount if paid within 70 days, net thereafter). When payments are made on terms and not anticipated, accounts payable often reach a relatively substantial figure. Normally a well-conducted business will have relatively low accounts payable, as it is customary to obtain loans from a commercial bank or trust company to discount trade invoices. Concerns in the smaller capital brackets, however, frequently have no lines of bank credit, and accounts payable then comprise all or the bulk of their current liabilities.

4. *Loans Payable.* A distinction is sometimes made by setting up notes payable to officers, directors, relatives, friends, and discount finance companies under the caption of *Loans Payable.* The distinction, however, does not have wide acceptance in accounting circles. Loans from officers, directors, relatives, or friends are often accepted as a friendly gesture to the creditor, the funds being used in place of bank borrowings. In other circumstances, if a concern were in an extended financial condition and unable to obtain credit from its bank or banks the last resort might be to borrow funds from someone already vitally interested in or particularly close to the business who was willing to take the risk.

Loans payable to a discount finance company are in a somewhat similar category. These loans are generally secured by the assignment of accounts receivable. In such cases, the loan made by the finance company would range from 70 to 90 per cent of the face value of accounts receivable. Under the notification plan the accounts receivable are collected by the finance company and the overage returned to the borrower. Under the nonnotification plan, the receivables are collected by the borrower who transmits on the day received all original checks, drafts, notes, or other payment instruments to the finance company. According to this plan of operation, the buyer of the merchandise never learns that his particular account receivable has been assigned to a finance company; at times the balance sheet of the borrower fails to disclose the fact that a valuable

Form CR 108
Statement Form Suggested By
FEDERAL RESERVE BANK OF NEW YORK

FINANCIAL STATEMENT

As of ....19......

CORPORATION
(LONG FORM)

NAME...

BUSINESS...INCORPORATED..........................UNDER.................LAWS
                                                (Date)   (State)

ADDRESS...

We make the following statement of all the assets and liabilities of this corporation at the close of business on the date indicated above

to...
                         (Name and Location of Financial Institution)

and give other material information for the purpose of obtaining advances on notes and bills bearing our signature, endorsement, or guaranty, and for obtaining credit generally upon present and future applications.

BALANCE SHEET

ASSETS		LIABILITIES and NET WORTH	
Cash on Hand	$	Notes Payable to Banks — Unsecured	$
		Direct borrowings only (Sch. No. 1)	
Cash in Banks		Notes Payable to Banks — Secured	
(Sch. No. 1)		Direct borrowings only (Sch. No. 1)	
Notes Receivable — Current & Collectible		Notes Payable to Trade Suppliers	
From customers, excl. subsidiaries & affiliates (Sch. No. 2)		Excluding subsidiaries & affiliates	
Accounts Receivable — Current & Collectible		Notes Payable for Machinery & Equipment	
From customers, excl. subsidiaries & affiliates (Sch. No. 3)		Due within one year	
Due from Subsidiaries & Affiliates —		Accounts Payable to Trade Suppliers	
Current & Collectible. For sale of goods on regular terms		Excluding subsidiaries & affiliates	
Inventories — Raw Materials		Advances & Deposits from Customers	
(Sch. No. 4)			
— Supplies		Due to Subsidiaries & Affiliates	
(Sch. No. 4)		For current purchases of goods, etc.	
— Goods in Process		Due to Subsidiaries & Affiliates	
(Sch. No. 4)		For loans, advances & other payables	
— Finished Goods		Due to Officers, Stockholders & Employees	
(Sch. No. 4)		For loans, advances & other payables	
Life Insurance — Cash Surrender Value		Loans against Life Insurance	
(Do not deduct loans) (Sch. No. 5)		(Sch. No. 5)	
Securities — Readily Marketable		Real Estate Mortgages Payable (Sch. No. 10)	
U. S. Govt. & listed on Stock Exchanges (Sch. No. 6)		Mortgages and installments due within one year	
		Federal Income Taxes	
		Real Estate Taxes & Assessments Payable	
		(Sch. No. 10)	
Total Current Assets	$	Accrued Liabilities	
		For other taxes, wages, interest, etc.	
Securities — Not Readily Marketable			
Unlisted stocks and bonds (Sch. No. 6)			
Investments in Subsidiaries & Affiliates		Total Current Liabilities	$
(Sch. No. 6)			
Due from Subsidiaries & Affiliates		Notes Payable for Machinery & Equipment	
Loans, advances & other receivables (Sch. No. 7)		Due after one year	
Mortgages Owned		Real Estate Mortgages Payable	
(Sch. No. 8)		Due after one year (Sch. No. 10)	
		Other Deferred Liabilities (Itemize)	
		Due after one year	
Land & Buildings — Used in Business			
(Do not deduct mortgages or deprec. reserve) (Sch. No. 9)			
Land & Buildings — Not Used in Business			
(Do not deduct mortgages or deprec. reserve) (Sch. No. 9)			
Leasehold Improvements		Total Liabilities	$
(Do not deduct amortization reserve)			
Machinery & Equipment		Depreciation Reserves-Buildings	
(Do not deduct mortgages or depreciation reserve)			
Furniture & Fixtures		-Machinery & Equipment	
(Do not deduct mortgages or depreciation reserve)			
Trucks, Automobiles, etc.		-Furniture & Fixtures	
(Do not deduct mortgages or depreciation reserve)			
Patterns, Tools, Dies, etc.		-Trucks, Automobiles, etc.	
		Amortization Reserve-Leasehold Improvements	
Notes Receivable		Other Reserves (Itemize)	
Past due or doubtful of collection (Sch. No. 2)			
Accounts Receivable			
Slow or doubtful of collection (Sch. No. 3)			
Due from Officers, Stockholders & Employees		Preferred Stock	
Loans, advances & other receivables (Sch. No. 11)		Dividend Rate .... %. Cumulative?	
Prepaid Expenses		Common Stock	
Taxes, insurance, interest, rent. etc.			
Goodwill, Patents, Trademarks, etc.		Unearned or Capital Surplus	
		Earned Surplus	
TOTAL ASSETS	$	TOTAL LIABILITIES AND NET WORTH	$

(Continued on Next Page)

CR. 108.4-12M-7-88

FORM 7. Long form of financial statement blank for corporations suggested by Federal Reserve Bank of New York (page 1).

— 2 —

BALANCE SHEET SCHEDULES

NOTE: The following data should be furnished as of the same date as this financial statement. Fill in all spaces; insert "NONE" where appropriate. If space is insufficient, separate schedules, which should be clearly identified as being part of this statement, may be attached hereto. Such schedules should be dated and signed in the same manner as this statement.

No. 1 — Banking Relations — List all bank accounts:

Name and Location of Bank	Cash Balance	Amount of Loan	Indicate How Loan is Endorsed, Guaranteed or Secured
	$	$	

No. 2 — Notes Receivable — Original Notes $................; Renewed Notes $................; Past Due Notes $................; Total $................; Less Reserve for Doubtful Notes $................; Net $................

Regular Selling Terms: ....

No. 4 — Inventory — Readily Saleable $................ ; Slow Moving & Obsolete $................; Total $................; Less Reserve (If Any) $................; Net $................ Inventory Pledged $................; On Consignment to Others $................ Goods on Consignment from Others $................

Basis of Inventory Valuation: ....

No. 3—Accounts Receivable—Not Due (Original Terms) $................; Past Due—less than 3 Months $................, 3 to 6 Months $................, more than 6 Months $................; Total $................; Less Reserve for Doubtful Accounts $................; Net $................

Inventory High & Low Points — During latest full fiscal year:

	High Point		Low Point	
	Date	Amount	Date	Amount
Raw Materials		$		$
Finished Goods				

No. 5 — Life Insurance — List all policies in names of officers for benefit of corporation:

Person Insured	Insurance Company	Type of Policy	Face Amount of Policy	Total Cash Surrender Value	Total Loans Against Policy	If Assigned, Indicate To Whom
			$	$	$	

No. 6 — Securities & Investments — List all stocks, bonds, etc.:

Face Value (Bonds) No. of Shares (Stocks)	Description of Security (Designate Readily Marketable "R.M." Not Readily Marketable "N.R.M." Subsidiaries "S." & Affiliates "A.")	Registered Owner	Cost	Market Value	Book Value	If Pledged, Indicate To Whom
			$	$	$	

No. 7 — Due from Subsidiaries & Affiliates —

Name of Subsidiary or Affiliate	Amount of Debt	Age of Debt	Nature of Debt	If Secured, Describe Security	Date Payment Expected
	$				

No. 8 — Mortgages Owned —

Location and Description of Mortgaged Property	Assessed Value	Market Value	Amount of Owned Mortgage	Mortgage Interest Due & Unpaid	Indicate if 1st or 2nd Mortgage	Amount of Prior Mortgage
	$	$	$	$		$

No. 9 — Land & Buildings —

Location and Description	Used in Business?	Cost with Improvements	Assessed Value	Market Value	Book Value	Annual Gross Rental Income	Annual Net Rental Income (Before Deprec.)
		$	$	$	$	$	$

The title to all of the above described properties is solely in the name of this corporation, except as follows: ....

(Continued on Next Page)

FORM 7. Long form of financial statement blank for corporations suggested by Federal Reserve Bank of New York (page 2).

— 3 —

BALANCE SHEET SCHEDULES (Continued) & SUPPLEMENTARY INFORMATION

No. 10 — Real Estate Mortgages Payable — List all mortgages on properties; follow same sequence as in Schedule No. 9:

First Mortgages		Second Mortgages		Mortgage Payments Due Within One Year	Mortgage Interest Due & Unpaid	Taxes and Assessments Due & Unpaid
Amount	Maturity	Amount	Maturity			
$		$		$	$	$

No. 11 — Due from Officers, Stockholders & Employees — List the largest amounts owed to the corporation:

Name of Debtor	Amount of Debt	Age of Debt	Nature of Debt	If Secured, Describe Security	Date Payment Expected
	$				

Notes & Accounts Payable — Renewed Notes $................; Past Due Notes $ .... ; Past Due Accounts $ ....

Regular Purchasing Terms: ....

Current Liabilities—High & Low Points—During latest full fiscal year:
High Point $................on................19....
Low Point $ ....on .. ..19....

Contingent Liabilities — As of the date of this financial statement, the corporation had no contingent liabilities, except as follows: Notes Receivable Discounted or Sold $. .... ; Accounts Receivable Assigned or Sold $........................; Accommodation Endorser, Guarantor or Surety $....................; Mortgage Bonds $....................; Leases $....................; Purchase Commitments for Merchandise $:....................; Contracts for Building Construction, Improvements or Equipment $....................; Claims for Taxes $....................; Other (describe): ....

Pledged, Assigned or Hypothecated Assets — Describe all assets not noted elsewhere in this statement as having been pledged, assigned or hypothecated and indicate the liabilities which they secure: ....

As of the date of this financial statement, this corporation had not pledged, assigned, hypothecated or transferred the title to any of its assets, except as noted on this form or on a supporting schedule, nor has any such action been taken since that date, except as follows (give details): ....

Legal Actions — No lawsuits, claims, judgments or other legal actions are outstanding or pending against this corporation and to the best of our knowledge no legal actions are to be started against this corporation, except as follows (give details): ....

Insurance Coverage — Fire Insurance: Inventory $................ ...., Buildings $...................., Machinery & Equipment $...................., Furniture & Fixtures $....................; Indicate if policies have extended coverage endorsement:....................; Use & Occupancy Insurance $....................; Liability Insurance: Autos & Trucks $. ...., General Public $....................; Burglary Insurance $....................; Fidelity Bonds — Officers & Employees $.............. ; Other Insurance (describe): ....

Date of latest independent analysis of insurance: ....; Indicate adequacy of coverage: .....

Capitalization —	Par Value	Number of Shares		**Preferred Stock Provisions**—Voting Rights, Preferences, Convertibility, etc.:
		Authorized	Outstanding	....
Common Stock	$			....
Preferred Stock				....

Dividend Policy — ....
....
....

Unpaid cumulative preferred stock dividends .... $....
Period of preferred dividend arrearage: ....

Management — List all Officers:			Current Annual Compensation from Corporation	Stockholdings in Corporation	
Name	Age	Title		No. of Shares of Common	No. of Shares of Preferred
			$		

Management Extra Compensation Plans — Bonus, Profit Sharing, Retirement, Stock Acquisition Plans, etc. (give details): ....
....

Subsidiaries & Affiliates — Give names, extent of interest, and nature of interrelations: ....

Accounting Data — Name of Independent Accountant ....; Indicate if Certified Public Accountant :....................;
Frequency of Independent Audits ....; Date of Latest Independent Audit ....
Date of Fiscal Year End .. ..; Date of Latest Physical Inventory ....

(Continued on Next Page)

FORM 7. Long form of financial statement blank for corporations suggested by Federal Reserve Bank of New York (page 3).

— 4 —

OPERATING STATEMENT

FOR THE .... MONTH PERIOD ENDED .... 19 ......

Gross Sales — To Regular Customers .... $...............

         — To Subsidiaries ....

         — To Affiliates .... $...............

     Less: Returns and Allowances (Do not deduct Cash Discounts) ....

Net Sales .... $...............

     Cost of Sales:

         Inventory at Beginning of Period .... $...............

         Purchases (Do not deduct Cash Discounts) ....

         Direct Labor ....

         Depreciation & Amortization ....

         Other Costs (Itemize):

         Less: Inventory at End of Period $.......... $...............

Gross Profit .... $...............

     Administrative and General Expenses (Schedule No. 1) .... $...............

     Selling Expenses (Schedule No. 2) ....

Net Operating Profit .... $...............

     Other Income (Schedule No. 3) ....

     Other Expense (Schedule No. 4) ....

Net Profit before Income Taxes .... $...............

     Provision for Income Taxes ....

Net Profit for the Period .... $...............

OPERATING STATEMENT SCHEDULES

No. 1 — ADMINISTRATIVE & GENERAL EXPENSES:	No. 2 — SELLING EXPENSES:
Officers' Salaries .... $...............	Salaries (Other than to Officers) .... $...............
Other Salaries	Commissions ....
Depreciation & Amortization	Traveling ....
	Advertising ....
Total .... $...............	Total .... $...............
No. 3 — OTHER INCOME:	**No. 4 — OTHER EXPENSE:**
Cash Discounts on Purchases .... $...............	Cash Discounts on Sales .... $...............
	Interest ....
	Bad Debts ....
Total .... $...............	Total .... $...............

RECONCILIATION OF EARNED SURPLUS

FOR THE .... MONTH PERIOD ENDED .... 19 ......

Earned Surplus — Beginning of Period .... $...............	Carried Forward .... $...............
Additions to Surplus (Itemize):	**Deductions from Surplus** (Itemize):
Net Profit for the Period .... $...............	Dividends—Common Stock . $...............
	Dividends—Preferred Stock..
Forward .... $...............	Earned Surplus—End of Period .... $...............

Certification — This is to certify that the foregoing figures were taken from the books and records of this corporation and that they and all other statements on this form and on any supporting schedules are true and give a correct showing of the financial condition of the corporation as of the date indicated. IN THE EVENT OF ANY MATERIAL ADVERSE CHANGE IN THE FINANCIAL CONDITION OF THIS CORPORATION, WE AGREE TO NOTIFY THE FINANCIAL INSTITUTION NAMED HEREIN IMMEDIATELY IN WRITING.

Signed this .... day of .... 19 ......

                          (Corporate Name)

         By ....

                        (Signature & Title of Authorized Officer)

IMPORTANT: If an audit was made as of the date of this statement, a copy of the accountant's report should be submitted herewith.

FORM 7. Long form of financial statement blank for corporations suggested by Federal Reserve Bank of New York (page 4).

asset or a part of it has been assigned as security and is out of reach of the general creditors.[48] Loans of this nature are generally obtained when a business enterprise is unable to borrow from its own bank, presumably because of a weakened financial condition. Interest and discount charges of finance companies are materially higher than the charges of commercial banking institutions.

5. *Accruals.* Accruals comprise amounts due but not yet paid for salaries, wages, rents, interest, and sometimes for taxes, although this item generally is a separate one. These items have been calculated up to the very day of the balance sheet. They would have to be met instantly in case of liquidation. Accruals are relatively small even for large corporations. Taxes may be an exception, or interest in those cases where a heavy funded debt is outstanding and an interest payment is shortly due. Often this item is omitted in unaudited figures and in smaller business enterprises where the amount is nominal.

Most businesses have a liability for accrued wages; larger corporations also often have accrued bonuses to officers and employees and accrued commissions to salesmen. Of even greater importance in the light of our current economic life is the item of accrued taxes, which for large corporations may amount to fantastic figures. This particular item of accruals has become so important in recent years that it is generally set up in the balance sheets of larger enterprises as a separate distinct item of accrued taxes, or, as outlined in a succeeding paragraph, as a reserve for or provisions for income taxes.

6. *Deposits.* Funds deposited with a concern as an evidence or a guaranty of good faith are generally carried in the liabilities as deposits. Such a situation arises where a deposit has been placed to bind a contemplated purchase. In such a case, the deposit becomes the initial or a part payment when the sale is consummated and so automatically is eliminated from the current liabilities. If the sale should not be consummated the deposit presumably would be returned on demand.

This item also arises when a deposit has been made to ensure the return of a container, a drum, a barrel, or a box. In such a case, the deposits are

---

[48] The state of Ohio took the lead in bringing this problem out into the open. The legislature of the state enacted a law which was signed by the governor on June 5, 1941, providing that an affidavit stating the name and address of the owner of the receivables, the name and address of the assignee, and the fact that an account or accounts had been assigned would have to be filed with the County Recorder of the county in which the owner resided or had its principal place of business. Such a filing is effective for a period of 3 years. The deposit of this affidavit constitutes a public notice that a particular business enterprise intends to assign certain receivables to the stated assignee until the filing has expired or has been canceled. Somewhat similar statutes have since been enacted by other states including Alabama, Arizona, California, Colorado, Florida, Georgia, Idaho, Iowa, Kansas, Nebraska, Oklahoma, South Carolina, Texas, Utah, Vermont, and Washington.

subject to repayment as the containers are returned. In many instances of this nature, the amount remains fairly stable as new deposits are received which offset the decrease from repayments. Even though the necessity of making more than a moderate repayment is somewhat remote, the item invariably is classified as a current liability.

7. *Advance Payments.* Advance payments from customers, when they occur, represent moderate amounts. This item arises when part of a sales price has been collected in advance, as when a department store sets aside a piece of merchandise on receipt of a payment, a process known as *layaways* or *will call.* The advance payment constitutes a liability until the sale is consummated, when it becomes part of the purchase price.

Advance payments[49] from the Federal government occurred on the balance sheets of prime contractors engaged in producing war materials, equipment, and supplies during the Second World War. In such situations the item at times was substantial, as the advance was the only means of financing the fulfillment of certain large contracts.

Occasionally, an advance payment is deducted from the inventory on the theory that an equivalent amount of inventory has been sold. The sale, however, has not been consummated. In these cases, the balance sheet must be adjusted when the item is posted, the inventory increased by the amount of advance payments, and the advance carried as a current liability.

8. *Reserves for Taxes.* As a result of changes in our Federal income tax laws in recent years, going down into lower and lower brackets, and the imposition of an increasing variety of supplementary taxes, nearly every business enterprise operating profitably and most commercial and industrial concerns operating unprofitably should show a provision for estimated taxes accrued to the date of a balance sheet. These obligations now include a wide variety of Federal, state, and local taxes. This item would also include liabilities such as sales taxes, social security tax, unemployment tax, and taxes on dividends paid to foreign stockholders, where it has become the duty of a concern to collect taxes from others and to remit to the appropriate governmental authority. In the case of large corporations, reserves or provisions for Federal income taxes often amount to many millions of dollars, which must be paid in cash or by tax-anticipation notes on definite, fixed dates.

9. *Dividends Declared but Not Paid.* Reserves for cash dividends declared but unpaid on the date of the balance sheet constitute a current liability and should always appear in the balance sheet. Not infrequently

[49] Advance payments were first authorized by the Federal government to prime contractors under an act of June 28, 1940, and then only up to 30 per cent of the contract when "in the interest of national defense." Subsequently, provisions under the First War Power Act of 1941 allowed advances "of any percentum of the contract price," that is, up to 100 per cent of a specific contract.

such an item is omitted altogether from unaudited financial statements, being mentioned solely in a footnote. In such cases the current liabilities, the apparent net working capital, the current ratio, and the surplus are distorted, and the analyst must make the necessary adjustments, even though they may be only estimated, when studying the figures.

10. *Reserves for Contingencies against Possible Losses.* An item of reserve for contingencies is exceeded in mystery only by the two items of investments and investments in and advances to subsidiaries and affiliates. What a reserve for contingencies represents no one outside the management staff or the accountant would know without a detailed explanation; that explanation the analyst must always seek.

It is not unusual for a reserve for contingencies to be set up in the balance sheet to obscure a definite liability or as a hidden valuation reserve. Where the item is an actual liability, as where a court suit has been lost and a stipulated sum must be paid, the reserve is a definite liability. Where the item is a valuation reserve, as against inventory revaluation, the sum should be deducted from the inventory figures in the assets, and the net inventory figure carried as a current asset. Where the item is, in reality, a real reserve for contingencies and not a cover for a liability which should and could be more adequately described under some more definite caption, it should be considered under deferred liabilities, which will be described later in this chapter.

11. *Current Maturity of a Funded Debt.* Whenever a funded debt of any kind matures within 1 year of the balance sheet date, the entire amount is a current liability. Some types of funded debts mature serially; that portion which is due within 1 year of the balance sheet date is a current debt. Funds are accumulated frequently by a business enterprise to meet a final maturity, and occasionally these funds are carried as a miscellaneous slow asset. Such funds, however, should be classified as a current asset.

At times, a serial maturity is met by an obligation to deposit a stipulated sum into a sinking fund. Such an obligation is a current liability, unless the corporation has the privilege and has already purchased and is carrying in its miscellaneous slow assets the stipulated number of bonds, debentures, or notes purchased in the open market. In this case the obligation has already been met.

Unfortunately there is no uniform practice among accountants in setting up as a current liability that portion of a funded debt due within 1 year. The analyst must always be alert to ascertain the terms of outstanding funded debts. He must be sure to adjust the figures to include all maturities due within 1 year of the balance sheet date when they have not been so included, as otherwise the current liabilities, the net working capital, the ratio of current assets to current liabilities, and the ratio of current liabilities to the tangible net worth will be distorted.

Deferred Liabilities

Deferred liabilities consist of one or several of the following four different types of items:

1. Long-term liabilities
2. Valuation reserves
3. Reserves for contingencies when a general reserve and not for a specific purpose
4. Unearned income

The great majority of business enterprises do not have deferred liabilities. It is in the balance sheets of medium-sized and large concerns that these items are occasionally found.

1. *Long-term Liabilities.* Long-term liabilities consist of mortgages, bonds, debentures, serial notes, purchase-money obligations, and occasionally long-term notes payable, all due more than 1 year from the statement date. "More than 1 year from the statement date" does not mean "a year and a day," as such an arrangement obviously is a subterfuge. From the point of view of the analyst, it is absolutely necessary to ascertain when a funded obligation is to mature, and, as the maturity date approaches, what provisions, if any, are being made to meet the maturity. In recent years, it has become the very desirable practice of accountants generally to state the maturity dates of outstanding issues of long-term liabilities in balance sheets, but this practice, unfortunately, is not uniformly followed.

Around 1953 a new type of corporate security, known as subordinated debentures, began to appear. In the immediately succeeding years a substantial number of representative corporations issued securities of this type. These issues are subordinated in principal and interest to what has come to be called "senior" or "prior" debt. Under typical provisions, subordinated debentures have more of the qualities of a preferred stock than a debt. They came into existence as a result of the fact that interest on debentures is a charge against earnings before Federal income taxes, while dividends on preferred stock are paid out of earnings after Federal income taxes. The qualities of a preferred stock are further accentuated where an indenture contains provisions that subordinated debenture holders "will not commence or join with any other creditor in commencing a bankruptcy, receivership, dissolution, or similar proceeding."

"Senior" or "prior" debt is defined in typical indentures as including the principal and interest on (a) indebtedness for money borrowed from or guaranteed to persons, firms, or corporations which engage in lending money, including, but without limitation, banks, trust companies, insurance companies, and other financing institutions, and charitable trusts, pension trusts, and other investing organizations, evidenced by notes or similar obligations, and/or (b) indebtedness evidenced by notes or debentures issued under the provisions of an indenture or similar instrument. Senior or prior debt, in other words, basically represents principal and interest on loans to banks, insurance companies, or other financial institutions, and similar obligations to other sources unless the instrument of indebtedness provides that such indebtedness is not superior in right of payment to the subordinated debentures. Some indentures also define senior or prior debt as including indebtedness incurred, assumed, or guaranteed in connection with the acquisition of businesses, properties, or other assets. Such provisions certainly cover a lot of ground, especially when trade creditors that, at times, furnish more credit than all other sources together are not even mentioned. Trade creditors are on a par with all unsecured creditors in case of financial difficulties. Trade creditors are no better off than subordinated debenture holders, although trade creditors rank ahead of stock. So the issuance of a subordinated debenture in lieu of preferred stock dilutes the assets in case of financial embarrassment, as far as trade creditors are concerned.

To the extent that such new obligations are specifically subordinated to senior or prior debts, the latter are in as strong a position as would be the case if there had been issued an equivalent amount of preferred stock. One must, however, keep in mind that interest on subordinated debentures must be paid as long as the business is solvent, and provisions are generally made to permit the partial and gradual retirement of principal by sinking fund operations, even though senior or prior obligations are outstanding. In other words, the gradual retirement of subordinated obligations, which often is provided for at the time of issuance, does gradually decrease the aggregate monetary strength, or slows up the growth of the aggregate monetary strength, behind senior or prior debts.

What is happening in this new look is that a new type of corporate obligation has come into use, and from different creditors' viewpoints, the possible effects of the creation of such subordinated debentures must be carefully appraised in each case.

In case of default in meeting interest or amortization, an acceleration clause generally provides that the entire outstanding amount of most issues of long-term liabilities becomes due and payable, and hence a current liability. Sometimes a yearly maturity is met ahead of time so that there is no current maturity. As previously mentioned, there is at times a provision whereby the current maturity may be met by the tendering of bonds, debentures, or notes at par value; if the corporation has been able to purchase the bonds or notes below par, a profit is earned by the transaction.

Quite extensive information regarding long-term liabilities is requested from registrants by the Securities and Exchange Commission. This information covers, among other points, the title of each issue, the amount of the issue authorized by the indenture, the amount issued and not retired or canceled, the amount in sinking and other special funds, and the amounts held by subsidiaries or affiliates.[50]

2. *Valuation Reserves.* In many balance sheets, valuation reserves for depreciation, obsolescence, and depletion are shown as a subdeduction under the related asset, and in other cases they are carried in the liabilities. Both practices are widely used although "writers in accounting theory are in practically universal agreement that valuation reserves should be deducted from the assets to which they apply."[51] To this theory and practice the analyst heartily agrees. In posting figures on a comparative statement blank, it is advisable for the analyst to deduct the valuation reserve from its related asset and to show the net value of the asset. Under this practice, fewer errors in analysis are likely to creep in, as the analyst then does not need to keep the existence of the offset items in the liabilities constantly in mind. A reserve for bad debts should likewise be deducted from the receivables in the current assets when posting to bring the value of the receivables to a net amount.

3. *Reserve for Contingencies*[52] *When a General Reserve and Not for a Specific Purpose.* As explained on page 108, a reserve for contingencies can never be properly classified unless the analyst has learned why such a sweeping generality has been used by a profession that prides itself on its exactness. Reserves for contingencies in substantial amounts have frequently been set up to keep stockholders and analysts in complete ignorance as to the real purpose of the reserve. Such a reserve lends itself to extremes such as covering up a liability, the amount of which may not be known within a few dollars, or evaluating some asset such as investments, so greatly overvalued that to acknowledge it might bring discredit upon the officer and directors, or appropriating surplus for the sole purpose of

---

[50] Regulation S-X, Rule 12-10, p. 50, Aug. 20, 1958.

[51] Fjeld, R. I., "Classification and Terminology of Individual Balance Sheet Items," *The Accounting Review*, Vol. XI, No. 4, p. 339, December, 1936. "As a general rule," state Lenhard and Defliese, "allowances for depreciation should be deducted from the costs of related assets, or the total of the allowances may be shown as a deduction from the total of depreciable assets. Where depletion is recognized in the accounts, the amounts for assets subject to depletion may be shown after deduction of these allowances, or the allowances may appear as deductions from related assets." —*Montgomery's Auditing*, p. 286.

[52] "The use of a reserve for contingencies appears to be a declining practice. In 1950, 155 out of 600 survey companies, or over 25 per cent, disclosed contingency reserves. The number of companies employing this type of account decreased each year since that time and in 1959 only 56 companies or less than 10 per cent reported reserves for contingencies."—*Accounting Trends and Techniques*, 14th ed., p. 99 (American Institute of Certified Public Accountants, New York, 1960).

misleading stockholders and others as to the true equity and the accumulated profits available for dividends.

When the item is actually a general reserve to meet some possible but not definite or too-clear obligation sometime in the future, such as a guaranty on the goodness, on the life, or on the performance of a product, then, and only then, is the item a deferred liability. If it is learned on investigation that the item is in reality a valuation reserve in disguise, it should, as already suggested, be deducted from the proper related asset, when posting. If the item is an actual, definite, known liability under camouflage, it should, of course, be classified as a current liability.

4. *Unearned Income.* Unearned income, often carried as deferred income, is the proportion of income which has been credited on the books as received, but which has not been earned up to the date of the balance sheet. A mercantile agency, for example, is paid in advance for 1 year of service. Such a payment increases the cash in the current assets and the unearned account in the liabilities. Each month, one-twelfth of the unearned income account is transferred to the income account as gross income to cover the cost of rendering service. The unearned income is the liability of the mercantile agency for the service still to be rendered.

Conservative furniture stores selling on the installment plan also set up *unearned* or *deferred* income. A three-piece set of furniture that costs $210 is sold for $390 with a down payment of $60 and the balance of $330 to be paid in 12 equal monthly installments. The $60 payment goes into cash, and $330 goes into installment receivables. The markup, which in this particular case is $180, does not go into gross profit until it is entirely collected, which on the selling terms will take 1 year. Accordingly, the $210 cost of the set goes into gross profit immediately and the remaining $180 goes into unearned income. The $180 is now reduced by $15 each month as the installment payments are received, and that $15 is credited to gross income. In other words, not until the entire $330 is collected is the full gross profit of $180 taken into account.

If this particular set of furniture had been sold for cash, the selling price in theory would have been $360, and not $390. The normal selling price was increased by $30 to cover interest, bad debts, and collection charges. Less conservative installment furniture stores probably would have transferred to unearned income not $180, but $30, representing the charge added to a cash price to create the installment price, which would then have been reduced monthly over the collection period of 12 months.

Unearned income is a natural item in the balance sheets of concerns selling on an installment basis with payments made over a period of 12 months or more, and on balance sheets of concerns that are paid for services to be rendered over a period of time in the future such as publishers of magazines, finance companies, and banking institutions.

Net Worth

Net worth may be considered a technical liability from a bookkeeping standpoint. It is a liability to a legal entity such as to a proprietor, to partners, or to stockholders who own the stock of a corporation. The net worth is the amount of funds invested at the risk of a business enterprise. More formally, it is a liability of a business enterprise to those interested in it after all debts of every description have been paid. The *net worth* is a single item with that exact caption in a proprietorship or partnership. Sometimes, however, it is also termed *proprietorship capital* or *partners' capital*. In a corporation, it consists of the sum of any or all of the following items that may be found in a particular balance sheet:

1. Preferred or preference stock
2. Common stock
3. Class A, B, and C stock
4. Capital surplus
5. Retained earnings (surplus)
6. Undivided profits

The balance sheets of the great majority of corporations have only two items in the net worth section, namely, common stock and retained earnings. The larger a corporation, the more likely it is to have in addition some form of preferred or preference stock.

1–3. *Preferred, Common, and Alphabet Stock.* As a corporation is a legal entity, it would upon liquidation or dissolution of its business owe to the holders of preferred or preference stock,[53] common stock,[54] and Class A, B, or C stock, in accordance with charter provisions, whatever remained after all obligations had been met. It is obvious that the amount that stockholders would receive would depend upon the character and the amount of the liabilities and upon the amount realized from the sale of the assets. Most industrial and commercial concerns realize little on their fixed assets under a forced sale. On the other hand, when the assets are purchased as a going business by some other active enterprise, the realization is generally greater and, at times, where valuable good will is involved and reflected in an earning record, may amount to several times the book value of the assets.

[53] For a comprehensive interesting listing of preferred stocks with various features which depart from the generally accepted pattern such as with and without par value, with detachable and nondetachable warrants, cumulative, noncumulative, convertible, and participating, see Benjamin Graham and David L. Dodd, *Security Analysis*, 1st ed., pp. 626–631 (McGraw-Hill Book Company, Inc., New York, 1934).

[54] A corresponding listing of common stocks which deviate from the standard pattern will also be found in *Security Analysis*, 1st ed., pp. 631–634.

STATEMENT MADE TO

STATEMENT FORM C

Credit -
MAN'S CONFIDENCE
IN MAN . . . . .

Dun & Bradstreet, Inc.

For the use of Subscribers as a Basis for Credit and Insurance

NOTE: Transmittal of financial statements on this particular form is optional. Financial statements on your own stationery or on that of your accountant will be equally useful. The full report of your accountant is preferred.

Business Name
Used for Buying..Street Address................................
Other Name or
Style Used, if any..City................................Zone........State............

Business..County............

FINANCIAL CONDITION AS OF..19....

IS THIS
FISCAL ☐
OR INTERIM? ☐

ASSETS		LIABILITIES	
CASH..$		DUE BANKS	$
GOVERNMENT SECURITIES............................		Unsecured ....$	
MARKETABLE SECURITIES............................		Secured	
NOTES RECEIVABLE (Customers)................		ACCOUNTS PAYABLE	
ACCOUNTS RECEIVABLE (Customers)		Not Due................$	
Not Due................$		Past Due................	
Past Due................		NOTES PAYABLE-TRADE ACCEPTANCES	
Less Reserves................		Merchandise................$	
INVENTORY		Machinery & Equip't........	
Finished Goods................$		Other	
In Process................		DUE RELATED CONCERNS	
Raw Materials................		Loans & Advances................$	
		Merchandise	
OTHER CURRENT ASSETS		LOANS & ADVANCES	
................$		From Officers................$	
....		Others	
TOTAL CURRENT ASSETS................		TAXES	
FIXED ASSETS		Federal Income................$	
Land ....$		Other	
Buildings		ACCRUALS	
Machinery and Equip't........		Salaries & Wages........$	
Furniture and Fixtures........		Other	
Less Depreciation........		MORTGAGES—DUE WITHIN 1 YEAR	
INVESTMENTS—RELATED CONCERNS		Real Estate................$	
Stocks & Bonds................$		....	
Loans & Advances................		....	
Accounts Receivable................		TOTAL CURRENT LIABILITIES................	
INVESTMENTS—OTHER		DEFERRED DEBTS—DUE AFTER 1 YEAR	
................$		Due Banks................$	
MISCELLANEOUS RECEIVABLES		Real Estate Mtg................	
Officers & Employees........$		....	
Other		....	
PREPAID—DEFERRED................		....	
DEPOSITS................		PREFERRED STOCK................	
SUPPLIES................		COMMON STOCK................	
		CAPITAL—PAID IN SURPLUS................	
		EARNED SURPLUS—RETAINED EARNINGS........	
		NET WORTH (Proprietor or Partners)........	
TOTAL ASSETS................$		TOTAL LIABILITIES AND CAPITAL...$	

SUMMARY STATEMENT OF INCOME

ABOVE FIGURES
PREPARED BY................................

NET SALES $..........—FROM..........TO..........

Name   Independent Accountant Yes ☐ No ☐

FINAL NET INCOME (LOSS) $................

DIVIDENDS OR WITHDRAWALS $................

BUSINESS NAME................

BASIS OF INVENTORY VALUATION................

SIGNED BY................

RECEIVABLES PLEDGED OR DISCOUNTED   YES ☐   NO ☐

TITLE................DATE................

CONTINGENT LIABILITIES $..........................(SEE OVER)

SG-10 (32198)   *(Use the reverse side of this form for submitting important supplementary details)*

FORM 8. Short form of financial statement used in mail requests by Dun & Bradstreet, Inc. (front).

STATEMENT OF INCOME

From............, 19....TO............, 19....

NET SALES.......................................$

COST OF GOODS SOLD.............................

GROSS PROFIT (LOSS) ON SALES...................

EXPENSES

    Selling ....$

    General ....

    Administrative ....

    ....

NET INCOME (LOSS) ON SALES.....................

OTHER INCOME

    ....$

OTHER EXPENSES

    ....$

NET INCOME (LOSS) BEFORE TAXES

    Federal Income Tax..........$

    Other Taxes on Income.......

FINAL NET INCOME (LOSS)........................$

SURPLUS OR NET WORTH RECONCILIATION

SURPLUS OR NET WORTH AT START............$

ADDITIONS

    Final Net Income............$

DEDUCTIONS

    Final Net Loss.............$

    Dividends ....

    Withdrawals ....

SURPLUS OR NET WORTH AT END............$

When financial statements prepared or certified to by independent accountants are transcribed to this form, indicate whether the statements transcribed are identical with the accountant's statement(s) Yes ☐ No ☐. If No, please describe adjustments. Attach copy of accountant's certificate.

THE FOREGOING STATEMENTS, IF CONSOLIDATED, INCLUDE THE FIGURES OF WHAT OTHER CONCERNS?........................

ANNUAL RENT $................... LEASE EXPIRES................... 19...... FIRE INSURANCE ON: Merchandise $................... Machinery & Equipment $................... Furniture & Fixtures $................... Bldgs. $................... ARE OFFICERS AND EMPLOYEES BONDED?...................
IS BUSINESS INTERRUPTION INSURANCE CARRIED?................... IS BODILY INJURY AND/OR PROPERTY DAMAGE INSURANCE CARRIED?...................
BASIS OF VALUATION OF: Fixed Assets........................Marketable Securities—Investments........................

ARE LIABILITIES SECURED IN ANY MANNER? Yes ☐ No ☐ If Yes, describe the security and the manner of payment........................

STATE AMOUNT OF EACH CONTINGENT LIABILITY: (Describe)........................

REAL ESTATE—LOCATION	Title—In Name Of	Value Mkt. ☐ Cost ☐	Mortgage	Due Date	Net Income—R. E.
		$	$		$

BRANCH LOCATIONS:........................

NOTE: Comments will be appreciated on any phase of your operations, including developments since the statement date.

Full Names of all Officers, Directors, Partners or Proprietor. If Partners, state if General, Special or Limited

FULL NAMES AND TITLES	% of Ownership	Year of Birth	Marital Status	Life Insurance Carried for the Benefit of the Business
A.				
B.				
C.				
D.				
E.				

FORM 8. Short form of financial statement used in mail requests by Dun & Bradstreet, Inc. (reverse).

The analyst is interested not only in the relationship between owned and borrowed funds, but also in any asset or dividend preferences that may affect the financial condition of a corporation; for example, knowledge of the dividend disbursements and of the amounts required to meet dividends on senior securities, quarterly and yearly, during the up-and-down phases of our economy, is pertinent information. The board of directors of a corporation might refuse to declare dividends if not earned, or, on the other hand, they might be less conservative and vote to continue to pay dividends on preferred stocks out of surplus, even if that policy might weaken the financial condition of the corporation. It has been no unusual occurrence for the principal stockholder or stockholders to be in such personal need of ready cash that they have insisted on the payment of dividends that have weakened a corporation. In other cases, one or several officers may have bonus arrangements whereby they receive a percentage of the net profits only after stipulated dividends have been paid. Dividends would then be disbursed so that the officers might obtain their higher recompense, even though the dividend policy weakened the net working capital appreciably.

Knowledge of sinking fund requirements, which may provide that a certain amount of preferred stock be retired yearly or that a certain percentage of the net profits be used for this purpose, is also highly desirable. Many corporations have failed to live up to the provisions under which preferred or preference stocks have been issued; others have attempted to do so even when it meant depleting the net working capital. The ability to meet and adequately to cover sinking fund and dividend requirements indicates the capacity of management, provided those requirements are reasonable.

4. *Capital Surplus.* Capital surplus results from funds paid into a business in excess of the par value of some one or several classes of stock, or in excess of the amount at which no-par-value stock is carried on the books, from a reappraisal and write-up of fixed assets, from a profit obtained in the retiring of securities, or from a scaling down of capitalization.[55] There is a current trend in accounting circles to get away from the use of *capital surplus* as a general term and to use more specific classifications in individual cases such as *additional paid-in capital, capital in excess of par or stated values, additional capital,* and *other capital.*[56]

[55] See Chap. XXIII, "Analyses of Surplus Accounts."

[56] *Accounting Terminology Bulletin,* No. 1, *Review and Résumé,* issued by the Committee on Terminology of the American Institute of Certified Public Accountants, reaffirmed an earlier recommendation made by the Committee that the use of the term "surplus" be discontinued in the balance sheet. This recommendation is applicable not only to the term surplus standing alone, but also in such combinations as "capital surplus," "paid-in surplus," "earned surplus," and "appraisal surplus."— pp. 28–31 (American Institute of Certified Public Accountants, New York, 1953). The term "capital surplus" is, however, still being widely used. For a list of substitute

5. *Retained Earnings.* When capital surplus, or a corresponding item, appears in a balance sheet, a supplementary item of *retained earnings* or *earned surplus* invariably appears. Where no capital surplus appears, the retained earnings generally represent the accumulation of earnings over and above the payment of dividends. To this item is transferred the final net profit or loss for the accounting period and to it is debited the payment of dividends, when made. Retained earnings represent the difference, as shown on the balance sheet, between the total assets of a corporation and the reported liabilities, including outstanding stock and any capital surplus.

6. *Undivided Profits.* The term *undivided profits* is found in the balance sheets of practically all commercial banks and trust companies but only occasionally in the balance sheets of commercial or industrial business enterprises. This item, when found, represents the accumulated net profits that have not been transferred to the retained earnings account. In this sense, the retained earnings become a somewhat more permanent segment of the capital funds, and dividends are declared and paid out of undivided profits.

Contingent Liabilities

Contingent liabilities are incurred whenever a concern has discounted any of its notes receivable or trade acceptances and then omitted these assets from the balance sheet, when it has endorsed or guaranteed for others, when contracts for the future have been made, and when commercial letters of credit have been obtained and only partly used. Such liabilities may or may not become a legal obligation sometime in the future for an indeterminate amount.

Seldom do contingent liabilities appear in the books of account, which makes it extremely difficult for the accountant to be sure he has covered the item adequately. Every contingent liability should appear in the balance sheet, either in a specific amount if such an amount may be determined, or in explanatory comments in a footnote if the nature of the possible liability cannot be put into actual figures.

Sale and Lease-back Obligations

The leasing of space in buildings, of land and buildings, and of land has long been a customary, normal process in carrying on business activity. Until shortly before the Second World War, such lease obligations were

terms which are being currently used, see *Accounting Trends and Techniques*, 14th ed., p. 11 (American Institute of Certified Public Accounts, New York, 1960).

FINANCIAL STATEMENT SUBMITTED TO **NATIONAL CREDIT OFFICE, INC.**

Name..Business................................

Street and No...City................Zone.........State..........

➡ **STATEMENT OF (DATE)**   **19**   ⬅

ASSETS		LIABILITIES	
CASH IN BANK........$_____		ACCOUNTS PAYABLE...............	$_____
ON HAND.....$_____	$_____	DUE CONTRACTORS (without offset)	_____
U. S. GOVERNMENT SECURITIES............		UNSECURED LOANS PAYABLE	
RECEIVABLES for Mdse. Sold to Customers (Age at Foot of Page)		To Banks...............	_____
ACCOUNTS ....$_____		To Partners or Officers...............	_____
		To Others...............	_____
Less Res. for Discounts ......$_____		SECURED LOANS PAYABLE	
Less Res. for Doubtful ....$_____		Owing to...............	_____
NOTES & TRADE ACCEPTANCES		ACCRUED WAGES & EXPENSES............	_____
(Less $_____ discounted)	_____	TAXES—Accrued and Payable: a. Withholding & Payroll...............	_____
DUE from FACTOR or FINANCE CO	_____	b. Federal & State Income...............	_____
		c. All Other...............	_____
PHYSICAL INVENTORY OF MDSE. (Valued at lower of Cost or Market)		RESERVE for Income Taxes since last closing	_____
Raw Materials......$_____		MORTGAGE—DEFERRED DEBT— Due within 12 mos...............	_____
In Process...........$_____			
Finished Mdse.......$_____		**CURRENT LIABILITIES**	_____
....	_____	MORTGAGE—DEFERRED DEBT— Due after 12 mos...............	_____
CURRENT ASSETS	_____		
Due from Partners, Officers, or Employees	_____	LOANS Subordinated until...........(date)	_____
Due from Affiliated or Assoc. Companies $	_____	....	
LAND & BUILDINGS $_____		**TOTAL LIABILITIES**	_____
Less Depreciation..$_____		IF CORPORATION	
MCHY., EQUIP., FURN., & FIXT....$_____		Capital Stock Pfd. $_____	
Less Depreciation..$_____		Capital Stock Common ....$_____	
INVESTMENTS (Describe on opp. page)		Capital Surplus......$_____	
PREPAID & DEFERRED............		Earned Surplus......$_____	
....		Deficit (red)........$_____	
		CORPORATE, PARTNERSHIP or INDIVIDUAL............**NET WORTH**	_____
TOTAL ASSETS		**TOTAL LIABILITIES & CAPITAL**	

ACCOUNTANT—Was above statement prepared by an outside accountant? Yes ☐ No ☐ Is he C.P.A.? ☐ Registered? ☐ Licensed? ☐	RECEIVABLES For goods shipped during months of:
Accountant's Name...............	a............... $_____
Address	b............... $_____
On what date are your books closed?...............	c............... $_____
MERCHANDISE—If not valued at Lower of Cost or Market, state	d. Prior Months............... $_____
basis used...............	Do these include any consigned goods, uncredited returns, or unshipped merchandise? Yes ☐ No ☐
Is original inventory record retained by you ☐ or outside auditor ☐	Have all bad accounts been charged off or reserved? Yes ☐ No ☐
Is any merchandise pledged as security for any debt? _____	During the past year have you sold, pledged, or assigned any receivables? Yes ☐ No ☐ If so, name financing concern and describe transaction...............
If so, state amount so pledged. $_____	
INSURANCE—Fire: Mdse. $_____, Bldg. & Fixt. $_____	....
Use & Occup. $_____; Burglary $_____; Life, Benefit Business $_____ on...............	....

FORM 9. Financial statement blank, used by National Credit Office, Inc. (front).

new form

PROFIT AND LOSS STATEMENT

FOR PERIOD FROM.................19....... TO.................19......

GROSS SALES................................. $_____

Less RETURNS......$_____

Less DISCOUNTS $_____ $_____

NET INCOME FROM SALES.................... $_____

Inventory—begin'g $_____

Purchases—Net ....$_____

Labor ....$_____

Factory Overhead .....$_____

Total $_____

Inventory at end........$_____

Cost of Goods Sold.................... $_____

GROSS PROFIT ON SALES.................... $_____

Selling & Ship. Exp. $_____

Salaries—Officers
or Principals ....$_____

Adm. & Gen. Exp......$_____

Bad Debts ....$_____

Depreciation ....$_____ $_____

INCOME or (LOSS) ON SALES.............. $_____

Other Income (exclude discount earned).. $_____

Total $_____

Deductions from Income........................... $_____

NET PROFIT or (LOSS) before Income
Taxes .... $_____

Provision for Fed. & State Income Taxes.. $_____

NET PROFIT or (LOSS)............................ $_____

RECONCILIATION OF SURPLUS OR NET WORTH

Beginning (date) .... $_____
ADD:
Profit for Period....$_____
Other Credits
to Surplus..........$_____ $_____
Total $_____
DEDUCT:
Loss for Period....$_____
Div. & Withdr'ls..$_____
Other Charges
to Surplus ....$_____ $_____
NET WORTH or SURPLUS. at end......... $_____
INVESTMENTS—Describe (If subsidiary or affiliated state % owned)
a... $_____
b. .... $_____
LIABILITIES—Merchandise received or charged to you but not in-
cluded in Assets or Liabilities $_____
Amount of Contingent Liabilities............ $_____
Are any liabilities secured in any way?........................ If so, state
amount, creditor, and nature of security...................................
....
Annual Rent $_____ Lease Expires...........................
NET WORTH—Has this been decreased since statement date by
withdrawal, retirement of capital, payment of dividends, bonuses,
or personal Income Taxes?...
If so, by what amount? $_____
TAXES—Have all Federal, State, and Local tax assessments been
paid or shown accrued on statement?...
Tax Closing date?... Date of latest return
examined by Internal Revenue Service?...

INDEPENDENT ACCOUNTANT'S OPINION

Accountants Signature... Address..
(Please use your own Letterhead if additional space is necessary)

TO **NATIONAL CREDIT OFFICE, INC.**
Two Park Avenue, New York 16, N. Y.

The undersigned warrants that the foregoing figures and answers are true and accurate in every respect and orders this statement mailed to you with the intention that it shall be relied upon in the extension of credit or insurance by such concerns, including factors or agents, who may subscribe to your service now or hereafter. My (Our) accountants are authorized to supply you with any supplementary information that may be required.

Dated at.................this.................day of...........................19.......
Signed in the presence of:

Name..

Address..

....
(Name of Corporation, Partnership or Proprietorship)

By...

....
(Signature of Officer, Partner or Owner)   (Title)

Please list officers, suppliers, and banks on reverse side

FORM 9. Financial statement blank, used by National Credit Office, Inc. (reverse).

ACCOUNTANT'S SUPPLEMENTARY INFORMATION

Relating to the attached financial statement as of_____(date)

Issued by_____Address_____

A. Do the figures on this statement agree with the figures in your report: Yes___ No___
Exceptions_____

B. Did you confirm the following items by direct correspondence:
   1. Cash _____Yes___ No___   4. Due from Contractors__Yes___ No___   7. Due to Contractors__Yes___ No___
   2. Accounts Receivable _____Yes___ No___   5. Accounts Payable ____Yes___ No___   8. Others (describe) __Yes___ No___
   3. Customers Notes and Acceptances__Yes___ No___   6. Notes Payable _____Yes___ No___
   Describe any other method used and relate to the item affected:_____

C. ACCOUNTS RECEIVABLE
   1. Does aging agree with your report? Yes___ No___ If not, give aging below for merchandise shipped to customers:
      Months   _____ $_____
      of   _____ $_____
      shipments   _____ $_____
                      Prior Months_____ $_____
                               Total $_____
   2. In your opinion, is provision for bad debts adequate: Yes___ No___ If no opinion, explain:_____
   3. In your opinion, is reserve for discounts adequate: Yes___ No___ If no opinion, explain:_____
   4. To your knowledge, have any receivables been sold, pledged or assigned during the year immediately preceding the statement date: Yes___ No___
      If yes, explain:_____
   5. To your knowledge, do Accounts Receivable include any amounts due from subsidiary or affiliated concerns: Yes___ No___
      Do Accounts Receivable include any individual accounts owing in excess of 25% of the net worth shown on attached financial statement: Yes___ No___
      If yes, state amount $_____ and number_____

D. MERCHANDISE INVENTORY
   1. Did you observe and test the count of the physical inventory quantities: Yes___ No___
      If no, state how verified_____
   2. If not verified, was detailed listing of inventory submitted to you: Yes___ No___   Is copy of original inventory listing in your possession: Yes___ No___
   3. How was the inventory priced?_____
   4. Did you test the inventory as to prices: Yes___ No___; Arithmetical Accuracy: Yes___ No___
   5. To your knowledge, has any merchandise been pledged as collateral during the year immediately preceding statement date: Yes___ No___
      If yes, explain:_____

E. INVESTMENTS — Describe_____

F. GENERAL
   1. Are you a Certified Public Accountant: Yes___ No___ What State_____ How often do you audit the books?_____
   2. Have all expenses and tax liabilities known to you been accrued: Yes___ No___
   3. Does the statement include all assets and liabilities known to you: Yes___ No___ Exceptions:_____
      Explain_____
   4. Do you know of any material contingent liabilities: Yes___ No___ Explain:_____
   5. Tax closing date:_____ Last taxable year examined by Internal Revenue Service:_____
   6. If client is not incorporated, state amount you believe will be withdrawn for personal income taxes of principal or partners on income earned to statement date and not shown in statement: $_____
   7. Other comments, if any_____

TO NATIONAL CREDIT OFFICE, INC.

   The above information is in answer to your inquiry regarding the attached financial statement of my/our client as of the date shown.

                                          _____
                                          (Firm Name of Accountant)

                                          _____
                                          (Signature of Individual Authorized to Sign)

                                          Dated_____

NATIONAL CREDIT OFFICE, INC. • TWO PARK AVE., NEW YORK 16, N. Y.

FORM 10. Accountant's supplementary information sheet used by National Credit Office, Inc.

Form 6W

Date_____ ___19____

INANCIAL STATEMENT OF_____

Kind of Business_____ Address _____

At Close of Business on _____19___ City_____ State _____

ISSUED TO_____ ←{ Name of firm asking for statement

[THIS FORM APPROVED AND PUBLISHED BY NATIONAL ASSOCIATION OF CREDIT MANAGEMENT]

For the purpose of obtaining merchandise from you on credit, or for the extension of credit, we make the following state-
ent in writing, intending that you should rely thereon respecting our exact financial condition.
[PLEASE ANSWER ALL QUESTIONS. WHEN NO FIGURES ARE INSERTED, WRITE WORD "NONE"]

ASSETS	Dollars	Cents	LIABILITIES	Dollars	Cents
ash In Bank			Accounts Payable (for Merchandise)		
On Hand			Notes & Acceptances Payable for Merchandise		
ccounts Receivable			Owe to_____ Bank		
(Amt. 60 Days Past Due $_____)			(When Due_____Secured) (Unsecured)		
(Amt. Sold or Pledged $_____)			Income Taxes, Accrued		
otes and Trade Acceptances Receivable			Other Taxes, Including Sales Taxes, Accrued		
(Amt. Sold or Pledged $_____)			Interest, Accrued		
erchandise Inventory, Not on Consignment or			Rental, Payrolls, etc., Accrued		
Conditional Sale, at Cost or Market which-			Payables to Partners, Relatives		
ever is lower			Other Current Liabilities (Describe)		
(Amount Pledged $_____)					
ther Current Assets (Describe)					
			TOTAL CURRENT LIABILITIES		
			Mortgage on Land and Buildings		
TOTAL CURRENT ASSETS			Chattel Mortgage on Mdse. or Equipment		
and and Buildings (Depreciated Value)			Liens on Mdse. or Equipment		
achinery, Fixtures and Equipment (Depreciated			Other Liabilities, No Current (Describe)		
Value)					
ue from Officers or Non-Customers					
ther Assets (Describe)			TOTAL LIABILITIES		
			Net Worth or {Capital $_____ {Surplus $_____}		
TOTAL ASSETS			TOTAL NET WORTH AND LIABILITIES		

BE SURE TO ANSWER ALL THESE QUESTIONS

ANNUAL NET SALES	COST OF GOODS SOLD	GROSS PROFIT	OPERATING EXPENSE	NET PROFIT FOR YEAR (Before Federal Taxes)

Amount you are liable for as endorser,
guarantor, surety $_____

Amount of delinquent taxes:
Sales tax $_____ Income tax $_____
Property tax $_____ Other taxes $_____

Amount of merchandise held on consignment $_____

Amount of machinery or equipment
held under lease $_____

Amount of machinery or equipment
under conditional sale $_____

Amount you pay per month on lease or
conditional sale contract $_____

What books of Account do you keep?

Date of latest inventory

Date of latest audit

Title to business premises is in name of

If premises leased state annual rental

Name of your bank(s)

INSURANCE CARRIED

Fire
Merchandise $_____
Furn. & Fixt. $_____
Building $_____
Extended Coverage $_____
U & O $_____

Liability
General $_____
Auto & Truck $_____
Burglary $_____
Life for Benefit
of Business $_____

SCHEDULE OF REAL ESTATE	TITLE IN WHOSE NAME	APPRAISED VALUE

BUY PRINCIPALLY FROM THE FOLLOWING FIRMS:

NAMES	ADDRESSES	AMOUNT OWING

The statement above and on the back of this form has been carefully read by the undersigned (both the printed and
written matter), and is, to my knowledge, in all respects complete, accurate and truthful. It discloses to you the true state of
my (our) financial condition on the _____day of_____19___ Since that time there has been no
material unfavorable change in my (our) financial condition, and if any such change takes place I (we) will give you notice.
Until such notice is given, you are to regard this as a continuing statement. **The figures submitted are not estimated.** They
have been taken from my (our) books and physical inventory taken as on date shown.

Name of Individual or Firm_____
{ Partnership. Name Partners }
{ Corporation. Name Officers }_____
How long established_____ Previous business experience_____
_____ Where_____

Date of Signing Statement_____ Street_____ City_____ State_____

Witness
Residence Address
of Witness_____ Signed by_____
OM_____ Title_____

RM 11. Financial statement blank, with flap for remailing, prepared by the National
sociation of Credit Men.

more or less of nominal importance in analyzing the financial condition of businesses, with two possible exceptions. These two exceptions were long-term leases—often for 99 years—on land on which buildings were erected by the lessee and leases on retail store properties of substantial aggregate size by several chain stores which became bankrupt during the Great Depression. No record of lease obligations, up to this time, appeared in the balance sheets or in notes appended to balance sheets of lessees.

Shortly before the Second World War contract lease obligations began to grow in size and importance as a result of the unprecedented demand for capital to finance expansion programs. There now developed the practice on the part of an increasing number of more responsible corporations of selling (later, of erecting structures to their own specifications, and then selling) certain real estate, that is, land and buildings, and in more recent years oil tankers and airplanes, and taking long-term leases (generally from 15 to 30 years, but in many cases with optional renewal clauses at lower rates at the expiration of the initial term of the lease) on those assets. As a result of this practice, lease obligations of individual businesses have increased very substantially over the years. Moreover, in the case of land and buildings, the lessee has in most cases become obligated to pay all real estate taxes, insurance costs, and upkeep of the buildings over the period of the lease. Such arrangements have come to be known as "net leases."

With this evolution the current lease has become a very flexible document. As one student of this subject has pointed out, there are at least four basic features common to every such lease.[57] These basic features are:

1. It provides for a basic term during which the lease is noncancelable, or cancelable only by the payment of a stipulated premium in excess of amortized cost. The length of this basic lease period is determined primarily by the economic life of the asset and is usually somewhat shorter than its expected life. Where the economic life of the asset is extremely long, the credit standing of the corporation may limit the length of this basic term.

2. The lease provides for periodic rental payments during this base period, which are calculated to return the original investment in the asset to the owner with a predetermined rate of interest. Occasionally, where the basic term is short in relation to the asset's economic life, or where land values represent a substantial portion of the investment, the amount repaid during the basic term of the lease may be something less than the original investment.

3. The rental payment so determined may be increased to cover the costs of maintenance, taxes, insurance, and other expenses directly related to the property. Usually, however, the arrangement is on a net lease basis, with the corporation assuming the obligation for these expenses as well as continuing reponsibility for the management of the property

[57] GANT, DONALD R., "Illusion in Lease Financing," *Harvard Business Review*, March–April, 1959.

GUIDE TO CLASSIFICATION OF BALANCE SHEET ITEMS   [Schedule 2]

Assets	Current	Slow	Intangible	Liabilities	Current	Slow	Net Worth
Accounts Receivable				Accounts Payable			
Customers (Less Reserves).	✓			For Merchandise..........	✓		
From Affiliate, if concern is in healthy shape and accounts are being paid on regular terms..........	✓			For Services..............	✓		
				To Directors.............	✓		
				To Employees............	✓		
From Affiliate, if concern is in unhealthy shape, or accounts are not being paid on regular terms........		✓		To Officers..............	✓		
				To Partners..............	✓		
From Directors...........		✓		To Related Concerns......	✓		
From Employees..........		✓		Sundry..................	✓		
From Officers............		✓		Accruals			
From Partners............		✓		Commission..............	✓		
From Subsidiary, if concern is in healthy shape, and receivables are being paid on regular terms........	✓			Interest..................	✓		
				Other Expenses...........	✓		
				Pay Rolls................	✓		
				Rent....................	✓		
				Salaries..................	✓		
				Taxes...................	✓		
From Subsidiary, if concern is in unhealthy shape, or accounts are not being paid on regular terms...		✓		Wages...................	✓		
				Advances from Customers...	✓		
Miscellaneous............		✓					
Other...................		✓		Bills Payable (*Same as* Notes Payable)................			
Advances				Bonds			
For Merchandise..........	✓			Amount Maturing within One Year..............	✓		
For Mining Royalties.....		✓		Amount Maturing after One Year..............		✓	
For Traveling............		✓		No Definite Maturity Date..................	✓		
To Affiliate..............		✓					
To Employees............		✓					
To Subsidiary............		✓					
Advertising...............			✓				
Assets, Miscellaneous........		✓		Capital (If Partnership or Proprietorship).........			✓]
Automobiles...............		✓		Capital Stock			
Bills Receivable (*Same as* Accounts Receivable)......				A, B, or C Stock.........			✓
Blending Rights...........			✓	Common Stock...........			✓
Bond Discount.............			✓	Minority Interest........		✓	
Bonds*...................	✓			Preferred or Preference Stock..................			✓
Bookplates				Capital Surplus..........			✓
At Cost.................			✓	Chattel Mortgage...........	✓		
Metal Value..............		✓		Common Stock............			✓
Bottling Rights............			✓	Conditional Bill of Sale......	✓		
Brands, Trade..............			✓	Contingencies, Reserve for†..			
Building and Loan Shares...	✓			Contracts Payable..........	✓		
Buildings.................		✓		Credit Balance.............	✓		
Canadian Government Securities..................	✓			Customers' Deposits........	✓		

Deferred Taxes on Income (handwritten)

Guide to Classification of Balance Sheet Items (*Continued*)

[Schedule 2 (*Cont.*)]

Assets	Current	Slow	Intangible	Liabilities	Current	Slow	Net Worth
Cash				Debentures...............			
In Bank.................	✓			Amount Maturing within			
In Closed Bank..........		✓		One Year..............	✓		
In Sinking Fund..........		✓		Amount Maturing after			
On Hand................	✓			One Year..............		✓	
Restricted..............		✓		Deferred Credits or Income..		✓	
Cash Value of Life Insurance.		✓		Deferred Income............		✓	
Catalogues.................			✓	Deposits			
Claims for Refunds under				From Customers..........	✓		
Carry-back Provisions of				From Employees..........	✓		
Tax Law...............	✓			From Officers............	✓		
Coal Lands.................		✓		From Salesmen..........	✓		
Contracts.................			✓	Depreciation (Deduct from			
Copyrights.................			✓	Related Asset)..........			
Debenture Discount.........			✓	Dividends Payable..........	✓		
Debtors, Sundry...........		✓		Donated Surplus............			✓
Deferred Charges (*See also*				Due Factor................	✓		
Prepaid Items).........		✓					
Deficit (Profit and Loss)....			✓	Earned Surplus.............			✓
Delivery Equipment........		✓		Earnings			
Deposits				Employed in Business.....			✓
With Factor.............	✓			Reinvested..............			✓
With Mutual Insurance				Retained................			✓
Company..............		✓		Employees' Deposits........	✓		
With Workmen's Compen-							
sation Commission......		✓		Federal Income Taxes.......	✓		
Designs...................			✓	Funded Debt			
Development Expense.......			✓	Amount Maturing within			
Dies.....................			✓	One Year..............	✓		
Docks....................		✓		Amount Maturing after			
Drawings..................			✓	One Year..............		✓	
Emergency Plant Facilities..		✓					
Equipment.................		✓		Income Deferred............		✓	
Experimental Expense.......			✓	Income Taxes..............	✓		
Exploration Expense........			✓				
Federal Government Securi-				Loan from Factor...........	✓		
ties (*see* United States				Loans Payable (*Same as*			
Government Securities).				Notes Payable)........			
Financing Expense..........			✓	Minority Interest...........		✓	
Fixed Assets..............		✓		Mortgages			
Fixtures...................		✓		Amount Maturing within			
Foreign Assets—Restricted..		✓		One Year..............	✓		
Formulas.................			✓	Amount Maturing after			
Franchises.................			✓	One Year..............		✓	
Furniture.................		✓		No Definite Maturity			
Good Will.................			✓	Date.................	✓		
Government Securities (*see*							
United States Govern-				Net Worth (If Partnership			
ment Securities)........				or Proprietorship).......			✓

GUIDE TO CLASSIFICATION OF BALANCE SHEET ITEMS (*Continued*)

[Schedule 2 (*Cont.*)]

Assets	Current	Slow	Intangible	Liabilities	Current	Slow	Net Worth
Improvements		✓		Notes Payable			
Insurance Deposits		✓		For Merchandise	✓		
Insurance Premium, Prepaid		✓		To Banks	✓		
Interest, Accrued		✓		To Individuals	✓		
Inventory				To Others	✓		
Advances on Merchandise	✓			To Partners	✓		
Finished Goods	✓			To Stockholders	✓		
In Transit	✓			Term Loans (*Same as* Bonds)			
On Consignment	✓						
Raw Materials	✓						
Supplies		✓		Officers' Deposits	✓		
Work in Process	✓						
Investments*		✓		Paid-in Surplus			✓
Investments in and Advances to Subsidiaries and Affiliates		✓		Preferred or Preference Stock			✓
				Provision for Income Taxes	✓		
Land		✓		Reinvested Earnings			✓
Lasts			✓	Rent, Unpaid	✓		
Leasehold Improvements		✓		Retained Earnings			✓
Leaseholds			✓	Reserves			
Licenses			✓	Bad Debts (Deduct from Accounts Receivable)			
Life Insurance Cash Surrender Value		✓		Contingencies†			
Listed Securities*	✓			Depletion (Deduct from Related Assets)			
Loan to Affiliate		✓					
Loan to Subsidiary		✓		Depreciation (Deduct from Related Assets)			
Machinery		✓					
Magazine Titles			✓	Discounts (Deduct from Accounts Receivable)			
Mailing Lists			✓				
Maintenance Materials and Parts		✓		Inventory Adjustments (Deduct from Related Assets)			
Marketable Securities*	✓						
Merchandise (*see* Inventory)				Obsolescence (Deduct from Related Asset)			
Mineral Land		✓					
Mines		✓		Retirement Capital Stock	✓		
Miscellaneous Assets		✓		Self-insurance		✓	
Miscellaneous Receivables		✓		Taxes	✓		
Models			✓	Unexpired Subscriptions		✓	
Mortgages Receivable		✓		Unrealized Profit		✓	
Municipal Bonds	✓						
Municipal Bonds in Default		✓		Salaries	✓		
Notes Receivable (*Same as* Accounts Receivable)							
Organization Expense			✓				
Packaging and Shipping Items	✓						
Patents			✓				
Patterns			✓				
Pension Funds	✓						

GUIDE TO CLASSIFICATION OF BALANCE SHEET ITEMS (*Continued*)
[**Schedule 2** (*Cont.*)]

(margin handwritten notes: "Shareholders' Equity", "Stockholders' Equity)")

Assets	Current	Slow	Intangible	Liabilities	Current	Slow	Net Worth
Plant		✓		Salesmen's Deposits	✓		
Prepaid Items				Sales Lien	✓		
Insurance			✓	Separation Allowances	✓		✓
Rent			✓	Social Security Taxes	✓		
Royalties			✓	Stock			✓
Supplies		✓		Stock Subscriptions	✓		
Taxes			✓	Subordinated Debentures			
Processes			✓	(*Same as* Debentures)			
Profit and Loss (Deficit)			✓	Sundry Accounts Payable	✓		
Property		✓		Surplus Account			
Quarries		✓		Capital Surplus			✓
Real Estate		✓		Deficit (*Deduct*)			✓
Refundable Federal Taxes on				Donated			✓
Income	✓			Earned			✓
Research Expense			✓	Paid-In			✓
Revenue Stamps	✓			Profit and Loss—If Red			
Rights, Publishing			✓	(*Deduct*)			✓
Royalty, Prepaid		✓		Surplus			✓
Savings and Loan Shares	✓			Surplus from Appreciation			✓
Securities*		✓		Undivided Profits			✓
Ships		✓					
Sight Drafts Outstanding	✓			Taxes, Unpaid	✓		
Sinking Fund		✓		Withheld at Source	✓		
State Bonds	✓			Term Loans (*Same as* Bonds)	✓		
Stocks and Bonds*		✓		Trade Acceptances Payable	✓		
Stock Subscriptions			✓				
Subscription Lists			✓	Unearned Income		✓	
Sundry Debtors			✓				
Surplus (Deficit)			✓	Wages, Unpaid	✓		
Timber (Standing or Uncut)		✓					
Tools		✓					
Tracings			✓				
Trade Acceptances	✓						
Trade Brand			✓				
Trade-marks			✓				
Trade Name			✓				
Treasury Bonds		✓					
Treasury Stock			✓				
Trucks		✓					
Unamortized Mortgage or							
Bond Expense			✓				
United States Government							
Securities	✓						
Agencies of the Federal							
Government	✓						
Unlisted Securities*		✓					
Vessels		✓					

* See pp. 84-85.   † See p. 108.

4. The lease customarily provides some means by which the corporation may continue to use the asset after the expiration of the basic lease term. This may take the form of renewal options for additional periods, usually at rentals substantially reduced from those paid during the initial term. The corporation may also be given an option to purchase the asset at the end of the basic lease period, or sometimes even during it.

In these transactions the lease creates a commitment on the part of the lessee to make a series of payments over a future period of time, which is as much a fixed obligation as the interest and sinking fund requirements of a long-term debt. The net lease arrangement, which has become so widely used, obviously is intended to assure the lessor of a fixed monetary return while relieving him of the responsibilities of ownership.

The sale and lease-back technique and the net lease type of obligation have grown by leaps and bounds in more recent years. It was originated for chain store operations, but it has spread into many areas of manufacturing and marine and air transportation. The technique provides a relatively easy means for corporate expansion. The alternative is a heavy direct investment in fixed assets financed by funded obligations or by the issuance of capital stock or both. Under the conventional method of expansion, the increase in fixed assets, funded debt, and capital stock would appear in the balance sheet. Under the existing conventions of accounting practice, a borrowing transaction is recorded in the balance sheet, a lease transaction is not; interest paid on debt is shown as a financial charge in the income statement; rental payments are generally buried among cost of sales and selling and administrative expenses.

In 1949, the Committee on Accounting Procedure of the American Institute of Certified Public Accountants, apparently motivated by the wave of sale and lease-back transactions then taking place, investigated the possible need for revised accounting standards which would in some way report details of existing lease obligations, where material. The recommendations adopted by the Committee at that time pictured the problem as follows: "One of the effects of the long-term lease as a substitute for ownership and mortgage borrowing is that neither the asset nor any indebtedness in connection with it is shown on the balance sheet. This has raised the question of disclosure in financial statements of the fixed amounts payable annually thereunder. . . . "[58] This Committee currently recommends that, where rentals or other obligations under long-term lease "are material in the circumstances":

(*a*) disclosure should be made in financial statements or in notes thereto of: (1) the amounts of annual rentals to be paid under such leases with some indication of the periods for which they are payable, and (2) any other important obligation

[58] *Accounting Research Bulletin*, No. 38 (American Institute of Certified Public Accountants, New York, October, 1949).

UNIFORM CONDENSED COMPARATIVE FINANCIAL STATEMENTS ☐			INDIVIDUAL ☐			CONSOLIDATED ☐		
NAME								
STATEMENT DATE								
1 CASH								
2 MARKETABLE SECURITIES								
3 NOTES RECEIVABLE								
4 ACCOUNTS RECEIVABLE								
5 INVENTORY								
6								
7 OTHER CURRENT ASSETS								
8 TOTAL CURRENT ASSETS								
9 FIXED ASSETS								
10 INVESTMENTS								
11 PREPAID–DEFERRED								
12								
13 OTHER ASSETS								
14 TOTAL ASSETS								
15 DUE BANKS								
16 NOTES PAYABLE								
17 ACCOUNTS PAYABLE								
18 ACCRUALS								
19 TAXES (Except Federal Income)								
20 FEDERAL INCOME TAXES								
21 LONG TERM LIABILITIES(Curr)								
22								
23 OTHER CURRENT LIABILITIES								
24 TOTAL CURRENT LIABILITIES								
25 LONG TERM LIABILITIES								
26								
27 RESERVES								
28 PREFERRED STOCK								
29 COMMON STOCK								
30 CAPITAL SURPLUS								
31 EARNED SURPLUS								
32 NET WORTH (Prop or Part)								
33 TOTAL LIABILITIES								
NET WORKING CAPITAL								
CURRENT RATIO								
TANGIBLE NET WORTH								

5G-62(31266)

FORM 12. Comparative statement form used by Dun & Bradstreet, Inc. (front).

INCOME STATEMENTS AND SURPLUS OR NET WORTH RECONCILIATIONS

FOR THE YEARS ENDED								
34 NET SALES								
35 COST OF GOODS SOLD								
36 GROSS PROFIT								
37 EXPENSES								
38 DEPRECIATION								
39 NET INCOME ON SALES								
40 OTHER INCOME								
41 OTHER EXPENSES								
42 FEDERAL INCOME TAXES								
43 OTHER TAXES								
44 FINAL NET INCOME								
45 SURPLUS OR NET WORTH START								
46 Add: Net Income								
47 Adjustments								
48 Deduct: Net Loss								
49 Adjustments								
50 Dividends—Withdrawals								
51 SURPLUS OR NET WORTH END								

FINANCIAL RATIOS

Net Profits on Net Sales	%		%		%		%
Net Profits on Tangible Net Worth	%		%		%		%
Net Profits on Net Working Capital	%		%		%		%
Net Sales to Tangible Net Worth	Times		Times		Times		Times
Net Sales to Net Working Capital	Times		Times		Times		Times
Average Collection Period	Days		Days		Days		Days
Net Sales to Inventory	Times		Times		Times		Times
Fixed Assets to Tangible Net Worth	%		%		%		%
Current Debt to Tangible Net Worth	%		%		%		%
Total Debt to Tangible Net Worth	%		%		%		%
Inventory to Net Working Capital	%		%		%		%
Current Debt to Inventory	%		%		%		%
Funded Debt to Net Working Capital	%		%		%		%

INSTRUCTIONS TO REPORTERS

A REGARDING CAPTIONS AT BEGINNING OF STATEMENTS:

1. Figures of a Corporation without Subsidiary(s), Proprietorship or Partnership: Check box after "Statements".

2. Figures of a Corporation showing Investment in Subsidiary(s): Check box after "Individual".

3. Figures of a Corporation consolidating figures of Subsidiary (s): Check box after "Consolidated".

4. If Statements are "mixed": Write in type of each statement above the date of that statement.

5. If necessary to show "Fiscal" or "Interim" Write in below the date of statements.

B Use lines 6,12,22, and 26 for significant items not otherwise provided for. Print title, using less than 25 characters including spaces.

C Use lines 7,13, and 23 for minor items and/or groups of miscellaneous items DO NOT write in title, If necessary, explain in Analysis.

D When there is more than one item for 25 or 27 group and explain in Analysis if necessary.

E When the same footnote symbols apply to all years place after the item; otherwise place before amount.

FORM 12. Comparative statement form used by Dun & Bradstreet, Inc. (reverse).

(000 OMITTED)	TYPE DATE	NAME					
1 CASH							
2 GOVTS. & MKT. SECURITIES							
3							
4 NOTES RECEIVABLE—TRADE							
5 ACCTS. RECEIVABLE—TRADE							
6 RESERVE FOR BAD DEBTS							
7 NET RECEIVABLES							
8 INVENTORY (153 /158 INCL.)							
9 CASH VALUE LIFE INS.							
10							
11 CURRENT ASSETS							
12							
13 PREPAID & DEFERRED CHARGES							
14 DUE FROM OFFICERS & EMPL.							
15 ADV. & INVEST.—AFFILIATES							
16 OTHER ASSETS							
17 FIXED ASSETS							
18 RESERVES FOR DEPRECIATION							
19 NET FIXED ASSETS							
20							
21							
22 INTANGIBLES—GOODWILL, ETC.							
23 TOTAL ASSETS							
24 NOTES PAYABLE—BANKS							
25 NOTES PAYABLE—OTHER							
26 ACCOUNTS PAYABLE—TRADE							
27 ACCRUALS							
28 FEDERAL & OTHER TAXES							
29							
30 CURRENT MATURITY TERM DEBT							
31 CURRENT LIABILITIES							
32 LONG TERM DEBT—BANK							
33 LONG TERM DEBT—OTHER							
34 SUBORDINATED DEBT							
35 TOTAL LIABILITIES							
36							
37							
38 SURPLUS RESERVES							
39 CAPITAL STOCK—PREFERRED							
40 CAPITAL STOCK—COMMON							
41 TREASURY STOCK (AT COST)							
42							
43 CAPITAL SURPLUS							
44 EARNED SURPLUS							
45 NET WORTH							
46 TOTAL LIAB. & NET WORTH							
47 CURRENT ASSETS							
48 CURRENT LIABILITIES							
49 WORKING CAPITAL							
50 CURRENT RATIO (11 ÷ 31)							
51 QUICK RATIO (1, 2, 7 ÷ 31)							
52 TANGIBLE NET WORTH							
53 WORTH X DEBT (52 ÷ 35)							
54 SALES							
55 NET PROFIT/ LOSS							
56 DIVIDENDS							
57 INC./ DEC.WORKING CAPITAL							
58 INC./ DEC.NET WORTH							
59 CONTINGENT LIABILITIES							

(Left margin section labels: ASSETS, LIABILITIES, NET WORTH, SUMMARY)

FORM 13. Comparative statement form used by First National Bank of Chicago (front).

balance sheet

		(000 OMITTED)	FROM TO					
	101	NET SALES						
	102	COST OF SALES						
	103	GROSS PROFIT						
O	104	SELLING & OPERATING EXP.						
P	105	GENERAL & ADMIN. EXP.						
E	106							
R	107	PROFIT FROM OPERATIONS						
A	108							
T	109	OTHER INCOME						
I	110	OTHER EXPENSE						
O	111							
N	112	PROFIT BEFORE TAX						
S	113	INCOME TAXES						
	114							
	115	NET PROFIT AFTER TAX						
S	116	EARNED SURPLUS—BEGINNING						
U	117	NET PROFIT/LOSS						
R	118	DIVIDENDS						
P	119							
L	120							
U	121							
S	122							
	123	EARNED SURPLUS—ENDING						
S	124	SOURCE OF FUNDS						
O	125	NET PROFIT						
U	126	DEPR. AMORT. DEPLETION						
R	127	INC.—TERM DEBT						
C	128							
E	129							
&	130	OTHER ACCOUNTS—NET						
A	131	SURPLUS ADJUSTMENTS						
P	132	DECREASE WORKING CAPITAL						
P	133	TOTAL						
L	134	APPLICATION OF FUNDS						
I	135	DIVIDENDS PAID						
C	136	INVESTED IN FIXED ASSETS						
A	137	REDUCTION—TERM DEBT						
T	138							
I	139							
O	140	OTHER ACCOUNTS—NET						
N	141	SURPLUS ADJUSTMENTS						
of	142	INCREASE WORKING CAPITAL						
FUNDS	143	TOTAL						
	144	% GROSS PROFIT (103 ÷ 101)	%	%	%	%	%	%
	145	% SELL & OPER. EXP. (104 ÷ 101)	%	%	%	%	%	%
%	146	% GENL. & ADM. EXP. (105 ÷ 101)	%	%	%	%	%	%
	147	% PROFIT BEFORE TAX (112 ÷ 101)	%	%	%	%	%	%
	148	% PROFIT AFTER TAX (115 ÷ 101)	%	%	%	%	%	%
	149	% RECEIVABLES CURRENT	%	%	%	%	%	%
	150							
I	151	INV. TURNOVER ON COST OF SALES						
N	152							
V	153	INVENTORY—FINISHED						
E	154	INVENTORY—PROCESS						
N	155	INVENTORY—RAW						
T	156	INVENTORY—OTHER						
O	157	RESERVE FOR INVENTORY						
R	158	NET INVENTORY						
Y		SPREAD BY						

FORM 13. Comparative statement form used by First National Bank of Chicago (reverse).

NAME

	BALANCE SHEET Source —	$	$	$	$	$
	ASSETS Date —					
1	Cash					
2	Securities					
3						
4	Receivables—Net (Reserve Below)					
5	Inventories—(See Below)					
6						
7						
8	Other Current Assets—Note (a)					
9	CURRENT ASSETS					
10	Investments & Advances—Affiliations					
11	" " —Others					
12						
13	Leasehold Improvements					
14	Land & Buildings					
15	Equipment, Etc.					
16	Reserves Applicable					
17	Fixed Assets—(Net)					
18	Deferred Charges, Etc.					
19	Intangibles					
20						
21						
22	Other Assets—Note (a)					
23	TOTAL					
24	LIABILITIES					
25	Notes Payable—Banks					
26	" " —Others					
27	Accounts Payable					
28	Accruals—Taxes & Misc. Expenses					
29	Provision For Income Taxes					
30	Current Portion—Long Term Debt					
31						
32						
33	Other Current Liabilities—Note (a)					
34	CURRENT LIABILITIES					
35	Other Liabilities—Note (a)					
36						
37	Reserves					
38	TOTAL DEBT					
39						
40	Subordinated Debt					
41	Capital St'k.—Preferred					
42	" " —Common					
43	Surplus —Capital					
44	" —Reserved					
45	" —Earned					
46	Treasury Stock					
47	NET WORTH PLUS SUBORDINATED DEBT					
48	TOTAL					
49	Reserve For Doubtful Receivables					
50						
51	Raw Materials					
52	Goods In Process					
53	Finished Goods					
54						

Analysis By—

FORM 14. Comparative statement form used by Mercantile Trust Company, St. Louis, Mo. (front).

NAME

INCOME AND SURPLUS	Period		Period		Period		Period		Period	
1 Sales—Gross	$		$		$		$		$	
2 Less—Returns, Allowances, etc.										
3 Sales—Net										
4										
5 Cost of Sales										
6										
7 Gross Profit										
8 Sales, Admin., & Gen'l. Expenses										
9 Salaries—Officers										
10 Salaries—Sales Employees										
11 Salaries—Other Employees										
12										
13										
14										
15										
16										
17										
18										
19										
20										
21										
22 Sundry										
23 TOTAL OPERATING EXPENSES										
24 Other Charges & Credits										
25										
26										
27										
28										
29										
30 Sundry										
31 Total—Other Inc. & Chg's.—Net										
32 Net Income—Before Fed. Taxes										
33 Prov. For Fed. Income Taxes										
34 Net Profit or Loss										
35	%		%		%		%		%	
36 Sales—(Net)										
37 Cost of Sales										
38 Operating Expenses										
39 Other Chg's. Net of Other Income										
40 Prov. For Fed. Inc. Taxes										
41 Net Profit or Loss										
42										
43 At Beginning	$		$		$		$		$	
44 Net Profit or Loss										
45										
46 Sundry										
47 Dividends—Cash										
48 " —Stock										
49 Withdrawals										
50										
51 Sundry										
52 At End										
53										
54										

Analysis By—

FORM 14. Comparative statement form used by Mercantile Trust Company, St. Louis, Mo. (reverse).

assumed or guarantee made in connection therewith; (*b*) the above information should be given not only in the year in which the transaction originates but also as long thereafter as the amounts involved are material; and (*c*) in addition, in the year in which the transaction originates, there should be disclosure of the principal details of any important sale-and-lease transactions.[59]

Rules of the Securities and Exchange Commission treat this subject in the following more general way, and as a result little pertinent data on leases are filed by registrants with the Commission: "Where the rentals or obligations under long-term leases are material there shall be shown the amounts of annual rentals under such leases with some indication of the periods for which they are payable, together with any important obligation assumed or guarantee made in connection therewith."[60] This subject of the disclosure of details of lease obligations, where lease obligations are material, is one which has continued and at this writing is still receiving considerable attention in recognized accounting circles.[61]

CLASSIFICATION OF BALANCE SHEET ITEMS

It is no wonder that many items in balance sheets are classified in different ways, considering the fact that balance sheets are prepared by thousands of certified public accountants with different degrees of training and experience, and by even more thousands of near-accountants, bookkeepers, and businessmen, generally with less understanding and less

[59] *Restatement and Revision of* Accounting Research *Bulletins,* Accounting Research Bulletin, No. 43, p. 126 (American Institute of Certified Public Accountants, 1953).
[60] Regulation S-X, Rule 3-18(*b*), p. 5, Aug. 20, 1958.
[61] For a history of the development of this form of financing and a detailed explanation of the many varied forms of sale-and-lease arrangements, and the accounting problems involved, see "Corporate Financing through the Sale and Lease-back of Property: Business, Tax, and Policy Considerations," *Harvard Law Review,* November, 1948, and "Sale and Lease-back of Corporate Property, *Harvard Business Review,* March, 1949, both studies by William L. Cary; "Danger Signals to Accountants in 'Net Lease' Financing," by Arthur M. Cannon, *The Journal of Accountancy,* April, 1948; *Long-term Leases: Problems of Taxation, Finance, and Accounting,* by Albert H. Cohen (Bureau of Business Research, University of Michigan, Ann Arbor, Mich., 1954); "Illusion in Lease Financing," by Donald R. Gant, *Harvard Business Review,* March–April, 1959; "The Financial Community Looks at Leasing," by Richard F. Vancil and Robert N. Anthony, *Harvard Business Review,* November–December, 1959; and "Recording of Lease Obligations and Related Property Rights," by John L. Hennessy, *The Journal of Accountancy,* March, 1961. The fourteenth edition of *Accounting Trends and Techniques* points out that for 1959, 224 out of 600 corporations surveyed "referred to, or implied, the existence of long-term leases in their 1959 reports [to stockholders]. One hundred and twenty of these companies merely mentioned or indicated that such leases existed but did not furnish any details with regard to them. The remaining 104 companies in this group provided in varying degrees and combinations such factual information as the amount of the annual rent, the aggregate rental, the term of the lease or its expiration date, the number of leases, information as to renewal options, and details as to sale-and-lease-back provisions. The foregoing information was usually presented in the footnotes to the financial statements."—p. 68.

knowledge of accounting principles and standards. Even among certified public accountants, the classification of items varies widely. One accountant will set up the cash surrender value of life insurance as a current asset while another accountant will consider this item as a miscellaneous slow asset; one accountant will set up receivables due from officers as a current asset, while another under similar circumstances will classify the item as a slow asset; and one accountant will treat the current serial maturity of a funded debt as a current liability, while another will leave this maturity lumped with the total funded debt as a deferred liability. In some cases, the difference is due to varying interpretation of management intentions and the various broad purposes for which financial statements are used. In most cases, the difference is a real difference in opinion, or even lack of opinion, among accountants.

Schedule 2 on pages 123–126 for classifying balance sheet items has been prepared from experience in posting thousands of financial statements in almost every line of commercial and industrial activity in every state of the Union. This classification shows not only which items are current (that is, a current asset or a current liability), which items are non-current, also termed slow (that is, fixed assets, miscellaneous assets, and deferred liabilities), but also which items are intangible. There are accountants, bankers, and business consultants who differ in their individual classifications of one or several of these items, or who might well differ in a particular case, but this classification has generally proved to be conservative, effective, and reliable from the viewpoint of bankers, credit men, accountants, security underwriters, brokers, investors, officials of business enterprises, and analysts.

TYPICAL FINANCIAL STATEMENT FORMS

Many of the larger commercial banking institutions and business corporations, as well as mercantile agencies, have their own specially prepared financial statement blanks. The simple short forms are printed on two pages, while the more elaborate long forms run to four pages. In the long forms, the first page is lined to receive the assets and the liabilities, and the second page generally to receive the income statement and the reconciliation of retained earnings (surplus). The third and fourth pages then contain such supporting schedules and supplementary information as a breakdown of receivables, details regarding life insurance carried, segregation of investments, real estate, and mortgages, and contingent liabilities.

The short forms are often printed on elongated sheets. The details of assets and liabilities are requested on the first page, and all other data on the reverse. The income statement and the reconciliation of retained earn-

RETAIL SPECIALTY SHOP, INC.　　　　Balance Sheet as of June 30, 19___　　　　Posting Sheet [Schedule 3]

ASSETS

Current Assets			
Cash in Banks		$ 5,747.32	
Cash on Hand		515.00	
Accounts Receivable		17,926.45	
Due from Lessors	$6,189.75		
Less: Reserve for Rent on Layaways	523.65	5,666.10	
Merchandise Inventory		36,696.55	
Notes Receivable		557.80	
Total Current Assets		$67,109.22	
Other Assets			
Fred Jacobs—Personal		$ 52.53	
State Sales Tax Stamps		5.74	
Defense Stamps Fund		50.00	
Deposits		75.00	
Claims Receivable		162.13	
Prepaid Expenses		887.50	
Total Other Assets		$ 1,232.90	
Fixed Assets			
Furniture and Fixtures		$14,866.06	
Less: Reserve for Depreciation		6,018.78	
Net Fixed Assets		$ 8,817.28	
TOTAL ASSETS		**$77,189.40**	

LIABILITIES AND CAPITAL

Current Liabilities			
Notes Payable to Bank		$11,000.00	
Accounts Payable—Merchandise	$2,433.39		
Less: Reserve for Discount	122.79	2,310.60	
Accounts Payable—Expense		1,545.81	
Federal Excise Tax		59.87	
Sales Tax		208.57	
Accrued Salaries, Expenses and Taxes		1,884.22	
Contingent Claim Liability		50.50	
Total Current Liabilities		$17,059.57	
5% Cumulative Preferred Stock		$27,000.00	
Common Stock		935.00	
Surplus		32,194.83	
Net Worth		$60,129.83	
TOTAL LIABILITIES AND CAPITAL		**$77,189.40**	

Posting Sheet — ASSETS

Cash	$ 6,262
Accounts Receivable	17,926
Due from Lessors	5,666
Inventory	36,697
Current Assets	$66,551
Fixed Assets	8,847
Miscellaneous Receivables	847
Prepaid Expenses	888
Other Assets	56
TOTAL	$77,189

LIABILITIES

Notes Payable to Bank	$11,000
Accounts Payable	3,856
Reserve for Taxes	268
Accruals	1,884
Other Liabilities	51
Current Liabilities	$17,059
5% Cumulative Pref. Stock	27,000
Common Stock	935
Surplus	32,195
TOTAL	$77,189

Net Working Capital	$49,492
Current Ratio	3.90
Tangible Net Worth	$60,130

From income statement

Net Sales	$206,911
Net Profits	6,810
Dividends	3,635

We have examined the Balance Sheet of Retail Specialty Shop, Inc, as of June 30, 19— and the statement of income and surplus for the period ending June 30, 19—; we have reviewed the system of internal control and the accounting procedures of the company, and have examined or tested accounting records and other supporting evidence by methods and to the extent we deemed appropriate.

In our opinion, and as a result of a continuous audit, the above Balance Sheet presents fairly the position of Retail Specialty Shop, Inc, as of June 30, 19—.

　　　　　　(Signed) _____
　　　　　　　　Certified Public Accountants

ings (surplus) are condensed into one continuous schedule. The other schedules and supplementary information also are briefed. These forms provide for all the information usually available on smaller business enterprises, as the schedules and the supplementary information requested on the typical long form rarely apply to small concerns. All blanks cover approximately the same essential ground, with particular emphasis on different items or phases of supplementary financial information. Illustrations of early financial statement forms appear on pages 11, 14, 16, 18, and 20. Illustrations of typical financial statement forms now in current use appear on pages 98–99, 102–105, 114–115, and 118–121.

Specialized Financial Statement Blanks

The statement form used by the National Credit Office, Inc., with the accountant's supplementary information sheet, are unique in their application and in their completeness. The statement of financial condition is mailed in an envelope to every concern in the industries upon which National Credit Office, Inc., issues a credit report. One page of this form requests the usual balance sheet information with supplementary information regarding qualifications of accountants, if any, inventory valuation, insurance, and condition of the receivables. The second page requests the profit and loss figures, the reconciliation of surplus or net worth, and the accountant's "opinion."

The *Accountant's Supplementary Information* sheet is mailed, whenever it is deemed necessary, to the accountant who audited the books to obtain information regarding the scope of his audit and the steps taken by the accountant to verify receivables and inventory, together with other pertinent data. These schedules are printed as received by the offset printing process, and are distributed immediately by the National Credit Office, Inc., to their interested members, banks, and mercantile houses.

Posting a Comparative Statement Blank

The first step which is taken with a balance sheet preparatory to analysis is to transpose the figures to a prepared comparative statement form technically known as a *posting sheet*, or a *spread sheet*. It makes no difference whether these were obtained from an accountant's report, from a financial statement blank of a banking institution or a mercantile creditor, from an annual report to stockholders, from an investment service, from a letterhead, or from a plain sheet of paper. If prepared comparative statement forms are not available, accountants' standard columnar paper or, as a last resort, plain paper may readily be used. The practical objective is to take any balance sheet, no matter how lengthy or how complicated,

WHOLESALERS OF TOBACCO PRODUCTS, INC.

Balance Sheet as of December 31, 19___

ASSETS

Current Assets

Cash in Banks and on Hand...		$242,450.46
Accounts Receivable—Trade Debtors...	$134,566.09	
Deduct: Reserve for Bad Debts...	10,000.00	
	$124,566.09	
Sundry Accounts Receivable...	19,936.53	
Merchandise Inventory (at lower of cost or market)...	236,997.21	
Total Current Assets...		$623,950.29

Investments

International Cigarettes, Inc., stock (quoted market value Dec. 31, 19— $8,700)...	$32,000.00	
Other—at Cost...	1,024.23	
		33,024.23
Due from Affiliated Company...		927.74
Due from Employees...		3,000.00
Furniture and Fixtures (Net)...		16,099.07
Deferred Charges...		5,421.52
		$682,422.85

LIABILITIES AND CAPITAL

Current Liabilities

Accounts Payable—Trade Creditors...	$94,907.93	
Sundry Accounts Payable (Commissions, Royalties, etc.)...	77,203.22	
Accrued Charges...	15,289.12	
Reserve for Federal Income Taxes...	29,593.00	
Total Current Liabilities...		$216,993.27
Reserve for Contingencies (see Note A)...		15,000.00

Capital Stock and Surplus

Capital Stock:		
Authorized and Issued—3,000 shares, par value $10.00 per share...	$30,000.00	
Capital Surplus...	720,000.00	
Deficit...	299,570.42	
Total Capital Stock and Surplus...		450,429.58
		$682,422.85

We have examined the balance sheet of Wholesalers of Tobacco Products, Inc., as of December 31, 19—, have reviewed the system of internal control and the accounting procedures of the company and, without making a detailed audit of the transactions, have examined or tested accounting records of the company and other supporting evidence, by methods and to the extent we deemed appropriate. Our examination was made in accordance with generally accepted auditing standards applicable in the circumstances and included all procedures which we considered necessary.

In our opinion, the above balance sheet presents fairly the position at December 31, 19—, in conformity with generally accepted accounting principles applied on a basis consistent with that of the preceding year.

_____ (Signed)

Certified Public Accountant

NOTE A: Claims have been made by the United States Government for additional duties on imports made during several years past, the amounts of which have, however, not yet been determined. The Company and its attorneys believe that claims in any substantial amount are not justified. A reserve in the amount of $15,000 has been provided in the Balance Sheet herein but whether this reserve is adequate or excessive cannot be presently determined.

---Posting Sheet   [Schedule 4]

ASSETS

Cash...	$ 242,450
Accounts Receivable...	124,566
Inventory...	236,997
Current Assets...	$ 604,013
Miscellaneous Receivables...	22,936
Investments...	33,024
Due from Affiliated Company...	928
Furniture and Fixtures...	16,099
Deferred Charges...	5,422
TOTAL...	$ 682,422

LIABILITIES

Accounts Payable...	$ 94,907
Accruals...	92,492
Reserve for Taxes...	29,593
Reserve for Contingencies...	15,000
Current Liabilities...	$ 231,992
Capital Stock...	30,000
Capital Surplus...	720,000
Deficit...	299,570
TOTAL...	$ 682,422

Net Working Capital...	$ 372,021
Current Ratio...	2.60
Tangible Net Worth...	450,430

From income statement

Net Sales...	$7,183,972
Net Profits...	23,334
Dividends...	None

and to combine similar items under the four primary groupings of the assets and the three primary groupings of liabilities described in this chapter. In this way, the figures to be analyzed will be relatively few in number and in a comparative form from one accounting period to another. In this process, as already mentioned, it is desirable to deduct valuation reserves for bad debts, depreciation, obsolescence, and depletion from related assets, so that these asset items will be carried net on the posting sheet.

Schedules 3, 4, and 5 are illustrative of this technique. Schedule 3 takes the balance sheet of a moderate-sized retail store and, by the use of arrows running from items in the audited balance sheet to a particular item on the posting sheet at the right of the page, shows how all the original items are arranged and combined in accordance with the classifications given on pages 123–126. *Cash in Banks* of $5,747.32 and *Cash on Hand* of $515, for example, are combined to create the one item of *Cash* $6,262 on the posting sheet. In a similar way *Notes Receivable* of $557.80, *Fred Jacobs—Personal* of $52.53, *Deposits* of $75, and *Claims Receivable* of $162.13 are combined into the one item of *Miscellaneous Receivables* carried on the posting sheet at $847. In this process the item *Notes Receivable* of $557.80, which is carried as a current asset by the accountant, becomes a slow asset on the posting sheet. The notes receivable are a miscellaneous asset in this case as a retail store has no occasion to accept notes in its normal business operations. Below the rearranged balance sheet figures on the posting sheet, three supplementary figures have been computed, *Net Working Capital* at $49,492, the *Current Ratio* of 3.90, and the *Tangible Net Worth* of $60,130. Below these figures, *Net Sales*, *Net Profits* (after Federal income tax), and *Dividends* have been inserted for ready reference.

Schedule 4 follows this same procedure for a wholesaler of tobacco products with a tangible net worth of $450,430. The audited figures show *Accounts Receivable—Trade Debtors* of $134,566.09 less a *Reserve for Bad Debts* of $10,000, giving net *Accounts Receivable* of $124,566.09. Only this net figure shows on the posting sheet. *Sundry Accounts Receivable* of $19,936.53 and *Due from Employees* of $3,000 are combined into the one figure of *Miscellaneous Receivables* of $22,936 on the posting sheet. In the liabilities, *Sundry Accounts Payable (Commissions, Royalties, etc.)* carried at $77,203.22 and *Accrued Charges* of $15,289.12 are combined into the one item of *Accruals* $92,492 in the posting sheet. In this process, *Sundry Accounts Receivable* $19,936.53 carried as a current asset by the accountant becomes a slow asset, and the *Reserve for Contingencies* $15,000 carried as a deferred liability by the accountant becomes a current liability. In the determination of the *Tangible Net Worth*, the *Deficit* of $299,570 is de-

[Schedule 6]

Posting Sheet

ASSETS	
Cash	$ 4,587,154
Marketable Securities	741,870
Accounts Receivable	4,568,280
Notes Receivable	
Inventory	7,831,410
Current Assets	$17,728,714
Investments	1,931,821
Fixed Assets	22,881,257
Miscellaneous Receivables	123,234
Deferred Charges	366,369
Patterns, Drawings, and Dies	2,100,000
Good Will	11,000,000
TOTAL	$56,131,395

LIABILITIES	
Accounts Payable	$ 1,844,595
Accrued Salaries and Wages	781,459
Accrued Taxes	223,774
Advance Payments	5,000
Contingency Reserves	877,699
Current Liabilities	$ 3,732,527
Accident Indemnity Reserves	755,156
5% Cumulative Pref. Stock	35,196,100
Common Stock	3,839,500
Capital Surplus	4,702,687
Earned Surplus	7,905,425
TOTAL	$56,131,395

From income statement:

Net Working Capital	$40,853,730
Current Ratio	4.75
Tangible Net Worth	$38,543,712
Net Sales	$13,996,187
Net Profits	2,321,576
Dividends	1,759,805

AMERICAN MACHINE CORPORATION AND SUBSIDIARY COMPANIES
Consolidated Balance Sheet, December 31, 19___

ASSETS

Current Assets

Cash		$ 4,587,154.24	
Marketable Securities (valued at market)		741,870.00	
Accounts and Notes Receivable—			
Trade	$ 4,698,803.88		
Less: Reserve for Doubtful Accounts and Notes	130,523.85	4,568,280.03	
Other Accounts and Notes Receivable		123,233.65	
Inventories—at lower of cost or market value			
Material and Supplies	$ 3,160,419.40		
Work in Process	2,952,918.90		
Finished Products	1,718,071.52	7,831,409.82	

Investments—at or below cost

Deposited with Workmen's Compensation Commissions	$ 486,677.81		
Other Investments	4,195,143.48		
	$ 4,681,821.29		
Less: Reserve for Possible Loss	2,750,000.00	1,931,821.29	

Fixed Assets—on basis of cost

Land	$ 2,119,390.00		
Buildings, Machinery, and Equipment, less Depreciation	20,585,905.93		
Unused Plant Sites, at estimated realizable values	175,961.00	22,881,256.93	
Deferred Charges		366,369.64	
Patterns, Drawings, and Dies		2,100,000.00	
Good Will		11,000,000.00	
		$56,131,395.60	

LIABILITIES AND CAPITAL

Current Liabilities

Accounts Payable	$ 1,844,595.27	
Accrued Salaries, Wages Expenses, etc.	781,458.77	
Accrued Taxes Other than Income	223,274.15	
Advance Payments Received on Contracts	5,000.00	
Total Current Liabilities		$ 2,854,828.19

Reserves

Contingency Reserves	$ 877,699.28	
Accident Indemnity Reserves	755,156.25	1,632,855.53

Capital Stock

Preferred—5% Cumulative, par value $100 per share	$35,196,100.00	
Common—no par, stated value $5 per share	3,839,500.00	39,035,600.00

Surplus

Capital Surplus	$ 4,702,686.79	
Earned Surplus	7,905,425.09	12,608,111.88
		$56,131,395.60

In our opinion, the accompanying consolidated balance sheet of American Machine Corporation at December 31, 19—, and related consolidated statements of profit and loss and of surplus present fairly the consolidated position of the companies at December 31, 19—, and the consolidated results of their operations for the fiscal year, in conformity with generally accepted accounting principles applied on a basis consistent with that of the preceding year.

_____ (Signed)

Certified Public Accountants

ducted from the sum of the *Capital Stock* $30,000 and the *Capital Surplus* $720,000, to give the figure of $450,430.

Schedule 5 for a large manufacturer of machines and tools with a tangible net worth of $38,543,712 has been treated similarly. As the *Reserve for Doubtful Accounts and Notes* of $130,523.85 is a valuation reserve, it has been deducted from the item of *Accounts and Notes Receivable—Trade* of $4,698,803.88 to give the net figure of $4,568,280.03 which is carried in the posting sheet. *Other Accounts and Notes Receivable* of $123,233.65, which the accountant has carried as a current asset, becomes a miscellaneous asset in the posting sheet. *Reserve for Possible Loss* of $2,750,000 set up against *Investments* has been deducted and only the net figure of *Investments* amounting to $1,931,821.29 is carried in the posting sheet. In the liabilities, the only change is the posting of the *Contingency Reserves* of $887,699.28 as a current liability. As a result of these modifications the *Current Assets* in the posting sheet amount to $17,728,714, compared with $17,851,947.74 in the audited figures, and the *Current Liabilities* to $3,732,527, compared with $2,854,828.19 in the audited figures. The *Tangible Net Worth* is computed by deducting *Patterns, Drawings, and Dies* valued at $2,100,000 and *Good Will* valued at $11,000,000 from the sum of the 5 *per cent Cumulative Preferred Stock, Common Stock, Capital Surplus*, and *Earned Surplus*.

If two or more balance sheets are being analyzed, the comparable items in each balance sheet are posted on the same line, thus making a running horizontal comparison relatively easy to follow. Many examples of this running comparison appear in succeeding chapters. Forms 12, 13, and 14 picture three such comparative statement blanks. The figures from the oldest balance sheet are posted in the first column for figures at the left, and succeeding balance sheets follow in chronological order to the right. The blank spaces in the extreme left-hand column are available for items peculiar to one concern, which may readily be inserted with ink in longhand.

No matter how complete a balance sheet may seem to be, additional information is almost always needed by the skilled analyst. The particular points upon which explanatory information is needed come to his mind as the analyst transfers the figures from the statement form to his posting sheet, particularly if he has figures for previous years. A noticeable increase or decrease in any item—receivables, merchandise, due from officers or employees, current liabilities, net sales, or net profits—or in important ratios between items calls for explanations. What caused the increase or the decrease? Then the policy which brought about the increase or the decrease must be evaluted. As a result of these changes in the financial setup, the concern is either stronger or weaker, a better or a poorer risk.

THEORY AND PROBLEMS

1. An examination of the balance sheet of an industrial company is made for credit purposes and the following conditions are discovered:

   a. Cash includes a substantial sum specifically set aside for the immediate reconstruction of plant and new machinery.

   b. Trade accounts receivable include a large amount of customers' notes of which a considerable number have been renewed continually. The interest is settled on each maturity date and the makers are in good credit standing.

   c. Inventory includes retired machinery, some at regularly depreciated book value, other at scrap or sales value.

   d. Surplus includes a sinking fund reserve, set up out of profits in accordance with the trust deed.

   How should each of the foregoing items be shown on the balance sheet? Gives reasons. [A.I.A. examination]

2. How would you suggest that the following items be presented in a balance sheet?

   a. Dividends in arrears on cumulative preferred stock.

   b. United States Treasury tax notes purchased for the payment of Federal income tax.

   c. Serial maturity of a funded debt falling due in 10 months.

   d. Cash surrender value of life insurance payable to the business.

   e. Municipal bonds.

3. Place the number of each item in the following consolidated balance sheet on a sheet of paper. Then classify each item in the assets as current, fixed, miscellaneous, or intangible, and each item in the liabilities as current, deferred, or net worth.

Machinery Manufacturing Corporation
Consolidated Balance Sheet, December 31, 19—
Assets

Current Assets
1. Cash... $2,197,523
2. Marketable securities (less reserve to reduce to value based upon market quotations, $8,381).......... 53,144
Receivables
3. Customers' notes, trade acceptances, and accounts.................. $ 2,357,439
4. Unbilled charges to customers for tools and dies................ 83,650
5. Sundry........................ 35,763
   Total...................... $ 2,476,852
6. *Less:* Reserve for doubtful receivables...................... 13,300   2,463,552
7. Inventories—Finished goods, work in process, materials, and supplies (at lower of cost or market). 2,646,488
   Total Current Assets..................... $ 7,360,707
Investments and Miscellaneous Assets
8. Notes and accounts receivable from employees..... $ 3,193
9. Mortgage receivable.......................... 25,229
10. Miscellaneous securities—at cost (less reserve for loss, $2,220)............................... 1,500
    Total Investments and Miscellaneous Assets. 29,922
Real Estate, Plants, and Equipment (net value based on sound values as appraised as of **August 1, 19—**, or at

MACHINERY MANUFACTURING CORPORATION (*Continued*)
various dates prior; with subsequent additions at cost
and less subsequent retirements and provision for
depreciation)

11. Land...		$ 855,608	
12. Buildings and building fixtures.......	$ 3,123,273		
13. Machinery and equipment...........	8,715,892		
Total......................	$11,839,165		
14. *Less:* Reserves for depreciation.......	6,604,696	5,234,469	
15. Construction in progress.........................		11,441	
Total Real Estate, Plants, and Equipment..			6,101,518
16. Patents and Good Will..............			1

Deferred Charges

17. Prepaid taxes and unexpired insurance premiums...	$ 120,600		
18. Deferred tool and die costs...............	42,850		
19. Miscellaneous...............................	29,247		
Total Deferred Charges...................		192,697	
Total...		$13,684,845	

LIABILITIES

Current Liabilities

20. Accounts payable for purchases and expenses.......	$ 746,207	
21. Accrued Federal and Dominion of Canada income taxes...	426,111	
22. Other accrued liabilities—Pay rolls, sundry taxes, royalties, and miscellaneous...................	397,854	
Total Current Liabilities.................		$ 1,570,172

Reserves

23. For possible additional Federal income taxes.......	$ 27,416	
24. Miscellaneous................................	13,576	
Total Reserves................................		40,992

Minority Interest in Motor Specialties Company, Inc.

25. Class A capital stock of no par value—52,090 shares.	$ 409,490	
26. Common capital stock of no par value—83 shares..	653	
Total Minority Interest.................		410,143

Capital Stock and Surplus

Capital stock of no par value................... $9,566,653
Represented by
Class A convertible preference—Entitled to
cumulative dividends of $2.50 per share
annually and in the event of redemption or
liquidation to $45.00 per share, plus accumu-
lated dividends (authorized, 500,000 shares;
issued, 174,480 shares).
Class B (authorized, 2,000,000 shares; issued,
802,087 shares).
Less: Capital stock in treasury—480 shares Class A
and 17,087 shares Class B
At cost................................. 282,487

27. Net capital stock (174,000 shares Class A; 785,-000 shares Class B)......................	$9,284,166	

Surplus—Including capital surplus

28. Unappropriated..................	$ 2,096,885		
29. Appropriated to cover cost of capital stock in treasury as deducted from capital stock above.............	282,487	2,379,372	
Total Capital Stock and Surplus...........		11,663,538	
TOTAL...		$13,684,845	

4. Revise the following balance sheet of the Star Manufacturing Co., Inc., as to form, content, and presentation of the items, based upon the information set forth below:

STAR MANUFACTURING CO., INC.
Balance Sheet, December 31, 19—
ASSETS

Current Assets
Cash on hand and in banks.............................	$137,500	
Notes receivable (less discounted notes $20,000)...........	60,000	
Accounts receivable (less reserve $8,500).................	247,800	
U.S. Govt. bonds (plus accrued interest, $420)............	42,350	
Total Current Assets...............................		$ 487,650

Working and Trading Assets
Raw materials and supplies............................	$ 92,440	
Work in process......................................	110,700	
Finished goods, including consigned merchandise, $21,670..	181,320	
Total Working and Trading Assets....................		384,460
Investment in the Capital Stock of Other Companies........		120,000

Capital Assets
Land and buildings at cost (less depreciation).............	$440,000	
Machinery and equipment (less depreciation, $162,800)....	332,000	
Furniture and fixtures (less depreciation, $3,200)..........	15,900	
Total Capital Assets................................		787,900
Sinking Fund for Retirement of First Mortgage Bonds.......		69,700
Treasury Stock.......................................		10,000
Prepaid Expenses and Deferred Charges..................		24,700
		$1,884,410

LIABILITIES

Current Liabilities
Accounts payable—trade..............................	$273,000	
Accrued pay rolls and interest........................	15,620	
Reserve for Federal income taxes......................	72,000	
Reserve for other taxes...............................	14,300	
Installment notes payable $12,000 on first of each month beginning Jan. 1, 19—, and accrued interest $4,500......	124,500	
Total Current Liabilities...........................		$ 499,420
Dividends payable Jan. 16, 19—........................		6,000
4% first mortgage bonds due at end of 20 years............		350,000

Capital Stock and Surplus
Capital stock
Preferred, 2,000 shares authorized; 1,800 shares issued...	$180,000	
Common, 3,000 shares authorized; 2,500 shares issued...	250,000	
Subscriptions to common stock, 400 shares.............	22,000	
Total Capital Stock..............................	$452,000	

Retained Earnings
Reserve for employees' pensions................	$ 14,000	
Free and available for dividends................	159,990	
Total Retained Earnings............................	173,990	
Capital surplus.......................................	403,000	
Total Capital Stock and Surplus....................		1,028,990
		$1,884,410

Through inquiry and investigation you obtain the following information with respect to items in the foregoing balance sheet:

1. Cash includes $14,000 in an employees' pension fund.
2. The U.S. Government bonds represent $42,000 face value 3½ per cent Treasury bonds valued at cost plus accured interest. The market value of such bonds on statement date was $44,700.
3. Accounts receivable include $8,400 of advances to employees.
4. Accounts receivable also include $15,000 advanced to suppliers of raw materials for materials neither received nor in transit. Since the placement of the orders, which are not subject to cancellation, the replacement cost of the materials has declined to 70 per cent of the commitment price.
5. Raw materials and supplies are stated at amounts lower than market and include invoices received, in the amount of $7,000, for materials shipped f.o.b. point of shipment and in the hands of common carriers on December 31, 19—. Excluded are $9,000 of raw materials received three days prior to statement date, for which invoices are dated fifteen days after statement date.
6. Work in process is valued at actual cost of direct materials and direct labor, plus a normal charge for manufacturing overhead based upon company experience, which is less than market value.
7. Finished goods are similarly valued, except for merchandise in hands of consignees, which is priced and billed on memorandum at 110% of cost. Finished goods valued at $140,000 are pledged against installment notes payable to bank.
8. Of the capital stock investments in other companies, $95,000 represents investments at cost in 50% or more of the stock of subsidiary companies. The realizable values of such investments exceed cost, and income therefrom is reduced as dividends are received.
9. The remaining investments represent small stock interests considered necessary for business operations, having an aggregate market value of $21,800 at statement date.
10. The land and buildings account, when analyzed, discloses the following—

Cost of land.	$ 75,000
Depreciated cost of buildings six years prior to statement date, established by revenue agent's report, adjusted for subsequent additions and retirements.	699,500
Accumulated depreciation.	304,500

11. The sinking fund consists of $19,700 in cash and $50,000 of the company's own first mortgage 4 per cent bonds.
12. The treasury stock represents 100 shares of preferred valued at par and acquired for resale to employees.
13. The preferred stock has a $100 par value. It is cumulative at the rate of 5 per cent, and is callable at 105 per cent of par value plus accumulated and unpaid dividends, if any. The 1,800 shares issued include the 100 shares in the treasury.
14. The common stock also has a $100 par value. The subscriptions to 400 shares of common stock are stated in the balance sheet net of $18,000 representing receivables from subscribers on their stock subscription contracts.
15. The reserve for employees' pensions of $14,000 offsets the amount of cash in the employees' pension fund. This fund was set up during the year as a result of a contract with employees.

[A.I.A. examination]

5. Give five factors that have influenced the increased publication of balance sheets during the past 75 years.

6. A stockholder who owns some stock in a listed corporation is concerned because he receives such small dividends. He has reviewed the last stockholders' report and has concluded there is ample cash available for larger dividends. In addition to cash in banks, the corporation's balance sheet shows the following items which he believes represent cash funds:

a. A large *Paid-in Surplus*
b. Plenty of *Undivided Profits*
c. A large *Reserve for General Contingencies*
d. A substantial *Reserve for Depreciation*

In simple nontechnical language, explain the nature of the items which the stockholder has confused with cash.

7. Set up the following two successive fiscal balance sheets of Regulator Machine Company, Inc., on a comparative statement form, making all necessary changes in the classification of items. Then compute the current assets, the current liabilities, the net working capital, the current ratio, and the tangible net worth from each balance sheet.

REGULATOR MACHINE COMPANY, INC.
Consolidated Balance Sheet, December 31, Year *B*
ASSETS

Current Assets

Cash (including $241,322.02 to be used on a government contract)..	$ 7,430,757
Dominion of Canada bonds—at cost..........................	72,072
Notes and accounts receivable (including unbilled charges for plant facilities)—less reserves for doubtful notes and accounts, $62,004.50	9,398,318
Accounts receivable from English and Swedish subsidiaries........	13,049
Sundry accounts receivable..................................	167,704
Inventories—raw materials, supplies, goods in process, and finished goods (at cost, not in excess of market)......................	12,603,425
Preliminary expenses incurred under a government contract........	1,343,000
Total Current Assets..................................	$31,028,325
Due Officers and Employees.................................	517,000
Investment in English and Swedish Subsidiaries....................	44,617
Cash Value of Life Insurance Policies...........................	233,619
Real Estate, Plant, and Equipment.............................	4,289,648
Patents—Less Amortization, $100,176..........................	200,100
Trade-marks and Good Will...................................	1
Deferred Manufacturing Expenses..............................	337,025
Other Deferred Charges, Etc.................................	191,250
TOTAL...	$36,841,585

LIABILITIES

Current Liabilities

Accounts payable..		$ 1,809,738
Advances against contract by United States government..........		2,204,322
Accrued expenses and taxes other than income and capital stock taxes		557,972
Federal capital stock, Canadian tax, and state taxes...	$ 1,091,040	
Federal income taxes..............................	13,468,024	
Total..	$14,559,064	

REGULATOR MACHINE COMPANY, INC. (*Continued*)

Less: United States Treasury notes available for payment of Federal income taxes....................	4,900,000	9,659,064
Notes payable—banks............................		6,000,000
Total Current Liabilities.................................		$20,231,096
Special Contingency Reserve...................................		500,000
4% cumulative convertible, Series B—30,700 shares.....	$ 3,070,000	
4¼% cumulative, Series C—25,000 shares..............	2,500,000	
Common (authorized, 750,000 shares without par value; issued, 621,963 shares, less 63 shares in treasury)......	3,291,499	
Total Capital Stock.....................................		8,861,499
Paid-in and other capital surplus......................	$ 914,531	
Retained Earnings.................................	6,334,459	
Total Surplus..		7,248,990
TOTAL...		$36,841,585

REGULATOR MACHINE COMPANY, INC.
Consolidated Balance Sheet, December 31, Year *A*

ASSETS

Current Assets		
Cash (including $574,078.75 to be used exclusively on a government contract)...		$14,054,669
Dominion of Canada bonds—at cost............................		90,090
Notes and accounts receivable (including unbilled charges for plant facilities)—less reserves for doubtful notes and accounts, $62,004..		6,808,259
Account receivable from English subsidiary.......................		12,941
Sundry accounts receivable (including employees' accounts of $84,466)		323,752
Inventories—raw materials, supplies, goods in process, and finished goods (at cost, not in excess of market)—(including $2,907,321 to be used exclusively on a government contract).....................		20,917,453
Preliminary manufacturing expenses incurred under a government contract..		1,744,784
Total Current Assets....................................		$43,951,948
Due Officers and Employees.......................................		1,064,318
Investment in English and Swedish Subsidiaries....................		44,617
Cash Value of Life Insurance Policies............................		251,296
Real Estate, Plant and Equipment...............................		4,545,188
Patents—Less Amortization, $118,403............................		194,911
Trade-marks and Good Will......................................		1
Deferred Charges, Etc..		225,993
TOTAL...		$50,278,272

LIABILITIES

Current Liabilities		
Accounts payable...		$ 2,526,961
Advances against contract by United States government..........		3,659,737
Accrued expenses and taxes other than income and capital stock taxes		1,404,566
Income and capital stock taxes		
Federal income and capital stock, Canadian tax, and state taxes...................................	$1,668,467	
Federal income taxes...........................	7,858,000	
Total.......................................		9,526,467
Notes payable—banks...		15,000,000
Total Current Liabilities.................................		$32,117,731
Reserves for Special Contingencies...............................		925,000

REGULATOR MACHINE COMPANY, INC. (*Continued*)

4% cumulative convertible, Series B—issued and outstanding, 30,700 shares............................	$3,070,000	
4¼% cumulative, Series C—issued and outstanding, 25,000 shares....................................	2,500,000	
Common (authorized, 750,000 shares without par value; issued, 621,963 shares, less 63 shares in treasury; outstanding, 621,900 shares).........................	3,291,499	
Total Capital Stock..................................		8,861,499
Paid-in and other capital surplus.................... $	914,530	
Retained Earnings.................................	7,459,512	
Total Surplus.......................................		8,374,042
TOTAL...		$50,278,272

8. For each of the following paragraphs state the letter and related number of the correct completing phrase.

    a. The M Company has under construction a large additional machine shop for its own use. Construction work in progress applicable thereto should appear on its balance sheet as

        (1) A current asset, a part of work-in-process inventory.
        (2) An intangible asset.
        (3) An investment.
        (4) A fixed tangible asset.
        (5) A part of surplus.

    b. The M Company's cash includes a sum of $1,000,000 appropriated by resolution of the board of directors for the construction of a new plant. On its financial statements this amount should be included

        (1) On the balance sheet as a current asset.
        (2) On the balance sheet as a non-current asset, specifically identified.
        (3) On the balance sheet as a fixed asset, included as part of plant cost.
        (4) On the income statement as a non-operating expense.
        (5) On the balance sheet as an allocation of surplus.

    c. The trial balance of the P Company as of June 30, Year (*A*), the end of its fiscal year, included opposite the title "Estimated Federal Income Taxes Accrued" the amount of $27,564.12, which included the company's estimate of the Federal income tax it would have to pay for its Year (*A*) fiscal year and the amount of an unpaid additional assessment for the Year (*C*) fiscal year. This amount should appear.

        (1) On the balance sheet as a general reserve.
        (2) On the balance sheet as a reduction of current assets.
        (3) On the balance sheet as a current liability.
        (4) On the balance sheet as an allocation of retained earnings.
        (5) On the balance sheet as an allocation of other surplus.

    d. The S Company leased space in a building for a period of 10 years from January 1, Year (*B*). It spent $25,000 for improvements to the space to adapt it to its needs, it being expected that such improvements would outlast the period of the lease. The improvements were completed and placed in service on January 1, Year (*A*). On the company's financial statements as of December 31, Year (*A*), and for the year then ended, the amount expended should be shown

    (1) On the balance sheet as a non-current asset.

    (2) On the income statement as an operating expense.

    (3) On the balance sheet as paid-in surplus.

    (4) On the balance sheet as a current asset.

    (5) Apportioned between the income statement and the balance sheet, the income statement portion appearing as an operating expense and the balance sheet portion as a non-current asset.

    e. The Y Company issued, on October 31, 19—, $1,000,000 of 20-year general mortgage bonds, at 105. The premium on these bonds should appear on the company's balance sheet at October 31, 19—, as

    (1) A part of capital surplus.

    (2) A part of retained earnings.

    (3) A part of the liability, "bonds payable."

    (4) A deferred credit.

    (5) An intangible asset.

[A.I.A. examination]

9. Select the current asset and current liability items from among the following list of debit and credit accounts and classify them in the manner in which they might respectively appear on the balance sheet of a large manufacturing company.

Debits	Credits
Plant and equipment	Accrued payroll
Cash in bank	Reserve for renegotiation of U.S. Government contracts
Inventory of operating parts and supplies	
Inventory of raw materials	Notes payable
Good will	Accrued interest on bonds
Cash and U.S. Government bonds set aside for property additions	Reserve for depreciation
	Accounts payable
Investment in subsidiary	Capital surplus
Accounts receivable:	Accrued interest on notes payable
U.S. Government contracts	5% 1st mortgage bonds to be redeemed
Regular	in ten years
Installments—due in Year (*C*)	Capital stock—preferred
Installments—due in Years (*B*)–(*A*)	Reserve for contingencies
Patent rights	4½% 1st mortgage bonds due in ten years
Inventory of finished goods	Reserve for doubtful accounts receivable
Inventory of work in process	Provision for Federal income taxes
Deficit	Customers, advances on contracts
Interest accrued on U.S. government securities	Reserve for raw materials inventory
	Premium on bonds to be redeemed in the
Notes receivable	coming year
Petty cash fund	Officers' bonus accrued
U.S. Government securities	[A.I.A. examination]
Treasury stock	

10. State (*a*) the relationship among business organizations which makes the preparation of consolidated financial statements advisable and (*b*) the purpose of preparing consolidated financial statements.

11. In August 19—, the Rex Corporation purchased for its use in manufacturing operations, at a cost of $200,000, real estate, consisting of land and a building erected thereon, subject to a mortgage of $125,000, but has not at any time assumed the mortgage. In preparing the company's financial statements as of August 31, 19—, the close of its fiscal year, the controller included the gross cost of the property, $200,000, in fixed assets and the amount of the mortgage, $125,000, in deferred liabilities. The company's treasurer objected, contending that the amount of the mortgage should be shown on the assets side of the balance sheet as a deduction from the gross cost of the real estate, and omitted from the liability side of the statement. Would you uphold the controller in his presentation or the treasurer in his contention? Give reasons for your answer.

[A.I.A. examination]

12. In response to a request from a prospective client, criticize briefly, item by item, the form and terminology of the following balance sheet:

Balance Sheet
ABC COMPANY
For the Year Ended December 31, 19—
ASSETS

Current:

Cash and related items	$ 11,000
Accounts and notes receivable	758,000
Raw material (market $100,000)	160,000
Work in process, cost	35,000
Finished goods, sales price	315,000
Supplies	78,000
Investments	155,000

Fixed:

Land, buildings, machinery, patents	1,500,000
Investments	300,000
Treasury Stock	18,000
Deficit	800,000
Total assets	$4,130,000

LIABILITIES

Current:

Miscellaneous current liabilities	$ 54,000
Accounts and notes payable	826,000

Fixed:

Mortgages and bonds	1,000,000
Preferred and common stock	1,700,000
Reserves for depreciation	200,000
Miscellaneous reserves	350,000
Total liabilities	$4,130,000

[A.I.A. examination]

PART II

Analysis of Small Business Enterprises

PART II *consists of one chapter on the analysis of small business enterprises by the breakdown of sales income. As approximately 82 per cent of all active commercial and industrial concerns have a tangible net worth of $35,000 or less, this technique of financial interpretation, known as sales analyses, has wide application. In this technique, the net sales of a particular business enterprise are broken down into three elements, namely, (1) cost of materials, (2) labor, and (3) other expenses plus net profit. That portion of the net sales income available monthly for the payment of materials is compared directly with the item of accounts payable in the current liabilities section of the balance sheet. If this portion of income available over the period covered by purchasing terms is equal to or greater than the accounts payable, trade obligations will probably be paid promptly or by discount. If, on the other hand, the income available for this purpose over the period of the purchasing terms is less than the accounts payable, some portion of the trade payments will run slow. This method of sales analysis has particular application to smaller business enterprises that make little or no use of bank credit and accordingly rely on merchandise suppliers for necessary credit. Where bank credit is used, this technique is not applicable as bank credit is obtained to meet seasonal current merchandise obligations and to tide over a period of inadequate cash income. The current assets of the typical small retail enterprise generally consist of cash and inventory. Small manufacturers and wholesalers also carry moderate receivables.*

CHAPTER V

Analysis of Small Business Enterprises

As stated in Chap. I, there were 1,855,000 active commercial and industrial business enterprises listed in the July, 1944, issue of the Reference Book of The Mercantile Agency and 2,708,000 in the July, 1960, issue. Between these two dates, there was an increase of 1,853,000, or approximately 100 per cent, in the number of listed business enterprises. Although no exact figures are available, it is known that a very high proportion of these new business ventures were started with moderate capital. There is no place in the world where it is so easy to go into business, or so easy to go out of business, as in the United States. A study of the age of business failures in 1950 showed that 68.2 per cent had been in existence five years or less, and of the failures for 1960, 57.9 per cent.

Studies made in recent years indicate that approximately 82 per cent of all commercial and industrial business concerns have a tangible net worth of $35,000 or less. As the tangible net worth grouping increases in size, a smaller and smaller percentage of all active business enterprises is represented. Concerns with a tangible net worth between $75,000 and $200,000 represent approximately 5.6 per cent; from $200,000 to $1,000,-000, 2.1 per cent; and above $1,000,000, only 0.7 per cent of listed businesses. These figures indicate the tremendous importance of small business enterprises in our economy.

Approximately 76 per cent of all active commercial and industrial concerns in the United States are retail enterprises. Bank credit is available to only a moderate portion of these smaller retailers, an occasional corner grocery store, shoe store, drugstore, or the delicatessen shop. Few of the owners of these smaller establishments realize that a bank relationship is one that may be cultivated into an eventual extension of modest credit; on the other hand, these smaller accounts are rarely the ones to invite a banker's sustained interest. Most small retailers are restricted in their use of credit to their merchandise suppliers, with some additional credit obtained now and then when a piece of machinery, a refrigerator, or a showcase is purchased on a moderate down payment with the balance in installments. With the growth in the number of city commercial banks and trust companies that have organized personal loan departments, and with the great increase in the volume of personal loans, this type of credit in small amounts represents an important growing source of loans to smaller businesses.

CHARACTERISTICS OF SMALL BUSINESS

Economic activity in the American capitalistic system is based upon the existence of this tremendous number of small establishments. Small businesses not only constitute a large segment of the entire business field, they also perform certain functions and services that are not duplicated elsewhere in our economy, and in so doing have a distinctive value in our national life. The first of these contributions represents the special services performed for the consumer, thus complementing and rounding out the production methods of big business. Second are the contributions made by the small business to big business where central industrial units receive the output of small concerns that have produced parts for assembly, and conversely, where small independent concerns carry on secondary and tertiary manufacturing processes for large corporations. Small business in the aggregate is an important customer of large business. Third is the fact that small business in many industries also competes with the large, the most impressive present-day example being provided by the transportation field. In this process the individual, small enterprise is the living expression of the initiative and individualism of the open competitive economic system. Fourth is the fact that small business supports a considerable part of the population. Fifth, the only way to obtain distribution of many commodities in rural and sparsely settled communities is through the small store.

Freedom in the economic world of a democracy is based upon the existence of a steady flow of business enterprises into and out of this group—the liquidation of tens of thousands[1] of these concerns each year as they are unsuccessful, as the owners die, voluntarily liquidate or sell their assets, retire, or move to some new location; and the starting of many thousands of new ventures. There is no other way, at this stage of economic development, to obtain the refined distribution of all kinds of merchandise into every community in the land, except by a gigantic development in the consumer cooperative movement; such an achievement would put hundreds of thousands of small retailers out of business even if it might otherwise be desirable.

[1] For the 3 years 1957 to 1959 inclusive, an average of 406,000 new businesses started operations yearly and an average of 343,000 discontinued operations yearly. For 1959, there were 423,000 new concerns and 347,000 discontinuances. These are preliminary figures quoted in "Growth in Business Concerns," *Survey of Current Business*, May, 1960, p. 13 (U.S. Department of Commerce, Washington). While no figures are currently available, in 1955 there were approximately 321,300 business transfers, that is, going businesses which were sold by the owners to others.

So, the fact must be stressed that small business enterprises are those which have a tangible net worth $35,000 or less, and as previously mentioned represent approximately 82 per cent of all active commercial and industrial concerns. This very percentage emphasizes the utmost importance of small business in the ~~existing~~ current economy of the United States.

Contrast between Small and Large Business

It is the unusual small retail business enterprise that sells merchandise on credit. Daily sales are made largely for cash. As a result, the current assets of the typical small retail enterprise generally consist of only two items, cash and inventory. Small wholesalers and small manufacturers make all or most of their sales on credit terms, and a representative proportion of their current assets consists of accounts receivable, notes receivable, and occasional trade acceptances, along with cash and inventory.

The principles described in succeeding chapters for the analysis of financial statements of larger commercial and industrial business enterprises also apply to these smaller concerns, but in a modified manner. An owner of a small business employing eight individuals can control the operations of his concern much more easily than the president of a corporation with 35,000 employees laboring in seven widely separated plants and in an excutive office located in New York City. If the inventory of an establishment with a tangible net worth of $35,000 or less is heavy, it can be reduced more readily than the inventory of a large corporation, because the amount to be assimilated by the market is relatively small, its forward commitments are fewer, for a smaller variety of items, and for smaller amounts. In case of absolute necessity, the small concern may even sell a substantial part of its inventory at wholesale without any appreciable lapse in time. If expenses must be cut by reducing the personnel, a reduction of 50 per cent may be made in a fraction of the time needed to accomplish the same objective by any large nationally known corporation.

A financial condition unbalanced by top-heavy investments in fixed assets, excessive funded liabilities, light working capital, heavy liabilities, or burdensome overhead may be as detrimental to the existence of the small as to the large business enterprise. There does exist, however, an ease of control and maneuverability that bears an inverse relationship to size.

TECHNIQUE OF SALES ANALYSIS

Income from net sales is the lifeblood of every commercial and industrial business. As in human life, the quality, the quantity, and above all the regularity of the flow govern the physical appearance and the internal condition of the business organism. The distribution of every dollar utilized in the operation of a commercial or industrial concern is regulated by the actual net sales or the expected sales volume. Consequently, every item in the balance sheet has a definite relationship to the net sales. In the sales analysis of balance sheets of small concerns, the relationship between the net sales and the current liabilities is of particular interest.

Income flows from inventory into receivables, where credit terms are used, from receivables into cash, and from cash back into inventory. Where sales are made only on a cash basis, the cycle is short-circuited by the elimination of the receivables. The inventory is accumulated in keeping with the expected sales demand, the receivables rise and fall with the flow of sales, except in those cases where sales are made only for cash, and the cash fluctuates with the income from net sales less the disbursement to create or replenish the inventory and to pay salaries, labor, and all overhead expenses.

Elements of Net Sales

The sales income of a commercial or industrial concern is distributed in many directions. It is used to purchase merchandise, to meet pay rolls, to pay rent, insurance, light, heat, telephone, taxes, and to take care of the many other debts of a going enterprise. These disbursements may be classified into several groups depending upon the purpose of the outlay. Purchases of merchandise by a wholesaler or a retailer, including transportation in, for example, may be grouped under cost of material; the relationship between cost of material and net sales is generally referred to as *percentage cost of sales*. The cash funds spent by a manufacturer for direct labor, maintenance, power, light, and heat to convert raw materials into finished goods may be grouped under manufacturing costs but with two primary subdivisions of labor and other expenses; and the costs incurred in distributing the finished products, such as salesmen's salaries and commissions and advertising, may be grouped under selling expenses. Similarly, the various other expenses, as explained in Chap. XVIII, may be classified according to the employment of the funds. After all disbursements have been accounted for, the residue of the net sales income is termed *operating profit*.[2]

To simplify the analysis of small business concerns, the term *element of net sales* is used to indicate each of the three general classes of disbursements into which closely related expenditures have been arbitrarily classi-

[2] *Operating profit* should not be confused with final net profit. Charges of various natures are often deducted from operating profit to arrive at a final net profit. At times, charges are made to retained earnings (surplus) which in reality should be taken into consideration before arriving at a final net profit. This subject is discussed in detail in Chap. XIX.

fied. These elements vary in their proportion to net sales, depending upon the method of operation of a particular concern, that is, whether it operates as a retailer, a wholesaler, or a manufacturer. For retail and wholesale concerns, the proportion of net sales represented by cost of materials (that is, cost of merchandise sold) invariably is greater than the proportion of net sales represented by the cost of raw materials used in manufacturing processes. Only with manufacturers do manufacturing labor costs appear. The three elements of disbursements and their respective proportions of net sales are grouped around the following general percentages:

Elements of Net Sales	Retailer	Wholesaler	Manufacturer
Cost of Materials.............	70	85	50
Manufacturing Labor..........	...	...	35
Expenses and Net Profits......	30	15	15
Net Sales....................	100	100	100

These percentages are approximate averages. Actually, a wide range of percentages exists for each element of net sales under each method of transacting business. The cost of raw materials for manufacturers may range from a low of approximately 54.7 per cent for manufacturers of "tobacco products" to a high of 81.6 per cent for textile mills;[3] for wholesalers, cost of sales runs from approximately 82.0 per cent for the distributors of machinery, equipment, and supplies to approximately 95.0 per cent for wholesalers of tobacco and tobacco products except leaf;[4] and for retailers, as will be seen in Schedule 6, it ranges from 52.5 per cent for installment jewelry stores to 85.0 per cent for automobile dealers. The cost of materials in each dollar of net sales is least in manufacturing, larger in retailing, and largest in wholesaling. Conversely, as a general rule, wholesalers use the greater part of their income from net sales to pay

[3] An analysis of corporation income figures covering the year 1956–1957 reveals the fact that manufacturers in 23 broad major lines of business expended $222,473,-601,000 for materials representing 72.7 per cent of the value of products shipped. *Statistics of Income 1956–1957, Corporation Income Tax Returns with Accounting Periods Ended July 1956–June 1957*, p. 26 (Internal Revenue Service, U.S. Treasury Department, Washington, 1959).

[4] See *Census of Business, 1954*, Vol. III, *Wholesale Trade—Summary Statistics*. This extensive study gives percentages of total operating expenses, exclusive of cost of merchandise, to net sales for all divisions of wholesale trade broken down by geographical districts and sales groups. The difference between 100 per cent and the percentage of total operating expenses to net sales gives the average percentage income available to pay merchandise invoices for each division of trade by sales groups. This study confirms the general impression that the percentage of operating expenses generally decreases as annual net sales increase. Total expenses, for example, of all wholesalers in the United States with sales below $50,000 amounted to 31.0 per

merchandise liabilities, retailers a smaller portion, and manufacturers the least.

Labor costs and overhead expenses, such as rent, light, heat, telephone, insurance, and taxes, invariably have first call on the income; merchandise indebtedness is paid only after these internal charges have been met. For this simple but very important everyday fact, the net sales income must be broken down into the above-mentioned broad elements of expense when determining by sales analysis the ability of a small concern to meet its merchandise obligations on time.

Typical Retail Operating Experience

Schedule 6 on page 159 gives typical operating experiences for 38 lines of retail trade based upon surveys of operating expenses conducted during the years given for respective lines of activity by various authorities. This schedule has been condensed into four columns of percentage figures for the particular use in sales analyses of smaller retail business enterprises. These four columns are cost of materials, net profit before income taxes, funds available for meeting merchandise obligations (representing the total of the first two columns), and total operating expenses.

The totals of the third and fourth per cent columns equal 100 per cent and represent the income from net sales. The third per cent column particularly affects the sales analyses of small retail enterprises. The operating expenses, as measured by the percentage of net sales income, are lowest with auto dealers at 13.6 per cent, followed by farm equipment dealers at 14.2 per cent, farm supply stores at 14.4 per cent, and grocery stores with 14.4 per cent, and the highest with bars and grills at 43.4 per cent.

cent of net sales for 1954 (p. 2-2). From this point the expense ratio decreased steadily with an increase in net sales:

Sales Group Wholesale Trade	Aggregate Sales	Expense Ratio
Under $50,000.................	$ 705,001,000	31.0
$ 50,000–$ 99,999...........	1,857,660,000	25.4
100,000– 199,999...........	4,532,948,000	22.5
200,000– 299,999...........	4,424,833,000	20.5
300,000– 499,999...........	7,656,795,000	18.9
500,000– 999,999...........	13,952,367,000	16.6
1,000,000– 1,999,999...........	16,741,594,000	13.8
2,000,000– 4,999,999...........	19,940,896,000	11.5
5,000,000– 9,999,999...........	11,223,011,000	9.3
10,000,000 and over.............	18,584,598,000	5.7
All wholesalers.................	101,100,941,000	13.2

ELEMENTS OF NET SALES FOR 38 RETAIL TRADES   [Schedule 6]

Line of Business	Year of Study	Cost of Materials	Net Profit before Income Taxes*	Available for Meeting Merchandise Obligations†	Total Operating Expenses
		Per Cent	Per Cent	Per Cent	Per Cent
Appliance; Radio; Television Dealers..	1959	64.6	1.0	65.6	34.4
Auto Accessory and Parts Stores.......	1955	65.6	2.7	68.3	31.7
Auto Dealers..................	1959	85.0	1.4	86.4	13.6
Bakeries.........................	1955	58.1	3.6	61.7	38.3
Bars and Taverns....................	1953	54.2	2.4	56.6	43.4
Book Stores.......................	1954	61.9	3.0	64.9	35.1
Camera and Photographic Supply Stores	1954	69.1	2.4	71.5	28.5
Candy, Nut, and Confectionery Stores.	1955	64.2	0.4	64.6	35.4
Children's and Infants' Wear Stores...	1957	67.5	1.7	69.2	30.8
Department Stores‡..................	1959	65.9	1.7	67.6	32.4
Drugstores........................	1959	64.4	5.7	70.1	29.9
Dry Goods and General Merchandise Stores...	1957	70.5	1.9	72.4	27.6
Family Clothing Stores..............	1956	69.4	2.7	72.1	27.9
Farm Equipment Dealers.............	1959	82.5	3.3	85.8	14.2
Farm Supply Stores.................	1956	84.1	1.5	85.6	14.4
Floor Coverings Stores..............	1954	64.3	1.7	66.0	34.0
Florists..........................	1953	52.6	3.3	55.9	44.1
Furniture Stores‡..................	1958	61.6	0.5	62.1	37.9
Gasoline Service Stations...........	1956	76.8	1.1	77.9	22.1
Gift, Novelty, and Souvenir Stores....	1957	60.0	1.9	61.9	38.1
Grocery Stores....................	1952	84.1	1.5	85.6	14.4
Hardware Stores...................	1959	69.5	1.3	70.8	29.2
Jewelry Stores (Primarily Cash and Open Credit)..................	1953	55.6	3.7	59.3	40.7
Jewelry Stores (Primarily Installment Credit)........................	1953	52.5	5.8	58.3	41.7
Juvenile Furniture Stores...........	1954	66.6	3.2	69.8	30.2
Liquor Stores (Package).............	1955	80.3	2.6	82.9	17.1
Lumber Dealers....................	1955	75.5	3.4	78.9	21.1
Meat Markets.....................	1954	79.3	1.4	80.7	19.3
Men's Furnishings Stores............	1952	67.2	3.5	70.7	29.3
Men's Wear Stores.................	1959	64.6	3.4	68.0	32.0
Music Stores......................	1956	64.2	2.5	66.7	33.3
Office Supply and Equipment Dealers..	1959	64.8	2.9	67.7	32.3
Paint and Wallpaper Stores..........	1956	66.9	3.0	69.9	30.1
Shoe Stores (Family)...............	1959	63.0	4.2	67.2	32.8
Sporting Goods Stores..............	1953	71.4	2.0	73.4	26.6
Women's Accessory and Specialty Stores	1954	66.3	2.2	68.5	31.5
Women's Ready-to-wear Stores.......	1953	67.7	2.9	70.6	29.4
Women's Wear Stores‡..............	1959	62.8	1.2	64.0	36.0

* In this table it would be preferable to use net profit *after* income taxes rather than net profit *before* income taxes. However, the various sources from which these figures have been compiled used both unincorporated businesses—partnerships and proprietorships—and corporations in their studies. Since income taxes paid by owners of unincorporated enterprises are not based on business profits alone, the figures of both unincorporated businesses and corporations can be utilized on a comparable basis only before income taxes.

† The figures in this column overstate the per cent of net sales "available for meeting merchandise obligations" by the typical per cent of income taxes to net sales for respective lines of business for the reason explained in the preceding footnote. In retail trades this typical per cent would be slight.

‡ Ratios shown are for stores in the following volume groups: department stores with annual sales volume under $1,000,000; furniture stores between $250,000 and $500,000; women's wear stores under $1,000,000.

The percentages in this schedule are typical for the retail trades that are listed. These percentages, however, vary from one locality to another, from a large city where rents and labor costs are high, to a country village where rents and labor costs are low. Moreover, these percentages vary from one store to another in the same locality depending upon the operating policies of the management, whether little or considerable advertising is used, whether rent expense is high or low, whether liberal or small salaries are taken out by the owner or the owners for their services. As a general rule, however, two characteristics are predominant regardless of the size of the city; the small retailer usually has a higher gross margin than the larger retailer, and retailers in large cities usually operate on a higher gross margin than those in small cities and towns.

ILLUSTRATIONS OF SALES ANALYSES

To make a sales analysis of any business enterprise it is absolutely essential to have a sales figure, preferably net sales, along with the balance sheet. If a figure is available for gross sales but not for net sales, a modest deduction may be made for returns and allowances to obtain an estimated net sales figure. It is also absolutely essential to know exact purchasing terms, and if several different terms are used by merchandise suppliers, to compute as closely as possible the weighted average purchasing term. Other information is desirable, as will be seen in the following examples, but if the additional facts are not available, fairly close estimates may be made to carry out this particular type of analysis of small business enterprises.

Haberdashery Shop

Fred A. Robbins owns and operates a retail men's furnishing shop in a densely populated tenement area in New York City. The business has been in operation 6 years and during that time the initial investment of $3,000 has grown to $8,964, partly out of earnings and partly by the investment of additional funds in the business. Between the last two fiscal years the net worth increased $1,695, but of this amount only $295 represented reinvested net profits for the year, after a modest salary to the owner. The difference of $1,400 represented additional funds invested in the business in year A. The comparative financial condition of the business as of the last two fiscal dates appears in Schedule 7.

Sales Analysis of Year B Figures. In year B, the current liabilities, which amounted to $5,621, were quite heavy; how heavy will be shown by a sales analysis. As a result of the net profit of $295 and the additional

$22,290 to $14,682, [handwritten]

2,800 [handwritten]

$1,400 invested in the business during year *A*, the financial condition was considerably improved. At the same time, the inventory was contracted from $11,145 to $7,341, bringing affairs even more into line. The current _5,914._ [handwritten] liabilities simultaneously were reduced to $2,957. To state the improvement in the form of a succinct comparison, the current liabilities at the end of *B* amounted to 77.7 per cent of the tangible net worth, and 1 year later to only 32.9 per cent.

FRED A. ROBBINS—PROPRIETOR　　　　　　　　　　　[Schedule 7]
Comparative Figures for Years Ended December 31, 19—

	(B) Two Years Ago	(A) One Year Ago	
ASSETS			
Cash	$ 1,084 2,168	$ 2,576	5,152
Inventory	11,145 22,290	7,341	14,682
Current Assets	$12,229 24,458	$ 9,917	19,834
Fixtures	211 422	1,613	3,226
Prepaid	318 636	286	592
Other Assets	132 264	105	210
TOTAL	$12,890 25,780	$11,921	23,842
LIABILITIES			
Accounts Payable	$ 5,347 10,694	$ 2,754	5,508
Accruals	274 548	203	406
Current Liabilities	$ 5,621 11,242	$ 2,957	5,914
Net Worth	7,269 14,538	8,964	17,928
TOTAL	$12,890 25,780	$11,921	23,842
Net Working Capital	$ 6,608 13,216	$ 6,960	13,920
Current Ratio	2.17 2.17	3.35	3.35
Tangible Net Worth	$ 7,269 14,538	$ 8,964	17,928
Net Sales	$28,176 56,352	$24,660	49,320
Net Profits	862 1,724	295	590
Withdrawals	None None	None	None

To make a sales analysis of the balance sheet for year *B*, it is necessary, first of all, to break certain figures down into average monthly periods. √6,352 [handwritten] For example, dividing the yearly net sales of $28,176 by 12 gives average monthly sales of $2,348. The average monthly net sales is the same as the average monthly income. Out of this average monthly income must come the funds to meet all operating expenses of every nature from day to day and from week to week, and then to meet invoices for merchandise on net buying terms, if not on discount terms.

By referring to the operating figures of men's furnishing shops in Schedule 6, it is seen that the total operating expenses in this line amount, on the average, to 29.3 per cent of net sales, leaving 70.7 per cent of the net income to pay merchandise invoices. On average monthly net sales of $2,348, 70.7 per cent or $1,660 is available on the average during each month throughout the year to pay merchandise invoices after $688 has been used during the month to meet all operating expenses such as salaries, wages, rent, light, heat, telephone, insurance, and taxes.

If $688, the average monthly expense, is now considered to be the absolute minimum cash requirement to be kept on hand, the excess of cash may be ascertained by deducting this figure from cash of $1,084 shown in the balance sheet of year B. The difference, which amounts to $396, may be applied immediately to reduce outstanding merchandise invoices.

If this excess cash of $396 is applied to the accounts payable of $5,347, a balance of $4,951 is owing to merchandise creditors. No consideration is given to other liabilities, which in this case represent accruals of $274, as payment of such an item is included in the gross expenses of 29.3 per cent which were immediately deducted from the average monthly income as a necessary prior expense. The balance of accounts payable of $4,951 can be met only out of that portion of the net sales income which is available to pay merchandise bills and which has been found by computation to be $1,660 monthly, on the average.

Dividing $4,951, the *net* accounts payable, by the average monthly income available to pay merchandise invoices, amounting to $1,660, gives 3 months, the length of time it would normally take to liquidate this outstanding net merchandise indebtedness. Merchandise is purchased by men's furnishing stores on net terms which average around 30 days.[5] The average net income to pay merchandise bills in 30 days or 1 month would be only $1,660, an amount insufficient to meet the outstanding net merchandise obligations, and payments to merchandise suppliers accordingly would run slow.

Sales Analysis of Year A Figures. The financial condition at the end of the following year A is materially different. On the basis of a similar sales analysis, the following computations may be made:

---

[5] Manufacturers of men's shirts, underwear, and pajamas, for example, sell to retail stores, exclusive of large chains and department stores, on terms of 2 per cent discount in 10 days, net 30 days; 3 per cent 10 days, EOM; and some few concerns on terms of 30 days net. Wholesalers of men's furnishings sell to retail men's furnishing shops on terms of 1 to 3 per cent discount in 10 days, EOM, the twenty-fifth of the month being considered the end of the month. Wholesalers of hoisery and underwear sell to retail stores on terms of net 30 days, but terms of 10 days, EOM, net 30 days, and 2 per cent discount in 10 days, net 30 days, are also used.

1. Yearly Net Sales... $24,660.00 *49,320.00*
2. Average Monthly Net Sales................................... 2,055.00 *4,110.00*
   (Divide 1 by 12 months)
3. Average Monthly Income to Meet Merchandise Obligations......... 1,452.88 *2,904.76*
   (Multiply 2 by 70.7 per cent)
4. Cash on Hand on Statement Date............................. 2,576.00 *5,152.00*
5. Average Monthly Income Needed to Cover Gross Expenses......... 602.12 *1,204.24*
   (Multiply 2 by 29.3 per cent)
6. Excess Cash on Hand...................................... 1,973.88 *3,947.76*
   (Subtract 5 from 4)
7. Accounts Payable on Statement Date......................... 2,754.00 *5,508.00*
8. Accounts Payable after Crediting Excess Cash on Hand........... 780.12 *1,560.24*
   (Subtract 6 from 7)
9. Number of Months to Liquidate Remaining Accounts Payable...... 0.53
   (Divide 8 by 3) *.590*

22,290

In year A, the inventory was materially reduced from $11,145 to $7,341; net profits of $295 were retained in the business; and $1,400 of *2,800* additional funds were invested in the business. These three features brought about a very material and healthy decrease in the current liabilities from $5,621 to $2,957, and improved the relationship between the *1,914* current liabilities and the tangible net worth. This improvement is now measured definitely by the sales analysis in the time it would take to liquidate the accounts payable. Whereas, at the date of the balance sheet in year B, it would have taken 3 months and payments would have been slow on typical buying terms of 30 days, at the date of the balance sheet in year A it would have taken only 0.53 of a month, or approximately 17 days, and all payments would certainly have been discounted or made promptly. By this technique, the ability of a concern to liquidate its obligations is put into the exact unit of days and is compared with typical or average purchasing terms. The technique is simple, logical, and reasonably accurate, particularly with smaller retail concerns.

Ladies Specialty Shop

In San Francisco 8 years ago, Marie Martel opened a small retail shop handling corsets, brassières, hosiery, lingerie, gloves, and accessories under the name of the Ladies Specialty Shop. The business was started *4* with a modest investment of $2,800. Operations were conducted with some moderate success, as the tangible net worth in year A amounted to $10,129, the increase having been gradually accumulated over the years from retained earnings. The comparative figures for year B and year A are shown in Schedule 8.

Very little difference appears in the figures between year B and year *1,468* A. The current assets expanded $734, represented partly by larger inventory and partly by greater cash; the current liabilities were almost identical for both years; the tangible net worth increased from $9,149 to

18,298

$10,129 as a result of keeping net profits of $980 in the business; the net working capital was moderately larger; and the net sales increased somewhat. The typical concern in this line of business utilizes 31.5 per cent of the annual net income from day to day to meet operating expenses and

[Schedule 8]

LADIES SPECIALTY SHOP

Comparative Figures for Years Ended August 31, 19—

	(B) Two Years Ago	(A) One Year Ago
ASSETS		
Cash	$ 227	$ 532
Accounts Receivable	1,835	1,802
Merchandise	10,961	11,423
Current Assets	$13,023	$13,757
Fixtures	2,752	2,710
Deposit	....	334
TOTAL	$15,775	$16,801
LIABILITIES		
Accounts Payable	$ 6,126	$ 6,047
Accrued Rent	500	500
Accrued Taxes	....	125
Current Liabilities	$ 6,626	$ 6,672
Net Worth	9,149	10,129
TOTAL	$15,775	$16,801
Net Working Capital	$ 6,397	$ 7,085
Current Ratio	1.96	2.06
Tangible Net Worth	$ 9,149	$10,129
Net Sales	$48,624	$52,432
Net Profits	1,109	980
Withdrawals	None	None

the remaining 68.5 per cent to cover merchandise purchases and net profits. Comparative sales analyses for year *B* and year *A* give the following results:

	Year B	Year A
1. Yearly Net Sales	$48,624	$52,432
2. Average Monthly Net Sales	4,052	4,371
3. Average Monthly Income to Meet Merchandise Obligations	2,776	2,994
4. Cash on Hand on Statement Date	227	532
5. Average Monthly Income Needed to Cover Gross Expenses	1,276	1,377
6. Excess Cash on Hand	(D)1,049	(D) 845
7. Accounts Payable on Statement Date	6,126	6,047
8. Accounts Payable after Debiting Lack of Cash Requirements on Hand	7,175	6,892
9. Number of Months to Liquidate Adjusted Accounts Payable	2.6	2.3

454

This enterprise had been operating with insufficient cash on hand. The balance sheet in year *B* disclosed cash of only $227, and in year *A* of $532. 1,064 Checks were drawn on balances in the depository bank just about as soon as the funds were deposited. On the basis that the minimum cash requirements should be sufficiently large to cover all operating expenses for 1 month, cash was short $1,049 in year *B*, and $845 in year *A*. If these 2,092 amounts are added to the respective accounts payable for both years,

WHOLESALE WOOLEN COMPANY   [Schedule 9]
Comparative Figures for Years Ended August 31, 19—

	(B) Two Years Ago	(A) One Year Ago
ASSETS		
Cash....................................	$ 2,225	$ 6,555
Accounts Receivable.....................	5,550	10,209
Merchandise............................	6,425	10,646
Current Assets........................	$14,200	$27,410
Fixtures...............................	750	712
Due from Partners......................	1,774	636
Prepaid Insurance......................	26	277
Securities.............................	....	204
TOTAL..............................	$16,750	$29,239
LIABILITIES		
Accounts payable......................	$......	$11,149
Accruals..............................	....	9
Current Liabilities..................	$......	$11,158
Net Worth.............................	16,750	18,081
TOTAL.............................	$16,750	$29,239
Net Working Capital..................	$14,200	$16,252
Current Ratio........................	....	2.45
Tangible Net Worth...................	$16,750	$18,081
Net Sales.............................	$......	$61,053
Net Profits...........................	....	1,331
Withdrawals...........................	None	None

and the average monthly incomes available to meet merchandise obligations are applied to these totals, 2.6 months for year *B* and 2.3 months for year *A* appear as the respective periods it would take to liquidate accounts payable on the basis of average monthly sales.

About one-third the annual purchases of the Ladies Specialty Shop are made on 30-day terms and the remaining two-thirds on 60-day terms, or weighted average purchasing terms of 50 days. Obviously trade obligations could not be met on these terms for either year, with average liquidating ability of 2.6 months and 2.3 months respectively. Subsequent trade investigations, made shortly after the statement dates, for both years verified these conclusions. Although some modest improvement was made during year A, the payments to three-quarters of the merchandise suppliers were running around 30 days slow after the end of year A.

Wholesaler of Woolen and Worsted Piece Goods

The Wholesale Woolen Company was organized in year B by two part ners. One of the partners had previously been a buyer for 10 years for a large representative jobber of woolen and worsted piece goods, while the other partner had been a salesman in the same line for 8 years with another concern. This enterprise started business with a paid-in capital of $16,750 as specialists in woolens and worsted piece goods selling to the ladies' dress trade. At the end of year B, operations had been carried on for about 3 months. No liabilities were outstanding on the statement date, all obligations having been met out of the paid-in tangible net worth.

The figures at the end of year A disclosed the results of an active busi ness. Net sales for the year had amounted to $61,053, quite a satisfactory volume for the first full year of operation. Net profits amounted to $1,331. The current liabilities now aggregated $11,158. The comparative figures for the 2 years are given in Schedule 9.

An income statement which accompanied the balance sheet for year A disclosed the fact that the cost of goods sold during year A amounted to $47,621, which was 78 per cent of the annual net sales. The cost of goods sold plus the net profits of $1,331 amounted to 80 per cent of the net sales, leaving 20 per cent for all expenses including salaries and wages, selling expense, shipping, general, taxes, and administrative expense. A sales analysis based on these percentages gives the following results as of the end of year A:

1. Yearly Net Sales... $61,053
2. Average Monthly Net Sales..................................... 5,088
   (Divide 1 by 12 months)
3. Average Monthly Income to Meet Merchandise Obligations........... 4,070
   (Multiply 2 by 80 per cent)
4. Cash on Hand on Statement Date................................ 6,555
5. Average Monthly Income Needed to Cover All Gross Expenses........ 1,018
   (Multiply 2 by 20 per cent)
6. Excess Cash on Hand.. 5,537
   (Subtract 5 from 4)
7. Accounts Payable on Statement Date............................ 11,149
8. Accounts Payable after Crediting Excess of Cash on Hand........... 5,612
   (Subtract 6 from 7)
9. Number of Months to Liquidate Remaining Accounts Payable......... 1.4
   (Divide 8 by 3)

Of the average monthly net sales of $5,088, 80 per cent, or $4,070, became available to meet merchandise obligations. The balance sheet showed an excess of cash of $5,537; applying this sum to the accounts payable of $11,149 brought the amount of accounts payable to be liquidated from net sales income down to $5,612. This amount on the average would be retired in 1.4 months on the basis of $4,070 being available monthly to apply to merchandise creditors. Purchases of woolen and worsted piece

BLANKBOOK MANUFACTURING COMPANY [Schedule 10]
Comparative Figures for Years Ended December 31, 19—

	(B) Two Years Ago	(A) One Year Ago
ASSETS		
Cash.................................	$ 10,484	$ 11,720
Accounts Receivable...................	13,620	14,432
Merchandise..........................	7,488	4,016
Current Assets.......................	$ 31,592	$ 30,168
Machinery...........................	10,400	10,000
Prepaid Insurance....................	328	296
TOTAL..........................	$ 42,320	$ 40,464
LIABILITIES		
Accounts Payable.....................	$ 14,612	$ 11,860
Accrued Taxes.......................	412	252
Current Liabilities...................	$ 15,024	$ 12,112
Net Worth...........................	27,296	28,352
TOTAL..........................	$ 42,320	$ 40,464
Net Working Capital..................	$ 16,568	$ 18,056
Current Ratio.......................	2.10	2.49
Tangible Net Worth..................	$ 27,296	$ 28,352
Net Sales............................	$144,856	$153,460
Net Profits..........................	1,552	1,056
Withdrawals..........................	None	None

goods are generally made on 60- or 70-day terms, so it is quite evident that affairs were in healthy shape and all obligations were being taken care of handily.

Manufacturer of Blankbooks

A small manufacturing business was organized 6 years ago by two brothers under the style of the Blankbook Manufacturing Company to produce blankbooks and binders. The business has remained continuously in their hands. Within a radius of 100 miles of the plant, sales are made to retail stationery stores, to printers, and to industrial enterprises. Comparative figures for the past 2 years appear in Schedule 10.

This firm is a relatively small enterprise, the balance sheet at the end of year *B* disclosing a tangible net worth of $27,296 and at the end of year *A*, a tangible net worth of $28,352. The volume of net sales increased moderately from $144,856 to $153,460 between the 2 years, and some profits were earned each year.

The internal financial condition improved somewhat between the two statement dates. The current liabilities were reduced from $15,024 in year *B* to $12,112 in year *A*. This reduction was brought about by retaining the net profits of $1,056 in year *A* in the current assets, by the reduction in the fixed assets through depreciation on the machinery account of $400, and by a decrease in the current assets reflected by the lower inventory. The net working capital increased from $16,568 to $18,056, the current ratio improved, and the other relationships which will be studied in succeeding chapters disclosed favorable trends.

A sales analysis will confirm this impression. There is no reliable estimate, based on a survey of a cross section of concerns in this line of activity, of the percentage of net sales income normally available to pay mercantile obligations. Attached to the balance sheet for year *A*, however was an income statement for the year reading as follows:

Gross Sales		$154,810
Less: Returns and Discounts		1,350
Net Sales		$153,460
Inventory, Jan. 1	$ 7,488	
Purchases, Manufacturing Labor, and Expense	114,468	
Total	$121,956	
Less: Inventory, Dec. 31	4,016	
Cost of Goods Sold		117,940
Gross Profit		$ 35,520
Deduct: Other Expenses	$ 15,984	
Salaries	18,480	$ 34,464
Net Profit		$ 1,056

The item in this schedule of particular interest is *Purchases, Manufacturing Labor, and Expense,* which totals $114,468. In this summarized condition the item is of very little value. A request for a breakdown of the item provided the following enlightening and helpful facts:

Pay Roll	$ 8,724
Ruling, Printing, and Numbering	27,480
Cost of Raw Material	78,264
Total	$114,468

From this segregation there is available the basic information needed for a sales analysis, the one figure of the cost of raw material, $78,264. To this figure must be added the net profits of $1,056, which gives a total of $79,320, or 51.7 per cent of the annual net sales, representing the percentage of income available to meet merchandise obligations. With the use of this percentage figure for year B as well as for year A, the same computation may now be made as has been made in the preceding cases:

	Year B	Year A
1. Yearly Net Sales...............................	$144,856	$153,460
2. Average Monthly Net Sales.......................	12,072	12,788
3. Average Monthly Income to Meet Merchandise Obligations......................................	6,240	6,608
4. Cash on Hand on Statement Date...................	10,484	11,720
5. Average Monthly Income Needed to Cover Gross Expenses	5,832	6,180
6. Excess Cash on Hand..............................	4,652	5,544
7. Accounts Payable on Statement Date...............	14,612	11,860
8. Accounts Payable after Crediting Excess Cash on Hand..	9,960	6,316
9. Number of Months to Liquidate Remaining Accounts Payable..	1.59	0.96

The raw materials of this concern consist of paper, cardboard, and some leather, all purchased from small jobbers on 30-day terms. In year B the accounts payable, after applying the excess cash of $4,652, amounted to $9,960. On the basis of average monthly sales of $12,072 and 51.7 per cent of the income being available to meet merchandise obligations, it would take 1.59 months, or 48 days, to liquidate merchandise obligations. On buying terms of 30 days, payments would run slow.

In year A, a material improvement had been brought about. The yearly net sales had expanded moderately from $144,856 to $153,460, and the average monthly net sales from $12,072 to $12,788. Accounts payable on the balance sheet had been reduced from $14,612 to $11,860 as a result of carrying a smaller inventory and, after applying the excess cash, amounted to $6,316. This sum could now be covered in 0.96 month, or 29 days, on the basis of 51.7 per cent of the income being available for this purpose. Payments accordingly would just be prompt on 30-day buying terms.

QUALIFICATIONS TO SALES ANALYSIS

The sales analyses described in the preceding pages are of a very precise, definite nature. The reasoning is based upon average monthly net sales because rarely is there available sufficient detailed information to show accurately the fluctuations in monthly net sales volume from the low point of a year to the peak of a season. At times this information is available in the form of exact monthly net sales figures for each month of the preceding year, and it is a simple mathematical procedure to obtain the percentage above and below the average monthly net sales for each specific month and then to adjust an analysis to the specific case to which these additional facts apply. Six additional qualifications also enter into sales analyses of this character:

1. Sales analysis applies more specifically to smaller industrial and commercial concerns, that is, manufacturers, wholesalers, and retailers where the tangible net worth does not greatly exceed $35,000 and that rarely, if ever, obtain short-term credit from a commercial bank. As a concern increases in size above $35,000 the technique of sales analysis loses its pure effectiveness, as seasonal fluctuations become greater and the use of bank credit cuts across the application of funds. Managements that utilize bank credit do so for the one reason that they are desirous of paying merchandise obligations promptly or by discount, and bank credit is needed, at the peak of a season, for that purpose.

2. Where *cost of merchandise sold* is available in the income statement of a wholesaler or a retailer, or *cost of raw material* in the detailed income statement of a manufacturer, those figures provide the exact percentages applicable to a specific case for sales analysis. The use of such a figure in a specific case is more exact than the use of a general or typical percentage or estimated percentage for that particular division of industry.

3. As a business concern grows in size, proportionally smaller inventory and receivables generally are carried, and larger investments are made in fixed assets, that is, in land, buildings, equipment, machinery, and fixtures. The accounts payable, by the same comparison, are often relatively smaller than notes payable to banks.

4. With progress come larger lines of bank credit. Bank loans often run proportionately higher with large enterprises than with smaller concerns in the same line of business and at a near-by location. These loans enable managements to keep trade indebtedness to fairly limited amounts, and to take advantage of anticipations and favorable discounts.

5. Sales analysis is based upon the relationship of available average monthly net income to pay only accounts payable for merchandise. All other liabilities are included in the gross overhead expenses, which are first deducted in the process of determining the typical average monthly net income available to retire merchandise invoices.

6. Every line of business activity has a season with a high and low point of liabilities. The date of a balance sheet should be correlated, wherever possible, with the season as outlined in Chap. VII. Sales analysis is based upon the computation of average monthly net sales and average monthly income available for specific purposes. If a season is known, the results of a sales analysis may be modified by that knowledge.

7. The credit manager of the Wholesale Shoe Corporation decided to extend credit up to $1,500 to the Retail Shoe Company after making a sales analysis of the fiscal figures at the end of year *B*. The Retail Shoe Company makes no use of bank credit. All shoes are purchased from wholesalers on the customary terms of 2 per cent discount in 30 days, net 60 days. The figures as of the end of year *A* have now been made available and have been posted on a comparative statement sheet beside the figures for *B*. If you were the credit manager would you increase your line of credit, decrease your line of credit, or leave your line at $1,500, after making a sales analysis of the year *A* figures?

RETAIL SHOE COMPANY
Comparative Figures for Years Ended December 31, 19—

	(B) Two Years Ago	(A) One Year Ago
ASSETS		
Cash...................................	$ 3,378	$ 3,828
Accounts Receivable.....................	3,942	2,892
Merchandise............................	26,250	21,564
Current Assets.........................	$33,570	$28,284
Furniture and Fixtures..................	2,916	3,078
Deposit................................	1,023	630
Deferred Items.........................	822	804
Other Assets...........................	306	222
TOTAL............................	$38,637	$33,018
LIABILITIES		
Accounts Payable.......................	$12,849	$ 5,604
Accrued Rent..........................	780	426
Accrued Wages.........................	264	294
Reserve for Taxes......................	1,047	939
Current Liabilities......................	$14,940	$ 7,263
Net Worth.............................	23,697	25,755
TOTAL............................	$38,637	$33,018
Net Sales..............................	$62,349	$68,040
Net Profits............................	2,340	2,058
Withdrawals...........................	None	None

8. A retail hardware store was opened in San Francisco by a veteran of the Second World War, who had saved $6,000. At the end of two years the business had a net worth of $7,240. During the second year net sales amounted to $23,460. Purchases of hardware, tools, twine, kitchen equipment, seeds, porch furniture, and cutlery are made largely on terms of 2 per cent discount in 10 days, net 30 days. Cash on hand at the end of the second year of the business amounted to $660, and accounts payable to $1,420. No bank credit was being used. You have received an order for paints and varnishes, which, if you ship, will involve the extension of credit for $480. Make a careful sales analysis and decide whether you would or would not fill this order.

9. The Curtain Mfg. Co., Inc., is engaged in the manufacture of curtains. No bank credit is used. All raw materials are purchased in the textile market on terms of 2–10–60 extra (that is, payments are net in 70 days). From the following balance sheet and related income statement make a sales analysis and ascertain whether payments will run prompt or slow on these purchasing terms.

CURTAIN MFG. CO., INC.
Balance Sheet, December 31, 19—

ASSETS

Cash..		$ 2,763
Accounts Receivable.................................	$ 7,539	
Less: Reserve for bad debts.........................	346	7,193
Inventory...		10,879
Notes receivable.....................................		1,200
Investments..		75
Machinery and fixtures..............................	$ 2,526	
Less: Depreciation...................................	1,353	1,173
TOTAL...		$ 23,283

LIABILITIES

Accounts payable.....................................	$ 7,165
Accrued taxes..	384
Accrued wages and expenses..........................	592
Common stock..	10,000
Retained earnings....................................	5,142
TOTAL...	$ 23,283

INCOME STATEMENT

Gross sales...		$126,552
Less: Returns and discounts..........................		7,762
Net sales...		$118,790
Inventory, Jan. 1.....................................	$ 12,517	
Purchases..	81,905	
Labor..	11,058	
Taxes on factory pay roll............................	553	
Total..	$106,033	
Inventory, Dec. 31...................................	10,879	
Cost of goods sold...................................		95,154
Gross profit on sales.................................		$ 23,636
Salaries..	$ 11,050	
Selling and shipping..................................	2,597	
General expense......................................	7,130	
Bad debts..	295	
Depreciation...	253	21,325
Net profit..		$ 2,311

10. If a small business enterprise makes use of bank credit, does that affect the conclusions arrived at by sales analysis to any appreciable extent? Explain your answer.

PART III

Internal Analyses of Balance Sheets

PART III *consists of 10 chapters on the discussion of 10 important financial ratios, one in each chapter. A ratio is a figure or a percentage representing the comparison of one dollar amount with some other dollar amount as a base. With a sound knowledge of typical financial ratios, one may determine whether a particular dollar amount representing receivables, inventory, fixed assets, current liabilities, funded liabilities, or net sales is relatively large, typical, or relatively small. The theory behind each ratio is discussed and then illustrated by three sets of comparative figures in each chapter. These comparative figures give the financial condition of many different lines of manufacturing, wholesaling, and retailing; they illustrate many different financial problems arising from diverse business enterprises. A condensed over-all analysis is made of each set of figures, pointing out not only how the particular ratio under discussion applies, but how other ratios also indicate fundamental strength or weakness. The ratios that are discussed and illustrated in these chapters have been studied and applied intensively for over 30 years to many tens of thousands of commercial and industrial situations; they are practical in every sense of the word.*

Balance sheets and income statements are historical rather than prophetic. They present a record of the financial performance of business enterprises. Comparative balance sheets and comparative income statements exhibit trends; a clear understanding of these trends based upon sound ratio studies may convey some premonition regarding the immediate future of a particular business enterprise, provided management policies do not radically change.

At the end of each of these 10 chapters there is included a schedule giving the typical ratios under discussion for various lines of business activity determined from figures for the years 1955 to 1959. These

These studies were initiated by the author while in the employ of Dun & Bradstreet, Inc. Since his retirement from that organization, the compilations have been carried on by the Industries Studies Department of Dun & Bradstreet, Inc.

ratios are medians. In addition to the median ratios for these years, a simple arithmetical 5-year average ratio of the medians for each line of business is given. These ratios have been determined on business concerns with a tangible net worth generally in excess of $75,000. ~~They are taken from pamphlets and studies written and compiled by the author and published by Dun & Bradstreet, Inc.~~ A table with the interquartile range of ratios, based on 1959 figures, for most of these lines of business, is included in the Appendix.

A ratio or a series of ratios that are good in one year may become poor in succeeding years under poor business management. Managements are constantly changing in ability, ingenuity, aggressiveness, and power, and in the relationship of these attributes as compared with competitive managements. A knowledge of the significance of important ratios will point out weaknesses and whether a financial condition is wholly or partly good, questionable, or poor, but the great unknown is always management, which has the power to improve the condition or hasten the ruin of any business. It is not the ratio or ratios, ipso facto, that mean a business concern is out of line. The ratio is the symptom, like the blood pressure, the pulse, or the temperature of an individual. Some managements can overcome or mitigate the symptoms; other managements fail to recognize the symptoms or lack the ability, the aggressiveness, and the knowledge to overcome or mitigate them.

CHAPTER VI

Current Assets to Current Liabilities

In the last few years of the nineteenth century when the number of financial statements available to creditors and to the public noticeably increased, there arose among commercial bankers and mercantile credit men the practice of comparing the amount of current assets of a commercial or an industrial business enterprise to the amount of its current liabilities, that is, of dividing the current assets by the current liabilities. By 1908 one author had written, " . . . Many good judges feel that the ratio of quick [current] assets to [current] liabilities should be about $2\frac{1}{2}$ to 1."[1] Gradually, 2 and not $2\frac{1}{2}$ dollars of current assets for each dollar of current liabilities came to be expected as a reasonable margin of protection. This comparison came to be known colloquially as the *current ratio*. In case of bankruptcy, falling prices, or inflated figures, the book value of the current assets could shrink 50 per cent in liquidation and current creditors, provided there were no long-term creditors, would still receive payment of their obligations in full. For many years this "two for one" current ratio was the alpha and omega of balance sheet analysis; even today the businessmen are legion who believe this single ratio to be the one infallible guide to balance sheet interpretation.

The early adoption of this one "ratio" represented fundamental progress in understanding the financial condition of balance sheets, particularly those of manufacturers, wholesalers, and retailers. On the other hand, the rapid growth in the use of this single comparison tended to blind many early analysts to the fact that a current ratio that was perfectly satisfactory for a factor[2] would be wholly inadequate for a manufacturer

---

[1] ROSENDALE, WILLIAM M., "Credit Department Methods," *Bankers Magazine*, Vol. LXXVI, No. 2, p. 187, February, 1908.

[2] A *factor* is a type of specialized banking institution which, until the Great Depression in the 1930's, specialized in financing cotton, woolen, silk, and acetate textile mills, selling agents, and converters selling primarily to manufacturers of apparel, and which had an extensive credit department whose members were especially trained for this purpose. In the Great Depression factors also began to finance concerns in widely different lines of business selling the retail trade. Factors have been in existence since early colonial days, but their method of operation has undergone gradual and steady change. (See FOULKE, ROY A., *The Story of the Factor*, Dun & Bradstreet,

of furniture, as inherent differences existed in the financial conditions of concerns in different lines of business activity. A current ratio that might be suitable for a well-established, soundly managed business concern might not be so safe for a relatively new, poorly managed, or rapidly expanding enterprise. Moreover, although a particular current ratio might be perfectly satisfactory for a corporation engaged almost exclusively in producing equipment and supplies directly as a prime contractor, or indirectly as a subcontractor, for the armed forces of the Federal government, it might well indicate that the wolf was lurking just around the corner for a corporation operating under different circumstances.

When credit men began to question the implicit efficacy of this single current ratio, a second, simple, supplemental comparison came into existence: the comparison of the total of cash, of marketable securities when they were known to be absolutely liquid, and of receivables,[3] with the current liabilities. If the current ratio was "two for one" or better and the total of cash, marketable securities, and receivables equaled or exceeded the current liabilities, a balance sheet was said to give double assurance of current credit soundness. Where cash, marketable securities, and receivables were less than the current liabilities, some doubt was thrown on the inherent *current* strength of the balance sheet no matter how high the current ratio happened to be. This second comparison came to be known as the "acid test." It gave added prestige to receivables as a realizable asset and less to inventory. This was a natural conclusion, as the inventory in all except those retail stores that transact business solely on a cash basis must first be converted by sales into receivables and then from receivables into cash.

An inventory may include a small or a large proportion of old, worthless, secondhand, or immovable merchandise. The valuation of the inventory, even though no deception is practiced, is a matter of individual judgment;[4] the active management often tends to view this portion of its

---

Inc., New York, 1953.) In its gradual evolution, the factor has come to have three distinct attributes: (1) advancing credit against finished merchandise as security, that is, acting as a bank; (2) passing upon the credits and in most cases cashing the sales, that is, buying the receivables of their customers outright without recourse and collecting those receivables direct from debtors; (3) in some cases performing a group of special services, such as providing space for the display and the storage of merchandise, handling insurance, billing, packing, shipping, and making city deliveries. For a condensed description of the day-to-day operation of a factor, see Raymond V. McNally, "The Factor at Work," *Credit and Financial Management*, Vol. 53, Nos. 3 and 4, March and April, 1951; Walter M. Kelly, "How to Meet Today's New Financing Requirements through Modern Factoring," *The Journal of Accountancy*, Vol. 99, No. 5, May, 1955; and Walter S. Seidman, *Accounts Receivable and Inventory Financing* (Mastero Press, Ann Arbor, Mich., 1957).

[3] These items came to be known as the *liquid* or *quick* assets.

[4] The important and fascinating subject of inventory valuation is considered in detail in Chap. XI.

assets with more optimism than do the creditors. Receivables, on the other hand, provided that they are not padded with intercompany transactions, personal loans, or questionable items, are a more definite quantity.

EVOLUTION OF CURRENT FIGURES

The evolution of the two expressions *current assets* and *current liabilities* in American accounting practice took place very gradually over a period of many years. No such classifications appeared in the first balance sheet blanks used by The Mercantile Agency in the 1870's, in the first financial statement blanks drawn up by the New York State Bankers' Association in 1894, or in the statement blank recommended by the National Association of Credit Men as late as 1906.[5] Each of these balance sheets carried only a limited number of items, all of equal value, with no subtotals of any kind.

Public Corporations

As early as the calendar year 1891, the Pennsylvania Railroad Company had divided the assets and the liabilities that appeared in its annual balance sheet into appropriate subdivisions. One of six broad classifications in the assets was *Current Assets;* under this division appeared such unusual items as *Advances to other roads for construction and for other purposes, Materials on hand,* and *Mortgages and ground-rents receivable.* On December 31, 1893, and December 31, 1894, the current assets included an additional item, *Appraised value of assets not disposed of, received with the lease of United New Jersey Railroad and Canal Company* consisting of both securities and equipment. The current assets in 1891, 1892, and 1893 did not include cash, which was another classification of equal value, or securities that presumably were more or less permanent investments. In the balance sheet of December 31, 1894, cash appeared for the first time in the figures of the Pennsylvania Railroad Company as a part of the current assets. The financial statement of December 31, 1891, of this railroad is the earliest balance sheet the author has seen that shows a trend toward the classification of assets.

The New York, New Haven & Hartford Railroad Co. apparently followed the lead of the Pennsylvania Railroad Company, as its balance

---

[5] PRENDERGAST, WILLIAM A., *Credit and Its Uses,* insert at p. 182, reprinted as Form 4, p. 18, in the present volume (D. Appleton-Century Company, Inc., New York, 1906). *Credit and Its Uses* also contains statement blanks then being used by the Fourth National Bank of the City of New York and the First National Bank of Chicago for (*a*) proprietorships and partnerships and (*b*) corporations. These blanks contained no classification of items by current assets or current liabilities.

sheet dated June 30, 1893, in its annual report to stockholders, showed a classification of *Cash and Current Assets* indicating the distinction, also implied in the earlier figures of the Pennsylvania Railroad Company, that current assets were not considered so liquid as cash. The Chesapeake and Ohio Railway Company first showed a classification of assets and liabilities as of June 30, 1897. Instead of using *current assets*, the term *total working assets* was used, but in the sense in which *current assets* is applied today. As of June 30, 1910, the Norfolk and Western Railroad Company also began to use the term *working assets*.

An examination[6] of the annual corporate reports to stockholders on file at the Baker Library of the Harvard Graduate School of Business Administration reveals that the following corporations, with the modifications described in the preceding paragraphs, first began to use the terms *current assets* and *current liabilities* in the year indicated:

Pennsylvania Railroad Co.	Dec. 31, 1891
New York, New Haven & Hartford Railroad Co.	June 30, 1893
Chesapeake and Ohio Railway Co.	June 30, 1897
New York Central & Hudson River Railroad Co.	June 30, 1898
Baltimore and Ohio Railroad Company	June 30, 1899
Cleveland, Cincinnati, Chicago and St. Louis Railway Company	June 30, 1900
Bangor and Aroostook Railroad Company	June 30, 1902
Union Pacific Railroad Co.	June 30, 1902
American Car and Foundry Company	Apr. 30, 1903
Allis-Chalmers Manufacturing Company	Apr. 30, 1904
Colorado Fuel & Iron Corporation	June 30, 1904
Lehigh Coal & Navigation Company	Dec. 31, 1905
National Lead Company	Dec. 31, 1913
Atchison, Topeka & Santa Fe Railway Co.	June 30, 1915
National Enameling & Stamping Co.	Dec. 30, 1916
United States Rubber Company	Dec. 31, 1917
General Electric Company	Dec. 31, 1917
National Biscuit Company	Dec. 31, 1928
American Tobacco Company	Dec. 31, 1934

From this enlightening tabulation, it is evident that the railroads were the first corporations to segregate assets and liabilities in order to present to those outside the active management a clearer picture of what might be called the *current financial condition*. The first eight corporations on this list, beginning with the Pennsylvania Railroad Company in 1891 and closely followed by the New York, New Haven & Hartford Railroad Co. in 1893, were rails. The first industrial on the list to adopt the change was the American Car and Foundry Company in 1903, followed by Allis-Chalmers Manufacturing Company in 1904. Of additional interest is the fact that such a well-known corporation as the National Biscuit Company

---

[6] This examination was carefully made for the author by Miss Ruth Crandall of the staff of the Baker Library.

Forty-fourth Annual Report, Pennsylvania Railroad Company.

GENERAL ACCOUNT.   *Cr.*

		DURING YEAR 1890.	
		INCREASE.	DECREASE.
By balance standing on the books of the Company for the construction of the railroad between Philadelphia and Pittsburgh, including the original cost of the Philadelphia and Columbia Railroad ($5,375,733.43), and the property of the Harrisburg, Portsmouth, Mt. Joy and Lancaster Railroad Company, represented by the guaranteed capital stock, and bonds of said company ($1,882,550); also, the branches to Indiana, Hollidaysburg, and Morrison's Cove; also, the branch to connect with the Pittsburgh, Virginia and Charleston Railway and branch at Tyrone; also, bridge over the Susquehanna River at Columbia, and branches from Columbia to York, and sundry other branches and extensions, including wharves and grain elevator, and cost of stations, warehouses, and shops, ...	$44,324,417 96	. . . . . .	$1,064,126 28
By balance to debit of equipment of road, consisting of locomotives, passenger cars, baggage, mail, and express cars, freight cars, and road cars, including shop machinery, steam-boats, and car-floats, and also including equipment of canal, consisting of schooners, barges, and tugs, ...	30,824,692 95	. . . . . .	1,940,135 85
By cost of real estate and telegraph line, ...	15,711,671 86	. . . . . .	652,314 46
Total amount charged to construction, equipment, and real estate, ...	. . . . . .	$90,860,782 77	
By Girard Life Insurance, Annuity, and Trust Company, trustee, special equipment account:			
Account Pennsylvania Railroad Company, ...	$1,465,000 00		
Account Pennsylvania Railroad Company, ...	1,610,000 00	3,075,000 00	75,000 00
OTHER ASSETS.			
By cost of bonds of railroad corporations, ...	$37,615,878 53	. . . . . .	1,696,065 37
By cost of capital stocks of railroad corporations, ...	66,982,746 26	. . . . . .	876,114 72
By cost of bonds and stocks of other corporations, coal companies, canal companies, bridge companies, and investments not otherwise enumerated, ...	8,585,109 44	. . . . . .	776,638 86
Total cost of bonds and stocks, ...	. . . . . .	113,183,734 23	
By Managers of Trust created by Pennsylvania Railroad Company, October 9th, 1878, ...	. . . . . .	4,065,694 86	87,433 45
By Pennsylvania Railroad consolidated mortgage, July 1st, 1873, Sinking Fund, ...	$3,715,900 00		
Less bonds redeemed and cancelled, ...	1,771,980 00	1,943,920 00	321,890 00
By freight balances due by other roads, account coal, ...	. . . . . .	565,162 86	359,972 50
By committee on insurance	. . . . . .	10,000 00	
By mortgages and ground-rents receivable, ...	. . . . . .	50,250 00	. . . . . .
By appraised value of securities owned by the United New Jersey Railroad and Canal Company, and transferred with the lease of the works of that Company, ...	. . . . . .	3,733,444 60	. . . . . .
By equipment of road and canal owned by the United New Jersey Railroad and Canal Company, and transferred with the lease of the works of that Company, ...	. . . . . .	931,921 37	. . . . . .
By amount of fuel and material on hand for repairs to locomotives, cars, and for maintenance of way, viz.:—			
For the Pennsylvania Railroad, ...	$2,877,753 61	. . . . . .	529,470 23
For the United New Jersey Railroad and Canal, ...	1,166,090 56	. . . . . .	
For the Philadelphia and Erie Railroad, ...	519,328 91	. . . . . .	105,523 64
By amount of bills and accounts receivable, and amounts due from other roads, including advances made to railroad corporations for construction, and purchase of equipment used on their lines, viz.:—		4,563,173 08	
United New Jersey Railroad and Canal construction, . .	$3,795,604 34	. . . . . .	871,605 59
United New Jersey Railroad and Canal sinking fund and redemption account, ...	2,237,780 00	. . . . . .	115,320 00
United New Jersey Railroad and Canal real estate, . . .	2,056,300 40	. . . . . .	183,238 56
Philadelphia and Trenton Railroad construction, ...	1,299,478 09	. . . . . .	65,796 24
Philadelphia and Trenton Railroad real estate, ...	289,108 83	. . . . . .	16,503 25
Other companies, ...	15,697,302 45	. . . . . .	1,799,748 27
By cash, balance in hands of the Joint Stock Bank, London, and other parties, to pay coupons due in January, 1891, . .	. . . . . .	25,375,574 11	
By cash, balance in hands of freight and passenger agents, &c.	. . . . . .	1,123,809 29	96,907 08
By cash, balance in hands of Treasurer, ...	$2,759,152 13	. . . . . .	217,588 85
	6,212,729 36	1,424,379 60	
		8,971,881 49	
Less amount of decrease, ...	$258,454,348 66	$12,961,276 87	$550,687 25
		550,687 25	
Total amount of increase, ...	. . . . . .	$12,410,589 62	

E. & O. E.   ROBT. W. SMITH,
December 31st, 1890.   *Treasurer.*

FORM 15. Asset side of the balance sheet of the Pennsylvania Railroad Company as of December 31, 1890. This is the last balance sheet of the Pennsylvania Railroad Company which gave no material segregation of the assets.

Forty-fifth Annual Report, Pennsylvania Railroad Company.

Dr. GENERAL BALANCE SHEET.

			DURING YEAR 1891.	
			INCREASE.	DECREASE.
ASSETS.				
Cost of road, including the cost of the Harrisburg, Portsmouth, Mt. Joy and Lancaster Railroad, represented by the guaranteed capital stock and bonds of said company, ($1,882,550.)		$49,326,681 74	. . . .	* $5,002,263 78
Cost of real estate,		15,842,666 40	. . . .	130,994 54
Cost of regular equipment, ... $33,629,454 06		. . . .	. . . .	2,804,761 11
Cost of trust equipment, covered by 4 per cent. Equipment Trust Gold Loan, Girard Life Insurance, Annuity and Trust Company, Trustee:—				
Account Penna. R. R. Co., . . $1,475,360 44				
Account Penna Co., ... 1,610,000 00				
	3,085,360 44			10,360 44
		36,714,814 50	. . . .	. . . .
			$101,884,162 64	
SECURITIES.				
Cost of bonds of railroad corporations, ...		$38,049,144 25	. . . .	433,265 72
Cost of capital stocks of railroad corporations, ...		68,021,735 34	. . . .	1,038,989 08
Cost of bonds and stocks of other corporations, coal companies, canal companies, bridge companies, and investments not otherwise enumerated, ...		8,528,902 19	. . . .	$56,207 25
Total cost of bonds and stocks, ...		. . . .	114,599,781 78	
CURRENT ASSETS.				
Advances to other roads for construction and other purposes :—				
United New Jersey Railroad and Canal Co. construction, .		$3,795,604 34	. . . .	. . . .
United New Jersey Railroad and Canal Co. real estate, . .		2,194,650 55	. . . .	138,350 15
United New Jersey Railroad and Canal Co. sinking fund and redemption account, ...		2,350,700 00	. . . .	112,920 00
Philadelphia and Trenton Railroad Co. construction, . . .		1,299,478 09	. . . .	. . . .
Philadelphia and Trenton Railroad Co. real estate, ...		326,529 24	. . . .	37,420 41
Other Companies, ...		13,587,320 76	. . . .	2,109,981 69
		23,554,282 98		
Materials on hand, ...		. . . .	4,314,050 20	249,122 88
Mortgages and ground-rents receivable, ...		. . . .	31,450 00	18,800 00
CASH.				
Balances with Superintendents and Agents, ...		$2,989,295 25	. . . .	230,143 12
In hands of London Joint Stock Bank and other parties to pay coupons due January 1st and March 1st, 1892, ...		1,220,331 49	. . . .	96,522 20
In hands of Treasurer, ...		7,109,552 59	. . . .	896,823 23
		11,319,179 33		
MISCELLANEOUS.				
Managers of Trust created October 9th, 1878, ...		$4,159,192 98	. . . .	93,498 12
Pennsylvania Railroad Consolidated Mortgage Sinking Fund, ... $4,040,680 00				
Less bonds redeemed and cancelled, . . . 1,771,980 00				
		2,268,700 00	. . . .	324,780 00
Insurance fund, ...		10,000 00		
Appraised value of assets not disposed of, received with the lease of United New Jersey Railroad and Canal Company, .				
Securities, ... $3,733,444 60				
Equipment, ... 853,626 37				
		4,587,070 97	. . . .	78,295 00
			11,024,963 95	
Total, ...		. . . .	$266,727,870 88	$11,351,091 90	$2,512,406 82
Less amount of decrease, ...		. . . .		2,512,406 82	
Amount of increase, ...		. . . .		$8,838,685 08	

* Of this increase $3,069,213.91 represents the amount expended in previous years on the Trenton Cut-off, and now charged to your construction account, as noted on page 33.

FORM 15a. Asset side of the balance sheet of the Pennsylvania Railroad Company as of December 31, 1891. This is the first balance sheet of the Pennsylvania Railroad Company which gave a material segregation of the assets.

did not make the change until 1928, and the American Tobacco Company waited until 1934. This change was certainly made gradually.

It was natural that the railroads should have taken the lead in evolving somewhat more comprehensive information for stockholders and investors, as the railroads had obtained tremendous sums from the public

---

General Balance Sheet.

April 30, 1902.

ASSETS.

Cost of Properties, Plants, and

Permanent Investments,	$55,127,132.88	
Stocks and Bonds of other companies at cost, . .	3,086,050.00	
New Steel Car Plant, Detroit, Mich., . . .	904,999.97	$59,118,182.85

Materials on Hand:

Inventoried at cost or less, about 75 per cent of which will be used on cars we have contracts to build.

BAR IRON, PIG IRON AND MISCELLANEOUS SUPPLIES	$9,248,281.20	
TIMBER AND LUMBER,	2,666,848.16	$11,915,129.36

Accounts Receivable.   7,461,950.47

Cash in Banks and on hand,   1,571,457.93

          $80,066,720.61

FORM 16. Asset side of the balance sheet of the American Car and Foundry Company as of April 30, 1902. This is the last balance sheet of the American Car and Foundry Company which contained no classification of items as current assets.

for construction and development purposes decades before industrial corporations obtained real public participation. On April 30, 1903, for example, when the first industrial in the list began to use subtotals for current assets and current liabilities, 116 railroads, 4 express companies, 15 street railways, 26 public utilities, and 64 industrials had their stocks listed on the New York Stock Exchange. There were more railroad companies with stocks listed on the New York Stock Exchange at this time than all the other corporations together, and the industrials comprised less than 28 per cent of the total.[7]

Certain early classifications of current assets and liabilities were quite naïve from the point of view of present-day accounting and financial

General Balance Sheet.

April 30, 1903.

ASSETS.

Cost of Properties, Plants, Etc.,

to April 30th, 1902, . .	$55,127,132.88	
Less: Stocks of other Companies included in Stocks and Bonds below, ...	760,137.53	
	$54,366,995.35	
Add: For cost of steel car plants at Detroit, Mich., Berwick, Pa., and Huntington, W. Va., and additional Real Estate, . .	2,693,770.19	$57,060,765.54

Current Assets:

MATERIALS ON HAND, inventoried at cost or less, about 75% of which will be used on cars we have contracts to build, ...	$13,133,803.62	
ACCOUNTS RECEIVABLE, .	9,613,587.09	
STOCKS AND BONDS of other Companies, at cost or less, .	1,813,863.05	
CASH IN BANKS AND ON HAND, . . .	2,463,056.54	27,024,310.30
		$84,085,075.84

FORM 16a. Asset side of the balance sheet of the American Car and Foundry Company as of April 30, 1903. This is the first balance sheet of the American Car and Foundry Company to have a segregation of current assets.

analysis. The Baltimore and Ohio Railroad Company, for example, in its June 30, 1899, balance sheet carried *B & O Common Stock in Treasury at par* $3,822,000 as a current asset; the Lehigh Coal & Navigation Company in its December 31, 1905, balance sheet carried *Prepaid Insurance*

[7] Final bid-and-asked quotation sheets for Thursday, Apr. 30, 1903, New York Stock Exchange.

BALANCE SHEET,

APRIL 30TH, 1903.

ASSETS.

Real estate, buildings, plant machinery, good-will, etc........................		$29,199,492 97
Bill and accounts receivable............................	$2,475,578 81	
Stocks of merchandise, materials and work in progress (at cost)...	5,131,800 00	
Cash...	1,628,009 45	9,235,388 26
Total...		$38,434,881 23

LIABILITIES.

Capital Stock:		
Preferred....................................	$16,250,000 00	
Common....................................	20,000,000 00	$36,250,000 00
Accounts payable................................	$1,079,670 66	
*Dividend No. 8................................	284,375 00	1,364,045 66
Surplus:		
Balance as at April 30, 1902......................	$304,759 51	
Profits for period................. $1,653,576 06		
Less: Dividends on Preferred Stock. 1,137,500 00		
	516,076 06	820,835 57
Total...		$38,434,881 23

STATEMENT OF PROFITS

For the Fiscal Year ending April 30, 1903.

Net profits, after deducting all expenses of manufacture and selling, and after making full provision for depreciation of buildings, plant and machinery and for possible bad debts...........................		$1,653,576 06
Deduct—Dividends declared on Preferred Stock:		
No. 5. 1¾% payable August 1, 1902.............	$284,375 00	
No. 6. 1¾% payable November 1, 1902............	284,375 00	
No 7. 1¾% payable February 2, 1903.............	284,375 00	
No. 8. 1¾% payable May 1, 1903................	284,375 00	1,137,500 00
Balance—Surplus carried to Balance Sheet...........................		$516,076 06

*Paid May 1, 1903.

FORM 17. Balance sheet and "statement of profits" of the Allis-Chalmers Manufacturing Company as of April 30, 1903. This is the last balance sheet of the Allis-Chalmers Manufacturing Company which gave no material segregation of the assets.

ALLIS-CHALMERS COMPANY.
OFFICE OF THE COMPTROLLER,

CHICAGO, ILL., JUNE 1, 1904.

BENJAMIN H. WARREN, ESQ.,
    President, Allis-Chalmers Company:

Herewith are submitted the Balance Sheet and the Profit and Loss Account of this Company on April 30, 1904, with statements showing the net profits for the fiscal year ending that date, and the provisions made for all known contingencies that may result in losses upon business carried over into the new year, but exclusive of the results of the business of the Bullock Electric Manufacturing Company, recently acquired.

Messrs. Jones, Caesar & Co., Chartered Accountants, have made quarterly examinations of the accounts of the Company, and have reported thereon regularly to the Board of Directors during the year.

BALANCE SHEET,

APRIL 30, 1904.

ASSETS.

CAPITAL ASSETS:		
Real estate, buildings, plant, machinery, good-will, etc..............		$30,246,084 59
CURRENT ASSETS:		
Bills and accounts receivable......................	$3,437,519 95	
Stocks of merchandise, material and work in process (less payments on account) at factory cost, not exceeding present market values.............	2,914,878 42	
The Bullock Electric Manufacturing Company of Ohio for working capital, and an interest in the Allis-Chalmers-Bullock Limited, of Canada..........	463,000 00	
Cash......................................	1,060,113 11	
		7,875,511 48
		$38,121,596 07

LIABILITIES.

CAPITAL LIABILITIES:		
Preferred Stock...............................	$16,150,000 00	
Dividends at the rate of 7% per annum cumulative from February 1, 1904............		
Common Stock...............................	19,820,000 00	
		$35,970,000 00
CURRENT LIABILITIES:		
Accounts payable.............................	$1,014,395 75	
Mortgage on Norwood Foundry, due March 22, 1905	34,000 00	
		1,048,395 75
FUNDS:		
Depreciation Reserves		478,364 75
SURPLUS		624,835 57
		$38,121,596 07

FORM 17a. Balance sheet of the Allis-Chalmers Manufacturing Company as of April 30, 1904. This is the first balance sheet of the Allis-Chalmers Manufacturing Company to include the terms *current assets* and *current liabilities*.

$19,475.80 as current; the Colorado Fuel & Iron Corporation in its June 30, 1904, balance sheet carried *Advance Royalties* $49,834.01 as current; and the National Enameling & Stamping Company in its December 31, 1916, balance sheet carried *Investments: Refunding First Mortgage Bonds of the Company at Cost and Accrued Interest to date* $148,721.25 as current. Today not one of these items would be considered a current asset by a qualified analyst or an experienced accountant.

Many of the balance sheets issued by corporations in the years immediately preceding the financial statements that first showed captions of *current assets* and *current liabilities* were quite abbreviated. The balance sheet of the Allis-Chalmers Manufacturing Company as of April 30, 1903, contained only four asset and seven liability items. Moreover, the very first item was the all-inclusive one of *Real estate, buildings, plant machinery, good will, etc.*, $29,199,492.97. The values at which "good will" and "etc." were carried in this total figure would be essential in any modest attempt to analyze the figures.

The financial statements of the railroads were in far greater detail and gave a more enlightening picture of their financial condition than did those of the industrial corporations. In the preparation of many of the early financial statements of industrial corporations, unusual efforts seem to have been expended to make it absolutely impossible for an analyst, no matter how skilled or experienced he might be, to understand and to interpret particular items. This was long before the days of the Securities and Exchange Commission. The December 31, 1917, balance sheet of the United States Rubber Company and Subsidiaries, for example, carried a picturesque item, *Securities, including Liberty Bonds, and stock of the U.S. Rubber Co., held by Subsidiary Companies* $7,937,920.06. What a perfect mystery!

Several of the early balance sheets contained classifications of asset items but none of liabilities. The Mergenthaler Linotype Company as of October 1, 1909, used the term *current assets*. The liabilities, however, consisted of five separate and distinct items with no subtotals. The balance sheet of the Diamond Match Co., as of December 31, 1910, similarly carried a subtotal for current assets but none for current liabilities.

By 1915 the value of classifying items as current assets and current liabilities was well established in credit circles, with both banking institutions and mercantile enterprises. Of the four financial statement forms prepared by the Federal Reserve Bank of New York in 1915 for the use of member banks, three—the forms for corporations, firms, and business proprietorships—had subtotals for *quick assets*[8] and *current liabilities*.

---

[8] The term *quick assets* was used in these early balance sheets with the connotation of present-day *current assets*. As explained on p. 179, the term *quick assets* has now come more specifically to mean cash, readily marketable securities, and receivables.

.ccounting Firms

records showing

'or the first edition of this volume, the author made a survey among 25 f the older firms of public accountants, practically all of which had been ctive prior to 1900, to ascertain when they began to use these two terms f *current assets* and *current liabilities* in their practices. Most of the firms ad no idea when they first began to use these classifications in drawing p balance sheets. The following six firms, however, were able to name the pproximate dates given below as the time when they first began to tilize subtotals for current assets and current liabilities in their account-ng practice:

Haskins & Sells	1898
Pogson, Peloubet & Co	1905
Peat, Marwick, Mitchell & Co	1906
Niles & Niles	1907
Leslie, Banks & Company	1910
F. W. Lafrentz & Co	Before 1914

One accountant who had had many years of experience, became inter-sted in the evolution of these classifications and searched the available ecords of his own firm. Subsequently, he unfolded the following interest-ng story: " . . . About the turn of the century, we sometimes used the lassification of current assets, but with a separate classification of current vorking assets, the latter including inventories, generally the major item, leferred charges, stores, and the like. In or about 1906 the classification nvolved into 'current and working assets,' the descriptive term for what s now simply 'current assets.' Two or three years later we find 'current ssets' and 'current liabilities' but 'current and working' was still good verbal mintage, and, as I recall it, the subject of intermittent informal liscussion. The decline and fall of the description 'working assets' either s a separate term, or as a constituent of 'current and working' dates, I vould say, from 1915 or thereabouts." Here is a general confirmation of he practice that seems to have been especially used by the railroads.

This episode in accounting evolution was supplemented by a second vell-known accountant: "I recall," he wrote, "that when I entered the mploy of my firm about 1914 [I noticed] in reviewing some of the old re-ports that the practice did not seem to be consistent. In some cases, cur-ent assets and liabilities were shown separately on the report and in other nstances they were not. In the cases where they were not shown, it may e that the accountant in charge was not sure that he could classify some f the items under current assets because they were what under present-lay practice [1945] would be termed borderline cases. However, I do recall hat about 1915 or 1916, while I was in the Richmond office of our company, our firm issued a form of balance sheet, profit and loss, and surplus statements, which contained approximately present-day classifications. These were issued with instructions to all offices that in the future, financial statements prepared by our firm must whenever possible show similar classifications. This form, of course, did require that sub-totals be shown for the figures of *current assets* and *current liabilities*."

Credit and Investment Services

In March, 1915, the Standard Statistics Service, Inc., now known as Standard & Poor's Corporation, broke away from an established tradition in the investment field and determined the *net working capital* on its card report on the United States Steel Corporation. This figure represented the difference between current assets and current liabilities and so was predicated upon the computation of one figure for current assets and of another for current liabilities. Card reports on all other important industrial corporations whose securities were held extensively by the public in 1922 were gradually modified to include the amount of net working capital.

In 1919 the Bank Service Department of the National Credit Office, Inc., was organized to investigate, analyze, and edit specialized credit reports on all concerns selling their commercial paper in the open market. These reports from their very inception contained a uniform, independent classification of balance sheet items that included current assets and current liabilities and the computation of the current ratio.

In 1922, Moody's Investors Service began to show under the balance sheets of large corporations, printed in its industrial manuals, footnotes giving the net working capital. Two years later, this practice was extended to the balance sheets of smaller industrial corporations. In 1925, the items in each balance sheet that were classified as current assets and current liabilities were set in italic. Here was a gradual realization of the importance of these two classifications in the analysis of balance sheets from the point of view of the investor.

In 1927, The Mercantile Agency prepared its first statement blank which gave a classification of items and subtotals for current assets and current liabilities. It was not until 1930, however, that arrangements were made to compute and quote current assets and current liabilities in all credit reports, whether balance sheets were received on the stationery of the concern, or the accountant's own paper, in an annual corporate report to stockholders, or on the statement blank of The Mercantile Agency In 1931 the ratio of current assets to current liabilities was computed on the larger commercial and industrial business enterprises in all parts of the country and included in the credit reports on these enterprises.

Evolution in the Use of Current Ratio

The use of the ratio of current assets to current liabilities by analysts has gone from one extreme to the other; it is now comfortably between the two. In the early days of this century, when analysts began their experimentations in the interpretation of balance sheets, this ratio, as already explained, was the only one in use and so was employed extensively. It was and is of considerable value. The ratio would hardly have been adopted so extensively as a standard if ordinary experience had not indicated its practical significance.

As other comparisons came into existence, the feeling developed widely that the current ratio is after all a generality, that no one ratio, no one comparison can possibly give a clear picture of the inherent soundness or weakness of a balance sheet. Other ratios came to have vital significance. Each ratio in turn tells its own story, and each ratio in conjunction with some other ratio and other facts then tells a supplemental story. At this intermediate stage in the evolution of analysis, the current ratio received less consideration, and other more specific ratios increased attention.

Now we are between these two extremes. The current ratio is valuable, particularly as an indication of the ability of a concern to meet its current obligations, but the fact must be kept in mind that, after all, it is only one ratio, and a generality at that. It does, however, give an indication of a condition that is timely and valuable. We shall find examples in other chapters of balance sheets which are strained but where the current ratio is above "two for one"; we shall find cases where this ratio is somewhat less than "two for one" but still the balance sheet is in healthy shape.

The current ratio is the reflection of a static condition, of a relationship at one date between two variables. This fact must constantly be kept in mind. A fundamental analysis is concerned more with understanding and interpreting the inherent financial condition of a business enterprise than its condition at a particular date. The current ratio changes daily as a concern enters its busy season, purchases merchandise, increases its inventory, sells its merchandise, expands its receivables, collects its receivables, increases its cash, pays down its liabilities, and finally reduces its cash to the low point of the season. The efficient management forecasts the current ratio of its business 1, 2, 3, and 6 months in the normal operations of its budgetary controls. It is often expedient for the outside analyst to do the same as the seasons roll around, and this can be accomplished if the knowledge of the seasons of a particular concern and the amount of its maximum liabilities during the previous fiscal year are obtained. This information is gradually becoming widely recognized as essential for the analyst. In recent years it has been requested on more and more balance sheet blanks.

ILLUSTRATIONS OF RELATIONSHIPS

The forceful manner in which the ratio of current assets to current liabilities exemplifies a changed financial condition is readily apparent from the following comparison:

	Year *B*	Year *A*
Current Assets	$600,000	$1,200,000
Current Liabilities	200,000	800,000
Net Working Capital	$400,000	$ 400,000
Current Ratio	3.00	1.50

In year *B* with current assets of $600,000 and current liabilities of $200,000, the net working capital amounts to the difference between the two figures, or $400,000, and the current ratio is 3.00. During year *A* operations were conducted on a break-even basis, but the inventory was increased by $600,000. The current liabilities expanded the same amount representing the purchase price of the increase in inventory. The current assets now total $1,200,000 and the current liabilities $800,000. The net working capital remains stationary at $400,000, but the current ratio becomes 1.50.

A changed condition similar to that which took place between year *B* and year *A* often happens during a period of rising prices. Now suppose the current assets, mostly inventory, shrank one-third in value as price dropped, after the close of both year *B* and year *A*. The current assets in year *B'* and in year *A'* would be respectively $400,000 and $800,000. There would be no change in the current liabilities. The comparison of the current condition under these circumstances in both years would then be as follows:

	Year *B'*	Year *A'*
Current Assets	$400,000	$800,000
Current Liabilities	200,000	800,000
Net Working Capital	$200,000	$. . . . . .
Current Ratio	2.00	1.00

Notwithstanding this shrinkage in values, the figures for year *B'* would disclose a net working capital of $200,000 and a ratio of current assets to current liabilities of 2.00. Here is a fairly satisfactory current financial condition. The one-third shrinkage in year *A'*, however, decreases the current assets from $1,200,000 to $800,000, an amount which is now just equal to the current liabilities. The net working capital is wiped out, and the ratio of current assets to current liabilities becomes 1.00. As a result of the smaller liabilities, the concern is much less vulnerable to such situation in year *B* than in year *A*.

In the computation of the current ratio the analyst must always include ɪny contingent liability for notes receivable discounted that have been ɪmitted from the balance sheet. Otherwise, the ratio will be determined on ɪgures of apparent current assets and current liabilities, neither of which ꜰill be accurate, and the resulting current ratio will be incorrect and ꜰisleading. If the contingent liability for notes receivable discounted is ˈ100,000, then this sum should be added to the receivables prior to the ɪomputation of the current assets and the same amount included as *Notes ꜰiscounted* in the current liabilities. The current ratio determined from ꜰhese adjusted totals will be accurate.

ꜰommercial Printer

ꜰhe Commercial Printing Corporation was incorporated in 1934 with an ɪuthorized and paid-in capital of $36,000, all common stock, to carry on a ꜰeneral jobbing and commercial printing business. In 1945 the authorized ɪapital was increased to $75,000, all 5 per cent cumulative preferred stock, ꜰnd to 100 shares of common stock of no par value but carried on the books ꜰt $1 per share. The business was organized and continuously operated ꜰy three men, all of whom had had extensive previous experience in the ꜰrinting business, two as production men and one as a salesman. The ꜰscal balance sheet as of year A disclosed a paid-in capital of $62,550 five ꜰer cent cumulative preferred stock, $100 common stock, and a deficit in ꜰhe retained earnings of $5,082.

The concern is located in Philadelphia. Its plant is equipped with six ꜰwo-color presses—two Harris, two Major, two Miehle—and six single-ɪolor presses—two Major, two Miehle, and two Simplex. The greater por-ɪion of the annual net sales consists of the printing of catalogues of the ꜰetter grade. Printing is handled on terms of 30 days net for about 125 ɪoncerns, all located within a radius of 100 miles of Philadelphia. Com-ꜰarative figures for the past three fiscal years appear in Schedule 11.

Up to year C, retained earnings of $11,914 had been accumulated. Of ꜰhis sum $2,268 had been earned during year C. For year B, a net loss of ˈ8,382 was sustained, and in year A, an additional net loss of $8,614 was ɪaken. As a result of these unfavorable operating results, a deficit of $5,082 ꜰas created in the retained earnings account by the end of year A, and ꜰhe tangible net worth decreased from $74,564 in year C to $57,568 in ꜰear A, or 22.8 per cent.

The fiscal figures for year C disclose a first mortgage on the real estate ꜰnd buildings of $16,457. By year B, the mortgage had been reduced to ˈ12,000, and during year A, 1 month before the close of the fiscal year, the ꜰntire $12,000 had been paid. In year D, two new printing presses had ꜰeen purchased at a cost of $28,000, of which $6,000 had been paid in cash

[Schedule 11]   COMMERCIAL PRINTING CORPORATIO;
Comparative Figures for Years Ended December 31, 19—

	(C) Three Years Ago	(B) Two Years Ago	(A) One Yea; Ago
ASSETS			
Cash..............................	$ 17,111	$ 16,409	$ 5,31
Accounts Receivable................	24,702	28,511	40,81
Inventory..........................	5,651	7,635	5,16
Current Assets.....................	$ 47,464	$ 52,555	$ 51,29
Fixed Assets, Net..................	72,560	74,924	64,17
Miscellaneous Receivables...........	5,715	1,566	82
Prepaid Insurance..................	743	113	78
Sundry Investments................	280	280	28
TOTAL......................	$126,762	$129,438	$117,35
LIABILITIES			
Notes Payable to Bank..............	....	$ 6,500	$ 6,00
Notes Payable for Presses...........	$ 17,400	8,874	8,26
Accounts Payable..................	8,218	12,251	18,74
Accruals..........................	5,099	7,037	5,83
Due to Officers....................	5,024	16,594	20,94
Current Liabilities..................	$ 35,731	$ 51,256	$ 59,78
First Mortgage....................	16,457	12,000	....
Total Liabilities....................	$ 52,198	$ 63,256	$ 59,78
5% Cumulative Preferred Stock.......	62,550	62,550	62,55
Common Stock, No Par.............	100	100	10
Retained Earnings.................	11,914	3,532	(D)5,08
TOTAL......................	$126,762	$129,438	$117,35
Net Working Capital................	$ 11,723	$ 1,299	$(D)8,48
Current Ratio......................	1.32	1.02	0.8
Tangible Net Worth.................	$ 74,564	$ 66,182	$ 57,56
Net Sales..........................	$138,645	$118,127	$104,93
Net Profit.........................	2,268	(L)8,382	(L)8,61
Dividends.........................	None	None	Nor

and the balance in installment notes, secured by a chattel mortgage, t
be paid in full over a period of 18 months, quite a customary method (
financing the purchase of presses. By year C, this particular debt had bee
reduced to $17,400. In year B, it became impossible to meet the instal
ments as they fell due, so part of the notes were renewed. The balanc
sheet at the end of year A showed $8,260 still due on the purchase pric
of these presses.

The effect on the current ratio of operating losses and the liquidation of the first mortgage is directly shown in the comparison of the current assets with the current liabilities for these 3 years.

	Year C	Year B	Year A
Current Assets...........................	$47,464	$52,555	$51,295
Current Liabilities.......................	35,741	51,256	59,783
Ratio of Current Assets to Current Liabilities....	1.32	1.02	0.86

Between year C and year A, the current assets increased moderately from $47,464 to $51,295. The cash went down while the receivables increased materially. At the same time, the current liabilities expanded from $35,741 in year C to $51,256 in year B, and then in year A to $59,783, an aggregate increase of 67 per cent. This steady increase in the current liabilities was due to the cumulative net losses from operations and from the liquidation out of current funds of the first mortgage which had been carried as a deferred debt in the balance sheets of year C and year B. For year A, current liabilities were in excess of current assets.

The net working capital amounted to $11,723 in year C, a comparatively moderate amount for a printing establishment of this size. In year B the net working capital had dropped to $1,299, and by year A, a deficit in net working capital to the extent of $8,488 had been created.

Between year C and year B the current ratio dropped from 1.32 to 1.02; in year A the drop continued to 0.86. Not only was each of these ratios low but the trend was steadily downward, an unfavorable feature that should never be overlooked. These relationships obviously were out of line. A comparison with the average ratio of current assets to current liabilities for job printers for the 5-year period given on page 202 will verify this conclusion, the 5-year average current ratio for this line of business activity being 2.35. /2.42.

Condensed Analysis. The comparative figures of the Commercial Printing Corporation reflect a chaotic condition. The net sales were lower for each succeeding year shown in Schedule 11; both the tangible net worth and the net working capital dropped steadily; the current liabilities were consistently heavy; the concern had had to request successive renewals on the notes given in year D for the payment of printing presses; the fixed assets were excessive; and the accounts receivable appeared to be heavy. The outlook of this business was about as rosy as the prospects of the submarine that broke through the surface of the ocean only to find a formation of enemy bombers directly overhead.

Of all these unfavorable characteristics, the one that was most immediately obvious was the heavy liabilities in relation to the current assets and the consequently low current ratio on each statement date. Second only to the heavy liabilities were the excessive fixed assets. The figures disclosed a net depreciated value of fixed assets which amounted to 97.3 per cent of the tangible net worth as of year C, and 113.2 per cent as of year A. As will be shown in Chap. X, rarely can a commercial or industrial concern operate successfully with such relationships. A basic error in management judgment had been made in some year prior to year C. As net profits were earned, they were immediately reinvested in real estate, buildings, and more presses. No adequate margin of net working capital had been maintained, an oversight of primary financial importance in a business world based upon competition and the profit motive.

Moreover, as the net sales decreased, the accounts receivable increased. Here was an anomaly. Something was rotten in Denmark. As will be explained in Chap. XIII, the receivables undoubtedly contained more than a reasonable proportion of uncollectible accounts.

Manufacturer of Furniture

The second example illustrative of an unbalanced condition between the current assets and the current liabilities is a manufacturer of furniture located in the furniture district of North Carolina. The Period Furniture Co., Inc., was incorporated in 1936 with an authorized capital of $140,000, of which $20,000 was immediately paid in, all common stock. The outstanding capital has remained unchanged from the inception of the business. The organizer, who was also the principal stockholder, died two years ago, and since that time the control and active management have rested in the hands of his one son.

This concern manufactures period furniture, including living-room, bedroom, dining-room, and kitchen suites. Pieces of occasional furniture are also manufactured, but in a small way. Sales are made only to retail furniture and department stores east of the Mississippi River, and on the customary terms of the furniture trade of 2 per cent discount in 30 days, net 60 days. Comparative figures for the past three fiscal years appear in Schedule 12.

Operations of the Period Furniture Co., Inc., have been conducted with some success. The net sales increased each year over this 3-year period, expanding from $289,622 in year C to $312,542 in year A. Quite a satisfactory net profit of $13,418 was recorded in year C, somewhat smaller but fairly satisfactory net profits of $6,700 in year B, and then very handsome net profits of $25,378 in year A. Dividends were paid only in year B, and then for the moderate sum of $3,000. By the time year A had ended, the financial condition was such that the entire net profits for the year were needed in the business to support the extended financial condition.

Between year C and year A, the tangible net worth expanded from $72,358 to $101,436. Of this increase, the greater part, or $25,378, was

PERIOD FURNITURE CO., INC.   [Schedule 12]
Comparative Figures for Years Ended December 31, 19—

	(C) Three Years Ago	(B) Two Years Ago	(A) One Year Ago
ASSETS			
Cash................................	$ 16,891	$ 15,568	$ 15,542
Accounts Receivable..................	12,603	12,912	15,940
Inventory............................	76,009	84,876	133,489
Current Assets........................	$105,503	$113,356	$164,971
Fixed Assets, Net....................	21,042	24,004	26,948
Leasehold Improvements..............	7,090	6,821	7,982
Miscellaneous Receivables............	1,026	7,235	23,325
Prepaid Expenses.....................	....	2,151	1,261
TOTAL........................	$134,661	$153,567	$224,487
LIABILITIES			
Notes Payable to Bank..............	$........	$ 20,000	$ 35,000
Due to Officers......................	....	5,992	10,240
Accounts Payable....................	45,083	28,642	52,022
Accruals............................	9,794	11,169	5,967
Reserve for Taxes...................	7,426	2,640	9,220
Customers' Deposits.................	....	9,066	10,602
Current Liabilities...................	$ 62,303	$ 77,509	$123,051
Common Stock......................	20,000	20,000	20,000
Earned Surplus.....................	52,358	56,058	81,436
TOTAL........................	$134,661	$153,567	$224,487
Net Working Capital..................	$ 43,200	$ 35,847	$ 41,920
Current Ratio.......................	1.70	1.46	1.34
Tangible Net Worth..................	$ 72,358	$ 76,058	$101,436
Net Sales..........................	$289,622	$292,976	$312,542
Net Profit..........................	13,418	6,700	25,378
Dividends..........................	None	3,000	None

earned in year A. As far as the expanding annual net sales, the net profits, and the growing tangible net worth are concerned, the comparative figures make an attractive showing. Now, however, let us turn to the current condition and to the ratio:

	Year C	Year B	Year A
Current Assets...........................	$105,503	$113,356	$164,971
Current Liabilities........................	62,303	77,509	123,051
Ratio of Current Assets to Current Liabilities.	1.70	1.46	1.34

During the 2 years ending year A, the current assets increased from $105,503 to $164,971, or 56.3 per cent. Practically all this increase was represented by heavier inventories, which were carried at $76,009 in year C and at $133,489 in year A. Of the net profits earned in year B and in year A, $29,078 had been retained in the business. Now, if we look at the slow assets, that is, the fixed assets, leasehold improvements, miscellane ous receivables, and prepaid expenses, in the comparative figures in Schedule 12, we shall see that the total of these items increased $30,35? during the 2-year period. In other words, the retained profits were no quite sufficient to offset the enlarged slow assets, so that greater curren liabilities, of necessity, had to be incurred to carry the increased curren assets. This is exactly what happened. The current liabilities amounted to $62,303 in year C. These liabilities increased to $77,509 in year B, and to $123,051 in year A. The result was a steady drop in the current ratio from 1.70 to 1.46 to 1.34.

That the current ratio for each of the 3 years was low, and the ratio of 1.34 for year A exceptionally low, may be confirmed in Schedule 14, on page 202, which shows the typical ratio for the furniture manufacturing industry. The 5-year average of the ratio of current assets to current liabilities for manufacturers of furniture is ~~3.06~~.

2.69.

Condensed Analysis. Here is a situation where net profits have been high but where, at the same time, affairs have become gradually more and more out of line with increasing current liabilities, insufficient net working capital, and a steadily decreasing current ratio. The liabilitie have become heavy with the greater expansion in the inventory. On each of the last two balance sheets the increase in inventory was substantial For a manufacturer of this size and with annual net sales in the neighbor hood of $300,000, the inventory on the fiscal date[9] should be betweer $40,000 and $50,000. If the inventory could have been reduced from $133,489 to this figure, funds would immediately have been freed to reduce the current liabilities a corresponding amount, which would have brought the debt into line with the current assets and resulted in an attractive current ratio.

Second, the item of miscellaneous receivables increased steadily from $1,026 to $7,235 to $23,325 over the 3-year spread. At this last figure the amount was obviously excessive. Profits had been lent to the officers who had used the funds in outside ventures. This money should be imme diately collected. If collected, the current assets and the net working capi tal would both expand a corresponding amount and the current ratio would improve accordingly. All other items appear to be in normal proportions.

Manufacturer of Paints and Varnishes

The Paint & Varnish Mfg. Co., Inc., was incorporated in 1892 with a paid-in capital of $50,000 to manufacture a full line of paints, varnishes

---

[9] Inventory and current liabilities of a manufacturer of furniture are normally at low points in November or December. See p. 215.

namels, and related products. From this relatively small start, the business expanded over a period of years and on December 30, 19—, had a
tangible net worth in the neighborhood of $2,125,000. Earnings retained
in the business during the immediately preceding years had been put into
fixed assets and into greatly increased inventories. Subsequently, prices
of paints, varnishes, and enamels had sustained a rapid and material drop,
necessitating drastic adjustments in the value of the inventory and write-
offs on the receivables. By year A the tangible net worth had been reduced
to $413,505, a shrinkage of over 80 per cent from the peak a few years
earlier. The comparative figures in Schedule 13 show this condition.

Every trend in these comparative figures is unfavorable. The net sales
went down steadily from $610,287 in year C to $357,262 in year A. Net
losses were assumed each year. The loss amounted to $46,541 for year C
and was climaxed with a loss of $255,514 in year A. As a result of these
steady losses, the tangible net worth reached a low point of $413,505 in
year A, and the net working capital, which amounted to $190,730 in year
C, was changed into a deficit of $12,993.

In year C the unbalanced financial condition was recognized by the
lending officer of the depository bank. The $30,000 due to this bank could
not be repaid and the bank officer handling the account refused to extend
additional credit. In this predicament, arrangements were made to borrow
funds from a finance company secured by the pledge of receivables. The
amount of these secured borrowings fluctuated on each of the three balance sheet dates, increasing to $200,606 in year B and decreasing to
$122,031 in year A. Funds were made available in this manner to meet
part of the current obligations, but the trend continued downward. In an
attempt to stem the outward tide, three of the larger merchandise creditors at this stage accepted a series of non-interest-bearing notes due in 5
years. In year B, these notes aggregated $112,000 and by year A had been
reduced nominally to $108,000. This downward trend is clearly evident
in the comparative condition:

	Year C	Year B	Year A
Current Assets	$573,402	$529,036	$354,626
Current Liabilities	382,672	479,820	367,619
Ratio of Current Assets to Current Liabilities	1.49	1.10	0.96

The current assets decreased from $573,402 to $529,036 between year
C and year B. Between year B and year A, the current assets now took
a substantial drop of 33 per cent, from $529,036 to $354,626. From year
C to year B the current liabilities increased from $382,672 to $479,820.
If the three merchandise creditors had not agreed to take the deferred
non-interest-bearing notes of $112,000 for their debts in year B, the current
liabilities would have been that much larger. In year A, when the net loss
amounted to $255,514, the current liabilities decreased along with the
current assets, but not in the same proportion. As a result the net working

capital of $49,216 in year B was turned into the deficit net working capital of $12,993 in year A.

This trend is epitomized in the ratio of current assets to current liabilities which decreased from 1.49 to 1.10 between year C and year B and then to 0.96 in year A. The figures of this corporation in year A indicate an approaching collapse in the near future.

[Schedule 13]   PAINT & VARNISH MFG. CO., INC
Comparative Figures for Years Ended December 31, 19—

	(C) Three Years Ago	(B) Two Years Ago	(A) One Year Ago
ASSETS			
Cash..........................	$ 26,834	$ 12,390	$ 5,86:
Notes Receivable..............	16,052	50,399	22,31'
Accounts Receivable...........	225,261	182,205	124,38:
Inventory.....................	305,255	284,042	202,06:
Current Assets................	$ 573,402	$ 529,036	$ 354,62
Fixed Assets, Net..............	526,425	514,612	490,74:
Investments...................	45,434	45,434	8,00
Miscellaneous Receivables.......	39,191	51,324	3,37:
Prepaid and Deferred..........	89,782	111,499	27,36:
Supplies......................	....	8,934	5,01:
TOTAL...................	$1,274,234	$1,260,839	$ 889,12
LIABILITIES			
Notes Payable to Bank.........	$ 30,000	$ 30,000	$ 30,00
Loans from Stockholders........	16,423	4,394	34,02
Trade Acceptances.............	3,546	9,140	12,52:
Accounts Payable.............	94,321	160,206	84,03:
Accruals.....................	45,702	75,474	85,00'
Advances from Finance Company	192,680	200,606	122,03
Current Liabilities.............	$ 382,672	$ 479,820	$ 367,61
Accounts Payable, Deferred.....	....	112,000	108,00
Total Liabilities...............	$ 382,672	$ 591,820	$ 475,61
5% Cumulative Preferred Stock.	100,000	100,000	100,00
Common Stock................	150,000	150,000	150,00
Retained Earnings............	641,562	419,019	163,50
TOTAL...................	$1,274,234	$1,260,839	$ 889,12
Net Working Capital...........	$ 190,730	$ 49,216	$(D)12,99
Current Ratio.................	1.49	1.10	0.9
Tangible Net Worth............	$ 891,562	$ 669,019	$ 413,50
Net Sales....................	$ 610,287	$ 443,507	$ 357,26
Net Profit...................	(L)46,541	(L)222,543	(L)255,51
Dividends....................	None	None	Non

Condensed Analysis. Only a miracle could save this concern, and mir-
acles rarely occur during rapid business tail spins. The troubles of the
Paint & Varnish Mfg. Co., Inc., started several years ago with inefficient
management. Its paints, varnishes, and enamels had had wide national
acceptance, but the products had not been kept up to date with the tremendous changes that had taken place in chemistry. The trend continued
downward with increased momentum from year *C*. At the same time
expenses—administrative, manufacturing, and selling—were high. The
treasurer, who had been with the business 18 years, had absolutely no
knowledge of budgetary control.

Suddenly the management was faced with a top-heavy inventory,
rapidly falling sales during a period of shrinking prices, and heavy overhead. That is a fatal combination of circumstances to all managements
except those few composed of supermen. These circumstances are reflected
in the comparative figures shown in Schedule 13 with a steadily and
rapidly shrinking current ratio. Each year the relationship between the
current assets and the current liabilities became more unfavorable. As
competitors one after another had developed and brought out modern
rapid-drying products, the sales had dropped, at first slowly and then
more rapidly. The experimental end of the business had ceased to function. By the time year *A* had come around, the figures were characterized
by excessive liabilities, heavy fixed assets, a deficit in net working capital,
and an obviously low current ratio.

TYPICAL RATIOS OF CURRENT ASSETS TO CURRENT LIABILITIES

Typical ratios of current assets to current liabilities for 70 lines of business activity—42 lines of manufacturing, 21 of wholesaling, and 7 of
retailing—are given the following two on pages. These ratios have been
computed from balance sheets for each year from 1955 through 1959, and
a final ratio has been computed as an arithmetical average for the 5-year
period.

The spread in the typical ratios of current assets to current liabilities
is narrow. Only nine lines of business in Schedule 14 show a 5-year average current ratio below the "two for one" standard. These nine ratios
range from 1.77 for building contractors to 1.95 for manufacturers of
women's coats and suits. On the other hand, 15 of the 42 manufacturing
lines, 9 of the 21 wholesaling lines, and 3 of the 7 retailing lines disclose
5-year average current ratios greater than "three for one."

The highest 5-year average current ratio among manufacturers is
shown by cotton cloth mills with 4.42 times, followed by manufacturers
of bedsprings and mattresses with 3.65 times. Among wholesalers, the
highest 5-year average current ratio is shown by wholesalers of hardware

[Schedule 14]   RATIOS OF CURRENT ASSETS TO CURRENT LIABILITIES

| Line of Business Activity | Number of Times | | | | | |
| | Median | | | | | Five-year Average |
	1955	1956	1957	1958	1959	
MANUFACTURERS						
Agricultural Implements and Machinery	3.38	3.73	3.83	3.68	3.21	3.57
Airplane Parts and Accessories	1.72	1.59	1.97	1.62	2.14	1.81
Automobile Parts and Accessories	2.50	2.54	3.01	2.80	2.69	2.71
Bakers	1.72	1.69	1.96	1.95	1.83	1.83
Bedsprings and Mattresses	3.41	3.61	3.71	4.03	3.50	3.65
Bodies, Auto, Bus, and Truck	2.32	2.53	2.81	3.68	2.40	2.75
Bolts, Screws, Nuts, and Nails	2.74	2.87	3.10	3.37	2.96	3.01
Breweries	2.20	2.32	2.71	2.71	2.34	2.46
Chemicals, Industrial	2.50	2.50	2.87	2.60	2.66	2.63
Coats and Suits, Men's and Boys'	2.39	2.41	2.48	2.53	2.15	2.39
Coats and Suits, Women's	2.00	1.92	2.15	1.84	1.83	1.95
Confectionery	2.97	3.05	2.72	2.83	2.97	2.91
Contractors, Building Construction	1.87	1.62	1.73	1.81	1.81	1.77
Contractors, Electrical	2.54	2.48	2.43	2.80	2.42	2.53
Cotton Cloth Mills	4.16	4.04	4.62	5.21	4.09	4.42
Cotton Goods, Converters, Non-factored	2.67	3.27	2.74	2.43	2.08	2.64
Dresses, Rayon, Silk, and Acetate	1.82	1.79	1.92	1.76	1.81	1.82
Drugs	3.02	3.22	2.85	3.15	3.25	3.15
Electrical Parts and Supplies	2.58	2.82	3.00	3.31	2.76	2.89
Foundries	2.82	2.71	3.41	3.63	3.19	3.15
Fruits and Vegetables, Canners	2.12	2.03	2.24	1.86	2.01	2.05
Furniture	3.12	2.94	3.17	3.24	2.82	3.06
Hardware and Tools	3.44	3.25	3.57	4.07	3.35	3.54
Hosiery	3.32	4.13	3.47	3.52	3.12	3.51
Lumber	3.54	3.31	3.63	3.51	3.04	3.41
Machine Shops	2.90	2.60	2.88	3.93	2.76	3.01
Machinery, Industrial	2.80	2.78	3.09	3.68	3.34	3.14
Meats and Provisions, Packers	2.13	2.23	2.42	1.99	2.34	2.22
Metal Stampings	2.62	2.80	3.04	3.31	2.97	2.95
Outerwear, Knitted	2.12	2.35	2.18	2.20	2.24	2.22
Overalls and Work Clothing	2.86	2.92	3.10	3.36	3.05	3.06
Paints, Varnishes, and Lacquers	3.20	3.43	3.40	3.55	2.95	3.31
Paper	2.46	2.66	2.79	2.80	2.66	2.67
Paper Boxes	2.66	2.67	2.52	2.75	3.14	2.75
Petroleum, Integrated Corporations	2.14	2.35	2.41	2.45	2.46	2.36
Printers, Job	2.44	2.17	2.38	2.48	2.27	2.35
Radio Parts and Supplies	2.23	2.21	2.33	2.49	2.46	2.34
Shirts, Underwear, and Pajamas, Men's	2.15	2.23	2.20	2.02	2.02	2.12
Shoes, Men's, Women's, and Children's	2.51	2.62	2.55	2.60	2.36	2.53
Soft Drinks and Carbonated Water, Bottlers	1.89	1.79	1.96	1.65	1.72	1.80
Steel, Structural Fabricators (Sell on Short Terms)	2.79	2.43	2.60	3.00	3.60	2.88
Stoves, Ranges, and Ovens	2.99	3.55	3.74	3.47	3.58	3.47

Ratios of Current Assets to Current Liabilities (*Continued*)

[**Schedule 14** (*Cont.*)]

Line of Business Activity	Number of Times					
	Median					Five-year Average
	1955	1956	1957	1958	1959	
Wholesalers						
Automobile Parts and Accessories....	3.00	2.98	3.15	3.14	2.84	3.02
Baked Goods......................	1.89	1.68	1.89	2.02	1.95	1.89
Cigars, Cigarettes, and Tobacco......	2.32	2.29	2.21	2.11	2.05	2.20
Drugs and Drug Sundries...........	2.41	2.40	2.42	2.62	2.66	2.50
Dry Goods.......................	2.86	3.15	3.17	2.94	2.62	2.95
Electrical Parts and Supplies........	2.16	2.23	2.79	2.68	2.43	2.46
Fruits and Produce, Fresh..........	3.54	3.12	2.77	3.30	2.84	3.11
Furnishings, Men's................	3.03	3.33	2.76	3.26	2.79	3.03
Gasoline, Fuel Oil, and Lubricating Oil...........................	1.82	1.90	1.98	2.01	1.95	1.93
Groceries........................	2.87	2.76	2.81	3.03	2.65	2.82
Hardware........................	3.42	3.40	3.92	3.50	3.42	3.53
Hosiery and Underwear...........	3.12	3.57	3.58	3.36	2.90	3.31
Household Appliances, Electrical.....	2.03	2.03	2.18	2.17	1.91	2.06
Lumber..........................	2.90	3.27	3.49	3.14	3.21	3.20
Lumber and Building Materials......	3.38	3.15	3.36	3.45	2.90	3.25
Meat and Poultry.................	2.46	2.05	2.29	2.50	2.28	2.32
Paints, Varnishes, and Lacquers......	2.70	3.59	3.44	3.37	3.54	3.33
Paper............................	2.57	2.70	2.99	2.83	2.71	2.76
Plumbing and Heating Supplies......	3.33	3.13	3.45	3.83	3.13	3.37
Shoes, Men's, Women's, and Children's...........................	2.47	2.56	2.15	2.39	2.30	2.37
Wines and Liquors.................	2.18	2.10	2.12	2.13	2.09	2.12
Retailers						
Clothing, Men's and Boys'..........	3.08	2.74	2.88	2.87	2.61	2.84
Department Stores.................	3.58	3.61	3.57	3.70	3.54	3.60
Furniture, 50 Per Cent or More Installment......................	3.84	3.58	3.46	3.27	3.71	3.57
Groceries and Meats, Independent...	1.76	1.79	1.79	1.89	1.80	1.81
Lumber and Building Materials......	3.02	3.24	4.21	3.66	3.48	3.52
Shoes............................	2.80	2.98	2.70	2.84	2.72	2.81
Women's Specialty Shops...........	2.52	2.50	2.52	2.26	2.41	2.44

with 3.~~53~~ 97, followed by wholesalers of plumbing and heating supplies with 3.3~~7~~. Among retailers, ~~department~~ hardware stores lead with ~~3.60~~, followed by ~~furniture stores with 50 per cent or more of their sales on installments with 3.57.~~

The three illustrations of unhealthy relationships between current assets and current liabilities used in this chapter are extreme. Balance sheets will reflect conditions from these extremes through fair to good, and finally there will be cases where there are absolutely no current liabilities. Examples of current ratios in somewhat more favorable categories will be found in illustrations in succeeding chapters.

Maxim

Over the years the practical standard of the ratio of current assets to current liabilities has come to be recognized as "two for one" for industrial and commercial business concerns. The current ratio is an indication of the current condition, which on further examination might or might not indicate strain. If a current ratio seems low, the reason should be ascertained. In other words, the analyst must look behind the ratio to find the reason for a condition. Further examination may verify or fail to verify a preliminary inference based solely on the relationship between the current assets and the current liabilities.

THEORY AND PROBLEMS

1. State briefly what information you would expect to obtain from the ratio of current assets to current liabilities.

2. The ratio of current assets to current liabilities of a manufacturer of office equipment is 1.82. How would each of the following transactions affect the current ratio?

Use the letters *I*, *D*, and *N* to indicate whether the current ratio would be increased, decreased, or unchanged.

a. Cash is increased $6,042 by the collection of outstanding receivables.
b. It is decided that U.S. Treasury tax notes of $50,000, which had been carried as a subdeduction from the item *Reserve for Federal income taxes* in the current liabilities, should now be carried in the current assets.
c. A bank loan of $100,000 is obtained.
d. An investment representing 51 per cent common stock interest in a subsidiary is sold for cash.
e. A dividend of $68,000 is declared and paid in cash.
f. A customer that was unable to make payment of $3,042 when his account fell due gave a promissory note payable in 30 days.
g. Some used equipment is sold on terms of 10 per cent cash and the balance in 12 equal monthly installments.
h. The president borrows $4,600 in cash from the corporation.
i. Common stock is split four for one.
j. Patents of $6,850 are written off the books.
k. Excess cash of $150,000 is being invested in marketable securities listed on the New York Stock Exchange.
l. Worn-out equipment is sold as scrap for cash.

3. When did it become customary for accountants to segregate the current assets in balance sheets? Describe briefly the evolution that took place in the years immediately preceding this change.

4. Two competing business enterprises in the same line of business show the following current positions. Which business enterprise is in the better current condition? Explain why.

	Company *A*	Company *B*
Current Assets..............................	$300,000	$500,000
Current Liabilities............................	100,000	300,000
Net Working Capital..........................	$200,000	$200,000

5. Post the following balance sheet on a comparative statement page and compute (*a*) net working capital, (*b*) current ratio, and (*c*) tangible net worth.

PURE DRUG CHAIN, INC.
Balance Sheet, December 31, 19—
ASSETS

Current Assets

Cash in banks, and in transit to banks................		$1,442,757
Checking accounts $1,439,693		
Savings deposit 3,064		
Cash on hand.......................................		117,354
Accounts receivable of customers.....................	$ 47,135	
Miscellaneous accounts receivable....................	89,984	
	$ 137,119	
Less: Reserve for doubtful accounts.................	2,500	134,619
Merchandise inventories, at the lower of cost or market..	$2,970,280	
Merchandise in transit..............................	122,594	3,092,874
Inventories of supplies..............................		29,229
Total Current Assets................................		$4,816,833
Cash in Closed Banks................................	$ 23,094	
Less: Reserve for losses............................	21,000	2,094
Contract Deposits...................................		10,180

Loans, Investments, Etc.

Note receivable, other than customer's note...........	$ 6,000	
Contracts of officers and employees for common stock		
purchases.......................................	5,848	
Loans to employees for educational training...........	21,328	
Cash surrender value of insurance on life of officer.......	38,013	
Miscellaneous investments...........................	15,272	86,461

Charges Deferred to Future Operations

Prepaid insurance, licenses, rents, etc.................	$ 102,559	
Premiums and commissions on leases, less proportion		
charged to operations...........................	47,879	150,438

Fixed Assets

Land.......................................		$ 348,804	
Buildings...............................	$ 972,625		
Less: Reserves for depreciation...........	248,892	723,733	
Store fixtures, warehouse, manufacturing,			
and office equipment....................	$3,010,806		
Less: Reserves for depreciation..........	1,486,391	1,524,415	
Automobiles and trucks....................	$ 82,189		
Less: Reserves for depreciation..........	55,346	26,843	
Improvements and alterations to buildings..	$ 938,048		
Less: Reserves for depreciation..........	523,089	414,959	3,038,754
Good Will..			3
			$8,104,763

PURE DRUG CHAIN, INC. (*Continued*)

LIABILITIES

Current Liabilities

Accounts payable, trade..............................	$ 998,822	
Accounts payable, miscellaneous.....................	17,213	$1,016,035
Salaries and wages, due and accrued..................		151,973
Accrued taxes, including state income taxes...........		132,948
Estimated bonuses payable to executives and store managers...		111,707
Total Current Liabilities.............................		$1,412,663
Reserve for Federal income tax.......................		229,824

Reserves

Reserve for unrealized profit on sale of treasury stock....	$ 49,400	
Group life insurance dividends held in reserve..........	29,990	
Reserve for contingencies............................	43,598	122,988

Capital Stock

Common, no par value

Authorized, 500,000 shares.

Issued and outstanding, 245,474 shares:

Stated value.................................	2,454,740	
Retained earnings............................	3,884,548	
Total Equity in Common Stock....................		6,339,288
		$8,104,763

6. What is the generally accepted standard for the ratio of current assets to current liabilities for industrial and commercial business enterprises? Is this standard open to fairly wide variations? Explain your answer.

CHAPTER VII

Current Liabilities to Tangible Net Worth

The only balance sheet relationship, other than the ratio of current assets to current liabilities, which seems to have had its origin in the relatively dim distant past rather than in more recent years when serious attempts have been made to evaluate effective standards of financial statement analysis, is the relationship between the liabilities and the tangible net worth of a commercial or industrial business enterprise. This relationship has always held significant implications as it contrasts the funds that creditors temporarily have at the risk of a concern in the form of its debts with the funds permanently invested by the owners. Since the invested funds, that is, the tangible net worth, serve to guarantee the liquidation of creditor liabilities, it is evident that the smaller the tangible net worth and the larger the liabilities, the less security do creditors normally have. A manufacturer of men's and boys' shoes with a tangible net worth of $78,000 and with liabilities twice as large, or $156,000, will, all else being equal, provide far less security to creditors than a second concern in the same line of business with a tangible net worth of $78,000 and with liabilities one-half as large, or $39,000.

As liabilities expand, the point finally arrives when an enterprise becomes more and more dependent in its daily operations upon the attitude of its creditors. In a very practical manner, as liabilities increase above a certain level, the management has more and more difficulty in meeting its financial obligations on scheduled time. Bank loans must be renewed and renewed. Trade payments drift from discount to prompt, then from prompt to a few days slow; finally, payments run 30, 60, and 90 or more days past due. Somewhere along this rocky route, with progress becoming ever more onerous, the banker, if he has a significant grasp of the situation, arranges to obtain adequate security to protect his extension of credit. The security might consist of stocks and bonds, the assignment of accounts receivable, the pledge of merchandise, the pledge of capital stock in subsidiaries, the assignment of the cash surrender value of life insurance, a mortgage on real estate, or any other asset of sufficient and realizable value. Then the mercantile creditors must decide, one by one, whether

207

they will continue to extend credit on the same basis which they have been using, give special terms, or petition the enterprise in bankruptcy.

A heavy debt is like high blood pressure. As the pressure goes up, a point is finally reached where the patient cannot survive. Every concern that is petitioned by creditors into involuntary bankruptcy inevitably reaches the point of excessive liabilities, just as surely as inflation materializes in a war economy. Sir Walter Scott learned this lesson when the publishing firm of which he was a partner failed with liabilities of £130,000. The relationship of liabilities to tangible net worth was far heavier than it should have been for the continued well-being of that historic enterprise. The Rothschilds had a significant motto based on long experience. It read, "Do not trust a man who owes too much."[1]

Sometime during the last quarter of the nineteenth century, the conception arose that the typical commercial or industrial business concern should not have liabilities in excess of the invested capital, that is, its tangible net worth. At this stage in our economic development, relatively few enterprises, except railroads, had long-term liabilities such as mortgages, bonds, debentures, or serial notes. The term *liabilities* carried the implication that is carried today by *current liabilities*. Such a situation would mean that all creditors, for their own protection, should have no more funds at stake in a particular endeavor than the owner or the owners of that business enterprise. That seemed a reasonable pragmatic proportion. Many early credit men, or those businessmen who performed the functions of present-day credit men, used this relationship literally, and would cut down their extension of credit when a balance sheet showed liabilities exceeding this very definite and recognizable limit.

In the more concentrated study that has been given to the analysis of financial statements in recent years, this one early relationship has been succeeded by two relationships. With the growth in the use of an almost infinite variety of funded obligations to finance commercial and industrial corporations, particularly after the organization of the United States Steel Corporation in 1901, a degree of analytical specialization became essential. A concern with modest current liabilities, but a substantial funded debt due 10 years in the future, would be a far better risk for current creditors than the relationship of total liabilities to tangible net worth would indicate. To differentiate these situations, two relationships have come to be used in the analyses of balance sheets of commercial and industrial business enterprises: (1) current liabilities to tangible net worth, and (2) total liabilities to tangible net worth. In this chapter the relationship of the current liabilities to the tangible net worth will be considered, and in the following chapter, the relationship of total liabilities to tangible net worth.

[1] WIMAN, ERASTUS, *Chances of Success*, p. 39 (F. R. James, Toronto, Canada, 1893).

SEASONAL OPERATIONS AND CURRENT LIABILITIES

Every business enterprise, large or small, has a current debt that fluctuates from day to day and from month to month during the year. The amplitude of this fluctuation depends upon the seasonal operations of a particular line of business and the closeness with which the activity of an individual concern in that line conforms to the typical pattern. The extreme importance of the date on which figures are drawn off in relation to the season of a business, and of the consequent size of liabilities, is explained in detail in the following paragraphs for three lines of business: manufacturers of fur coats, department stores, and manufacturers of furniture.

Manufacturers of Fur Coats

A manufacturer of fur coats produces sample coats during the months of March and April. These samples, representing the ultimate in new styles, are exhibited at the June fashion shows, where orders for the new fur coats are booked. These orders go into immediate production in June and July, to provide merchandise for the August fur-coat promotion sales which are featured by department stores and the retail fur specialty shops in the larger cities. To carry out these operations, the manufacturer makes heavy purchases of skins during the first half of the year. Inventories, consisting of skins, work in process, and finished coats, continue to increase until a peak is reached in either October or November.

The finished fur coats are sold to department stores on terms of 8 per cent discount, 10 days EOM, and to retail fur specialty shops on terms of 10 days, EOM, or payment by promissory notes ranging up to 4 months maturity. As a result of these selling terms, the receivables of fur coat manufacturers are not liquidated until November and December.

From this picture of typical seasonal operations, it is evident why the current liabilities of a manufacturer of fur coats gradually expand to a peak during September, October, or November, then suddenly drop to a low point in January, when receivables have been largely collected and the proceeds applied to reduce the current debt. The seasonal operation then starts over once again.

Department Stores

A department store annually has two peaks in sales, a primary top peak in December caused by Christmas buying, and a secondary peak in the spring caused by purchases for Easter and for the summer. Between these two seasons, sales decline to low valleys in January and February, and again in July, August, and the early part of September.

The inventory of a department store fluctuates in anticipation of sales, but with smaller seasonal swings. From a low point in July, the inventory gradually rises to a maximum early in December. By the end of January, Christmas shopping and January clearance sales have reduced merchandise to the lowest level of the year. The renewal of merchandise stocks for the spring demand now brings the inventory to a modified plateau in March and in April. Stocks again become low in July and in August.

Approximately 40 per cent of all department store sales are made on a cash basis, less than 10 per cent are installment sales, and the remainder are on open-book account. In these operations, current liabilities thus reach a peak early in December when the inventory is at the high point and receivables are expanding, a secondary peak around Easter, and the basic low point for the year in the latter part of January or early February when collections from Christmas receivables have been applied to reduce the debt.

Manufacturers of Furniture

A manufacturer of furniture, like a department store, has two peaks annually in sales. Shipments begin to expand in July following the summer furniture shows and rise to their peak in September and October in anticipation of the general increase in the furniture sales of retail stores which take place in October, November, and December. Shipments fall off to a minimum in December and begin to build up in January in preparation for February retail sales. A secondary peak now materializes in February, March, and early April, following the introduction of new lines in the January furniture shows.

In preparation for the June and January furniture showings, the manufacturer makes up samples of new styles of furniture and attempts to reduce the inventory of finished goods left from the previous season. Raw materials tend to follow the shipment curve rather closely and ordinarily are not accumulated far in advance of current needs. Inventories of raw materials and finished goods drop to a low point in December.

The usual terms of sale used by the manufacturer of furniture are 2 per cent discount in 10 days, net 30 days. Receivables which are created from fall shipments thus are largely liquidated by the end of December or early in January. In these seasonal operations, the current debt reaches a low point in December or January, with a modified dip in June or July.

Natural Business Year

The natural business year of a business enterprise is the period of 12 consecutive months that ends when the business activities of the concern have reached the lowest point in their annual cycle. This principle has been widely recognized in business practice for many years. General use of the calendar year for fiscal purposes began with the enactment of the Federal corporate tax law of 1909, which required all corporations to file returns as of December 31.[2] This statute remained in force for 4 years. The law was repealed in its entirety in 1913 when the first Federal income tax law was enacted. The present law provides that the taxpayers may file returns as of the close of a fiscal year of their own selection.[3]

The Natural Business Year Council was created in November, 1935, to represent businessmen, bankers, credit men, accountants, and trade associations in the study of seasonal operations and the recommendation of the low points of the business years of particular lines of activity as the most logical fiscal dates for those lines. In the early 1950's the activities of the Council were taken over by the Committee on Natural Business Year of the American Institute of Certified Public Accountants. The

---

[2] " . . . Said tax shall be computed upon the remainder of said net income of such corporation, joint stock company, or association, or insurance company for the year ending December 31, 1909, and for each calendar year thereafter. . . . "—36 U.S. Stat. at Large 114, Chap. 6. Poor's Industrial Manual for 1909 contained 211 industrial corporations which took their inventories and closed their books in 1908 at the end of months other than December. Only two of the 12 corporations listed on p. 181 whose balance sheets were studied at a date prior to 1909 used the end of the calendar year as their fiscal date, namely, the Pennsylvania Railroad Company and the Lehigh Coal & Navigation Company.

[3] Tax regulations allow corporations to change their annual accounting period *without advance permission* if they meet the following requirements: (1) the corporation has not changed its annual accounting period at any time within the ten calendar years ending with the calendar year which includes the beginning of the short period required to effect the change of annual accounting period; (2) the short period required to effect the change of annual accounting period is not a taxable year in which the corporation has a net operating loss; (3) the taxable income of the corporation for the short period required to effect the change of annual accounting period is, if placed on an annual basis, 80 per cent or more of the taxable income of the corporation for the taxable year immediately preceding such short period; and (4) if a corporation had a special status (described in the following sentence) either for the short period or for the taxable year immediately preceding such short period, it must have the same special status for both the short period and such taxable year. For the purpose of the preceding sentence, special status includes only: a personal holding company, a foreign personal holding company, a corporation which is an exempt organization, a foreign corporation not engaged in trade or business within the United States, a Western Hemisphere trade corporation, and a China Trade Act corporation. In establishing a new corporation, the desired fiscal year is simply written in the by-laws. All other taxpayers *must request permission* within 1 month after their new closing dates by filing Form 1128 with the Commissioner of Internal Revenue, Washington 25, D.C. Requests for such permission, when based upon sound reasons, are generally approved without further inquiry. State tax authorities generally give permission for a change in fiscal year approved by the Federal government. In general, the change to a natural business year presents few problems. The by laws of the corporation may have to be amended, the tax regulations must be observed, and corporations regulated by the Securities and Exchange Commission must file interim reports when the period between fiscal years is 3 months or more.

analyst finds many advantages in studying the financial statements of a business taken off at the low point of operations, in contrast to the necessity of obtaining the amount of maximum and minimum liabilities during the year from trial balances, and then placing the concern as of December 31 (if it uses the calendar year as its fiscal date) in the proper part of its season, as is done on page 219 with the Men's Clothing Company, Inc.

The U.S. Treasury Department reported that the number of corporations which changed from the calendar to the natural fiscal year was increasing up to the time when the United States actively entered the Second World War: 3,265 changes in 1938, 3,291 in 1939, 3,916 in 1940, and 4,812 in 1941. During the war the number of annual changes dropped to 576 in 1945. After that the trend went up to a high of 3,366 in 1950. There were 1,482 changes in 1953, 1,315 in 1954, and 1,132 in 1955. For the tax year which ended June 30, 1956, 48 per cent of the corporate returns filed with the Internal Revenue Service were on a "fiscal" (*i.e.*, natural business) year basis compared with 41 per cent in 1953 and 13 per cent in 1930. At the low point of the natural business year the inventory is more easily taken, the accounts are closed and year-end financial statements prepared more rapidly, and operations may be more accurately analyzed.[4] At the same time, there has taken place a quickening of interest

---

[4] A clear explanation of the specific reasons for the change in fiscal date to the low point of the natural business year, as applied to his own business, was made in an address by A. R. M. Boyle, treasurer of Lehn & Fink Products Corporation, New York: "We are manufacturers of nationally advertised brands of consumer products sold by us chiefly to wholesale and retail druggists, department stores, 5 and 10 cent and other general merchandise chains, etc. These products include disinfectants, tooth pastes, tooth powders, face, hand and body lotions, cosmetics, and other toilet articles. Many of these items are highly seasonable. For example, all lotions are used in substantially greater volume in the winter than in the summer because of their great use for chapped skin and other similar discomforts due to winter weather. Perfumes, colognes, cosmetics, and toilet articles generally are winter sellers with many special packings and gift sets made especially for the Christmas trade. Christmas items begin moving to the trade around October and shipments continue into the Christmas week. Due to certain trade practices, net results of Christmas business are not known until January. By far the greater portion of our business consists of items which have a greater volume during the winter months than during the summer." Special promotion deals such as two for one sales, half-price sales, and combination offers designed to stimulate the sale of a particular product to the wholesaler, retailer, and consumer affect the sales curve so much that monthly comparisons with prior years become meaningless. Boyle then continued, "I have in mind a series of promotions of this kind which were scheduled to break at retail the beginning of January. All of this merchandise was shipped and billed by us in December. It was not, however, legitimate December business, it was January, February, and March business because these were the months when we would have sold that merchandise in the ordinary course. On a calendar year basis either one year's profits would have been inflated by several hundred thousand dollars and the following year's profit would have suffered accordingly or else deferred income reserves in some form would have been necessary. If these profits had been taken in the calendar year in which the shipments were made, stockholders and the public would have been grossly deceived as to the true earning power of the business. If, on the other hand, reserves had been

among accountants, reflected by the enlarged committee of the American Institute of Certified Public Accountants on the natural business year and the increase in the number of state societies of certified public accountants that now have committees on the subject.[5]

Inventory. The taking of inventory at the end of a natural business year has the following four distinct advantages from an accounting and analysis point of view:

1. As the normal activities of a business enterprise have substantially decreased, or in some cases have even temporarily ceased, the inventory may be taken with less interference to the productive operations of manufacturers and to the daily operations of wholesalers and retailers than at any other time during the year.

2. Stock of merchandise is greatly reduced and is moving slowly, if at all. It may be counted with greater ease and in less time than at any other date.

3. Members of the staff are relieved to some extent of the pressure of their normal duties and are available to assist in taking inventory. Expense of employing additional assistants who are not so well acquainted with the stock, which is often necessary when inventory is taken at a busier season, is thus eliminated.

---

provided with respect to such earnings the difficulty of determining what portion of many operating expenses and overhead had been incurred with respect to these sales would have been considerable. In an annual statement such estimates are not desirable, and they are not necessary where the fiscal year ends at a time when such conditions do not exist. Another large factor entering into our decision was the importance of our advertising expenditures. We spend large sums of money on this item. These are planned on an annual basis but the greatest expenditures are made during the period of greatest consumer purchases, namely the fall, winter and spring. Obviously these are more properly charged to the year in which they belong when the year closes after the cycle has been completed and not right in the middle of it. In short, our business year comes to a more natural end in June than it does in December. At that time there is less room for errors of judgment or differences of opinion in all of the steps which have to be taken in determining the financial position and the earnings of the company for a twelve-month period."—*Problems of Financial Reporting under Wartime Conditions*, pp. 12–13 (New York State Society of Certified Public Accountants, 1942).

[5] "Insurance companies have in many instances designated certified public accountants as 'preferred risks.' It is possible that the new group insurance plan now being promulgated may dispel this illusion. Be that as it may, it now appears that the life expectancy of the average certified public accountant is alarmingly short. . . . In my opinion the greatest contributing factor is the tension caused by meeting deadlines and the physical and mental strain caused by our so-called 'peak season,' or to state it more simply, just plain overwork. To get down to the meat of the situation, this matter of overwork is a life-and-death issue with us. Analyze the causes of overwork and the principal one must inevitably be the 'peak season' caused by the press of work due to the use of the calendar year for determining profits. There the natural business year concept is not just a theory to be weakly expounded, but . . . a matter of life and death. . . . "—YEAGER, L. C. J., *Case Studies on the Natural Business Year*, a paper presented at the Sixtieth Annual Meeting of the American Institute of Certified Public Accountants, Miami Beach, Fla., November, 1947. Reprinted in *Challenges to the Accounting Profession*, pp. 57–58 (American Institute of Certified Public Accountants, New York, 1947).

4. The margin of error in the valuation of inventory is reduced with the quantity at the low point of the year. Accuracy of valuation is one of the fundamental advantages in taking inventory at the end of a natural business year.

Annual Closing of Accounts and Preparation of Financial Statements. The low point of operations for the year is the most advantageous date for closing accounts for the preceding 12 months and for the preparation of financial statements for the following four reasons:

1. Just as the inventory may be more conveniently taken at this time of the year, so may the books of account be closed most conveniently and with least interference with other activities.

2. The resulting financial statements reflect the outcome of one complete cycle of operations. The results of policies and programs initiated at the beginning of a period are clearly shown by financial statements prepared as of the end of the natural business year. As of any other date, financial statements reflect the results partly of one season and partly of another.

3. The items which make up financial statements may be more readily and accurately determined because the inventory may be taken with greater efficiency, and because receivables and liabilities are generally at a minimum.

4. The actual worth of a business enterprise is more readily discernible when the concern is in its most liquid condition. At the end of a natural business year, financial statements invariably show the greatest normal liquidity attainable.

Analysis on Natural Business Year Basis. To analyze the results of a season of business operations, an analyst should be able to view the season as a unit, to begin with causes and follow through the sequence of events to the effects. If annual financial statements are prepared as of any date other than at the end of a natural business year, they include the results of the latter portion of one season and the beginning of a subsequent season. Under those conditions, it is difficult at times to obtain a clear picture of either period. Moreover, the recurring ability of a concern to liquidate to the seasonal low point at the close of its natural business year is a sound indication of whether the investment in receivables and inventory at the peak was profitable or unprofitable. The orderly conversion of trading assets into cash is the conclusive test of asset soundness.

A flour milling concern with a statement date of May 31 will generally have a minimum of inventory and few or only nominal liabilities. The same situation applies to a rice milling business with a statement dated July 31. Concerns in these lines have highly seasonal operations. Financial statements drawn off at the low point show the ability or inability of the management to bring affairs into liquid shape after each season. In every case where possible, it is also expedient and desirable to ascertain the amounts and the dates for both maximum and minimum liabilities, as that

Trade or Industry	Closing Date, Last Day of:
Advertising Agencies	December
Agricultural Implements, Manufacturers	August to October
Air Transportation	April
Aircraft, Manufacturers	November
Airports	April
Automobile, Manufacturers	September
Automobile, Retailers	October
Automotive Accessories, Manufacturers	July or August
Automotive Accessories, Wholesalers	January
Awnings and Sunshades, Manufacturers	August
Bakeries	June
Barber Shop and Beauty Parlor Supplies, Manufacturers	September
Beverages, Carbonated, Manufacturers	September
Books, Publishing	June
Book Stores	June
Breweries	October
Bricks, Manufacturers	March or October
Brooms and Brushes, Manufacturers	June
Building Contractors	February
Candy, Manufacturers	June
Candy, Wholesalers	July
Canning, Vegetables and Fruits	January or February
Cement, Manufacturers	January
Clay Products, Manufacturers	March or October
Cleaning and Dyeing Establishments	November
Clocks and Watches, Manufacturers	March
Clothing, Men's, Retailers	January
Coal, Mining	March
Coal, Retailers	May
Coal, Wholesalers	April
Coats and Suits, Women's, Manufacturers	November
Containers, Paper, Manufacturers	April
Corsets and Brassières, Manufacturers	December
Crockery and Glassware, Manufacturers	January
Dairy and Produce Companies	February or March
Department Stores	January
Distillers	August
Drugs, Retailers	January
Drugs, Wholesalers	June
Dry Goods, Wholesalers	November or December
Electrical Appliances, Retailers	June
Electrical Parts and Supplies, Manufacturers	September
Filling Stations	September
Florists, Retailers	September
Flour Milling	March to June
Foundries and Machine Shops	January
Fruit and Vegetable Brokers	June
Furniture, Manufacturers	November or December
Furniture, Retailers	June

Trade or Industry	Closing Date, Last Day of:
Garages	September
Gasoline, Refining	October
General Merchandise, Retailers	January
Gift Shops	May
Glass, Manufacturers	June
Gloves, Manufacturers	November
Grain Dealers	June
Grain, Mills and Elevators	May or June
Groceries, Retailers	June
Groceries, Wholesalers	June
Hardware, Manufacturers	June
Hardware, Retailers	January
Hats, Manufacturers	October
Heating and Plumbing Contractors	December
Hotels, Residential	June or July
Hotels, Resort	Last month of season
Ice, Artificial	October
Ice Cream, Manufacturers	December
Insecticides, Manufacturers	October
Jewelry and Silverware, Retailers	January
Jewelry and Silverware, Wholesalers	February
Laundries	June
Leather Goods, Retailers	January
Lime, Production	November
Lumber Products, Manufacturers	October
Lumber and Building Materials, Retailers	November to February
Mail-order Houses	January
Mattresses, Manufacturers	July
Meat, Packing	October
Millinery, Retailers	June
Newspapers	August
Office Buildings	May
Office Supplies, Retailers	May
Oil Production	June
Oil Well Suppliers, Manufacturers	December
Paints, Varnishes, and Lacquers, Manufacturers	November
Paper Mills	July
Paper, Wholesalers	June
Paving Contractors	March
Photographers	April
Plumbers' Materials, Wholesalers	February
Poultry Farms	September
Public Utilities	December
Radio and Television, Wholesalers	January
Radio and Television, Retailers	January

Trade or Industry	Closing Date, Last Day of:
Ready-to-wear, Ladies', Retailers	January
Refrigerator, Manufacturers	July
Restaurants	June
Roofing and Waterproof Paper, Manufacturers	June
Rubber Goods, Manufacturers	October
Rubber Tires, Manufacturers	October
Salt, Miners and Refiners	June
Seeds, Wholesalers and Retailers	June
Sheet Metal, Manufacturers	March
Shoes, Manufacturers	November or December
Stationery, Retailers	June
Steel and Iron Products, Manufacturers	June
Stoves and Furnaces, Manufacturers	June
Sugar, Beet, Manufacturers	June
Sulfur, Refining	March
Wallpaper, Manufacturers	June
Warehouse, Cold Storage	March
Work Clothing, Manufacturers	November

information gives a supplementary picture of the extent of the swing of seasonal operations in each individual enterprise.

Suggested Closing Dates

The fiscal closing dates listed on pages 215–217 are recommended by the Committee on the Natural Business Year of the American Institute of Certified Public Accountants. These dates represent the low points of the seasons in the respective lines of business activity; receivables have been largely collected, inventories sold, and liabilities paid.

ILLUSTRATIONS OF RELATIONSHIPS

The unfavorable relationship of excessive current liabilities to tangible net worth is illustrated in three different situations on the following pages. These examples are a manufacturer and retailer of men's clothing, a wholesale dealer in liquors, and a builder of yachts and launches.

Manufacturer and Retailer of Men's Clothing

Two young men, one twenty-eight years of age and the other thirty-one years of age, organized the Men's Clothing Company, Inc., 15 years ago in New York, with a paid-in capital of $16,500 to manufacture men's suits, topcoats, and overcoats. Both men had spent their entire business careers as employees in this field, one as a designer and the other as a salesman. Their new enterprise, however, did not begin operations in a particularly propitious manner. The concern earned a little profit or showed a

[Schedule 16]   MEN'S CLOTHING COMPANY, INC.

Comparative Figures for Years Ended December 31, 19—

	(C) Three Years Ago	(B) Two Years Ago	(A) One Year Ago
ASSETS			
Cash...........................	$ 6,618	$ 8,246	$ 13,807
Layaways.......................	13,862	20,079	13,514
Inventory......................	86,928	120,952	183,311
Current Assets..................	$107,408	$149,277	$210,632
Fixed Assets, Net..............	4,790	6,593	6,270
Miscellaneous Receivables......	10,116	7,739	22,872
Deferred Charges..............	100	100	5,591
TOTAL......	$122,414	$163,709	$245,365
LIABILITIES			
Notes Payable to Bank.........	$ 5,261	$.......	$ 5,771
Notes Payable for Merchandise..	....	4,602	3,280
Accounts Payable..............	47,181	68,688	132,087
Accruals......................	3,694	3,856	875
Reserve for Taxes..............	6,117	7,402	14,914
Due to Contractors............	10,517	19,456	18,432
Current Liabilities..............	$ 72,770	$104,004	$175,359
5% Cumulative Preferred Stock..	20,000	20,000	20,000
Common Stock.................	26,100	26,100	26,100
Earned Surplus................	3,544	13,605	23,906
TOTAL......................	$122,414	$163,709	$245,365
Net Working Capital.............	$ 34,638	$ 45,273	$ 35,273
Current Ratio...................	1.47	1.43	1.20
Tangible Net Worth..............	$ 49,644	$ 59,705	$ 70,006
Net Sales.....................	$650,568	$762,482	$798,523
Net Profit....................	169	10,061	10,301
Dividends.....................	None	None	None

little loss each year for the first 6 years of its existence. By that time the tangible net worth stood at $17,242.

The management 5 years ago decided to discontinue sales to retail stores, to enlarge its quarters, and to sell on the premises direct to the consumer, in other words, to combine manufacturing and retailing operations, a trend which was becoming recognized as sound and profitable in the clothing industry. The plan was successful and sales exceeded all expectations. The enterprise began to do better, net profits were largely retained in the business, and 3 years ago the tangible net worth showed a remarkable increase to $49,644. The comparative financial condition for the past 3 years is shown in Schedule 16.

Each of the financial statements in the comparative figures is dated December 31. This date was in the middle of the season for a concern carrying on both manufacturing and retailing operations. The current debt would normally fall to a low point in June, which would be just prior to the receipt of substantial quantities of piece goods to be cut up for fall garments. The peak debt would be reached 4 months later in October, which would be the top of the autumn manufacturing season.

Operations during year A were typical of these seasonal fluctuations with a minimum current debt, as shown in monthly trial balances, of $96,-660 in June, and a maximum current debt of $225,000 in October. On the statement date for year A the current liabilities of $175,359 were on the way down. During year B, the minimum current debt amounted to $76,920, and during year C, to $59,170, both in June.

Not only were the current liabilities on each fiscal statement date considerably in excess of the respective tangible net worth, but even at the low point of the season for each of these 3 years, when liabilities normally should have been almost completely liquidated, the debt was greater than the tangible net worth. At all times during these 3 years, the creditors in the aggregate actually had more funds at stake in this enterprise than the two owners of the entire outstanding stock of the corporation. The following schedule shows not only how heavy the current liabilities had been on each statement date for these 3 years, but how the relationship with the tangible net worth had been going up, not down.

	Year C	Year B	Year A
Current Liabilities................	$72,770	$104,004	$175,359
Tangible Net Worth................	49,644	59,705	70,006
Ratio of Current Liabilities to Tangible Net Worth................	146.5%	174.2%	250.5%
Minimum Current Debt................	$59,170	$ 76,920	$ 96,660
Ratio of Minimum Current Debt to Tangible Net Worth................	119.1%	128.8%	138.0%

Between year C and year A, the current liabilities on the statement date expanded from $72,770 to $175,359, or 131 per cent. At the same time, the tangible net worth increased from $49,644 to $70,006, or 40 per cent. This disproportionate and steady increase in the current liabilities on the respective balance sheets is readily seen in the direct relationship between the two items, the ratio of the current liabilities to tangible net worth heading skyward from 146.5 per cent to 174.2 per cent between year

C and year B, and then to 250.5 per cent in year A. This last ratio is in the stratosphere.

Further substantiation of the fact that the current liabilities were heavy is found in the increasing figure of minimum debt for each of these three years. This figure expanded from $59,170 in year C to $76,920 in year B, and then to $96,660 in year A. The relationship between these debt figures and the tangible net worth likewise was augmenting. This ratio rose from 119.1 per cent, to 128.8 per cent, to 138.0 per cent. Although operations had been extremely profitable over these years, the financial condition had been getting more and more out of line. Any appreciable increase in these liabilities could very easily cause financial jitters for the management.

Condensed Analysis. The comparative figures in Schedule 16 disclose the typical condition of a concern which is overtrading, that is, handling a volume of business that is large in relation to its net working capital and its tangible net worth. This situation had become more and more aggravated on each of the three fiscal dates, and in year A was very materially out of line. Such a condition, as explained in Chap. XV, results in heavy current liabilities, which become a critical burden in a period of suddenly falling prices or in a period of difficult collections. There is no room for turning around. There is no reserve in the balance sheet and any slight disturbance to the income makes it impossible to meet obligations on schedule. In this particular case, the financial condition was characterized by a heavy inventory, excessive current liabilities, and a substantial, uncalled-for item of miscellaneous receivables.

Three steps could be taken to remedy this situation, all of which would center around a reduction in the current liabilities. First, the miscellaneous receivables of $22,872 could be collected. This step would provide cash to reduce the current liabilities a corresponding amount. If carried out in year A, the net working capital would have been $58,145 instead of $35,273. Second, the net sales could be reduced approximately 65 per cent or brought down to the neighborhood of $275,000. Many managements have the predominant idea that large sales are the objective of the business enterprise. Not sales, but net profit is the real objective. For year A, net profits amounted to only $10,301, or 1.29 per cent on sales. The sales could be reduced by raising prices; undoubtedly equal dollar profits would be earned by raising the percentage of net profit on net sales. Net sales of $275,000 would give approximately four times turnover of tangible net worth and five times turnover of the enlarged net working capital of $58,145, fairly rapid but satisfactory turnover relationships. Third, if the annual volume was reduced 65 per cent, the inventory could be reduced to around $55,000. The difference between the inventory of $183,311 at the end of year A and $55,000 would then be applied to reduce the current liabilities, and the balance sheet as a whole would then reflect quite a normal financial condition.

If by any chance the miscellaneous receivables or any reasonable part of it could not be collected, then the figures suggested in the preceding paragraph would need to be adjusted accordingly.

LIQUOR WHOLESALE CORPORATION   [Schedule 17]
Comparative Figures for Years Ended February 28, 19—

	(C) Three Years Ago	(B) Two Years Ago	(A) One Year Ago
ASSETS			
Cash..........................	$ 23,200	$ 35,089	$ 37,936
Notes Receivable..............	43,861	56,656	36,182
Accounts Receivable...........	317,651	371,560	283,163
Inventory.....................	421,020	338,350	454,605
Current Assets...............	$ 805,732	$ 801,655	$ 811,886
Furniture & Fixtures, Net.......	13,390	15,716	16,685
Cash Value of Life Insurance....	....	240	250
Due from Officers and Employees	3,714	3,157	2,048
Deferred Charges..............	14,006	17,052	13,533
TOTAL...................	$ 836,842	$ 837,820	$ 844,402
LIABILITIES			
Notes Payable to Bank.........	$ 99,281	$ 31,190	$ 23,282
Other Loans Payable, Secured...	175,758	160,164	51,441
Trade Acceptances............	29,083	41,416	4,613
Accounts Payable.............	233,296	271,346	438,244
Accruals and Taxes............	72,908	93,638	95,832
Current Liabilities.............	$ 610,326	$ 597,754	$ 613,412
5% Cumulative Preferred Stock.	75,000	75,000	77,500
Common Stock...............	95,070	95,070	95,070
Retained Earnings............	56,446	69,996	58,420
TOTAL...................	$ 836,842	$ 837,820	$ 844,402
Net Working Capital...........	$ 195,406	$ 203,900	$ 198,474
Current Ratio.................	1.32	1.34	1.32
Tangible Net Worth............	$ 226,516	$ 240,066	$ 230,990
Net Sales....................	$2,962,554	$3,261,522	$3,555,915
Net Profit...................	1,424	18,800	(L)6,326
Dividends...................	5,250	5,250	5,250

Wholesaler of Liquor

Shortly after the repeal of the eighteenth amendment to the Federal Constitution, the Wholesale Fruit & Produce Company, Inc., Philadelphia, organized a department to distribute wines and liquors. The department expanded rapidly and profitably. This department was separately incorporated 6 years ago as the Liquor Wholesale Corporation. The outstanding preferred stock was retained by the Wholesale Fruit & Produce Company, Inc., while the common stock was distributed as a stock dividend to the common stockholders of that corporation. Operations were continued on a very profitable basis until 3 years ago when retained earnings of $56,446 had been accumulated. Since that time, net profits have been neither as large nor as steady. Net profits for year C amounted to $1,424, for year B to $18,800, while for year A a loss of $6,326 was assumed. The comparative figures for these 3 years are exhibited in Schedule 17.

The outstanding characteristic of these comparative figures is the consistently heavy current liabilities. In this case the liabilities did not go up steadily with an ever more disproportionate relationship, as took place with the Men's Clothing Company, Inc. In fact they dipped from $610,326 to $597,754 between year C and year B, and then increased to $613,412 in year A.

Wholesale enterprises generally have a somewhat smaller seasonal fluctuation in liabilities than do manufacturers. Wholesalers of liquor invariably have their heaviest debt in December when many retail stores are owing for holiday purchases; their minimum liabilities occur in June or July as a result of the summer liquidation of inventory. With these seasonal operations in mind, it is evident that the ratio between the current liabilities and the tangible net worth of the Liquor Wholesale Corporation was heavy for each of the 3 years.

	Year C	Year B	Year A
Current Liabilities.........................	$610,326	$597,754	$613,412
Tangible Net Worth........................	226,516	240,066	230,990
Ratio of Current Liabilities to Tangible Net Worth.................................	269.4%	248.9%	265.5%

In year C, the ratio of the current liabilities to tangible net worth was 269.4 per cent. In the following year, the current liabilities dropped $12,572 and the tangible net worth swelled $13,550, causing a moderate drop in this ratio to 248.9 per cent. In year A, the current liabilities increased from $597,754 to $613,412 and the tangible net worth decreased from $240,066 to $230,990, moving the ratio upward to 265.5 per cent.

This is another case of overtrading, that is, the annual volume of business was very substantial for the net working capital. Consequently heavy liabilities were the result, with creditors providing more than twice as much funds to operate the business from day to day as was actually invested in the enterprise.

The fact that the current debt was obviously heavy was verified by the nature of three of the five items that comprised the current liabilities in the comparative figures shown in Schedule 17, (1) *Notes Payable to Bank*, (2) *Other Loans Payable, Secured,* and (3) *Trade Acceptances.* The notes payable were in odd rather than in round numbers, which is unusual for bank borrowings. Odd numbers would indicate that the borrowings in year *B* and in year *A*, and at least part of the borrowings in year *C*, were represented by discounted customers' notes receivable, and were not customary borrowings on the straight note of the corporation, a fact that implies some modest lack of confidence on the part of the lending bank. On investigation, this inference was verified. Secondly, the existence of such an item as *Other Loans Payable, Secured* would indicate that the concern had been finding it necessary for at least 3 years to borrow funds to help pay overhead and some trade obligations by pledging certain of its assets. On investigation, it was learned that some accounts receivable (chosen by the lender and so presumably the best) were assigned to a finance company with a margin in favor of the lender of 33⅓ per cent for the loan. Third was the item of *Trade Acceptances*, which are generally given to obtain more time to pay an obligation. Trade acceptances are used extensively in the liquor trade, but they are never given by a concern that is in an easy financial position and rarely by any except those in a somewhat strained financial condition.

Condensed Analysis. The answer to this problem is similar to the analysis of the figures of the Men's Clothing Company, Inc. An excessive volume of business was being handled. The annual sales should be reduced from approximately $3,500,000 to $2,500,000 as an outside limit, and the lines of merchandise with the smallest markup eliminated. Such a reduction would allow a decrease of $125,000 in the inventory and approximately $100,000 in the receivables. This $225,000 reduction in the current assets would provide the funds to reduce the current liabilities to $488,000 on the statement date, and to a somewhat larger figure at the peak in December. Current liabilities of $488,000 would still be quite heavy, but in view of the ready marketability of the inventory, concerns in this line have been able to incur heavier liabilities than most other lines of wholesaling. At the same time the income figures would need to be studied. The loss in year *A* would indicate that the business was being handled on an insufficient markup in order to gain volume at competitively low prices, or that certain items of expense had been excessive. The suggested reduction in volume would simultaneously call for this examination.

Builder of Yachts and Launches

The Shipbuilding Corporation, located in Seattle, was incorporated in 1896 by Fred S. Adams to build small pleasure sailboats. From its very inception, the control of the corporation has remained in the hands of the

Adams family, the enterprise today being actively managed by a grandson of the founder.

From a very modest beginning, the business was built up out of retained earnings to a tangible net worth of $990,000 and annual sales of $1,600,000 at the peak of "good times." Activity spread to the construction of larger and larger boats, contracts being accepted to construct diesel-propelled

[Schedule 18]   SHIPBUILDING CORPORATION
Comparative Figures for Years Ended December 31, 19—

	(C) Three Years Ago	(B) Two Years Ago	(A) One Year Ago
ASSETS			
Cash	$ 91,301	$ 89,474	$ 49,609
Accounts Receivable	36,995	28,169	44,366
Inventory	245,059	185,325	158,016
Govt. Contracts in Process	....	....	184,031
Current Assets	$373,355	$302,968	$436,022
Real Estate	190,872	190,872	192,563
Plant, Net after Depreciation	92,684	90,342	100,572
Machinery and Equipment, Net	47,043	42,435	60,332
Miscellaneous Receivables	2,590	4,178	....
Prepaid Expenses	7,486	5,029	5,593
Patents	1	1	1
TOTAL	$714,031	$635,825	$795,083
LIABILITIES			
Notes Payable to Bank	$100,000	$100,000	$300,000
Customers' Deposits	52,768	28,035	....
Accounts Payable	12,761	9,598	112,316
Accruals	7,113	3,029	19,275
Reserve for Taxes	....	4,572	10,007
Current Liabilities	$172,642	$145,234	$441,598
Common Stock	525,000	525,000	525,000
Surplus	16,389	(D)34,409	(D)171,515
TOTAL	$714,031	$635,825	$795,083
Net Working Capital	$200,713	$157,734	$(D)5,576
Current Ratio	2.16	2.08	0.98
Tangible Net Worth	$541,388	$490,590	$353,484
Net Sales	$426,364	$663,715	$722,918
Net Profit	15,328	(L)50,798	(L)137,106
Dividends	None	None	None

private ocean-going yachts which cost up to $265,000. As a depression developed, less and less business materialized, the annual volume dropping in one disastrous year to $283,000, with consequent heavy losses reflected in successive income statements. By the end of year C the tangible net worth had dropped to $541,388 and by year A, to $353,484. Comparative figures for the past 3 years disclose the unique financial conditions shown in Schedule 18.

recession

The figures for year C reflect a satisfactory financial condition, although the tangible net worth at \$541,388 was materially below the peak figure of \$990,000. A net profit of \$15,328 was earned for this year.

During the latter part of year B, contracts were obtained from the United States Navy to construct five harbor tugboats. Now the financial condition began to head downward. A loss of \$50,798 was assumed on operations for this year. During year A, three of the tugboats were completed and delivered. They failed to come up to specifications, and change after change had to be made, involving very substantial additional expenditures. The tugboats had been constructed with steel hulls whereas the experience of the management had been largely with wooden hulls. The three tugs were finally accepted by the Navy Department, but operations on the increased volume showed a heavy loss of \$137,106, increasing the deficit in the surplus account during the year from \$34,409 to \$171,515 and turning a net working capital of \$157,734 into a deficit of \$5,576. In this process, the current liabilities, which had been quite modest in comparison to the tangible net worth in year C and in year B, became very heavy, as the following comparison clearly shows:

	Year C	Year B	Year A
Current Liabilities	\$172,642	\$145,234	\$441,598
Tangible Net Worth	541,388	490,590	353,484
Ratio of Current Liabilities to Tangible Net Worth	31.9%	29.5%	124.9%

Between years C and B, the current liabilities were reduced from \$172,642 to \$145,234. Simultaneously, the tangible net worth dropped moderately from \$541,388 to \$490,590, bringing about a reduction in the ratio of the current liabilities to the tangible net worth from 31.9 per cent to 29.5 per cent. A spectacular change now took place between year B and year A. As a result of the net loss of \$137,106, the tangible net worth dropped from \$490,590 to \$353,484 and the current liabilities rose like an interceptor airplane from \$145,234 to \$441,598. The ratio of the current debt to tangible net worth became 124.9 per cent. Another year like year A would bankrupt this enterprise.

Condensed Analysis. For many years up to and through year C, the fundamental problem of this corporation had been to obtain an adequate volume of business. Additional sales were obtained in year B and in year A, but losses were assumed instead of profits earned, merely because the management had not been sufficiently trained or skilled to handle the new type of business that it had secured. If its products fail to meet contract specifications in the year or two following year A, or if its manufacturing expenses and overhead are too high, losses will continue, the disparity between current liabilities and tangible net worth will increase, and the final curtain will be rung down on this venture. On the other hand, if the management has learned from its recent experiences how to handle the production of new types of boats more efficiently, if profits are earned and retained in the business, the situation may be gradually but slowly improved. A long difficult row is ahead.

TYPICAL RATIOS OF CURRENT LIABILITIES TO TANGIBLE NET WORTH

Thousands of business enterprises become financially embarrassed each year because of the receipt of too liberal extension of credit. For many years, students of business failures classified a large percentage of these annual difficulties as being due to "lack of capital." It is probable that a more careful study of these situations would have developed a modified classification of the "unsound or inexperienced use of capital" rather than "lack of capital." Concerns that need the excessive use of too liberal credit are generally those which overtrade, that is, handle a volume of business that is too large in relation to the net working capital. The managements of such enterprises seize upon every source of available credit; the more pressing the need for more credit, the more vital seems to be the so-called "lack of capital." From an analyst's point of view, this excessive use of credit becomes nothing more than heavy liabilities, generally current liabilities. The measure of that use is the relationship between (1) the current assets and the current liabilities, (2) the current liabilities and the tangible net worth, and (3) the minimum current liabilities during the year, as shown from monthly trial balance figures, and the tangible net worth.

The figure of minimum current liabilities needed for this third comparison is never readily available, as it appears in no financial statement normally issued to those outside the management of a business enterprise. However, it is a figure that is often extremely helpful in analysis and is now being requested on the financial statement blanks of an increasing number of financial institutions, mercantile creditors, and mercantile agencies. The figure never appears in annual corporate reports to stockholders. It can generally be obtained in a direct personal interview with a member of the management staff. However, as more and more business enterprises use the natural business year for fiscal purposes, this figure in an increasing number of situations will be the current liabilities that appear on the statement date.

Typical ratios of current liabilities to tangible net worth for 42 lines of manufacturing activity, 24 lines of wholesaling, and 7 lines of retailing appear in Schedule 19. These ratios are given for 70 lines of commercial and industrial activity for each year from 1955 through 1959, based upon operations for the respective years, and then a final ratio representing an average for the 5-year period.

The variations are broad in the typical (median) ratios of current lia-

Ratios of Current Liabilities to Tangible Net Worth   [Schedule 19]

Line of Business Activity	Percentage					
	Median					Five-year Average
	1955	1956	1957	1958	1959	
Manufacturers						
Agricultural Implements and Machinery	24.4	21.3	27.6	30.7	32.8	27.4
Airplane Parts and Accessories	64.6	111.7	75.4	75.7	59.7	77.4
Automobile Parts and Accessories	40.3	38.3	29.2	29.5	32.8	34.0
Bakers	30.0	33.7	25.5	30.0	28.3	29.5
Bedsprings and Mattresses	26.1	27.9	24.4	22.1	23.3	24.8
Bodies, Auto, Bus, and Truck	48.3	38.5	37.5	21.1	39.6	37.0
Bolts, Screws, Nuts, and Nails	32.5	28.3	22.5	21.1	29.2	26.7
Breweries	23.4	22.2	18.5	18.4	23.3	21.2
Chemicals, Industrial	35.5	29.8	26.3	31.2	29.3	30.4
Coats and Suits, Men's and Boys'	64.6	62.4	57.8	57.8	71.9	62.9
Coats and Suits, Women's	75.6	83.9	71.3	94.2	93.7	83.7
Confectionery	24.3	24.6	26.0	23.6	30.2	25.7
Contractors, Building Construction	59.9	91.1	81.1	75.2	75.7	76.6
Contractors, Electrical	48.3	58.1	53.9	44.3	48.0	50.5
Cotton Cloth Mills	18.9	18.2	16.9	13.7	17.0	16.9
Cotton Goods, Converters, Non-factored	55.1	46.4	45.2	40.7	78.0	53.1
Dresses, Rayon, Silk, and Acetate	94.2	102.4	89.2	90.2	92.3	93.7
Drugs	28.5	31.4	34.1	27.5	26.8	29.7
Electrical Parts and Supplies	41.6	37.4	30.1	30.2	38.2	35.5
Foundries	26.7	30.8	23.1	20.1	25.1	25.2
Fruits and Vegetables, Canners	49.2	50.7	43.7	53.0	58.1	50.9
Furniture	30.6	33.0	29.8	28.8	33.6	31.2
Hardware and Tools	29.2	29.1	24.9	23.5	28.2	27.0
Hosiery	23.3	15.9	19.6	20.4	23.0	20.4
Lumber	19.4	16.2	17.3	18.9	20.6	18.5
Machine Shops	28.7	35.5	28.2	17.8	31.4	28.3
Machinery, Industrial	37.1	36.9	31.2	25.5	29.5	32.0
Meats and Provisions, Packers	34.0	35.2	31.7	41.0	34.2	35.2
Metal Stampings	31.3	32.5	25.6	22.5	27.7	27.9
Outerwear, Knitted	58.8	54.8	61.2	55.5	56.8	57.4
Overalls and Work Clothing	42.7	39.1	35.4	31.4	39.0	37.5
Paints, Varnishes, and Lacquers	27.6	25.4	24.2	24.5	29.6	26.3
Paper	25.8	23.9	17.6	19.6	18.4	21.1
Paper Boxes	26.8	26.1	24.5	22.8	21.7	24.4
Petroleum, Integrated Corporations	21.3	19.5	18.4	19.0	19.9	19.6
Printers, Job	30.7	34.5	31.3	28.0	29.4	30.8
Radio Parts and Supplies	51.2	58.0	44.0	41.0	45.5	47.9
Shirts, Underwear, and Pajamas, Men's	57.8	70.5	66.8	77.0	84.2	71.3
Shoes, Men's, Women's, and Children's	48.7	48.0	49.5	49.4	59.1	50.9
Soft Drinks and Carbonated Water, Bottlers	26.9	28.5	22.3	33.2	29.8	28.1
Steel, Structural Fabricators (Sell on Short Terms)	32.7	42.2	36.0	29.5	24.7	33.0
Stoves, Ranges, and Ovens	35.5	27.6	28.9	27.2	30.0	29.8

RATIOS OF CURRENT LIABILITIES TO TANGIBLE NET WORTH (*Continued*)
[**Schedule 19** (*Cont.*)]

Line of Business Activity	Percentage					
	Median					Five-year Average
	1955	1956	1957	1958	1959	
WHOLESALERS						
Automobile Parts and Accessories....	38.2	43.3	36.2	38.7	42.1	39.7
Baked Goods......................	27.3	37.1	27.4	29.4	27.8	29.8
Cigars, Cigarettes, and Tobacco......	54.5	58.1	63.5	68.3	75.0	63.9
Drugs and Drug Sundries...........	62.7	62.9	64.0	53.8	51.6	59.0
Dry Goods.......................	43.1	38.9	38.2	43.4	51.7	43.1
Electrical Parts and Supplies........	70.4	65.7	43.4	45.2	58.8	56.7
Fruits and Produce, Fresh...........	22.9	23.1	34.9	25.6	34.0	28.1
Furnishings, Men's................	32.7	31.8	50.8	42.5	50.9	41.7
Gasoline, Fuel Oil, and Lubricating Oil....	63.5	45.0	41.8	49.7	48.0	49.6
Groceries.........................	41.4	46.3	47.6	42.5	48.7	45.3
Hardware.........................	34.7	34.5	29.5	33.1	34.4	33.2
Hosiery and Underwear............	41.0	42.7	38.2	41.1	46.3	41.9
Household Appliances, Electrical.....	78.8	80.9	74.6	68.6	97.4	80.1
Lumber...........................	43.4	33.6	28.9	33.2	39.7	35.8
Lumber and Building Materials......	31.2	32.5	30.8	27.1	38.8	32.1
Meat and Poultry.................	42.6	62.4	57.7	39.1	48.3	50.0
Paints, Varnishes, and Lacquers......	33.3	27.5	33.6	31.8	32.0	31.6
Paper............................	48.7	48.7	42.9	45.6	51.2	47.4
Plumbing and Heating Supplies......	36.3	37.9	30.6	29.7	36.9	34.3
Shoes, Men's, Women's, and Children's....	52.4	55.8	72.4	63.0	68.1	62.3
Wines and Liquors.................	66.2	67.6	62.4	69.8	69.1	67.0
RETAILERS						
Clothing, Men's and Boys'..........	36.9	47.6	41.6	39.2	48.8	42.8
Department Stores.................	27.1	27.3	27.4	26.8	27.2	27.2
Furniture, 50 Per Cent or More Installment....	34.5	35.8	37.7	42.5	38.2	37.7
Groceries and Meats, Independent...	58.7	50.3	46.5	48.7	50.5	50.9
Lumber and Building Materials......	34.5	30.9	25.4	27.8	31.3	30.0
Shoes............................	38.9	35.9	38.9	55.5	45.3	39.5
Women's Specialty Shops...........	41.2	41.4	46.9	54.4	50.8	46.9

bilities to tangible net worth between different lines of industry and commerce. Cotton cloth mills had the lowest 5-year average of 16.9 per cent, followed by lumber mills with 18.5 per cent and integrated petroleum corporations with 10.6 per cent. At the other extreme are manufacturers of rayon, silk, and acetate dresses with 93.7 per cent, manufacturers of women's coats and suits with 83.7 per cent, and wholesalers of electrical

household appliances with a 5-year average ratio of 80.1 per cent. In 19 23
instances out of the 70 lines of industry and commerce included in this
table—14 lines of manufacturing, 7 of wholesaling, and 1 of retailing—the
5-year averages of this ratio equal or exceed 50 per cent; in other words,
the current liabilities are equal to or greater than one-half of the tangible
net worth. The highest 5-year average ratio of current liabilities to tangible net worth among the 7 retail trades is shown by the independent
grocery and meat stores with 50.9 per cent. *wholesalers of cigars
cigarettes, and tobacco with 77.8 per cent*

Maxim

The commercial or industrial business enterprise that has heavy current
liabilities needs considered attention. The time always comes when a liability must be paid. Experience in the analysis of many thousands of
balance sheets in all lines of business activity in good times and in poor
has indicated that when a commercial or industrial concern has a tangible
net worth between $50,000 and $250,000, its operations should be carefully analyzed if the current liabilities exceed two-thirds the tangible net
worth; if the tangible net worth is greater than $250,000, its affairs should
be studied closely if the current liabilities exceed three-quarters of the tangible net worth.

THEORY AND PROBLEMS

1. Discuss the evolution of and the theory behind the ratio of current liabilities to
   tangible net worth.

2. Define the term *natural business year*, and explain how you would determine it for
   (a) a retailer, (b) a wholesaler, (c) a manufacturer.

3. Describe the natural business year of (a) a manufacturer of fur coats, (b) a department store, and (c) a manufacturer of furniture.

4. State at least three advantages (a) in taking inventory and (b) in closing accounts
   and preparing financial statements on a natural business year basis.

5. Below are given the ratios of current liabilities to tangible net worth for 10 lines
   of business. After each item place the capital letter which describes that particular ratio: G, good; F, fair; P, poor.

   a. Manufacturer of auto parts and accessories......... 42.2
   b. Manufacturer of confectionery.................... 23.8
   c. Manufacturer of drugs........................... 87.7
   d. Packer of meats and provisions................... 92.4
   e. Manufacturer of paper boxes...................... 36.7
   f. Manufacturer of stoves, ranges, and ovens......... 25.7
   g. Wholesaler of butter, eggs, and cheese............. 58.9
   h. Wholesaler of lumber............................ 88.8
   i. Wholesaler of plumbing and heating supplies........ 48.5
   j. Retailer of furniture............................ 23.5

6. The following schedule gives the comparative figures of the Chain Retail Grocery Corporation over a 3-year period. From these figures compute for each year (*a*) the net working capital, (*b*) the current ratio, (*c*) the tangible net worth, and (*d*) the ratio of current liabilities to tangible net worth. Assume you are a mercantile creditor; interpret briefly the variations in the ratio of current liabilities to tangible net worth over the 3 years.

CHAIN RETAIL GROCERY CORPORATION
Comparative Figures for Years Ended December 31, 19—

	(C) Three Years Ago	(B) Two Years Ago	(A) One Year Ago
ASSETS			
Cash.........................	$ 51,439	$ 100,974	$ 76,109
Accounts Receivable...........	17,090	24,726	19,292
Merchandise..................	283,796	209,726	215,096
Current Assets................	$ 352,325	$ 335,426	$ 310,497
Fixed Assets, Net..............	119,459	97,094	82,379
Miscellaneous Receivables.......	577	....	....
Prepaid and Deferred...........	31,369	28,816	27,013
Organization Expense..........	24,874	24,874	24,874
TOTAL..................	$ 528,604	$ 486,210	$ 444,763
LIABILITIES			
Bills Payable to Bank..........	$........	$ 16,400	$ 5,600
Trade Acceptances.............	8,804	....	....
Accounts Payable..............	327,837	311,827	293,174
Accruals.....................	5,189	1,866	8,110
Reserves for Taxes............	20,845	18,666	....
Other Liabilities...............	3,392	....	5,832
Current Liabilities..............	$ 366,067	$ 348,759	$ 312,716
Minority Interest..............	16,437	13,728	13,195
$3.50 Cumulative Pref. Stock....	5,800	5,800	5,800
Common Stock, No Par.........	973,841	973,841	973,841
Deficit.......................	*833,541*	*855,918*	*860,789*
TOTAL..................	$ 528,604	$ 486,210	$ 444,763
Net Sales.....................	$2,621,920	$3,075,361	$3,027,380
Net Profits...................	3,781	(L)*22,377*	(L)*4,871*
Dividends....................	None	None	None

7. The treasurer of the Cylinder Gas Corporation called on his banker to negotiate for a 6 months' loan of $500,000. Among the papers that the treasurer turned over to the banker after their discussion was the following balance sheet as of Dec. 31, 19—. The banker posted these figures accurately on a comparative balance sheet form and then computed (*a*) the net working capital, (*b*) the current ratio, (*c*) the tangible net worth, and (*d*) the ratio of current liabilities to tangible net worth. Assume you are the banker; post the figure, make these four computations, and then from the ratio of current liabilities to tangible net worth that you obtain explain whether you would be inclined to grant the loan or not. Give your reasons.

CYLINDER GAS CORPORATION
Balance Sheet, December 31, 19—
ASSETS

Cash in banks and on hand.............................		$ 882,663
Notes receivable.....................................		6,857
Accounts receivable, less allowances aggregating $181,143		
Trade debtors.....................................	$ 215,946	
Miscellaneous.....................................	51,154	267,100
Installment accounts receivable, less unearned income, financing charges, insurance, etc., aggregating $1,507,861.		702,609
Inventories at cost (not in excess of market)		
Parts..	$ 250,451	
Materials and supplies.............................	54,197	
Work in process and finished products................	59,938	
Other apparatus...................................	4,925	369,511
Total Current Assets...........................		$2,228,740

Plant and equipment	Costs	Allowances for Depreciation	
Land and building........................	$ 63,489	$ 53,979	
Machinery and equipment.................	168,434	135,196	
Automobiles.............................	54,241	22,732	
Furniture and fixtures....................	32,007	13,088	
	$ 318,171	$ 224,995	
Equipment leased to customers............	1,880,629	796,032	
	$2,198,800	$1,021,027	$1,177,773

Sundry prepayments and deferred charges................		10,645
Patents at cost in cash or in capital stocks of corporation..	$2,856,553	
Less: Provision for amortization based upon life of patents.	2,365,396	491,157
		$3,908,315

LIABILITIES

Accounts payable, including sundry accruals..............	$ 358,473
Provision for United States income taxes................	446,560
Total Current Liabilities........................	$ 805,033
Deferred income, representing advance rental charges for equipment leased to customers, less provision of $227,000 for estimated Federal taxes applicable thereto..........	133,391

CAPITAL

Capital stock		
Common of no par value; authorized, issued, and outstanding 478,518 shares...........................	$ 853,755	
Earned surplus......................................	2,210,989	
	$3,064,744	
Less: Cost of 3,300 shares of the corporation's common stock held by subsidiary companies.................	94,853	2,969,891
		$3,908,315

8. In your own words, give the general ratio to keep in mind when studying the relationship between the current liabilities and tangible net worth of a commercial or industrial business enterprise when (a) the tangible net worth is below $250,000 and (b) above $250,000.

CHAPTER VIII

Total Liabilities to Tangible Net Worth

For the vast majority of commercial and industrial business enterprises, the figures of current liabilities and total liabilities are one and the same, absolutely identical. Only when a mortgage, an issue of bonds, debentures, serial notes, or other obligations with a maturity of more than 1 year from the statement date appear in a balance sheet is there a difference between the current and the total liabilities. Small business enterprises occasionally have a mortgage outstanding, but rarely any other form of deferred liabilities. Railroads and public utilities have extensive and often complicated issues of deferred liabilities outstanding. Some large commercial and industrial corporations also owe substantial funded obligations, the amount of these obligations depending upon the views of the financial management of the corporation and the conditions under which the financing arrangements were determined.

EVOLUTION OF LONG-TERM OBLIGATIONS

During the eighteenth century, it had become quite customary for the colonial importer-wholesalers located in the Atlantic seacoast cities and towns to extend credit for the sale of merchandise to their retail customers, shopkeepers, storekeepers, and country general stores on terms of approximately 12 months. Similar terms were granted by English merchants in their extensive trade with colonial importers. Colonial correspondence, as preserved in the letter books of these early merchants, contains plenty of evidence that creditors had their full share of collection difficulties on these long terms.

Long-term Liabilities during the Colonial Era

One of the well-known business houses in New York City just prior to the Revolutionary War was that of John & Henry Cruger. This house transacted extensive business with the help of foreign branches managed by the sons of Henry, John Harris Cruger on the island of Jamaica, Telemon at Curaçao, Nicolas at St. Croix, and Henry, Jr., at Bristol, England. One of the large accounts of Henry, Jr., was with Aaron Lopez of Newport, R.I. Extensive correspondence between these two men from 1765 to 1772 indicates the difficulties involved in collection during this period. In April, 1766, Lopez was indebted to Cruger for the very substantial sum of £10,784.8.4. As his own liabilities increased, Cruger began to wonder if he, himself, would not become bankrupt before Lopez would appreciably reduce his account. By May, 1771, the balance had been brought down slowly to £4,047.9.1, but in July, 1772, it still amounted to £2,452.15.11 exclusive of interest.[1]

Obligations for the payment of merchandise in these early years of our history often ran on and on. From the extensive mercantile correspondence that has come down to us, it is quite evident that creditors in the colonial period, and in the early days of our national life, were more worried as to how long they might be called upon to wait for payment, than that they would not be paid at all. Eventually, most debts were liquidated with the payment of interest on overdue accounts.[2] One of the most exaggerated examples of this prevailing tendency appeared in a letter written in 1783 by Philip Cuyler of Albany to a Mrs. Catherine Wendell of Schenectady regarding a debt of 12 years' standing. Cuyler meticulously and quaintly wrote, "I have Repeatedly Inclosed you, your Dec^d Husband's acc^t requesting the payment of it, to which I have had no Answer, so find inclose you the same with my—Ernest Request you would with Speed discharge it as Really think its time after Cred^t of more than Twelve Years.—being much pressed for Cash puts it Out of my power to waite any longer." Shortly after this unique letter was mailed, the payment was received and the account closed.[3]

During the days of the colonies, most of the debts were eventually collected. The fact remains, however, that a considerable portion of normal mercantile credit became long-term liabilities of the debtor. Over all the years of existence of the colonies, mortgage liabilities were also quite widely used.

Preceded in the extent of usage only by the long terms of mercantile obligations and by mortgages came two types of obligations, now virtually unknown but used extensively in American commerce throughout the eighteenth and well into the nineteenth century, namely, bottomry and

---

[1] *Commerce of Rhode Island*, Vol. I, pp. 155, 368, 405, Massachusetts Historical Society Collections, 7th ser., Vol. IX, 1914.

[2] FOULKE, ROY A., *The Sinews of American Commerce*, p. 360 (Dun & Bradstreet, Inc., New York, 1941).

[3] Letter inserted in the Ledger of Philip Cuyler, 1763–1794 (New York Public Library).

respondentia. During these early years of our economic history, manu-facturing was of relatively little importance compared with the volume of foreign and domestic commerce. *Bottomry*, according to maritime law, was a legal instrument by which a ship was pledged as security for a loan. This form of obligation was widely used prior to the earliest development of the railroad. Transportation was largely by water, and ships repre-sented the great capital investment of the day. Overland traffic was slow and difficult, as there was little conception of good roads as we know them today.[4]

Respondentia represented a supplementary process by which a ship-owner would borrow funds upon the security of a cargo, agreeing to repay within a stipulated period of time, such as 24 months, or 60 days after the return of the vessel to its home port. The original sum together with a sub-stantial increment, usually 24 per cent, was paid for the use of the money, but if the vessel and the cargo were lost, then no payment was made either on the principal or the increment.[5] A supplementary provision of the charter of the Insurance Company of North America, Philadelphia, the oldest stock fire and marine insurance company in America, organized in November, 1782, provided that money could be loaned "upon bottomry and respondentia."[6]

---

[4] "The construction and care of roads was generally left to the local authorities who were not particularly interested in the development of through routes. The prevailing ignorance of the principles of road engineering and the lack of capital were additional hampers upon improvement. In its elemental form a road consisted of a cleared path through the trees and nothing else. If further refinement was demanded, the road was crowned high with dirt and edged by a gutter. Over such roads the transportation of passengers was alone profitable. Freight commerce was confined either to short dis-tances or to products such as whiskey and peltries, whose value was high in proportion to the bulk. A wagonload of goods could be sent overland at the time of the War of 1812 from Augusta, Maine, to Savannah, Georgia, but the journey required 115 days and the freight charges on the road were $1,000. . . . To move a barrel of flour from Pittsburgh to Philadelphia cost $13.00. Off the main roads it probably cost, according to McMaster's careful estimate, 'ten dollars per ton per hundred miles.' Very few bulky articles could stand such freight charges. Although manufactured articles might pay for their transportation, agricultural ones like wheat and flour could not be gain-fully carried more than one hundred and fifty miles. A ton of goods could be moved across the Atlantic almost as cheaply as from Philadelphia to Lancaster."—KIRKLAND, EDWARD C., *A History of American Economic Life*, 3d ed., pp. 228–229, 231 (Appleton-Century-Crofts, Inc., New York, 1951). In 1803, Thaddeus Mason Harris made a journey through the Northwest Territory. Thirty-one miles was a long distance to be covered in a carriage in one day. At one point Harris summarized, "After many a wearisome ascent, we arrive at Seybour's on the top of the Alleghany; and, having ridden thirty-one miles, were sufficiently tired to accept even of the miserable accom-modations this Inn afforded for the night."—*The Journal of a Tour into the Territory Northwest of the Alleghany Mountains*, p. 21 (Manning & Loring, Boston, 1805).

[5] PORTER, KENNETH WIGGINS, *The Jacksons and the Lees*, Vol. I, pp. 52, 672 (Har-vard University Press, Cambridge, Mass., 1937).

[6] *The Sinews of American Commerce*, p. 125. Also see JAMES, MARQUIS, *Biography of a Business, 1792–1942*, pp. 53–54 (Bobbs-Merrill Company, Indianapolis, 1942).

Early Long-term Railroad Securities

The first railroads in the United States were financed solely by funds obtained by the sale of capital stock. The Boston & Lowell Railway issued no bonds for 20 years; in fact, none of the smaller railroads radiating from Boston issued bonds for many years after their organization. The Boston & Providence Railway, constructed in 1849, after a time issued bonds aggregating one-fourth of its share capital, and by 1865 had practically extinguished this mortgage indebtedness. As late as 1855, the capital stock of all railroads in the United States exceeded the total bonded indebtedness by 42 per cent.[7]

In 1833 the Baltimore and Susquehanna Rail Road Co. sold an issue of $350,000 five per cent bonds, the payment of the interest but not the principal being guaranteed by the State of Maryland. Apparently this was the first issue of bonds to be sold by a railroad in the United States. The state insisted the railroad issue a blanket mortgage upon all of the road, then constructed or to be constructed, and "the real and personal property belonging to said company of every sort and description." In 1845 the Chesapeake and Ohio Canal Company issued $1,700,000 six per cent income bonds, probably the first of their type to be issued in the United States.[8]

In 1846, it became necessary for the Baltimore & Ohio Rail Road Co. to reconstruct the entire 81 miles of the road from Baltimore to Harpers Ferry and to lay the new edge rail in place of the antiquated plate rail. The road had no funds. In this situation, the company received the privilege by legislation of the General Assembly of the State of Maryland dated December, 1845, to sell an issue of bonds, not to "exceed in amount one million dollars" and to bear interest at the rate of 6 per cent per annum secured by the pledge of the property of the road.[9] These bonds, dated January 1, 1846, were sold as favorable financial conditions permitted, but the total amount was not outstanding until 1852. The bonds matured on January 1, 1867. In order to effect the sale, they were sold at a discount of 10 per cent.[10]

After managing a bank in Madison, Ind., J. F. D. Lanier came to New York City in 1849 and formed a partnership with Richard H. Winslow,

---

[7] RIPLEY, WILLIAM Z., *Railroads, Finance and Organization*, p. 10 (Longmans, Green & Co., Inc., New York, 1927).

[8] BLANDI, JOSEPH G., *Maryland Business Corporation*, pp. 35–38 (The Johns Hopkins Press, Baltimore, Md., 1934).

[9] This obligation is carried on the books of the Baltimore and Ohio Railway Company as Loan No. 2. Loan No. 1 amounted to $1,000,000 and was obtained from the Union Bank of Maryland, bearing interest at the rate of 6 per cent per annum. This bank loan was obtained Oct. 1, 1833, and was paid at maturity, Jan. 1, 1854.

[10] CARTER, CHARLES FREDERICK, *When Railroads Were New*, p. 59 (Simmons-Boardman Publishing Corporation, New York, 1926).

mainly for the distribution of railway securities. In his reminiscence
Lanier tells how his firm was the first one to distribute the mortgage bond
of small western railroads in the New York security market. This occurred
only a few years after the Baltimore & Ohio Rail Road Co. had begun to
sell its initial issue of 6 per cent bonds to the public. "Commencing with
the bonds of the Madison and Indianapolis Railroad, which were the first
securities of the kind ever brought out in the New York market," wrote
Lanier, "we followed them with the bonds of the little Miami; Columbus
and Xenia; Cleveland, Columbus and Cincinnati; Cleveland, Painesville
and Ashtabula; Ohio and Pennsylvania; Michigan Southern and other
important lines. We not infrequently negotiated a million of bonds daily.
The aggregate for the year was enormous. We were without competitor
for a business we had created, and consequently made money very rapidly. The commissions for the negotiations of bonds averaged at first five
per cent."[11]

In 1854 six issues of railroad bonds were quoted daily in the trading on
the New York Stock Exchange, "Harlem Bonds, Erie 1st Mtge. Bds.
Erie Income Bonds, Hudson Convertible Bds., Ill. Cen. R. R. Bonds, and
N. Y. Cen. R.R. Bds." No industrial or public utility bonds were quoted.[r]
Within 10 years there were 68 bond issues of 31 railroads listed on the New
York Stock Exchange.[13] By January 6, 1900, 758 bond issues of 346 rail-
roads were being quoted on the Big Board.[14]

By 1862, the technique of railroad building had been radically changed
from the conservative original pattern whereby funds were obtained solely
or largely by the issue of common stock. Under the revamped technique
the railroad was first organized by the projectors upon a blueprint, and
a charter obtained involving free grants of land, sometimes in alternate
sections running from 6 to 10 miles on either side of the line. Then a land
company, owned by the directors of the railroad, was incorporated to
develop and to sell its land. With the proceeds from the sale of the land
in addition to that from government subsidies and from the extensive sale
of mortgage bonds in Europe undertaken simultaneously, building was
begun. This was done by a construction company, also owned by the
directors. In this process extensive quantities of railroad bonds, and in
later years railroad stocks, were placed with European investors. By 1914
securities and direct investments by Europeans in the United States

[11] Quoted by Henry Wyshane Lanier, in *A Century of Banking in New York, 1822-
1922*, p. 210 (The Gilliss Press, New York, 1922).
[12] Record book of the New York Stock Exchange, *Stock Reports Apr. '54 to Jan. '55.*
[13] Quotation Sheet of Nov. 25, 1864; Vol. 1 of *Quotations, Nov. 25, 1864 to Nov. 8*
1865, New York Stock Exchange.
[14] Quotation Sheet of Jan. 6, 1900; Vol. 36 of *Quotations, Jan. 1, 1900 to Dec. 31*
1900, New York Stock Exchange.

otaled $6,700,000,000, well over half of which was represented by rail-
oad stocks and bonds.[15]

Early Industrial and Public Utility Bonds

While the number of bond issues of railroads listed on the New York
Stock Exchange was going up by leaps and bounds, industrials and public
utility long-term securities were virtually unknown. Not until June 20,
1868, did either an industrial or a public utility bond appear in the daily
quotations. On that date the bonds of the Long Dock Company and the
Western Union Company appeared for the first time in the "free list."[16]
On October 9, 1868, the bonds of the American Dock & Improvement
Company appeared;[17] on November 21, 1868, the bonds of the Iron Moun-
tain Company;[18] and on December 26, 1868, the bonds of the Oil Creek
Company.[19]

By January 6, 1900, when there were 758 bond issues of 346 railroads
listed on the New York Stock Exchange, there were listed only 33 bond
issues of 22 gas and electric companies. There was no segregation of bond
issues of industrial companies. There were, however, 68 bond issues of 48
miscellaneous companies, and more than half these corporations probably
were industrials.[20]

ILLUSTRATIONS OF RELATIONSHIPS

Total liabilities consist of all current liabilities, together with all actual
long-term financial liabilities which must be paid sometime in the future.
Important features of long-term liabilities are described in the early pages
of Chap. IX. Total liabilities do not include technical liabilities in a bookkeeping sense, such as minority interest in subsidiaries, unearned income,
or valuation reserves. The maturity date of every long-term liability, as
carefully explained in Chap. IV, must always be obtained prior to posting
a balance sheet; many funded debts have serial maturities and the amount
which is due and payable within 12 months after the statement date must
always be classified as a current liability. This information should appear
in the balance sheet, either in the financial statement or as a footnote.
Unfortunately, this information often is omitted from balance sheets. No

---

[15] *A History of American Economic Life*, p. 541.

[16] Quotation Sheet of June 20, 1868; Vol 4 of *Quotations, Nov. 16, 1867 to Nov. 18,
1868*, New York Stock Exchange.

[17] Quotation Sheet of Oct. 9, 1868.

[18] Quotation Sheet of Nov. 21, 1868; Vol. 5 of *Quotations, Nov. 19, 1868 to Nov. 26,
1869*, New York Stock Exchange.

[19] Quotation Sheet of Dec. 26, 1868.

[20] Quotation Sheet of Jan. 6, 1900.

balance sheet with any long-term debt can be properly posted or intell
gently analyzed until this preliminary information is obtained.

For large corporations that have several mortgage loans and man
different issues of bonds or debentures outstanding, where the accountar
makes no attempt to segregate or to list the serial maturities during th
year following the statement date, this information is difficult to obtaii
However, it constitutes an initial step in analysis. Often, one or more c
the mortgage obligations, issues of bonds, or debentures also mature i
the year following the statement date. In such a situation that maturit
as well as any serial maturities due during the year must be classified a
current liabilities. Difficulties in refunding such issues may be forecas
in many cases as soon as the schedule of maturities is learned.

Department Store

The Resort Department Store, Inc., is located in a large Atlantic seacoas
resort community. Unlike most summer resort centers where the popula
tion increases in the summer like the doubled and redoubled score of a
bridge player, the number of residents in this community increases only
moderately and does not shrink greatly in the autumn months. A con
siderable population lives the year round in the city; in addition, the per
manent residents within a radius of 50 miles number approximately
800,000 and are well able to support a representative department store

The business was established as a small local venture in 1878. In 1896
the proprietorship was incorporated with an authorized and paid-in capi
tal of $100,000, which was subsequently increased to $500,000, consisting
of $250,000 five per cent cumulative preferred stock and $250,000 com
mon stock, both classes of stock with a par value of $100. At the end of
year A, $237,800 of the 5 per cent cumulative preferred stock and $11,300
of the common stock were outstanding.

An extensive line of medium to better grade men's, ladies', and children's wearing apparel, furniture, rugs, and house furnishings is carried.
About 2 per cent of the annual net sales is made on a deferred payment
basis with down payments ranging from 10 to 15 per cent, and with
monthly installments running up to 3 years. The comparative financial
condition for the past three fiscal years appears in Schedule 20.

Each of the three comparative balance sheets contains an item of good
will carried at the same figure of $155,826. The tangible net worth as of
each statement date was obtained by deducting this item of good will
from the sum of outstanding 5 per cent cumulative preferred stock, the
common stock, and the respective retained earnings. This computation
gave a tangible net worth of $190,455 in year C, a decrease to $182,888 in
year B, and then an all-time high figure of $234,684 in year A.

RESORT DEPARTMENT STORE, INC.   [Schedule 20]
Comparative Figures for Years Ended January 31, 19—

	(C) Three Years Ago	(B) Two Years Ago	(A) One Year Ago
ASSETS			
Cash	$ 18,113	$ 13,452	$ 65,093
Notes Receivable	496	2,123	1,687
Accounts Receivable	95,281	123,810	162,897
Inventory	300,436	262,998	309,954
Current Assets	$ 414,326	$ 402,383	$ 539,631
Fixed Assets, Net	219,204	200,861	203,450
Investments	3,330	3,667	3,023
Cash Value of Life Insurance	7,296	10,097	10,185
Prepaid Items	15,575	13,842	13,024
Miscellaneous Receivables	4,566	5,875	3,764
Good Will	155,826	155,826	155,826
TOTAL	$ 820,123	$ 792,551	$ 928,903
LIABILITIES			
Notes Payable to Bank	$ 40,000	$ 10,000	$ 20,000
Other Notes Payable	5,584	950	5,800
Accounts Payable	160,029	182,674	200,752
Accruals	32,867	28,656	40,380
Reserve for Taxes	1,612	2,807	47,711
Cur. Maturity of Debentures	5,000	5,000	5,000
Current Liabilities	$ 245,092	$ 230,087	$ 319,643
$4\frac{1}{2}\%$ Debentures	228,750	223,750	218,750
Total Liabilities	$ 473,842	$ 453,837	$ 538,393
5% Cumulative Preferred Stock	237,800	237,800	237,800
Common Stock	11,300	11,300	11,300
Retained Earnings	97,181	89,614	141,410
TOTAL	$ 820,123	$ 792,551	$ 928,903
Net Working Capital	$ 169,234	$ 172,296	$ 219,988
Current Ratio	1.69	1.74	1.69
Tangible Net Worth	$ 190,455	$ 182,888	$ 234,684
Net Sales	$1,310,116	$1,361,220	$1,513,748
Net Profit	1,956	(L)7,567	51,796
Dividends	None	None	None

The net sales increased moderately between year C and year B, and
then quite considerably from $1,361,220 to $1,513,748, or 11.2 per cent,
between year B and year A. Nominal net profits amounting to $1,956
were recorded in year C, a loss of $7,567 was assumed in year B, and most
satisfactory net profits of $51,796 were earned in year A. No dividends
were paid during any of these years; as a result both the net working capi-

tal and the tangible net worth increased quite materially between year B and year A.

Net fixed assets, after accumulated depreciation, exceeded the tangible net worth at the end of year C and also at the end of year B. The balance sheet at the end of year A disclosed a slightly improved condition as a result of the retained profits; the net fixed assets now amounted to $203,450 and were moderately less than the tangible net worth of $234,684. As will be discussed in Chap. X, such a financial condition is basically unsound; for a typical department store, the net fixed assets, after depreciation, should represent approximately 25 per cent of the tangible net worth. Where the fixed assets closely approximate the tangible net worth there would normally be little or no net working capital. It fortunately happened, however, that several years ago the management of this enterprise sold an issue of 4½ per cent debentures to a life insurance company that was looking for investments in industrial securities. In year C, the outstanding portion of this issue amounted to $233,750, of which $5,000 was carried as a current liability as that installment matured during the following 12 months, and the balance of $228,750 was carried as a deferred liability. In each succeeding balance sheet, the deferred amount was reduced by the $5,000 which had matured and had been paid.

For each of the 3 years the outstanding debentures made up the difference by which the fixed assets and the miscellaneous assets exceeded the tangible net worth, and so provided the funds to furnish the net working capital. The result was a continuously heavy total debt over the 3-year spread:

	Year C	Year B	Year A
Current Liabilities	$245,092	$230,087	$319,643
4½ Per Cent Debentures	228,750	223,750	218,750
Total Liabilities	$473,842	$453,837	$538,393
Tangible Net Worth	190,455	182,888	234,684
Ratio of Total Liabilities to Tangible Net Worth	248.8%	247.0%	229.4%

Between the two years from year C to year A, the current liabilities increased from $245,092 to $319,643, while the deferred liabilities decreased $5,000 each year. The total liabilities expanded from $473,842 to $538,393, or 13.5 per cent, with a modest dip in year B. Simultaneously, the tangible net worth increased from $190,455 to $234,684, or 23.2 per cent. Because of the proportionately smaller increase in the amount of the total liabilities, the ratio of the total debt to the tangible net worth showed a moderate but steady reduction for each year from 248.8 to 247.0 per cent between year C and year B, and from 247.0 to 229.4 per cent between year B and year A. Although the downward trend was a favorable one, the relationship even in year A was high. Schedule 23, on pages 251 and 252, shows a 5-year average ratio of total liabilities to tangible net worth for department stores of 60.0 per cent, considerably less than one-third of this particular ratio of the Resort Department Store, Inc., in year A.

Condensed Analysis. A fundamental error in management judgment had been made sometime prior to year C, when funds had been invested in fixed assets in excess of the tangible net worth. There is little excuse except financial ignorance for such a policy. To provide net working capital an issue of debentures had to be floated. The result had been a fluctuating but constantly heavy total debt. At the time when the funds were put into fixed assets, additional money should have been invested in capital stock to have kept a well-balanced financial condition, or else a considerably smaller sum should have been put into the fixed assets.

There are only two ways to improve this heavy total liability condition, to invest additional funds in one or both forms of capital stock and use that new cash to reduce the outstanding debentures, or to earn profits and then keep these net profits in the business in the current assets and gradually retire the debentures. If losses are assumed instead of net profits earned, not only will no progress be made, but affairs will become more and more extended, ending in a reorganization or in bankruptcy.

A second criticism of the figures will be found in the increasing accounts receivable which amounted to $95,281 in year C, $123,810 in year B, and $162,897 in year A. These accounts receivable appear heavy for a department store transacting the volume of the Resort Department Store, Inc. Quite possibly, they include at least a reasonable amount of past-due accounts for which reserves should be set up. A thorough analysis should be made by obtaining a breakdown of the annual net sales into cash, 30-day charge accounts, and installment sales; also a breakdown of the accounts receivable into those made on a 30-day charge basis, and those on installment terms. The average collection period should then be determined for both classes of charge accounts as explained in Chap. XIII. If the average collection periods determined in this way should appear excessive, and probably that would be the situation, then an aging of charge accounts into the amount now due and 30, 60, and 90 days or more past due would be needed to understand the exact picture. To the extent that the accounts receivable might contain bad debts, the tangible net worth is inflated and the ratio of total liabilities to tangible net worth, particularly in year A, is actually heavier than it appears.

A third criticism is the fact that the inventory has been consistently large. This important feature of balance sheet analysis is examined in Chaps. XI and XII. At this point, however, it may be stated that the inventory carried at $309,954 in year A could be reduced by $75,000, which would bring it into line. Such a reduction would release a corresponding amount of funds to reduce the total liabilities. The lower the liabilities can be maintained while transacting a normal volume of business, the healthier is any business enterprise.

Notwithstanding the fine net profits earned in year A, the affairs of this concern were not in good shape. The ratio of current assets to current liabilities was low in each of the three comparative balance sheets, the relationship between the current liabilities and the tangible net worth was heavy for each year, and the relationship between the total liabilities and the tangible net worth on each statement date was even more out of line. In other words, the management had failed to operate the business with a real degree of foresight and knowledge.

Manufacturer of Electrical Products

The Electrical Specialty Corporation was incorporated in 1919 with an authorized and paid-in capital of $1,000,000 six per cent cumulative preferred stock and 20,000 shares of common stock of no par value but carried on the books at $150,000. For some years prior to year C, preferred stock was being reacquired and carried in the assets of the annual balance sheet as treasury stock. In year B, this treasury stock was retired reducing the outstanding preferred capital from $1,000,000 to $857,538. The outstanding common stock remained unchanged.

This concern manufactures electrical equipment, including lighting fixtures, switches, outlet boxes, portable lamps, reflectors, wiring devices, and panel switchboards. Operations were conducted at a substantial net loss of $105,652 in year C. In addition to this loss, affairs were in an unhealthy state; the ratio of current assets to current liabilities was obviously low, and the inventory was more than twice as large as it should have been. The principal stockholder, who was a director in the corporation, suddenly became aware of the situation and proceeded to clean house in blitz fashion. Early in year B, the president and the executive vice-president were released and two new officers took over the active management of the business. The first move of the new management to obtain a breathing spell was to arrange with creditors to accept notes for $402,633 payable after 5 years in settlement of long past due mercantile claims.

The loss for year B amounted to $104,356, only slightly below the loss for the preceding year. The new management now made arrangements with creditors holding claims for an additional $210,059 also to accept 5-year notes, so that at the end of year A the deferred liabilities aggregated the substantial sum of $612,692. Notwithstanding an increase in net sales from $1,060,611 to $1,284,748 between year B and year A, operations resulted in a red figure to the extent of $264,194, a triple-threat loss with almost a knockout punch. For the entire 3-year period, operating losses

ELECTRICAL SPECIALTY CORPORATION   [Schedule 21]
Comparative Figures for Years Ended December 31, 19—

	(C) Three Years Ago	(B) Two Years Ago	(A) One Year Ago
ASSETS			
Cash..........................	$ 27,486	$ 50,660	$ 55,483
Notes Receivable..............	22,143	17,120	25,200
Accounts Receivable...........	84,141	70,011	102,301
Inventory.....................	611,763	666,375	471,323
Current Assets................	$ 745,533	$ 805,166	$ 654,307
Fixed Assets, Net.............	737,958	727,636	688,863
Investments...................	115	114	114
Miscellaneous Receivables......	835	2,598	3,790
Prepaid Expenses..............	56,146	17,627	18,618
Development Expense..........	40,122	119,734	135,712
Patents.......................	1	1	1
Treasury Stock................	102,340	....	....
TOTAL....................	$1,683,050	$1,671,876	$1,501,405
LIABILITIES			
Notes Payable for Merchandise..	$ 322,393	$ 52,728	$ 40,143
Accounts Payable..............	128,525	217,735	121,241
Accruals......................	14,891	28,357	21,100
Current Liabilities............	$ 465,809	$ 298,820	$ 182,484
Notes Payable, Deferred........	....	402,633	612,692
Total Liabilities...............	$ 465,809	$ 701,453	$ 795,176
6% Cumulative Preferred Stock.	1,000,000	857,538	857,538
Common Stock................	150,000	150,000	150,000
Retained Earnings............	67,241	(D)37,115	(D)301,309
TOTAL....................	$1,683,050	$1,671,876	$1,501,405
Net Working Capital...........	$ 279,724	$ 595,346	$ 471,823
Current Ratio.................	1.60	2.70	3.59
Tangible Net Worth............	$1,074,778	$ 850,688	$ 570,516
Net Sales.....................	$1,080,306	$1,060,611	$1,284,748
Net Profit....................	(L)105,652	(L)104,356	(L)264,194
Dividends....................	None	None	None

aggregated $474,202. Comparative figures showing this depressing panorama appear in Schedule 21.

The tangible net worth of $1,074,778 in year C was arrived at by deducting the sum of development expenses $40,122, patents $1, and treasury stock $102,340, a total of $142,463, from the sum of the 6 per cent cumulative preferred stock $1,000,000, common stock $150,000, and retained earnings $67,241. In year B, the sum of development expenses $119,734, patents $1, and the deficit in retained earnings of $37,115, a total of $156,850, was deducted from the total of the preferred and common stock of $1,007,538, to give a tangible net worth figure of $850,688. In year A, development expense now amounted to $135,712, patents $1, and the deficit $301,309, a total of $437,022, which was deducted from the sum of the outstanding preferred and common stocks to arrive at a tangible net worth figure of $570,516.

As a result of the steady heavyweight yearly losses, the tangible net worth dropped from $1,180,440 to $570,516, or 51.8 per cent between year D and year A, a space of 3 years. This rate of decline approximates the speed of the newest dive bombers. As $402,633 of the liabilities became deferred in year B, the net working capital increased from $279,724 to $505,346. In other words, the net working capital showed improvement while the financial condition of the business was becoming more and more strained with steadily increasing total liabilities. The current ratio along with the net working capital improved during this period. Here is a typical case indicating the necessity of studying all features of a financial statement rather than just one.

Between years B and A, the net working capital decreased moderately from $505,346 to $471,823, but the current ratio continued to improve as payment of $210,059 additional current liabilities was deferred. The current liabilities continued to decrease. In this year, the business became even more strained, but again the strain was not reflected in the current ratio or in the continued improvement in the relationship of the current liabilities to the tangible net worth; it appeared chiefly in the increasingly unfavorable ratio between the total liabilities and the tangible net worth. The comparative relationships between these two major items appear as follows over the 3 years:

	Year C	Year B	Year A
Current Liabilities	$465,809	$298,820	$182,484
Notes Payable, Deferred	....	402,633	612,692
Total Liabilities	$465,809	$701,453	$795,176
Tangible Net Worth	1,074,778	850,688	570,516
Ratio of Total Liabilities to Tangible Net Worth	43.3%	82.5%	139.6%

These figures show a steady and material reduction in the current liabilities for each year. From year C to year B the current debt was reduced from $465,809 to $298,820 and then in year A to $182,484. With these reductions, the ratio between the current assets and the current liabilities was improved gradually from 1.60 in year C, to 2.70 in year B, and then to 3.59 in year A. An analyst unfamiliar with other supplementary relationships who based his analysis largely on the showing and the trend of the current ratio would be basically and entirely misled in this case. He would likewise be misled if his repertoire went no further than the supplementary relationship between the current liabilities and the tangible net worth, as this relationship also improved for each of these 3 years.

The ratio of the total liabilities to the tangible net worth holds the key to this picture. While the reduction in the current liabilities gives the appearance of an improving condition, actually the business was becoming more and more distressed. The total liabilities increased each year, going from $465,809 to $701,453 to $795,176. At the same time, the tangible net worth dropped each year, falling from $1,074,778 to $850,688 to $570,516. The relationship between these two unfavorable trends is shown in the rapidly increasing ratio of total debt to tangible net worth. From 43.3 per cent in year C, the ratio skipped to 82.5 per cent in year B, and then jumped to 139.6 per cent in year A. Here was the tip-off to a trend that had reached a basically unsound condition.

Condensed Analysis. The balance sheet of the Electrical Specialty Corporation as of the end of year C indicated a bad case of inventory indigestion. On the basis of an annual net sales volume of $1,080,306 and a net working capital of $279,724, the inventory should have been in the neighborhood of $200,000, instead of $611,763. A reduction of approximately $400,000 in this one item would have freed the necessary funds to have brought the current liabilities down to a moderate amount.

The operating management prior to year C had been absolutely lax. In a specialty line of highly competitive nature where research must be carried on and where up-to-the-minute new products had constantly to be developed, the president had had no conception of the expediency of inventory turnover that will be discussed in a subsequent chapter. When the inventory piled up as a result of the drop in net sales in year D and in year C because of the improved products of competitive manufacturers, the management had no workable policy to relieve the situation. For the first time in his career the president realized the truth of the modern axiom that a business enterprise, to succeed, must always be prepared for the unexpected. There must always be an ace in the hole. He had none.

The new management that came into power in year B realized the full importance of research and proceeded to capitalize part of the funds expended in this manner, as shown by the increase in the item of development expense from $40,122 to $119,734 between year C and year B. The downward momentum, however, could not be stopped overnight. The liabilities continued their upward climb while losses continued at approximately the same rate. By the time year A had come around the corner, the net sales were increasing and the inventory was decreasing, but the disastrous policies of the earlier years had now culminated in the heavy unbalanced relationship between the increasing total liabilities and the shrinking tangible net worth.

This situation would be relieved (1) by investing additional funds in the business which could be used to pay off part or all the deferred notes payable, (2) by operating profitably and using the net profits for the same purpose, or (3) by converting the deferred notes payable into a prior preferred stock. None of these alternatives would probably be followed unless it became clearly evident that operations could be conducted on a profitable basis. Then which policy could or would be followed would be a matter of expediency. In the other hand, further material losses would result in bankruptcy.

Manufacturer of Boilers

Here is a somewhat larger business enterprise than the two concerns whose total liabilities have just been examined. The Power Boiler Corporation was organized in 1938 to acquire the business and the assets of a manufacturing enterprise that had been operated by receivers for 3 years. This corporation is engaged in designing, manufacturing, selling, and installing complete plants for the production of steam, including both stationary and marine boilers. At the time of the reorganization, the creditors of the predecessor corporation received first mortgage bonds, common stock in the new corporation in varying proportions for their claims, together with some cash realized from the sale of $3,500,000 five per cent debentures to a close group of five interested concerns.

The interesting picture of the comparative financial condition of this manufacturer for the past 3 years appears in Schedule 22. For year C, net sales of $13,683,013 were recorded and handsome net profits of $694,048 were earned. Of this amount $309,660 was paid out in dividends and the difference retained to build the retained earnings account. The net sales then decreased in year B to $11,937,725 and a net loss of $72,030 was assumed. In year A, the volume reached a high point of $15,762,193, and net profits advanced to the phenomenal amount of $1,308,467. The entire net profits for this year were retained in the business.

Between year C and year B, the net working capital shrank from $4,361,774 to $4,014,456 as a result of (1) the net loss of $72,030 for that year, (2) the increase in prepaid expenses in the assets from $118,900 to $207,560, and (3) the redemption of $187,200 of the 5 per cent debentures. In year A the trend was reversed; the net working capital jumped to $5,032,141 as a result of the substantial amount of retained net profits for the year. The tangible net worth on each balance sheet consisted of the sum of the outstanding common stock, the capital surplus, and the retained earnings, less $2. The $2 represented the value at which the two

POWER BOILER CORPORATION [Schedule 22]
Comparative Figures for Years Ended December 31, 19—

	(C) Three Years Ago	(B) Two Years Ago	(A) One Year Ago
ASSETS			
Cash......................	$ 1,272,364	$ 1,167,605	$ 1,069,839
Notes Receivable...........	209,143	352,346	800,526
Accounts Receivable........	2,030,133	2,123,352	4,200,432
Inventory.................	2,390,849	3,088,659	4,645,802
Marketable Securities.......	....	....	23,158
Current Assets..............	$ 5,902,489	$ 6,731,962	$10,739,757
Property, Plant & Equipment	3,511,392	3,508,091	3,619,284
Miscellaneous Receivables....	16,931	19,660	11,612
Prepaid Expenses..........	118,900	207,560	207,997
Patents...................	1	1	1
Trade marks...............	1	1	1
TOTAL.................	$ 9,549,714	$10,467,275	$14,578,652
LIABILITIES			
Notes Payable to Banks.....	$ 188,000	$ 1,186,000	$ 2,447,000
Advance Pay. on Contracts..	229,899	298,912	104,951
Accounts Payable...........	496,505	570,572	1,239,144
Accruals..................	262,672	430,842	591,877
Reserves for Taxes.........	176,439	43,980	1,137,444
Cur. Maturity of Debentures.	187,200	187,200	187,200
Current Liabilities...........	$ 1,540,715	$ 2,717,506	$ 5,707,616
First Mortgage 4% Bonds...	2,000,000	2,000,000	2,000,000
5% Debentures.............	3,256,800	3,069,600	2,882,400
Minority Interest..........	89,501	89,501	89,501
Total Liabilities............	$ 6,887,016	$ 7,876,607	$10,679,517
Common Stock.............	154,830	154,830	154,830
Capital Surplus............	2,000,000	2,000,000	2,000,000
Retained Earnings..........	507,868	435,838	1,744,305
TOTAL.................	$ 9,549,714	$10,467,275	$14,578,652
Net Working Capital........	$ 4,361,774	$ 4,014,456	$ 5,032,141
Current Ratio..............	3.83	2.48	1.88
Tangible Net Worth..........	$ 2,662,696	$ 2,590,666	$ 3,899,133
Net Sales.................	$13,683,013	$11,937,725	$15,762,193
Net Profit................	694,048	(L)72,030	1,308,467
Dividends.................	309,660	None	None

items, one of *Patents* and the other of *Trademarks*, were carried in the assets of each of the three balance sheets.

The comparative figures represent the consolidated financial condition of the Power Boiler Corporation and its four subsidiaries. Three of the subsidiaries are wholly owned, while in the fourth 70 per cent of the capital stock is owned. The 30 per cent interest in this subsidiary owned by others is carried as the item minority interest at $89,501 on each of the three comparative balance sheets. This particular subsidiary has been virtually inactive for 5 years.

The first mortgage bonds and the 5 per cent debentures issued at the time of reorganization are carried in the comparative figures as deferred liabilities. The first mortgage bonds amounting to $2,000,000 bear 4 per cent interest and mature 25 years after issuance. No change took place in this liability over the 3 years covered by the comparative figures. The debentures bear 5 per cent interest and mature at the rate of $187,200 annually, and so that amount must be carried each year as a current liability while the deferred portion of the debentures decreases by the same amount simultaneously. Now, let us look at the relationship of the total debt to the tangible net worth on the successive statement dates:

	Year C	Year B	Year A
Current Liabilities	$1,540,715	$2,717,506	$ 5,707,616
First Mortgage 4% Bonds	2,000,000	2,000,000	2,000,000
5% Debentures	3,256,800	3,069,600	2,882,400
Total Liabilities	$6,797,515	$7,787,106	$10,590,016
Tangible Net Worth	2,662,696	2,590,666	3,899,133
Ratio of Total Liabilities to Tangible Net Worth	255.3%	300.6%	271.6%

The total liabilities for each of the 3 years in the above schedule are $89,501 smaller than the total liabilities for each year as shown in the comparative balance sheet figures on page 247. This difference is due to the fact that the *Minority Interest*, which is carried at $89,501, is a technical "accounting" liability in the balance sheets but not an actual liability that must be paid.

In the case of the Electrical Specialty Corporation we found a steady increase in the total liabilities with, at the same time, a steady decrease in the tangible net worth in the three comparative balance sheets. With the Power Boiler Corporation we also find a steady increase in the total liabilities, but with the difference that here we have some fluctuation with an upward trend—not a steady decrease—in the tangible net worth over the 3-year period, a somewhat more favorable sign.

Each year the current liabilities expanded very substantially. In year C the current debt amounted to $1,540,715. Two years later in year A, the current liabilities were more than three times as large, amounting to the impressive sum of $5,707,616. The first mortgage bonds remained unchanged, and a relatively nominal yearly reduction of $187,200 took place in the 5 per cent debentures. The net result was an increase in the total debt from $6,797,515 to $10,590,016, or 55.8 per cent. During the same period of time the tangible net worth expanded from $2,662,696 to $3,899,133, or 46.4 per cent, out of retained earnings.

The ratio of total liabilities to tangible net worth was 255.3 per cent for year C, 300.6 per cent for year B, and then dropped to 271.6 per cent for year A. These relationships are too heavy, far too heavy for a healthy financial condition. At the end of year A, outside creditors had $2\frac{3}{4}$ times as much money at stake in this corporation as the stockholders, which represented a very unbalanced financial condition.

Condensed Analysis. Many reorganizations like this one, or the Chicago, Milwaukee, and St. Paul Railway Company in 1925, which was the greatest receivership at that time in the up-and-down economic history of our country, are made on an unsound basis. The new corporation is too often saddled with a tremendous debt and everyone concerned hopes for the best, but hopes have never yet placed a business enterprise in a sound financial condition. It takes sound managerial guidance. The balance sheet of year C of the Power Boiler Corporation typifies this exact condition. The fixed assets at net depreciated value of $3,511,392 were appreciably in excess of the tangible net worth of $2,662,696. To make up this difference of $848,696 and to provide net working capital without which no commercial or industrial concern can operate for any reasonable length of time, the funded debt consisting of first mortgage bonds and 5 per cent debentures was created.

The figures for year B gave little prospect that the reorganized business would work out. The corporation was saddled with interest on its funded debts in excess of $250,000, which had to be met along with all operating expenses before a profit could be earned. Both the tangible net worth and the net working capital were reduced because of the unprofitable operations. At the same time, the total debt had increased. Here were two most unfavorable trends, reflected in the ratio of total liabilities to tangible net worth, which ballooned from 255.3 to 300.6 per cent.

The figures of year A showed a different story as a result of the handsome profits of $1,308,467 which were earned and retained in the business. This enterprise, under resourceful management, has a chance to work out if a very unbalanced condition is overcome. On the other hand, it would not be unexpected if affairs went from bad to worse. Because of the complete lack of any liquid reserves, affairs will fluctuate upward and downward from year to year, depending upon operating results, until such a time, if ever, as affairs are put into a balanced condition. Competitively, the concern is operating at a handicap with depreciation charges and interest on borrowed funds both far heavier than similar expenses of competitors. This situation is epitomized in the relationship of the total liabilities to the tangible net worth. The normal condition would be for the total debt to approximate, as a maximum, the tangible net worth. The relationship in this case in year A is just about $2\frac{3}{4}$ times as high, and so correspondingly unfavorable.

TYPICAL RATIOS OF TOTAL LIABILITIES
TO TANGIBLE NET WORTH

In credit practice a liability, provided it matures more than 1 year after the statement date, is posted as a deferred debt, that is, it is omitted from the total which comprises the current liabilities. A number of bonds issued, in particular of railroads, have remote liquidation dates. Most funded obligations, however, are due from 5 to 30 years after issuance and many have serial maturities due from year to year. *from the balance sheet data*

The fact that a funded debt must mature more than 1 year ~~in the future~~ to be classified as a deferred liability has become ~~widely known~~ in financial ~~and business~~ circles. As a result, the analyst occasionally will run across a situation where a funded debt matures 1 year and 1 day from the statement date. Obviously this technique is a subterfuge used by the management to exceed the "1-year" period; under these circumstances the entire amount should be classified as a current liability.

In many instances, mortgages are not paid off when they mature but are carried "open." Payment of such a mortgage may be demanded by the mortgagee on any interest date. It is a rare occurrence when such a demand is made if taxes, insurance, upkeep, and interest are taken care of promptly. The fact that such a contingency may occur, however, does make it necessary that the entire amount be carried in the current liabilities when figures are posted on a comparative statement blank. If an investigation indicates that no demand for payment will probably be made, the analysis of the figures should, of course, be made on the basis that the mortgage, to all intents and purposes, is really a deferred liability.

Schedule 23 contains the typical ratios of total liabilities to tangible net worth for 42 lines of manufacturing, 21 of wholesaling, and 7 of retailing. This particular ratio could be determined only for those lines of business and for those years in which a reasonable number of concerns had outstanding deferred liabilities. ~~For certain of these lines of industrial and commercial activity, this ratio is available for the entire 5-year spread which has been used in earlier chapters, and for other lines for only some of these years.~~

Of the 42 divisions of manufacturing activity for which average ratios of total liabilities to tangible net worth over a spread of years have been

RATIOS OF TOTAL LIABILITIES TO TANGIBLE NET WORTH   [Schedule 23]

Line of Business Activity	Percentage					
	Median					Five-year Average
	1955	1956	1957	1958	1959	
MANUFACTURERS						
Agricultural Implements and Machinery	50.4	44.4	78.0	58.2	59.0	58.0
Airplane Parts and Accessories	81.0	160.2	95.5	105.0	68.0	101.9
Automobile Parts and Accessories	62.0	52.5	52.5	45.8	56.3	53.8
Bakers	45.9	55.4	48.9	47.0	39.9	47.4
Bedsprings and Mattresses	50.2	56.0	47.6	54.3	62.2	54.1
Bodies, Auto, Bus, and Truck	79.7	74.2	79.3	54.6	88.9	75.3
Bolts, Screws, Nuts, and Nails	62.2	48.0	79.6	48.5	52.2	58.1
Breweries	40.9	32.0	33.4	37.5	48.1	38.4
Chemicals, Industrial	65.2	66.9	53.6	59.0	65.2	62.0
Coats and Suits, Men's and Boys'	123.8	123.9	108.0	84.9	134.4	115.0
Coats and Suits, Women's	95.0	121.3	114.7	130.9	141.2	120.6
Confectionery	49.8	55.5	52.9	48.5	42.8	49.9
Contractors, Building Construction	106.3	132.3	148.4	82.9	120.0	118.0
Contractors, Electrical	79.6	77.3	116.3	68.4	114.1	91.1
Cotton Cloth Mills	59.2	36.6	39.7	35.0	45.6	43.2
Cotton Goods, Converters, Non-factored	.....	118.4	.....	135.9	108.3	120.9
Dresses, Rayon, Silk, and Acetate	157.7	.....	144.6	112.2	97.3	128.0
Drugs	59.4	56.6	52.7	51.7	55.9	55.3
Electrical Parts and Supplies	66.4	69.7	62.7	65.0	68.3	66.4
Foundries	51.9	55.4	47.3	40.6	56.5	50.3
Fruits and Vegetables, Canners	111.7	77.5	73.4	125.3	93.9	96.4
Furniture	57.7	68.8	59.7	54.8	66.8	61.6
Hardware and Tools	46.9	46.0	43.5	52.0	44.6	46.6
Hosiery	49.7	53.9	52.2	92.4	53.4	60.3
Lumber	39.1	48.5	49.5	56.4	59.7	50.6
Machine Shops	65.4	64.1	49.8	33.8	60.4	54.7
Machinery, Industrial	65.5	68.5	60.3	49.3	54.9	59.7
Meats and Provisions, Packers	70.9	65.7	66.7	71.7	73.7	69.7
Metal Stampings	63.7	68.3	54.5	59.1	66.5	62.4
Outerwear, Knitted	78.6	80.8	86.7	82.7	76.4	81.0
Overalls and Work Clothing	79.6	63.0	86.0	73.0	92.6	78.8
Paints, Varnishes, and Lacquers	49.3	46.1	44.0	47.3	43.9	46.1
Paper	51.2	48.4	35.6	46.8	41.1	44.6
Paper Boxes	55.1	63.5	62.8	48.0	60.7	58.0
Petroleum, Integrated Corporations	45.0	50.7	51.5	47.1	50.2	48.9
Printers, Job	55.3	58.8	41.9	45.3	62.8	52.8
Radio Parts and Supplies	96.9	98.7	74.8	74.0	70.9	83.1
Shirts, Underwear, and Pajamas, Men's	82.4	80.5	81.3	105.6	113.5	92.7
Shoes, Men's, Women's, and Children's	73.7	68.6	74.0	65.5	84.9	73.3
Soft Drinks and Carbonated Water, Bottlers	43.8	59.8	68.6	66.1	62.2	60.1
Steel, Structural Fabricators (Sell on Short Terms)	77.4	86.5	82.1	64.3	25.9	67.2
Stoves, Ranges, and Ovens	51.4	63.6	56.7	42.4	67.7	56.4

RATIOS OF TOTAL LIABILITIES TO TANGIBLE NET WORTH (*Continued*)

[Schedule 23 (*Cont.*)]

Line of Business Activity	Percentage					
	Median					Five-year Average
	1955	1956	1957	1958	1959	
WHOLESALERS						
Automobile Parts and Accessories....	58.2	73.3	64.9	66.4	76.3	67.8
Baked Goods....................	54.4	59.5	57.9	54.6	48.0	54.9
Cigars, Cigarettes, and Tobacco......	115.2	108.9	77.5	102.6	103.1	101.5
Drugs and Drug Sundries..........	71.5	93.7	79.5	64.9	70.7	76.1
Dry Goods......................	64.5	70.3	61.8	65.8	59.8	64.4
Electrical Parts and Supplies........	87.0	105.4	66.6	87.0	82.5	85.7
Fruits and Produce, Fresh..........	53.7	84.4	122.5	89.3	119.3	93.8
Furnishings, Men's................	42.7	72.4	74.1	79.6	65.1	66.8
Gasoline, Fuel Oil, and Lubricating Oil	110.6	126.5	71.2	67.5	74.9	90.1
Groceries......................	85.5	93.6	88.1	90.5	96.0	90.7
Hardware....	61.0	61.5	54.2	66.0	74.0	63.3
Hosiery and Underwear.............	.....	56.0	.....	88.4	78.6	74.3
Household Appliances, Electrical.....	133.0	127.9	103.9	117.3	134.2	123.3
Lumber........................	86.1	77.9	91.5	72.3	74.3	80.4
Lumber and Building Materials......	66.6	51.6	63.1	66.5	80.3	65.6
Meat and Poultry...	53.9	78.7	58.1	78.6	100.3	73.9
Paints, Varnishes, and Lacquers......	60.0	59.1	45.3	61.9	73.0	59.9
Paper..........................	88.5	93.6	68.6	72.0	86.0	81.7
Plumbing and Heating Supplies......	68.1	74.8	59.2	66.7	75.5	68.9
Shoes, Men's, Women's, and Children's......................	92.4	82.7	101.8	110.6	107.6	99.0
Wines and Liquors...	118.9	95.2	130.9	121.2	129.3	119.1
RETAILERS						
Clothing, Men's and Boys'..........	67.6	89.6	98.9	94.0	96.9	89.4
Department Stores................	61.1	59.7	61.5	60.7	57.1	60.0
Furniture, 50 Per Cent or More Installment........................	70.0	83.9	81.9	83.6	85.4	81.0
Groceries and Meats, Independent...	97.8	81.8	96.8	89.4	91.8	91.5
Lumber and Building Materials......	70.9	62.9	71.7	58.7	54.3	63.7
Shoes..........................	74.8	54.1	66.1	55.5	63.6	62.8
Women's Specialty Shops...........	79.1	87.7	85.6	95.8	98.1	89.3

determined, the highest ratio is shown by manufacturers of rayon, silk, and acetate dresses with 128.0 per cent, followed by non-factored cotton goods converters with 120.9 per cent, and manufacturers of women's coats and suits with 120.6 per cent. Wholesalers of electrical household appliances top the wholesale trades with a 5-year average of 123.3, followed by wholesalers of wines and liquors with 119.1 per cent, and wholesalers of cigars, cigarettes, and tobacco with 101.5 per cent. Independent grocery

[handwritten marginalia: "per cent", "and contractors of building construction with 140.6 per cent", "5-year average", "179.7", "150.5", "124.0", "116.4", "Discount stores", "cigars, cigarettes and tobacco", "wholesalers of household electrical appliances"]

and meat stores have the highest 5-year average among the retail lines with 91.5 per cent, followed by men's and boys' clothing stores with 89.4 per cent. Breweries have the lowest ratio of total liabilities to tangible net worth with a 5-year average of 38.4 per cent, followed by cotton cloth mills with 43.2 per cent and manufacturers of paints, varnishes, and lacquer with 46.1 per cent. Of the 70 lines in Schedule 23, 9 have an average relationship between these two balance sheet items over the spread of years in excess of 100 per cent and 28 in excess of 75 per cent.

Maxim

From the figures in the preceding paragraph it is obvious that a ratio of total liabilities to tangible net worth in excess of 100.0 per cent is unusual. Rarely, if ever, should total liabilities of a commercial or industrial concern exceed the tangible net worth, as in such cases creditors have more at stake in a business enterprise than the stockholders or the owners. The handicap of interest charges, especially where competitors have no such expenses, may become a critical burden. Where liabilities are in excess of tangible net worth, the management is proportionately handicapped.

This maxim is a corollary to the one in the preceding chapter regarding the relationship between current liabilities and tangible net worth. If a commercial or industrial business enterprise has deferred liabilities, the total liabilities that may practically be carried may be moderately greater in the same line of business than another concern with only current liabilities, as the management has a longer period in which to make plans to meet or to solve its financial problems.

THEORY AND PROBLEMS

1. Give your interpretation of the term *total liabilities* as applied to a balance sheet. After you have given your interpretation, state for each of the following items whether it would or would not be included in the computation of total liabilities:

    a. Minority interest
    b. Purchase money mortgage
    c. Accrued wages
    d. Unearned income
    e. Depreciation on fixed assets
    f. Notes payable to bank
    g. Surplus

2. Define (a) bottomry and (b) respondentia.

3. Describe briefly the highlights in the evolution of long-term obligations from colonial days to recent times.

4. Would the following ratios of total liabilities to tangible net worth for the lines of business indicated be high, medium, or low?

    a. Manufacturer of industrial chemicals.............. 42.3
    b. Electrical contractor........................... 72.5
    c. Manufacturer of knitted outerwear.............. 113.8
    d. Wholesaler of men's furnishings................. 36.3
    e. Department store............................ 147.6

5. The Oil Refining Corporation has been engaged in manufacturing lubricants and greases for 18 years. From the following comparative figures compute the ratio of total liabilities to tangible net worth and give your interpretation of this ratio for each year.

OIL REFINING CORPORATION
Comparative Figures for Years Ended April 30, 19—

	(C) Three Years Ago	(B) Two Years Age	(A) One Year Ago
ASSETS			
Cash.........................	$ 16,972	$ 11,588	$ 244,873
Accounts Receivable............	190,824	130,202	124,286
Inventories...................	127,203	138,344	36,876
Marketable Securities..........	120,750	....	....
Current Assets................	$ 455,749	$ 280,134	$ 406,035
Plants Property Account, Net...	556,083	421,248	497,668
Investments...................	....	300	300
Prepaid and Deferred..........	11,455	13,272	12,825
TOTAL...................	$1,023,287	$ 714,954	$ 916,828
LIABILITIES			
Notes Payable, Bank..........	$ 108,725	$ 33,366	$........
Notes Payable, Other..........	76,002	20,697	....
Long-term Notes, Current.......	....	12,500	49,000
Accounts Payable.............	90,302	71,322	68,756
Accruals.....................	....	....	5,384
Reserves for Fire Loss Replace- ment........................	....	....	222,404
Reserve for Contingency.......	15,000	15,000	15,000
Current Liabilities............	$ 290,029	$ 152,885	$ 360,544
Long-term Notes..............	133,000	112,500	106,450
Total Liabilities...............	$ 423,029	$ 265,385	$ 466,994
Common Stock, Class A........	870,000	870,000	870,000
Surplus.....................	(D)269,742	(D)420,431	(D)420,166
TOTAL...................	$1,023,287	$ 714,954	$ 916,828
Net Working Capital...........	$ 165,720	$ 127,249	$ 45,491
Current Ratio................	1.56	1.86	1.07
Tangible Net Worth...........	$ 600,258	$ 449,569	$ 449,834
Net Sales....................	$1,138,751	$1,137,357	$1,123,903

6. The Building Products Corporation is engaged in manufacturing and selling various kinds and types of building products used in construction and in the fabrication of many allied products. Post the following balance sheet on a columnar sheet of paper. In this process compute accurately (*a*) the current assets, (*b*) the current liabilities, (*c*) the net working capital, (*d*) the current ratio, (*e*) the tangible net worth, (*f*) the ratio of current liabilities to tangible net worth, and (*g*) the ratio of total liabilities to tangible net worth. Then give your interpretations of the ratios that you obtain in your computation of current liabilities to tangible net worth, and total liabilities to tangible net worth.

BUILDING PRODUCTS CORPORATION
Balance Sheet, December 31, 19—
ASSETS

Current Assets

Cash in banks and on hand...........................		$	920,248
Notes and accounts receivable			
Notes receivable—customers.......................	$	169,459	
Accounts receivable—customers....................		1,931,459	
Other notes and accounts receivable...............		136,258	
Salesmen's traveling advances and employees' accounts		22,116	
		$2,259,292	
Less: Reserves for bad debts and allowances.........		163,118	
			2,096,174
Advances (secured) and charges in respect to merchandise received on consignment for resale.................			155,928
Raw materials, products and supplies—at lower of cost or market...			1,778,828
Total Current Assets..........................			$ 4,951,178
Investment in Subsidiary.............................			
Class A and Class B preferred and common stock—at cost (no quoted market value available; equity based on balance sheet at Dec. 31, 19—).................			3,336,805
Miscellaneous Investments, less reserve................			26,672
Statutory Deposits (cash and securities at cost) with state and provincial authorities...........................			50,090
Prepaid Expenses and Deferred Charges...............			202,695
Property, Plant and Equipment			
Operating plants and facilities:			
Land...	$	818,869	
Buildings, machinery, and operating equipment—at cost, less reserve for depreciation ($8,104,590.44)...		5,921,834	
Nonoperating plants and abandoned departments			
Land...		431,864	
Buildings, machinery and equipment—at cost or written down value, less reserve for depreciation ($140,907.80).................................		130,518	
Gypsum deposits—as appraised, less reserve for depletion ($106,906.71)...............................		3,489,088	
Timber concessions—at cost, less reserve for depletion ($173,585.37)...................................		879,770	
Water-power rights................................		1	
			11,671,944
Good will, Trade marks, and Other Intangibles..........			1
			$20,269,385

BUILDING PRODUCTS CORPORATION (*Continued*)
LIABILITIES

Current Liabilities

Accounts payable and accrued expenses..............	$	666,229
Interest accrued on funded debt......................		167,125
Taxes due and accrued...............................		122,023
Provision for income and capital stock taxes..........		51,601
Total Current Liabilities.......................	$	996,978
Reserve for Contingencies............................		25,011

Funded Debt

20-year 4½% sinking fund debentures due in 10 years (sinking fund requirements $200,000 principal amount semiannually have been satisfied to and including next year)......................................	$9,100,000	
Purchase money mortgage bonds 4½%, due in 2 years .	19,500	
		9,119,500

Capital Stock

5% cumulative prior preference stock Authorized, 186,996 shares of $100 each Outstanding, 73,069.3 shares......................	$7,306,930	
Common Authorized, 1,000,000 shares of $1 each Outstanding, 625,340 shares......................	625,340	
		7,932,270

Surplus

Capital Surplus.............................	$2,477,406	
Less: Deficiency on earned surplus...................	*281,780*	
		2,195,626
		$20,269,385

7. From the point of view of creditors, can a business enterprise carry somewhat heavier liabilities if part of those liabilities represent some form of funded debt, than if all liabilities are current? Explain your answer.

8. In a highly competitive business world, why does a substantial funded debt represent a competitive handicap?

9. Discuss the complementary character of the following three ratios, pointing out the lack of effectiveness in obtaining the complete picture in particular situations by the use of only one of these ratios: (*a*) current assets to current liabilities, (*b*) current liabilities to tangible net worth, and (*c*) total liabilities to tangible net worth.

10. What maxim regarding total liabilities is to be followed generally in analyzing the affairs of commercial and industrial concerns?

CHAPTER IX

Funded Debt to Net Working Capital

As explained in the previous chapter, for the purposes of analysis a funded debt comprises all debts the maturities of which are more than 1 year distant from the date of the balance sheet. An open mortgage with no maturity is a current liability. A funded debt is also popularly termed a deferred or long-term liability.

A promissory note running for 2 years would be a funded debt during the first year and a current liability during the second year. Probably the most common form of funded debt is the mortgage on land and buildings, a form of long-term liability used by individuals and small business enterprises as well as by large corporations. Technically, the instrument is more properly called a bond and mortgage, the bond being the promise to pay and the mortgage being the security for the funds borrowed.

Most funded obligations of large business enterprises are known as corporation bonds. They are of wide and infinite varieties. Corporation bonds are instruments promising to pay a stipulated sum of money at a definite future time. They are essentially long-term promissory notes. In the eyes of the law, a bond is a contract setting forth the terms and the conditions under which an obligation is assumed. Corporation bonds generally are transferable although it is not unusual for registration to be necessary to prove ownership. Moreover, a corporation bond, in contrast to a real estate mortgage, is usually divisible into small parts.

IMPORTANT FEATURES OF LONG-TERM SECURITIES

Funded or long-term liabilities are classified according to underlying security as unsecured, first mortgage, second mortgage, third mortgage, general mortgage, guaranteed, collateral trust, debenture, income, land grant, prior lien, convertible, and subordinated. They are also classified according to the payment of interest as unconditional, registered, registered coupon, participating, and income.[1]

[1] For a comprehensive and interesting list of long-term securities with features which depart from the generally accepted pattern, such as modifications of the unqualified right to a fixed interest payment on fixed dates, modification of the unqualified right

It is extremely important for the analyst to ascertain what security, if any, is pledged to secure a long-term liability. The pledge of any assets, in case of financial difficulty, means that certain creditors have prior claims over others, and the understanding of these various claims, before an involved situation arises, is the basis of many analyses. Often the land and buildings are so pledged as underlying security. Of less frequency, all or part of the current assets are also pledged; unfortunately, this information does not always appear in the balance sheet, in a footnote, or, in audited figures, in the certificate. It can always be secured by a study of the indenture. The pledge of current assets to secure long-term creditors is of particularly vital interest to current creditors, who must look primarily to the current assets for repayment.

Indentures covering many long-term issues of commercial and industrial corporations also contain supplementary provisions to the effect that the debtor must maintain a certain minimum ratio of current assets to current liabilities, a certain minimum ratio of total liabilities to net worth, or a certain minimum ratio of funded debt to net working capital. Where any such provision is included, the indenture also contains very carefully worded definitions for computing the current assets, the current liabilities, the total liabilities, or the net worth.

In case any provision in an indenture is broken, intentionally or unintentionally, then the trustees of the funded debt may take appropriate action to protect the interests of the owners of the obligations. In years gone by such action was rarely taken except at the request of holders of a certain percentage of the issue, but under the sponsorship of the Securities and Exchange Commission, there has developed an attitude that trustees may well be held responsible if they fail to take appropriate action to protect the interests of the owners of such securities. The existence of these provisions has a distinct bearing on the analysis of the figures of a particular business where a receiver might suddenly be appointed to protect the interests of all creditors. The majority of funded obligations also contain provisions which accelerate the maturity, after proper legal action, if interest, indenture provisions, sometimes a serial maturity, or a sinking fund provision is in default.

Most long-term securities of commercial and industrial business enterprises have a life ranging from 5 to 25 years, and many issues are reduced by yearly serial maturities. If operations are sufficiently profitable and all or the greater part of the profits are kept in current assets, serial maturities are met from year to year without difficulty. When, however, sub-

---

to repayment of a fixed principal amount on a fixed date, participating and convertible issues, long-term securities with stock purchase warrants, and issues with a voice in the management, see Benjamin Graham and David L. Dodd, *Security Analysis*, 1st ed., pp. 619–626 (McGraw-Hill Book Company, Inc., New York, 1934).

stantial losses are assumed or net profits are reinvested in fixed or miscellaneous assets, the ability to meet serial maturities tends to become more and more strained. When the balance of a serial issue, or the entire principal of a funded debt, falls due after several years of unprofitable operations, the problems of meeting, extending, or renewing the obligation are sufficient to test the ingenuity of any management.

Railroads and public utilities have outstanding issues of funded obligations that are far longer than any issue of commercial and industrial corporations. The West Shore Railroad Co., for example, authorized an issue of $50,000,000 four per cent first mortgage bonds in 1886, due 475 years later, in the year 2361. On December 31, 1959, $43,647,500 of this issue was in the hands of the public. The Elmira & Williamsport Railroad Company authorized an issue of $570,000 five per cent income bonds in 1863 due 999 years later, in the year 2862. On December 31, 1959, $550,000 of this issue, the interest of which in the meantime had been guaranteed by the Pennsylvania Railroad Company, was outstanding.

Even these rather distant maturities are exceeded by an outstanding issue of 4 per cent consolidated debentures authorized by an act of the Canadian Parliament passed in 1899 and subsequent acts in the name of the Canadian Pacific Railway Company which are perpetual and noncallable. The total authorized amount of this perpetual issue is $471,171,-229; of this amount $292,558,888 was in the hands of the public on December 31, 1959, and $158,171,700 was pledged to secure other issues.

ILLUSTRATIONS AND RELATIONSHIPS

Occasional issues of funded debt are convertible into preferred or common stocks at certain rates of conversion for definite periods of time, a feature which may turn a debt into capital under the right price relationship of the particular securities and so create a stronger corporate financial structure. Other issues occasionally are sold with stock purchase warrants attached, a feature which under the right price relationship with the stock would not convert the debt into stock, but would provide additional capital funds.

The study of these features, along with explicit information regarding various assets pledged as security to a particular issue of funded securities and full information regarding restrictive provisions in the indenture and serial maturities, if any, are pertinent features[2] in the analysis of a balance

[2] See GUTHMANN, HARRY G., and HERBERT E. DOUGALL, *Corporate Financial Policy*, 3d ed., pp. 98–158 (Prentice-Hall, Inc., Englewood Cliffs, N.J., 1956); HOAGLAND, HENRY E., *Corporation Finance*, 3d ed., pp. 169–219 (McGraw-Hill Book Company, Inc., New York, 1947); DEWING, ARTHUR STONE, *The Financial Policy of Corporations*, 3d rev. ed., pp. 68–124 (The Ronald Press Company, New York, 1934).

sheet. Situations of this nature will not arise in the cases to be considered in this chapter; they exist only with the larger issues of securities which have been distributed to the public or have been acquired by one or more life insurance companies or pension trusts. For every issue of this nature, the analyst will run across 100 situations where a simple real estate mortgage will be the only funded debt in the balance sheet.

Manufacturer of Kitchen Equipment

The Kitchen Equipment Manufacturing Corporation is engaged in manufacturing ranges, ovens, and cooking apparatus. For its type of business it is a relatively small enterprise. Sales are made to institutions, colleges, hospitals, clubs, steamship companies, and various divisions of the Federal armed services, generally on open account terms of 30 days net.

The business was established in 1871. Over the years, substantial net profits were realized and the tangible net worth was increased by the reinvestment of a representative part of the earnings. Several years ago the tangible net worth decreased from $205,671 to the $50,021 reflected in the balance sheet of year C. During these difficult years, several of the officers died, some dividends were paid, and other concerns in the same industry developed competitive lines of merchandise which seemed more adapted to the changing needs of the times. By year A, the new young management had brought about some change. The comparative financial condition for the last 3 years is shown in Schedule 24.

For year C a net loss of $1,396 was sustained. For year B the loss had decreased nominally to $1,090. For year A a remarkable change took place. Net sales increased from $168,167 in year B to $274,346 in year A, bringing about surprising net profits of $18,270, of which $15,270 was retained in the business and $3,000 was paid out in dividends. In the latter part of year B a contract for $150,000 of equipment had been obtained from the Defense Department. This contract was completed in year A and was the basic reason for the successful operations.

The figures disclosed current liabilities at the end of year C of $19,104 and at the end of year B of $16,417. Current liabilities of these amounts were moderate compared with the current assets and as a result the current ratio was quite satisfactory for both years. The current debt was also in satisfactory relationship with the tangible net worth; in year C the current liabilities amounted to 38.2 per cent of the tangible net worth, and in year B to 33.5 per cent.

In addition to the current liabilities, however, a mortgage debt of $58,200 in year C, and of $56,400 in year B, appeared in the figures. Of the funded debt $1,200 was due and payable yearly, and that sum accordingly was included in the current liabilities. Between these 2 years $1,800

KITCHEN EQUIPMENT MANUFACTURING CORPORATION   [Schedule 24]
Comparative Figures for Years Ended December 31, 19—

	(C) Three Years Ago	(B) Two Years Ago	(A) One Year Ago
ASSETS			
Cash..............................	$ 6,813	$ 6,374	$ 5,914
Notes Receivable....................	1,242	2,110	821
Accounts Receivable.................	18,309	17,111	65,113
Inventory..........................	13,609	13,949	27,178
Current Assets......................	$ 39,973	$ 39,544	$ 99,026
Plant and Equipment, Net............	81,820	75,838	71,582
Cash Value of Life Insurance..........	3,802	4,334	4,618
Prepaid Expense....................	1,730	2,032	1,670
TOTAL......................	$127,325	$121,748	$176,896
LIABILITIES			
Notes Payable for Merchandise........	$ 4,270	$ 2,277	$ 8,101
Accounts Payable...................	8,704	7,974	44,083
Accruals including Taxes.............	2,855	2,891	4,111
Mortgage Payable, Current...........	1,200	1,200	1,200
Rent Payable.......................	2,075	2,075	....
Current Liabilities...................	$ 19,104	$ 16,417	$ 57,495
First Mortgage.....................	58,200	56,400	55,200
Total Liabilities.....................	$ 77,304	$ 72,817	$112,695
Common Stock.....................	58,820	58,820	58,820
Retained Earnings..................	(D)8,799	(D)9,889	5,381
TOTAL........................	$127,325	$121,748	$176,896
Net Working Capital..................	$ 20,869	$ 23,127	$ 41,531
Current Ratio.......................	2.09	2.41	1.72
Tangible Net Worth..................	$ 50,021	$ 48,931	$ 64,201
Net Sales..........................	$176,515	$168,167	$274,346
Net Profit.........................	(L)1,396	(L)1,090	18,270
Dividends.........................	None	None	3,000

was actually retired. In year *A*, this long-term debt was reduced by the customary $1,200. The deferred debt was very heavy for both of these years. The 3-year comparison of the first mortgage debt with the net working capital appears as follows:

	Year C	Year B	Year A
First Mortgage Debt........................	$58,200	$56,400	$55,200
Net Working Capital........................	20,869	23,127	41,531
Ratio of Funded Debt to Net Working Capital...	278.4%	243.8%	132.9%

In year *C*, comparison of the deferred portion of the first mortgage debt to the net working capital of $20,869 was materially out of line, the funded debt being 278.4 per cent of the net working capital. Obviously, if the Kitchen Equipment Manufacturing Corporation had been unable to obtain a mortgage loan during the immediately preceding difficult years, the net working capital would have disappeared and the business would have faded from the industrial picture.

By the end of year B, the mortgage debt had been decreased by the stipulated yearly payment of $1,200 and an additional $600, reducing the deferred portion of the funded debt to $56,400. At the same time the net working capital increased moderately from $20,869 to $23,127, notwithstanding the net loss for the year, by the earned depreciation which reduced the net valuation of the plant and equipment from $81,820 to $75,838. The trend of these two items reduced the ratio of the funded debt to the net working capital from 278.4 per cent to 243.8 per cent.

In year A, great improvement took place. The funded debt was reduced by the annual installment of $1,200 while the net working capital expanded from $23,127 to $41,531 as a result of the earnings of $15,270 retained in current assets and the earned depreciation for the year. The ratio of the two critical items now dropped to 132.9 per cent and, although still heavy, was finally on the way to make a fairly respectable comparison.

Condensed Analysis. This concern had run into a difficult period of several years when three officers had died and the management had devolved on inexperienced young men who had failed to realize the necessity of constant research to keep its products competitively attractive. Losses were assumed on operations year after year. During the first 2 years of these losses, the seriousness of the situation had not been realized and $16,000 had also been paid out in dividends. These payments naturally aggravated the downward trend of the business. The losses for these 2 years alone, together with the dividends, resulted in a shrinkage of $28,000 in the tangible net worth.

At this stage in the life history of the corporation, the directors decided that no more dividends would be paid until operations were on a profitable basis. The management took hold in the traditional manner by reducing wages, cutting salaries, and keeping expenses down in every possible manner. This program meant almost the complete elimination of the research so essential in any progressive manufacturing business. Operations continued on an unprofitable basis and in year F the concern was unable to meet its merchandise invoices, as the net working capital had been almost eliminated. In this situation a first mortgage loan of $61,800 was obtained from a life insurance company on the real estate, plant, and equipment, repayable $1,200 each year for 10 years and the balance at maturity. The mortgage loan was granted by the insurance company, not on the financial responsibility of the corporation, but on the security of the real estate, plant, and fixtures, as the real estate was centrally located and would amply protect the lender if it became necessary to foreclose on the property.

With these funds the net working capital of the Kitchen Equipment Manufacturing Corporation was temporarily rehabilitated, but by year C affairs had drifted into an even more serious state. The net depreciated value of the fixed assets was carried at \$81,820, which was \$31,799 in excess of the tangible net worth, a relationship, described in Chap. X, which is very much out of line. The current liabilities of \$19,104 and the mortgage debt of \$58,200 amounted to total liabilities of \$77,304, which was 54.6 per cent in excess of the tangible net worth and, as explained in Chap. VIII, also very much out of line.

The outlook was dark and gloomy. Year B provided no encouragement; the downhill trend continued. Net sales amounted to \$168,167 and on this low volume was below the break-even point even on the reduced expenses. Current liabilities of \$16,417 appeared to be in a satisfactory relationship with the current assets and with the tangible net worth. But this was only part of the picture. Total liabilities amounted to \$72,817 and represented 148.8 per cent of the tangible net worth of \$48,931. The unbalancing features were heavy fixed assets, excessive total liabilities, and unprofitable operations on shrinking sales. In view of the low volume of business, it is obvious that current liabilities would not fluctuate greatly during these particular years as there would be no particular season of heightened activity.

Suddenly a substantial order was obtained from the Defense Department; net sales spurted to \$274,346 in year A and on this increased activity an exceptional profit was recorded. Fortunately all but \$3,000 of the earnings was retained in the business. It would have been sounder policy to have paid no dividends, to have kept even the \$3,000 in the business, or possibly to have used it to anticipate payments on the funded debt.

As a result of the increased net sales, the current liabilities increased between year B and year A from \$16,417 to \$57,495 to carry the increased receivables. An aging of these receivables indicated that they were in healthy shape, an indication which was confirmed by the fact that \$52,914 was collected during the first month following the date of the fiscal balance sheet of year A. The heavy current liabilities were thus in the nature of a seasonal liability, and as the peak of the season passed and the receivables were collected, the funds were used to reduce the current debt to a normal amount.

Over the years of the comparative figures, no funds were borrowed from any bank and a representative item appeared on each financial statement of *Notes Payable for Merchandise*. In the investigation it was learned that the depository bank considered the risk unsound on any basis and would grant no credit. To finance itself in the absence of bank credit, it had been necessary to purchase some merchandise on long terms of 4 to 6 months, and notes were accepted by certain friendly suppliers. Here was a further indication of the financial weakness.

At the end of year A, the figures presented a striking improvement compared with the condition at the end of the two preceding fiscal years. Much, however, still needed to be done to bring affairs into a really healthy shape. Not until the fixed assets represent no more than 50 per cent of the tangible net worth, the total liabilities no more than 100 per cent of the tangible net worth, and the funded debt no more than the net working capital, should the management cease to worry. The basic problem was one of obtaining an annual volume of business in excess of $225,000, as on sales of that amount profits could be earned and, if retained in the business, would continue to improve the internal financial structure.

Finisher of Piece Goods

In 1908 the Dye Works Company, Inc., was organized in New Jersey as a merger of two established corporations. Five other competitors were taken over from time to time until year H, when the corporation was operating on a paid-in capital of $7,500,000 six per cent cumulative preferred stock, par value of $100, and $1,125,000 common stock par value of $25. By year D, a tremendous deficit in the surplus account had been built up; to eliminate this deficit, the value at which the outstanding preferred stock was carried on the books was reduced from $7,500,000 to $1,000,000 and the par value changed from $100 per share to no par.

This business is fundamentally a service enterprise. Operations consist of dyeing, printing, finishing, and weighting silk, rayon, nylon, orlon, cotton, and mixed fabrics and yarns. In recent years approximately 75 per cent of the goods processed has consisted of mixed acetates, and the remainder, of silks with some cotton goods. Comparative figures which indicate that operations have been carried on under evident financial handicaps appear in Schedule 25.

No sales figures were available for any of these 3 years. Tremendous losses were incurred, ranging from $1,743,032 for year C to $540,045 in year A. As a result, the tangible net worth shows a steady reduction between year C and year A from $2,704,030 to $1,611,259, or 40.5 per cent. For each of the 8 years ending year A, moreover, a loss had been assumed. Aggregate losses for this decade amounted to somewhat over $7,000,000. Here is an outstanding example of unprofitable operations due to the single fact that the management signally had failed to keep up with the times.

In year E, the tangible net worth dropped below the net depreciated

Dye Works Company, Inc.   [Schedule 25]

Comparative Figures for Years Ending December 31, 19—

	(C) Three Years Ago	(B) Two Years Ago	(A) One Year Ago
Assets			
Cash...................... $	48,514	$ 59,067	$ 20,556
Accounts Receivable.........	267,718	136,664	156,877
Inventory..................	250,800	233,681	221,811
Current Assets............ $	567,032	$ 429,412	$ 399,244
Land, Buildings, and Machinery, Net after Deprec......	3,171,193	2,921,190	2,689,903
Miscellaneous Receivables...	25,949	7,412	9,054
Investments................	876,250	698,952	604,621
Deferred Charges...........	23,251	27,502	4,036
Good Will.................	1	1	1
Total................ $	4,683,676	$4,084,479	$3,706,859
Liabilities			
Notes Pay. for Equipment... $	15,600	$ 5,437	$.........
Other Notes Payable........	....	11,458	12,437
Accounts Payable...........	173,850	86,177	164,451
Accruals...................	263,185	75,917	112,436
Current Liabilities........... $	452,635	$ 178,989	$ 289,324
First Mortgage Loan........	1,527,010	1,754,185	1,806,275
Total Liabilites............ $	1,979,645	$1,933,174	$2,095,599
Preference Stock............	1,000,000	1,000,000	1,000,000
Common Stock.............	1,125,000	1,125,000	1,125,000
Retained Earnings..........	579,031	26,305	(D)513,740
Total................ $	4,683,676	$4,084,479	$3,706,859
Net Working Capital......... $	114,397	$ 250,423	$ 109,920
Current Ratio...............	1.25	2.40	1.37
Tangible Net Worth.......... $	2,704,030	$2,151,304	$1,611,259
Net Sales.................. $	....	$.........	$.........
Net Profit.................	(L)1,743,032	(L)552,726	(L)540,045
Dividends..................	None	None	None

value of the fixed assets. These assets consisted largely of five separate plants, all of which had been operated at the peak of activity. Now only one plant is in use. A 10-year loan secured by a first mortgage on real estate, plants, and equipment was obtained from a Federal lending agency in year *E* to keep the business in operation. If that loan had not been obtained the corporation would have been forced into bankruptcy and liquidated. Additional long-term loans were also obtained from the same source in year *D* and year *C*. Since year *C*, the corporation has found it impossible to meet the interest charges at the rate of 3½ per cent per annum, and these charges have been deferred and added to the outstanding mortgage loan. The deferred debt accordingly increased from $1,527,-010 in year C to $1,754,185 in year B, and finally to $1,806,275 in year A.

For each of the 3 years under review the net working capital had been nominal, reaching a low point of $109,920 in year A. If the interest charges on the outstanding mortgage debt for year B and year A had not been deferred, the net working capital would have been wiped out and a deficit would have appeared. The relationship between the funded debt and the net working capital for these 3 years is as follows:

	Year C	Year B	Year A
First Mortgage Loan and Deferred Interest	$1,527,010	$1,754,185	$1,806,275
Net Working Capital	114,397	250,423	109,920
Ratio of Funded Debt to Net Working Capital	1334.8%	700.5%	1643.5%

Many business enterprises, as we have learned, make a gradual reduction in the amount of outstanding funded debt with serial maturities or payments on account. It is sound business policy to do so. Here we find not a reduction but a steady increase in the funded debt as the financial situation became more and more embarrassed. The Dye Works Company, Inc., is actually being kept alive at the pleasure of the mortgage holder. The deferred debt of $1,806,275 in year A is outstandingly excessive.

Between year C and year B, the net working capital increased from $114,397 to $250,423 as a result of obtaining an increase in the mortgage loan and deferring the interest charges for the year. Between year B and year A the net working capital decreased from $250,423 to $109,920. If the interest charges on the mortgage loan for year A had not been deferred, the net working capital would have decreased an additional $52,090.

Because of the very small net working capital, the ratio of funded debt to net working capital is extremely high, probably as high as will ever be seen in the examination of financial statements of industrial and commercial businesses. The ratio was 1334.8 per cent for year C, 700.5 per cent for year B, and 1643.5 per cent for year A. Generally, before a financial condition has reached such an extreme stage, a business enterprise will have ended its useful career.

Condensed Analysis. The fundamental trouble with this corporation was a confident overexpansion program carried out by the operating management many years ago. In that expansion program the officers received liberal salaries and paid little attention to budgetary operations. Suddenly depressed conditions materialized in this industry and the annual volume of business shrank approximately 80 per cent within a 2-year period. The officers continued to draw their high salaries determined in a more rosy ra and to give little attention to expenses, as there was a feeling that the epressed conditions would be short-lived.

At the same time that the volume of business decreased, problems of andling certain mixed synthetic fabrics arose. The transition to synthetic abrics required no additional equipment in the operation of the business. Research and experimental costs, however, were involved in developing ew processes to handle some of the mixed synthetics. While all silk and otton fibers react in the same way to specific dyes and processes, synhetic fibers, which themselves are a product of chemistry, vary in types nd have different reactions to a particular dye or process. Thus it became ecessary for finishers and dyers to develop their own dyes for each type f synthetic fiber, and this could only be done through extensive research nd experimentation.

Each of the three comparative balance sheets contains an item of *nvestments* which decreased from $876,250 in year C to $604,621 in year A. In this case, the investments presented no complications in the analyis. The item in each balance sheet represented the book value of four wholly owned but inactive subsidiaries, each of which in earlier and more ffluent years had operated separate finishing plants. None of the subidiaries had any liabilities. Each year the investment was progressively educed as it became evident that the plants probably would not be repened and that if they were sold, it would only be at considerable loss and o concerns in other lines of business that could not use the buildings until xtensive alterations had been made.

The tangible net worth as determined on the comparative balance heets included the investments on each statement date at their face value. t is probable that the investments were worth only a fraction of each gure in each balance sheet; to the extent that this item might have been vervalued, the tangible net worth was inflated. Even on this possibly nflated size of the tangible net worth, the fixed assets were excessive. In ear C the net depreciated value of the fixed assets exceeded the book angible net worth by 19.1 per cent, in year B by 35.8 per cent, and in year A by 66.9 per cent. The proportions were becoming steadily more excesive. The total liabilities represented 73.2 per cent of the probably inflated angible net worth in year C, 89.8 per cent in year B, but by the time A ad come around, 130.1 per cent. No proportion, however, was as excesively out of balance as the direct relationship between the funded debt nd the net working capital.

After several years had passed in careless wishfulness, the management woke to its predicament. A heavy toll had been taken in the meantime, nd the financial condition was clearly top-heavy with fixed assets that ould only partially be used. The annual volume of business continued ow, and it was apparent that the management was using oxygen to keep

the business alive. This had been done with the aid of loans obtained in
directly from an agency of the Federal government. Without these funds
the corporation would long ago have joined the great number of busines
enterprises whose managements have been unable to keep up to date with
revolutionary and evolutionary technological changes.

Manufacturer of Pipe Fittings

Here is a business founded in 1846 at Providence, R.I., and in 1876 in
corporated as the Valve & Pipe Manufacturing Co., Inc. Over the year
operations were successful and the corporation became one of the leader
in the manufacture of pipe fittings in steel, malleable iron, cast iron
bronze, and nickel alloy, as well as extensive producers of valves and pipe
tools of the Stillson wrench type. Operations became affected by the
steady drop in sales. Inability to earn carrying charges on $9,000,000 c
outstanding 6 per cent first mortgage bonds eventually culminated in th
filing of a petition in bankruptcy under Section 77b of the Bankruptcy
Act.

A reorganization subsequently took place under which the holders o
the outstanding 6 per cent first mortgage bonds were given 4 per cent firs
mortgage bonds for both principal and unpaid interest. New managemen
assumed control of operations, aggressiveness was put into the sales force
and expenses were radically reduced. Earnings began to materialize on the
steadily increasing volume of sales, so that not only were funds available
to pay the interest on the new bonds but substantial net profits were avail
able to pay dividends to stockholders, and to build the net working capi
tal. These trends are readily recognizable in the comparative figures in
Schedule 26.

The tangible net worth figure of $4,503,292 in year C was arrived at by
adding together the outstanding 5 per cent cumulative preferred stock o
$614,110, the common stock of $3,394,080, the capital surplus of $912,187
and deducting from that total the item of *Patents and Good Will* carried a
$23,693 in the assets, and the deficit in the retained earnings account o
$393,392. In year B the deficit in retained earnings was changed into an
actual surplus of $586,034. Consequently the only deduction from the
sum of capital stocks, capital surplus, and retained earnings to determin
the tangible net worth in year B and year A was the item of *Patents and
Good Will*, carried at $21,950 and at $20,205, respectively.

Between year C and year B the net sales increased from $14,472,514 to
$17,721,928, or 22.5 per cent. Between year B and year A the volume in
creased from $17,721,928 to $31,845,178, or 79.7 per cent. With the ex
panding volume came expanding net profits, $250,192 in year C, $1,089,
426 in year B, and $1,994,808 in year A. For these 3 years the net profit

VALVE & PIPE MANUFACTURING CO., INC.   [Schedule 26]
Comparative Figures for Years Ended December 31, 19—

	(C) Three Years Ago	(B) Two Years Ago	(A) One Year Ago
ASSETS			
Cash	$ 458,612	$ 456,068	$ 854,099
Notes Receivable	212,324	270,330	220,320
Accounts Receivable	1,226,231	1,803,311	4,001,340
Inventory	4,354,359	5,573,251	6,812,107
Current Assets	$ 6,251,526	$ 8,102,960	$11,887,866
Plants and Equipment, Net	6,990,474	7,014,068	7,121,502
Miscellaneous Receivables	200,887	180,175	114,879
Suspense Debits	....	154,019	69,336
Investments	42,438	28,888	....
Prepaid Expenses	198,252	67,595	102,571
Patents and Good Will	23,693	21,950	20,205
TOTAL	$13,707,270	$15,569,655	$19,316,359
LIABILITIES			
Due to Banks	$ 700,000	$ 1,200,000	$..........
Accounts Payable	503,451	762,921	2,086,763
Accruals	395,459	580,140	1,076,973
Reserve for Federal Taxes	33,000	347,772	2,395,000
Current Liabilities	$ 1,631,910	$ 2,890,833	$ 5,558,736
4% First Mortgage Bonds	7,548,375	7,148,075	6,610,480
Total Liabilities	$ 9,180,285	$10,038,908	$12,169,216
5% Cumulative Pref. Stock	614,110	619,120	619,120
Common Stock	3,394,080	3,394,870	3,395,395
Capital Surplus	912,187	930,723	931,786
Retained Earnings	(D)393,392	586,034	2,200,842
TOTAL	$13,707,270	$15,569,655	$19,316,359
Net Working Capital	$ 4,619,616	$ 5,212,127	$ 6,329,130
Current Ratio	3.83	2.80	2.14
Tangible Net Worth	$ 4,503,292	$ 5,508,797	$ 7,126,938
Net Sales	$14,472,514	$17,721,928	$31,845,178
Net Profit	250,192	1,089,426	1,994,808
Dividends	None	110,000	380,000

aggregated $3,334,426 and all but $490,000 was retained in the business. The deficit of $393,392 in retained earnings in year C was turned into a black figure of $2,200,842 by the end of year A.

The tangible net worth increased 58.3 per cent between year C and year A. The net working capital increased a somewhat smaller percentage, as part of the retained net profits was used to reduce the outstanding amount of first mortgage bonds. Over these 3 years the financial condition showed a steady increase in the current liabilities and the total liabilities. At the same time, a consistent decrease took place in the outstanding first mortgage debt. As a result, the relationship between the funded debt and the net working capital improved steadily. Here is the trend in this interesting relationship:

	Year C	Year B	Year A
4% First Mortgage Bonds	$7,548,375	$7,148,075	$6,610,480
Net Working Capital	4,619,616	5,212,127	6,329,130
Ratio of Funded Debt to Net Working Capital	163.4%	137.1%	104.4%

The fiscal figures for year C revealed $7,548,375 of outstanding 4 per cent first mortgage bonds. By the end of year B this deferred debt had been reduced to $7,148,075, a difference of $400,300; and by the end of year A to $6,610,480, a further difference of $437,595. Over these 2 years the total reduction in the funded debt had amounted to $837,895, or 11.1 per cent. Simultaneously the net working capital expanded from $4,619,-616 to $6,329,130, or 37.0 per cent.

The trends in these two items show perfect improvement, a combination that only occasionally takes place. The funded debt was steadily reduced and the new working capital was steadily increased. The relationship of the funded debt to net working capital was heavy in year C with a ratio of 163.4 per cent. The improvement in both items is reflected in the reduction in this ratio to 137.1 per cent for year B, and in the still further reduction to 104.4 per cent for year A.

At year C this ratio was so heavy that a fundamental question existed regarding the financial soundness of this corporation. The improvement in year B was somewhat reassuring but not until the figures for year A became available, showing that additional progress had been made instead of a slide backwards, was real evidence available that the new management had guided the affairs of the corporation almost out of the wilderness.

Condensed Analysis. From the time of the reorganization of this corporation to the end of year C, operations had not been successful. Interest had been met on the outstanding 4 per cent first mortgage bonds, but after making these payments, a deficit had been created to the extent of $393,392. In year C net profits had amounted to $250,192 after all charges including interest, so it is evident at the end of year D the deficit in the retained earnings account had amounted to $643,584.

This reorganization, like so many others, had represented a compromise between conflicting interests. The result was a situation unbalanced by heavy fixed assets and a very substantial funded debt. The current debt was kept to a moderate figure over all these years, an absolute necessity in any serious attempt to work out such an unbalanced situation. Suddenly, in year B very substantial orders were obtained from the Federal government. These expanding orders now provided the net profits to improve the basic financial condition rapidly and materially by redeeming a portion of the funded debt, and by keeping the greater portion of the remaining net profits in the business to increase the net working capital. At the end of year C, the outlook was not particularly bright; at the end of year A, the sky was rosy with only a few fleecy clouds.

The one large fleecy cloud was the relationship between the total liabilities and the tangible net worth. The relationship between the current assets and the current liabilities was satisfactory on each statement date. Likewise, the relationship between the current liabilities and the tangible net worth was satisfactory. As the volume of sales increased, the current liabilities increased at a much faster rate than the decrease in the funded debt. Consequently the total liabilities expanded from $9,180,285 in year C to $10,038,908 in year B, and finally to $12,169,216 in year A. As the tangible net worth was expanding at a faster rate than the total liabilities, a gradual improvement was taking place in the relationship between these two items. In year C, the ratio of total liabilities to tangible net worth was 204.0 per cent, in year B 182.3 per cent, and in year A 170.8 per cent. At this figure the relationship was still excessive, but the trend was in the right direction.

This is a splendid example of how a capable management under propitious circumstances is able to make a real improvement in a weak financial situation. Many corporations which come out of a reorganization with a financial condition as unbalanced as this concern go downhill steadily and become bankrupt a second time. This case is a worthy example of a corporation that had a hard struggle for several years to keep its head above water because of the handicap of an unsound financial structure and then under favorable circumstances made real progress, although the condition is still unbalanced with excessive fixed assets and heavy total liabilities.

TYPICAL RATIOS OF FUNDED DEBT TO NET WORKING CAPITAL

Where long-term liabilities exist, the funded debt of a commercial or industrial business enterprise should not exceed the net working capital if the financial condition is to be considered sound. The Kitchen Equipment Manufacturing Corporation, for example, at the end of year C, had a competitive disadvantage measured by the extent of interest charges on its funded debt plus depreciation charges on the proportion of its fixed assets which were heavier than the typical concern in its line. The entire interest charge on the funded debt was a competitive handicap, as the typical commercial or industrial business enterprise has no funded debt. In this case the interest charge had to be earned by the turnover of a net working capital of $20,869, which was only 35.8 per cent as large as the funded debt. It is frequently difficult to earn these interest charges, together with amortization, year after year, but particularly so when the net working capital is less than the funded debt. A top-heavy funded debt generally insinuates itself surreptitiously into the financial condition of a commercial or industrial business enterprise.

This situation is exemplified by the unprofitable operations of the Kitchen Equipment Manufacturing Corporation for the 5 years up to year A, by the unsound operations of the Dye Works Company, Inc., over an even longer period, and by the operations of the Valve & Pipe Manufacturing Co., Inc., for a series of years up to year C. Even paper mills, which traditionally have been financed substantially with funded obligations, cannot stand the strain if the funded debt becomes excessive. The measure of excessiveness is not a comparison of the funded debt with the depreciated book value of fixed assets or with current earnings, which often fluctuate widely from one year to another, but with the net working capital.

The managements of many business enterprises, particularly retail stores, feel that taxes on real estate and improvements, depreciation on buildings, and the interest charges on a funded debt that was issued to provide part of the funds to acquire the property are payments that are made in lieu of rent. Whether these aggregate charges are in excess of what would be a normal rent is a matter of comparing operating costs under both situations. The amount of the rent on leased quarters can, however, be revamped at the end of a lease. Where property is owned in fee, the above-mentioned charges are fixed.

Land and buildings fluctuate in market value like all other commodities, and many business enterprises have become financially embarrassed by the drop in the value of land and buildings below the amount at which these assets were mortgaged. The only remedy to such a situation is a preventive one; the investment in fixed assets should never exceed a certain percentage of the tangible net worth, and a funded debt should never exceed a certain definite fixed percentage of the net working capital. Then, although a loss may be taken if an unexpected situation arises, rarely is the loss so great as to force the concern into bankruptcy. Moreover, if these relationships are adhered to, a margin exists so that the management will have a leeway for a reasonable period of time to change policies and to work out an unfavorable situation.

Typical relationships of funded debt to net working capital are given in Schedule 27 for 42 lines of manufacturing, 21 of wholesaling, and 7 of retailing. In several of the lines, a sufficient number of concerns with

RATIOS OF FUNDED DEBT TO NET WORKING CAPITAL   [Schedule 27]

Lines of Business Activity	Percentage					
	Median					Five-year Average
	1955	1956	1957	1958	1959	
MANUFACTURERS						
Agricultural Implements and Machinery	26.8	30.2	39.1	26.2	32.6	31.0
Airplane Parts and Accessories	41.6	57.6	36.6	56.1	23.2	43.0
Automobile Parts and Accessories	28.2	22.6	26.8	30.8	35.0	28.7
Bakers	74.3	77.6	76.3	84.2	74.0	77.3
Bedsprings and Mattresses	20.9	22.1	21.9	32.7	23.9	24.3
Bodies, Auto, Bus, and Truck	30.2	22.7	26.8	24.0	30.9	26.9
Bolts, Screws, Nuts, and Nails	43.7	38.4	54.2	36.7	35.7	41.7
Breweries	60.3	53.9	44.2	53.8	65.6	55.6
Chemicals, Industrial	43.5	57.4	43.4	53.2	54.4	50.4
Coats and Suits, Men's and Boys'	23.3	23.5	25.6	17.5	16.3	21.2
Coats and Suits, Women's	32.3	24.4	32.9	25.7	29.9	29.0
Confectionery	44.9	35.7	27.1	24.1	35.7	33.5
Contractors, Building Construction	21.9	21.8	18.6	17.9	21.8	20.4
Contractors, Electrical	23.1	23.6	29.2	24.2	20.1	24.0
Cotton Cloth Mills	37.1	28.3	24.1	27.1	27.8	28.9
Cotton Goods, Converters, Non-factored	....	34.8	....	25.4	24.5	28.2
Dresses, Rayon, Silk, and Acetate	30.8	....	44.1	39.9	23.6	34.6
Drugs	39.8	30.8	26.4	19.4	19.5	27.2
Electrical Parts and Supplies	25.2	24.7	26.9	30.4	31.6	27.8
Foundries	35.4	29.6	34.4	26.2	29.6	31.0
Fruits and Vegetables, Canners	44.4	34.1	27.6	40.4	29.4	35.2
Furniture	28.0	24.6	23.0	26.9	22.7	25.0
Hardware and Tools	19.8	28.2	24.8	34.8	26.8	26.9
Hosiery	41.0	35.6	27.5	45.6	52.3	40.4
Lumber	44.9	44.1	38.8	51.4	62.8	48.4
Machine Shops	30.0	34.6	31.8	34.4	42.1	34.6
Machinery, Industrial	24.6	22.8	25.6	23.0	26.2	24.4
Meats and Provisions, Packers	45.7	43.5	50.2	52.2	60.5	50.4
Metal Stampings	34.4	39.9	32.1	34.1	31.4	34.4
Outerwear, Knitted	19.7	18.2	14.9	27.4	20.4	20.1
Overalls and Work Clothing	27.8	26.1	22.2	22.8	23.6	24.5
Paints, Varnishes, and Lacquers	21.3	19.1	23.6	21.9	17.6	20.7
Paper	63.1	56.2	50.4	66.4	65.7	60.4
Paper Boxes	66.9	60.7	67.3	61.7	56.2	62.6
Petroleum, Integrated Corporations	82.9	66.0	109.7	96.6	78.7	86.8
Printers, Job	33.8	56.4	27.9	43.2	57.4	43.7
Radio Parts and Supplies	31.5	38.0	25.8	25.1	27.0	29.5
Shirts, Underwear, and Pajamas, Men's	17.5	20.4	19.6	19.8	11.4	17.7
Shoes, Men's, Women's, and Children's	22.6	19.5	24.6	23.5	21.6	22.4
Soft Drinks and Carbonated Water, Bottlers	80.9	87.4	81.3	129.9	113.1	98.5
Steel, Structural Fabricators (Sell on Short Terms)	26.2	23.3	31.2	24.6	33.0	27.7
Stoves, Ranges, and Ovens	28.6	27.3	27.8	17.4	22.9	24.8

RATIOS OF FUNDED DEBTS TO NET WORKING CAPITAL (*Continued*)
[**Schedule 27** (*Cont.*)]

	Percentage					
Lines of Business Activity	Median					Five-year Average
	1955	1956	1957	1958	1959	
WHOLESALERS						
Automobile Parts and Accessories....	18.0	23.4	18.9	18.9	17.7	19.4
Baked Goods......................	125.9	101.6	106.8	82.1	58.4	95.0
Cigars, Cigarettes, and Tobacco......	21.5	21.8	19.6	24.2	24.8	22.4
Drugs and Drug Sundries...........	20.3	21.5	18.6	15.9	20.9	19.4
Dry Goods.......................	20.7	18.5	17.4	14.8	17.0	17.7
Electrical Parts and Supplies........	14.1	14.2	12.8	18.8	17.4	15.5
Fruits and Produce, Fresh...........	39.3	48.7	50.9	39.1	67.9	49.2
Furnishings, Men's.................	21.2	16.4	14.9	20.6	16.8	18.0
Gasoline, Fuel Oil, and Lubricating Oil..........................	43.5	29.9	36.0	31.3	18.7	31.9
Groceries........................	24.8	26.5	22.8	28.9	29.3	26.5
Hardware........................	16.5	17.0	20.5	17.8	20.7	18.5
Hosiery and Underwear.............	....	20.3	....	29.9	18.6	22.9
Household Appliances, Electrical.....	20.0	20.4	22.3	17.9	18.2	19.8
Lumber..........................	18.6	29.3	34.7	20.8	22.5	25.2
Lumber and Building Materials......	20.4	20.9	23.7	21.3	21.1	21.5
Meat and Poultry.................	33.2	28.6	33.8	51.5	34.0	36.2
Paints, Varnishes, and Lacquers......	24.0	32.9	26.2	23.8	17.6	24.9
Paper...........................	16.5	20.1	18.7	16.4	18.4	18.0
Plumbing and Heating Supplies......	14.1	19.9	16.7	14.9	20.1	17.1
Shoes, Men's, Women's and Children's.........................	18.5	14.5	17.6	25.8	24.2	20.1
Wines and Liquors.................	21.0	15.2	13.7	17.2	11.5	15.7
RETAILERS						
Clothing, Men's and Boys'..........	23.9	35.6	36.5	37.4	37.6	48.2
Department Stores.................	25.7	24.7	32.7	34.2	27.3	28.9
Furniture, 50 Per Cent or More Installment......................	19.3	19.8	23.2	22.2	23.7	21.6
Groceries and Meats, Independent...	46.7	52.5	60.2	69.0	74.8	60.6
Lumber and Building Materials......	21.9	26.9	25.2	21.4	15.4	22.2
Shoes...........................	27.1	27.4	21.1	21.4	25.5	24.5
Women's Specialty Shops...........	30.4	23.9	32.0	29.8	31.1	29.4

funded obligations have been studied only in certain years over the 5-year period, and not in all the years, to determine these ratios.

Of the 42 lines of manufacturing activity listed, for which the average ratios of funded debt to net working capital have been determined over the spread of years, the highest ratio is shown by bottlers of soft drinks

manufacturers of industrial chemicals

107.5

and carbonated water with a 5-year average of 98.5 per cent. This state-ment does not mean that most bottlers show this relationship. Many bottlers, as a matter of fact, have no long-term liabilities whatsoever. This particular relationship was determined only from the figures of those particular bottlers which did have outstanding funded debts. Next highest were ~~integrated petroleum corporations~~ with a 5-year average *paper mills* ~~68.3~~ of 86.8 per cent, followed by ~~bakers~~ with ~~77.3~~ per cent. Wholesalers ~~67.3~~ ~~of baked goods~~ lead the wholesale trades with a 5-year average of ~~95.0~~ per cent, followed by wholesalers of ~~fresh fruits and produce~~ with ~~49.2~~ per ~~46.4~~ cent, and ~~wholesalers of meat and poultry~~ with 36.2 per cent. ~~Independent~~ *55.1* ~~grocery and meat stores with~~ 60.6 per cent have the highest 5-year average among the retail lines. *32.5*

groceries   *gasoline, fuel oil and lubricating oil*

Maxim

The examination of thousands of balance sheets yearly in all lines of industrial and commercial activity has led to the conclusion that rarely, if ever, should the aggregate of funded liabilities exceed the net working capital. Where the funded debt is heavier, the relationship invariably is unbalanced. Under such circumstances, the entire capital of a business enterprise is tied up in noncurrent (slow) assets, and the concern must operate currently, from day to day, on long-term borrowed funds. Interest and amortization become a burden, often too great a burden to be carried in a world of competitive capitalism, fluctuating sales, and constantly varying gross margins of profit.

THEORY AND PROBLEMS

1. The Screw & Bolt Corporation manufactures an extensive line of screw and bolt products. Set up the following balance sheet on a columnar sheet of paper, com-puting (a) current assets, (b) current liabilities, (c) total liabilities, (d) net working capital, (e) current ratio, and (f) ratio of funded debt to net working capital. Then give your interpretation of the ratio of funded debt to net working capital.

SCREW & BOLT CORPORATION
Balance Sheet, December 31, 19—
ASSETS

Current Assets
Cash in banks and on hand.......................... $1,423,665
Marketable securities, at cost.............. $ 359,510
    Less: Reserve for excess of cost over quoted
      market values...................... 310,267   49,243
Accounts receivable—Trade.............. $ 361,419
    Less: Reserves....................... 5,703   355,716

SCREW & BOLT CORPORATION (*Continued*)

Inventories, certified by officials as to quantities and condition

Raw materials—lower of cost or market.	$ 742,047		
Supplies—lower of cost or market......	191,749		
Finished and semifinished products— normal cost, less than market........	1,103,328	2,037,124	
Miscellaneous accounts receivable....................		7,548	
Receivable from employees...........................		14,175	$3,887,471
Amount Receivable from Officers and Directors...........			56,600

Fixed Assets, at cost

Land...		$ 842,757	
Buildings................................	$2,876,158		
Machinery, equipment, and fixtures........	3,646,759		
	$6,522,917		
Less: Reserve for depreciation..............	3,595,412	2,927,505	
Uncompleted construction............................		18,937	3,789,199
Patents, at cost..		$ 50,009	
Less: Amortization................................		28,420	21,589

Deferred Charges

Prepaid insurance, taxes, expenses, etc.................			63,096
			$7,817,955

LIABILITIES

Current Liabilities

Accounts payable—Trade............................		$ 199,054	
Accrued liabilities			
Pay rolls..		63,894	
Taxes, other than income taxes....................		102,346	
Interest...		10,200	
All other..		59,248	
Sinking fund payment..............................		60,000	
Reserve for Federal income taxes......................		22,535	$ 517,277

Funded Debt

Eleven-year first mortgage 4¼% bonds due May 1, 19— Authorized and issued.................			$1,500,000	
Less: Redeemed and canceled..........	$ 60,000			
Sinking fund payment due—trans- ferred to current liabilities........	60,000	120,000	1,380,000	

Capital Stock and Surplus

Capital stock				
1,500,000 shares, stated at........................			$1,500,000	
Surplus				
Paid-in surplus...........................	$3,823,994			
Retained earnings.......................	596,684	4,420,678	5,920,678	
				$7,817,955

2. Give a definition or a comprehensive explanation of the meaning of *funded debt* as used in everyday practical financial statement analysis.

3. State briefly what information you would obtain from the ratio of funded debt to net working capital.

4. Funded debts, at times, are secured. Give the principal assets that are often pledged as security. Why is it essential to ascertain whether a funded debt is secured and what that security represents?

5. Why is it desirable to study the indentures covering long-term issues of funded obligations of commercial and industrial corporations?

6. The treasurer of the Cement Manufacturing Co., Inc., called on the vice-president of a bank in a central reserve city with the idea of opening an account by obtaining a loan from the bank. Among the financial schedules that the treasurer turned over to the banker was the following fiscal balance sheet. The vice-president asked the credit manager of the bank to post the figures on a comparative statement blank, make the following computations, and return the balance sheet with a brief interpretation of these four computations: (*a*) current ratio, (*b*) current liabilities to tangible net worth, (*c*) total debt to tangible net worth, and (*d*) funded debt to net working capital. Assume you are the credit manager of the bank. Post the figures, make the necessary computations, and, by interpreting the above four ratios, write your memorandum for the use of the vice-president in deciding whether the account should or should not be opened with a loan.

CEMENT MANUFACTURING CO., INC.
Balance Sheet, December 31, 19—
ASSETS

Current Assets

Cash in banks and on hand			$ 3,320,409
Notes and accounts receivable			
Customers	$288,907		
Others	12,660		
	$301,567		
Less: Reserves	63,693	237,874	
Inventories, at cost or market, whichever is lower			
Cement	$756,695		
Process stocks	227,124		
Bags	259,157		
Supplies	177,298	1,420,274	
			$ 4,978,557
U.S. Government Securities, on deposit with State Workmen's Compensation Commission, at face value			35,000
Sundry Investments and Deferred Receivables, at estimated realizable values			26,326
Fixed Assets, at reproduction cost, less depreciation, as appraised, plus subsequent additions at cost, and less depletion and depreciation provided			
Land, buildings, machinery, equipment, etc	$34,799,834		
Less: Reserves for depletion and depreciation	19,902,865		
	$14,896,969		
Less: Balance of special reserve created out of capital surplus for elimination of appreciation	7,859,902		
	$ 7,037,067		
Investment in a foreign subsidiary (50% owned) whose only asset is land	225,000		
		7,262,067	
Deferred Charges to Future Operations		40,759	
		$12,342,709	

CEMENT MANUFACTURING CO., INC. (*Continued*)
LIABILITIES

Current Liabilities
Accounts payable (trade).......................... $ 72,389
Accrued liabilities
Salaries and wages.................... $ 28,204
Taxes...............................   93,121
Interest............................   125,422
All other...........................   36,393   283,140
Provision for Federal Income Taxes..................   106,087 $ 461,616
First Mortgage Sinking Fund 4% Gold Bonds, Series A,
Due September 15, 19—:
Issued.. $14,515,000
Redeemed and canceled.........................   5,228,000
                                                 $ 9,287,000
Less: Held in treasury (of which it is estimated
$449,000 principal amount will be retired through
sinking fund during the next fiscal year).......   2,120,000
                                                                  7,157,000
Reserve for Self Insurance (Workmen's compensation)...............   149,335
Capital Stock and Surplus
Preferred stock
Authorized—125,000 shares without par value, enti-
tled to $100 per share and accumulated dividends
on involuntary liquidation......................
Issued—121,200 shares Series A, Convertible $5
Cumulative (redeemable at $110 per share) stated
at $25 per share............................. $ 3,030,000
Common stock
Authorized—587,500 shares without par value
Issued—400,000 shares stated at $1 per share......   400,000
                                                 $ 3,430,000
Capital surplus..................................   951,935
Retained earnings................................   182,823
                                                                  4,564,758
                                                                 $12,342,709

7. When is a funded debt heavy in relation to the net working capital of a commercial
or industrial business enterprise?

CHAPTER X

Fixed Assets to Tangible Net Worth

In the development of accounting and credit practices a certain group of items in the balance sheet has come to be known as fixed assets. These assets, as explained in Chap. IV, consist primarily of land and buildings but also include many other items generally of a depreciable or depletable nature, such as machinery, equipment, tools, furniture, fixtures, leasehold improvements, pipe lines, and rolling stock. These items represent a very substantial part of the tangible net worth of railroads, public utilities, pipe lines, and mining corporations. Although a somewhat smaller percentage, they still represent a substantial part of the tangible net worth of manufacturers; they are a much smaller percentage of the tangible net worth of retailers, and an even smaller percentage in the case of jobbers, wholesalers, and financial institutions.[1]

Modern life has been so influenced by the results of the industrial revolution that it is well-nigh impossible to conceive of a world without the machine. An era in which goods were produced by families in their homes, by artisans in their small shops, by small mills with the crudest of simple machinery "is more unreal in retrospect than the extravagances forecast for the coming centuries by writers of science fiction."[2] Economic wealth through the colonial era and well into the nineteenth century was measured primarily by actual material possessions, of which the most important were fixed assets represented first by land (mostly farm lands), and then by buildings, and in the world of business by ships, which were so absolutely essential in transportation and commerce.

---

[1] *Statistics of Income 1957–58* contains combined balance sheet figures for all corporations engaged in (1) manufacturing processes, (2) retailing, and (3) wholesaling. Computations from these combined balance sheets and supplementary tables indicate that all *manufacturing* corporations (133,558) showed a ratio of depreciated capital assets, that is, fixed assets to net worth of 56.5 per cent; all *retail* corporations (167,054), a ratio of 39.7 per cent; and all *wholesale* corporations (100,338), a ratio of 25.1 per cent. Computed from *Statistics of Income 1957–58, Corporation Income Tax Returns*, pp. 32, 35 (Internal Revenue Service, U.S. Treasury Department, Washington, D.C., 1960).

[2] KIRKLAND, EDWARD C., *A History of American Economic Life*, 3d ed., p. 80 (Appleton-Century-Crofts, Inc., New York, 1951).

Until after the War of 1812 up-country freighting, that is, from the seaport cities and towns inland, was by pack horses and wagons; down-country freighting, that is, from inland settlements to the coasts, was mostly by various types of vessels such as arks, sloops, barges, and keel-boats. Shortly after 1815, steamboats and canals transformed inland transportation in three ways: they cheapened the cost and shortened the time for carrying bulky freight to the interior; they connected formerly isolated transportation systems; and they opened to settlement country that had been previously unavailable because it was not accessible to natural waterways. Waterways were comparatively smooth avenues for commerce, while transportation over primitive roads offered daily adventures in which human ingenuity was tested by a constant variety of problems in getting freight over boggy roads and fords.

So long as pack horses and wagons remained the only means of transporting merchandise inland, overland freight cost from 20 to 40 and even 60 cents a ton-mile, according to the condition of the roads and the distance covered. The saving effected by railways is sufficiently indicated by the single fact that transportation charges fell to 3 cents a ton-mile, or to about one-tenth the cost of wagon carriage. This radical revolution in transportation was accomplished within a single generation. The consequent sudden enlarging of markets gave a powerful incentive to the growth of manufacturing businesses with their relatively large investments in fixed assets.[3]

Evolution of the Factory System

The factory system of manufacture, with its large investment in fixed assets, obtained its first real foothold in the United States following the passage of the Embargo Act in December, 1807. Factories appeared in the textile industry, initially in the spinning of yarn, and then in 1814 in the weaving of cloth. Shortly before the Civil War, this factory system had spread into the manufacture of wood and metal products which required the mechanical production of uniform and interchangeable parts such as the manufacture of firearms, agricultural implements, sewing machines, clocks, and watches. As the system spread, factory towns such as Lowell, Lawrence, Holyoke, Fall River, Cohoes, and Paterson sprang up along the streams of New England and the Middle Atlantic States.

With the early consolidation of railroads, headed by the New York

[3] In a volume of striking insight, *The Coming Struggle for Power* (Covici, Friede, Inc., New York, 1933), John Strachey argues with convincing logic that the basic reason for the growth of the capitalistic system and the waging of important wars over the years has been the growth in and the struggle for the constant enlargement of the market. In this theory, Strachey would certainly have included the Second World War, which he forecast by clear implications.

Central and the Hudson River lines in 1869 by Commodore Vanderbilt, impetus was given to large-scale production and commerce under the corporate enterprise which provided a medium of wealth in the form of corporate securities, stocks, and evidences of debts which, together with government securities of all classes, gradually appeared more interesting to the investing layman than real estate. The widespread colonial policy of investing in land now came to be represented by the broader investment in corporate securities; the corporations in turn proceeded to invest in fixed assets in the broad connotation of that term. In this development, the value of fixed assets in industry and commerce increased by leaps and bounds.

Value of Fixed Assets

In the following chapter we shall learn the various formulas and the very different dollar amounts at which the same physical quantity of inventory may be valued and carried in the balance sheet. In Chap. XXIV, we shall learn the reasons why many assets, including fixed assets, are often carried in balance sheets at figures above or below their "actual" value. At this point, the analyst should be cautioned that the dollar amounts at which the various items comprising the fixed assets are carried in the balance sheet are relative and not absolute values, depending upon the method of valuation, that is, depreciated cost, market, replacement less depreciation, or liquidation value.

Cost Less Depreciation.[4] The most general method of valuing fixed assets is cost or a modification of cost, that is, land at cost; machinery, tools, equipment, furniture, and fixtures at cost less depreciation; and buildings at cost plus capitalized improvements less depreciation. While this method of valuation has the virtue of consistency and is hallowed by precedent, the analyst must keep in mind that the basis is an accounting convention which signally fails to measure current economic value.

Cost might have been an inflated cost, or a deflated cost compared with the economic value at the date of the balance sheet. Improvements or betterments, instead of being capitalized, may have been charged to expense, while repairs and ordinary maintenance customarily charged to

---

[4] Depreciation is not a method of valuation. This fact is emphasized in the definition prepared by the Committee on Accounting Procedure of the American Institute of Certified Public Accountants. That definition reads as follows: [*depreciation accounting* is] "a system of accounting which aims to distribute the cost or other basic value of tangible capital assets, less salvage (if any), over the estimated useful life of the unit (which may be a group of assets) in a systematic and rational manner. It is a process of allocation, not of valuation." *Restatement and Revision of Accounting Research Bulletins, Accounting Research Bulletin No. 43*, p. 76 (American Institute of Certified Public Accountants, New York 1953).

expense may have been partly or largely capitalized. Depreciation of depreciable assets may be too low, which would inflate the value of the fixed assets, or too high, which would mean that the item had a higher value than that carried on the books. Moreover, the technique or the standard of depreciation in use by a particular concern would affect book value.

Market. Whereas merchandise is quite generally valued at "cost or market, whichever is lower," fixed assets are rarely if ever valued on this basis. When a small or moderate-sized business enterprise is purchased, quite often the market value of the fixed assets is one of the components that go to make up the aggregate price to be paid for the business. In practically all active business enterprises there is absolutely no connection between the value at which fixed assets are carried in the balance sheet and actual market value.

Replacement Less Depreciation. When larger business enterprises are purchased, merged, or consolidated, it is often highly desirable as a practical business policy to ascertain the existing replacement value, less depreciation, of the fixed assets. Work of this nature is undertaken by appraisal companies. Quite often this valuation appears in the initial balance sheet after control has changed hands, or a merger or a consolidation has taken place. Subsequent valuations as carried in succeeding balance sheets might depart from their economic value for the very same reasons that the valuation of cost less depreciation is different from economic value.

The fact that fixed assets are often carried on the books at a figure below replacement less depreciation provides a realistic advantage, as in theory depreciation costs charged into the income statement would be less than corresponding charges of competitors that might be carrying their fixed assets at a figure closer to actual replacements less depreciation. Conversely, where fixed assets are carried at a higher figure, depreciation charges in theory are greater and, to that extent, increase accounting cost.

Liquidation. The above three bases of valuation are predicated on the assumption that a particular business enterprise is a going concern. When a business enterprise is in a very extended financial condition and bankruptcy looks inevitable in the near future, the fixed assets might be appraised for valuation, not as a going concern but as a liquidated business. A building which might be valued at $100,000 by a going concern might be worth only $26,000 if the concern becomes bankrupt and the building must be sold. Machinery, equipment, tools, furniture, and fixtures, likewise, would have only a fraction of their value to a going business, if liquidation were anticipated. This is the rock-bottom basis, the minimum that might be raised by forced sale under the most unfavorable circumstances.

Comparative Relationship of Fixed Assets

For every line of commercial and industrial business activity, there is a certain proportion of the tangible net worth that may typically be invested in fixed assets. A smaller proportion is a favorable feature. A higher proportion is unfavorable for two simple reasons: first, the annual depreciation charge that must be assumed in the income statement is proportionately heavier than for competitors; and second, if the fixed assets are very heavy, the concern has either a low net working capital with subsequent overtrading, as will be outlined in Chap. XV, or a funded debt to furnish adequate net working capital, as analyzed in Chap. IX.

Consider the case of two department stores in the same city, each on opposite corners of the same block and each handling an annual volume of business in the neighborhood of $2,500,000 on a tangible net worth of approximately $1,000,000. One store operates from a five-story structure, which is twenty-three years old but which had been kept modern and in fine condition by constant repairs and improvements. The land, building, furniture, and fixtures are carried on the books at a net depreciated value of $300,000. The management of the second store erected an up-to-the minute structure of six stories 3 years ago. The net depreciated value of its land, building, furnishings, and fixtures is carried at $700,000. For the first store the land is carried on the books at $100,000, and for the second store at $150,000. The respective value of the remaining fixed assets subject to yearly depreciation in the two cases is $200,000 and $550,000, respectively. The rates of depreciation on the structure, furnishings, and equipment are approximately the same for both stores. It is obvious that the dollar depreciation to be taken into the income account as an item of yearly expense of the second concern is $2\frac{1}{4}$ times as large as that taken by the first concern. Here is the proportionate handicap that must be overcome in a highly competitive market where prices are fundamentally the same.

Presumably, in the second case the management took extreme pride in having the most modern department store in the state. The management hoped and assumed that such a structure would have a competitive advantage in increasing its volume of sales, and that the increased volume would provide sufficient additional profit to offset the additional depreciation charges and even earn a larger final net profit on the tangible net worth. Frequently such reasoning does actually work out in practice; often, however, the handicap of the additional charges and the necessity of operating on a lower net working capital and consequent heavier liabilities do not work out successfully. Such managements are dominated more by enthusiasm and prospects for the future than by realities in a competitive world where price so often makes the market. It is more a question of the desires and hopes of management, and less a question of what is sound financial policy for the business.

ILLUSTRATIONS OF RELATIONSHIPS

No situations are more disappointing or more unsound than those resulting from a management's belief that a larger and better plant, store, or home office is desirable. Accordingly, it invests a substantial proportion of the tangible net worth in fixed assets. Too late does the management learn from experience that the move was financially unsound. Capital once invested in fixed assets is there to stay, except insofar as yearly depreciation is earned. Interest, dividends, salaries, wages, and burden cannot be paid by excessive investments in bricks, mortar, or beautiful furnishings.

Wholesaler of Fuel and Oil

In 1928 the Wholesale Fuel & Oil Corp. was incorporated under the laws of the State of New York to acquire the assets and the businesses of six concerns operating in near-by cities and towns as wholesalers of coal and fuel oil. At its inception this corporation was a representative enterprise, operating on a paid-in capital of $2,600,000, consisting of $1,250,000 of 5 per cent prior preferred stock, $1,250,000 of 5 per cent cumulative preferred stock, and $100,000 of common stock. Against this tangible net worth of $2,600,000 the corporation carried in its balance sheet fixed assets consisting of land, buildings, machinery, equipment, and delivery trucks at $5,000,000, or 192.3 per cent of its tangible net worth. In order to carry fixed assets of this excessive size, it was necessary for the concern to have a substantial outstanding funded debt. This debt amounted to $3,000,000, consisting of $1,500,000 four per cent first mortgage bonds and $1,500,000 five per cent convertible debentures.

The annual interest charges on the funded debt, amounting to $135,000, and the substantial depreciation charges on the top-heavy fixed assets resulted in net losses from the very first year. The business was basically unbalanced with excessive fixed charges and from the inception the result was tragically expressive. The business became more and more cramped for working funds. The struggle to provide income to meet outgo ended after 6 years. Funds were not available to meet the interest charges and the corporation was petitioned into bankruptcy.

In the reorganization, the holder of each $1,000 of 4 per cent first mortgage bonds received $1,000 in 4 per cent first mortgage cumulative income bonds. The holder of each $1,000 of 5 per cent convertible debenture received in exchange $675 in 4 per cent convertible income debentures and

WHOLESALE FUEL & OIL CORP.   [Schedule 28]
Comparative Figures for Years Ended December 31, 19—

	(C) Three Years Ago	(B) Two Years Ago	(A) One Year Ago
ASSETS			
Cash.	$ 58,649	$ 53,767	$ 36,331
Notes Receivable.	14,320	10,226	6,182
Accounts Receivable.	112,556	110,271	90,005
Inventory.	117,888	94,383	73,549
Current Assets.	$ 303,413	$ 268,647	$ 206,067
Fixed Assets, Net.	2,871,905	2,812,165	2,755,880
Miscellaneous Receivables.	....	6,673	2,924
Deferred Charges.	30,100	17,406	10,789
Good Will.	1	1	1
TOTAL.	$3,205,419	$3,104,892	$2,975,661
LIABILITIES			
Notes Payable for Merchandise.	$ 7,722	$ 13,372	$ 46,028
Accounts Payable.	148,025	131,227	128,419
Accruals.	10,699	11,950	12,084
Due to Officers.	21,921	18,430	18,079
Current Liabilities.	$ 188,367	$ 174,979	$ 204,610
Real Estate Mortgages.	107,250	102,050	102,820
1st Mtge. 4% Cum. Inc. Bonds.	1,390,300	1,390,300	1,215,000
4% Convertible Income Deben.	987,220	987,220	982,780
Accrued Bond Interest.	111,737	168,300	206,827
Total Liabilities.	$2,784,874	$2,822,849	$2,712,037
Common Stock.	21,005	21,005	20,870
Capital Surplus.	100,000	100,000	100,000
Retained Earnings.	299,540	161,038	142,754
TOTAL.	$3,205,419	$3,104,892	$2,975,661
Net Working Capital.	$ 115,046	$ 93,668	$ 1,457
Current Ratio.	1.61	1.54	1.01
Tangible Net Worth.	$ 420,544	$ 282,042	$ 263,623
Net Sales.	$1,464,992	$1,422,960	$1,236,575
Net Profit.	(L)107,150	(L)138,502	(L)18,284
Dividends.	None	None	None

five shares of common stock. Interest on both issues of funded debt became payable only out of income but before depreciation. The financial condition for 3 years appears in Schedule 28.

These three sets of comparative figures disclose a condition radically different from that which existed at the inception of the enterprise. Instead of a tangible net worth of $2,600,000, at year *C* the tangible net worth was $420,544, and at year *A*, only $263,623. What a magnificent shrinkage! Losses had been assumed for each of the intervening years. The net working capital in year C amounted to $115,046, in year B to $93,668, and at year A had finally dropped to the nominal figure of $1,457. Hard times again were a-knockin' at the door.

These balance sheets are of interest because the financial condition of this enterprise is characterized by very heavy fixed assets. It is a rare occurrence to run across a commercial or industrial business enterprise where the fixed assets are as relatively heavy as with the Wholesale Fuel & Oil Corp. This condition is readily seen in the following direct comparison of the net depreciated value of these assets with the tangible net worth on the successive statement dates:

	Year C	Year B	Year A
Fixed Assets, Net after Depreciation....	$2,871,905	$2,812,165	$2,755,880
Tangible Net Worth..................	420,544	282,042	263,623
Ratio of Fixed Assets to Tangible Net Worth.........................	682.9%	997.2%	1045.5%

These figures show an exceptionally exaggerated condition, one that is very rarely approached unless bankruptcy is around the corner. That was the situation in year A, as the corporation was just tottering on the verge of a second collapse. Rarely will a going concern show a financial condition even approximating this unusual but not exactly unprecedented comparison.

Between year C and year A the fixed assets, net after depreciation but including the capitalization of moderate improvements, dropped nominally from $2,871,905 to $2,755,880. During the same period the tangible net worth shrank from $420,544 to $263,623. Railroads and public utilities often operate with fixed assets in excess of their tangible net worth but this condition does not apply where competition is the life of trade, as in commerce and industry. In year C the fixed assets were 682.9 per cent of the tangible net worth, in year B, 977.2 per cent, and by year A the comparison had increased to 1045.5 per cent. The typical business enterprise would have been petitioned into bankruptcy long before this condition had been approximated.

Condensed Analysis. This corporation has practically no chance to survive. At the reorganization, the interested parties were concerned with keeping the enterprise alive instead of calling it a day and liquidating the business. To keep the head of the enterprise above water, two classes of income securities were issued, first mortgage 4 per cent cumulative income bonds and 4 per cent convertible income debentures. In other words, the interest on the first mortgage income bonds accumulated if not paid, but the interest on the debentures did not accumulate. The accrued bond interest, which increased from $111,737 in year C to $206,827 in year A, represented this accumulated interest on the first mortgage income bonds.

The original reorganization was basically unsound for three reasons: (1) the tangible net worth and (2) the net working capital were both too small to carry on the business, and (3) the fixed assets were out of all proportion, being excessively large for the tangible net worth and for the annual sales of this enterprise. No one with an understanding of the basic reasoning behind reasonable balance sheet proportions would ever have reorganized this business on the existing basis. With the value of fixed assets so greatly in excess of the tangible net worth, there was no possibility that the enterprise would live more than a few gasping years. The successive yearly net losses and vanishing net working capital were foreordained.

Department Store

The Midwestern Department Store, Inc., was incorporated in 1904 with an authorized and paid-in capital of $10,000. Control of the enterprise has remained continuously in the hands of one family. Today, the business is actively managed and controlled by two sons of the founder. For several years prior to 1929 operations were conducted on a high margin of profit. With a bright outlook ahead, the management purchased a parcel of land on the most prominent corner in the business section of the city. Real estate was selling at the highest price in the history of the city.[5] The cost of the real estate, after paying for the demolition of the old structures on this parcel of land, was $302,000. That same piece of real estate today has an assessed valuation of $62,000 and a market value in the neighborhood of $108,000.

A four-story building, a practical attractive structure, was erected to carry on department store operations. Three years ago, year C, the land and building, net after accumulated depreciation, were being carried on the books at $535,345, an amount that was appreciably in excess of the tangible net worth of $352,282. Operations have been conducted profitably for each of the past 3 years and the profits have been retained entirely in the business. This additional support, together with the decrease in the book value of the fixed assets as a result of earned yearly depreciation, show an improving trend but the fixed assets continue to be heavy. This condition is reflected in the comparative figures in Schedule 29.

The trend of operations shown by these figures is generally favorable. The annual net sales increased each year from $606,831 to $631,746 to $679,107, and the net profits went up at the same time. No dividends were paid. The management realized the fundamental problem which was on

---

[5] For a comparative, dramatic story of land speculation from the earliest colonial days down through the Florida boom, see A. M. Sakolski, *The Great American Land Bubble* (Harper & Brothers, New York, 1932).

[Schedule 29]   MIDWESTERN DEPARTMENT STORE, INC.
Comparative Figures for Years Ended January 31, 19—

	(C) Three Years Ago	(B) Two Years Ago	(A) One Year Ago
ASSETS			
Cash.............................	$ 30,598	$ 21,843	$ 26,970
Accounts Receivable.................	83,047	93,940	99,621
Inventory.........................	83,308	82,072	102,763
Current Assets.....................	$196,953	$197,855	$229,354
Fixed Assets, Net...................	535,345	526,806	514,740
Cash Value of Life Insurance..........	12,133	13,558	14,983
Investments.......................	2,075	2,075	3,216
Deferred Charges..................	5,373	7,428	4,125
TOTAL.......................	$751,879	$747,722	$766,418
LIABILITIES			
Due to Banks.......................	$ 1,627	$ 1,403	$ 3,141
Accounts Payable...................	29,853	35,388	30,172
Accruals..........................	7,789	5,796	24,665
Current Maturity of Bonds............	16,043	16,653	5,125
Due to Officers.....................	14,000	11,000	9,000
Other Payables.....................	3,055	7,280	6,263
Current Liabilities...................	$ 72,367	$ 77,520	$ 78,366
First Mortgage Bonds...............	327,230	295,540	275,800
Total Liabilities.....................	$399,597	$373,060	$354,166
Common Stock.....................	300,000	300,000	300,000
Earned Surplus....................	52,282	74,662	112,252
TOTAL.......................	$751,879	$747,722	$766,418
Net Working Capital.................	$124,586	$120,335	$150,988
Current Ratio......................	2.72	2.55	2.92
Tangible Net Worth.................	$352,282	$374,662	$412,252
Net Sales.........................	$606,831	$631,746	$679,107
Net Profit........................	4,402	22,380	37,590
Dividends.........................	None	None	None

their hands and kept all net profits in the business. In year *B* the net working capital decreased $4,251 as a result of the retirement of $31,690 of the first mortgage bonds, but in year *A* the net working capital increased appreciably by the sum of $30,653.

Between year *C* and year *A* the net depreciated value of the fixed assets decreased from $535,345 to $514,740, or 3.9 per cent, while the tangible net worth increased as a result of retained profits from $352,282 to $412,-252, or 17 per cent. The balance sheet as of January 31, year *A*, however, disclosed a relationship where fixed assets were 24.8 per cent in excess of the tangible net worth, an abnormal and unbalanced condition for a department store.

Shortly after the figures for year *A* were issued, the president of the Midwestern Department Store, Inc., came in to see the author. He had tentative plans to spend $25,000 to modernize the front of the store and to revamp and to modernize one of the departments. From these expenditures, he felt sure that net profits would increase $5,000 yearly which would mean, according to the logic of the hour, that the contemplated expenditure would be repaid out of earnings within 5 years. The plan sounded perfectly simple and fascinating.

After he had finished, I asked how the figure of $5,000 additional net profit was determined. The answer, of course, was based upon anticipated additional net sales. Actually, the anticipated sales might or might not materialize; even if they did materialize, the additional net profits might or might not amount to $5,000. The founder of the business had followed somewhat similar reasoning when he purchased the real estate and erected the existing building several years ago. If there is one fact to be learned from the constant study of the problems of business enterprise in a world of fluctuating values, it is that a concern must always be prepared, not for the expected, but for the unexpected.

The direct comparison of the net depreciated value of the fixed assets with the tangible net worth for the last 3 years discloses the following figures:

	Year *C*	Year *B*	Year *A*
Fixed Assets, Net after Depreciation........	$535,345	$526,806	$514,740
Tangible Net Worth......................	352,382	374,662	412,252
Ratio of Fixed Assets to Tangible Net Worth	151.9%	140.6%	124.8%

The analogy struck home. My visitor decided that until the existing fixed assets could be brought more into line with the tangible net worth, it would certainly be inexpedient to invest more money in improvements that were not absolutely essential. Every possible cent of economy which could be brought about was needed. The only solution to this picture is to earn profits and to keep these profits in the business. This program will increase the tangible net worth as depreciation is taken on the existing fixed assets, gradually bringing about a financial condition that will be more typical of a department store.

In year *C* the fixed assets amounted to $535,345 and the tangible net worth to $352,382, giving a relationship of fixed assets to tangible net worth of 151.9 per cent. Depreciation brought the fixed assets down to $526,806 in year *B* and retained profits, which amounted to $22,380, increased the tangible net worth to $374,662, bringing the ratio down to 140.6 per cent. The higher net profits of $37,590 in year *A* and continued depreciation now improved the ratio still more to 124.8 per cent. Even this ratio is high, the 5-year average for department stores, as shown in the table at the end of this chapter, being 25.4 per cent. The trend of this ratio has been downward over the 3 years, reflecting moderate but gradual improvement, but it is still a long way from par.

Condensed Analysis. Here was a situation which was badly out of line a few years ago but which now seems to be on the mend. If the management had failed to realize the predicament at the time, this business could easily have joined the parade of the wooden soldiers. When the financial condition of the business became tight several years ago, the management cut the salaries of every officer to the bone; they received barely enough for living expenses. Every other possible expense was reduced. Scrap paper was used on both sides in the office. As profits were earned, these profits were kept wholly in the business. If expenses had not been radically reduced and if some of the net profits had been paid out in dividends, the outlook of this business would not even have provided a gambling chance to Lloyd's.

Even now the business is not out of the woods but progress has been made, and the management clearly understands its predicament. Not until this ratio of fixed assets to tangible net worth approximates the typical percentage for its line of business, and not until the first mortgage bonds have been reduced to a point below the net working capital, will the management of this store be able to relax for a few moments and take their eyes off the cash register.

Wholesaler of Lumber

On the other side is the picture of the financial condition of the West Coast Wholesale Lumber Co., Inc. There are thousands of retail lumber yards in the United States but relatively few wholesalers of lumber. This concern was organized in 1906 with an authorized and paid-in capital of $500,000. Operations have been conducted profitably in all except three of the intervening years, and in many years with unusually high profits. The business has been a very successful one.

In 1912 the paid-in capital was increased by the issuance of $1,000,000 of 6 per cent cumulative preferred stock. Over the intervening years some of this stock has been retired. In year *A*, operations were being conducted on an outstanding capital of $908,000 six per cent cumulative preferred stock, $461,800 common stock, a capital surplus of $385,200, and retained earnings of $1,321,744. The company handles Pacific Coast fir, hemlock, and spruce, selling primarily to retail lumber yards, railroads, and larger industrial users of lumber in the West North Central states of Minnesota, Iowa, Missouri, North Dakota, South Dakota, Nebraska, and

WEST COAST WHOLESALE LUMBER CO., INC. [Schedule 30]
Comparative Figures for Years Ended December 31, 19—

	(C) Three Years Ago	(B) Two Years Ago	(A) One Year Ago
ASSETS			
Cash	$ 251,462	$ 289,065	$ 363,096
Notes receivable	82,032	60,055	102,405
Accounts Receivable	702,037	707,132	905,425
Inventory	1,460,249	1,629,901	1,427,307
Current Assets	$2,495,780	$2,686,153	$2,798,233
Land	376,003	376,003	376,003
Roadways and Docks, Net	90,467	81,692	72,183
Buildings, Net	194,863	174,954	142,650
Machinery and Equipment, Net	60,294	45,526	35,681
Cash Value of Life Insurance	84,340	85,904	87,267
Miscellaneous Receivables	18,156	23,719	28,355
Deferred Charges	12,027	10,630	13,200
Investments	1,000	896	75,896
TOTAL	$3,332,930	$3,485,477	$3,629,468
LIABILITIES			
Notes Payable to Banks	$ 300,000	$ 350,000	$ 300,000
Trade Acceptances	5,012	5,012	7,562
Accounts Payable	73,196	35,097	39,080
Accruals	5,108	17,401	22,520
Reserve for Taxes	130,000	145,000	180,000
Dues to Officers	2,960	1,446	3,562
Current Liabilities	$ 516,276	$ 553,956	$ 552,724
6% Cumulative Preferred Stock	956,600	940,500	908,000
Common Stock	462,800	462,800	461,800
Capital Surplus	385,200	385,200	385,200
Retained Earnings	1,012,054	1,143,021	1,321,744
TOTAL	$3,332,930	$3,485,477	$3,629,468
Net Working Capital	$1,979,504	$2,132,197	$2,245,509
Current Ratio	4.83	4.86	5.06
Tangible Net Worth	$2,816,654	$2,931,521	$3,076,744
Net Sales	$5,271,128	$6,619,408	$8,048,542
Net Profit	192,748	224,890	270,881
Dividends	94,931	93,923	92,158

Kansas. Selling terms are 2 per cent discount in 10 days, net 60 days. The comparative figures of this successfully operated corporation for the last three fiscal years appear in Schedule 30.

From these comparative figures it is evident that the West Coast Wholesale Lumber Co., Inc., is a representative distributor in its field. Operations for the 3-year period disclose steadily increasing net sales from

$5,271,128 in year C, to $6,619,408 in year B, and to $8,048,542 in year A, with expanding net profits for each of these years. The net profits show a return of 6.8 per cent on the tangible net worth in year C, 7.6 per cent in year B, and 8.8 per cent in year A. A moderate portion of the net profits for each year was paid out in dividends so that both the tangible net worth and the net working capital have shown steady progress.

The fiscal figures for year A reflect a tangible worth of $3,076,744. Each of the three sets of figures discloses well-balanced conditions with moderate liabilities, inventories in proportion, healthy receivables, and generally all-round healthy successful operations. The fixed assets are also in sound proportion. The comparisons of the fixed assets with the tangible net worth on each statement date bring this fact out clearly.

	Year C	Year B	Year A
Land................................	$ 376,003	$ 376,003	$ 376,003
Roadways and Docks................	90,467	81,692	72,183
Buildings.........................	194,863	174,954	142,650
Machinery and Equipment...... *......	60,294	45,526	35,681
Total of Fixed Assets, Net after Depreciation............................	$ 721,627	$ 678,175	$ 626,517
Tangible Net Worth.................	2,816,654	2,931,521	3,076,744
Ratio of Fixed Assets to Tangible Net Worth...........................	25.6%	23.1%	20.4%

The ratio of fixed assets to tangible net worth was outstandingly excessive for each of the 3 years for the Wholesale Fuel and Oil Corp. They were also excessive in the case of the Midwestern Department Store, Inc., even though the trend indicated moderate but steady improvement. For the West Coast Wholesale Lumber Co., Inc., however, the ratios are very much in line. In year C, the net depreciated value of the fixed assets amounted to $721,627. In year B, the value had decreased to $678,175, and in year A, to $626,517. At the same time the tangible net worth increased steadily as a result of the retained net profits after depreciation; from $2,816,654 in year C, the tangible net worth expanded to $3,076,744 in year A. With decreasing fixed assets and increasing tangible net worth, the ratio of fixed assets to tangible net worth over these 3 years has shown constant improvement. In year C, this ratio was 25.6 per cent, in year B 23.1 per cent, and in year A 20.4 per cent.

The 5-year average ratio of fixed assets to tangible net worth of wholesalers of lumber as given in Schedule 31, page 296, is 11.6 per cent, which is somewhat less than the 20.4 per cent shown in year A. The interquartile range of this ratio for wholesalers of lumber given in the Appendix discloses ratios that are in fairly close proximity. There is no doubt that the fixed assets of this corporation are in healthy proportion, that the enterprise is in sound financial condition, and that the relationship of the fixed assets to tangible net worth is one of the contributing factors to that sound financial condition.

Condensed Analysis. This business has been operated by unusually capable and experienced management. In seven ways the comparative figures in Schedule 30 disclose conditions substantially better than those typical for wholesalers of lumber: higher ratios of current assets to current liabilities, lower ratios of current liabilities to tangible net worth, no funded debt, higher ratios of net sales to inventory, shorter average collection periods, higher net profits to tangible net worth, and higher net profits to sales. A financial condition characterized by these favorable features is impressive. These are the results of operating policies based on sound financial insight.

In two respects, the financial condition is moderately below that which is typical for its division of commerce. These are the relationship between net sales and tangible net worth, and the relationship between net sales and the net working capital. The turnover of tangible net worth and the turnover of net working capital are both a trifle low, as are the annual sales for a concern of this size. To one familiar with this field of endeavor, this fact is due to the rather heavy investment in this business; wholesalers of lumber in the larger capital brackets do not obtain quite as rapid turnovers as do those in lower brackets. A wholesale lumber dealer with a tangible net worth of $3,076,744 is quite a substantial enterprise. These two points are of minor significance compared with the favorable features mentioned in the preceding paragraph. Moreover, even with somewhat smaller turnovers of tangible net worth and of net working capital, the net profits on both the net sales and the tangible net worth are impressively high and steady.

TYPICAL RATIOS OF FIXED ASSETS TO TANGIBLE NET WORTH

The ratio of fixed assets to tangible net worth is obtained by dividing the depreciated book value of all fixed assets by the tangible net worth. Generally, the funds invested in fixed assets show a slight downward tendency in successive fiscal balance sheets, as yearly depreciation charges on the depreciable assets are usually greater than the capitalized improvements. When the sale of a piece of property or other fixed asset is made, there is a sudden drop, and when a new store is opened or a new factory erected, there is a sudden increase. Such cases are constantly occurring but compared with those situations where no sudden change takes place, they are few and far between.

The tangible net worth of a business enterprise increases moderately from year to year as net profits are earned and some portion of the profits is retained in the business, or decreases in those years when losses are assumed or dividends in excess of earnings are paid. When additional funds are invested in a business, or when very substantial losses are assumed, the yearly change covers more ground.

Most wholesalers, and manufacturers in the needle industries, invest lightly in fixed assets. Larger manufacturers and retailers have substantial properties and equipment. As a concern increases in size, the tendency to place a greater proportion of its funds in land, buildings, improvements, equipment, and expansion programs becomes stronger.

The ratio of current assets to current liabilities is a ratio between two variables; accordingly, it often changes considerably from year to year in the same concern. The ratio of current liabilities to tangible net worth is between one variable and the tangible net worth, which is fairly static. The ratio of fixed assets to tangible net worth, except in abnormal situations, is between two fairly static items; therefore, this relationship in a particular business enterprise usually will change relatively little from one year to another.

Desirability of Low Ratio

Keep the investment in fixed assets as low as possible is sound advice to organizers of new business concerns. This advice is just as applicable to the management of established commercial and industrial business enterprises as it is to organizers of new business concerns. Rent buildings and real estate whenever practicable until such time as the future of the business is ensured, as a result of its past financial success. The building and equipment of a manufacturing concern may be utterly useless for any other type of business. Hence, the fixed assets may have only scrap value, if for some reason the business must cease to operate. After a time it may be found that it is desirable to change the location of the plant. This can be done only with great expense and loss when substantial capital has been already sunk in fixed assets. The competitive disadvantage of heavy fixed assets is measured by the yearly depreciation charges on that portion of fixed assets which is above the average ratio to tangible net worth, plus interest charges on borrowed money, plus any inability to take discounts on purchases because of the consequent low net working capital.

The median ratios of fixed assets to tangible net worth for 70 lines of industrial and commercial activity—42 lines of manufacturing, 21 of wholesaling, and 7 of retailing—appear in Schedule 31. These ratios have been computed over the 5-year spread of 1955 through 1959 inclusive, with an arithmetical average for the 5 years.

From the point of view of the relative size of fixed assets, manufacturers present greater problems than wholesalers and retailers. The three lines of manufacturing activity with the highest 5-year average ratio of fixed

Ratios of Fixed Assets to Tangible Net Worth   [Schedule 31]

Lines of Business Activity	Percentage					
	Median					Five-year Average
	1955	1956	1957	1958	1959	
Manufacturers						
Agricultural Implements and Machinery	34.0	31.4	29.5	29.7	28.0	30.5
Airplane Parts and Accessories	37.2	59.2	49.8	40.6	40.6	45.5
Automobile Parts and Accessories	41.0	39.9	35.8	43.7	36.8	39.4
Bakers	77.6	74.9	63.6	71.7	71.7	71.9
Bedsprings and Mattresses	26.9	29.3	26.9	25.0	22.8	26.2
Bodies, Auto, Bus, and Truck	38.2	42.9	40.3	38.1	35.1	38.9
Bolts, Screws, Nuts, and Nails	51.7	42.2	45.7	55.4	56.4	50.3
Breweries	76.0	66.9	68.5	67.6	77.0	71.2
Chemicals, Industrial	59.7	44.8	56.6	55.0	58.0	54.8
Coats and Suits, Men's and Boys'	7.9	7.7	6.1	6.6	6.6	7.0
Coats and Suits, Women's	6.9	7.4	7.6	7.3	7.4	7.3
Confectionery	41.0	40.7	42.4	39.8	43.2	41.4
Contractors, Building Construction	21.7	23.5	22.8	20.0	20.4	21.7
Contractors, Electrical	14.8	16.2	13.8	19.9	15.0	15.9
Cotton Cloth Mills	51.8	47.1	50.0	47.4	48.1	48.9
Cotton Goods, Converters, Non-factored	1.7	1.1	1.1	1.2	1.3	1.3
Dresses, Rayon, Silk, and Acetate	9.1	8.5	7.7	9.0	9.2	8.7
Drugs	39.2	37.3	34.3	37.4	34.1	36.5
Electrical Parts and Supplies	32.5	34.1	35.9	34.7	40.0	35.4
Foundries	46.3	47.4	48.4	47.3	47.2	47.3
Fruits and Vegetables, Canners	50.0	47.2	45.3	50.3	42.4	47.0
Furniture	32.5	33.0	31.5	29.8	33.8	32.1
Hardware and Tools	33.6	35.5	36.8	37.0	33.6	35.3
Hosiery	49.6	44.8	42.1	41.8	42.5	44.2
Lumber	39.0	33.0	31.1	37.0	44.7	37.0
Machine Shops	42.8	44.5	45.2	44.8	51.8	45.8
Machinery, Industrial	34.4	35.1	32.6	32.4	32.3	33.4
Meats and Provisions, Packers	57.7	63.1	58.4	62.9	60.4	60.5
Metal Stampings	42.8	45.3	43.7	42.3	40.3	42.9
Outerwear, Knitted	14.5	13.8	11.4	14.3	17.7	14.3
Overalls and Work Clothing	15.3	16.4	16.6	15.7	14.8	15.8
Paints, Varnishes, and Lacquers	32.0	31.8	34.9	33.5	31.8	32.8
Paper	71.6	67.3	71.3	76.7	72.2	71.8
Paper Boxes	55.6	50.1	58.3	54.7	50.6	53.9
Petroleum, Integrated Corporations	83.6	86.2	89.0	90.1	89.6	87.7
Printers, Job	48.9	62.1	60.0	59.3	59.5	58.0
Radio Parts and Supplies	32.9	41.9	37.6	39.2	38.1	37.9
Shirts, Underwear, and Pajamas, Men's	8.5	6.1	5.9	6.1	5.2	6.4
Shoes, Men's, Women's, and Children's	17.3	16.2	17.9	17.7	18.5	17.5
Soft Drinks and Carbonated Water, Bottlers	70.6	72.1	70.1	66.5	75.9	71.0
Steel, Structural Fabricators (Sell on Short Terms)	35.1	32.9	32.9	32.6	33.7	33.4
Stoves, Ranges, and Ovens	31.8	31.0	29.4	29.6	31.6	30.7

RATIOS OF FIXED ASSETS TO TANGIBLE NET WORTH (*Continued*)
[Schedule 31 (*Cont.*)]

Lines of Business Activity	Percentage					
	Median					Five-year Average
	1955	1956	1957	1958	1959	
WHOLESALERS						
Automobile Parts and Accessories....	15.4	13.9	13.1	13.5	12.9	13.8
Baked Goods......................	78.8	72.8	69.4	71.8	80.0	74.6
Cigars, Cigarettes, and Tobacco......	11.7	12.4	11.8	12.2	11.7	12.0
Drugs and Drug Sundries...........	10.5	11.7	13.0	15.3	17.4	13.6
Dry Goods........................	4.3	4.4	4.8	4.9	4.9	4.7
Electrical Parts and Supplies........	10.6	11.2	10.4	10.9	11.9	11.0
Fruits and Produce, Fresh...........	18.9	19.7	18.5	21.0	26.5	20.9
Furnishings, Men's.................	5.4	3.9	4.0	2.5	3.7	3.9
Gasoline, Fuel Oil, and Lubricating Oil	46.4	38.4	40.2	42.4	44.1	42.3
Groceries.........................	15.1	13.7	14.4	13.9	14.8	14.4
Hardware.........................	14.6	12.9	14.0	14.9	16.3	14.5
Hosiery and Underwear.............	3.9	3.5	3.7	4.5	2.7	3.7
Household Appliances, Electrical.....	11.1	9.3	9.5	7.0	7.8	8.9
Lumber...........................	12.3	9.2	10.8	12.0	13.8	11.6
Lumber and Building Materials......	19.0	16.8	20.4	19.9	20.5	19.3
Meat and Poultry..................	21.7	29.1	22.8	34.1	21.4	25.8
Paints, Varnishes, and Lacquers......	21.7	19.5	17.9	13.3	15.0	17.5
Paper............................	12.4	11.9	10.9	10.2	10.4	11.2
Plumbing and Heating Supplies......	15.8	15.1	14.7	15.2	14.6	15.1
Shoes, Men's, Women's, and Children's................................	3.8	4.6	4.6	3.8	3.7	4.1
Wines and Liquors.................	21.9	18.6	14.6	14.0	11.4	16.1
RETAILERS						
Clothing, Men's and Boys'..........	11.4	13.4	14.0	11.6	13.8	12.8
Department Stores.................	25.4	26.5	25.0	24.5	25.7	25.4
Furniture, 50 Per Cent or More Installment........................	13.1	10.2	14.2	13.4	9.2	12.0
Groceries and Meats, Independent....	63.3	58.9	51.4	54.9	41.6	54.0
Lumber and Building Materials......	22.8	20.5	25.1	17.7	19.2	21.1
Shoes............................	15.4	14.5	15.2	13.0	14.0	14.4
Women's Specialty Shops...........	23.3	21.1	22.3	21.4	21.1	21.8

assets to tangible net worth are: integrated petroleum operators with 87.7 per cent, bakers with 71.9 per cent, and manufacturers of paper with 71.8 per cent. The lowest 5-year average ratio for a manufacturer is 1.3 per cent for non-factored cotton goods converters.

Among wholesalers, the highest 5-year average ratio of fixed assets to tangible net worth is disclosed by wholesalers of baked goods with 74.6

per cent, and the lowest by wholesalers of ~~hosiery and underwear~~ *whole* with 3.7 per cent. Among the retail lines, the highest 5-year average ratio is *√9.9* shown by ~~independent~~ grocery and meat stores with 54.0 per cent, and the lowest by furniture stores with ~~12.0~~ *10.2* per cent.

By and large, it is an exceptional wholesaler or jobber that develops a financial problem as a result of excessive fixed assets. Combined balance *1961–1962* sheets of all wholesale corporations in ~~1957–1958~~, as set forth in footnote 1 *0* on page 279, show approximately 25.1 per cent of their aggregate net worth on the average invested in fixed assets. As will be seen in Schedule 31, in only 4 of the particular ~~21~~ *18* wholesale lines which have been studied over the 5-year period does the average 5-year investment in fixed assets exceed 20 per cent of the tangible net worth. These four lines are ~~wholesalers of baked goods with 74.6 per cent,~~ wholesalers of gasoline, fuel oil, and lubricating oil with ~~42.3~~ per cent, ~~wholesalers of meat and poultry with 25.8 per cent,~~ and wholesalers of fresh fruits and produce with ~~20.9~~ *28.5* per cent, *wholesalers of meat and meat products with 2.29 per cent, and wholesalers of lumber and building materials with 20.2 per cent.*

Maxim

When a business enterprise has a tangible net worth between $50,000 and $250,000, experience has shown that its condition should be carefully analyzed if the depreciated book value of its fixed assets is more than two-thirds of its tangible net worth. When the tangible net worth exceeds $250,000 the affairs of the concern should be followed closely if the depreciated book value of its fixed assets is more than three-quarters of its tangible net worth. *66*

Only 11 of the ~~70~~ important lines of industrial and commercial activity that have been analyzed show a 5-year average ratio where the fixed assets amount to more than one-half the tangible net worth. Ten of them are manufacturing lines of activity and one a wholesale line. Only ~~five~~ *three* lines show 5-year averages in which the investments in fixed assets exceed two-thirds of the tangible net worth. A ratio of 66⅔ to 75 per cent of the tangible net worth is more than a fair leeway as a reasonable business guide for the percentage of funds to be invested in fixed assets. Smaller percentages are proportionately more favorable.

THEORY AND PROBLEMS

1. Explain what is meant by the term *fixed assets*. State four ways by which fixed assets may be valued and explain each method of valuation.

2. If two competing concerns have approximately the same tangible net worth, but one concern has a substantially greater investment in net depreciated fixed assets, why is that concern often unable to earn as large net profits as the one with smaller net depreciated fixed assets?

3. The Beer Brewing Co., Inc., is a brewer of beer in a Midwestern city. From the following comparative figures compute (*a*) net working capital, (*b*) tangible net worth, (*c*) current ratio, (*d*) ratio of current debt to tangible net worth, and (*e*) ratio of fixed assets to tangible net worth. Then give your interpretation of each of these particular ratios for each year.

BEER BREWING CO., INC.

Comparative Figures for Years Ended December 31, 19—

	(B) Two Years Ago	(A) One Year Ago
ASSETS		
Cash..	$ 13,151	$ 30,864
Accounts Receivable............................	45,179	51,936
Merchandise...................................	97,530	107,386
Beer Stamps...................................	4,717	9,753
Current Assets................................	$160,577	$199,939
Fixed Assets, Net after Depreciation..................	449,169	509,459
Investments...................................	2,000	5,726
Deferred.....................	1,903	2,003
Miscellaneous Receivables.........................	1,350	6,708
Good Will.....................................	189,639	189,707
TOTAL.....................................	$804,638	$913,542
LIABILITIES		
Notes Payable to Bank............................	$ 74,000	$ 50,000
Accounts Payable................................	56,650	34,036
Accruals......................................	39,266	47,417
Dividend Payable.............................	....	27,000
Other Liabilities................................	18,610	4,289
Current Liabilities.............................	$188,526	$162,742
Preferred Stock.................................	300,000	300,000
Common Stock..................................	150,000	150,000
Capital Surplus.................................	4,033	4,033
Retained Earnings...............................	162,079	296,767
TOTAL.....................................	$804,638	$913,542

4. The Machine Manufacturing Corporation was recently reorganized. The balance sheet which follows is the first to be issued after the reorganization. The president of the corporation took these figures with the accompanying notes to a financial consultant for his analysis. The financial consultant proceeded to post the figures carefully and then to make the following computations:

   a. Net working capital
   b. Tangible net worth
   c. Current ratio
   d. Ratio of current liabilities to tangible net worth
   e. Ratio of total liabilities to tangible net worth
   f. Ratio of funded debt to net working capital
   g. Ratio of fixed assets to tangible net worth

Assume you are the financial consultant. Post the balance sheet, make the above computations, and then give your interpretation of the ratio of fixed assets to tangible net worth.

MACHINE MANUFACTURING CORPORATION
Balance Sheet, December 31, 19—
ASSETS

Current Assets			
Cash on hand and on deposit......................			$ 233,864
Trade accounts receivable.........................	$ 414,395		
Less: Reserves..................................	43,580		370,815
Inventories—Note *A*			
Finished product................................	$ 556,223		
Work in process.................................	83,484		
Raw materials, supplies, etc.....................	80,772		720,479
Incompleted construction contract			
Labor, material, and other costs....................			3,377
Total Current Assets.......................			$1,328,535
Investments and Other Assets			
Investments in and advances, etc., to affiliates			
Canadian Company (60% owned)—capital stock at par value ($180,000) and advances, etc. ($29,923)..............	$ 209,923		
Domestic Company (74.30% owned) preferred (voting) capital stock at par value.............................	28,220		
	$ 238,143		
Less: Reserves......................	52,055	186,088	
Other investments at cost (no quoted market).........		2,634	
Sundry claims, deposits, receivables, etc...............		17,136	
Sinking and property release funds in connection with first mortgage bonds..................................		4,922	210,780
Property, Plant, and Equipment—Note *B*			
Subject to mortgage securing first mortgage 5½% bonds			
Real estate, mineral lands, rights, etc....	$ 2,459,236		
Buildings, machinery, equipment, etc....	7,771,499		
	$10,230,735		
Less: Reserves for depreciation and depletion.............................	4,057,570	$6,173,165	
Not subject to mortgage securing first mortgage 5½% bonds—Note *C*			
Real estate, mineral lands, rights, etc..	$ 861,999		
Building, machinery, equipment, etc...	2,219,420		
	$ 3,081,419		
Less: Reserves for depreciation and depletion.......................	1,173,063	1,908,357	8,081,522
Good Will.....................			1
Deferred Charges			
Unamortized portion of bond discount and expense......	$ 10,961		
Prepaid insurance...................................	9,358		
Other deferred expense..............................	48,366		68,685
			$9,689,523

MACHINE MANUFACTURING CORPORATION (*Continued*)

LIABILITIES

Current Liabilities
  Accounts payable

Trade accounts...................................	$	137,753	
Salaries, wages, commissions, and bonuses...........		62,477	
Pay roll and withholding taxes.....................		33,159	
Employees' deposits..............................		6,707 $	240,096

Accrued

Local taxes.....................................	$	28,043	
Interest on first mortgage bonds, etc................		6,112	
Sundry taxes, insurance, and other expenses..........		18,794	52,949

Advance billing on uncompleted construction contract

Advance billings.................................	$	4,941	
Less: Labor, material, and other costs...............		4,557	384
Purchase money mortgage installments due—Note *D*....			14,200
Total Current Liabilities....................		$	307,629

Funded and Other Long-term Debt
  First mortgage convertible 5½% bonds
    Series A—due Nov. 1, 19—Note *E*
      Authorized $1,000,000

Issued.............................	$	800,000	
Less: Retired ($572,500) and in treasury			
($2,000).........................		574,500 $	225,500

16-year 5% cumulative convertible income
  debentures—due May 1, 19—
    Issued or to be issued under plan of reor-

ganization........................	$2,636,900		
Less: In treasury....................	83,600	2,553,300	
Purchase money mortgages—Note *D*.......	$	605,200	
Less installments due as shown above.......		14,200	591,000	3,369,800

Deferred Liability

Accumulated interest on 16-year 5% cumulative converti-		
ble income debentures...........................		851,100

Reserves

For new dies and repairs...........................		5,544

Capital Stock and Surplus
  Capital stock
    Common—par value $5 per share
      Authorized 750,000 shares
      Reserved for conversion of funded debt (186,005
      shares)
      Issued or to be issued under plan of reorganization

approved June 8, 19—489,782 shares............	$2,448,910		

Surplus

Capital surplus.........................	$3,235,800		
Retained earnings—deficit...............	*529,260*	2,706,540	5,155,450
		·	$9,689,523

NOTES TO FINANCIAL STATEMENTS

Note *A*. Inventory amounts are based upon book records of the corporation which were adjusted to reflect physical determinations of quantities made by employees during the latter part of the year. In-process and finished products are priced at standard costs (approximating actual costs but not including depreciation charges) not in excess of the lower of average cost or market prices, and raw materials, supplies, etc., are priced on the basis of the lower of first-in first-out cost or replacement market prices.

Note *B*. $1,909,551 of the net amount of $8,081,522 stated for property, plant, and equipment represents the net book carrying amount applicable to plants and equipment not operated since reorganization of the corporation as of June 8, 19—. Provision for depreciation of such plants and equipment amounted to $56,860 for the current fiscal year.

Note *C*. Property, plant, and equipment of a net book carrying amount of $647,469 (not subject to the mortgage securing the first mortgage 5½ per cent bonds) are subject to purchase money mortgages payable of $605,200.

Note *D*. Under the terms of a modification agreement, $603,000 of the amount stated for purchase money mortgages payable is due $12,000 next year, and $8,750 quarterly thereafter until payment is made in full.

Note *E*. The terms of the first mortgage convertible 5½ per cent bond indenture require the payment into a sinking fund for the purchase or redemption of said bonds on April 1 of each year during which the bonds are outstanding of 25 per cent of the "available net earnings" (as defined in the indenture) of the corporation for the preceding calendar year. The corporation had no "available net earnings" for the current year.

5. What maxim should be followed in deciding whether the net depreciated value of fixed assets of a commercial or industrial business enterprise is reasonable or excessive?

CHAPTER XI

Net Sales to Inventory

From a very practical viewpoint, the size and balance of the inventory of every business enterprise are of great importance. For years it has been almost standard practice for managements to value inventories of commercial and industrial concerns at *cost or market, whichever is lower*. The early concept of *cost or market, whichever is lower*, however, made little headway in this country until the advent of the Federal income tax law. Originally it was not officially recognized as a sound practice by the Treasury Department. Subsequent enthusiasm for this accounting convention was engendered by the fact that taxable income was reduced by its use.[1]

The practical business theory was then evolved that, in those cases where the market value of the inventory was higher than cost, profits should not be anticipated but that losses, if probable even though not actually incurred where the market was lower than cost, should be anticipated. This principle is partly a matter of valuation, but also a recognition of the principle of the balance of recoverable cost.

The cost of purchased articles is generally understood to be the purchase price plus transportation charges incurred for delivery to the purchaser. In addition, other costs, such as import duties, insurance, warehousing and handling costs may be proper additions to purchase price. . . . Manufacturers not only must account for purchased materials costs but also must determine the cost of finished and semifinished products including material, labor, and a reasonable allocation of manufacturing overhead.[2]

COST OR MARKET, WHICHEVER IS LOWER

There is probably no term in accounting in greater need of clarification than the constantly used phrase *cost or market, whichever is lower*. The words *cost* and *market* carry an absolute meaning to the layman and to the young analyst. Actually, however, each term may have several meanings,

[1] PATON, WILLIAM A., "Comments on 'A Statement of Accounting Principles,'" *Journal of Accountancy*, Vol. 65, No. 3, p. 202, March, 1938.

[2] LENHART, NORMAN J., AND PHILIP L. DEFLIESE, *Montgomery's Auditing*, 8th ed., pp. 193–194 (The Ronald Press Company, New York, 1957).

each interpretation giving a different value to the inventory. Should this phrase, for example, apply to each item in the inventory or to the inventory in the aggregate? Notice the difference in the following illustration:

Item	Cost	Market	Lower of Cost or Market
A	$ 1,800	$ 2,200	$ 1,800
B	1,050	1,650	1,050
C	3,200	3,100	3,100
D	3,500	3,800	3,500
E	1,425	1,125	1,125
	$10,975	$11,875	$10,575

In this schedule the cost of the five items is $10,975. The market value of the five items is $11,875. At the lower of cost or market for each individual item the value is $10,575. If the phase *cost or market, whichever is lower* should apply to the inventory in the aggregate, the inventory would then be carried at $10,975. If the phase should apply item by item, the inventory would be carried in the balance sheet at $10,575. Today, the item-by-item process is generally but by no means exclusively used.[3]

Suppose a business concern enters its fiscal year with 1,000,000 pounds of copper purchased at 24 cents per pound, or an inventory of $240,000. Suppose the first purchase during the year, amounting to 1,000,000 pounds, is made at 30 cents per pound, and additional copper is purchased during the remainder of the year at prices ranging up to 33 cents per pound, at which price the market closes at the end of the fiscal year. Now, suppose that an inventory of 1,100,000 pounds of copper is on hand when the year closes. In this case, the market price on the statement date obviously is 33 cents per pound. But what is *cost* for the 1,100,000 pounds of copper, and what is *cost or market, whichever is lower?* Is it 24 cents per pound, the starting cost for the 1,000,000 pounds on hand when the year

[3] "The purpose of reducing inventory to *market* is to reflect fairly the income of the period. The most common practice is to apply the *lower of cost or market* rule separately to each item of the inventory. However, if there is only one end-product category, the cost utility of the total stock—the inventory in its entirety—may have the greatest significance for accounting purposes. Accordingly, the reduction of individual items to *market* may not always lead to the most useful result if the utility of the total inventory to the business is not below its cost. This might be the case if selling prices are not affected by temporary or small fluctuations in current costs of purchases or manufacture. Similarly, where more than one major product or operational category exists, the application of the *cost or market, whichever is lower* rule to the total of the items included in such major categories may result in the most useful determination of income."—*Restatement and Revision of Accounting Research Bulletins, Accounting Research Bulletin* No. 43, p. 32 (American Institute of Certified Public Accountants, New York, 1953).

opened, and 30 cents per pound for the 100,000 additional pounds, or $270,000? Is it the last cost of 33 cents per pound for the entire 1,100,000 pounds, or $363,000? Is it 24 cents per pound for the 1,000,000 pounds on hand when the year opened and 33 cents per pound for the last 100,000 pounds purchased, or $273,000? Is it the cost of the last 1,100,000 pounds of copper purchased? Or is it a weighted average cost throughout the year that would rest somewhere between these varied figures?

There are six widely known and used methods of valuing inventory that approach this problem in different ways, namely, first-in first-out, base stock, average cost, retail method, standard costs, and, of the widest current interest, last-in first-out.[4]

It is an axiom of accounting that the basis of valuing inventory should be consistently applied from one accounting period to another and should be disclosed in the balance sheet. When a significant change in the method is made, such as changing from first-in first-out to last-in first-out, that fact also should be disclosed and, as accountants say, "if material," the effect that the change had upon the income should be fully explained.[5] This practice is customarily followed by independent accountants, and the significance of the change is quite generally outlined by chief executive officers of larger corporations in their annual reports to stockholders.

Retailers and wholesalers purchase finished products to which they add a distributing service in the process of reselling. Manufacturers purchase raw materials, to which they add labor and overhead to produce finished products. The finished products of one manufacturer often are raw materials for another. The raw material, together with the material partly or wholly manufactured but yet unsold, is inventory. When part of the inventory is sold it must be replaced if a business is to continue. In other words, some inventory is always on hand in all but very unusual business enterprises. Now, let us compare the various well-known ways by which inventory may be valued, keeping in mind that, insofar as possible, the practice should be consistent from year to year.

First-in First-out

First is the first-in first-out method, the process that has been and still is more widely used than all others in the valuation of inventories. Under

[4] The fourteenth annual edition of *Accounting Trends and Techniques* lists seven additional methods of inventory valuation used by 600 representative corporations in 1959, namely, approximate cost, actual cost, invoice cost, production cost, estimated cost, replacement cost, and job-order method.—p. 51 (American Institute of Certified Public Accountants, New York, 1960).

[5] *Restatement and Revision of Accounting Research Bulletins, Accounting Research Bulletin No. 43*, pp. 33–34 (American Institute of Certified Public Accountants, New York, 1953).

this method, the cost of any article in the inventory is assumed to be the latest cost of the corresponding quantity purchased or produced. It is based on the assumption that the oldest material or finished goods are used or sold before using or selling any later purchases or productions, an assumption most applicable to concerns whose merchandise is subject to deterioration. This is predicated on the theory that inventory costs move toward expiration in the chronological order in which they are incurred.

Under this first-in first-out method, the 1,100,000 pounds of copper on hand at the end of the year would be valued at the cost of the last 1,100,000 pounds purchased. If that cost was 31 cents per pound for 400,000 pounds, 32 cents per pound for 500,000 pounds, and 33 cents per pound for 200,000 pounds, the cost by this most widely used method would be $124,000 plus $160,000 plus $66,000, or $350,000. If the cost was 33 cents per pound for the last 1,100,000 pounds of copper purchased during the year, the inventory would be carried at $363,000.

During a period of rising prices there is included in income, under first-in first-out, unrealized appreciation in the value of inventories; during a period of falling prices, operating profits are reduced or wiped out by unrealized inventory losses. Inventories often are highest, not only in value but also quantitatively, at the peak of a price cycle. Price appreciation on goods remaining in the inventory may never be realized because a period of rising prices is always followed, some time or other, by a period of falling prices. Where inventories have been materially increased by deliberate buying for a rise, or where inventories normally constitute an important part of the assets of a business enterprise, their valuation under first-in first-out may represent the most important factor in the determination of profit or loss during the up-and-down phases of the price cycle, inflating true profits in years of rising prices, and understating true profits when prices recede.

Industries where the first-in first-out method of valuing inventory clearly distorts income and fails to picture the correct cost of goods produced and sold are characterized by one or more of the following conditions:

1. The inventory turnover consumes a relatively long period of time because of either the length of processing or conditions of merchandising, thus necessitating the maintenance at all times of a substantial inventory.

2. The average investment in inventory is relatively large compared with other assets.

3. The inventory consists of a few basic and imperishable commodities which are subject to wide price fluctuation.

4. The cost of raw materials constitutes a substantial part of the cost of the finished product, and increases in the prices of raw materials are promptly reflected in the price of the product.

Base Stock

The second way by which inventory may be valued is known as the *base stock* or *normal stock* method of control. This method is predicated on the theory that the only real costs are replacement costs, and that a fixed, or a relatively fixed, permanent quantity of inventory, analogous to a reservoir, without which operations would not be continued, must be maintained at all times. This essential supply, or base stock, is valued at a fixed price, usually so low that actual prices will never fall below it. This part of the inventory is treated as though it were never sold, despite the fact that it is mixed with incoming inventory and physically, more or less, does get processed and is used. Inventory purchased during a given year, or during other accounting periods, in excess of this base stock, is generally valued in inventory on the basis of cost or market whichever is lower, by the first-in first-out method, or by averaging.

While the physical volume of inventory actually on hand may sometimes fall below the base stock quantity, this fact does not interfere with the base price. When replacements are made and the physical stock again is brought to its predetermined normal size, any excess cost is written off against earnings. If the market value breaks through the price at which the base inventory is carried, then the value of the base inventory is continued permanently at this lower level until another break-through.

If 500,000 pounds of copper should be the base stock, then the inventory of the 1,100,000 pounds would be valued: (1) 500,000 pounds at a base price, say, of 10 cents per pound, or $50,000, and (2) 600,000 pounds at first-in first-out basis, 400,000 pounds at 32 cents per pound, and 200,000 pounds at 33 cents per pound, or $194,000, giving an inventory valuation of $244,000.

The base stock method of inventory valuation has been used in Scotland, Wales, England, and Holland for more than half a century, although it is not generally accepted even in those countries. The American Smelting & Refining Company was the first large corporation in the United States to adopt base stock method of control. That took place in 1903. The National Lead Company[6] followed suit in 1913, the American Can Company in 1917, Endicott-Johnson Corporation in 1936, and the Corn Products Refining Company in 1939.

The United States Treasury Department has consistently refused to

---

[6] Since 1932 the National Lead Company has carried its base stock of lead at 3 cents per pound. Inventories in excess of base stock on Dec. 31, 1960, were carried at the lower of cost (on various "averages," "first-in first-out," or "last-in first-out" bases) or market. The Dec. 31, 1960, annual report gives the physical quantity and price of base stock as follows: 49,687½ short tons of lead at 3 cents per pound, 1,124½ short tons of tin at 21 cents per pound, and 1,400 short tons of antimony at 5 cents per pound.

recognize the use of base stock accounting in corporate income tax returns. ~~Under these circumstances, it hardly seems likely that there will be any material growth in the use of base stock in corporation accounting except as a protection for stockholders and for the investing public.~~

Average Cost

Third is the average cost method of pricing inventory, a method which is peculiarly suitable to the tobacco industry. Fluctuations in the price of the various kinds of tobacco entering into the inventory are ironed out to a very material extent by this method of costing. The average cost is a "moving average" and is figured from additions to and subtractions from stocks on hand each month over, roughly, a 3-year period.[7] Market quotations for raw tobacco are entirely ignored. At times, inventory valuations on the balance sheet bear little relation to the immediate market prices.

To use average cost it is quite necessary for a concern to have a complete cost system with perpetual inventory records kept in both dollars and quantities. The weighted average for an item is computed by adding the purchases to the beginning inventory and dividing the total dollar amount by the total quantity. This weighted average cost is used in pricing the closing inventory. This method eliminates much of the detailed pricing; it spreads the effect of price fluctuations; and it is more satisfactory from the managerial point of view where costs on the average are of greater importance than are costs of a particular lot. Quite a number of companies in other industries have borrowed the average cost system from the tobacco processors, and its use is fairly general at the present time.[8]

[7] From the point of view of regularity of yearly income, it is doubtful if the record of the three leading tobacco concerns, often referred to as "The Big Three"—American Tobacco, Liggett & Myers, and R. J. Reynolds—can be equaled by comparable corporations in any other industry. What their stockholders and the investing public generally have failed to realize, however, although there has been no effort to conceal the fact, is that this unusual showing has been due in great part to the manner in which they have valued their inventories. Had these three corporations reported inventory on the usual "cost or market, whichever is lower" basis, using "first-in first-out," it is certain that their earnings would have been a great deal more erratic, that in some years one or more of them would have shown either a small profit or possibly a loss, while in other years reported income would have been swollen by high-priced inventories. Inventories constitute an exceptionally large percentage of all assets—more than 75 per cent on the average—and moreover, tobacco must be kept for approximately 3 years for "aging," increasing the impact of price changes upon the value of stocks on hand. In 1957 a radical change occurred when R. J. Reynolds Tobacco Company changed from average cost to last-in first-out in valuing its inventory. This change was made since substantial savings could be made in Federal income taxes by using last-in first-out.

[8] A survey by the National Industrial Conference Board in 1938 revealed the fact that 39 per cent of 826 *manufacturers* that replied to a questionnaire employed average cost in valuing all or part of their inventories. The ~~fourteenth~~ nineteenth edition of *Account-*

Retail Method

Fourth, is the retail method of inventory valuation. This method values the inventory at average cost or market, whichever is lower (on a rising market the value will be essentially cost; on a falling market, cost or market whichever is lower). It is considered to be the most scientific and satisfactory method of valuing inventories for retail enterprises, although in recent years many of the larger department stores have superimposed last-in first-out on the retail method.

All purchases are entered in the merchandise record at cost and at predetermined selling prices. The difference between the cost of all items in the inventory and the total predetermined selling prices of all items represents the anticipated gross profit. This percentage of mark-on, with necessary adjustments for discounts, sales, and allowances, is applied to the ending inventory at the aggregate selling price, yielding the inventory at computed "cost," which may be cost or market whichever is lower depending on price revisions on purchases, and price changes made on merchandise in stock. By this method, cost is a direct derivative of the price at which merchandise is currently being offered for sale.

By use of the retail inventory method of valuation, the laborious process of inventorying and costing thousands of items to obtain an inventory figure for balance sheet purposes is eliminated. Balance sheets may be prepared monthly or as often as desired by using the book inventories obtained from the merchandise record or stock ledger. Like all book inventories, the retail book inventory must be checked periodically by physical inventories. This inventorying may be done for the store as a whole at one time or by departments or subdivisions of departments throughout the year.

Standard Cost

Fifth, is the standard cost method of inventory valuation used in valuing finished products of a manufacturer. Standard cost has been defined as predetermined cost computed on the specifications of the product and predetermined manufacturing methods, which include specific amounts of raw material, direct labor, and burden; it is more a theory of what cost should be than what cost really is. Standard raw material is obtained from an itemized schedule of the various kinds, grades, and sizes of mate-

---

ing Trends and Techniques showed that in 1950, 136 out of 521 corporations disclosing their method of inventory valuation in their annual corporate reports, used average cost, and for 1959, 161 out of 645 corporations used average cost. In 1959 average cost was exceeded in use only by last-in first-out and first-in first-out by this particular group of 645 representative corporations.—p. 51 (American Institute of Certified Public Accountants, New York, 1960).

rials used. Standard labor is obtained from an itemized schedule of operations necessary for the manufacture of the product, computed at current labor rates. Standard burden rates are established by means of a budget of the manufacturing expenses considered appropriate to a normal level of operating capacity. The difference between standard costs and actual costs is usually reflected in overabsorbed and underabsorbed accounts which are used in making actual adjustment at the time of the physical inventory.

Last-in First-out

Sixth is the last-in first-out method of inventory valuation. Last-in first-out, unlike the base stock method of pricing inventory, disregards the necessity of any given volume of inventory. It assumes that real costs of goods are those of replacement, as nearly as possible at the time of sale, and, therefore, sales are costed on the basis of inventory latest acquired, or *last-in*, while *first-in* inventory is treated as unsold, or, in effect, a tool for future operations, and is thus reported on the balance sheet.[9] Since this method of interpreting cost does not necessarily require any fixed amount of stock, first-in inventory at the end of any given year will be affected by the volume of purchases and sales. It assumes that the 100,000 pounds of copper added to the inventory was the first purchased at 30 cents, while the copper later purchased, being last-in, was first-out, or sold. On this basis the 1,100,000 pounds would be valued at $270,000, or an average of approximately 24.55 cents per pound.

As in the case of base stock, successful operation of last-in first-out presupposes that first-in stocks will be carried at a conservative price level.

[9] "Petroleum, one of the greatest American industries, may claim the honor of being the leader, as an industry, in advocating and putting into practice itself the 'last-in first-out' method of inventory valuation. A number of oil companies have been costing their inventories on the current basis—using this method—for years, and in 1934 the American Petroleum Institute recommended the general adoption of the system by all producers and refiners. . . . The reasons for this lie in the nature of the petroleum industry itself. In the first place, inventory is a serious problem. Values of stocks carried sometimes run as high as one-third of all invested capital, and there have been times when crude oil prices have declined as much as 50 per cent within the space of a few months. The impact of such large stocks subject to such wide price variations upon assets and profits is only too plain."—COTTER, ARUNDEL, *Fool's Profits*, p. 134 (Barron's Publishing Company, Inc., New York, 1940). A study made by the American Institute of Certified Public Accountants disclosed that a marked increase in the use of the last-in first-out method of cost determination occurred in 1950 and 1951, such method of cost determination being used since 1950 more often than any other method. Prior to 1950, average cost was most frequently used, with first-in first-out and last-in first-out alternating in second and third places from 1946 through 1949. In the 1960 study, last-in first-out was used by 202 of 645 corporations whose annual reports were examined, Fourteenth edition of *Accounting Trends and Techniques*, p. 51 (American Institute of Certified Public Accountants, New York, 1960).

It is not essential, however, that low market quotations prevail at the time of the change to last-in first-out. It is probable that most of the companies using this system originally made some adjustment by writing down inventory values to what they considered conservative levels, and that these adjustments were charged to the income statement or to the surplus account. For the average manufacturing or processing concern the last-in first-out method of inventory valuation comes closer to revealing to management, stockholders, and creditors the true condition of the business and the real profits or losses than any other accounting formula that has yet been devised.

Over a sufficiently long period of time—a complete economic cycle—aggregate net operating results should be exactly the same, whether last-in first-out, first-in first-out, or any other approved method of valuing inventory is employed. The net profits before taxes of respective years within the cycle may vary considerably, depending upon which method is employed, and under present tax laws, net profits after taxes over a complete cycle will vary considerably. Last-in first-out tends to level off the annual net income by lowering the peaks and raising the valleys.

This system of inventory valuation was first recognized by statutory provision of the Revenue Act of 1939. The fact that many important corporations had adopted this interpretation of cost before it was permitted for tax purposes indicates that in some cases benefits other than those arising from income tax reasons were responsible for its adoption.

NEED FOR INVENTORY CONTROL

Inventories have been called the "graveyard of American business" because they have so frequently been the prime cause of business failures. Inventories that have been allowed to become unwieldy often contain an ill assortment of poorly chosen or obsolete goods, or the management has speculated on rising prices. When prices fall, losses are assumed; if both the inventory and the liabilities are heavy, bankruptcy often results. The inventory is one of the more important balance sheet items because of its direct relation to the profit and loss for two successive periods, the year just closed, and the following year. The importance of the inventory increases as the dollar volume of the inventory rises in relation to other assets.

Losses from Falling Prices

No one factor has such an immediate effect upon the well-being of a business enterprise as the level of prices of the raw material which a manufacturing concern uses, or the level of wholesale prices of the products which a wholesale or a retail concern handles. If the general level of prices of the products which a concern is handling goes up, its own selling prices may be raised and an unexpected profit may be obtained on the inventory purchased at lower prices and already on hand. To a marginal enterprise balancing itself on the brink of uncertainty, that means renewed vigor and a somewhat longer lease on life. The time always comes, however, when the rise in prices ceases, hesitates, and then turns downward. When the downward trend sets in, the inventory on hand must be marked with lower prices in order that it may be sold in a competitive market, and a loss is taken in that very process, a process which ends only in a permanent blackout for many marginal concerns.[10]

It should also be kept in mind that every dollar added to or subtracted from the value of the inventory is reflected in a like amount in the income statement. The size of net profits depends upon the validity of the inventory values shown in the balance sheet. We have seen what a wide range in bases exists for this valuation.

Losses from Obsolescence

Second in importance to falling prices in the effect upon inventory losses is obsolescence, particularly where the inventory is not turned over as rapidly as is typical for a division of industry or commerce. Style, design, color, utility, and price play important parts not only in the retail trade, but also in manufacturing and wholesaling. To cope with these trends the manufacturer is faced with two major conditions. An adequate stock of the right merchandise must be maintained at the right time if a business is to progress, yet, at the same time, the inventory must be under constant control to avoid excessive stocks with consequent losses from obsolescence. In spite of seasonal demand, the production program of a manufacturer must be planned so that a relatively even flow will continue throughout the year to obtain maximum benefits of plant, equipment, and labor utilization. If sales and production are carefully coordinated with effective controls, obsolescence in inventory will be kept to a minimum, except where market studies for the demand of a particular product, or the judgment of those responsible for style, design, color, utility, and price, have been in error.

Aging of Inventory

There has been developing a technique of inventory control similar to the technique which has long existed in accounts receivable control. The objectives of inventory control are the keeping of the inventory in a defi-

[10] The correlation between price levels and failures is discussed in *Peaks and Valleys in Wholesale Prices and Business Failures* by Roy A. Foulke (Dun & Bradstreet, Inc. New York, 1950).

nite relationship with net sales and with net working capital, the conversion of inventory into cash in the shortest possible time, the minimizing of losses through obsolescence, depreciation, and expenses resulting from excessive inventory, and the developing of records to give a constant aging of inventory similar to an aging of receivables.

The age of inventory is important from the financial point of view as it indicates the rate at which materials and merchandise are being converted into cash; simultaneously, it emphasizes the cost of carrying goods in stock. A large inventory increases the current assets, but it also increases the current liabilities. In a manufacturing concern if the raw material does not find its way into salable finished merchandise in a reasonable length of time, its actual value may be much less than that carried on the books.

Products in the inventory that have not been moved for a relatively long period may prove to be an unprofitable investment; they may eventually be sold at a loss or scrapped because of a change in design or in the line of products, because the items were not suitable or actually needed, or because the goods had been damaged or allowed to deteriorate. The most unsatisfactory products would be disposed of as obsolete, damaged, or deteriorated. An aging of inventory items, however, would furnish the information to management to forestall such losses.

Moreover, it is costly to carry in stock goods for which there is no immediate use. If money is being borrowed at the rate of 5 per cent per annum, then the cost of goods lying in a warehouse or a store for a year is increased by that percentage. An exaggerated example of this situation was disclosed by a company that had on hand enough of certain standard kinds of wood screws to fill its normal needs for 20 years. Had these wood screws been held until they were used, the last of them would have cost more than twice the original price.

There are certain times when it may be economical to add goods to the inventory even though they may not be used for a long period. When only a few pieces of a certain part are used in an assembly, when the setup for the manufacture of the part is expensive, and when the material is relatively inexpensive, it may pay to make a sufficient quantity at one time to last for a long period. In some types of manufacture, the time that is taken to prepare the machine and produce the first piece to pass inspection may justify the production of a large number once the setup is made. In such exceptional cases it is economical to carry relatively large stocks of certain slow-moving items.

The turnover of inventory is a means to an end, the end of earning the maximum of net profits. Heavy inventories involve losses from obsolescence and depreciation, and expense in carrying. Light inventories bring about lessening of profits through higher costs in fractional buying and loss of sales through incomplete stocks. In other words, an Aristotelian sense of proportion must come into play; the minimum inventory consistent with sound operations is the desired objective. That objective differs widely in different divisions of industry and commerce, and often within departments of the same concern. The only real bargain in inventory is as small a stock as circumstances will warrant with a rapid turnover of that stock, never the purchase of merchandise merely because it seems to be offered at a low price.

Inventory Partially a Purchasing Problem

The purchasing problems of a manufacturer are usually somewhat more complicated than those of a distributing business because of the greater fluctuations in raw material prices and because orders must often be placed months ahead of delivery. The larger manufacturing concerns, in particular, must generally place orders for their requirements well in advance of their needs to be sure that there will be no interruption in production.

Once purchase commitments are made and orders are placed, it is extremely difficult and sometimes impossible to cut down on the growth of inventories with sufficient speed to keep a financial condition thoroughly sound. In fact it is no unusual occurrence for the market value of goods on order to drop before the goods are even shipped. The handling of such situations became so important that the subject received the attention of the Committee on Accounting Procedure of the American Institute of Certified Public Accountants in 1947. It is evident that the recognition in the current accounting period of such potential losses which are expected from firm, uncancelable, and unhedged commitments is essential in analyzing the financial condition of a business. The losses on such commitments should be measured in the same way as are inventory losses and, if material, should be separately disclosed in the income statement. The utility of such commitments, however, is not impaired, and there is no loss, when the amounts to be realized from the disposition of the future inventory items are adequately protected by firm sales contracts.[11]

This problem grows in importance with the size of the business. Inventories which are reasonable in one month may, within a very few months, become excessive and dangerous as a result of a sharp decline in the rate of sales. The only possible way to avoid or to alleviate headaches which result from undigested inventories is to plan far ahead and, with large concerns, to build up efficient internal controls.

[11] *Restatement and Revision of Accounting Research Bulletins, Accounting Research Bulletin* No. 43, pp. 34–35 (American Institute of Certified Public Accountants, New York, 1953).

ILLUSTRATIONS OF RELATIONSHIPS

There are two practical guides to the size of inventories in commercial and industrial businesses, the relationship between the net sales and the inventory, and the relationship between the inventory and the net working capital. This chapter is concerned with the first of these two relationships. The ratio of net sales to inventory, or a qualification of this ratio—the relationship of cost of sales to inventory, which tends to give a turnover rate—has been used for many years by progressive business executives.

Retail Men's Clothing Store

James Cluff started a small retail men's furnishing shop 26 years ago in Jersey City, N.J., with a moderate investment of $5,600. At that time Cluff was a young man twenty-two years of age. He discontinued this business 4 years later and opened a slightly larger store in Newark, N.J., to retail men's clothing, principally suits, topcoats, and overcoats but with a side line of furnishings and shoes. Each of these units was operated as a proprietorship.

The Newark business was incorporated 11 years ago under the style of Retail Men's Clothing, Inc., with an authorized and paid-in capital of 25 shares of common stock of no par value. In the years immediately following the incorporation, sales declined and the financial condition of the business became involved. An involuntary petition in bankruptcy was filed 9 years ago against the corporation by three creditors. Assets amounted to $17,555 and liabilities to $28,336. Claims were subsequently settled by the payment of 25 per cent in cash. The business was then resumed and operations have continued with more or less success up to the present time. The comparative figures for the past 3 years appear in Schedule 32.

At the end of year C and of year B operations were being conducted on a paid-in capital of $20,820. On the first day of year A, the paid-in capital was increased to $40,000 by the payment in cash of $19,180 into the business by friends of James Cluff. The retained earnings at the end of year C amounted to $189, at the end of year B to $1,846, and at the end of year A to $3,495. Largely as the result of the issuance of the additional common stock for cash, the tangible net worth increased from $22,666 at the end of year B to $43,495 at the end of year A.

During year C, net sales amounted to $52,498 and a net loss of $576 was incurred. During year B, net sales dropped to $46,497 but a net profit of $1,657 was earned on the smaller volume. During year A, net sales expanded to $65,462 and a net profit of $1,649 was recorded. No dividends were paid during any of these 3 years.

The sales of the Retail Men's Clothing, Inc., are made largely on a cash basis. As a result, the receivables represent a nominal proportion of the current assets in each of the three balance sheets, ranging from a low of

RETAIL MEN'S CLOTHING, INC. [Schedule 32]
Comparative Figures for Years Ended March 31, 19—

	(C) Three Years Ago	(B) Two Years Ago	(A) One Year Ago
ASSETS			
Cash	$ 709	$ 1,402	$ 1,238
Accounts Receivable	1,344	1,496	1,644
Inventory	29,161	32,447	54,502
Current Assets	$31,214	$35,345	$57,384
Fixed Assets, Net	350	518	683
Loans Receivable	1,872	2,459	3,964
Deposits	175	176	185
TOTAL	$33,611	$38,498	$62,216
LIABILITIES			
Loan from Bank	$ 500	$ 200	$ 600
Accounts Payable	8,497	13,072	16,871
Accruals	103	240	216
Due to James Cluff	3,502	2,320	1,034
Current Liabilities	$12,602	$15,832	$18,721
Common Stock	20,820	20,820	40,000
Retained Earnings	189	1,846	3,495
TOTAL	$33,611	$38,498	$62,216
Net Working Capital	$18,612	$19,513	$38,663
Current Ratio	2.48	2.23	3.06
Tangible Net Worth	$21,009	$22,666	$43,495
Net Sales	$52,498	$46,497	$65,462
Net Profit	(L)576	1,657	1,649
Dividends	None	None	None

$1,344 in year C to a high of $1,644 in year A. Cash was also low on each statement. Under these circumstances the current assets over the years consisted primarily of inventory. The relationship of the net sales to the inventory on each of these statement dates gave the following picture:

	Year C	Year B	Year A
Net Sales	$52,498	$46,497	$65,462
Inventory	29,161	32,447	54,502
Ratio of Net Sales to Inventory	1.8	1.4	1.2

While the net sales were fluctuating down and then up over this 3-year period, the inventory went up steadily. At the end of year C, the inventory stood at $29,161. One year later the inventory amounted to $32,447, and at the end of year A, to $54,502. As soon as the additional funds had been invested in the business early in year A, the management used those funds to increase the stock of merchandise which fluctuated around this higher level throughout that fiscal year.

The ratio between the net sales of $52,498 for year C and the inventory of $29,161 shown in the balance sheet at the end of year C amounted to 1.8 times. On the lower net sales of $46,497 for year B and the higher inventory of $32,447, the ratio dropped to 1.4 times. The net sales expanded to $65,462 for year A, but the inventory went up more than a proportionate amount and the ratio now dropped to 1.2 times. Here is a steady downward trend in the ratio of net sales to the inventory for these 3 years.

Condensed Analysis. The balance sheet figures for year C would, at a superficial glance, seem to disclose a satisfactory financial condition. The ratio of current assets to current liabilities was satisfactory, the relationship between the current liabilities and the tangible net worth was satisfactory, fixed assets were nominal, receivables were small, and there was no funded debt. Only two minor features gave an unfavorable picture: the cash of $709 was certainly low, and a bank debt of only $500, in contrast to $8,497 owing for merchandise and $3,502 due to the president, would seem to indicate some reticence on the part of the bank to extend what might be termed reasonable credit. On the basis of the sales analysis as described in Chap. V, it would have taken 2.34 months to have liquidated the accounts payable, and on buying terms of 30 days, payments would certainly have been slow. This was later verified by an investigation; trade payments were running up to 60 days slow. Apparently Cluff had had to make advances to the corporation in order to meet the more extended trade obligations.

A similar condition was reflected by the figures for both year B and year A. In both years, the cash was nominal, bank loans were small, accounts payable were progressively larger, the amounts due James Cluff grew smaller as payments were made on this indebtedness, receivables were small, and fixed assets were nominal. Loans receivable amounting to $1,872 in year C represented loans to two friends of Cluff. This item expanded to $2,459 in year B, and to $3,964 in year A, as additional funds were lent to these two friends and a new loan made to a third friend.

When a study of relationship is made between the net sales of $52,498 and the inventory of $29,161 for year C, the picture becomes decidedly more unfavorable. Here we have a ratio of only 1.8 times compared with a 5-year average ratio of net sales to inventory for retail men's and boys' clothing stores of 3.5 times. In other words, in year C this particular ratio was about one-half as high as it should have been as a minimum. This ratio now became progressively more unfavorable with 1.4 times in year *B* and 1.2 times in year *A*. The ratio of 1.2 times for year *A* is approximately one-third as large as the 5-year average, indicating how poorly this business is being managed from a merchandising point of view.

With the relationship of net sales to inventory so greatly out of line in year *A*, two conclusions would seem obvious: (1) the inventory over the years has probably included a steadily increasing proportion of soiled, out-of-style, or unsalable merchandise which presumably is being carried at cost and not at marked-down values, and (2) the management, even though it has operated this business and its predecessor for 15 years, knows little about merchandising and the desirability, even the necessity, of inventory turnover. The inventory had become so greatly excessive by the end of year *A* that probably both conclusions are valid.

On the net working capital of $38,663 for year *A*, an inventory no greater than this amount should be carried. Net sales of a retail concern in this line of business and of this size under fairly capable management should amount to approximately $155,000. By obtaining the typical ratio of net sales to inventory of 3.5 times, a reduction could be obtained in the inventory from $54,502 to around $44,000, which would release $10,502 to reduce liabilities and to increase cash to a reasonable amount.

If the inventory at the end of year *A* actually contained out-of-style merchandise which was unsalable except at a considerable markdown, then the figure of $54,502 is inflated. If that inflation existed to an amount greater than $1,657 in year *B* and greater than $1,649 in year *A*, then losses were actually assumed in those years instead of the net profits that were recorded. What is actually needed in this situation is (1) a physical inventory of every piece of merchandise by competent outside appraisers, (2) a policy of weeding out and reducing inventory to an amount not greater than the net working capital, at the same time keeping the inventory well balanced, and (3) an operating policy that would build up net sales. That policy might involve increased advertising, a lower markup, or a change in the type and price level of merchandise to cater more nearly to the requirements of available customers.

Manufacturers of Men's Clothing

The Men's Suit Co., Inc., was incorporated 3 years ago under the laws of the State of New York with an authorized capital of 200 shares of preferred stock, par value of $100, and 400 shares of common stock of no par value. At the end of the first year of operations, the paid-in capital, consisting of the 400 shares of common stock, was carried in the balance sheet at $113,000. No preferred stock was outstanding. In year *B*, 120 shares of preferred stock, carried at $12,000, were issued for cash. No further change was made in the capitalization.

This business is controlled by one Fred Solomon, the president of the corporation. At the end of year A, Solomon was forty-nine years of age. In his business career he had been employed first as a salesman for a manu-

[Schedule 33]   MEN'S SUIT CO., INC.
Comparative Figures for Years Ended June 30, 19—

	(C) Three Years Ago	(B) Two Years Ago	(A) One Year Ago
ASSETS			
Cash	$ 68,178	$ 43,760	$ 35,447
Notes Receivable	2,216	2,102	4,110
Accounts Receivable	98,110	121,043	181,496
Inventory	140,002	146,201	279,896
Current Assets	$308,506	$313,106	$500,949
Furniture and Equipment	255	201	2,870
Miscellaneous Receivables	594	....	158
Deferred Assets	206	85	107
TOTAL	$309,561	$313,392	$504,084
LIABILITIES			
Due to Banks	$ 60,000	$100,000	$ 80,000
Due to Contractors	22,105	24,565	23,912
Accounts Payable	114,171	60,220	252,401
Accruals	77	1,191	5,158
Current Liabilities	$196,353	$185,976	$361,471
6% Cumulative Preferred Stock	....	12,000	12,000
Common Stock	113,000	113,000	113,000
Surplus	208	2,416	17,613
TOTAL	$309,561	$313,392	$504,084
Net Working Capital	$112,153	$127,130	$139,478
Current Ratio	1.57	1.68	1.39
Tangible Net Worth	$113,208	$127,416	$142,613
Net Sales	$718,624	$606,943	$801,625
Net Profit	1,696	2,928	15,917
Dividends	None	720	720

facturer of men's clothing, and then as a principal in three successive concerns engaged in manufacturing men's clothing. None of these three concerns had been successful. Creditors, however, had assumed no losses in these ventures. As each concern had been liquidated all obligations had been paid in full.

Men's Suit Co., Inc., manufactures medium and better priced men's suits, topcoats, and overcoats. Sales are made on 60-day terms to department stores and retail men's clothing stores in the Midwestern states. Garments are cut on the premises but are completed by outside contractors. The comparative fiscal figures for the 3 years that the business has been in existence appear in Schedule 33.

These balance sheets are dated June 30, which is normally the date after spring inventories have been liquidated and just prior to the receipt of piece goods to be made into autumn and winter garments. The typical concern in this line of business would normally close its fiscal year with an inventory that would be approximately one-sixth as large as its annual net sales. In this case the inventory was materially greater on each statement date, with an upward tendency.

Net sales in year C amounted to $718,624. For year B, the net sales dropped to $606,943, and then in year A expanded to a high point of $801,625. Net profits were earned each year. The net profits for year C amounted to only $1,696, which was 0.23 per cent on the net sales. For year B, the net profits increased to $2,928, which was 0.48 per cent on the net sales. For year A a more satisfactory return of $15,917 was recorded, representing 1.98 per cent on the net sales.

Over these 3 years the minimum of dividends were paid, none in year C, $720 on the preferred stock in year B, and $720 on the preferred stock in year A. As a result of these minimum dividend payments, a very substantial portion of the earnings was reinvested in the business. Between year C and year A, the tangible net worth increased from $113,208 to $142,613, partly from retained earnings and partly from the sale of the preferred stock for cash.

In several ways, these balance sheets are unusual. Among these features is the ratio of the net sales to the inventory. These two items give the following relationship over the 3 years:

	Year C	Year B	Year A
Net Sales	$718,624	$606,943	$801,625
Inventory	140,002	146,201	279,896
Ratio of Net Sales to Inventory	5.1	4.2	2.9

While the net sales were fluctuating, first down, and then up, the inventory showed a steadily upward growth on each statement date. The inventory at the end of year C was $140,002, at the end of year B $146,-201, and at the end of year A $279,896. Between year C and year A the inventory went up 99.9 per cent. As a result of this upward trend in the inventory, the relationship between the two items became more and more unfavorable. Whereas the typical concern in this line has a ratio of net sales to inventory of 5.8 times, this ratio for Men's Suit Co., Inc., dropped from 5.1 times in year C to 4.2 times in year B, and to 2.9 times in year A.

In year A the relationship was just one-half what would normally be expected.

Condensed Analysis. There are several situations which are not conducive to confidence in these comparative figures. The ratio of current assets to current liabilities was low on each of the three balance sheets and particularly so on the balance sheet at the end of year A. That the current liabilities were very heavy is also evident by the ratio of the current liabilities to the tangible net worth. Whereas the typical ratio of current liabilities to tangible net worth for a manufacturer of men's suits and coats is around 62.9 per cent on the fiscal date, here the ratio was 173.4 per cent in year C, 145.8 per cent in year B, and 253.5 per cent in year A.

To ascertain why the current liabilities were so heavy, the analyst must look to the current assets. The explanation must rest in the current assets in view of the fact that such a nominal proportion of the tangible net worth, only 2.01 per cent in year A, was represented by fixed assets. When fixed assets are heavy, often the current liabilities are also heavy to carry a normal volume of business for the tangible net worth. The situation which predominates here is very different.

The current assets in this case consisted of four items, or if we consider the notes receivable and accounts receivable together as one, of three items. The cash, with the exception of year C, was reasonable; at least there was no excess. The accounts and notes receivable gave an average collection period based on net sales of 51 days, 74 days, and 84 days, respectively. On selling terms of 60 days, the collection periods in year C and in year B were well in proportion. The average collection period of 84 days in year A, as will be seen from Chap. XIII, was only slightly in excess of a normal leeway. So, even though the collection period had been going up, it had just reached the point in year A where some attention was needed to see that no further expansion took place. This conclusion was then verified by obtaining the following aging of the receivables:

June shipments	$113,339
May shipments	41,199
April shipments	19,382
March shipments	10,305
February shipments	3,147
Total	$187,372
Less: Reserve for Discounts	1,766
Accounts and Notes Receivable, Net	$185,606

Of the total accounts and notes receivable, 82.5 per cent represented shipments within 60 days, and 92.9 per cent shipments within 90 days. Only $13,452, or 7.1 per cent, represented shipments more than 90 days old, which is quite a satisfactory showing.

For an explanation of the heavy current liabilities we are now left to the last item in the current assets, namely, the inventory. In the comparison which has already been made between the net sales and the inventory, we found a gradual but steadily downward trend in the relationship from 5.1 times in year C, to 4.2 times in year B, and, although it is almost unbelievable, to 2.9 times in year A. The verification of the heaviness of the inventory is also found in the relationship between the inventory for each year and the respective net working capital. This relationship is discussed in Chap. XII.

The typical manufacturer of men's suits and overcoats has a rather moderate inventory on June 30; spring merchandise has been made up and largely or completely sold, unless there is a carry-over; piece goods generally are on order for delivery in July and August to be made into autumn and winter clothing. Under these operations, the inventory on June 30 for a concern of this size might range normally somewhere between $50,000 and $125,000. For each year the inventory exceeded this maximum outside limit, and at the end of year A it was more than twice as large.

An explanation was in order. The heaviness of the inventory in year A might have been caused by the inability to liquidate spring suits. If so, the concern was headed for trouble; those suits would have to be sold at a sacrifice to raise cash, or, if the bank were particularly friendly and liberal, be carried until the next spring season, which would mean excessive bank borrowings to carry this merchandise and to finance the heavier winter business. On the other hand, the heaviness might be due to the fact that the management had completed its spring season and had ordered and received early shipments of piece goods for autumn and winter garments in order to start cutting early. Such a situation would be extremely favorable. Which interpretation of the figures was correct could be obtained only from an explanation by the management.

That explanation fortunately turned out to be the favorable one. A breakdown of the inventory carried at $279,896 in the balance sheet for year A disclosed a nominal carry-over of spring suits as follows:

Finished suits, spring season	$ 12,360
Finished suits, autumn and winter	110,311
In process	90,570
Piece goods	41,734
Trimmings	24,921
Total	$279,896

So, here is a concern which apparently has had a heavy financial condition over the 3 years, with a very unbalanced condition at the end of the fiscal year A. However, the financial condition as of the end of year A was quite satisfactory. It is a fact that current liabilities were far heavier than normal, but the assets supporting these liabilities were sound. With such heavy liabilities the financial condition was one which would need to be followed closely. If the autumn and winter season should not work out as budgeted, if net sales should drop off, if the piece goods which had been purchased represented "fancies" and the clothing made with it would not sell easily, if a substantial loss should be taken on any one or on several accounts, if returns should be heavy as a result of poor manufacturing, in short, if any situation should arise where the business did not function on schedule, the heavy liability condition could very well become a vulnerable one. On the other hand, if sales held up well for the fall season, a normal seasonal liquidation would take place and everything would be rosy.

Manufacturer of Heavy Chemicals

Industrial Chemicals, Inc., was incorporated under the laws of Delaware in 1939 as a consolidation of two successful corporations, both of which had been engaged in the manufacture of heavy chemicals. At the end of year A, operations were being conducted on a paid-in capital of $157,614 of 6 per cent cumulative preferred stock, $1,650,000 of common stock, capital surplus of $366,126, and retained earnings of $828,600.

Among the heavy chemicals which this concern manufactures are sulfuric, nitric, hydrochloric, chlorsulfonic, and acetic acids, chlorine, caustic soda, alum, niter coke, sodium sulfate, sodium sulfite, and sodium sulfide. In recent years, experimentation has also led to the production of specialties such as coal-tar intermediates, phosphoric acid compounds, plastics, and rubber chemicals. Some products are sold on 30-day net terms and others on 60-day net terms.

Operations were conducted profitably during each of the 3 years under review, but with decreasing profits. For year C, the net profits were $308,-792, or 10.54 per cent on the tangible net worth; for year B $205,131, or 6.85 per cent on the tangible net worth; and for year A $133,106, or 4.44 per cent on the tangible net worth. Dividends of 6 per cent on the outstanding preferred stock, amounting to $9,457, were paid each year. In year C and in year A, dividends of 7 per cent, amounting to $115,500, were paid on the outstanding common stock, and in year B 8 per cent, amounting to $132,000. As the earnings exceeded the dividends each year, retained earnings increased from year to year, but very moderately in year A. The comparative figures for the 3 years appear in Schedule 34.

While the net profits were decreasing from year to year, most of the other items were increasing. The current assets expanded from $1,963,977 in year C to $2,805,262 in year A, the current liabilities from $479,417 to $1,203,160, the net working capital from $1,484,560 to $1,602,102, and the net sales from $3,834,615 to $4,395,546.

The increase in the current assets was brought about by the steady

INDUSTRIAL CHEMICALS, INC.   [Schedule 34]
Comparative Figures for Years Ended December 31, 19—

	(C) Three Years Ago	(B) Two Years Ago	(A) One Year Ago
ASSETS			
Cash........................	$ 291,283	$ 323,149	$ 295,374
Notes Receivable..............	23,702	41,212	32,261
Accounts Receivable...........	576,210	642,512	352,621
Inventory....................	1,028,095	1,550,213	2,025,006
Marketable Securities..........	44,687	....	100,000
Current Assets................	$1,963,977	$2,557,086	$2,805,262
Real Estate...................	117,452	117,452	117,452
Buildings, Net................	618,777	610,627	590,624
Machinery and Equipment, Net.	646,043	635,941	595,041
Miscellaneous Receivables.......	10,285	3,561	14,277
Deferred Charges..............	53,399	61,092	61,843
Postwar Refund...............	....	....	21,000
Patents......................	1	1	1
TOTAL...................	$3,409,934	$3,985,760	$4,205,500
LIABILITIES			
Notes Payable to Banks........	$ 200,000	$ 500,000	$ 500,000
Due to Officers................	22,480	6,500	....
Accounts Payable.............	13,105	120,299	116,585
Accruals.....................	92,778	74,770	70,575
Reserves for Contingencies......	....	50,000	150,000
Dividends Payable.............	....	30,000	30,000
Reserve for Taxes.............	151,054	210,000	336,000
Current Liabilities.............	$ 479,417	$ 991,569	$1,203,160
6% Cumulative Pref. Stock.....	157,614	157,614	157,614
Common Stock................	1,650,000	1,650,000	1,650,000
Capital Surplus...............	366,126	366,126	366,126
Retained Earnings.............	756,777	820,451	828,600
TOTAL...................	$3,409,934	$3,985,760	$4,205,500
Net Working Capital............	$1,484,560	$1,565,517	$1,602,102
Current Ratio..................	4.10	2.58	2.33
Tangible Net Worth.............	$2,930,516	$2,994,190	$3,002,339
Net Sales.....................	$3,834,615	$4,036,726	$4,395,546
Net Profit....................	308,792	205,131	133,106
Dividends....................	124,957	141,457	124,957

expansion in one item, the inventory. With the increase in current assets,
the current liabilities, likewise, had to expand, less the retained net profits
and less the amount of the earned depreciation on the fixed assets. In other
words, the changes from year C to year B to year A in this particular case
had been brought about largely by carrying a steadily increasing inven-

tory to take care of the increasing sales. The relationship between these two items gives the following interesting pictures for the 3 years:

	Year C	Year B	Year A
Net Sales........................	$3,834,615	$4,036,726	$4,395,546
Inventory........................	1,028,095	1,550,213	2,025,006
Ratio of Net Sales to Inventory........	3.7	2.6	2.1

The net sales increased from $3,834,615 for year C to $4,036,726 for year B, an increase of 5.2 per cent. Net sales then expanded to $4,395,546 for year A, an increase of 14.6 per cent over the net sales for year C.

The inventory increased at a much more rapid rate. At the end of year C the inventory amounted to $1,028,095. By the end of year B, the inventory amounted to $1,550,213, representing an increase of 50.8 per cent. By the end of year A the inventory amounted to $2,025,006, an increase of 96.9 per cent over year C.

Because of the more rapid increase in the inventory, the ratio between the net sales and the inventory went downward steadily. At the end of year C, this ratio was 3.7 times. At the end of year B it was 2.6 times, and at the end of year A only 2.1 times.

Condensed Analysis. The figures as of the end of year C disclosed an all-round healthy condition. The ratio of current assets to current liabilities was 4.10 times and was high, well above most concerns in this line. The current liabilities amounted to $479,417 and represented only 16.3 per cent of the tangible net worth. The fixed assets represented 47.2 per cent of the tangible net worth and were just about average. The receivables and the inventory were likewise in satisfactory proportion.

In one respect, however, the figures were open to real improvement. The net sales for the year amounted to $3,834,615 and were low. These sales were low from three relationships: with the tangible net worth, with the net working capital, and with the inventory. Net sales would have been more in line if the volume had ranged in the neighborhood of $5,000,000.

In year B the net sales increased moderately, indicating that the active managerial staff was on the way to the objective of $5,000,000. All the proportions of the business remained in healthy shape, with this one exception. The management apparently believed that the way to obtain the increased sales was to expand its products substantially so that customers would have wider choice, and consequently the inventory expanded from $1,028,095 to $1,550,213 and became excessive. The net sales of $5,000,000 under proper inventory control could easily have been obtained on the inventory of $1,028,095 of year C. At the end of year B, the management now had two problems instead of one: to increase the net sales, and at the same time to reduce what had become an excessive inventory during the year.

As we have seen, the net sales increased to $4,395,546 in year A, on the way to that $5,000,000 mark but still quite far from it. The inventory, instead of being reduced, continued to expand to $2,025,006 and at that figure was almost one-half as large as the net sales, whereas the typical inventory in the industrial chemical field on the fiscal statement date is in the neighborhood of one-sixth of the annual net sales. The fixed assets continued in proportion, the receivables were in excellent shape with an average collection period of only 32 days, the current debt was not excessive, but the inventory was out of all reasonable proportion.

The problem of the analyst now became one of learning, if possible, by a skilled survey or by an explanation from the management, how the inventory was valued, to be sure that it had not been inflated in any way or that no part that had deteriorated was being carried at the full value of first-class merchandise. If any such program had been followed purposely or accidentally, the real value of the inventory was less than the stated amount, and the retained earnings likewise. In such a predicament, the analyst would need to adjust the inventory figure, retained earnings, and also the reported net profit downward to the extent of the reevaluation.

If no such situation existed, the analyst would be faced with an unsound picture with an inventory twice as large as it should be at the end of year A for this particular business. Under these circumstances, a considerable loss would materialize in the liquidation of slow-moving items in the inventory during any period of falling prices, a contingency that must always be anticipated. So, although this business is not in financial difficulty and headed for obvious bankruptcy, the situation is one which is open to improvement, and well worth the ingenuity of skilled capable management to earn more reasonable, let alone maximum, profits.

TYPICAL RATIOS OF NET SALES TO INVENTORY

Before excessive inventories are appreciably reduced, losses are often involved. If a business enterprise has both an excessive inventory and top-heavy liabilities, financial embarrassment is often the result before the inventory can be brought into line. Comparatively few managements, however, recognize an excessive inventory condition during its early stage because they have no measuring stick; they have no means of setting a definite figure that the inventory in their particular business should not exceed. Their individual experience has been inadequate to provide the answer. No management ever planned deliberately to build up an excessive inventory except for speculation. When the products or materials which comprise a heavy inventory were ordered, there was no expectation that the inventory would become excessive; it became so only in the course of time and in the light of conditions which later arose, or by failure to recognize the condition. Inventory problems are thus the results of human errors or mistakes in judgment. In this chapter one method of measuring the relative size of inventory, the ratio of net sales to inventory, has been discussed; in the following chapter a supplementary measuring unit, the relationship of inventory to net working capital, will be taken up.

The relationship between net sales and inventory may be increased in three ways: by maintaining net sales at a constant level with a decreasing inventory, by expanding net sales on the same inventory, and by increasing net sales and reducing the inventory simultaneously. All else being equal, turnover and net profits will increase slightly in the first situation, and more in the second and third situations.

A business enterprise operating in a line of activity where the inventory has a high degree of price responsiveness, where the turnover of inventory is low, and where the inventory represents a high percentage of the net working capital is very much at the mercy of fluctuating prices. On the basis of first-in first-out cost, without making any inventory write-down, a period of rising prices will show exceedingly gratifying net profits. When the economic cycle enters its price-declining phase, the net profits, if there are any at all, will be exceedingly ungratifying.

A second concern in the same line of business with a rapid turnover of inventory will enjoy prosperity on the upswing also, but will not suffer as much on the downswing. Moreover, as between two concerns with approximately similar rates of turnover, the one with the largest investment in inventories will experience a far greater spread between the upgrade and downgrade movements than will the one with the smaller inventory. A rapid turnover of stock indicates sound controls and good financial management. The business with a quick turnover naturally ties up a smaller proportion of capital in inventory than does the concern whose turnover is slower. In some lines of business, however, profits are high even though turnover is slow.

It must not be supposed that by merely increasing the turnover of inventory, net profits expand. It must be remembered that net profits are actually not earned until bills are paid, nor is a profit earned unless the cost of goods and all expenses of conducting the business have been more than covered by the price received. It is possible to speed up the turnover by selling merchandise at a low price. It is also possible to increase the turnover by intensive and extensive methods of selling. Obviously, there is in each business a point beyond which it is not financially profitable to attempt to secure a larger volume of net sales. Perhaps the surest and easiest method of increasing turnover is to buy "light" and carry at all times only the amount of inventory absolutely necessary.

Turnover of Inventory

The *turnover of inventory* is a term meaning the ratio of *cost of sales* to the inventory. In a trading business, it is desirable to compare the cost of sales with the average merchandise throughout the year based upon monthly inventory figures. In a manufacturing business, the ratio is usually computed by dividing the cost of sales by the average monthly inventory. It is evident that even this computation is not altogether accurate since the average inventory may be composed of varying quantities of finished merchandise, goods in process, and raw material. The most exact step would be to compare the average monthly volume in units of inventory with the actual volume in units sold, whether or not in the original form. This would give a true comparison of physical quantities which would unmistakably show the turnover of goods. However, such figures are rarely available to the analyst.

From the study of a balance sheet it is impossible to ascertain the average value of inventory carried during the year unless the business is largely free from seasonal fluctuations, a situation which is rarely true. Often stock is taken and financial returns are made when the inventory is low, and hence the balance sheet figure may be somewhat misleading. Sometimes a fair approximation may be arrived at by taking the mean of the high and low figures for the year, or by an average of the inventory at the beginning and the end of the year. These various methods of obtaining an inventory figure to compare with cost of sales are available to the operating management but rarely to the outside analyst. Even when no wholly accurate or absolute inventory figures are available, it is still very useful to compare the inventory reported in the annual balance sheet with the annual net sales. In this manner, light may be thrown upon the comparative conditions and policies of different establishments in the same industry.

The table at the end of this chapter was obtained by dividing annual net sales by the inventory item appearing on the year-end balance sheet. Inventory is generally carried at the lower of cost or market, while net sales represent the value of merchandise sold during the period at selling prices, which includes the markup over cost. Consequently, this ratio is not actually a turnover such as would be obtained by dividing cost of sales by the inventory, or net sales by the aggregate selling price of the inventory. It is, however, a relationship that has become widely used over the years, as these two figures are more readily available to provide standards.

When this ratio is high, it is evidence of the generally high quality of the inventory and of the ability of the management to move its merchandise quickly. Conversely, when the ratio is low, the inclusion of slow moving, possibly obsolete or shopworn items of questionable value may be suspected, and some doubt may be raised regarding the efficiency and merchandising ability of the management.

It is extremely difficult to establish the full importance of a current act in its place, its respective niche, in history. Likewise it is difficult to orient a business in the current movements and trends of economic activity When prices are falling, a rapid turnover of inventory is a matter of basic importance in restricting losses. When prices are rising, the turnover of inventory and its size contribute much toward keeping a business in healthy condition. A heavy or an excessive inventory, purchased for a speculative profit, decreases the turnover. Changes in style, customs needs, and new competitive products result in hazardous complications particularly in those concerns where inventories are excessive and, at the same time, current liabilities are heavy.

Schedule 35, on the following pages, gives the typical ratios of net sale to inventory for 67 lines of business activity—39 manufacturers, 21 whole salers, and 7 retailers—each year for the 5 years from 1955 to 1959 and a 5-year average for this spread of years. Of the 39 lines of manufacturing activity which comprise this running study, bakers show the highest 5 year average ratio of net sales to inventory with 26.2 times, packers of meats and provisions are second with 25.6 times, and breweries are third with 18.2 times. Manufacturers of ladies' apparel such as dresses, coats suits, and underwear from piece goods also show a relatively high relationship, as inventories in these lines invariably are at a low point of the year on the balance sheet date. Canners of fruits and vegetables show the lowest 5-year average with 3.5 times, followed by manufacturers of agricultural equipment and machinery with 3.6 times, and manufacturers of overalls and work clothing with 4.4 times.

Of the 21 lines of wholesaling, wholesalers of fresh fruits and produce have the highest 5-year average with 54.3 times, the wholesalers of mea and poultry are second with 40.2 times, and wholesale distributors of baked goods are third with 26.0 times. The lowest ratio among the whole sale trades is contributed by wholesalers of hardware with 4.1 times.

The 5-year average ratios among the retailers range from a high of 17.1 times of the independent grocery and meat stores to a low of 3.5 times by retailers of men's and boys' clothing, and retail furnishing stores

Maxim

Heavy or excessive inventories are to be avoided just as much as over investment in fixed assets and large liabilities. Constant attention to these

RATIOS OF NET SALES TO INVENTORY   [Schedule 35]

| Lines of Business Activity | Number of Times | | | | | |
| | Median | | | | | Five-year Average |
	1955	1956	1957	1958	1959	
MANUFACTURERS						
Agricultural Implements and Machinery	3.5	3.3	3.5	4.2	3.7	3.6
Airplane Parts and Accessories	6.4	4.7	6.0	6.4	4.9	5.7
Automobile Parts and Accessories	6.1	5.8	5.8	5.9	6.4	6.0
Bakers	31.2	22.7	23.4	25.7	28.1	26.2
Bedsprings and Mattresses	8.1	8.0	7.2	8.1	8.1	7.9
Bodies, Auto, Bus, and Truck	6.4	7.5	6.3	4.8	6.5	6.3
Bolts, Screws, Nuts, and Nails	6.5	6.4	5.1	5.5	6.3	6.0
Breweries	18.8	19.3	19.5	16.8	16.7	18.2
Chemicals, Industrial	7.7	7.5	6.7	7.5	7.1	7.3
Coats and Suits, Men's and Boys'	5.6	6.0	5.4	6.8	5.2	5.8
Coats and Suits, Women's	11.5	8.8	14.0	9.4	9.5	10.6
Confectionery	6.3	8.6	6.8	10.7	8.5	8.2
Cotton Cloth Mills	5.2	4.6	4.2	4.5	5.5	4.8
Cotton Goods, Converters, Non-factored	6.1	5.7	5.0	4.7	7.1	5.7
Dresses, Rayon, Silk, and Acetate	23.0	17.7	19.7	14.8	14.0	17.8
Drugs	5.9	5.2	5.5	5.8	6.0	5.7
Electrical Parts and Supplies	4.7	4.8	5.2	4.7	4.8	4.8
Foundries	8.1	8.0	7.5	7.2	8.6	7.9
Fruits and Vegetables, Canners	3.6	3.7	3.6	3.5	3.1	3.5
Furniture	8.1	6.4	5.9	6.2	6.3	6.6
Hardware and Tools	4.2	4.7	4.8	4.6	4.7	4.6
Hosiery	5.8	5.3	5.8	5.2	5.4	5.5
Lumber	5.8	4.6	5.5	5.9	5.2	5.4
Machine Shops	5.8	5.4	8.5	4.9	7.1	6.3
Machinery, Industrial	4.6	4.4	4.6	4.6	4.3	4.5
Meats and Provisions, Packers	25.6	23.6	24.7	26.0	28.2	25.6
Metal Stampings	7.1	6.3	6.2	6.8	6.2	6.5
Outerwear, Knitted	7.6	7.8	6.2	7.4	8.5	7.5
Overalls and Work Clothing	4.3	4.3	4.4	4.4	4.7	4.4
Paints, Varnishes, and Lacquers	5.6	6.7	6.9	7.0	6.1	6.5
Paper	7.6	7.2	7.0	6.1	6.8	6.9
Paper Boxes	9.4	10.2	10.0	9.2	9.3	9.6
Petroleum, Integrated Corporations	9.4	8.0	7.6	8.2	9.0	8.4
Radio Parts and Supplies	5.3	4.8	4.8	5.6	4.6	5.0
Shirts, Underwear, and Pajamas, Men's	5.9	4.6	5.4	4.9	5.4	5.2
Shoes, Men's, Women's, and Children's	4.9	4.8	5.2	4.8	5.1	5.0
Soft Drinks and Carbonated Water, Bottlers	10.5	12.5	14.4	15.6	17.4	14.1
Steel, Structural Fabricators (Sell on Short Terms)	6.7	6.8	6.2	6.4	5.7	6.4
Stoves, Ranges, and Ovens	5.0	5.0	5.2	5.3	5.7	5.2

Lines of Business Activity	Number of Times					
	Median					Five-year Average
	1955	1956	1957	1958	1959	
WHOLESALERS						
Automobile Parts and Accessories....	5.1	5.3	4.5	4.7	4.5	4.8
Baked Goods.....................	25.0	25.0	25.5	23.5	31.2	26.0
Cigars, Cigarettes, and Tobacco......	26.4	22.1	27.0	23.1	22.6	24.2
Drugs and Drug Sundries..........	7.3	7.8	6.6	7.5	7.2	7.3
Dry Goods.......................	6.3	5.9	6.2	6.1	6.1	6.1
Electrical Parts and Supplies........	8.5	7.6	6.2	6.3	5.9	6.9
Fruits and Produce, Fresh..........	40.3	45.8	66.7	66.5	52.3	54.3
Furnishings, Men's................	5.2	4.4	5.1	5.9	4.0	4.9
Gasoline, Fuel Oil, and Lubricating Oil	19.8	20.8	18.2	16.4	14.2	17.9
Groceries........................	10.5	10.2	10.9	11.2	11.2	10.8
Hardware........................	4.0	4.4	4.1	4.0	3.8	4.1
Hosiery and Underwear............	6.3	5.9	5.2	6.3	6.3	6.0
Household Appliances, Electrical.....	7.0	6.9	6.5	7.7	7.0	7.0
Lumber..........................	12.9	9.3	7.6	5.4	6.4	8.3
Lumber and Building Materials......	6.5	6.2	5.2	5.6	7.3	6.2
Meat and Poultry.................	36.4	35.5	38.1	46.8	44.1	40.2
Paints, Varnishes, and Lacquers......	5.5	4.2	5.8	4.9	5.1	5.1
Paper............................	7.5	7.0	7.8	7.5	7.7	7.5
Plumbing and Heating Supplies......	5.5	5.9	5.9	5.2	5.8	5.7
Shoes, Men's, Women's, and Children's........................	7.3	7.9	7.6	6.9	7.0	7.3
Wines and Liquors................	7.5	8.0	6.9	9.9	8.6	8.2
RETAILERS						
Clothing, Men's and Boys'..........	3.7	3.6	3.3	3.3	3.7	3.5
Department Stores................	6.2	5.8	5.7	5.8	5.8	5.9
Furniture, 50 Per Cent or More Installment......................	5.9	4.5	4.9	4.5	4.4	4.8
Groceries and Meats, Independent....	14.0	16.3	17.5	19.9	18.3	17.2
Lumber and Building Materials......	5.7	5.6	5.5	4.7	5.0	5.3
Shoes............................	3.6	4.0	3.9	4.1	3.9	3.9
Women's Specialty Shops...........	7.0	6.9	6.6	6.1	6.5	6.6

three items is of the utmost importance in the continuous successful operation of every commercial and industrial business enterprise. The same yearly depreciation charges must be taken when a plant is operating at 25 per cent capacity as at 100 per cent, and the same interest charges must be paid on funded obligations in a depression as in good times. A heavy or excessive inventory likewise is a drag upon the business concern and results in heavy losses due to obsolescence, changes in style, perishability, and constant price fluctuations.

Even though several of the ratios that have been described in earlier chapters vary widely for different divisions of industry and commerce, it has been possible to supplement the relationships for particular divisions with broad over-all standards. No such maxim, however, can be formulated for the ratio of net sales to inventory. Standards for each division of manufacturing and trade are essential as separate and distinct bases. Where they are not available, the similarity of a line of activity with some other line for which this particular ratio has been studied over the years may be used. Naturally, any ratio higher than the individual yearly medians and the 5-year average given in Schedule 35 would represent a better showing.

The interquartile range of ratios quoted in the Appendix gives the more desirable upper-quartile ratios of net sales to inventory in contrast to the median. This schedule also shows the less desirable lower-quartile relationship between net sales and inventory.

THEORY AND PROBLEMS

1. What are the chief reasons why certain businesses have adopted for the valuation of inventory the so-called "last-in first-out" method?

2. State clearly the information you would expect to obtain from the ratio of net sales to inventory.

3. You are an accountant. One of your clients requests information about the retail method of valuing inventory: (a) what it is, (b) what advantages, if any, it has over his practice of inventorying at cost or market, and (c) whether it will facilitate the preparation of income tax returns. What information would you give concerning each of these three points?

4. Of each of the following inventory cost determination methods, (a) describe the principal features; (b) give at least one situation, business, or industry in which it is used to advantage and considered good accounting practice; and (c) give the reason for its selection in each case:

Retail method
Using a constant price for so-called "normal" quantity of materials or goods in stock (base stock method)
Last-in first-out
First-in first-out
Average cost
Standard costs

5. The Wholesale Paper Company has been in existence many years in a Southern city. Audited balance sheets and income statements have been submitted yearly to a mercantile agency. The principal creditor ordered a mercantile agency credit report. In that report the audited figures for the last 3 years had been set up in comparative columns as shown. Assume that you are the credit manager of the paper manufacturing company that is the principal creditor. From these comparative figures compute the ratio of net sales to inventory for each of the 3 years and give your interpretation of each ratio.

WHOLESALE PAPER COMPANY
Comparative Figures for Years Ended December 31, 19—

	(C) Three Years Ago	(B) Two Years Ago	(A) One Year Ago
ASSETS			
Cash..............................	$ 3,201	$ 1,726	$ 2,578
Accounts Receivable.................	50,242	50,217	55,028
Inventory..........................	67,008	58,634	68,071
Current Assets	$120,451	$110,577	$125,677
Fixed Assets, Net....................	1,918	1,586	2,118
Miscellaneous Receivables.............	....	....	4,858
Deposits...........................	20	23	22
TOTAL........................	$122,389	$112,186	$132,675
LIABILITIES			
Notes Payable to Bank...............	$ 13,500	$ 7,500	$ 15,000
Loans Payable, Other................	10,920	16,943	16,609
Accounts Payable....................	31,206	16,700	29,114
Current Liabilities....................	$ 55,626	$ 41,143	$ 60,723
Common Stock.....................	50,000	50,000	50,000
Surplus............................	16,763	21,043	21,952
TOTAL........................	$122,389	$112,186	$132,675
Net Working Capital..................	$ 64,825	$ 69,434	$ 64,954
Current Ratio.......................	2.16	2.68	2.07
Tangible Net Worth..................	$ 66,763	$ 71,043	$ 71,952
Sales..............................	$197,766	$282,051	$287,023
Net Profits.........................	3,642	4,280	909
Dividends..........................	None	None	None

6. The audited balance sheet of the Auto Accessories Manufacturing Corp. as of December 31, 19—, is given below. For the fiscal year net sales aggregated $2,661,580. Post the figures on a columnar sheet of paper computing accurately (a) net working capital, (b) tangible net worth, (c) current ratio, (d) ratio of current liabilities to tangible net worth, (e) ratio of fixed assets to tangible net worth, and (f) ratio of net sales to inventory. Then give your interpretation of each of these ratios for a manufacturer of automobile parts and accessories.

AUTO ACCESSORIES MANUFACTURING CORP.
Balance Sheet, December 31, 19—
ASSETS

Current Assets
Cash on deposit and on hand........................ $ 579,606
Accounts receivable—trade debtors......... $ 462,989
Less: Reserve for doubtful accounts......... 31,718   431,271
Other receivables.................................   6,477
Inventories—at standard costs
  Raw materials....................... $ 53,990
  Work in process and finished parts....... 280,214
  Finished merchandise.................. 662,362   996,566
    Total Current Assets........................... $2,013,920

AUTO ACCESSORIES MANUFACTURING CORP. (*Continued*)

Slow and Inactive Receivables

Sundry receivables and claims....................	$ 35,151	
Less: Reserve for doubtful accounts..............	27,853	
Slow and Inactive Receivables—Net.............		7,298

Fixed Assets

Land......................................		$ 69,833	
Buildings and fixed equipment............	$ 292,730		
Machinery, equipment, and tools..........	394,250		
Dies, jigs, fixtures, and gauges...........	308,227		
Office furniture and equipment............	61,093		
	$1,056,300		
Less: Reserve for depreciation.............	567,018	489,282	
Construction work in progress...................		2,815	
Net Fixed Assets............................			$ 561,930

Patents

Issued patents and applications..................	$ 316,223	
Less: Reserve for amortization.................	227,368	
Net Patents..................................		88,855

Deferred Expenses

Prepaid insurance and taxes, factory supplies, etc.......	31,495
	$2,703,498

LIABILITIES, CAPITAL, AND SURPLUS

Current Liabilities

Accounts payable—trade creditors..................	$ 27,449	
Provision for Federal income tax..................	90,596	
Accrued wages and commissions..................	65,927	
Patent purchase contract.........................	9,900	
Other accruals and payables.....................	44,353	
Total Current Liabilities......................		$ 238,225
Reserve for Contingencies......................		202,072

Capital and Surplus

Preferred stock

5% cumulative, $10 par; 25,000 shares authorized

Issued...............	24,900.0 shares	
Held in treasury.......	3.9 shares	
Outstanding...........	24,896.1 shares	
Stated value...................................		$ 249,000

Common stock

$5 par; 300,000 shares authorized

Issued...............	232,378.0 shares	
Held in treasury.......	5,735.6 shares	
Outstanding...........	226,642.4 shares	
Stated value...................................		1,161,890
Total Stated Capital............................		$1,410,890

Surplus

Reduction surplus.......................	$173,395	
Paid-in surplus..........................	408,600	
Retained earnings.......................	270,316	
Total Surplus.................................	852,311	
Total Capital and Surplus.....................		2,263,201
		$2,703,498

CHAPTER XII

Inventory to Net Working Capital

The fundamental theory of the business enterprise is based upon the conception and the performance of a service. The performance of a service was the major characteristic in the early European economic history when Rome, Venice, Amsterdam, and then London became successively the trading centers for the merchandise of the world. Business then was almost synonymous with commercial activity. Service included the taking of a large monetary risk. Water transportation was the only business activity that involved a material investment, and because of the nature of the times, shipping in small vessels was a most precarious undertaking, comparable today only with agriculture, which depends so greatly upon the whims of nature—storms, sun, rain, hail, snow, and frost. The early European businessman, under these circumstances, was more of a speculator and took a far greater risk of pecuniary loss or gain than the wholesaler and the retailer of today.

In this country before the Civil War, it was the custom of retail merchants, outside the principal cities in the South and in the West, to obtain credit from their suppliers for a period long enough to provide for the complete turnover of their merchandise and the actual cash liquidation from the proceeds of local crops. The usual terms were 6 and 8 months and only one or two liquidations were expected each year.[1] Under this system, the wholesaler virtually acted as the banker for the retailer; banks were relatively few[2] and as a general rule extended credit only against security or two-name trade or accommodation paper.

The retailer rarely had wide credit in his own name. Generally he established relations with a limited number of wholesalers who acquired intimate knowledge of his character, personality, ability, financial responsibility, and outlook from season to season. Under this early nineteenth century system of commercial operation which now seems so unique, no large turnover of inventory was obtained by either the city wholesaler or

---

[1] For a discussion of early terms of sale in the United States, see Chaps. IV and V of *The Sinews of American Commerce* by Roy A. Foulke (Dun & Bradstreet, Inc., New York, 1941).

[2] In 1830 there were 329, in 1840, 901, and in 1850, 824 commercial banks in the United States.—*Report of the Comptroller of the Currency*, Vol. II, pp. 846–847, 1920.

the city or country retailer. Competition was limited, profits were liberal, and merchandise was largely staple goods, whether dry goods, leather, hardware, or groceries. Fashion and perishability had still to become factors in merchandising.

Then came the Civil War, bringing in its train unprecedented changes in the methods of transacting everyday business. Both manufacturers and wholesalers gradually cut their terms to 30 days. Later, as railroads opened up new territories, as telegraph lines were laid, as steamboat transportation improved, and as better roads were constructed, revolutionary changes in buying methods took place. Where the retailer had formerly visited the wholesaler and purchased the exact merchandise he wanted at a warehouse, now salesmen began to visit him with samples and to guarantee quality, style, appearance, and performance.

The manufacturer, importer, and wholesaler were brought closer to the market; fashion and style became so increasingly important that merchandise left over at the end of one season depreciated greatly in value and often was worth little at the beginning of the next season. Mail-order houses and national chains came into existence. Retailers increased the variety of their stocks and carried smaller amounts of each number as orders could readily be placed and merchandise could readily be obtained on short notice. Extensive national advertising programs in newspapers and magazines, and on radio and television, arranged by agencies, became the vogue. More and more emphasis was placed upon having the right merchandise to please old customers and to draw new ones.

The measures of successful merchandising now became the turnover of merchandise and the resulting net profits. A business enterprise that obtained six turnovers per annum, on the same or even a slightly lower markup, and with the same capital as a competitor that obtained only four, had the better merchandising policies and earned the greater net profits. Skill in merchandising became a specialized field of business acumen, recognized particularly by department stores, chain stores, manufacturers of consumer goods, and graduate schools of business administration.

RESPONSIBILITY FOR INVENTORY VALUATION

Along with the development of the theory of merchandise turnover came a wider realization of the importance of the valuation of inventory because of the effect upon turnover as well as the effect upon the determination of the amount of net profit or loss. The predominating practice among accountants continued to be that of accepting the certificate of the management as to the valuation of inventory, subject to the verification of the clerical accuracy of the figures.

A feeling gradually developed among progressive accountants, however, that while responsible employees of a business enterprise should continue to take the inventory, they should take it under the direction of the accountant who should set up the routine and supervise the actual job. Under this practice the management would continue to certify to the accuracy of the inventory as they had been doing. This procedure gave the accountant more responsibility and naturally added to his confidence in the final figure of the inventory, which was so important for the accurate presentation of the balance sheet and the income statement.[3]

This entire problem broke open with widespread discussion upon the discovery of the fradulent inventory figures used in the financial statements of McKesson & Robbins, Inc., over the years through 1937. The Securities and Exchange Commission summarized the gradual but by no means radical change in the point of view of the accounting profession toward the verification of inventories: "We find that a substantial difference of opinion existed among accountants during this time as to the extent of the auditor's duties and responsibilities in connection with physical verification of quantities, quality, and condition." The accounting firm that audited for McKesson & Robbins, Inc., "in common with a substantial portion of the profession, took the position that the verification of quantities, quality, and condition of inventories should be confined to the records. There was, however, a substantial body of equally authoritative opinion which supported the view, which we endorse, that auditors should gain physical contact with the inventory either by test counts, by observation of the inventory taking, or by a combination of these methods. Meticulous verification of the inventory was not needed in this case to discover the fraud. . . . We commend the action of the profession in subsequently adopting, as normal, procedures requiring physical contact with clients' inventories."[4]

A smaller group of accountants have become advocates of an even more advanced view. They maintain that the nonverification of inventories by accountants constitutes a lax point in auditing procedure and they contend that it is highly desirable for them to assume full responsibility for inventory verification in a direct and unequivocal manner.[5]

---

[3] An interesting description of the accountant's part in the taking of inventory is discussed extensively and practically by the twelve experts, all well-known members of representative firms of practicing accountants, in the volume of 638 pages entitled *Testimony of Experts in the Matter of McKesson & Robbins, Inc.* (Securities and Exchange Commission, 1939).

[4] *Report on Investigation in the Matter of McKesson & Robbins, Inc.*, p. 12 (Securities and Exchange Commission, 1940).

[5] This subject is discussed in a survey undertaken by Roy A. Foulke and summarized in *The Balance Sheet of the Future*, pp. 25–31 (Dun & Bradstreet, Inc., New York, 1941).

SERVICE ELEMENT IN MODERN BUSINESS

When a manufacturing concern sells its products, it receives payment for turning raw material into a finished product, for taking a risk in judging the need and the style that will be demanded by the market when the product is finished, and for keeping a stock of merchandise, often with a wide range of sizes, styles, colors, and grades, available until such time as particular products are needed or are in demand by customers. A wholesaler receives payment for distributing merchandise between the manufacturer and the retailer, which involves keeping an inventory on hand and judging future demands; the retailer for having merchandise available and distributing it to the consumer, which also involves the risk of keeping the right inventory on the shelves.

The net profit for the performance of these services is rarely large or abnormal. Competition tends to keep such profit within reasonable limits. However, the profit from a single speculative transaction, or from a series of speculative transactions, may at times be immense. It is because of the possibility of unusual profits that speculative excesses so often reach tragic heights. This is also the reason why business enterprises sometimes carry top-heavy inventories. It should be remembered, however, that the possibility of loss is at least slightly greater than the possibility of profit in most speculative operations.

The business enterprise that is unusually successful, year after year, is the one that performs its fundamental services in a manner superior to competition in its field. It is the concern whose management is able to discern general economic trends, anticipate the changing needs of customers, understand to a degree the forces affecting the market value of its primary commodities, and take advantage, somewhat earlier than others, of any unusual variations in prices. These are legitimate business functions, but they are qualifications only of managements of the highest order. It does not follow that indiscriminate speculation (that is, purchasing an excessive inventory in expectation of higher prices and consequently bringing about a strained financial condition characterized by heavy liabilities) should be carried on, as the risk involved is outside the legitimate field of the typical commercial and industrial business enterprise. The value of inventory is particularly susceptible, it has been aptly said, "to changing price levels, fluctuations in business activity, variations in consumer demand, obsolescence, depreciation, supersession, and all the other unpredictable factors that enter into the determination of marketing conditions."[6]

[6] GEE, EDWARD F., *The Evaluation of Receivables and Inventories*, p. 135 (Bankers Publishing Company, Cambridge, Mass., 1943).

NEED FOR A SUPPLEMENTARY INVENTORY RELATIONSHIP

The relationship between net sales and inventory, which was described in the preceding chapter, is between two variables, two items that often change considerably from one year to another. If both items increase in the same proportion, the ratio remains unchanged, and a situation may develop that may innocently lead to an unsound financial condition.

A wholesaler of paper, for example, handled an annual volume of business in year C of \$1,309,006 on an ending inventory of \$184,367, giving a ratio of net sales to inventory of 7.1 times. A ratio of 7.1 times is quite good for wholesalers of paper. In year B, the net sales jumped to \$2,290,-240 and the ending inventory amounted to \$322,569, giving the same ratio of 7.1 times. By maintaining this ratio, the president of the corporation felt he was keeping in line with the typical concerns in his division of business. In year A, net sales expanded to \$3,084,750 and the inventory at the end of the year amounted to \$434,472. Again the ratio of net sales to inventory was 7.1 times. This 3-year comparison is as follows:

	Year C	Year B	Year A
Net Sales...........................	\$1,309,006	\$2,290,240	\$3,084,750
Inventory...........................	184,367	322,569	434,472
Ratio of Net Sales to Inventory........	7.1	7.1	7.1

It is quite apparent that the management of this business realized the importance of the turnover of inventory, so much so that it made every effort to keep this ratio as stable as possible and in no case to allow it to fall below the typical ratio for wholesalers of paper. This point of view was admirable, but it certainly needed tempering. It is quite obvious that if this single ratio were followed implicitly, both the net sales and the ending inventory would remain in line, provided they both continued to increase at the same rate. It is also perfectly obvious that, somewhere in this upward trend of net sales and inventory, the inventory would become excessive for the size of the business, perhaps at \$200,000, maybe \$300,-000, or possibly at \$500,000. If the inventory were excessive, any sudden drop in inventory values would involve losses; if the inventory were very excessive, it could result in bankruptcy. Where is the danger point, and how may it be discerned?

At the end of year C, this concern was operating on a tangible net worth of \$265,516 and on a net working capital of \$244,106. At the end of year B, the tangible net worth amounted to \$276,692 and the net working capital to \$252,121. At the end of year A, the tangible net worth had increased to \$291,426 and the net working capital to \$258,762. By correlating these figures for the 3 years with the respective ending inventory, we obtain the following running picture:

	Year C	Year B	Year A
Tangible Net Worth......................	$265,516	$276,692	$291,426
Net Working Capital....................	244,106	252,121	258,762
Inventory...............................	184,367	322,569	434,472

For year C with net sales of $1,309,006, this enterprise was turning its tangible net worth 4.93 times, its net working capital 5.36 times, and the ratio of net sales to inventory, as we have seen, was 7.1 times. The ratio of net sales to tangible net worth was close to par, the ratio of net sales to net working capital was a little low, and the ratio of net sales to the ending inventory a trifle low. The management of this corporation was composed of aggressive young men, all of whom had come up through the sales end of competing concerns and who had organized this enterprise on their ability to get sales. They got the sales. There was no mistake about that.

As the net sales expanded, the inventory went up. Since the president was following the guide of net sales to inventory, he felt that everything was shipshape because that single ratio was in line. As the net sales expanded, the receivables also went up. With the increase in inventory and in receivables, the current liabilities likewise had to expand. At the end of year B and at the end of year A, the current liabilities were excessive, very excessive, in comparison with either the current assets or the tangible net worth.

Ratio of Inventory to Net Working Capital

The ratio of net sales to inventory must be supplemented by the ratio of inventory to net working capital to prevent situations just like this one from arising. The relationship between the inventory and the net working capital is between one variable, the inventory, and one item that generally changes very moderately from one year to another, the net working capital, so that here is a relatively fixed basis for comparison which has unusual significance.

In this case of the wholesaler of paper, the ending inventory should not have been allowed to exceed appreciably three-quarters of the net working capital. This proportion existed in year C at the same time that the ratio of net sales to inventory of 7.1 times was reasonably in line. In year B, as the net sales increased, the objective of the management should not have been to have the inventory equal 1/7.1 of the net sales, but to have it no more than three-quarters of the net working capital. An inventory equal to no more than three-quarters of the net working capital would have meant a much higher ratio of net sales to the closing inventory. In other words, for every line of business there is a normal volume of sales in relation to net working capital, and a normal relationship of net sales to inventory. When, however, a concern begins to handle a greater volume of business than might be considered normal, then those greater sales must be obtained on a proportionately smaller inventory; the size of the inventory must bear a certain definite relationship to the net working capital.

The reason for this supplementary relationship is very sound. Suppose there were a sudden drop of 50 per cent in the wholesale value of paper. During any such period, sales would decrease rapidly, but purchase commitments which had been placed with mills would be accepted as the paper was delivered. The wholesaler would be faced with increasing inventories on decreasing sales and with falling prices. This situation is no figment of the imagination. It is exactly what enterprises face continuously, although at certain phases of the economic cycle the situation is spread through more industries, with more rapidly falling prices, than at other times. Let us forget about the fact that inventories would increase during such a period and see what would happen in theory to the wholesaler of paper if the value of the inventory should shrink 50 per cent. We would then have the following situations:

	Year C	Year B	Year A
Net Working Capital	$244,106	$252,121	$258,762
Inventory	184,367	322,569	434,472
Loss with 50 Per Cent Drop in Inventory Value	92,183	161,284	217,236

In these hypothetical situations, the loss of the inventory at the end of year C would be $92,183, at the end of year B $161,284, and at the end of year A $217,236. The loss naturally increases in proportion to the size of the inventory. Now, let us relate these respective losses to the respective amounts of net working capital and see the result.

	Year C	Year B	Year A
Net Working Capital	$244,106	$252,121	$258,762
Loss with 50 Per Cent Drop in Inventory Value	92,183	161,284	217,236
Final Net Working Capital	$151,923	$ 90,837	$ 41,526

In year C, the resulting net working capital after the inventory loss of $92,183 would have been $151,923. In year B, the resulting net working capital after the inventory loss of $161,284 would have been $90,837, and in year A the final net working capital would have been only $41,526. In other words, the larger the inventory, the larger the loss taken during a period of falling prices and the greater the inroad on net working capital. The only managements that would allow an inventory to reach the proportions described in this case would be those who were misguided, who were ignorant of sound finance, or who were speculating in inventory for a rise. Some definite, fairly fixed relationship is desirable between the net working capital and the inventory.

Price fluctuations are familiar phenomena to businessmen, all of whom recognize price oscillations as a profit factor, serving at times to expand profits and at other times constituting a source of major loss. That was the sole reason for the development of the base stock method, average cost, and last-in first-out method of valuing inventory. Nevertheless, the large part that fluctuating prices play as a daily factor in total profits is not so widely recognized as it should be, for the simple reason that the amount of profit that can be directly traced to price changes is rarely determinable.

Overbuying of merchandise is one of the worst evils that can befall a business enterprise. Yet each year thousands of business concerns are ruined by such a policy. Some managements are utterly unable to resist what seems to be a bargain, although the common testimony of successful businessmen is to the effect that bargains rarely exist in raw materials to such a degree that a concern in normal times is warranted in locking up its capital in excess inventory. The more effective and the only sure way to save money in buying is to purchase reasonable quantities under the most favorable market conditions. It never pays to load up with excess quantities.

ILLUSTRATIONS OF RELATIONSHIPS

These principles are illustrated in the operations of three different business enterprises, a cotton goods converter, a corporation operating a chain of retail drugstores, and a canner of fruits and vegetables.

Cotton Goods Converter

Cotton goods converters have no mills. Their headquarters are located in important textile markets such as New York City; their investments in fixed assets represent only furniture and fixtures in their offices and so are always small in relation to the tangible net worth. Operations consist in buying grey goods direct from cotton mills or in the open market, creating the designs to be printed on the grey goods in colors, called "fancies," and having the fabrics dyed in single colors, generally called "staples," unless the shades are unusual and delicate.

This work of printing and dyeing is handled for the converter by textile mills known as "finishers," which have extensive machinery and equipment for finishing the grey goods according to the specific instructions of each converter. Converters have built up large annual sales by handling that portion of the cotton textile industry concerned with styling, a part of the industry that previously had been handled by the weaving mills on their own account and that they still handle to a moderate extent. As a result of this method of operation, converters handle a far greater volume of sales on their tangible net worth than do weaving mills,

The Cotton Goods Converting Company has been in existence 12 years, having operated continuously as a partnership with the same three partners. Sales are made largely to the dress trade on the typical terms of 2 per cent 10 days, 60 days extra. At the present time the concern has 260 active accounts on its books. Comparative figures for the last three fiscal years appear in Schedule 36.

[Schedule 36]   COTTON GOODS CONVERTING COMPANY
Comparative Figures for Years Ended July 31, 19—

	(C) Three Years Ago	(B) Two Years Ago	(A) One Year Ago
ASSETS			
Cash	$ 25,567	$ 24,337	$ 11,828
Notes Receivable	6,201	16,102	488
Accounts Receivable	64,601	121,011	215,223
Inventory	85,623	77,506	195,833
Current Assets	$181,992	$238,956	$423,372
Furniture and Fixtures, Net	3,968	5,675	7,414
Miscellaneous Receivables	2,151	469	13,654
Prepaid Expense	404	751	1,275
TOTAL	$188,515	$245,851	$445,715
LIABILITIES			
Notes Payable to Bank	$.......	$.......	$ 50,000
Due to Partners	7,000	5,690	19,192
Accounts Payable	91,335	129,787	240,889
Accruals	6,251	7,145	13,449
Reserve for Taxes	....	....	8,257
Current Liabilities	$104,586	$142,622	$331,787
Tangible Net Worth	83,929	103,229	113,928
TOTAL	$188,515	$245,851	$445,715
Net Working Capital	$ 77,406	$ 96,334	$ 91,585
Current Ratio	1.74	1.67	1.28
Tangible Net Worth	$ 83,929	$103,229	$113,928
Net Sales	$502,633	$522,184	$598,927
Net Profit	16,944	24,300	20,699
Withdrawals	10,000	5,000	10,000

This enterprise has operated profitably every year since its inception. In those years when net profits were small, withdrawals were even smaller, so that the business has a record of continuous although at times rather moderate growth. For year C net profits were $6,944 in excess of withdrawals, for year B $19,300, and for year A $10,699. As a result of the retained earnings, the tangible net worth at the end of year C amounted to

$83,929, and at the end of year A to $113,928. The net working capital increased quite substantially from $77,406 to $96,334 between year C and year B, and then dropped to $91,585 in year A as a result of an increase in miscellaneous receivables from $469 to $13,654 and the moderate increase in furniture and fixtures from $5,675 to $7,414.

These changes, however, were all of minor significance. Two other changes were of considerably more importance: the steady increase in the accounts receivable from $64,601 in year C, to $121,011 in year B, to $215,223 in year A, and almost as large an increase in the inventory from $85,623 in year C to $195,833 in year A, although a dip did take place in this item in year B. Because of the very substantial expansion in these two items, there was a concomitant expansion in the current liabilities from $104,586 to $142,622 to $331,787 over the 3-year period.

Of these three items, the one that is of especial interest is the inventory. By relating this item to the net working capital we obtain the following yearly comparisons:

	Year C	Year B	Year A
Inventory	$85,623	$77,506	$195,833
Net Working Capital	77,406	96,334	91,585
Ratio of Inventory to Net Working Capital	110.6%	80.4%	213.8%

These relationships show some fluctuation. Between year C and year B, the net working capital expanded from $77,406 to $96,334. At the same time the inventory was reduced from $85,623 to $77,506. The trends of both items were in favorable directions, bringing about an improved relationship from 110.6 per cent to 80.4 per cent.

But between year B and year A affairs headed skyward with no real control at the helm. Both items turned in the wrong direction. The net working capital decreased from $96,334 to $91,585, or 4.9 per cent, and the inventory expanded from $77,506 to $195,833, or 152.7 per cent. Year A closed with the very extended relationship of 213.8 per cent between the closing inventory and the net working capital, a condition far out of line for a cotton goods converter.

Condensed Analysis. The figures for year C disclosed a fairly satisfactory internal financial condition. The notes and accounts receivable aggregating $70,802 indicated an average collection period of 51.5 days compared with the selling terms of 70 days. The inventory of $85,623 gave a ratio of 5.9 times when compared with the net sales of $502,633, which was fairly satisfactory for this line of business, as evidenced by the schedule at the end of Chap. XI. The current liabilities of $104,586 were somewhat larger than the tangible net worth of $83,929, but this condition is not abnormal for a concern with nominal investments in fixed assets where the receivables and the inventory are in healthy proportion. If the inventory had been lower than the net working capital, the current liabilities would have been correspondingly smaller and a somewhat higher ratio would have been obtained with the net sales. The financial condition then might have been characterized as quite satisfactory instead of fairly satisfactory.

In year B one important change took place. The notes and accounts receivable increased from $70,802 to $137,113, or 93.6 per cent. As the net sales for year B increased only $19,551, or 3.9 per cent, over the net sales for year C, the average collection period went up from 51.5 days to 95.8 days. On selling terms of 70 days an average collection period of 95.8 days would seem to be somewhat extended with past-due accounts, especially in view of the increase in the average collection period from 51.5 days in year C. While the receivables appeared to be in somewhat poorer shape, the inventory appeared to be in better shape. The inventory had been reduced to $77,506. At this figure it was materially below the net working capital of $96,334 and showed an improved relationship of 6.7 times when compared with the net sales of $522,184. As a result of the larger current assets represented by the expanded receivables, the current liabilities were larger. All in all, the condition was somewhat less favorable than at the end of the previous fiscal year.   •

In year A the downward trend continued as far as the internal condition of the business was concerned, even though net profits were recorded. The notes and accounts receivable continued to expand and now amounted to $215,711. On the basis of the net annual sales of $598,927 the average collection period was 131.5 days. No aging of the receivables could be obtained, but the management did indicate that sales had not bulked heavily during the 2 months preceding the statement date. Under these circumstances a collection period of 131.5 days on selling terms of 70 days certainly indicated a vulnerable condition with a considerable portion of the receivables past due.

On top of this unfavorable condition, the inventory had expanded out of all reasonable proportions. Prices had risen during the year and the management had decided to buy a little extra quantity of grey goods. They had. Not only a little but a great deal. Moreover, as the concern used the first-in first-out method of taking inventory, there was no reserve in the item and any drop in market prices would find this enterprise off-balance. At $195,833 the inventory showed a relationship with net sales for the year of only 3.1 times, about one-half the typical turnover of cotton goods converters. Instead of being less than the net working capital as in year B, the inventory now became 213.8 per cent of the net working capital, a double check indicating the heaviness of this item. With both heavy receivables and heavy inventory, the current liabilities were also excessive, amounting to 291.3 per cent of the tangible net worth.

This enterprise has a hard year ahead. Its financial condition at the end of year A was very extended. If the receivables can be reduced approximately $100,000 and the inventory reduced another $100,000 during the year following year A without loss, a miracle will have taken place. A situation such as this is wide open for a considerable use of red ink, even if it should be the first in the history of the enterprise. It is most likely that a substantial loss in bad accounts is hidden in the receivables. Often by the time it becomes imperative to reduce inventories, as in this case, a falling market has developed. However, if prices of grey goods and finished cotton goods should remain firm, the situation would not be so vulnerable. In this predicament the management is trusting to fortuitous circumstances and not consciously guiding its affairs. As the situation remains, a minimum of $200,000 must be raised by liquidating receivables and merchandise to bring the liabilities reasonably into line, and with no loss in time.

Chain Drug Stores

The business now known as Chain Drug Stores, Inc., was organized 28 years ago with an authorized and paid-in capital of $50,000. The enterprise became financially embarrassed 9 years ago and affairs were revamped. Under the plan of reorganization stockholders authorized an issue of $250,000 five per cent cumulative preferred stock, par $50, of which $212,600 was issued. The plan provided that one share of this 5 per cent cumulative preferred stock be issued for each $50 of indebtedness, fractional liabilities to be liquidated by cash. Over the intervening 9 years the outstanding 5 per cent cumulative preferred stock had been reduced to $181,800 by buying in occasional shares of the outstanding stock at a fraction of the book value and retiring them.

From time to time, unprofitable stores have been closed and new stores have been opened. At the end of year A, 16 units were in operation, all at strategic locations, and all in the one city of Chicago. All stores carried a complete line of drugs, drug sundries, cosmetics, candy, and tobacco, soda and luncheonette departments, and facilities for handling prescriptions. Three of the stores also carried extensive lines of ladies' gloves and hosiery.

A small wholesale department was conducted for the purpose of disposing of surplus stocks of tobacco, candy, and supplementary miscellaneous merchandise when acquired in quantities beyond immediate requirements. Normally, chain drugstores sell entirely for cash. The comparative figures in Schedule 37 show accounts receivable outstanding on each statement date. These receivables arise partly from sales of the wholesale department, and partly from specialized prescription business that had been built up by catering especially to doctors.

Comparative figures indicate a steady downward trend over the 3-year period. Unless some radical change is instituted in the very immediate future, the management will awake some cloudy morning to find that the business is ready for its second reorganization, or possibly this time bankruptcy with liquidation.

[Schedule 37]   CHAIN DRUG STORES, INC.

Comparative Figures for Years Ended September 30, 19—

	(C) Three Years Ago	(B) Two Years Ago	(A) One Year Ago
ASSETS			
Cash.........................	$ 38,343	$ 15,489	$ 25,443
Accounts Receivable...........	22,858	19,855	19,214
Inventory....................	276,129	258,775	238,252
Current Assets.................	$ 337,330	$ 294,119	$ 282,909
Fixed Assets, Net..............	208,612	242,113	250,412
Investments..................	6,282	5,622	5,051
Prepaid Expenses.............	3,798	5,023	4,677
Deposits.....................	4,795	4,795	4,795
TOTAL...................	$ 560,817	$ 551,672	$ 547,844
LIABILITIES			
Notes Payable for Merchandise..	$ 1,360	$ 10,709	$ 10,593
Accounts Payable..............	155,714	201,217	204,614
Accruals.....................	19,079	10,995	8,155
Reserve for Taxes.............	6,304	5,479	5,307
Current Liabilities..............	$ 182,457	$ 228,400	$ 228,669
5% Cumulative Preferred Stock.	185,300	182,950	181,800
Common Stock................	130,000	130,000	130,000
Earned Surplus...............	63,060	10,322	7,375
TOTAL...................	$ 560,817	$ 551,672	$ 547,844
Net Working Capital............	$ 154,873	$ 65,719	$ 54,240
Current Ratio..................	1.85	1.29	1.24
Tangible Net Worth.............	$ 378,360	$ 323,272	$ 319,175
Net Sales.....................	$1,526,187	$1,442,910	$1,433,572
Net Profit....................	3,218	(L)52,738	(L)2,947
Dividends....................	None	None	None

While nominal net profits of $3,218 were recorded in year *C*, a loss of $52,738 was assumed in year *B*, and a loss of $2,947 in year *A*. No dividends were paid over these years, even on the outstanding 5 per cent cumulative preferred stock. The net sales have decreased, not greatly but still on the downward side each year; they amounted to $1,433,572 for year *A*, which was 6.1 per cent below the net sales for year *C*.

Along with the downward trend in net sales and the unprofitable operations for year *B* and for year *A*, was the same but a more exaggerated trend in net working capital. From $154,873 in year *C*, the net working capital dropped to $65,719 in year B, and to $54,240 in year A. As the net working capital shrank, the inventory was reduced from year to year but much less moderately. The relationship between these two items shows the following unfavorable trend:

	Year C	Year B	Year A
Inventory...............................	$276,129	$258,775	$238,252
Net Working Capital.....................	154,873	65,719	54,240
Ratio of Inventory to Net Working Capital...	178.3%	378.5%	439.2%

Between year C and year A the inventory was reduced from $276,129 to $238,252, or 13.7 per cent. At the same time, the net working capital shrank from $154,873 to $65,719 to $54,240, or 65.0 per cent. As a result of this proportionately more rapid drop in the net working capital the ratio between these two items went steadily upward. At the end of year C, the ratio of 178.3 per cent was heavy. At the end of year B the ratio had increased to 378.5 per cent and the business was becoming hard pressed. At the end of year A, the ratio continued upward to 439.2 per cent and the business was being kept alive by the grace of creditors.

Condensed Analysis. The figures for year C disclosed a fairly satisfactory condition with one exception, and that one exception was the relationship between the inventory and the net working capital. The net sales for the year were 5.5 times the inventory, the fixed assets were 55.2 per cent of the tangible net worth, and the ratio of current assets to current liabilities was 1.85. These relationships were all a trifle out of line, but not sufficiently so to cause any vital concern. But the comparison between the inventory and the net working capital with a ratio of 178.3 per cent, a ratio almost twice as large as it should have been, was clear evidence that something basically was wrong.

If $125,000 could have been cut off the inventory, then the inventory would have approximated the net working capital, and by freeing funds the current liabilities would have been reduced the same amount, that is, from $182,457 to approximately $57,000. But the inventory could not be reduced this amount without keeping the stores understocked. In other words, with an investment of $378,360 the company was operating too many large stores; at this particular stage, the management was reluctant to close any of them. To have operated this number of stores adequately $125,000 additional funds should have been invested in the business to furnish additional net working capital.

During year B the fixed assets increased from $208,612 to $242,113, an expansion of $33,501. This sum is not large, but it was relatively large at the time for this business. The additional investment of such a sum in fixed assets together with the net loss of $52,738 for the year was tragic. The current liabilities increased from $182,457 to $228,400 and the net working capital was reduced from $154,873 to $65,719.

Whereas the answer to the problem of this corporation at the end of year C had been the investment of \$125,000 to be kept in liquid assets and to furnish additional net working capital, or the closing of certain stores to bring the inventory into line, the answer at the end of year B was the investment of approximately \$195,000 to increase net working capital which no one, not even the stockholders, would invest in an extremely unprofitable venture. The ratio of current assets to current liabilities dropped from 1.85 to 1.29, and the current liabilities now reached 70.3 of the tangible net worth.

The figures for year A showed a condition which had gone from bad to worse. The investment in fixed assets continued to increase, the net sales continued to drop, a loss was assumed, the net working capital continued to shrink, and the relationship between the inventory and the net working capital was out of all reasonable proportion. The graveyard was just around the corner.

Canner of Fruits and Vegetables

Fruit & Vegetable Canners, Inc., was organized as a partnership by two brothers 43 years ago. The partnership was incorporated 22 years ago, and 3 years ago the business was reincorporated under the laws of another state to merge the enterprise with four smaller successful canners. The partners in the original enterprise have since died and the business for the past 4 years has come under the direct management of the president, a son of one of the original partners, who is now only 28 years of age.

As will be seen by the figures in Schedule 38, this corporation is a representative enterprise in its field, operating at the end of year A on a tangible net worth of \$5,663,674. The business is both a holding and an operating company. As an operating company, the corporation and its subsidiaries are engaged in preparing, packing, and distributing nationally under its own well-advertised brands vegetables, fruits, and condiments. It has 32 packing and canning plants located in the Middle West. As a holding company it owns the entire outstanding stock of six direct subsidiaries.

For a thorough analysis of the affairs of this corporation, the analyst, as outlined in Chap. IV, would obtain, if possible, comparative individual financial statements of the parent corporation and each of the six subsidiaries as well as comparative consolidated financial statements of the seven corporations together, with all intercompany relations eliminated. He would also need full information covering intercompany loans and intercompany debts for the sale of merchandise. Supplementing this information it would be desirable to know whether intercompany loans were of a seasonal nature to cover an operating peak or had been running several years and were quite permanent; how long each outstanding loan had been on the books; and what was the possibility of repayment in the near future where the loan was of long standing. In the case of intercompany receivables similar information would assist in the analysis. The analyst would also learn whether intercompany purchases were made on regular terms and whether the liabilities so created were retired on those terms; or, if purchases were made on special terms, what those terms were and whether they were respected.

After obtaining as complete information as possible, the analyst would then proceed to analyze the affairs of each subsidiary. If the analyst represented a bank or a merchandise creditor he might, after determining that a particular subsidiary in which he was interested was in a weak financial condition, obtain a guaranty from the parent company to cover obligations of this particular subsidiary. Then the analyst would study the comparative consolidated financial statement to obtain an over-all picture.

For the purpose of this study we shall pass over the intermediate phases of the analysis and take up the consolidated figures, which appear in Schedule 38.

For year C a loss of $335,592 was sustained and dividends of $307,500 were paid. As a result of these two features, the tangible net worth dropped $643,092 and the net working capital approximately the same amount. Notwithstanding the loss and the payment of dividends, the consolidated figures as of the end of year C disclosed a fairly satisfactory condition, with two exceptions. The receivables reflected an average collection period of 26 days based on the net sales, the fixed assets represented 52 per cent of the tangible net worth, and the current assets disclosed a healthy margin over the current liabilities.

The two exceptions were the heavy inventory and the rather substantial total debt of $6,625,976. The net sales of $16,586,249 were only 2.3 times the inventory of $7,189,656, a rather low relationship for this line of business. Moreover—and more obvious—was the fact that the inventory was appreciably larger than the net working capital of $5,992,378.

Operations went from bad to worse in year B. The inventory at the end of year C had been valued at first-in first-out and in a rising market was clearly heavy. As so often happens with a heavy inventory valued on this basis, a loss is immediately incurred in a falling market. That happened here, and although the inventory was reduced from $7,189,656 to $5,932,-026 at the end of year B, operations were conducted at a loss of $712,404. This loss, together with dividends of $61,250, the reduction of $1,000,000 in the term loan, and the additional expenditure of $101,160 for fixed assets, brought about a further reduction in the net working capital to $3,878,356. The inventory, notwithstanding its decrease, continued to be materially out of line. The total debt increased as the tangible net worth decreased. Affairs became very extended.

Year A shows real improvement, but the company was still not out of

Comparative Consolidated Figures for Years Ended May 21, 19—

	(C) Three Years Ago	(B) Two Years Ago	(A) One Year Ago
ASSETS			
Cash......................	$ 651,779	$ 500,860	$ 538,074
Notes Receivable...........	160,110	110,201	100,452
Accounts Receivable........	1,021,113	1,910,100	1,810,221
Inventory..................	7,189,656	5,932,026	5,409,997
Advances on Growing Crops..	293,246	245,283	311,547
Current Assets.............	$ 9,315,904	$ 8,698,470	$ 8,170,291
Fixed Assets, Net...........	3,404,238	3,505,398	3,595,547
Cash Value of Life Insurance.	49,874	60,261	70,894
Investments...............	35,073	25,001	4,502
Miscellaneous Receivables....	105,020	65,031	215,108
Deferred Assets.............	228,988	232,478	200,207
Good Will.................	1	1	1
TOTAL.................	$13,139,098	$12,586,640	$12,256,550
LIABILITIES			
Notes Payable to Banks.....	$ 2,000,000	$ 3,500,000	$ 2,750,000
Due to Officers and Employees	83,867	52,577	37,985
Accounts Payable...........	890,675	976,084	990,422
Accruals..................	140,782	182,708	158,448
Advance Payments..........	147,719	92,244	139,285
Due on Stock Subscription...	37,151	....	....
Reserve for Taxes...........	23,332	16,501	125,000
Current Liabilities...........	$ 3,323,526	$ 4,820,114	$ 4,201,140
Term Loan.................	3,000,000	2,000,000	2,000,000
Mortgages.................	302,450	406,866	391,635
Total Debt.................	$ 6,625,976	$ 7,226,980	$ 6,592,775
4% Cumulative Pref. Stock..	3,500,000	3,500,000	3,500,000
Common Stock.............	550,242	552,500	552,500
Capital Surplus.............	689,208	307,642	282,016
Retained Earnings..........	1,773,672	999,518	1,329,259
TOTAL.................	$13,139,098	$12,586,640	$12,256,550
Net Working Capital.........	$ 5,992,378	$ 3,878,356	$ 3,969,151
Current Ratio...............	2.81	1.80	1.94
Tangible Net Worth..........	$ 6,513,121	$ 5,359,659	$ 5,663,774
Net Sales..................	$16,586,249	$18,269,811	$20,337,746
Net Profit.................	(L)*335,592*	(L)*712,404*	329,741
Dividends.................	307,500	61,250	None

the woods. Net profits of $329,741 were earned, current liabilities and total liabilities were moderately reduced, the net sales were increased, the net working capital was increased, and the inventory was reduced, all favorable features as far as the trends were concerned, but the improvements in the aggregate were only moderate. These trends need to be continued in a marked manner. The relationship between the inventory and the net working capital for the 3 years was as follows:

	Year C	Year B	Year A
Inventory	$7,189,656	$5,932,026	$5,409,997
Net Working Capital	5,992,378	3,878,356	3,969,151
Ratio of Inventory to Net Working Capital	119.9%	152.9%	136.3%

In year C the inventory of $7,189,656 was 119.9 per cent of the net working capital of $5,992,378. In year B the inventory was reduced to $5,932,026, and in year A still further reduced to $5,409,997. In year B the net working capital decreased 35.3 per cent to $3,878,356 and then in year A increased moderately to $3,969,151. Because of the very substantial shrinkage in the net working capital in year B, the relationship with the inventory went up to 152.9 per cent, and then as a result of the improved trend in both items in year A, the relationship decreased to 136.3 per cent.

Condensed Analysis. In year C, as we have seen, the inventory was heavy and the total liabilities were greater than the tangible net worth, always a vulnerable combination; the operations for year B showed just how vulnerable. The inventory was heavy in relation to both the net sales and the net working capital. The net sales were only 2.3 times the inventory, when the relationship should have been quite materially higher. Moreover, the inventory was 19.9 per cent in excess of the net working capital.

Here was the situation for the first full year after merging with the four smaller concerns. Whereas the management had planned to close the year with an inventory of $4,000,000, the inventory had reached $7,189,656, and, to carry the excess, a term loan of $3,000,000 had been obtained just prior to the statement date. The internal management had become disorganized during the year. Possibly the president of the corporation had been too inexperienced to realize the unfavorable trend, possibly too ineffectual to hold a firm hand over others in the management who wanted to speculate for a rise in values. At any rate the year closed with a fever.

From this point on, the fundamental policy should have been one of making the most out of a bad situation, reducing the inventory and liabilities as fast as possible, yet not assuming unnecessary losses. Year B closed with a serious heart attack and peak liabilities of $7,226,980, well in excess of the tangible net worth.

During year A net profits of \$329,741 were finally earned, a heartening sign after the substantial losses of year C and year B. Liabilities and merchandise were reduced moderately but both items continued heavy; the total liabilities were 16.4 greater than the tangible net worth, and the inventory was 36.3 per cent greater than the net working capital. To bring this situation into reasonable proportions, the inventory should be reduced \$1,500,000 from the figure at the end of year A and those funds used to reduce current liabilities. Moreover, several years of profitable operations are needed with the retention of all the profits in the business in liquid form to increase the net working capital to a figure between \$5,000,000 and \$5,500,000. Future operations should keep the year-end inventory constantly below the net working capital even if it means that the net sales will represent six or eight times the closing inventory. With capable strong management, the financial condition of this corporation probably can be brought into line.

TYPICAL RATIOS OF INVENTORY TO NET WORKING CAPITAL

Schedule 39 gives the typical ratios of closing inventory to net working capital for 39 lines of manufacturing, 21 of wholesaling, and 7 of retailing for the years 1955 through 1959 with a 5-year arithmetical average. Breweries have the lowest 5-year average among the 39 manufacturing lines with 49.6 per cent; foundries have the second best 5-year average with 55.2 per cent; and manufacturers of drugs are third with 60.5 per cent. Canners of fruits and vegetables are at the bottom of the list with a 5-year average ratio of inventory to net working capital of 153.2 per cent. Manufacturers of airplane parts and accessories are next to the bottom with a 5-year average of 110.2 per cent.

Among the wholesale lines, wholesalers of fresh fruits and vegetables with a 5-year average ratio of 28.4 per cent make the best showing of inventory to net working capital, followed by wholesalers of meat and poultry with a 5-year average of 52.5 per cent, and wholesalers of gasoline, fuel oil, and lubricating oil with 56.9 per cent. The poorest showing is made by wholesalers of groceries with a 5-year average of 98.1 per cent, and wholesalers of drugs and drug sundries with 90.7 per cent.

Among the seven retail trades, the best showing is made by furniture stores making at least half of their sales on installment with a 5-year average of 42.3 per cent, and the poorest showing by independent grocery and meat stores with 128.0 per cent.

Maxim

When a manufacturer or a wholesaler is operating on a tangible net worth between \$50,000 and \$250,000, wide practical experience has indicated

RATIOS OF INVENTORY TO NET WORKING CAPITAL   [Schedule 39]

Lines of Business Activity	Percentage					
	Median					Five-year Average
	1955	1956	1957	1958	1959	
MANUFACTURERS						
Agricultural Implements and Machinery............................	81.6	82.7	80.3	69.3	75.0	77.8
Airplane Parts and Accessories.......	120.0	122.9	105.1	118.2	84.8	110.2
Automobile Parts and Accessories....	77.5	79.2	79.0	77.7	82.7	79.2
Bakers.............................	80.0	78.9	65.1	59.1	62.3	69.1
Bedsprings and Mattresses..........	62.0	64.0	59.4	64.7	68.4	63.7
Bodies, Auto, Bus, and Truck........	87.6	72.6	98.1	71.4	94.2	84.8
Bolts, Screws, Nuts, and Nails.......	76.4	78.7	75.7	69.9	83.4	76.8
Breweries...........................	50.0	50.8	46.8	47.4	53.2	49.6
Chemicals, Industrial...............	64.0	58.9	65.3	63.8	61.5	62.7
Coats and Suits, Men's and Boys'....	89.4	88.4	81.9	73.8	84.2	83.5
Coats and Suits, Women's...........	81.0	67.5	72.7	76.9	88.3	77.3
Confectionery......................	75.1	70.0	74.8	70.7	77.0	73.5
Cotton Cloth Mills.................	78.8	74.6	81.0	78.5	60.6	74.7
Cotton Goods, Converters, Non-factored............................	76.5	79.2	77.4	78.0	86.8	79.6
Dresses, Rayon, Silk, and Acetate....	71.4	66.9	61.6	76.1	86.7	72.5
Drugs..............................	58.2	71.2	62.8	54.6	55.6	60.5
Electrical Parts and Supplies.........	83.4	83.2	75.2	77.8	83.4	80.6
Foundries..........................	55.9	64.6	56.3	48.9	50.4	55.2
Fruits and Vegetables, Canners......	144.4	155.0	147.7	153.1	165.6	153.2
Furniture..........................	67.5	69.4	68.7	68.2	79.3	70.6
Hardware and Tools.................	79.6	80.7	75.7	67.6	77.4	76.2
Hosiery............................	79.4	68.6	72.3	68.3	76.5	73.0
Lumber............................	69.1	74.7	77.8	75.3	75.8	74.5
Machine Shops.....................	70.6	76.8	69.2	60.2	66.2	68.6
Machinery, Industrial...............	76.1	79.5	74.6	63.7	71.4	73.1
Meats and Provisions, Packers.......	73.0	76.4	64.4	87.0	68.0	73.8
Metal Stampings...................	70.5	75.9	71.8	60.6	67.3	69.2
Outerwear, Knitted.................	68.3	76.3	76.1	72.3	80.2	74.6
Overalls and Work Clothing.........	92.6	86.7	92.0	80.5	87.6	87.9
Paints, Varnishes, and Lacquers......	69.4	68.7	67.7	64.2	67.1	67.4
Paper..............................	70.9	65.6	69.6	73.5	68.9	69.7
Paper Boxes.......................	72.5	68.1	55.7	66.7	65.6	65.7
Petroleum, Integrated Corporations..	68.3	69.9	71.2	62.7	63.9	67.2
Radio Parts and Supplies............	75.3	92.5	90.3	71.2	82.6	82.4
Shirts, Underwear, and Pajamas, Men's............................	94.1	95.1	102.2	102.9	111.1	101.1
Shoes, Men's, Women's, and Children's............................	81.2	79.8	84.4	74.3	91.1	82.2
Soft Drinks and Carbonated Water, Bottlers........................	59.2	54.3	55.6	52.8	81.9	60.8
Steel, Structural Fabricators (Sell on Short Terms)....................	75.2	77.3	81.3	65.9	64.5	72.8
Stoves, Ranges, and Ovens..........	76.4	82.5	72.6	66.6	68.4	73.3

RATIOS OF INVENTORY TO NET WORKING CAPITAL (*Continued*)
[Schedule 39 (*Cont.*)]

Lines of Business Activity	Percentage					
	Median					Five-year Average
	1955	1956	1957	1958	1959	
WHOLESALERS						
Automobile Parts and Accessories....	87.9	89.0	88.6	84.6	93.4	88.7
Baked Goods......................	75.3	83.9	73.6	58.6	68.6	72.0
Cigars, Cigarettes, and Tobacco......	73.4	80.3	74.0	79.8	82.1	77.9
Drugs and Drug Sundries...........	95.7	89.4	89.2	89.7	89.6	90.7
Dry Goods.......................	67.9	69.9	68.6	69.5	76.6	70.5
Electrical Parts and Supplies.........	78.1	82.8	75.7	75.8	82.9	79.1
Fruits and Produce, Fresh...........	25.0	30.1	28.9	27.2	30.7	28.4
Furnishings, Men's................	67.7	68.6	69.9	55.7	70.3	66.4
Gasoline, Fuel Oil, and Lubricating Oil	57.5	58.4	55.0	50.8	62.9	56.9
Groceries........................	99.6	96.9	98.2	94.8	100.8	98.1
Hardware........................	91.1	88.0	83.9	83.7	85.6	86.5
Hosiery and Underwear.............	80.2	72.1	76.0	68.2	72.3	73.8
Household Appliances, Electrical.....	87.1	89.4	91.5	85.5	93.9	89.5
Lumber..........................	67.2	67.0	66.6	68.3	71.0	68.0
Lumber and Building Materials......	71.4	73.9	70.2	73.9	76.8	73.2
Meat and Poultry.................	57.9	70.7	54.3	40.8	38.8	52.5
Paints, Varnishes, and Lacquers......	77.0	69.3	76.8	68.9	72.9	73.0
Paper...........................	77.5	81.4	79.5	76.3	75.9	78.1
Plumbing and Heating Supplies......	81.0	81.8	77.2	74.1	76.5	78.1
Shoes, Men's, Women's, and Children's.........................	64.5	69.2	69.3	61.2	76.7	68.2
Wines and Liquors................	85.2	83.1	88.2	84.3	84.2	85.0
RETAILERS						
Clothing, Men's and Boys'..........	87.7	89.6	97.1	90.9	95.6	92.2
Department Stores.................	65.5	67.7	67.1	63.7	64.8	65.8
Furniture, 50 Per Cent or More Installment......................	38.2	41.4	42.6	44.2	45.0	42.3
Groceries and Meats, Independent...	133.7	130.0	132.8	124.4	119.0	128.0
Lumber and Building Materials......	76.4	68.7	66.3	67.7	67.4	69.3
Shoes...........................	122.2	117.4	117.9	104.5	116.4	115.7
Women's Specialty Shops...........	72.4	67.3	68.2	71.2	71.9	70.2

that extreme care should be exercised in the analysis, even though the ratio of net sales to inventory is in satisfactory relationship, if the inventory is greater than three-quarters of the net working capital. When the tangible net worth exceeds $250,000, the inventory should be no greater than the net working capital. In a retail business with a tangible net worth in excess of $50,000, the inventory should be no greater than the net working capital.

THEORY AND PROBLEMS

1. Describe the trend that has taken place in recent years as to who should be responsible for the inventory figure used in the balance sheet.

2. If you were operating a business enterprise would you be inclined to purchase an excessive quantity of merchandise because you believed prices would rise in the near future and you would make a great profit? Explain your answer.

3. Why will the ratio of net sales to inventory sometimes give the analyst a false sense of security?

4. To ascertain whether the inventory is excessive or not, what ratio should be used to supplement the ratio of net sales to inventory?

5. The Airplane Parts Manufacturing Co., Inc., submitted the following comparative balance sheets to its investment banker. The manager of the statistical department of the investment banking house posted these figures on a comparative statement sheet. He computed the net working capital and the tangible net worth for both years. He then determined the following ratios for both years: (a) current assets to current liabilities, (b) current liabilities to tangible net worth, (c) total liabilities to tangible net worth, (d) funded debt to net working capital, and (e) fixed assets to tangible net worth. Assume you are the manager of the statistical department. Make the computations, interpret each ratio, and render a brief report of your analysis to the senior partner of your firm.

AIRPLANE PARTS MANUFACTURING CO., INC.
Comparative Balance Sheets, December 31, 19—

ASSETS	(B) Two Years Ago		(A) One Year Ago	
Current Assets				
Cash......................	$ 203,123		$ 162,829	
U.S. Treasury tax notes.......	2,009,035		451,260	
Notes and accounts receivable, less allowances.............	1,841,126		1,820,217	
Due from U.S. government....	223,037	$ 4,276,321	....	$2,434,306
Inventory				
Finished product.............	$ 211,626		$ 233,068	
Raw material and in process...	2,683,542	2,895,168	2,268,731	2,501,799
		$ 7,171,489		$4,936,105
Investment and Other Assets				
Investment in associated company pref. and com. stock...	$ 138,076		$ 138,075	
Sundry notes, accounts, and advances.................	215,413	$ 353,489	28,794	$ 166,869
Factory Plant and Equipment				
Factory real estate...........		509,006		499,004
Buildings, sidings, yards......	$1,674,438		$1,671,641	
Less: Reserve for depreciation.	1,027,081	647,357	985,053	686,588
Equipment................	$7,588,936		$7,030,284	
Less: Reserve for depreciation	6,087,922	1,501,014	5,634,542	1,395,742

AIRPLANE PARTS MANUFACTURING CO., INC. (*Continued*)

	(B) Two Years Ago		(A) One Year Ago	
Foundry				
Real estate...............				155,75
Buildings, sidings, yards....			$ 562,602	
Less: Reserve for depreciation			163,529	399,07
Equipment................	$ 556,141		$ 531,751	
Less: Reserve for depreciation	296,105	260,036	266,870	264,88
Warehouse				
Real estate...............		49,339		49,33
Building.................	$ 128,891		$ 128,891	
Less: Reserve for depreciation	19,320	109,571	16,098	112,79
		$ 3,076,323		$3,563,17
Building under construction.		152,720		
Deferred Charges				
Unexpired insurance premiums, prepaid...................		94,224		113,32
Patents, Trademarks, and Good Will......................		1		
		$10,848,246		$8,779,47

LIABILITIES

Current Liabilities				
Notes Payable..............	$ 805,000		$ 966,000	
Real estate notes maturing in 12 months................			10,000	
Accounts payable and accrued pay roll, interest, and taxes..	863,925		949,466	
Federal and state income taxes	2,775,000	$ 4,443,925	1,100,000	$3,025,46
Long-term Debt..............		45,000		55,00
Debenture Notes..............		173,500		144,80
Reserves				
For contingencies............	$ 430,000		$ 250,000	
For injuries to employees.....	33,279		24,737	
For guaranty expense........	75,000	538,279	15,000	289,73
Capital Stock and Surplus				
Authorized.................	$7,500,000		$7,500,000	
Less unissued...............	2,681,200		2,681,200	
Less in treasury.............	284,700		284,700	
	$4,534,100		$4,534,100	
Retained Earnings..........	1,113,442	5,647,542	730,372	5,264,47
		$10,848,246		$8,779,47

6. Study the ratios of inventory to net working capital for the following six lines o business. After each ratio place the capital letter which best describes that particular ratio: *G*, good; *F*, fair; *P*, poor.

    a. Cotton cloth mills................. 60.2
    b. Manufacturer of furniture.......... 122.3
    c. Manufacturer of paper............. 84.5
    d. Wholesaler of groceries............. 118.9
    e. Wholesaler of hardware............ 146.7
    f. Retailer of shoes.................. 94.3

7. Retail Drug Chain, Inc., operates a chain of 12 drug stores in a prominent Southern city. From the following comparative figures compute for both years (a) the ratio of net sales to inventory, and (b) the ratio of inventory to net working capital. Give your interpretation of the four ratios that you obtain, and also the trend in each ratio for the 2 years.

RETAIL DRUG CHAIN, INC.
Comparative Figures for Years Ended December 31, 19—

	(B) Two Years Ago	(A) One Year Ago
ASSETS		
Cash...	$ 7,416	$ 3,428
Notes Receivable............................	200	175
Accounts Receivable.........................	9,277	12,255
Inventory....................................	86,937	115,554
Current Assets................................	$103,830	$131,412
Fixed Assets, Net............................	60,507	77,982
Bank Stock..................................	210	210
Miscellaneous Receivables....................	549	2,271
Prepaid Items...............................	2,909	5,397
Supplies....................................	874	....
Good Will...................................	1,002	13,534
TOTAL..................................	$169,881	$230,806
LIABILITIES		
Notes Payable to Bank.......................	$.......	$ 40,000
Notes Payable for Equipment.................	....	4,623
Accounts Payable............................	28,282	48,033
Accruals....................................	1,899	958
Due to Affiliate.............................	1,001	2,153
Current Liabilities............................	$ 31,182	$ 95,767
Common Stock, No Par.......................	142,590	152,590
Deficit......................................	*3,891*	*7,551*
TOTAL..................................	$169,881	$230,806
Net Working Capital...........................	$ 72,648	$ 35,644
Current Ratio................................	3.32	1.38
Tangible Net Worth...........................	$137,697	$121,505
Sales.......................................	$458,017	$567,487
Net Profits..................................	$ 2,525	(L)*3,660*
Dividends...................................	None	None

CHAPTER XIII

Average Collection Period

Quality and quantity are attributes that the natural scientist tells us are of unusual importance. "Indeed, the qualitative," Alexis Carrel meticulously summarized, "is more difficult to study than the quantitative." These two attributes are equally significant in analyzing the total of notes and accounts receivable in a balance sheet. Are the receivables in healthy shape or not? Do they contain a substantial proportion of past-due accounts? Are some accounts carried in the receivables ledger even though they are worth no more than ice in Iceland? That it is of the utmost importance to analyze the receivables is evident from the fact that only the cash and readily marketable securities in a balance sheet are more liquid

A member of the management staff of a business enterprise, a lending banker, the accountant on the books, and occasionally a mercantile credit manager may obtain an *aging* of the receivables of a concern, that is, a breakdown showing the amount not due on a particular date, the amount up to 30 days past due, 31 to 60, 61 to 90, 91 to 180, and over 180 days past due on original terms of sale. In particular situations it is pertinent that the aging be made on the original terms of sales, as past-due accounts receivable might have been closed out with notes receivable, and the notes receivable in the usual aging would be considered not due if the notes had not matured. This detailed information, together with a knowledge of the amount recently charged off for bad debts, is of the greatest help in determining the condition of the receivables, but in too few cases is this information available. Under the circumstances, the analyst is left to his own ingenuity, which invariably means a study of the receivables by means of the average collection period.

NEED OF SELLING TERMS

The one immediate measure of the qualitative condition of receivables is to compare the average collection period, based upon the volume of net sales, with the terms of sale used by the particular business enterprise whose figures are being analyzed. If a wholesaler of groceries is selling merchandise on terms of 2 per cent discount in 10 days, net 30 days, the average collection period, if the receivables are sound, should be only slightly in excess of 30 days, at the most, not more than 40 days. If the average collection period were 54 days, something would be radically off color and an aging would be essential for further careful study. Without an aging, the analyst would be forced to assume that a large portion of the receivables were uncollectible.

No item of receivables can be analyzed without ascertaining the exact terms of sale used by a particular business enterprise. An average collection period of 60 days would carry one meaning on net selling terms of 30 days and another implication on net selling terms of 60 days. Where a concern uses different selling terms for different trades or for different products, such as cash, 30 days open account, and an installment basis, the analysis of receivables becomes almost as complicated as the study of an item of investments. It is also important that the accounts and notes receivable represent only merchandise sales and that they do not include receivables for the sales of real estate, fixtures, machinery, and equipment, or loans to officers, to directors, or to others.

COMPUTATION OF AVERAGE COLLECTION PERIOD

What is an average collection period based upon the volume of net sales? There is a simple mathematical formula for obtaining this figure so essential in a study of the quality of receivables. The first step in that formula is to divide the annual net credit sales by 365 days to obtain the average amount of credit sales per day. Then the total of the accounts and notes receivable (together with any discounted notes) is divided by the average net credit sales per day to obtain a figure which represents the average collection period. The term *annual net credit sales* is used, as, in the case of a retail store which sells both for cash and on charge accounts, the cash sales must be deducted from the annual net sales to obtain the volume of *annual net credit sales;* in case installment sales are also made, the entire selling price of such sales, including the down payment, must also be deducted. No loss is assumed on cash sales and they do not figure in the process of determining an average collection period. Installment sales are deducted because a separate computation must be made to determine the average collection period of the long-term receivables created by sales of this type. The formula for computing the average collection period for the typical business enterprise is as follows:

$$\frac{\text{Net credit sale for 1 year}}{365 \text{ days}} = \text{net credit sales per day}$$

$$\frac{\substack{\text{Accounts receivable} + \text{notes receivable} \\ \text{(including discounted notes receivable)}}}{\text{Net credit sales per day}} = \text{average collection period}$$

If the net credit sales used in this formula are for a period of 6 months then the denominator of the first fraction is 182.5 days instead of 365 days if the net credit sales used are for a 3 months' period, then the denominator is 91 days. Any reserves for bad debts should be deducted from the accounts and notes receivable to obtain a net figure of accounts and notes receivable to be used in this formula. By substituting the fraction

$$\frac{\text{Net credit sales for 1 year}}{365 \text{ days}}$$

for *net credit sales per day* in the second equation, at the bottom of the preceding page, we arrive at the following formula:

$$\frac{\text{Accounts receivable} + \text{notes receivable (including discounted notes receivable)}}{1} \times \frac{365}{\text{net credit sales for 1 year}}$$

$$= \frac{\text{accounts receivable} + \text{notes receivable (including discounted notes)} \times 365}{\text{net credit sales for 1 year}} = \text{average collection period}$$

Illustration 1

A manufacturer of women's full-fashioned hosiery sells direct to retail stores. For the last fiscal year net sales amounted to $1,500,880; the total of accounts and notes receivable in the fiscal balance sheet amounted to $140,230. To obtain the average collection period according to the first formula given above, $1,500,880, the annual net sales, is divided by 365 days which gives an average of $4,112 net credit sales per day. The total receivables of $140,230 is now divided by $4,112 and we obtain 34 days as the average collection period. If we use the second formula given above the receivables of $140,230 are multiplied by 365 days to give a figure of $51,183,950 and this amount is divided by $1,500,800, the annual net sales, giving the same average collection period of 34 days.

These detailed mathematical processes are streamlined by the use of Schedule 40. In the horizontal line of figures on the top of this schedule, in bold face type, we find the first three digits of the sales figures, 150. This figure appears on page 363. Then we find the first three digits of the receivables, 140, in the vertical column either at the extreme right or the extreme left of the table. Where the projected series of figures from these two points intersect is the number 34.1, which is our average collection period.

Illustration 2

A department store has net annual sales of $8,642,000. Of this amount $5,042,000 represents cash sales and the difference of $3,600,000 repre sents charge accounts payable on the first of the following month. The fiscal balance sheet of January 31 shows accounts receivable of $340,000.

The volume of cash sales of $5,042,000 plays no part in determining the average collection period; only the charged sales of $3,600,000 are used. As in the preceding case, net credit sales per day are determined by dividing the charged sales by 365 days, which gives a figure of $9,863. This amount is then divided into the accounts receivable of $340,000 to arrive at the average collection period of 34.5 days.

This process again is simplified by using the accompanying table. The first three digits of the charged annual volume, namely, 360, are located in the top line of Schedule 40 on page 365, and the first three digits of the receivables, namely, 340, are found in the vertical column at the right side of the page. The two projected lines cross at 34.5, which is the average collection period.

Illustration 3

Probably the most complicated situation in which to determine an average collection period is in the case of a business enterprise, such as a furniture store, that sells merchandise on three different terms of sale at the same time, for cash, on charge accounts payable on the first of the following month, and on installment terms payable monthly over a period of 1 to 3 years. In such a situation, the net sales must be broken down into the volume handled (1) for cash, (2) on an open-account charge basis, and (3) on installment terms; and the receivables must be broken down into those representing (4) sales on an open-account charge basis and (5) sales on an installment basis.

Here, for example, is a retailer of furniture that transacted an annual volume of net sales of $640,000. The last fiscal balance sheet showed accounts receivable of $18,046, installments receivable of $220,780, and a contingent liability of $100,000 for installment accounts discounted at a local banking institution. In the thorough investigation and study of such an enterprise it is necessary to obtain a breakdown of the annual net sales into the three categories described in the preceding paragraph. Upon request, the treasurer of the corporation furnished the following segregation of the annual volume of business:

Net Sales for Cash..	$ 90,000
Net Sales on Open Account...	160,000
Net Installment Sales on Average Terms of 18 Months, Payable Monthly..	390,000
Annual Net Sales..	$640,000

The determination of a single average collection period based upon net credit sales would be absolutely useless in the study of the receivables of this enterprise. A concern that sold 20 per cent of its annual net credit

Table for Determining Average Collection Period

Receivables	Annual Net Credit Sales: 101	102	103	104	105	106	107	108	109	110	111	112	113	11
102	369	365	362	358	355	351	348	345	342	338	335	332	330	32
104	376	372	369	365	362	358	355	351	348	345	342	339	336	33
106	383	379	376	372	368	365	362	358	355	352	349	345	342	33
108	390	387	383	379	375	372	368	365	362	358	355	352	349	34
110	398	394	390	386	382	379	375	372	368	365	362	359	355	35
112	405	401	397	393	389	386	382	378	375	372	368	365	362	35
114	412	408	404	400	396	392	389	385	382	378	375	372	368	36
116	419	415	411	407	403	400	395	392	388	385	381	378	375	37
118	427	422	418	414	410	406	403	399	395	392	388	385	381	37
120	434	430	425	421	417	413	410	406	402	398	395	391	388	38
140	506	501	496	492	487	482	478	473	469	465	461	457	452	44
160	579	573	567	562	556	551	546	541	536	531	526	522	517	51
180	605	644	638	632	626	620	614	609	603	598	592	587	582	57
200	723	716	709	702	696	688	682	676	670	664	658	652	646	64
220	795	788	780	773	765	758	750	744	737	730	724	717	711	70
240	868	859	851	842	834	826	818	811	804	797	789	783	775	76
260	940	931	921	913	904	897	886	879	871	863	854	847	840	83
280	101	100	992	983	974	954	955	946	937	929	920	913	904	89
300	108	107	106	105	104	103	102	101	100	996	987	978	969	96
320	116	114	113	112	111	110	109	108	107	106	105	104	103	10
340	123	122	121	119	118	117	116	115	114	113	112	111	110	10
360	130	129	127	126	125	124	123	122	121	119	118	117	116	11
380	137	136	135	133	131	130	129	128	127	126	125	124	123	12
400	144	143	142	140	139	138	136	135	134	133	131	130	129	12
420	152	150	149	147	146	144	143	142	141	139	138	137	136	13
440	159	157	156	154	153	152	150	149	147	146	145	143	142	14
460	166	165	163	162	160	158	157	155	154	153	151	150	149	14
480	173	172	170	168	167	165	164	162	161	159	158	156	155	15
500	181	179	177	175	174	172	170	169	168	166	165	163	161	16
520	188	186	184	182	181	178	177	176	174	172	171	170	168	16
540	195	193	191	189	188	186	184	182	181	179	178	176	174	17
560	202	200	198	197	195	193	191	189	187	186	184	182	181	17
580	210	207	206	203	201	200	198	196	194	192	191	189	187	18
600	217	215	213	211	209	206	205	203	201	199	197	195	194	19
620	224	222	220	217	215	214	211	209	208	206	204	202	200	19
640	231	229	227	225	223	220	218	216	214	212	210	208	207	20
660	238	236	234	232	229	227	225	223	221	219	217	215	213	21
680	246	243	241	238	236	234	232	230	228	225	223	221	220	21
700	253	250	248	245	243	241	239	236	234	232	230	228	226	22
720	260	257	255	253	250	248	246	243	241	239	237	234	232	23
740	267	265	262	260	257	255	252	250	248	245	243	241	239	23
760	274	272	269	267	264	262	259	257	254	252	250	248	245	24
780	282	279	276	274	271	268	266	263	261	259	256	254	252	25
800	289	286	283	281	278	275	273	270	267	265	263	261	258	25
820	296	293	290	288	285	282	280	277	275	272	270	267	265	26
840	303	300	298	295	292	290	287	284	281	279	276	273	271	26
860	311	307	305	302	299	296	293	291	288	285	283	280	278	27
880	318	315	312	309	306	303	300	297	294	292	289	287	284	28
900	325	322	319	316	313	310	307	304	301	298	296	293	291	28
920	332	329	326	323	320	317	313	310	308	305	302	300	297	29
940	340	336	333	330	326	323	320	318	315	312	309	307	304	30
960	347	343	340	337	334	331	327	324	321	318	316	313	310	30
980	354	350	347	344	341	337	334	331	328	325	322	319	316	31
1000	361	358	354	351	348	344	341	338	335	332	329	326	323	32

———————————Annual Net Credit Sales———————————

115	116	117	118	119	120	130	140	150	160	170	180	190	200	
324	321	318	315	313	310	287	266	248	233	219	207	196	186	102
330	327	324	322	319	316	292	271	253	236	223	211	200	190	104
336	333	331	328	325	323	298	276	258	241	227	215	204	193	106
343	340	337	334	331	329	303	282	263	246	232	219	208	197	108
349	346	343	340	337	335	309	287	268	251	236	223	211	201	110
355	352	349	346	344	341	314	292	273	255	240	227	215	204	112
362	358	355	352	350	347	320	297	277	260	245	231	219	208	114
368	365	362	359	355	353	326	302	282	265	249	235	223	212	116
375	371	368	365	362	359	331	308	287	269	253	239	227	215	118
381	377	374	371	368	365	337	313	292	274	258	243	230	219	120
444	440	437	433	430	426	393	365	341	320	301	284	269	255	140
508	504	500	495	491	487	450	418	390	365	344	324	307	292	160
572	566	562	557	552	548	505	469	438	411	387	365	346	328	180
634	630	624	618	614	609	562	521	487	456	430	405	384	365	200
699	693	686	681	675	670	618	574	535	502	473	446	423	402	220
762	755	749	742	736	730	674	626	584	547	515	487	461	438	240
825	818	811	804	797	791	730	678	633	593	558	527	500	475	260
889	881	874	865	859	852	786	730	682	639	601	568	538	511	280
953	944	936	929	920	913	843	783	730	685	644	608	577	548	300
102	101	999	990	982	954	899	835	779	730	687	649	625	584	320
108	107	106	105	104	103	955	887	828	776	730	690	654	621	340
114	113	112	111	110	109	101	938	876	821	773	730	692	657	360
121	120	118	117	116	115	107	992	926	867	816	771	730	694	380
127	126	125	124	123	122	112	104	975	913	859	812	769	730	400
133	132	131	130	129	128	118	109	102	958	902	852	807	767	420
140	138	137	136	135	134	123	115	107	100	944	892	846	804	440
146	145	143	142	141	140	129	120	112	105	988	934	884	840	460
152	151	150	148	147	146	135	125	117	109	103	974	922	876	480
158	157	156	155	153	152	140	130	122	114	107	101	961	913	500
165	164	162	161	159	158	146	135	126	119	111	105	100	948	520
171	170	168	167	166	164	152	141	131	123	116	109	104	985	540
177	176	174	173	172	170	157	146	136	128	120	113	107	102	560
184	182	181	180	178	176	163	151	141	132	124	117	111	106	580
190	189	187	185	184	182	168	156	146	137	129	122	115	110	600
197	195	193	192	190	188	174	162	151	141	133	126	119	113	620
203	201	200	198	196	195	180	167	156	146	137	130	123	117	640
209	208	206	204	202	201	185	172	161	151	142	134	127	120	660
216	214	212	210	209	207	191	177	165	155	146	138	131	124	680
222	220	218	216	214	213	196	183	170	159	150	142	134	128	700
228	227	225	223	221	219	202	188	175	164	154	146	138	131	720
235	233	231	229	227	225	207	193	180	169	159	150	142	135	740
241	239	237	235	233	231	213	198	185	173	163	154	146	139	760
247	245	243	241	239	237	219	203	190	178	167	158	150	142	780
254	252	249	247	245	243	225	209	195	183	172	162	154	146	800
260	258	256	254	251	249	230	214	199	187	176	166	157	150	820
266	264	262	260	257	255	236	219	204	192	180	170	161	153	840
273	270	268	266	263	261	241	224	209	196	185	174	165	157	860
279	277	274	272	270	268	247	229	214	200	189	178	169	161	880
285	283	280	278	276	274	252	235	219	205	193	182	173	164	900
292	289	286	284	282	280	258	240	224	210	197	186	177	168	920
298	296	293	291	288	286	264	245	229	214	202	191	180	172	940
305	302	299	297	294	292	269	250	233	219	206	195	184	175	960
311	308	305	303	301	298	275	255	238	223	210	199	188	179	980
318	315	312	309	307	304	281	261	243	228	215	223	192	183	1000

Receivables

Table for Determining Average Collection Period (*Continued*)

Receivables	210	220	230	240	250	260	270	280	290	300	310	320	330	34
102	177	169	162	155	149	143	138	133	128	124	120	116	113	11
104	181	172	165	158	152	146	141	136	131	126	122	119	115	11
106	184	176	168	161	155	149	143	138	133	129	125	121	117	11
108	188	179	171	164	158	152	146	141	136	131	127	123	120	11
110	191	183	175	167	161	154	149	143	138	134	129	125	122	11
112	195	186	178	170	163	157	151	146	141	136	132	128	124	12
114	198	189	181	173	166	160	154	149	143	139	134	130	126	12
116	202	193	184	177	169	163	157	151	146	141	137	132	128	12
118	205	196	187	179	172	166	160	154	149	144	139	135	131	12
120	209	199	190	182	175	168	162	156	151	146	141	137	133	12
140	243	232	222	213	204	197	189	182	176	170	165	160	155	15
160	278	265	254	243	234	225	216	208	202	195	188	183	177	17
180	313	299	286	274	263	253	243	235	227	219	212	205	199	19
200	348	332	317	304	292	281	270	261	251	243	235	228	221	21
220	382	365	349	335	321	309	297	287	277	268	259	251	243	23
240	417	398	381	365	350	337	325	313	302	292	283	274	265	25
260	452	432	413	395	380	365	351	339	327	316	306	297	288	27
280	487	465	445	426	409	393	379	365	352	341	330	319	310	30
300	522	498	477	456	438	421	406	391	378	365	353	343	332	32
320	556	531	508	487	467	450	433	418	403	390	377	365	354	34
340	591	564	540	527	497	477	460	443	428	414	400	388	376	36
360	626	597	571	548	526	506	487	470	453	438	424	411	398	38
380	661	631	603	578	555	534	514	496	478	463	447	433	420	40
400	698	664	635	609	584	562	541	522	504	487	471	457	443	43
420	730	696	666	639	613	590	568	548	529	511	494	479	465	45
440	765	730	699	669	643	618	595	574	554	536	518	502	487	47
460	800	763	731	700	672	646	622	600	579	560	542	525	509	49
480	835	797	762	730	701	674	649	626	604	584	565	548	531	51
500	869	830	794	761	730	702	676	652	630	609	589	571	554	53
520	904	863	825	791	759	730	703	678	654	633	612	593	575	55
540	938	896	857	822	788	758	730	704	680	657	636	616	597	58
560	973	930	889	853	817	786	757	730	704	681	659	638	619	60
580	101	963	920	883	848	814	784	756	730	705	683	662	642	62
600	104	994	952	913	876	842	811	782	755	730	707	684	664	64
620	108	103	984	944	905	870	838	808	780	754	730	707	685	66
640	111	106	102	974	934	899	865	834	806	779	754	730	708	68
660	115	108	105	100	964	927	893	861	832	803	777	753	730	70
680	118	113	108	103	994	955	920	886	856	828	802	776	753	73
700	122	116	111	106	102	984	946	914	881	852	826	798	775	75
720	125	119	114	109	105	101	974	939	906	877	848	821	797	77
740	129	123	117	114	108	104	100	965	931	901	872	844	819	79
760	132	126	121	116	111	107	103	990	956	925	895	867	841	81
780	135	129	124	119	114	109	105	102	982	949	918	890	863	83
800	139	133	127	122	117	112	108	104	101	974	942	913	886	85
820	142	136	130	125	120	115	111	107	103	100	965	936	907	88
840	146	139	133	128	123	118	114	109	106	102	989	958	930	90
860	149	143	136	131	126	121	116	112	108	105	101	981	952	92
880	153	146	140	134	128	123	119	115	111	107	104	100	974	94
900	156	149	143	137	131	126	122	117	113	109	106	103	995	96
920	160	153	146	140	134	129	124	120	116	112	108	105	102	98
940	163	156	149	143	137	132	127	123	118	114	111	107	104	101
960	167	159	157	146	140	135	130	125	121	117	113	109	106	103
980	170	163	155	149	143	138	132	128	123	119	115	112	108	105
1000	174	166	159	157	146	140	135	130	126	122	118	114	111	107

————————————Annual Net Credit Sales————————————

350	360	370	380	390	400	410	420	430	440	450	460	470	480	
106	103	101	970	954	932	908	886	866	846	828	810	792	776	102
108	105	103	100	974	950	926	904	884	863	844	826	808	791	104
111	108	105	102	997	968	946	922	900	880	860	842	824	807	106
113	109	106	104	101	986	962	940	917	896	877	858	839	822	108
115	111	109	106	103	100	979	956	934	913	892	873	854	837	110
117	113	111	107	105	102	999	974	952	929	909	889	870	852	112
119	116	112	110	107	104	101	991	969	948	926	905	886	867	114
121	118	114	111	109	106	103	101	985	952	941	921	901	883	116
123	120	117	113	110	108	105	103	100	980	957	937	918	898	118
125	122	118	115	112	109	107	104	102	100	964	953	933	914	120
146	142	138	134	131	128	125	122	119	116	114	111	109	106	140
167	162	158	154	150	146	143	139	136	133	130	127	124	122	160
188	182	178	173	169	164	160	156	153	149	146	143	140	137	180
209	203	197	192	187	182	178	174	170	166	162	159	155	152	200
230	223	217	211	206	201	196	191	187	183	179	175	171	167	220
250	243	237	230	225	219	214	209	204	199	195	190	186	183	240
271	263	256	250	243	237	231	226	221	216	211	206	207	198	260
292	284	276	269	262	255	249	243	238	232	227	222	218	213	280
313	305	296	288	281	274	267	261	255	249	243	238	233	228	300
334	325	316	307	300	292	285	278	272	265	260	254	249	243	320
355	345	336	326	318	310	303	295	289	282	276	270	264	258	340
376	365	355	346	337	329	321	313	306	299	292	286	280	274	360
396	385	375	365	356	347	339	330	322	315	308	302	296	289	380
418	406	395	384	375	365	356	348	340	332	325	317	311	304	400
438	426	415	403	393	383	374	365	357	348	341	333	326	320	420
459	446	434	423	412	402	392	382	374	365	357	349	342	335	440
480	467	454	442	431	420	410	400	391	382	373	365	358	350	460
501	487	474	461	449	438	428	417	407	398	389	381	373	365	480
522	507	493	481	468	457	445	435	425	415	406	397	388	380	500
542	527	513	499	487	475	463	452	442	431	422	412	404	395	520
564	547	533	519	505	493	481	469	458	448	438	429	420	411	540
584	568	552	538	524	511	498	487	475	465	454	445	435	426	560
605	588	572	557	543	529	516	504	493	481	471	460	451	442	580
626	608	592	576	562	548	534	522	510	497	487	476	466	456	600
648	629	612	596	581	566	552	549	526	514	503	492	482	472	620
668	649	632	615	599	584	570	556	544	531	519	508	498	487	640
688	669	652	634	618	603	588	574	560	548	536	524	512	502	660
710	690	671	654	637	621	606	592	578	564	552	540	528	517	680
730	710	690	672	655	639	624	609	594	581	568	556	544	533	700
752	730	710	692	674	657	641	636	611	598	584	571	559	548	720
772	750	730	710	693	675	659	644	628	614	600	588	575	563	740
793	771	750	730	711	694	677	660	645	631	616	603	590	578	760
814	791	769	750	730	712	694	678	652	647	633	619	606	593	780
845	812	790	769	748	730	712	695	679	664	649	635	622	609	800
855	832	809	788	768	749	730	713	696	681	665	651	636	624	820
876	852	829	807	786	767	748	730	713	697	682	667	652	639	840
896	872	849	826	805	785	766	747	730	714	698	683	668	654	860
918	882	867	846	824	803	784	765	747	730	714	698	684	669	880
938	913	887	865	842	821	801	782	764	747	730	714	699	685	900
960	933	907	884	862	840	820	800	781	764	748	730	714	700	920
981	953	928	904	880	858	837	817	798	780	762	746	730	715	940
100	974	947	922	898	877	855	834	815	796	779	762	745	730	960
102	994	967	942	928	895	873	852	832	814	795	778	761	745	980
104	101	988	961	936	914	891	870	850	830	812	794	777	760	1000

Receivables

TABLE FOR DETERMINING AVERAGE COLLECTION PERIOD (*Continued*)

Annual Net Credit Sales

	490	500	510	520	530	540	550	560	570	580	590	600	610
102	760	745	730	718	703	690	677	665	654	642	631	621	610
104	775	760	744	731	716	703	691	678	668	655	644	633	622
106	790	774	759	745	730	717	704	692	679	667	656	645	635
108	805	789	774	758	744	730	717	702	692	680	668	658	646
110	820	804	788	772	758	744	730	717	705	692	681	670	658
112	834	818	802	786	772	757	744	730	717	705	693	682	670
114	850	833	816	801	785	771	757	743	730	718	706	694	682
116	864	848	830	815	799	784	770	756	743	730	718	705	694
118	880	852	845	829	814	798	784	770	756	744	731	718	706
120	894	877	860	843	827	812	797	783	769	755	743	731	719
140	104	102	100	983	965	946	929	913	897	882	866	852	838
160	119	117	115	112	110	108	106	104	102	101	990	974	957
180	134	131	129	126	124	122	120	117	115	113	111	110	108
200	149	146	143	140	138	135	133	130	128	126	124	122	120
220	164	161	158	155	152	149	146	143	141	138	136	134	132
240	179	175	172	169	165	162	160	157	154	151	149	146	143
260	194	190	186	182	179	176	173	170	164	163	161	158	155
280	209	204	200	196	193	189	186	182	179	176	173	170	168
300	224	219	215	211	207	203	200	196	193	189	186	183	170
320	238	234	230	225	221	216	213	209	205	201	198	195	192
340	253	248	243	239	234	230	225	221	218	214	210	207	204
360	269	263	258	252	247	243	239	235	231	227	223	219	216
380	284	278	273	267	262	257	253	248	243	239	234	231	228
400	298	292	287	281	276	270	266	261	256	252	248	243	239
420	314	307	301	295	290	284	279	274	270	265	260	255	251
440	328	321	315	309	304	298	293	287	282	277	273	268	264
460	343	336	330	323	317	311	306	300	295	290	285	280	275
480	358	350	343	337	331	324	319	313	308	302	297	292	287
500	372	365	358	351	345	338	332	326	321	315	310	304	300
520	387	380	372	365	359	352	346	339	333	327	322	317	312
540	402	395	387	379	372	365	359	352	346	340	335	329	324
560	417	409	401	393	386	379	372	365	359	352	347	341	336
580	432	423	415	307	400	392	385	378	372	365	359	353	348
600	447	438	429	421	413	405	398	391	384	377	371	365	359
620	462	453	444	436	427	420	412	405	397	391	384	377	371
640	477	468	458	449	441	433	425	417	410	403	396	390	383
660	492	482	472	463	454	446	438	430	423	415	408	402	395
680	507	496	487	478	468	460	452	444	436	428	421	414	407
700	522	511	501	492	483	473	465	456	448	441	433	426	419
720	536	526	515	506	496	487	478	470	461	453	446	438	431
740	552	541	530	520	510	500	491	483	474	466	458	451	443
760	566	555	544	533	523	514	504	495	487	478	470	463	455
780	581	570	558	548	537	527	518	508	500	491	483	475	467
800	596	584	573	562	551	541	531	522	512	503	495	487	479
820	611	598	587	576	565	544	554	535	526	516	507	599	491
840	626	613	601	590	578	568	557	547	538	529	519	511	502
860	641	628	616	604	592	582	581	561	551	542	532	524	515
880	655	643	630	618	606	595	584	574	563	554	545	536	527
900	671	657	644	631	620	608	597	586	576	566	557	548	538
920	685	671	659	646	634	622	610	600	589	579	569	560	550
940	700	686	673	660	648	636	624	613	602	592	582	572	563
960	715	701	687	674	661	649	638	626	615	604	594	584	575
980	730	715	701	688	675	663	650	639	628	617	606	596	585
1000	745	730	716	702	689	676	664	652	640	629	619	608	598

Receivables

[Schedule 40 (*Cont.*)]

					—Annual Net Credit Sales—								
620	630	640	650	660	670	680	690	700	710	720	730	740	
601	591	582	573	564	556	548	540	532	525	517	510	504	**102**
613	603	594	584	576	567	559	550	543	535	528	520	514	**104**
624	615	605	595	586	578	569	561	553	545	537	530	523	**106**
636	626	616	607	598	589	580	572	564	555	548	540	533	**108**
648	637	628	618	608	599	590	582	574	565	558	550	542	**110**
660	649	639	629	620	610	601	593	584	576	568	560	553	**112**
672	661	650	641	631	621	612	604	595	586	578	570	562	**114**
684	672	662	652	642	632	623	614	605	597	588	580	572	**116**
695	684	674	663	654	644	634	625	616	607	599	591	583	**118**
707	696	685	674	664	654	645	635	626	617	609	600	592	**120**
824	811	799	787	775	763	752	742	730	720	710	700	691	**140**
943	927	913	898	885	872	859	846	835	823	812	800	789	**160**
106	104	103	101	996	982	967	953	939	926	913	901	888	**180**
118	116	114	112	110	109	107	106	104	103	101	100	987	**200**
130	127	125	123	122	120	118	116	115	113	112	110	109	**220**
141	139	137	135	133	131	129	127	125	123	122	120	118	**240**
153	150	148	146	143	141	139	137	136	134	132	130	128	**260**
165	162	159	157	155	153	150	148	146	144	142	140	138	**280**
177	174	171	169	166	164	161	159	157	155	152	150	148	**300**
188	186	183	180	177	175	172	170	167	165	162	160	158	**320**
200	197	194	191	188	185	182	180	177	175	172	170	168	**340**
212	209	205	202	199	196	193	190	188	185	182	180	178	**360**
224	221	217	214	210	207	204	201	198	196	193	190	187	**380**
235	232	228	225	221	218	215	212	208	206	203	200	197	**400**
247	244	240	236	232	229	225	222	219	216	213	210	207	**420**
259	255	251	247	243	240	236	233	230	227	223	220	217	**440**
271	267	263	259	255	251	247	244	240	237	233	230	227	**460**
282	278	274	270	265	262	258	254	250	247	243	240	237	**480**
295	290	285	281	277	273	268	264	261	258	254	251	247	**500**
306	302	297	293	288	284	279	275	271	268	264	260	256	**520**
318	313	308	304	299	295	290	286	282	278	274	271	267	**540**
330	325	320	315	310	305	300	296	292	288	284	280	276	**560**
342	337	331	326	321	316	311	307	303	299	294	290	286	**580**
353	348	342	337	332	327	322	318	313	309	304	300	296	**600**
365	360	354	349	343	338	333	329	324	319	314	310	306	**620**
377	371	365	360	354	349	344	339	334	330	325	321	316	**640**
388	382	376	371	365	360	355	350	344	340	335	331	326	**660**
401	394	388	382	376	371	365	360	355	350	345	340	335	**680**
412	406	399	393	387	382	376	371	365	360	355	351	346	**700**
424	417	411	405	398	392	387	381	376	370	365	360	355	**720**
436	429	423	416	410	403	398	392	386	381	375	371	365	**740**
447	440	433	427	420	414	407	402	396	391	385	380	375	**760**
460	452	445	438	432	425	419	413	407	401	395	390	385	**780**
471	463	456	449	442	436	430	423	417	412	406	400	395	**800**
483	476	468	461	453	447	440	434	428	422	416	410	405	**820**
495	487	479	472	464	458	451	444	438	432	426	420	414	**840**
506	498	491	483	476	468	462	455	448	443	436	430	424	**860**
518	510	502	494	487	480	473	466	458	452	446	440	434	**880**
530	522	514	506	498	491	483	476	470	463	457	450	444	**900**
542	533	525	517	509	501	494	487	480	473	467	460	454	**920**
554	545	536	528	520	512	505	497	490	483	477	470	464	**940**
565	556	548	539	530	523	515	508	500	493	487	480	473	**960**
577	568	559	550	542	534	526	518	511	504	497	490	483	**980**
589	580	571	561	553	545	537	529	521	514	505	500	493	**1000**

Receivables

TABLE FOR DETERMINING AVERAGE COLLECTION PERIOD (*Continued*)

Annual Net Credit Sales

	750	760	770	780	790	800	810	820	830	840	850	860	87
102	497	490	484	478	472	466	460	454	449	444	438	433	42
104	506	500	493	487	481	475	469	463	458	452	447	442	43
106	516	509	503	497	490	484	478	472	467	462	455	450	44
108	526	519	512	506	499	493	487	481	475	470	464	459	45
110	536	529	522	515	509	502	496	490	484	478	473	467	46
112	546	538	531	524	517	511	505	498	492	486	482	475	47
114	555	548	541	534	527	520	514	508	502	496	490	494	47
116	565	557	550	543	536	530	523	517	510	504	498	493	48
118	575	567	560	552	546	539	532	526	520	513	507	501	49
120	584	577	570	562	555	548	541	535	528	522	516	510	50
140	682	673	664	655	647	639	632	624	616	609	602	594	58
160	779	768	759	749	740	731	721	713	704	695	688	679	67
180	877	865	854	843	832	822	812	802	792	783	773	764	75
200	974	961	949	937	924	913	902	891	880	870	859	849	83
220	107	106	104	103	102	100	992	979	968	956	945	934	92
240	117	115	114	112	111	110	109	107	106	104	103	102	10
260	127	125	124	122	121	119	118	116	115	113	112	110	10
280	136	134	133	131	130	128	127	125	124	122	121	119	11
300	146	144	142	140	139	137	136	134	132	130	129	127	12
320	156	154	152	150	148	146	144	142	141	139	138	136	13
340	166	163	161	159	157	155	153	151	150	148	146	144	142
360	176	173	171	168	166	164	162	160	158	156	155	153	151
380	185	182	180	178	176	173	171	169	167	165	163	161	160
400	195	192	190	187	185	183	181	178	176	174	172	170	168
420	204	202	199	196	194	192	190	187	185	183	181	178	176
440	214	211	209	206	203	201	199	196	194	191	189	187	185
460	224	221	218	215	213	210	208	205	203	200	198	195	193
480	234	230	228	225	222	219	217	214	211	208	206	204	202
500	244	240	237	234	231	228	225	223	220	217	215	212	210
520	253	250	247	243	240	237	234	231	229	226	223	221	219
540	264	260	257	253	250	247	244	240	238	235	232	229	227
560	273	269	265	262	259	255	252	249	246	243	241	238	235
580	282	278	275	271	268	265	262	258	256	252	249	246	243
600	292	288	285	281	278	274	271	268	265	261	258	255	252
620	302	298	294	290	287	283	280	276	273	270	267	263	260
640	312	307	303	299	296	292	289	285	282	278	275	272	269
660	322	317	313	309	305	301	298	294	291	287	284	280	277
680	331	327	323	318	314	310	307	303	300	296	293	289	286
700	342	337	333	328	324	320	316	312	308	304	301	298	295
720	351	346	342	337	333	329	325	320	317	313	310	306	303
740	360	355	351	346	342	338	334	330	326	322	318	314	311
760	370	365	360	356	351	347	343	338	334	330	326	323	319
780	380	375	370	365	361	356	352	347	343	339	335	331	327
800	390	384	379	374	370	365	361	357	352	348	343	340	336
820	399	394	389	384	379	374	370	365	361	357	352	348	344
840	409	403	398	393	388	383	378	374	370	365	361	357	352
860	419	413	408	403	398	392	388	383	378	374	370	365	361
880	428	423	417	412	407	402	396	392	387	382	378	373	369
900	438	432	427	421	416	411	406	400	396	392	387	382	378
920	448	442	436	431	425	420	415	410	405	400	395	390	386
940	457	452	446	440	434	429	423	418	413	408	404	399	394
960	467	461	455	449	444	438	433	427	423	417	412	407	403
980	477	471	465	458	553	447	442	436	431	426	421	416	411
1000	487	481	474	468	462	457	451	445	440	435	429	424	420

Receivables

———————Annual Net Credit Sales———————

880	890	900	910	920	930	940	950	960	970	980	990	1000	
423	419	414	410	405	401	396	392	388	384	380	376	372	**102**
432	427	422	417	413	408	404	400	396	392	388	384	380	**104**
440	435	430	426	421	416	412	407	403	399	395	391	387	**106**
448	443	438	434	428	424	420	415	411	407	402	399	394	**108**
456	452	447	442	437	432	427	423	418	414	410	406	402	**110**
465	459	455	449	444	440	435	430	426	421	417	413	409	**112**
473	467	463	458	453	448	443	438	434	429	425	420	416	**114**
482	476	471	466	461	455	451	446	441	437	432	428	424	**116**
490	484	479	474	469	464	459	454	449	445	440	435	431	**118**
498	493	487	482	477	472	467	461	457	452	447	443	438	**120**
581	575	568	562	555	550	544	538	532	527	522	516	511	**140**
664	656	649	642	635	628	622	615	608	602	596	590	584	**160**
747	739	730	722	715	707	700	692	685	678	671	664	657	**180**
830	821	812	802	794	785	777	769	761	753	745	738	730	**200**
913	903	893	883	874	864	855	845	837	828	820	811	803	**220**
995	985	974	964	953	943	932	923	913	904	894	885	877	**240**
108	107	105	104	103	102	101	100	989	989	969	959	949	**260**
116	115	114	113	111	110	109	108	106	105	104	103	102	**280**
125	124	122	121	119	118	117	116	115	114	112	111	110	**300**
133	132	130	129	127	126	124	123	122	121	119	118	117	**320**
141	140	138	137	135	134	132	131	129	128	127	126	124	**340**
149	148	146	145	143	142	140	139	137	136	134	133	131	**360**
158	156	154	153	151	150	148	146	144	143	142	141	139	**380**
166	164	162	161	159	157	155	154	152	151	149	148	146	**400**
174	172	170	169	167	165	163	162	160	159	157	156	154	**420**
183	181	179	177	175	173	170	169	167	166	164	163	161	**440**
191	189	187	185	183	181	179	177	175	174	172	170	168	**460**
199	197	195	193	190	188	186	184	182	181	179	177	175	**480**
207	205	203	201	198	196	194	192	190	188	186	184	182	**500**
216	214	211	209	206	205	203	201	198	196	194	192	190	**520**
224	222	219	217	214	212	210	208	205	203	201	199	197	**540**
232	230	227	225	222	220	218	216	213	211	209	207	204	**560**
240	238	235	233	230	228	225	223	220	218	216	214	212	**580**
249	247	244	241	238	236	233	231	228	226	224	222	219	**600**
257	254	251	249	246	244	241	239	236	234	231	229	226	**620**
266	263	260	257	254	252	249	246	243	241	238	236	234	**640**
274	271	268	265	262	259	256	253	251	249	246	244	241	**660**
282	279	276	273	270	267	264	262	259	256	253	251	248	**680**
291	288	284	281	278	275	272	270	267	264	261	259	256	**700**
299	296	292	289	286	283	280	277	274	271	268	266	263	**720**
307	304	300	297	294	291	288	286	282	279	276	273	270	**740**
315	312	308	305	302	298	295	292	289	286	283	280	277	**760**
323	320	316	313	310	306	303	300	296	294	290	288	285	**780**
332	328	325	321	318	314	311	307	304	301	298	295	292	**800**
340	336	333	329	326	322	318	315	312	309	305	302	299	**820**
348	345	341	337	333	330	326	323	320	316	313	310	307	**840**
357	353	349	345	341	338	334	331	327	324	320	317	314	**860**
365	361	357	353	349	345	342	338	335	331	328	325	321	**880**
373	369	365	361	357	353	350	346	342	339	335	332	329	**900**
381	377	373	369	365	361	357	354	350	346	343	339	336	**920**
390	386	382	377	373	369	365	361	357	354	350	347	343	**940**
398	394	389	385	381	377	372	368	365	361	357	353	350	**960**
407	402	398	393	389	385	381	377	373	369	365	362	357	**980**
415	410	406	401	397	392	388	384	381	377	373	369	365	**1000**

Receivables

sales on open account terms and 80 per cent on installment terms would naturally have a radically different average collection period, if only one collection period were determined, than a concern that sold 40 per cent of its annual net credit sales on open account terms and 60 per cent on installment terms. Moreover, an average collection period would be radically different even if the percentage of sales on these two bases were the same, but in one case the installment sales were made principally on terms of 18 equal monthly payments, and in the second case on terms of 24 equal monthly payments.

So we come to a situation where two average collection periods must be determined, (1) on the relationship between the annual net credit sales made on end-of-the-month terms and the specific accounts receivable outstanding on the fiscal date from these particular sales, and (2) on the relationship between the annual net installment sales and the installments receivable outstanding on the fiscal date plus the amount of installments receivable discounted. Cash sales do not enter into the computation.

On the basis of the volume of net credit sales made on end-of-the-month terms amounting to $160,000, and the accounts receivable outstanding of $18,046 on these sales, the average collection period is 41 days, determined as in the preceding illustrations.

When we come to the determination of the average collection period on the installment accounts, the first step is to deduct the aggregate of down payments received during the year on the volume of the installment sales. If the typical terms of sale are 10 per cent down and the remainder payable in 18 equal monthly installments, we must first deduct $39,000 from the annual installment sales of $390,000, to arrive at a figure of $351,000 which we might term *net credit installment sales*. This figure is now used along with the installments receivable of $220,780 plus the discounted installments receivable of $100,000, or a total of $320,780, to obtain an average collection period of 333 days, or 11 months.

The average collection period on installment sales should be only slightly greater than one-half the terms of installment sales as, on the average, approximately one-half the installment accounts should always have been collected. So here the average collection period of 11 months is compared not with the selling terms of 18 months but with one-half of those terms, or 9 months.

USE OF COLLECTION TABLE

Instead of carrying out the mathematical calculations used in these illustrations by longhand, by cancellation, or by means of a slide rule, the collection period may be found by ready reference to Schedule 40. Like all computations with tables of this nature, the place where the decimal point is to be inserted must be determined mentally. In the first illustration the answer, as far as the table is concerned, might have been 341 days, 34.1 days, or 3.41 days. Actually, however, a quick glance at the figures representing the net sales and the receivables would show that 34.1 days was the answer.

Also, where the exact figure in the formula cannot be located on the table, such as sales of $55,500, interpolation must be used to place the collection period for that figure halfway between the collection period found for the particular amount of receivables under the two sales figures of 550 and 560. Three cautions must be kept constantly in mind in determining an average collection period under any method. These are:

1. Discounted notes or discounted installments receivable which create contingent liabilities must always be added to the total of accounts and notes receivable or installments receivable, as the case may be, to obtain the figure of total outstanding receivables which must be used in the computation.

2. As already emphasized, cash sales must always be deducted from the total annual net sales of a retail store to obtain the figure of annual net credit sales on the basis of which the average collection period must be determined.

3. If a retail store transacts a substantial volume of business on an installment basis, the annual net sales must be separated into the volume of business transacted on (a) cash terms, (b) regular open-account credit terms, and (c) installment terms; and the receivables carried in the balance sheet separated into sales made (d) on regular open-account terms, and (e) on installment terms. Then separate average collection periods must be computed upon the net credit sales on open-account terms, and upon the net installment sales after the deduction of the aggregate of all down payments. The results, that is, the average collection periods, must then be compared with the net selling terms used on open-account sales and one-half of the net selling terms used on installment sales.

ILLUSTRATIONS OF RELATIONSHIPS

From the earliest colonial days until the beginning of the nineteenth century it was customary to charge more for merchandise sold on credit terms than for cash. In fact, during the colonial period, selling prices often depended upon the length of terms requested by the buyer.[1]

Among the failures that received wide publicity in New York City during the panic of 1837 was that of the well-known business of Arthur Tappan & Co., wholesale and retail dealers in dry goods, largely imported from France and India. Walter Barrett in one of his volumes succinctly described this concern as "doing the largest silk business in the City . . . in 1826. It was a better class store than any of its neighbors, being built of

[1] FOULKE, ROY A., *The Sinews of American Commerce*, pp. 69–70 (Dun & Bradstreet, Inc., New York, 1941).

granite."[2] Liabilities at the time of the failure amounted to what was then, and still is, the very impressive sum of $1,000,000. The obligations comprising this debt were renewed by notes falling due in 6, 12, and 18 months, and were promptly met and paid as they fell due. When this energetic Yankee merchant had opened this business in New York City, he had, contrary to all established business practices, decided to sell merchandise only for cash, "or short notes, as they were called, payable, with interest, at some bank," and at one price. As his business expanded Tappan continued to sell at one price but he gradually departed from cash terms as more and more sales were made on credit. Here was a radical departure of the day; whether a customer purchased merchandise from Arthur Tappan & Co. for cash or on 6 months' terms, he obtained the same price.[3]

Gouge explained the custom of the day in 1833, "Whoever sells on trust, puts on his goods an additional price, equivalent to the interest for the time to which payment is deferred. Sellers may persuade purchasers to the contrary, and, in some cases, capital may be so plentiful that the amount of interest on a small sum, for a short period, may be scarcely appreciable. In other cases, the increase of price is greater than the amount of interest; as with fashionable tailors and shoemakers, who are forced to charge *insurance* on each item, and make the honest pay for themselves and the dishonest also."[4]

With the exception of installment sales, where a finance and interest charge is added today, and the customary exception where anticipation is allowed by distributors of woolen and worsted piece goods at the rate of 6 per cent per annum, and by more recently established retail "discount" stores, business in the United States is transacted quite generally in the manner stated by Arthur Tappan & Co. The price is the same whether payments are made immediately by cash or on open-book charge account.

Wholesaler of Electrical Supplies

In 1944 the Electrical Supply Wholesale Corp. was organized as a proprietorship to distribute electrical parts and supplies to retail stores, industrial concerns, and electrical contractors. In 1953 the business was incorporated under the present style, all the common stock except qualifying director shares being owned by the former proprietor. The business had been started with a moderate capital of $5,000. From this beginning

[2] BARRETT, WALTER, *The Old Merchant of New York City*, Vol. I, p. 229 (Worthington Co., New York, 1885).

[3] TAPPAN, LEWIS, *The Life of Arthur Tappan*, pp. 60–61, 73 (Hurd and Houghton, New York, 1870).

[4] GOUGE, WILLIAM M., *A Short History of Paper Money and Banking in the United States*, p. 22 (T. W. Ustick, Philadelphia, 1833).

the tangible net worth had grown to $100,306 in year A, all coming from retained earnings except the initial $5,000 and an additional $25,000 which was subsequently paid in.

Since the incorporation, net profits have been earned yearly with the exception of 2 years. The variety of electrical parts and supplies handled has kept growth with the expansion in this type of activity. Approximately 80 per cent of the annual volume of sales during the past 3 years has been transacted with retail stores and the remaining 20 per cent with industrial concerns and contractors. All sales are made on the standard terms in this line of business of 2 per cent discount in 10 days, net 30 days. Except for a slight increase in sales during the spring months, the volume is quite steady throughout the year. The comparative figures of this corporation for the last three fiscal years appear in Schedule 41. The tangible net worth for each year represents the sum of the common stock and surplus, less the $12,000 carried as good will in each of the balance sheets.

The comparative figures disclose a drop in net sales from $460,856 to $410,498 between year C and year B, and then an increase to $526,751, or 27.2 per cent, in year A. Net profits amounted to $4,346 in year C, dropped to $2,760 in year B, and then expanded on the increased volume to $13,350 in year A. Dividends were paid during each year but were somewhat less then the net profits. Tangible net worth accordingly grew from $90,196 to $100,306 over these years.

Along with the expansion in tangible net worth came a more rapid growth in current liabilities. From $80,188 in year C, the current debt increased to $94,386 in year B, and then to $177,117 in year A. The current liabilities expanded to carry the larger current assets, which increased from $160,764 in year C to $259,518 in year A. Between these 2 years all the items in the current assets increased. The two items which are of particular interest in this chapter are the notes receivable and the accounts receivable. The fluctuation in these two items will readily be seen in the following table:

	Year C	Year B	Year A
Notes Receivable............................	$ 2,122	$ 2,080	$ 5,256
Accounts Receivable........................	95,706	90,959	125,050
Total Receivables...........................	$ 97,828	$ 93,039	$130,306
Net Sales..................................	460,856	410,498	526,751
Average Collection Period, in Number of Days.	77	83	90

As the net sales decreased between year C and year B, the total of notes and accounts receivable dropped from $97,828 to $93,039. As the net sales expanded to $526,751 in year A, the total of notes and accounts receivable increased from $93,039 to $130,306. The fluctuating trend of outstanding receivables would naturally be expected to follow the trend in the volmue of net sales, but when an analysis is made, it is evident that the trend of the receivables was a modified trend and that the receivables were noticeably heavy.

[Schedule 41] ELECTRICAL SUPPLY WHOLESALE CORP.
Comparative Figures for Years Ended June 30, 19—

	(C) Three Years Ago	(B) Two Years Ago	(A) One Year Ago
ASSETS			
Cash..................................	$ 4,102	$ 17,287	$ 12,623
Notes Receivable.....................	2,122	2,080	5,256
Accounts Receivable..................	95,706	90,959	125,050
Inventory............................	58,834	67,379	116,589
Current Assets.......................	$160,764	$177,705	$259,518
Fixed Assets, Net....................	6,302	5,599	6,616
Miscellaneous Receivables............	1,905	1,555	9,957
Prepaid Expense......................	1,413	483	1,332
Good Will............................	12,000	12,000	12,000
TOTAL............................	$182,384	$197,342	$289,423
LIABILITIES			
Notes Payable to Bank................	$ 7,000	$ 15,000	$ 23,500
Accounts Payable.....................	61,763	48,884	107,897
Accruals.............................	5,781	5,442	4,154
Due to Officers......................	5,644	18,862	25,543
Due to Others........................	....	6,198	16,023
Current Liabilities..................	$ 80,188	$ 94,386	$177,117
Common Stock.........................	100,000	100,000	100,000
Surplus..............................	2,196	2,956	12,306
Total............................	$182,384	$197,342	$289,423
Net Working Capital..................	$ 80,576	$ 83,319	$ 82,401
Current Ratio........................	2.00	1.88	1.47
Tangible Net Worth...................	$ 90,196	$ 90,956	$100,306
Net Sales............................	$460,856	$410,498	$526,751
Net Profit...........................	4,346	2,760	13,350
Dividends............................	2,000	2,000	4,000

On the basis of the yearly net sales of $460,856, the total of notes and accounts receivable of $97,828 outstanding at the end of year C gave an average collection period of 77 days. The decrease in the total receivables between year C and year B was only 4.9 per cent, while the drop in net sales was 10.9 per cent. As a result of this smaller decrease, the average collection period of the outstanding receivables increased to 83 days in year B. This trend continued to a collection period of 90 days in year A.

In other words, the average collection period went steadily upward, indicating that an increasing proportion of the receivables was becoming more and more past due.

Not only had the average collection period been heading in the wrong direction but the period of 77 days reflected by the figures for year C was heavy. This is evident as soon as one learns that sales of the Electrical Supply Wholesale Corp. were made entirely on terms of 2 per cent discount in 10 days, net 30 days. In theory, the average collection period on these terms should be somewhat less than 30 days, depending upon the proportion of sales which were paid on discount terms. On the general assumption that all payments were being made promptly on net terms the average collection period would be exactly 30 days.

Instead of 30 days, we have 77 days for year C, 83 for year B, and 90 for year A. On this basis at least 61 per cent of the receivables in volume were past due in year C, at least 63 per cent in year B, and at least 66 per cent in year A. The receivables were noticeably weak and undoubtedly have included over the years an increasing proportion of worn-out, useless, and uncollectible accounts.

Condensed Analysis. The figures for year C disclosed an apparently satisfactory financial condition, with one exception. The current liabilities were in satisfactory proportion with the current assets, the inventory was moderate when compared with both the net sales and the net working capital, the fixed assets were relatively nominal, operations were profitable, and the current ratio was just two for one. The one exception was the total of notes and accounts receivable which at $97,828 gave the average collection period of 77 days, as computed above. This collection period was more than twice as long as the net selling terms of 30 days and indicated that a very substantial proportion of the receivables was long past due and undoubtedly uncollectible, especially as no material increase in sales took place in May and June of year C. In this situation, an attempt was made to secure an aging of the receivables which would show the exact amount not due, and the amounts past due for various stipulated periods of time. This information would have given an accurate picture of the receivables. The fact that the figures were unaudited and that the management refused to make this detailed aging available would seem to confirm the fact that heavy uncollectible accounts were included.

During year B, the current assets increased as a result of carrying larger cash and a larger inventory. The current liabilities expanded from $80,188 to $94,386 and the current ratio dropped. Although the inventory went from $58,834 to $67,379 it continued in satisfactory proportion. In these figures, the receivables again represented the fly in the ointment. With total notes and accounts receivable of $93,039 and net sales for the year of $410,498, the average collection period went up from 77 to 83 days.

Apparently the receivables for year B included a somewhat higher proportion of uncollectible accounts.

By the time the figures for the end of year A were put together, the situation had degenerated quite considerably. Now we find four loopholes. The inventory suddenly jumped from $67,379 to $116,589 and was at least $40,000 too high. Miscellaneous receivables, which represented a loan to a vice-president of the business, increased from $1,555 to $9,957. These funds were needed in the business and the loan should never have been made. The current liabilities at $177,117 were excessive compared with (a) the current assets and (b) the tangible net worth. To carry the growing current assets, the president had gradually increased his loan to the business to $25,543, and $16,023 had been borrowed from his brother-in-law. The current ratio was low. Last but not least was the problem of receivables which had persisted over the years and now showed an average extended collection period of 90 days. Somewhat over half of the receivables would probably never be collected. No aging was available.

What was needed here was a good public accountant on the books, someone who knew receivables and who would charge off or set up reserves on all questionable accounts. If half the receivables were worthless, that would mean that approximately $70,000 in valueless assets were being carried on the books, and instead of $100,306 the concern had a tangible net worth of approximately $30,000. If the real tangible net worth was in the neighborhood of $30,000 it was hardly sufficient to support current liabilities of $177,117 and the corporation was in financial trouble whether the management was or was not aware of the facts of life.

The only way to work this establishment out of its morass, after charging off or setting up reserves against all questionable accounts, would be for the president to accept stock for the $25,543 due to him, for his brother-in-law to do the same for the $16,023 due to him, for the inventory to be liquidated down to a figure between $50,000 and $60,000, to collect whatever amount was possible from the vice-president who owed $9,957, and for credit to be extended in future operations with extreme care. If some such policies were not followed, the concern would probably be able to liquidate its affairs and pay creditors close to 100 cents on the dollar at this time; continued unsound operations for 2 or 3 additional years might well impair the capital, and in such a situation the stockholders might be wiped out and creditors would take a considerable loss in the final liquidation.

Wholesaler of Toys

The business now known as the Wholesale Toy Corporation was organized in 1920 as a proprietorship with an initial tangible net worth of $15,000.

At the end of year A, operations were being conducted on an authorized capital of $250,000 five per cent cumulative preferred stock of which $210,700 was paid in, and 1,000 shares of common stock, no par, carried at $56,015. The difference between the original tangible net worth of $15,000 and the present net investment of $266,715 had come entirely from retained earnings. The organizer of the business died shortly after the incorporation. The present staff of officers are all experienced men in this field who have grown up with the business.

Activity consists of wholesaling toys, dolls, games, and sporting goods. Sales are made primarily to retail toy, department, and sporting goods stores throughout the country, on terms of 2 per cent discount in 10 days, net 30 days. The business is highly seasonal with the peak in shipments being reached in September or October.

Schedule 42 shows the comparative figures for the last 3 years. Operations were conducted profitably over this period. Cash dividends, amounting to $10,535, were paid only during year A. During year A, however, there was also declared and paid a dividend of $20,600 in 5 per cent cumulative preferred stock. The tangible net worth expanded steadily from $237,945 in year C to $266,715 in year A, and the net working capital from $168,800 in year C to $199,680 in year A. In addition, a desirable "reserve" was carried among the other assets in the form of the cash surrender value of life insurance on the lives of the officers. In year A, this item amounted to the appreciable sum of $27,609.

Over the years, the inventory had been brought to a low amount on each fiscal date, the fixed assets had been very moderate, the amounts due from officers had not been large, and the net sales expanded each year. The only two items which appeared heavy were the receivables and the current liabilities. If the receivables were extended and included a substantial amount of past-due and uncollectible accounts, then the current liabilities, as well as appearing heavy, would actually be heavy. On the other hand, if the receivables should be in healthy shape, then the current liabilities would not be out of line, and along with all the other favorable features, the figures would represent an attractive financial condition.

With this obvious fact in mind, let us analyze the accounts and notes receivable. The comparative pertinent figures are as follows:

	Year C	Year B	Year A
Notes Receivable...................	$ 5,159	$ 6,780	$ 8,816
Accounts Receivable..............	332,754	371,020	401,161
Total Receivables................	$ 337,913	$ 377,800	$ 409,977
Net Sales........................	1,385,464	1,483,670	1,552,517
Average Collection Period, in Number of Days.....	89	93	96

On selling terms of 2 per cent discount in 10 days, net 30 days the average collection periods, based on the respective annual net sales, were 89 days, 93 days, and 96 days. Here was a slow but steady increase in the average collection period. The probable conclusion would be that

[Schedule 42]   WHOLESALE TOY CORPORATION
Comparative Figures for Years Ended January 1, 19—

	(C) Three Years Ago	(B) Two Years Ago	(A) One Year Ago
ASSETS			
Cash	$ 19,834	$ 25,877	$ 24,960
Notes Receivable	5,159	6,780	8,816
Accounts Receivable	332,754	371,020	401,161
Inventory	67,659	103,238	116,056
Current Assets	$ 425,406	$ 506,915	$ 550,993
Fixed Assets, Net	13,316	14,891	11,343
Investments	7,284	3,000	3,000
Due from Officers	6,109	4,165	8,918
Miscellaneous Receivables	9,682	1,850	5,912
Deferred Items	10,287	14,645	10,253
Cash Value of Life Insurance	22,467	23,483	27,609
TOTAL	$ 494,551	$ 568,949	$ 618,028
LIABILITIES			
Notes Payable to Banks	$ 75,500	$ 67,750	$ 93,750
Accounts Payable	173,576	238,143	241,045
Accruals	4,019	6,369	8,446
Reserves for Taxes	3,511	7,704	8,072
Current Liabilities	$ 256,606	$ 319,966	$ 351,313
5% Cumulative Preferred Stock	190,100	190,100	210,700
Common Stock, No Par	47,845	58,883	56,015
TOTAL	$ 494,551	$ 568,949	$ 618,028
Net Working Capital	$ 168,800	$ 186,949	$ 199,680
Current Ratio	1.65	1.58	1.57
Tangible Net Worth	$ 237,945	$ 248,983	$ 266,715
Net Sales	$1,385,464	$1,483,670	$1,552,517
Net Profit	2,759	11,038	28,267
Dividends	None	None	10,535

between one-half and two-thirds of the receivables on the consecutive fiscal dates were extended. But in this particular situation, the obvious conclusion might possibly be incorrect.

Notice that the fiscal date of the figures was January 1, namely, prior to the receipt of payment for the heavy December sales, and in many cases for November sales. In a case like this, either one or both of two schedules are desirable. The first schedule would be an aging of the receivables on the statement date showing the amount not due, and the amounts 30, 31 to 60, 61 to 90, 91 to 120, and more than 120 days past due. The second schedule would show the exact amount of the receivables collected during the month of January, and, if the auditors did not get on the books until March, then the amount of receivables in the fiscal balance sheet also collected in the month of February. With a highly seasonal business such as a wholesaler of toys, either one or both of these schedules would throw additional light on an average collection period.

In this case, we do not have the first schedule, but we do have the second schedule. Of the accounts and notes receivable aggregating $409,977 at the end of year A, a total of $249,950, or 60.9 per cent, was collected during the single month of January. By February 28 an additional $133,595 of these particular receivables had been collected, leaving only $26,432 outstanding on the books. In the 2 months following the statement date 95.5 per cent of the receivables had been collected, a splendid record. Similar information available for year C and year B showed corresponding collectibility of the receivables in the balance sheets of those years.

The cash realized from these collections in January and February following the year A balance sheet was immediately used to reduce the current liabilities. The accounts payable of $241,045 shown in the balance sheet at the end of year A had been paid in full, and by March 1 the notes payable of $93,750 had also been retired. From this additional information it is clearly evident that the fiscal figures were at a peak, but a controlled peak, on the statement date and that affairs were really in healthy shape at all times notwithstanding what appeared, at first glance, to be heavy collection periods.

Condensed Analysis. This analysis indicates that the Wholesale Toy Corporation has been a well-managed, aggressive, successful enterprise. Not only has progress been made from year to year, but, of fully equal importance, the financial condition has been kept uniformly in well-balanced condition.

The one place open for real improvement is in the operating results. Over the 3 years net profits fluctuated from $2,759 in year C to $28,267 in year A. Over these years the net profits averaged $14,021, or 5.59 per cent on the average tangible net worth and 0.95 per cent on the average yearly net sales. Profit margins of these percentages were low and would indicate that a careful analysis of the income statement was most essential. Either the markup on cost of sales had been competitively low giving a low gross profit, or some items of expense had been relatively heavy, cutting in on a normal percentage of gross profit. The correction of either one or both of these situations would increase the net profits to a percentage more commensurate with this field of activity.

Manufacturers of Plumbers' Specialties

In 1912 this enterprise was incorporated with an authorized and paid-in capital of $250,000 all common stock as the Royal Foundry Co., Inc. Operations were conducted over the years with widely fluctuating results; net profits were earned in some years and losses were assumed in others. The net sales, however, expanded quite steadily and the net working capital increased in a satisfactory proportion. Profits were retained in the business in certain years, and when more funds were needed than the reinvested net profits furnished, additional funds were obtained by the sale of stock and first mortgage bonds for cash.

In 1930 a sharp decline in net sales led into several years of heavy losses. By 1938 the shrinkage in the tangible net worth and the burden of interest charges on the first mortgage bonds forced the filing of a voluntary petition for reorganization under Section 77b of the Bankruptcy Act. The plan for reorganization approved during the following year provided for a change in style to the Plumbers Specialty Mfg. Corp. and for the issuance of new 10-year 5 per cent first mortgage bonds and common stock to all creditors.

Upon reorganization the manufacture of several of the old lines such as radiators, boilers, and synthetic marble was discontinued. Operations were concentrated on the production of soil pipes and fittings, pressure pipes and fittings, steam fittings, and brake shoes. Four plants are now operated in different sections of the country and five warehouses are maintained in centers to handle distribution. Sales are made to jobbers, municipalities, public utility companies, and the plumbing supply trade on regular terms of 30 days net. Figures over the past 3 years disclose the comparative condition shown in Schedule 43.

At each successive fiscal year, the current assets increased. Between year C and year B, for example, the current assets expanded from $1,634,313 to $1,984,581 and from year B to year A from $1,984,581 to $2,368,156. As the current assets expanded the current liabilities and the total liabilities expanded. From year C to year A, the current liabilities went up from $344,833 to $978,846 and the total liabilities from $1,343,633 to $1,853,756.

Net sales likewise increased each year. For year C the net sales aggregated $4,060,369, for year B $4,961,842, and for year A $5,234,218. As the net sales expanded, the operating results improved. A very substantial loss of $351,898 recorded on operations for year C was changed to a net profit of $88,102 on operations for year A.

PLUMBERS SPECIALTY MFG. CORP.   [Schedule 43]
Comparative Figures for Years Ended December 31, 19—

	(C) Three Years Ago	(B) Two Years Ago	(A) One Year Ago
ASSETS			
Cash.........................	$ 156,245	$ 135,133	$ 138,967
Notes Receivable...............	21,321	60,622	62,150
Accounts Receivable............	411,310	740,171	1,055,226
Inventory.....................	1,045,437	1,048,655	1,111,813
Current Assets................	$1,634,313	$1,984,581	$2,368,156
Land.........................	402,487	402,487	402,487
Buildings, Net.................	1,023,350	1,022,302	1,032,554
Machinery and Equipment, Net.	1,300,552	1,298,809	1,303,305
Investments....................	49,302	49,302	36,000
Prepaid Expenses.............	56,874	58,281	31,253
Unamortized Bond Discount....	29,576	2,059	....
Patents.......................	1	1	1
TOTAL...................	$4,496,455	$4,817,822	$5,173,756
LIABILITIES			
Notes Payable to Banks........	$ 150,000	$ 300,000	$ 500,000
Notes Payable to Trade........	2,800	....	....
Accounts Payable.............	92,256	91,931	200,628
Accruals......................	99,777	109,573	111,897
Reserves for Taxes.............	....	....	11,021
Mortgage Bonds, Due..........	....	....	155,300
Current Liabilities.............	$ 344,833	$ 501,504	$ 978,846
5% First Mortgage Bonds......	998,800	1,095,800	874,910
Total Liabilities................	$1,343,633	$1,597,304	$1,853,756
5% Cumulative Pref. Stock.....	370,300	370,300	370,300
Common Stock................	632,793	633,348	637,683
Capital Surplus...............	2,085,762	2,088,074	2,095,119
Retained Earnings............	63,967	128,796	216,898
TOTAL...................	$4,496,455	$4,817,822	$5,173,756
Net Working Capital...........	$1,289,480	$1,483,077	$1,389,310
Current Ratio..................	4.74	3.96	2.42
Tangible Net Worth............	$3,123,245	$3,218,458	$3,319,999
Net Sales.....................	$4,060,369	$4,961,842	$5,234,218
Net Profit....................	(L)351,898	64,829	88,102
Dividends....................	None	None	None

Net working capital fluctuated over the 3-year period. Between year *C* and *B*, the net working capital increased from $1,289,480 to $1,483,077 as a result of the net profits retained in the business and the increase in the outstanding 5 per cent first mortgage bonds of $97,000. The net working capital then dropped to $1,389,310 by the end of year *A* as a result primarily of retiring a block of first mortgage bonds materially in excess of the retained net profits of $88,102.

As the net sales increased, the inventory expanded moderately while the receivables expanded very rapidly. This one item appeared to be getting somewhat out of line. Let us analyze the receivables and see:

	Year C	Year B	Year A
Notes Receivable	$ 21,321	$ 60,622	$ 62,150
Accounts Receivable	411,310	740,171	1,055,226
Total Receivables	$ 432,631	$ 800,793	$1,117,376
Net Sales	4,060,369	4,961,842	5,234,218
Average Collection Period, in Number of Days	39	59	78

In year C the total of notes and accounts receivable amounted to $432,631, in year B to $800,793, and in year A to $1,117,376. The net sales expanded at the same time, but at a much slower rate. In other words, while the receivables increased 158.3 per cent between year C and year A, the net sales expanded only 29 per cent. As a result, the average collection period, which was 39 days in year C, became 59 days in year B, and then 78 days in year A.

In conversation with the treasurer, it was learned that no changes had been made in selling terms, and sales had been fairly steady throughout the year as the result of national distribution. On selling terms of net 30 days, the collection period of 39 days for year C allowed a reasonable leeway and was about normal. But with collection periods of 59 days for year B and 78 days for year A, the obvious conclusion was that an increasing proportion of uncollectible accounts was being carried in the receivables without adequate reserves against them. In year A, approximately one-half the receivables would appear to be very extended. On this basis, the current assets, the net working capital, and the tangible net worth, if adjusted, would each show a drop of approximately $558,000, or one-half the receivables, and the financial condition instead of being fairly satisfactory would certainly be somewhat extended.

Condensed Analysis. Like so many larger corporations that go through reorganization, the new enterprise started operations with disproportionately heavy fixed assets and a substantial funded debt. The annual depreciation charges, to the extent that they were on that part of the depreciable fixed assets which represented a greater percentage of the tangible net worth than the average manufacturer in this line of business, plus the interest on the funded debt, represented a competitive handicap in expenses. There were losses or only nominal net profits from the time of the reorganization up to year B, indicating that these handicaps had been real and not theoretical.

These two operating handicaps, together with the rather moderate volume of net sales compared to the tangible net worth, were the unfavorable features of the financial condition of the Plumbers Specialty Mfg. Corp., until the receivables became heavy in year B. By the time year A had ended, the heavy receivables was the outstanding single unfavorable feature which needed immediate correction. If approximately one-half the receivables were worthless, which might well be indicated by the average collection period of 78 days in year A, then the current assets really amounted to $1,809,468 instead of $2,368,156, and the net working capital to $830,622 instead of $1,389,310. These adjustments would put a radically different complexion on the face of the balance sheet. Moreover, if this were true, instead of net profits being earned in year B and year A as the figures showed, actual losses had been assumed for both years and the losses had been covered, purposely or inadvertently, by carrying an increasing amount of bad debts in the receivables.

In this situation it would seem that an immediate examination of all receivables was in order, that all accounts long past due should be written off the books or adequate reserves set up against them. That policy would be necessary to obtain a clear picture of the exact financial condition of the corporation. Then it would seem that a revamping of personnel was needed in the credit department to be assured that thorough investigations and analyses of all risks would be made in the future, and that a prompt, energetic, collection policy would be immediately instituted. After these steps had been taken, then the basic management policy should be one of earning real profits and keeping those profits in the business. A substantial increase in tangible net worth is needed to bring the relationship with the fixed assets down to a reasonable proportion.

TYPICAL AVERAGE COLLECTION PERIODS

When merchandise is sold, the gross profit is generally taken into the income statement simultaneously. This accounting practice is followed in every line of business, with the exception of those concerns that sell machinery, equipment, or furniture on the deferred payment plan, magazine publishing houses, and service organizations that are paid in advance and that make a practice of setting up all or some portion of the payment as unrealized profit or deferred income. Actually the gross profit in these situations is not earned unless and until the account is fully and

Lines of Business Activity	Number of Days					
	Median					Five-year Average
	1955	1956	1957	1958	1959	
MANUFACTURERS						
Agricultural Implements and Machinery	26	26	38	41	43	35
Airplane Parts and Accessories	39	55	40	43	56	47
Automobile Parts and Accessories	33	40	32	42	42	38
Bakers	10	12	15	13	14	13
Bedsprings and Mattresses	40	42	44	37	35	40
Bodies, Auto, Bus, and Truck	37	31	29	35	43	35
Bolts, Screws, Nuts, and Nails	29	29	24	35	31	30
Breweries	20	23	18	22	18	20
Chemicals, Industrial	39	39	37	39	40	39
Coats and Suits, Men's and Boys'	46	47	46	53	48	48
Coats and Suits, Women's	28	40	30	39	45	36
Confectionery	17	22	18	26	19	20
Cotton Cloth Mills	34	33	37	38	35	35
Cotton Goods, Converters, Non-factored	58	50	38	45	37	46
Dresses, Rayon, Silk, and Acetate	33	35	32	34	28	32
Drugs	41	45	38	44	44	42
Electrical Parts and Supplies	42	39	32	41	46	40
Foundries	42	33	30	36	38	36
Fruits and Vegetables, Canners	21	16	21	20	21	20
Furniture	43	42	41	48	41	43
Hardware and Tools	37	38	34	42	40	38
Hosiery	34	30	31	41	38	35
Lumber	29	26	32	38	36	32
Machine Shops	38	37	33	40	43	38
Machinery, Industrial	48	46	44	47	52	47
Meats and Provisions, Packers	12	13	11	10	12	12
Metal Stampings	35	34	35	37	33	35
Outerwear, Knitted	35	26	36	28	20	29
Overalls and Work Clothing	43	39	33	38	30	37
Paints, Varnishes, and Lacquers	34	36	36	36	36	36
Paper	29	27	26	33	30	29
Paper Boxes	27	24	29	29	28	27
Petroleum, Integrated Corporations	36	38	38	41	41	39
Printers, Job	38	36	37	41	39	38
Radio Parts and Supplies	39	44	37	43	43	41
Shirts, Underwear, and Pajamas, Men's	50	45	50	41	47	47
Shoes, Men's, Women's, and Children's	44	46	49	55	54	50
Soft Drinks and Carbonated Water, Bottlers	14	15	13	14	17	15
Steel, Structural Fabricators (Sell on Short Terms)	48	49	47	43	48	47
Stoves, Ranges, and Ovens	43	41	41	47	50	44

AVERAGE COLLECTION PERIODS (*Continued*)   [**Schedule 44** (*Cont.*)]

Lines of Business Activity	Number of Days					
	Median					Five-year Average
	1955	1956	1957	1958	1959	
WHOLESALERS						
Automobile Parts and Accessories....	37	39	34	38	38	37
Baked Goods.....................	10	13	12	12	14	12
Cigars, Cigarettes, and Tobacco......	16	15	17	17	18	17
Drugs and Drug Sundries..........	28	32	31	33	35	32
Dry Goods.....................	43	46	49	54	49	48
Electrical Parts and Supplies........	47	42	42	44	44	44
Fruits and Produce, Fresh..........	15	19	15	17	20	17
Furnishings, Men's..........	46	52	43	49	42	46
Gasoline, Fuel Oil, and Lubricating Oil	35	33	36	34	33	34
Groceries.......................	15	16	15	16	15	15
Hardware......................	35	34	33	41	36	36
Hosiery and Underwear............	41	39	43	50	45	44
Household Appliances, Electrical.....	38	41	40	49	41	42
Lumber.......................	36	38	42	44	41	40
Lumber and Building Materials......	39	38	43	40	34	39
Meat and Poultry.................	15	13	17	11	12	14
Paints, Varnishes, and Lacquers.....	39	32	42	40	35	38
Paper.........................	34	34	32	38	37	35
Plumbing and Heating Supplies......	46	38	45	49	43	44
Shoes, Men's, Women's, and Children's..................	55	56	53	58	62	57
Wines and Liquors...............	30	35	28	41	33	33
RETAILERS						
Furniture, 50 Per Cent or More Installment.....................	177	171	153	148	161	162
Lumber and Building Materials......	53	58	67	59	64	60

finally collected in the case of installment sales, and the service rendered in the case of advance payments. "Distance lends enchantment" is no adage to describe length of terms of sale.

It is evident that the average collection period must be compared with the net selling terms of a particular business enterprise. Typical (median) ratios have, however, been computed for many years for 40 lines of manufacturing, 21 wholesalers, and 2 retail lines which sell substantially on credit terms. These figures, based on operations in each of the 5 years from 1955 through 1959, with the 5-year arithmetical average, appear in Schedule 44. The figures in this schedule, while not directly applicable as standards, as are corresponding schedules in other chapters, do give an idea of the wide differences in average collection periods between different lines of commercial and industrial activity.

Maxim

Extensive experience in the analysis of financial statements indicates that the average collection period should be no more than one-third greater than the *net* selling terms of a particular business enterprise that normally sells its merchandise on open book account. With selling terms, for example, of 2 per cent discount in 10 days, *net* 30 days, the average collection period should not exceed 40 days. With selling terms of 2 per cent discount in 10 days, *net* 60 days, the average collection period should not exceed 80 days.

If the average collection period is more than one-third greater than the average net selling terms, then additional information should be obtained to ascertain if sales were bulked more than normally during the 30 or 60 days preceding the statement date, or an aging obtained to ascertain exactly what portion of the receivables are past due and for how long. If this supplementary information cannot be obtained, the analyst must assume that the receivables are in an unhealthy state, the exact condition depending upon the relationship between the average collection period and the net selling terms. If supplementary information is obtained that shows a different condition than the results of the average collection period, often the discrepancy may be due to the bulking of sales immediately preceding the statement date, as described in the financial condition of the wholesaler of toys.

For concerns normally selling on an installment basis, the average collection period of the installment accounts, based on the net sales after deducting the aggregate down payments, should be no more than one-third greater than one-half of the average selling terms. If the average selling terms are 18 equal monthly installments, for example, one-half those terms would be 9 months, and one-third increase would give a standard of 12 months.

The maxims described in the immediately preceding paragraphs allow leeway for a normal volume of slow but generally good accounts.

THEORY AND PROBLEMS

1. In analyzing the condition of receivables, why should the average collection period be compared with net terms of sale?

2. State and explain the formula for the computation of the average collection period.

3. Assume that the net sales of a particular department store are made partly for cash, partly on charge accounts payable on the tenth of the following month, and

partly on installment terms. Explain what computations you would need to make in studying the condition of the receivables by obtaining average collection periods.

4. Should discounted notes receivable or discounted installment notes be added to the receivables prior to the computation of an average collection period? Explain.

5. What significance is attached to the following changes in receivables between two fiscal balance sheet dates:

	Two Years Ago	One Year Ago
Accounts Receivable............	$265,000	$135,000
Notes Receivable..............	105,000	285,000

6. Describe a situation in which the average collection period might give a misleading idea that a substantial portion of the receivables is past due.

7. A manufacturer of stoves, ranges, and parts sells to retail hardware and retail furniture stores on terms of 2 per cent discount in 30 days, 60 days net. The accounts receivable and notes receivable as of the fiscal date for each of the past 3 years and the net sales for these years are as follows:

	Three Years Ago	Two Years Ago	One Year Ago
Accounts Receivable............	$ 27,421	$ 16,966	$ 42,791
Notes Receivable..............	2,106	1,843	4,621
Net Sales....................	$134,233	$168,696	$221,563

Determine the average collection period for each of the 3 years and then give your interpretation of those figures and of the trend.

8. Northern Chemicals, Inc., is engaged in manufacturing an extensive line of heavy chemicals. Net sales for the last fiscal year totaled $39,621,730 on terms of 1 per cent discount in 10 days, net 30 days. Post the following fiscal balance sheet on a columnar sheet of paper, then make the following computations: (a) net working capital, (b) tangible net worth, (c) current ratio, (d) ratio of current liabilities to tangible net worth, (e) ratio of fixed assets to tangible net worth, (f) ratio of net sales to inventory, (g) ratio of inventory to net working capital, and (h) the average collection period. Interpret each of the ratios.

NORTHERN CHEMICALS, INC.
Balance Sheet, December 31, 19—
ASSETS

Current Assets

Cash..	$ 5,229,119	
United States Treasury notes—at approximate market value..	1,005,177	
Receivables, less reserves..........................	3,913,992	
Inventories—at the lower of cost or market...........	9,171,997	$19,320,285
Cash Appropriated for Property Additions.............		5,450,000

Other Assets

Due from officers and employees on purchases of capital stock, etc......................................	$ 113,855	
Investments in associated companies—at cost or less..	702,223	
Miscellaneous investments, deposits, etc.............	350,452	1,166,530

NORTHERN CHEMICALS, INC. (*Continued*)

Property
Land.. $ 1,782,079
Buildings...................................... 9,586,994
Machinery..................................... 28,826,444
Phosphate deposits, less depletion.................. 396,371   40,591,888
Patents and Processes............................ 1
Deferred Charges................................ 209,199

    TOTAL..................................... $66,737,903

LIABILITIES

Current Liabilities
Accounts payable and accruals.................... $ 2,997,747
Estimated income taxes.......................... 889,024
Dividends on preferred capital stock............... 217,000
Deposits for returnable containers .... 408,471 $ 4,512,242

Reserves
Depreciation and obsolescence..................... $14,534,684
Fluctuations of exchange......................... 140,258
Contingencies.................................. 238,123   14,913,065

Minority Interest in Subsidiary Companies
Preference shares of British subsidiary—5½%, cumulative and redeemable—authorized, 500,000 shares of £1 each; outstanding, 400,000 shares............. $ 1,940,000
Beneficial shares and surplus of American subsidiary. . 362,215   2,302,215

Capital Stock and Surplus
Preferred stock—authorized, 275,000 shares without par value, issuable in series by board of directors; outstanding, 100,000 shares, $4.50 cumulative dividend—at $100 a share:
    Series A................................ $ 5,000,000
    Series B................................ 5,000,000
Common stock—authorized 1,725,000 shares, par value $10 each; issued, 1,262,957 shares, less 21,141 shares in treasury; outstanding, 1,241,816 shares............ 12,418,160
Surplus:
    Paid-in................................ 11,322,148
    Retained earnings....................... 11,270,073   45,010,381

    TOTAL................................. $66,737,903

9. State a maxim to keep in mind when analyzing the average collection period.

10. If the average collection period is heavy, and it is possible to obtain additional information from the management, for what information would you ask to supplement the average collection period?

CHAPTER XIV

Net Sales to Tangible Net Worth

The ratio of net sales to tangible net worth indicates the activity of the investment in a business. A high ratio may indicate an excessive volume of business on a thin margin of invested capital and the consequent overuse of credit. On the other hand, until a dangerous point is reached, it may indicate considerable economy and skill in operation. The problem of overtrading is as old as business itself. To overtrade, an excessive use must be made of outside credit; in that process, liabilities reach high proportions. Creditors furnish more funds to carry on operations from day to day than do the owners of the business. We have learned how a concern becomes more and more vulnerable as its liabilities expand.

The larger business enterprises grow, the more conservative their financial policies tend to become. Managements of corporations in the top brackets operate with a relatively larger investment in relation to the volume of business. Hence, even under efficient management, it is not surprising that the turnover of tangible net worth in the larger business units tends to be at a lower rate than in the smaller ones.

In the early days of financial statement analysis, the problem of overtrading was presented to the credit world but no attempt was made to study or to solve the problem. As long ago as 1903, the following observations were published in the *Monthly Bulletin* of the National Association of Credit Men:

We very frequently see a statement, or hear an assertion that So and So failed in business because he was trying to do more business than his capital warranted, in other words, that he had insufficient capital for the amount of business transacted. This was brought out in one of the addresses at the St. Louis Convention of the National Association of Credit Men. I have often wondered if there was any rule that could be laid down to indicate when a man was doing more business than his capital warranted. After a man has failed, and the post-mortem examination is held, it is very easy to say that he died of under capitalization, but what are the symptoms that indicate this disease? How are we to distinguish it when it first makes its appearance? These are questions I am unable to answer, and if any of our friends are familiar enough with the disease, for it surely is a disease, I should very much like to have the symptoms described.[1]

This interesting query appeared in the early days of what we might term scientific credit investigation and analysis. Relatively few financial statements were making their appearance, and a rather substantial proportion of those that were being made available to bankers, credit men, and analysts were balance sheets without supplementary net sales figures, which are essential to an analysis of the phenomenon of overtrading. It is only in recent years, after typical relationships between net sales and tangible net worth had been set up for different lines of commercial and industrial activity, that the problem of overtrading has been clearly understood, forecast, and interpreted.

OVERTRADING AND UNDERTRADING

Overtrading is the process of handling an excessive volume of net sales in relation to the tangible net worth, as compared with similar concerns of the same approximate size in the same or similar lines of commercial or industrial activity. Undertrading is just the opposite situation; a far smaller volume of net sales in comparison with the tangible net worth is handled than by similar business enterprises.

The phenomenon of overtrading generally is easily recognized. Creditors, such as banking institutions and suppliers of merchandise, are alive to such situations because, not infrequently, in case of trouble the tangible net worth is completely wiped out and a partial loss is assumed by creditors. Investment bankers are on the lookout for such situations as they give a clear indication for the need of additional capital where the concern has a satisfactory earning record.

Undertrading is probably far more widespread at all times in our economy than overtrading. This condition, however, receives little attention from creditors, as in case of financial difficulty debts are light and invariably are paid in full. Undertrading is more a problem of management. Sometimes new advertising methods and mediums solve the problem; a new sales manager with more aggressiveness may change the outlook; or handling supplementary lines of merchandise may often help. For a retailer, a more advantageous location may be the answer.

Where the lack of ingenuity, aggressiveness, and skill of the management cannot solve undertrading, operating losses are assumed, year after year. These losses finally lead to the voluntary liquidation of the enterprise, generally with all obligations paid in full. Or they may lead to the sale of the business or its assets to a competitor, or to some new

---

[1] BADGER, MINOR C., "Thoughts on Many Topics," *Monthly Bulletin of the National Association of Credit Men*, p. 9, August, 1903.

management that either has failed to realize the condition, or believes it knows how to expand the volume. Thousands upon thousands of business enterprises go out of existence every year because their managements have been unable to develop an adequate volume of net sales for the size of the investment.

Volume of Net Sales

Overtrading, and incurring top-heavy liabilities in the process, are conditions that often go unrecognized by management. This is particularly true of those managements that are essentially sales-minded, that believe in developing more and more sales. Is not the purpose of a business enterprise to sell merchandise in order to earn a profit? If that is so, will not steadily increasing sales give greater profits? The answer to both of these questions is "Yes," but within reasonable limits, as we shall see.

On the other hand, a situation may arise where a management is fully aware that it is handling a heavy and perhaps excessive volume of net sales. It has incurred an extended condition with its eyes open believing (1) that it can keep its current assets so clean and active that it is well able to protect itself in any emergency (a very difficult thing for even the most expert management to work out), and (2) that the overtrading is only temporary, due to external or internal factors, and in the not too distant future the volume will shrink to a more reasonable proportion.

Size of Tangible Net Worth

The solution to overtrading exists in the investment of additional funds in a business enterprise to bring the tangible net worth more into line, as well as in reducing the net sales. This policy of investing additional money is followed by many active managements that realize and understand the condition and that have or can obtain the funds. Many managements which realize the condition of their business lack additional funds to invest in capital stock and are unable or unwilling to sell an interest in the business to others. In this predicament, where the condition gives evidence of being no passing phenomenon, the only alternatives are to reduce sales by setting higher credit standards and occasionally by raising prices, or to allow the condition to exist but to pay particular attention to collections so that receivables will be maintained in the best possible condition, and to keep the inventory to the smallest possible amount.

Undertrading and overcapitalization are two terms which, at times, explain a somewhat similar condition; at other times, they have quite different implications. Business enterprises occasionally are overcapitalized; the answer is to reduce the capitalization, thus obtaining a satisfactory and normal relationship between net sales and the tangible net worth. But the answer to undertrading is rarely as simple as this explanation. Only in an occasional instance, depending upon the distribution of the assets, is a reduction in capital the answer.

Reduction in capitalization is a sound policy only where the net sales being handled are sufficient to give a satisfactory net profit to support the business. In most cases of undertrading, the reduction in capitalization would be ineffective, as the volume is inadequate to return a profit on any capitalization; the volume is literally too small to support even the most rigid management expenses. Whether a business is overcapitalized or is undertrading because of inadequate net sales may readily be determined by an analysis of the income statement.

ILLUSTRATIONS OF RELATIONSHIPS

Three very different situations, all involving a high relationship of net sales to the tangible net worth, appear in the following pages. The first is a manufacturer of women's coats and suits, the second a manufacturer of commercial automobile trucks, and the third a converter of specialty cotton cloth with two subsidiaries.

Manufacturer of Women's Coats

There is no line of business where the tendency to overtrade is so widespread as in the manufacture of ladies' outer garments such as dresses, coats, and suits. This tendency is disclosed by a high relationship between the net sales and the tangible net worth, and between the net sales and the net working capital. These two ratios are supplementary. If the turnover of tangible net worth is low and the turnover of net working capital is high, the slow assets should be carefully studied to ascertain whether any of the items classified as slow are worthless or close to worthless, and whether any of the items, under immediate pressure, might be readily converted into needed cash.

The manufacturers of ladies' outer garments are concentrated in New York City, although a few concerns are located in other large cities. The Ladies' Coat Company, Inc., was organized in 1949 with a paid-in capital of $25,000. The increase in tangible net worth to $201,767 in year A was accrued over the years entirely from retained profits. The capital structure was revamped 5 years ago. At the present time, operations are being conducted on a paid-in capital of $113,000 in 5 per cent cumulative preferred stock, par $100, and 150 shares of common stock of no par value carried on the books at $150.

This concern produces women's and misses' untrimmed coats and suits priced from $24.75 to $49.75 in the spring, and from $24.75 to $59.75 in the autumn. Sales are made to department stores, chain clothing stores, and specialty shops throughout the country on the regular terms

LADIES' COAT COMPANY, INC.   [Schedule 45]
Comparative Figures for Years Ended May 31, 19—

	(C) Three Years Ago	(B) Two Years Ago	(A) One Year Ago
ASSETS			
Cash.........................	$ 9,208	$ 78,942	$ 48,208
Notes Receivable..............		27	40
Accounts Receivable...........	43,376	48,999	237,206
Inventory.....................	72,862	81,263	255,726
Current Assets................	$ 125,446	$ 209,231	$ 541,180
Fixed Assets, Net..............	15,321	11,106	12,358
Cash Value of Life Insurance....	15,760	18,336	21,459
Investments...................	2,240	2,240	2,240
Miscellaneous Receivables......	4,284	9,875	18,882
Due from Officers.............	5,689	887	2,389
Deferred Charges.............	3,070	2,484	9,612
TOTAL...................	$ 171,810	$ 254,159	$ 608,120
LIABILITIES			
Contractors Payable...........	$ 2,514	$ 2,270	$ 27,096
Accounts Payable..............	26,106	57,004	286,304
Accruals......................	5,245	7,503	11,044
Credit Balances...............	520	1,118	645
Reserve for Taxes.............	11,720	23,403	81,264
Current Liabilities.............	$ 46,105	$ 91,298	$ 406,353
5% Cumulative Preferred Stock.	113,000	113,000	113,000
Common Stock.................	150	150	150
Surplus.......................	12,555	49,711	88,617
TOTAL...................	$ 171,810	$ 254,159	$ 608,120
Net Working Capital...........	$ 79,341	$ 117,933	$ 134,827
Current Ratio..................	2.72	2.29	1.33
Tangible Net Worth............	$ 125,705	$ 162,861	$ 201,767
Net Sales.....................	$1,797,306	$1,937,892	$2,962,945
Net Profit....................	(L)8,077	37,156	38,906
Dividends....................	25,000	None	None

in this line of business of 8 per cent discount within 10 days after the end of the month (8-10 EOM). The comparative figures for the last three fiscal years appear in Schedule 45.

These figures reflect an interesting condition, not so much because of their trends as because of the magnitude of the trends. The current assets, for example, increased from $125,446 in year C to $209,231 in year B, an expansion of 66.8 per cent. Notwithstanding the extent of this increase, it was dwarfed by the continued expansion of the current assets between year B and year A, an increase from $209,231 to $541,180, or 163.5 per cent. Between year C and year A, the current assets expanded $415,734.

As the current assets climbed upward on the successive statement dates, so did the current liabilities. From $46,105 in year C, a very moderate debt, the current liabilities increased to $91,298 in year B, and then to $406,353 in year A. Between year C and year A, the current liabilities expanded a total amount of $360,248. This increase was somewhat less than the growth in the current assets over the same period of time because all of the net profits earned in year B and in year A were retained in the business, and largely in the current assets.

For year C a loss of $8,077 had been assumed. Dividends of $25,000 had been paid earlier in that year before the final results of operations had been known. The result was a decrease in the tangible net worth of $33,077. In year B, this decrease was recovered by net profits of $37,156, all of which was reinvested in the business. Still more headway was made in year A, when net profits aggregated $38,906 and this entire amount was also retained in the business. Over the spread of these comparative figures, the tangible net worth grew from $125,705 to $201,767, or 60.5 per cent, and the net working capital from $79,341 to $134,827, or 69.9 per cent.

With this background, let us compare the relationship between the net sales and the tangible net worth over the 3-year spread:

	Year C	Year B	Year A
Net Sales	$1,797,306	$1,937,892	$2,962,945
Tangible Net Worth	125,705	162,861	201,767
Ratio of Net Sales to Tangible Net Worth	14.29	11.90	14.69

The changes between the current assets and the current liabilities in year C and in year B were largely due to the accumulation of cash of $78,942 in year B. If a part of this cash had been used to release a corresponding portion of the current liabilities, the difference between the current liabilities on the two financial statements would have been nominal. The considerable changes, when compared with the figures of year A, were partly the result of swelling net sales and partly the result of a different season in year A than in the two earlier years. Large receivables totaling $237,246 were on the books in year A, and heavy purchases of piece goods for fall garments had been made earlier in the spring than usual. The net sales had grown from $1,797,306 to $1,937,892, between year C and year B, and then had jumped most spectacularly to $2,962,945 in year A.

For year C, the turnover of the tangible net worth was 14.29 times. While the net sales increased to $1,937,892 in year B, the tangible net worth increased in a somewhat higher proportion from $125,705 to $162,861, and the turnover accordingly dropped to 11.90 times. The net sales for year A bounded to $2,962,945. The tangible net worth continued its growth, but with a more modest increment, so that the relationship between these two figures now went up to a peak of 14.69 times.

That the ratio between net sales and the tangible net worth was very high for each of these 3 years is clearly evident from the typical ratios for manufacturers of ladies' coats and suits given in Schedule 49. The 5-year average of the median turnover of tangible net worth produced a ratio of 5.88 times, with the low median figure of 5.18 in 1955 and the high median figure of 6.53 in 1957. In fact, the turnover of tangible net worth of the Ladies' Coat Company, Inc., for each of these 3 years was materially higher than the 75th percentile for this line of business as quoted in the 1959 ratios, given with the interquartile range in the Appendix.

A substantial volume of business necessitates large purchases of raw materials and correspondingly heavy costs of production in the case of manufacturers, and large purchases of finished merchandise in the case of wholesalers and retailers. When a business enterprise in a normal season has high liabilities on the statement date, then, if the ratio of net sales to tangible net worth is high, the current liabilities at the peak of the preceding season would have been appreciably greater. When a business enterprise in a normal season has only a moderate amount of liabilities on the statement date, then, if the ratio of net sales to tangible net worth is high, the current liabilities probably will have been fairly heavy throughout the year. The analyst, under these circumstances, must be sure to consider the crucial importance of the size of current liabilities as explained in Chaps. VI and VII.

Condensed Analysis. The internal relationships shown by the balance sheets for year C and year B disclose all-round healthy conditions. Both sets of figures were dated May 31, the end of the spring season. Receivables were low on both dates, the inventories were liquidated at the end of the season to moderate amounts, fixed assets were nominal, current liabilities were moderate, and quite a desirable reserve was available in the form of the cash surrender value of life insurance.

The investment of $2,240 which appeared unchanged in each of the balance sheets represented cost for 100 shares of stock in a specialty store to which Ladies' Coat Company, Inc., was selling considerable merchandise. There was no market for the stock, and the book value was appreciably higher, around $5 per share, or approximately $4,500. The value at which this item appeared in the balance sheet was quite reasonable.

In each of the three balance sheets there appeared an item of miscellaneous receivables. This item was quite moderate in year C, amounting to $4,284. In year B, it had expanded to a figure of $9,875. In year A the item increased to $18,882 and was out of all reasonable proportions for a concern of this size. An explanation was sought. Miscellaneous receivables in year C represented eight different loans of moderate amounts, two of which were advances to salesmen. Of the increase between year C and year B, $5,000 had been lent to a mutual friend of the officers to purchase a minority interest in a retail women's wear shop in Reading, Pa. This business was being operated profitably. Instead of insisting upon a partial repayment of this loan, the officers now advanced $10,000 during year A to the same individual to purchase complete ownership of the business. The capital stock of this corporation had been pledged as collateral to secure the loan. In the meantime, two of the eight smaller loans had been repaid, and the other six greatly reduced.

There was a real question regarding the soundness of the judgment of the officers in granting this business loan, which in year A aggregated $15,000. Some increased sales were obtained by the connection but if there was an attribute in year B and year A that this concern did not need, it was increased sales. To support the growing volume, every possible cent should have been used to build up the net working capital. If this loan had not been made, the net working capital in year B would have been $5,000 greater, and in year A $15,000 greater.

When a comparison was made of the net sales to the tangible net worth, a condition with high turnovers was found, a condition that was quite abnormal. With a turnover of 14.29 times in year C, and 11.90 times in year B, it became immediately evident that at some point during each of these fiscal years current liabilities had been very high. A heavy peak liability is associated with a high turnover of tangible net worth just as the automobile is associated with the name of Ford. This conclusion was subsequently verified when it was learned that the peak liabilities as shown in the monthly trial balances during year C were $439,000, and during year B $493,000, both in February of their respective years.

For year A, the financial condition became appreciably and more noticeably aggravated. The current liabilities at $406,353 were clearly heavy when compared with both the current assets of $541,180 and the tangible net worth of $201,767. With current liabilities heavy in the month of May, which is normally the low point of the season, they

Supplementary Sources of Elements of Sales

The sales analysis of the men's furnishing shop was based upon the one figure that 70.7 per cent of the average monthly net sales income was available to retire merchandise invoices; the analysis of the ladies' specialty shop was based on the figure that 68.5 of the income was available. *63.9* Suppose, however, a concern in a retail trade not listed in Schedule 6 were being analyzed and that the typical breakdown of net sales income was not readily available. Then what could be done?

There are three other possibilities. The first and most accurate approach would be to secure an income statement of the concern which is under the fluoroscope, as was done with the wholesaler of woolen and worsted piece goods and the manufacturer of blankbooks. An exact percentage of net sales income to pay merchandise obligations generally would be available in the income schedule, a percentage which in each individual case would be far more exact than a percentage obtained from any broad survey of operating expenses. Secondly, an estimate might be secured from others, from accountants who specialize in or are familiar with the particular line of business under analysis, from bankers, from trade associations, from mercantile credit men in concerns actively selling that line of business, from managements of concerns in the same line of activity that might even be competitors of the enterprise whose figures are being analyzed. In the third place, a close estimate might be made by the analyst if he were familiar with the operations of the particular line of business. If he were not familiar with the line of activity, his last resort would be to make an estimate which might or might not be close to the actual situation but which would provide a basis of reasoning.

If the concern were a manufacturer or a wholesaler, and no income statement were available, a typical percentage of net sales income available on the average to pay merchandise obligations, in addition to the sources mentioned in the preceding paragraph, might also be computed from the census figures as outlined in footnotes 3 and 4 on pages 157 and 158. Census figures are in great detail, being broken down into refined lines of business activity, by location, and by sales groupings.

THEORY AND PROBLEMS

1. Outline the principal sources of credit to small business enterprises. Which of these sources is the most widely used?

2. Give four functions and services performed by small business. Discuss the one that you believe to be the most important in the economy of our country.

3. Name the three elements of net sales used to indicate three general classes or disbursements used in sales analysis. Give the approximate percentages of each of these elements for (*a*) retailers, (*b*) wholesalers, and (*c*) manufacturers.

4. Describe fully the technique known as *sales analysis*, being sure to mention two essential pieces of information not included in the balance sheet. What final conclusion can be drawn from this technique of analyzing balance sheets of small business enterprises?

5. Arthur Sinclair operates a small neighborhood grocery store. All merchandise is purchased on regular terms of 2 per cent discount in 10 days, net 30 days. Net sales for the year ended Dec. 31, 19—, amounted to $94,622. No bank credit has been established. With this information, make a sales analysis of the following balance sheet and indicate whether, in your opinion, trade obligations are being retired on time or are running slow.

Balance Sheet, December 31, 19—

ASSETS

Cash	$1,242	
Inventory	9,156	
Current assets		$10,398
Store fixtures and showcases	$2,864	
Prepaid expenses	203	
Miscellaneous	207	
Other assets		3,274
Total Assets		$13,672

LIABILITIES

Accounts payable for merchandise	$3,621	
Accrued wages	68	
Current liabilities		$ 3,689
Net worth		9,983
Total Liabilities and Net Worth		$13,672

6. A retail book store has been in operation in an Eastern city for 12 years. The last fiscal year ended 2 months ago. Financial statements which have just become available show net sales for the last year of $122,642. Purchases are made on terms of 1 per cent discount in 10 days, net 30 days, 2 per cent discount in 10 days, net 30 days, and net 30 days. Accounts payable appear in the year-end balance sheet at $8,340. There is sufficient cash on hand for 1 month's need. No bank credit is available. Will payments of the accounts payable be made promptly or will payments be slow?

would naturally have been materially more out of line at the peak of the season. They were. The maximum current liabilities during the fiscal year *A*, also in the month of February, amounted to $638,000, or more than three times the tangible net worth.

In probably no line of manufacturing activity does successful operation over the years depend so little upon excellent workmanship and price, as it does with manufacturers of ladies' coats and suits. Style is almost supreme. If a manufacturer misses the current style, a loss will almost always be assumed. If he hits the current style squarely, his orders will skyrocket overnight, and he will do everything in his power to fill those orders. The clear-cut result is overtrading, with consequent heavy current liabilities. In such a situation, the manufacturer's financial condition will become extended; if he is skilled in financial matters he will realize his predicament; if he is unskilled, he will have absolutely no idea that his financial condition is unsound until his banker or some mercantile creditor asks if he is trying to corner the market on sales. If everything works out, if his styles continue to be in demand, if his customers pay reasonably on time, if his banker understands the situation and lends support through the peak, and if trade creditors do not press unduly, profits will be high. But if styles suddenly change in the middle of the season, if his inventory must be liquidated at a sacrifice, he will have difficulty in bringing his current debt into line, a loss will be assumed, and it is entirely possible that the loss will be so great that the business may join the never-ending ranks of the bankrupt.

The only answer to overtrading is for the management to plan and to budget its operations so that net sales will not exceed a certain amount, that amount to be predicated upon the level of liabilities that will be incurred during the high point of a season, and the income to meet obligations on time with a reasonable margin. Such a policy, while sound and followed in many lines of business activity, is rarely, if ever, followed by manufacturers of coats and suits. It is almost inherent in this type of business activity for managements to transact as large a volume as possible, and to pay little or no attention to the normal safeguards of sound business policies.

Manufacturer of Commercial Trucks

Two brothers organized a business in St. Louis 20 years ago to manufacture automobile trucks. The process of manufacturing auto trucks is largely a matter of assembly; engines, steering apparatus, lighting systems, panel boards, and wheels are purchased ready to be put together. Almost the only parts of the product manufactured on the premises are the chassis and the body of the truck itself. About 18 months after its inception, this enterprise became overloaded with liabilities, a creditors' committee was set up, and the business was reorganized. This same process was repeated 2 years after the reorganization. Since that time operations have been carried on steadily, through good times and poor, although with no great financial success.

The Commercial Truck Corporation had been under the same management since its last reorganization, which occurred approximately 16 years ago. Operations gradually were enlarged from the "manufacture" of trucks alone to include busses, tractors, and motor fire apparatus to meet particular specifications. Over one-half of the annual volume of business in recent years has come from municipalities, and the percentage has been slowly but steadily increasing. The comparative figures showing the financial condition of this corporation over the past 3 years appear in Schedule 46.

Competition in the production of automobile trucks has always been keen. For the fiscal year C, net sales were $575,355, and net profits amounted to the nominal sum of $1,972, no part of which was paid out in dividends. At the end of the year C, the surplus account disclosed an accumulated deficit of $28,884 because of the unprofitable operations in 6 out of the 8 years immediately preceding. At the same time, however, the figures seemed to indicate a satisfactory internal financial condition. The liabilities were moderate, the receivables and the inventory were in satisfactory proportion, and the fixed assets comprised only 20.2 per cent of the tangible net worth, quite a low percentage. The only fly in the ointment was the item of investments carried at $21,201, which was a trifle heavy for an enterprise of this size. We shall come to this item a little later in the condensed analysis of this situation.

For year B, the net sales jumped from $575,355 to $1,076,813, quite a substantial increase of 87.2 per cent. Net profits for the year expanded to $14,127, reducing the deficit in the surplus account to $14,757. As the sales increased, the receivables and the inventory went up. As the receivables and the inventory went up, the current liabilities dilated. With enlarged current assets of $624,009, and enlarged current liabilities of $477,-622, the current ratio in year B dropped from 3.38 times to 1.39 times, notwithstanding the increase in the net working capital. The inventory exceeded the net working capital, and the current liabilities were 70.2 per cent greater than the *apparent* tangible net worth. The expression *apparent* tangible net worth is used advisedly, as we shall see shortly that this figure needs some adjustment.

The trends that became evident in year B continued through year A. The net sales increased to $1,904,666, or 331.6 per cent of the net sales in year C. Net profits amounted to $38,801, which was sufficient to convert the surplus deficit into a black figure of $24,044. As far as the management

COMMERCIAL TRUCK CORPORATION   [Schedule 46]
Comparative Figures for Years Ended December 31, 19—

	(C) Three Years Ago	(B) Two Years Ago	(A) One Year Ago
ASSETS			
Cash........................	$ 24,292	$ 102,828	$ 192,171
Notes Receivable.............	9,368	26,385	37,214
Accounts Receivable...........	78,552	277,202	281,745
Inventory....................	119,781	217,594	1,088,540
Cash Advs. Rec. on Contracts...	....	....	381,860
Current Assets................	$ 231,993	$ 624,009	$1,981,530
Fixed Assets, Net.............	50,207	53,538	60,041
Investments..................	21,201	19,043	19,043
Miscellaneous Receivables......	2,208	208	....
Due from Officers.............	4,117	7,861	6,583
Deferred Items...............	9,498	8,863	7,090
Good Will....................	1	1	1
TOTAL...................	$ 319,225	$ 713,523	$2,074,288
LIABILITIES			
Notes Payable to Banks........	$ 20,400	$ 210,900	$ 613,953
Notes Payable for Merchandise..	....	....	4,732
Accounts Payable.............	35,204	225,067	620,323
Accruals.....................	4,026	7,176	13,794
Advances on Contracts.........	....	....	420,000
Reserves for Taxes............	....	....	82,255
Credit Balances...............	3,343	2,311	5,426
Due to Officers...............	5,614	2,168	10,081
Current Liabilities.............	$ 68,587	$ 447,622	$1,770,564
Deferred Income..............	1,647	2,783	1,805
Common Stock, Class A........	102,875	102,875	102,875
Common Stock, Class B........	175,000	175,000	175,000
Surplus......................	(D)28,884	(D)14,757	24,044
TOTAL...................	$ 319,225	$ 713,523	$2,074,288
Net Working Capital...........	$ 163,406	$ 176,387	$ 210,966
Current Ratio..................	3.38	1.39	1.12
Tangible Net Worth.............	$ 248,990	$ 263,117	$ 301,918
Net Sales.....................	$ 575,355	$1,076,813	$1,904,666
Net Profit....................	1,972	14,127	38,801
Dividends.....................	None	None	None

was concerned, the business was going along swimmingly. Receivables
continued to increase, but only nominally when compared with the great
expansion in the net sales. The inventory now swelled to $1,088,540 and
was out of all reasonable proportion for a concern of this size. An item of
Cash Advances Received on Contracts of $381,860 made its appearance in

the current assets, representing cash advances on certain large orders. Because of these changes, the current assets totaled the impressive sum of $1,981,530, and the current liabilities totaled $1,770,564, leaving a net working capital of $210,966 and a current ratio of 1.12 times. The current liabilities were more than five times as large as the tangible net worth, a clearly evident extended condition.

The *Deferred Income,* which amounted to $1,647, $2,783, and $1,805 in the respective balance sheets, represented unearned finance charges on sales made on the installment basis. The rather small amount of this item, if correctly figured, would indicate that only a moderate portion of the annual volume called for monthly payments on the installment basis.

With this trend of the business in mind, let us compare the net sales with the apparent tangible net worth for the 3 years.

	Year C	Year B	Year A
Net Sales	$575,355	$1,076,813	$1,904,666
Tangible Net Worth	248,990	263,117	301,918
Ratio of Net Sales to Tangible Net Worth	2.31	4.09	6.31

Between year *C* and year *A*, the net sales expanded from $575,355 to $1,904,666, while the tangible net worth increased much more moderately from $248,990 to $301,918. In other words, the net sales expanded 231.1 per cent and the tangible net worth only 21.3 per cent. The result was the steady widening in the direct relationship between net sales and the tangible net worth from 2.31 to 4.09 to 6.31 times.

The importance of this relationship was shown in the study of the financial condition of the Ladies' Coat Company, Inc. As the turnover of tangible net worth increases, the current assets and the current liabilities expand more and more disproportionately to reach an abnormal and weakened condition at the peak of the season. If a subsequent liquidation takes place in an orderly manner, affairs are brought into line at the low point of the season. If the liquidation during the down part of the season becomes forced because of the need of funds; if the liquidation does not take place; if the market value of the inventory drops suddenly in this process; or if a substantial portion of the receivables become extended, an embarrassed financial condition may readily occur.

In the case of a manufacturer of motor trucks, the seasonal peak is less apparent than with a manufacturer of ladies' coats. A low point is generally reached around the end of September or October, and a high point of operations in March or April. With figures dated December 31, liabilities would usually be increasing. For manufacturers of trucks operating in a normal profitable manner the turnover of tangible net worth would range between 3 times to 3.50 times. In contrast to this normal relationship, the turnovers in year *B* at 4.09 times, and in year *A* at 6.31 times, were appreciably faster than for typical concerns in this line of business.

With moderate seasonal fluctuations in this division of manufacturing activity, the effect of a faster turnover of tangible net worth becomes clearly evident in the comparative fiscal figures. Increased sales up to a certain point, a point which is moderately greater than the typical volume per invested dollar for the industry, are desirable to produce a greater margin of profit. Increased sales above this point place increasing strain on a business, like an increasing air strain on the wings of an airplane as its speed increases. The sequence of reasoning behind this growing strain is as follows: to handle increasing net sales (and management invariably is under the illusion that the increase will be sustained), larger inventories generally must be built up, the increasing net sales bring increasing receivables, the increasing inventory and larger receivables necessitate increasing liabilities. Every business enterprise that becomes involved in financial difficulties has heavy liabilities. In this process more and more opportunities for an unbalanced financial condition come up; increased sales are often obtained by selling to poorer credit risks; the resulting receivables may easily get out of line with selling terms, the inventory may get out of line with net working capital and net sales, and the current liabilities out of line with current assets and with the tangible net worth. Such a situation is just too bad!

Condensed Analysis. The comparative figures of the Commercial Truck Corporation were unaudited figures as issued by the treasurer of the corporation. As previously mentioned, these balance sheets contained an item of investments which amounted to $21,201 in the balance sheet for year C, and to $19,043 in the balance sheets for year B and year A.

An item of investments, no matter how small, should never be overlooked by the analyst. An explanation of this item accordingly was sought from the treasurer to ascertain whether the amount represented marketable securities, miscellaneous investments, or capital stock interest in one or more subsidiaries, and how each part was valued. The explanation was simple and enlightening. In year C, the investments consisted of five different items, all of which were carried at cost; in year B and in year A, it consisted of four different items, all of which were carried at cost. In year B, an investment in a tire-recapping business that had been carried at cost of $2,158 was written off the books at a total loss. This little venture had gone bankrupt in year D, but no thought had been given to taking the loss on the books of the Commercial Truck Corporation until year B. The four remaining items represented minority stock interests ranging from 18 to 37 per cent in corporations that acted as selling agents for the Commercial Truck Corporation in different parts of the country. Outstanding capitalization of these four corporations consisted only of common stock, no preferred stock. The cost values of these four investments and their respective book values on the three fiscal dates, as determined from their individual balance sheets, disclosed the following interesting conditions:

	Per Cent of Stock Owned	Cost	Book Value		
			Year C	Year B	Year A
Corporation 1............	18	$ 4,526	$ 3,820	$ 2,276	$1,096
Corporation 2............	20	5,490	5,362	4,884	3,624
Corporation 3............	26	2,840	2,260	1,257	(D)526
Corporation 4............	37	6,187	5,878	5,270	2,863
		$19,043	$17,320	$13,687	$7,057

At the end of year C, the book value of the stock interest held in these four distributing agencies was $17,320, at the end of year B, it was $13,687, and by the end of year A, the book value had dropped to $7,057. Each of the four concerns had operated unprofitably for each of the 3 years; in fact, for Corporation 3, the 26 per cent stock interest had fallen from a book value of $2,260 in year C, to a book deficit in tangible net worth of $526 in year A. For each year the item of investments in the balance sheets of the Commercial Truck Corporation, and also the surplus, were accordingly inflated by the difference between the cost value of the investments and the actual book value on the respective statement dates, that is, by a difference of $1,723, $5,356, and $11,986 respectively.

A computation of the average collection period for the total of accounts and notes receivable gave 56 days for year C, 103 days for year B, and 61 days for year A, based on the figures in Schedule 46. Such a wide fluctuation in average collection periods for a 3-year spread is very unusual. Moreover, sales in this line of business often are made on terms that call for monthly payments for from 1 to 3 years; even the longer collection period of 103 days for year B accordingly seemed rather short. This subject was discussed with the treasurer to ascertain the typical terms of sale. Some sales, the treasurer explained, were made on cash terms with part payment advanced with the order. Other sales were made on 30- and 60-day net terms; still others called for one-fourth down payment and the remainder in 24 equal monthly installments. The selling terms were so varied that they were of no use unless a detailed breakdown of the receivables could have been obtained on the specific respective terms of sale.

At this stage, the treasurer was asked why the Commercial Truck Corporation carried all its own notes receivable and installment accounts when most truck manufacturers had an arrangement with a sales finance company whereby the finance company advanced from 80 to 90 per cent of notes receivable and installment paper. "That is the finance policy we follow too," replied the treasurer. "We borrow from our banks on our note bearing the endorsement of our officers but we also discount our notes receivable and installment paper with a well-known finance company." The treasurer was asked why the liability to the finance company was not shown in the balance sheet as a direct liability, or in a footnote to the balance sheet as an indirect liability, to which he exclaimed that he did not think "that was necessary." The amount of the contingent liability for notes receivable discounted in this manner on each of the fiscal dates was then learned to have been as follows:

> Year C............ $102,517
> Year B........... 137,986
> Year A........... 172,273

Analysis of Adjusted Figures. To obtain an accurate picture of the financial condition of this concern over the 3-year period it now became necessary to adjust the figures shown in Schedule 46, decreasing the investment on each balance sheet to the actual book value of the investments on each statement date, decreasing the surplus accounts similar amounts, increasing notes receivable to the respective amounts which were discounted, and increasing liabilities on each statement date the same amount. With these adjustments, the comparative figures would be changed as they appear in Schedule 47.

No change took place in the net working capital or in the net sales as a result of these adjustments. However, most of the other important figures used in studying the financial condition of a business enterprise were modified—the current assets, the current liabilities, the surplus, the tangible net worth, the net profits, and the current ratio.

The most evident changes were in the net profit figures. As a result of taking the respective yearly losses on the investments into the income statement, the net profit of $1,972 in year C became a loss of $1,909; the net profit of $14,127 in year B became $12,652, and the net profit of $38,801 in year A was reduced to $32,171. The surplus and the tangible net worth on each statement were reduced the same respective yearly amounts.

The notes receivable in each balance sheet were increased to the extent of the respective contingent liabilities, $102,517 for year C, $137,986 for year B, and $172,273 for year A. The current assets and the current liabilities were expanded each year by the same amounts. The result was a reduction in the current ratio from 3.38 to 1.95 in year C, from 1.39 to 1.30 in year B, and from 1.12 to 1.11 in year A. The average collection periods now became 121 days, 150 days, and 94 days respectively.

The original figures showed an extended financial condition from over-

[Schedule 47]   COMMERCIAL TRUCK CORPORATION

Comparative *Adjusted* Figures for Years Ended December 31, 19—

	(C) Three Years Ago	(B) Two Years Ago	(A) One Year Ago
ASSETS			
Cash................... $	24,292	$ 102,828	$ 192,171
Notes Receivable...............	111,885	164,371	209,487
Accounts Receivable...........	78,552	277,202	281,745
Inventory....................	119,781	217,594	1,088,540
Cash Advs. Rec. on Contracts...	....	....	381,860
Current Assets................. $	334,510	$ 761,995	$2,153,803
Fixed Assets, Net..............	50,207	53,538	60,041
Investments..................	17,320	13,687	7,057
Miscellaneous Receivables.......	2,208	208	....
Due from Officers..............	4,117	7,861	6,583
Deferred Items................	9,498	8,863	7,090
Good Will....................	1	1	1
TOTAL.................. $	417,861	$ 846,153	$2,234,575
LIABILITIES			
Due to Finance Company....... $	102,517	$ 137,986	$ 172,273
Notes Payable to Banks........	20,400	210,900	613,953
Notes Pay. for Merchandise.....	....	....	4,732
Accounts Payable..............	35,204	225,067	620,323
Accruals.....................	4,026	7,176	13,794
Advances on Contracts........	....	....	420,000
Reserves for Taxes............	....	....	82,255
Credit Balances...............	3,343	2,311	5,426
Due to Officers...............	5,614	2,168	10,081
Current Liabilities.............. $	171,104	$ 585,608	$1,942,837
Deferred Income..............	1,647	2,783	1,805
Common Stock, Class A.......	102,875	102,875	102,875
Common Stock, Class B.......	175,000	175,000	175,000
Surplus......................	(D)32,765	(D)20,113	12,058
TOTAL.................. $	417,861	$ 846,153	$2,234,575
Net Working Capital........... $	163,406	$ 176,387	$ 210,966
Current Ratio..................	1.95	1.30	1.11
Tangible Net Worth............. $	245,109	$ 257,761	$ 289,932
Net Sales.................... $	575,355	$1,076,813	$1,904,666
Net Profit....................	(L)1,909	12,652	32,171
Dividends....................	None	None	None

trading. The adjusted figures threw that condition into more relief. Whereas the current liabilities in year B and year A in the original figures were \$447,622 and \$1,770,564, respectively, in the adjusted figures they became \$585,608 and \$1,942,837, respectively. At the same time the *apparent* tangible net worth dropped from \$263,117 and \$301,918 to \$257,761 and \$289,932, respectively. As a result of the increase in current liabilities and the shrinkage in the real tangible net worth, the relationship of the current debt to tangible net worth expanded from 170.1 per cent to 227.3 per cent in year B, and from 586.2 per cent to 670.2 per cent in year A. Simultaneously the relationship between the net sales and the tangible net worth increased moderately from 4.09 to 4.18 times in year B, and from 6.31 to 6.57 times in year A.

This corporation was in an unbalanced financial condition in year B, and obviously so in year A. Not only were the inventory and the current liabilities most excessive, but it was evident that the concern was having some difficulty in financing itself. This is clear from three items in the balance sheet. The first item is the *Notes Payable to Banks* of \$613,953. Of this amount \$600,000 was being lent on the endorsement of the officers who were reputed to have large outside means. When an additional loan was sought from one of the depository banks, only \$13,953 could be obtained, and that was secured by the pledge of the notes receivable which had not already been discounted with the finance company. The second item is *Notes Payable for Merchandise* of \$4,732. This amount is small, but to obtain extra time a promissory note running for 3 months was given in payment instead of buying on discount or open account net terms. Third are the two items, one in the assets of *Cash Advances Received on Contracts* of \$381,860, and the other in the current liabilities of *Advances on Contracts* of \$420,000. One very substantial business corporation had placed a heavy order; to see that order through, it had been necessary for the corporation to make cash advances totaling \$420,000. Each of these practices is out of the ordinary and would not be followed by concerns in healthy financial condition.

There was absolutely no question about the fact that the Commercial Truck Corporation was overtrading, and that this was the fundamental reason for the extended financial condition. The figures as of year B and year A, both the original and adjusted figures, left no basis for any other conclusion, even though the original figures were slightly less heavy than the adjusted figures. The only solution to a condition of this nature is to reduce the volume as rapidly as is reasonably possible in accordance with a carefully planned policy. An annual volume of business in the neighborhood of \$950,000 would be sufficient to keep all facilities occupied at capacity and provide a handsome profit, if the management were well-rounded, capable, aggressive, and imaginative.

Converters of Specialty Cotton Cloth

This business enterprise has had quite a record of continuous operations. It was organized in 1892 to process specialty cloth for bookbinders; that is, to buy grey goods in the open market from cotton cloth mills and then to treat that grey goods in a variety of special ways and processes. Since that time, many supplementary products had been added so that today it produces starch-filled, pyroxylin-impregnated, and pyroxyl-coated fabrics, shoe fabrics, tracing cloth, rubber holland gumming, holland cloth, and backing cloth for the photographic trade. Control of the business remained in the hands of the same family until year A, when the control was purchased by a group of employees. Operations have been conducted under the style of the Book Cloth Manufacturing Corporation with the manufacturing plant located in Connecticut.

The corporation has two subsidiaries. Control of the first subsidiary, the Bleachery & Finishing Co. Inc., also located in Connecticut, was acquired 7 year ago. This concern bleaches and finishes all the grey cotton cloth purchased in the open market and used by the parent company. The subsidiary is in a very extended financial condition, operating with a deficit in tangible net worth of $173,624. It is kept in existence by advances from the parent company, which totaled $546,822 at the end of year A. The deficit in the tangible net worth and the advances are washed out in the consolidated balance sheets which the management releases on the financial condition of the parent corporation and the two subsidiaries. This subsidiary is wholly owned.

A 75 per cent interest was acquired 3 years ago in the second subsidiary, Book Mills, Inc., located in South Carolina. This enterprise has been operated profitably and its affairs are in healthy shape. At this plant specialty cotton cloth is woven. This subsidiary operates on its own responsibility and receives no advances from the parent company. The minority interest representing the one-quarter interest in this mill owned by others is carried at $56,808 in the consolidated balance sheet of the parent corporation and the two subsidiaries in year C, at $56,005 in year B, and at $66,864 in year A.

The comparative consolidated financial conditions of the Book Cloth Manufacturing Corporation and its two subsidiaries for the last three consecutive years appear in Schedule 48. These figures disclose several rather unusual and interesting situations.

During 6 of the 7 years preceding year C, consolidated operations were conducted unprofitably. Over this period, it became increasingly difficult for the Book Cloth Manufacturing Corporation to obtain bank loans on its straight unsecured note without the endorsements of the owners of the business. Although the owners were willing to lend funds directly to the

BOOK CLOTH MANUFACTURING CORPORATION
Comparative Consolidated Figures for Years Ended September 30, 19—

	(C) Three Years Ago	(B) Two Years Ago	(A) One Year Ago
ASSETS			
Cash.........................	$ 29,169	$ 18,347	$ 18,942
Notes Receivable...............	....	1,070	1,387
Accounts Receivable...........	11,954	19,916	7,754
Due from Factor..............	80,533	61,445	252,497
Inventory...................	781,344	735,526	699,745
Current Assets................	$ 903,000	$ 836,304	$ 980,325
Fixed Assets, Net..............	966,427	955,068	917,305
Investments..................	492	350	350
Miscellaneous Receivables.......	31,565	29,249	23,749
Prepaid Expenses..............	13,877	9,411	4,962
Good Will....................	100,000	100,000	100,000
Trade-marks..................	58,960	58,932	58,932
TOTAL...................	$2,074,321	$1,989,314	$2,085,623
LIABILITIES			
Notes Payable for Machinery...	$.........	$.........	$ 6,000
Accounts Payable.............	214,814	192,322	163,902
Accruals.....................	48,978	28,224	24,735
Deferred Notes Payable—Current Maturity..............	20,000	20,000	20,000
Current Liabilities.............	$ 283,792	$ 240,546	$ 214,637
Reserves for Contingencies......	22,000	22,000	....
5% First Mortgage Bonds.......	....	....	800,000
Real Estate Mortgage..........	25,000	25,000	25,000
Deferred Notes Payable........	235,000	215,000	195,000
Total Liabilities................	$ 565,792	$ 502,546	$1,234,637
Minority Interest..............	56,808	56,005	66,864
Common Stock................	1,150,000	1,150,000	7,000
Capital Surplus...............	....	....	343,000
Earned Surplus...............	301,721	280,763	434,122
TOTAL...................	$2,074,321	$1,989,314	$2,085,623
Net Working Capital...........	$ 619,208	$ 595,758	$ 765,688
Current Ratio..................	3.18	3.48	4.57
Tangible Net Worth...........	$1,292,761	$1,271,831	$ 625,190
Net Sales....................	$2,984,508	$3,968,531	$4,426,952
Net Profit...................	(L)*13,505*	(L)*20,958*	153,359
Dividends....................	None	None	None

business itself, they did not care to endorse bank borrowings. These owners extended loans on an open account basis, gradually increasing in amount to $275,000 in year D. At this point it was decided to fund the loans over a period of years, $5,000 to mature quarterly during each succeeding year until the entire amount was paid. This item appears as *Deferred Notes Payable* in the comparative figures ranging from $235,000 in year C to $195,000 in year A, bearing interest at 4 per cent per annum. Each balance sheet includes the $20,000 due quarterly in the ensuing year in the current liabilities.

In the early part of year A, several of the employees decided to attempt to acquire control of the business. They believed that they could operate the enterprise for themselves more profitably than the absentee owners had been able to operate it. Among themselves they were able to collect a pool of cash of an undisclosed amount. They went to the owners, offering this cash as a down payment for the entire outstanding stock, the balance of the purchase price to be an issue of 5 per cent first mortgage bonds to run for 15 years but with serial maturities to begin within 3 years, the serial maturity to be a minimum of $50,000 but to be increased by a certain fixed percentage of net earnings.

The sale of the entire outstanding capital stock was made on this basis. The common stock of $1,150,000 in year C and year B now became an issue of first mortgage bonds of $800,000, common stock of $7,000, and capital surplus of $343,000. By this change $800,000 of the tangible net worth in year B became a definite fixed liability of the same amount in year A with immediate yearly interest charges of $40,000. The new owners realized what an added obligation the business was assuming but they felt that more than the $40,000 could be saved by the elimination of unprofitable lines, by a reduction in personnel, by a gradual strengthening in prices, and by more efficient production methods.

In addition to this issue of first mortgage bonds aggregating $800,000 and deferred notes payable of $195,000, the figures as of year A disclose a real estate mortgage of $25,000, or total slow liabilities of $1,020,000. The mortgage was on one piece of the plant property, bore interest at the rate of 5 per cent per annum, and was due 6 years in the future.

In year E the business had been very heavily indebted to the owners for loans. Arrangements had been made with a factor at that time to check the credits, and to guarantee and cash the sales.[2] Under this arrangement, receivables as created were immediately sold to the factor without recourse and the corporation received cash for its sales without any delay. This arrangement is quite typical in various divisions of the textile industry. The item *Due from Factor*, which amounted to $80,533 in year C, $61,445 in year B, and $252,497 in year A, represented cash for the sale

[2] For information regarding the operations of factors, see footnote 2, pp. 178–179.

of receivables without recourse which was still in the hands of the factor and which could be drawn on a moment's notice. The sale of receivables to a factor is a very different financing arrangement from the discounting of notes receivable with a finance company, as the sale is made without recourse and there is no contingent liability such as exists with the discounting of notes receivable.

The tangible net worth represented the sum of the outstanding common stock and earned surplus in year C and year B, and of the common stock, capital surplus, and earned surplus in year A, less good will carried at $100,000 in each of the consolidated balance sheets, and trademarks carried at $58,960 in year C and at $58,932 in year B and in year A.

For year C the consolidated income statement disclosed a loss of $13,505, and for year B a loss of $20,958. For year A, a very substantial net profit of $153,359 was recorded. The profits for year A together with the earned depreciation on the fixed assets brought about a very material increase in the net working capital from $595,758 in year B to $765,688 in year A. Now let us examine the relationship between the net sales and the tangible net worth over these 3 years:

	Year C	Year B	Year A
Net Sales........................	$2,984,508	$3,968,531	$4,426,952
Tangible Net Worth................	1,292,761	1,271,831	625,190
Ratio of Net Sales to Tangible Net Worth........................	2.31	3.12	7.08

For year C, net sales amounted to $2,984,508 on a tangible net worth of $1,292,761, giving a turnover of 2.31 times. During year B, the net sales increased to $3,968,531 or 32.9 per cent, while the tangible net worth decreased to $1,271,831, or 1.7 per cent. With the spread in these two figures the turnover for year B became 3.12 times.

For year A, the net profits amounted to $153,359. The change in capitalization had taken place as of April 1, so that interest for 6 months on the newly created issue of first mortgage bonds of $800,000, amounting to $20,000, had been charged to expense. In year A, net sales expanded to $4,426,952, the highest annual sales in the history of the business. To support this greater volume, the tangible net worth should have increased in proportion. However, it had actually decreased well over 50 per cent with the conversion of $800,000 of the tangible net worth into a funded liability. On the greatly reduced tangible net worth of $625,109, the turnover was 7.08 times, out of all reasonable proportion for this line of business.

Condensed Analysis. In this case the investment item, amounting to $492 in year C, and to $350 in year B and in year A, carried no significance. This item represented a few shares of stock in two corporations in which the Book Cloth Manufacturing Corporation had been a creditor.

These shares of stock had been received in reorganizations of the two corporations.

The figures as of year C and year B both disclosed attractive current conditions. The current liabilities in both years were moderate. In other respects, however, the figures of both years were heavy. In the first place, the inventory exceeded the net working capital. In the second place, the net depreciated value of the fixed assets represented 74.8 per cent and 75.1 per cent of the respective tangible net worth. In the third place, operations had been conducted at a loss in 8 out of the preceding 10 years.

Then the changes which have already been described took place in year A, and the financial condition was transposed overnight. As a result of the increase in net working capital and a reduction in inventory, the inventory was now in line. The current liabilities were low. Operations were changed from the red to the black. Notwithstanding these improvements, four other relationships were now so very much out of line that the business was in a very critical financial condition. The fixed assets were 46.7 per cent in excess of the tangible net worth. Funded obligations aggregated the substantial sum of $1,020,000 and were materially greater than the net working capital. Total liabilities amounted to $1,234,637 and were almost twice as large as the tangible net worth. Finally, the turnover of tangible net worth was 7.08 times as compared with a normal turnover of 2.75 to 3.00 times for this type of operation.

The consolidated financial condition as of year A was so mixed up that it would be difficult to unscramble. In the two preceding cases studied in this chapter, overtrading was the clear explanation of the unbalanced condition, and the solution was a reduction in the volume of net sales to reasonable limits. The problem here was quite different. If the financial capitalization had been the same in year A as in year B, the volume of $4,426,952, while a trifle heavy, could have been carried by the tangible net worth.

To decrease the volume of business to the amount that should be handled by the reduced tangible net worth of $625,190 was not the sound solution here. Such a program would mean that the plants would be operated at a low percentage of capacity; the increased operating expenses would invite unprofitable operations. The basic solution really called for the investment of at least $1,000,000 in cash in capital stock. Of that sum $800,000 should be used to pay off the first mortgage bonds; and the remaining $200,000 to increase the working capital. This solution was not a feasible one, as the new owners did not have the funds and they did not want outside interests in the business.

With the financial condition so obviously unbalanced in year A, there is just a bare chance that this enterprise may be pulled out of the hole over a period of years by exceptionally keen, aggressive, economical management. Every penny that can be saved must be saved and be used to reduce liabilities. There is absolutely no chance for dividends. The $1,000,000 which is needed to put the business in sound shape must be earned. That will be a difficult job with expenses higher than competitors' to the extent of the interest and amortization on the funded obligations, and to the extent that the depreciation must be earned on the excessive amount of the fixed assets.

TYPICAL RATIOS OF NET SALES TO TANGIBLE NET WORTH

From the gross income, that is, the actual receipts from the net sales of a business, come the funds to repay bank loans, to pay merchandise invoices, salaries, wages, rent, light, heat, transportation, insurance, and other expenses. Net sales are to a business enterprise what oxygen is to the human being. They both support life. A very material increase in the volume of net sales has the same effect upon the business organism as an increase in the quantity of inhaled oxygen has upon the human organism. The business operates with greater profits and effectiveness, operations are speeded up, but the apparent ease of accomplishment is based upon a strain that must be kept in delicate balance. The more net sales expand above a certain point, the greater the strain becomes. That strain is measured by two valuable comparisons, one of net sales to tangible net worth discussed in this chapter, and the other of net sales to net working capital discussed in the following chapter.

What is meant by the "delicate balance" that controls the strain when a concern is transacting a heavy volume of business? Merely the relationship between the income and the outgo of funds. The lapse of time between the day when funds are taken in and the day when those same funds are disbursed is very short, and nothing can disturb that balance without having a vital effect upon the business.

The operation of a commercial or industrial business enterprise which is trading heavily is based upon an anticipated volume of business. Forward commitments invariably are placed for its requirements of raw material or finished merchandise to be shipped at some near future date. If anticipated orders now fail to materialize; if certain important orders already confirmed and on the books are canceled and for business reasons the cancellations must be accepted; if a strike occurs in a plant and the inventory continues to pile up with the receipt of raw material; if any unexpected factor happens to materialize and to last for a period of 1 to 3 months, then the liabilities, already heavy, must continue to expand just at the time when the income to meet these larger obligations is rapidly dropping. That is an almost ideal combination for financial embarrassment. Funds to meet the increasing liabilities are lacking.

Small business enterprises have a better chance of getting away with overtrading than larger concerns. The resources of small concerns may be managed more readily, the problems are smaller and less widely scattered, the decisions are less important, the necessary controls are fewer, and the knowledge of the business is greater. Overtrading becomes increasingly hazardous as size mounts.

The momentum of a concern that is overtrading carries the business forward on its path in the same way that a moving automobile continues to plunge ahead notwithstanding pressure on its brakes. The faster a business concern is moving, the more chance there is for vital mistakes, and the more difficult it is to change its direction. Speed is a difficult reality to control. The greater the speed, the greater the possibility of a critical accident!

Maxim

As with the ratio of net sales to inventory, no broad maxim can be given as a guide to the safe limits of the ratio of net sales to tangible net worth. As a general rule, if this ratio is more than twice as large as the median for the particular division of commerce or industry, as given in Schedule 49, on the following two pages, the analyst may well feel that overtrading is taking place.

Schedule 49 lists the typical ratios of net sales to tangible net worth for 42 divisions of manufacturing, 21 of wholesaling, and 7 of retailing each year for the 5 years from 1955 to 1959 inclusive, with a 5-year arithmetical average for each division. The ratio of net sales to tangible net worth for any of these lines of activity, to disclose undertrading, would probably be below the figure representing the lower quartile in the table in the Appendix.

Manufacturers of dresses with a 5-year average of 10.78 times have the highest turnover of tangible net worth, packers of meats and provisions are second with a ratio of 7.83 times, and building construction contractors are third with a 5-year average ratio of 6.25 times. The lowest ratio of net sales to tangible net worth among manufacturers is shown by the integrated petroleum operators with their tremendous investments, with a 5-year average of 1.21 times, followed by lumber producers with a ratio of 1.79 times, and of cotton cloth mills with 1.93 times.

Wholesalers as a class naturally have a faster turnover of tangible net worth than manufacturers or retailers. Wholesalers of cigars, cigarettes, and tobacco with a 5-year average ratio of net sales to tangible net worth of 14.36 times lead the parade. Wholesalers of meat and poultry are second with a 5-year average of 10.63 times, and wholesalers of fresh fruits and produce third with a 5-year average of 10.12 times. The slowest

RATIOS OF NET SALES TO TANGIBLE NET WORTH [Schedule 49]

Lines of Business Activity	Number of Times					
	Median					Five-year Average
	1955	1956	1957	1958	1959	
MANUFACTURERS						
Agricultural Implements and Machinery	2.07	1.95	1.76	2.73	2.53	2.21
Airplane Parts and Accessories	2.80	4.75	3.83	4.37	3.23	3.80
Automobile Parts and Accessories	2.73	2.62	2.45	2.02	2.65	2.48
Bakers	4.96	5.00	4.43	4.80	4.77	4.79
Bedsprings and Mattresses	3.30	3.22	2.71	2.80	2.76	2.96
Bodies, Auto, Bus, and Truck	2.82	3.09	3.26	3.03	3.40	3.12
Bolts, Screws, Nuts, and Nails	2.56	3.03	2.80	2.24	2.52	2.63
Breweries	2.51	2.35	2.36	2.41	2.35	2.40
Chemicals, Industrial	1.96	2.19	1.94	2.06	2.29	2.09
Coats and Suits, Men's and Boys'	4.31	4.72	4.39	4.04	4.86	4.46
Coats and Suits, Women's	5.18	6.01	6.53	5.20	6.50	5.88
Confectionery	2.93	2.92	3.02	2.96	2.83	2.93
Contractors, Building Construction	6.09	6.79	5.98	6.52	5.85	6.25
Contractors, Electrical	4.35	4.37	5.05	4.91	4.31	4.60
Cotton Cloth Mills	2.25	1.97	1.63	1.73	2.08	1.93
Cotton Goods, Converters, Non-factored	4.28	3.00	2.99	3.20	6.38	3.97
Dresses, Rayon, Silk, and Acetate	11.78	10.97	11.47	11.22	8.48	10.78
Drugs	2.01	2.07	2.08	2.01	1.99	2.03
Electrical Parts and Supplies	2.79	2.98	2.75	2.48	2.89	2.78
Foundries	2.48	2.76	2.68	2.20	2.28	2.48
Fruits and Vegetables, Canners	2.98	2.77	2.60	3.39	3.04	2.96
Furniture	3.25	3.08	2.97	2.78	3.05	3.03
Hardware and Tools	2.06	2.30	2.30	2.03	2.53	2.24
Hosiery	2.21	2.31	2.58	2.20	2.09	2.28
Lumber	1.68	1.61	1.66	2.29	1.72	1.79
Machine Shops	2.07	2.43	2.28	1.56	1.84	2.04
Machinery, Industrial	2.51	2.62	2.50	2.04	2.06	2.35
Meats and Provisions, Packers	8.05	7.29	7.36	9.68	6.76	7.83
Metal Stampings	2.73	2.85	2.49	2.33	2.40	2.56
Outerwear, Knitted	4.51	5.81	3.98	5.46	5.16	4.98
Overalls and Work Clothing	3.60	3.70	3.61	3.40	3.71	3.60
Paints, Varnishes, and Lacquers	2.58	2.69	2.64	2.50	2.69	2.62
Paper	1.73	1.77	1.64	1.57	1.56	1.65
Paper Boxes	2.39	2.72	2.54	2.05	2.35	2.41
Petroleum, Integrated Corporations	1.26	1.27	1.18	1.18	1.17	1.21
Printers, Job	2.61	2.84	2.65	2.49	2.54	2.63
Radio Parts and Supplies	3.10	3.21	3.24	2.78	2.99	3.06
Shirts, Underwear, and Pajamas, Men's	4.51	4.48	5.40	4.38	5.46	4.85
Shoes, Men's, Women's, and Children's	3.60	3.46	3.54	3.32	3.60	3.50
Soft Drinks and Carbonated Water, Bottlers	2.17	2.62	1.74	2.06	2.61	2.24
Steel, Structural Fabricators (Sell on Short Terms)	3.50	3.24	3.24	2.97	2.72	3.13
Stoves, Ranges, and Ovens	2.94	2.81	3.09	2.87	2.89	2.92

[Schedule 49 (*Cont.*)]

RATIOS OF NET SALES TO TANGIBLE NET WORTH (*Continued*)

Lines of Business Activity	Number of Times					
	Median					Five-year Average
	1955	1956	1957	1958	1959	
WHOLESALERS						
Automobile Parts and Accessories....	3.56	3.81	3.19	3.25	3.21	3.40
Baked Goods.....................	5.18	5.07	5.00	4.08	4.09	4.68
Cigars, Cigarettes, and Tobacco......	14.06	13.48	13.27	14.38	16.59	14.36
Drugs and Drug Sundries..........	5.51	5.38	5.57	5.45	5.26	5.43
Dry Goods......................	3.97	4.09	4.17	4.21	4.52	4.19
Electrical Parts and Supplies.......	5.57	5.70	4.60	4.56	5.07	5.10
Fruits and Produce, Fresh..........	10.37	10.15	10.25	10.45	9.40	10.12
Furnishings, Men's................	2.82	2.84	2.65	2.59	2.78	2.74
Gasoline, Fuel Oil, and Lubricating Oil	5.26	6.44	6.23	5.91	4.51	5.67
Groceries.......................	7.76	8.31	8.57	8.24	8.67	8.31
Hardware.......................	3.12	3.35	3.02	2.91	2.87	3.05
Hosiery and Underwear............	3.64	3.51	4.62	4.18	3.77	3.94
Household Appliances, Electrical.....	7.37	7.19	5.91	6.82	7.00	6.86
Lumber.........................	6.84	4.80	4.98	4.15	4.57	5.07
Lumber and Building Materials......	4.91	3.95	3.37	4.52	4.16	4.18
Meat and Poultry.................	9.57	9.56	9.51	11.83	12.69	10.63
Paints, Varnishes, and Lacquers......	3.00	2.91	3.30	3.20	3.27	3.14
Paper..........................	5.05	4.95	5.04	4.77	5.01	4.96
Plumbing and Heating Supplies......	3.96	3.97	3.72	3.24	3.65	3.71
Shoes, Men's, Women's, and Children's......................	4.52	5.09	4.07	4.00	5.05	4.55
Wines and Liquors................	6.09	6.49	5.74	7.76	5.92	6.40
RETAILERS						
Clothing, Men's and Boys'.........	2.48	2.57	2.54	2.38	2.50	2.49
Department Stores................	2.87	2.76	2.83	2.88	3.04	2.88
Furniture, 50 Per Cent or More Installment.....................	1.82	1.91	2.03	1.92	1.80	1.90
Groceries and Meats, Independent...	10.45	9.29	9.89	9.01	9.27	9.58
Lumber and Building Materials......	3.10	2.85	2.49	2.14	2.36	2.59
Shoes...........................	3.46	3.58	3.48	3.69	3.31	3.50
Women's Specialty Shops..........	2.97	3.40	3.29	3.10	3.40	3.23

turnover of tangible net worth among wholesalers is contributed by
wholesalers of ~~men's furnishings~~ with a 5-year average of 2.74 times, followed by wholesalers of hardware with 3.05 times.

The highest ratio of net sales to tangible net worth among the retail
lines is shown by ~~independent~~ grocery and meat stores with a 5-year
average of 9.58 times, and the lowest by ~~furniture~~ stores with more than
~~half of their sales made on installment~~ with 1.90 times.

THEORY AND PROBLEMS *retail hardware*

1. What information would you expect to obtain from the relationship of net sales to
tangible net worth?

2. Compute the ratio of net sales to tangible net worth of the following two business
enterprises:

	Company A	Company B
Net Sales	$423,620	$561,432
Total Assets	360,140	480,670
Intangible Assets	50,100	1
Total Liabilities	$155,622	$378,462

Does the higher ratio indicate which of these two business enterprises is using its
assets with greater efficiency, its investment in the business with greater efficiency,
or both, or neither? Explain.

3. Describe what is meant by overtrading; by undertrading.

4. What is an indication of overtrading? of undertrading? Give two solutions to a
financial condition characterized by overtrading.

5. Are liabilities light or heavy in cases of overtrading? Explain your answer.

6. Determine the ratio of net sales to tangible net worth of the Wholesale Hosiery
Co., Inc., from the following figures and give your interpretation of the trend:

	Year C	Year B	Year A
Net Sales	$226,710	$310,886	$401,972
Tangible Net Worth	67,264	71,790	76,687

7. The audited figures of Style Dress Manufacturers, Inc., for the past three fiscal
years have been posted on a comparative statement page. These figures are given
on page 416. You are an industrial engineer. These figures have been turned over
to you for your analysis and criticism. The management is anxious to obtain from
you an objective toward which its financial condition should be headed. Give your
interpretation of the following ratios for each year and the trend of each of these
ratios over the 3 years. Sales are made on terms of 8 per cent discount on the tenth
of the following month:

   a. Current assets to current liabilities
   b. Current liabilities to tangible net worth
   c. Fixed assets to tangible net worth
   d. Net sales to inventory
   e. Inventory to net working capital
   f. Average collection period
   g. Net sales to tangible net worth

STYLE DRESS MANUFACTURERS, INC.
Comparative Figures for Years Ended October 31, 19—

	(C) Three Years Ago	(B) Two Years Ago	(A) One Year Ago
ASSETS			
Cash.	$ 4,607	$ 7,134	$ 13,562
Accounts Receivable.	33,282	78,290	71,356
Merchandise.	56,202	105,461	87,655
Current Assets.	$ 94,091	$190,885	$ 172,573
Fixed Assets.	35,328	35,331	43,828
Miscellaneous Receivables.	15,484	7,657	10,913
Prepaid Assets.	101	538	1,118
TOTAL.	$145,004	$234,411	$ 228,432
LIABILITIES			
Notes Payable.	$.......	$.......	$ 7,500
Bills Payable to Officers.	....	....	2,590
Accounts Payable.	32,778	92,055	71,845
Accruals.	9,551	16,368	11,479
Reserves.	....	4,000	2,000
Current Liabilities.	$ 42,329	$112,423	$ 95,414
Reserves for Depreciation.	25,971	27,146	27,961
Preferred Stock.	27,000	27,000	27,000
Common Stock and Surplus.	49,704	67,842	78,057
TOTAL.	$145,004	$234,411	$ 228,432
Net Working Capital.	$ 51,762	$ 78,462	$ 77,159
Current Ratio.	2.22	1.70	1.81
Tangible Net Worth.	$ 76,704	$ 94,842	$ 105,057
Net Sales.	$414,242	$640,000	$1,302,000
Net Profits.	22,577	18,138	10,215
Dividends.	None	None	None

8. The following audited balance sheet was rendered in an annual report by the Candy Manufacturing Corporation to its stockholders. The accompanying income statement disclosed net sales for the year of $2,434,000. These sales were made on terms of 2 per cent discount in 10 days, net 30 days. As a substantial stockholder you are interested in analyzing these figures to ascertain the basic condition of the corporation. Post the figures on a columnar sheet of paper and make the following computations:

a. Net working capital
b. Tangible net worth
c. Current ratio
d. Ratio of current liabilities to tangible net worth
e. Ratio of fixed assets to tangible net worth
f. Ratio of net sales to inventory

g. Ratio of inventory to net working capital
h. Average collection period
i. Ratio of net sales to tangible net worth

Interpret each of the above ratios for a manufacturer of confectionery.

CANDY MANUFACTURING CORPORATION
Balance Sheet, December 31, 19—
ASSETS

Current Assets			
Cash..			$ 614,074
Accounts receivable—*Less:* Reserve for doubtful accounts			
Customers.......................................		$ 226,915	
Others...		1,448	228,363
Inventories (at cost or market, whichever is lower)......			709,114
Total Current Assets..........................			$1,551,551
Investments			
Real estate mortgage.................................		$ 105,806	
Real estate acquired through foreclosure of mortgages...		100,017	
		$ 205,823	
Less: Reserve for possible losses...................		173,884	
		$ 31,939	
Cash surrender value of life insurance policies..........		148,062	
Stocks and notes......................................		11,086	191,087
Deferred Charges.....................................			35,863
Fixed Assets..			
Land, buildings, machinery, and equipment at cost......		$4,721,297	
Less: Reserve for depreciation and reduction of cost			
values......................................		3,472,544	1,248,753
Trademarks and Good Will			2
			$3,027,256

LIABILITIES AND CAPITAL

Current Liabilities			
Accounts payable.....................................			$ 140,376
Accruals and Reserves			
Salaries and commissions...........................		$ 28,746	
Real estate and personal property taxes.............		23,676	
Federal income taxes.............................		33,625	
Other accruals and reserves.......................		28,887	114,934
Total Current Liabilities........................			$ 255,310
Reserve for Prior Years' Taxes.........................			15,620
Capital Stock	*Shares*		
4% Cumulative preferred, $100 par value			
Authorized...............................	4,176		
Issued....................................	3,621		
Less: In treasury...........................	454		
Outstanding...............................	3,167		316,700
Common $10 par value			
Authorized and issued.....................	88,518		
Less: In treasury.........................	850		
Outstanding..............................	87,668		876,680
Earned Surplus.......................................			1,562,946
			$3,027,256

CHAPTER XV

Net Sales to Net Working Capital

It is not unusual to come across a situation where the relationship of net sales to tangible net worth is in satisfactory proportion, but the relationship of net sales to net working capital is excessive. Such a condition is the concomitant result of a top-heavy investment in fixed or slow assets, leaving a rather moderate net working capital position. As a business concern with this financial condition goes into the peak of its season, the relationship between net sales and net working capital becomes more and more exaggerated. Any reasonable volume of sales on a low or nominal net working capital condition results in relatively heavy current liabilities in relation to the current assets, and a consequent low current ratio. Where the portion of the tangible net worth invested in fixed or slow assets is reasonable, the ratio of net sales to net working capital parallels the ratio of net sales to tangible net worth, and if over-trading or undertrading exists, that condition is reflected simultaneously in both relationships.

There is a tendency among analysts to follow one or the other of these two ratios. The more thorough analyst, however, will follow both comparisons, as they are complementary and at times one will indicate a condition which is not quite so evident from the other. A high ratio of net sales to net working capital may be the result of overtrading, permanent or temporary, or may indicate the need of additional capital to support a structure unbalanced by top-heavy investment in fixed property. A careful study of the figures will always give the correct answer for the particular situation. A low ratio may be the result of undertrading, or may be a result of the fact that more funds are invested in a particular business enterprise than can be used to reasonable advantage.

ILLUSTRATIONS OF RELATIONSHIPS

The following three examples are illustrative of the importance of understanding the significance of the relationship between net sales and net working capital. The three situations are a Southern wholesaler of wines and liquors, a manufacturer of men's shirts, and a manufacturer of woolen cloth. In the first two cases, the investments in fixed assets were heavy over the 3-year period. In the case of the manufacturer of woolen cloth, the investment in fixed assets became particularly heavy in year A.

Wholesaler of Wines and Liquors

A wholesale business handling tobacco, drugs, and confectionery, with an authorized and paid-in capital of $10,000, was started in Atlanta, Ga., 16 years ago. From the inception of the business, the distribution of tobacco and tobacco products became far more important than either drugs or confectionery. Ten years ago, when the tangible net worth had been increased to approximately $38,000, the concern began to distribute wines and liquors. Within 2 years this division of the business became the most important. Eight years ago, the name was changed to Wholesale Liquor Distributors, Inc., and the authorized capital, all common stock, was increased to $100,000, of which $90,000 is now paid in.

At the present time exclusive distribution rights are held for certain nationally advertised brands of wines, liquors, and beer. In year A, less than 10 per cent of the annual volume of business was presented by the sale of tobacco, drugs, and confectionery. Comparative figures for the past three fiscal periods appear in Schedule 50.

An increasing volume of net sales was handled each year over the 3-year period. For year C, the net sales amounted to $2,650,522 and on this volume a net profit of $6,194 was earned. For year B, the net sales expanded to $2,882,433, an increase of 8.75 per cent, but the net profit dropped to $3,075. For year A, the net sales jumped to $4,583,313, an increase of 72.93 per cent when compared with the volume for year C. On these substantially expanded net sales, the net profits amounted to $49,861, materially greater than had ever been earned by this enterprise in any single previous year.

It is very evident, in the light of Chap. XIV, that the Wholesale Liquor Distributors, Inc., had been overtrading for many years, and clearly so over this 3-year spread. On the net sales of $2,650,522 handled in year C, the ratio of net sales to tangible net worth was 23.29 times, for year B, 24.66 times, and for year A, 21.14 times.

The great extent to which this concern had been overtrading may readily be seen by Schedule 49, page 414, showing the 5-year average ratio of net sales to tangible net worth of wholesalers of wines and liquors at 6.40, which is somewhat less than one-third the ratios disclosed by the figures of this wholesaler for any one of these 3 years.

That the management was aware the business was handling an excessive volume of sales was evident from two policies. First, was the fact that no dividends were declared over the 3 years, even in year *A* when net profits aggregated $49,861. The earnings over the 3 years totaled $59,130 and every single penny was retained in the business to support the

[**Schedule 50**]   WHOLESALE LIQUOR DISTRIBUTORS, INC.
Comparative Figures for Years Ended December 31, 19—

	(C) Three Years Ago	(B) Two Years Ago	(A) One Year Ago
ASSETS			
Cash..........................	$ 50,733	$ 123,692	$ 230,661
Notes Receivable..............	8,604	12,271	24,262
Accounts Receivable...........	154,968	275,422	404,324
Inventory.....................	144,751	276,030	391,029
Current Assets.................	$ 359,056	$ 687,415	$1,050,276
Fixed Assets, Net.............	53,449	58,533	56,592
Prepaid......................	3,363	3,038	7,835
TOTAL..................	$ 415,868	$ 748,986	$1,114,703
LIABILITIES			
Notes Payable for Merchandise..	$ 40,610	$ 78,650	$ 275,990
Due to Officers................	25,592	56,874	21,092
Accounts Payable.............	218,447	464,849	545,697
Accruals......................	14,187	25,431	38,745
Reserve for Taxes.............	3,158	6,233	16,369
Current Liabilities.............	$ 301,994	$ 632,037	$ 897,893
Common Stock................	40,000	40,000	90,000
Retained Earnings............	73,874	76,949	126,810
TOTAL..................	$ 415,868	$ 748,986	$1,114,703
Net Working Capital...........	$ 57,062	$ 55,378	$ 152,383
Current Ratio.................	1.19	1.08	1.17
Tangible Net Worth........... ...	$ 113,874	$ 116,949	$ 216,810
Net Sales......................	$2,650,522	$2,882,433	$4,583,313
Net Profit....................	6,194	3,075	49,861
Dividends....................	None	None	None

heavy volume. Second, was the sudden jump in the outstanding common stock from $40,000 to $90,000 in year *A*. The reinvested net profits of $59,130 had been insufficient to support the expanding volume in year *A*, even though the management apparently believed in overtrading. To support this sudden increase in sales, the management had put $50,000 additional funds in the business in the form of common stock; of this sum $25,000 represented actual cash and $25,000 represented stock taken in payment of funds due to the officers. If the common stock had not been increased the relationship of the net sales to the tangible net worth would have exceeded materially the 21.14 times shown in year A.

The typical concern in this line of business has approximately 16 per cent of its tangible net worth invested in fixed assets. In the case of Wholesale Liquor Distributors, Inc., the percentage was materially greater. In year C, the net depreciated value of the fixed assets consisting of a warehouse, office furniture, fixtures, equipment, and a fleet of delivery trucks amounted to 46.9 per cent of the tangible net worth, in year B, 50.1 per cent, and in year A, 26.1 per cent. The percentage change between year B and year A was due to the increase in the tangible net worth from the added $50,000 common stock, and the $49,861 of net profits retained in the surplus account.

Because of the relatively large investment in fixed assets, the net working capital was considerably smaller than it should have been. The relationship between the net sales and the net working capital accordingly resulted in high turnovers:

	Year C	Year B	Year A
Net Sales............................	$2,650,522	$2,882,433	$4,583,313
Net Working Capital.................	57,062	55,378	152,383
Ratio of Net Sales to Net Working Capital..........................	46.49	52.12	30.94

While the net sales were expanding steadily and rapidly over these 3 years, the net working capital was fluctuating. Between year C and year B, the net working capital dropped from $57,062 to $55,378, notwithstanding the fact that the net profits of $3,075 had been retained in the business. This drop was occasioned by an increase in the net depreciated value of the fixed assets from $53,449 to $58,533 in year B when several new delivery trucks had been purchased. In year A, the net working capital came into its own by a terrific expansion to $152,383 as the new funds, both earned and invested, were largely retained in current assets.

In year C, the ratio of net sales to net working capital was 46.49 times. In year B, this ratio increased to 52.12, and then in year A dropped to 30.94 on the enlarged net working capital. That the ratio for each of these 3 years was very much out of line is evident from the fact that the 5-year average of the median ratio for this line of business was 9.27 times, with a high of 10.35 in 1959 and a low of 8.51 in 1957.

Condensed Analysis. As we learned in the last chapter, overtrading results in heavy current liabilities. That situation was only too true here. The ratio of current assets to current liabilities was 1.19 times in year C, 1.08 in year B, and 1.17 in year A, all exceptionally low ratios, because of the heavy liabilities. The same fact is emphasized by the relationship of the current liabilities to the tangible net worth, ratios of 265.4 per cent, 540.2 per cent, and 414.2 per cent, respectively.

The liabilities had been so palpably heavy that the depository bank would grant no loan. The lending officer who handled the account was afraid that the concern might become financially involved at any time, and even if a loan was secured by the assignment of receivables or the pledge of warehouse receipts covering wines and liquors in a bonded warehouse, the risk was hardly worth the bother. Because of the lack of bank credit, some portion of the merchandise was paid by promissory notes running for 3 months. These notes amounted to $40,610 in year C, increased to $78,650 in year B, and then expanded to the quite substantial sum of $275,990 in year A.

A splendid turnover of the inventory had been consistently obtained. The relationship of the net sales to the inventory was 18.3 times, 10.5 times, and 11.7 times, respectively. At the same time the inventory on each statement date was several times as large as the net working capital. On the basis of the existing volume it would be practically impossible to operate with a smaller inventory. The inventory had been taken on December 31, the time when it would normally be low and the receivables high for a wholesale distributor.

In this situation the following seem to have been the high lights of the financial condition of the figures in year A, based on the volume of net sales of $4,583,313: The inventory was heavy compared with the net working capital; the net depreciated value of the fixed assets was about twice as large as normal for a concern of this size in this line of business; the current liabilities were exceptionally heavy from every viewpoint; and the net working capital was low.

There are three answers to this situation. On the assumption that the volume of sales reached in year A would be maintained or increased only moderately in the immediate future, $250,000 or $300,000 additional money could be invested in the business in the form of preferred or common stock. With this amount of new money the various relationships would still be a little below normal, but affairs would be in healthy shape and the business would be sound. The second answer would be to keep the present capitalization and reduce the net sales to a proportionate amount for this line, or down to between $1,750,000 and $2,000,000, that is, somewhat more than one-half. All items in the current liabilities would be reduced proportionately. The third answer would be to combine these two solutions in a proportionate manner, reducing the volume somewhat, depending upon how much new money could be obtained for investment in the business.

As a practical matter, in a situation of this character, the volume is rarely reduced consciously. If funds are available, or can be obtained on terms which are satisfactory to the owners of a business, then such funds are often invested to support the growing operations. If no funds are available from any source to invest in preferred or common stocks, the owners generally go along their beaten path of overtrading, often to end in financial trouble, but occasionally, when they have had the full support of creditors, to keep going and reinvesting profits until affairs are gradually worked into better shape.

Manufacturer of Men's Shirts

A small enterprise with a paid-in cash capital of $25,000 was organized 14 years ago in an eastern Pennsylvania city to manufacture men's shirts under the name of Shirt Mfg. Co., Inc. The owner was a young man from New York who had spent six years as a salesman, and a very successful salesman, for a large corporation in this line of business. He was sure he could keep a small factory going with orders, and as the records show, he has been well able to keep a larger and larger factory constantly busy filling orders. His one purpose in life was sales, and from the measure of steadily increasing net sales, he has done well.

As the business expanded, additional funds were invested from time to time in the corporation and a large part of the earnings were kept in the business. At the end of year A, operations were being carried on with a paid-in capital of $55,000 of 5 per cent cumulative preferred stock, $175,000 common stock, and retained earnings of $110,199, giving a tangible net worth of $340,199.

Over the years a wide variety of shirts had been designed. About 75 per cent of the annual volume consisted of men's dress shirts, and the other 25 per cent of sport shirts, sport clothes, jackets, and summer ensembles. Sales gradually spread from a local Eastern market to national distribution into every state.

The financial condition of this corporation has changed in many ways over the past three fiscal years. These figures are shown in Schedule 51.

Here again, as with so many concerns that overtrade, net sales increased every year, from $1,277,675 in year C, to $1,518,494 in year B, and to $2,078,946 in year A. The net sales between year C and year A showed an increase of 62.7 per cent. Net profits disclosed a very satisfactory return for each year, $32,413 in year C, a drop to $19,971 in year B, and then spectacular profits of $58,108 in year A. All earnings were retained in the business to support the growing volume of sales.

An interpretation of the financial condition of this business involves a clear understanding and explanation of several points that would be raised by a normal study of these comparative figures: (1) the policies responsible for the steady increase in dollars and in percentage of the

[Schedule 51] SHIRT MFG. CO., INC.

Comparative Figures for Years Ended December 31, 19—

	(C) Three Years Ago	(B) Two Years Ago	(A) One Year Ago
ASSETS			
Cash........................	$ 3,333	$ 7,787	$ 12,370
Notes Receivable..............	10,064	10,121	....
Accounts Receivable...........	188,035	240,113	37,325
Inventory....................	193,007	186,666	497,139
Current Assets.................	$ 394,439	$ 444,687	$ 546,840
Fixed Assets, Net..............	20,954	61,066	173,988
Cash Value of Life Insurance....	2,847	4,473	6,127
Miscellaneous Receivables.......	1,749	4,840	5,857
Deferred Items................	3,144	2,332	4,099
Investment...................	....	4,000	....
Due from Affiliated Company...	....	28,923	....
TOTAL...................	$ 423,133	$ 550,321	$ 736,911
LIABILITIES			
Notes Payable to Banks........	$ 79,000	$ 135,500	$ 5,000
Notes Payable for Merchandise..	....	11,578	42,932
Other Notes Payable...........	....	1,692	6,767
Accruals.....................	19,516	6,273	7,977
Accounts Payable..............	110,865	107,225	56,375
Due to Factor.................	....	....	151,944
Reserve for Taxes.............	6,632	5,962	50,930
Mortgage—Current Maturity...	....	....	32,570
Current Liabilities..............	$ 216,013	$ 268,230	$ 354,495
Mortgages....................	....	....	42,217
Total Liabilities................	$ 216,013	$ 268,230	$ 396,712
5% Cumulative Preferred Stock.	....	55,000	55,000
Common Stock................	75,000	175,000	175,000
Retained Earnings............	132,120	52,091	110,199
TOTAL...................	$ 423,133	$ 550,321	$ 736,911
Net Working Capital...........	$ 178,426	$ 176,457	$ 192,345
Current Ratio..................	1.82	1.65	1.54
Tangible Net Worth............	$ 207,120	$ 282,091	$ 340,199
Net Sales....................	$1,277,675	$1,518,494	$2,078,946
Net Profit...................	32,413	19,971	58,108
Dividends...................	None	None	None

tangible net worth represented by the net depreciated value of the fixed assets; (2) the origin of the $55,000 of 5 per cent cumulative preferred stock and the increase of $100,000 in the common stock in year B; (3) the steady increase in the miscellaneous receivables; (4) the investment item carried at $4,000 in year B, with the reason why it did not appear in year A; (5) the item *Due from Affiliated Company* $28,923 in year B; (6) the reason why no notes receivable appeared in year A, and why the accounts receivable were so greatly reduced; (7) the item *Due to Factor* which suddenly appeared for the first time in year A and at the quite substantial figure of $151,944; and (8) the reason for the decrease between year B and year A in *Notes Payable to Banks* and an understanding of the basis on which these loans were obtained. Let us examine these points, one by one, in the order they have been mentioned. We shall find that explanations of certain items involve other items.

The net depreciated value of the fixed assets amounted to $20,954 in year C. During the following year, this item had increased to $61,066 and by the end of year A to $173,988, a very material increase. Not only did the net depreciated value of these assets steadily increase from year to year, but the increase was at such a rate that it represented each year a larger portion of the tangible net worth. In year C, for example, the fixed assets of $20,954 represented the very modest 10.1 per cent, in year B they had advanced to 21.6 per cent, and in year A, notwithstanding the handsome profits largely retained in surplus, to 51.2 per cent, slightly more than one-half the tangible net worth. During the last week of year B, the president of this concern had sold to the corporation for $40,000 a shirt manufacturing plant that he had owned personally in a neighboring city; he took in payment, not $40,000 in cash, but $40,000 in 5 per cent cumulative preferred stock. The increase in the fixed assets from $20,954 in year C to $61,066 in year B was represented almost entirely by this one transaction. During year A, a new plant, the third now in operation, was constructed in another city at a cost of approximately $80,000. Finally, the plant of the affiliated company, valued at approximately $35,000, was taken over in a manner described a little later. In year C, at 10.1 per cent of the tangible net worth, the fixed assets were in splendid proportion; in year A, at 51.2 per cent, they absorbed an excessive portion of the tangible net worth and by so doing kept the net working capital relatively low for the high turnover of business.

We have seen that $40,000 of the $55,000 outstanding 5 per cent cumulative preferred stock which appeared for the first time in the balance sheet for year B was issued in payment for a plant which previously had been owned personally by the president of the corporation. The remaining $15,000 represented stock sold at par for cash to three interested local individuals. The increase in the outstanding common stock from $75,000 to $175,000, also in year *B*, represented the capitalization of $100,000 of the surplus account; not one penny represented new money. The surplus accordingly showed a decrease during that year, representing the difference between this $100,000 and the earnings for the year of $19,971.

The miscellaneous receivables amounted to the nominal sum of $1,749 in year *C*. By the end of year *B*, the item had grown to $4,840 and at the end of year *A* to $5,857. Even at $5,857 the item was relatively small but the upward trend represented a cause for inquiry. A continuation of this trend would shortly involve a representative sum. The management explained that no single receivable in this item was greater than $425; that all items were due from employees, that little care until recently had been taken in handling these accounts, and that only 3 months ago a plan calling for weekly or monthly payments on account had been instituted. By the end of the next fiscal year, the item would be materially smaller.

The item of *Investment* carried at $4,000 in year *B* represented a 50 per cent stock interest at cost in a corporation engaged in manufacturing a line of men's pajamas. This enterprise was financed by cash advances from the Shirt Mfg. Co., Inc. These advances at the end of year *B* amounted to $28,923 and represented the item *Due from Affiliated Company*. This affiliated concern was operating unprofitably. In year *A*, the Shirt Mfg. Co., Inc., purchased the other 50 per cent stock interest and then dissolved that corporation, merging its assets and liabilities with its own. In this process the Shirt Mfg. Co., Inc., acquired the plant of this affiliated concern, valued at approximately $35,000; simultaneously the investment item and the amount due from the affiliated company were eliminated.

It is one of the cardinal principles of banking, that when a concern borrows from two or more commercial banks or trust companies all loans shall be on the same basis so that each bank will share equally with the others in case of financial difficulties. This principle meant very little to the management of this concern, as up to year *B* loans from one bank were on the straight unsecured note of the corporation, loans from another bank were secured by a mortgage on one of the plants, and loans from a third institution had been secured by the pledge of the cash surrender value of life insurance and the assignment of part of the receivables. In other words, to obtain sufficient credit to overtrade and still not run slow in meeting trade bills for the purchase of cotton piece goods bank credit was obtained in any and every possible way; and even this amount of bank credit was insufficient. It became necessary to pay for some merchandise with promissory notes; such notes amounted to

$11,578 in year B, and to $42,932 in year A. In this predicament, the management finally made arrangements to do business with a factor. Notes and accounts receivable for the sale of merchandise as they arose were now sold without recourse, to the factor. With these funds bank loans were reduced to $5,000 in year A, and shortly afterward that $5,000 was retired. It was as a result of these new factoring arrangements that no notes receivable appeared in the balance sheet for year A, and the accounts receivable were reduced from $240,113 to $37,325.

In the liabilities for year A there now appeared an item *Due to Factor* amounting to $151,944. Such an item rarely appears in the financial statement of a concern being factored, as receivables are generally sold without recourse. Factors, however, at times do lend against the pledge of merchandise and under such an arrangement a liability to a factor would appear in the liabilities side of the balance sheet. When this item was investigated it was learned that no merchandise was pledged to secure this loan, but that the factor in a unique arrangement was extending credit for seasonal operations secured not by assets of the business, but partly by the pledge of $4,000 of the outstanding 5 per cent cumulative preferred stock, and $125,000 of the common stock in the name of the president, as well as buying the receivables outright, as is the customary practice, without recourse.

With this background of constantly shifting changes in financial condition and make-up of the balance sheet, and the difficulty that the management had undergone in financing its operations, it is quite clear that the volume of business had been high in relation to the net working capital. Here is that relationship over the 3-year period:

	Year C	Year B	Year A
Net Sales.........................	$1,277,675	$1,518,494	$2,078,946
Net Working Capital................	178,426	176,457	192,345
Ratio of Net Sales to Net Working Capital.........................	7.16	8.61	10.81

With net sales of $1,277,675 on a net working capital of $178,426 in year C, the ratio between these two items was 7.16 times. The 5-year average for manufacturers of shirts, underwear, and pajamas is 6.15 times. In year B, the net working capital decreased nominally to $176,457 because of the relatively substantial increase in the fixed assets, the rise of the investment item, and the slow receivables of $28,923 due from the affiliated company. With the expansion in net sales to $1,518,494, the relationship between these two items rose to 8.61 times. In year A, the net working capital increased to $192,345, an increase of 9.0 per cent, but the net sales expanded to $2,078,946, or 36.8 per cent. With the greater proportionate increase in net sales, the ratio with the net working capital continued to go up to 10.81 times, approximately 1.75 times as large as the 5-year average of the median for this particular line of business.

Condensed Analysis. The condition of this concern in year *A* may be studied from two different angles: What should be the normal financial condition of a manufacturer of shirts with a tangible net worth in the neighborhood of $340,000, what volume of net sales should be sustained, what should be a typical amount of receivables, inventory, current assets, current liabilities, and fixed assets? Or, on the assumption that net sales should be sustained around $2,078,000, how much additional funds should be invested in the business to support this volume?

The 5-year average for manufacturers of men's shirts, underwear, and pajamas gives a turnover of tangible net worth of 4.85 times and a turnover of net working capital of 6.15 times. On the basis of a tangible net worth of $340,199 and of a net working capital of $192,345, we would estimate normal annual net sales of $1,650,000 and $1,183,000 respectively, or an average volume between these two estimates of $1,417,500.

The 5-year average of net sales to inventory in this line is 5.2 times, which, on the basis of typical net sales of $1,417,500, would allow a year-end inventory of approximately $272,500. On the basis that the inventory would represent 101.1 per cent of the net working capital, we would have an inventory figure of $194,000. An average of these two estimated inventory figures would give typical inventory of approximately $233,250 for a concern in this line of business with a tangible net worth of $340,000 and net sales of $1,417,500.

The actual inventory at the end of year *A* was $497,139. If the inventory were reduced to $233,250 on the smaller volume, the difference of $263,889 would be released. Part of this sum would be offset by receivables if the concern were operating without the services of a factor. How much? The receivables in year *C* disclosed an average collection period of 56 days and in year *B* of 63 days. If the receivables based on sales of $1,417,500 disclosed an average collection period of 60 days, they would amount to $236,000. The difference between the reduction in inventory of $263,889 and the increase in the receivables from $37,325 to $236,000, or $198,675, would provide increased cash of $65,214 to reduce current liabilities. On this basis the current assets consisting of cash of $12,376, receivables of $236,000, and inventory of $233,250 would amount to $481,626, and the current liabilities to $289,281, which would give a current ratio of 1.66, representing a somewhat improved financial condition.

A reduction in net sales from $2,078,946 to $1,417,500 would be a reduction of 31.9 per cent. In fact, the suggested normal sales would be lower than the actual net sales for year *B*. While this reduction from overtrading to a normal volume would automatically bring the current assets and the current liabilities into somewhat better line, one problem would not be solved, the problem of the heavy fixed assets. The typical concern in this line has 6.4 per cent of its tangible net worth invested in fixed assets; on a tangible net worth of $340,199 that would amount to only $21,770. Instead of this sum, the Shirt Mfg. Co., Inc., in year A had over 8 times this dollar amount, or actually $173,988 invested in fixed assets, representing 51.2 per cent of the tangible net worth. As early as year B, the management had overinvested in fixed assets, and in year A the greatly expanded investment in plant facilities exaggerated this overbalance. The error in judgment had already been made. Little could be done about this feature unless part of the facilities could be sold from time to time.

The second problem is the problem of pricing, which would need careful study and analysis. Prices presumably were set low on the large anticipated volume of overtrading; that policy certainly showed handsome net profits, amounting to $58,108 in year A. If the volume of sales were consciously reduced so that the internal financial condition would be reasonably more stable, then it might be necessary, expedient, and practical to raise prices moderately. Without some such change, the net profits would greatly decrease and possibly evaporate.

That is one way to analyze this picture. How about the other—on the assumption that the existing volume of $2,078,946 should be sustained, how much additional money should be invested in the business? With the typical 5-year average turnover of 4.85 times for the tangible net worth and 6.15 times for net working capital, the tangible net worth to support this volume of net sales would be $434,000, and the net working capital would be $338,000. The difference between adequate tangible net worth of $434,000 and the actual tangible net worth of $340,199 is in the neighborhood of $90,800. The difference between the adequate net working capital of $338,000 and the actual net working capital of $192,345 is approximately $146,000. The average between these required sums, $90,800 and $146,000, would give $118,400, the amount of funds needed to be invested in the tangible net worth and kept in liquid assets to support the approximate existing volume of business.

Whether additional funds of $118,400 could be raised and invested in the business, provided the management could be made to realize the practicability and desirability of a change in policies, is another problem. If the management could be so convinced or educated, then the other question to be answered would be whether the management had all or part of the necessary funds. If the management had no additional funds or only a portion of them, then it would be a question of selling either 5 per cent cumulative preferred stock or common stock to friends or to local businessmen interested and willing to put funds into the venture.

Even on this basis the investment in fixed assets would be top-heavy.

Fixed assets of $173,988 would represent 35.8 per cent of the enlarged tangible net worth of $458,599, a percentage materially higher than is typical in this line of business.

As a matter of practical business judgment, the chances are 99 out of 100 that the management would not deviate one iota from the policy it had pursued in operating this concern. Managements who overtrade are convinced in their own minds that a large volume of business is the only way to operate successfully—and by successfully they mean the maximum of profits in the immediate future, which is a different matter from the more far-sighted policy of the maximum profits over several years in the future. Overtrading puts great strains on operations, and these strains are disclosed by the unbalanced financial condition of the balance sheet. It is a real management that recognizes how crucial these strains are and operates accordingly; most managements realize only in a general way that a business is being operated under some difficulty but they have no clear idea of the exact reason for the difficulties until liabilities become so burdensome that financial embarrassment is around the corner.

Manufacturer of Woolen Cloth

Woolen Cloth Mills, Inc., was organized 37 years ago with a paid-in capital of $500,000 in the state of Rhode Island. Over the years the capitalization has been changed several times. At the end of year A, operations were being conducted on a paid-in capital of $198,000 six per cent cumulative preferred stock, $1,500,000 common stock, and a surplus of $1,925,619. Operations are centered in a series of plants located on an 80-acre plot of land, the mill buildings having an aggregate floor area of 1,000,000 square feet. Approximately 2,000 employees are on the pay roll when the mill is operating at capacity.

Products consist of woolen piece goods for men's and boys' suits, topcoating, mackinaws, and blankets. The principal product is woolen piece goods which are sold to manufacturers of men's and boys' suits and coats. The comparative figures for the past three fiscal years appear in Schedule 52.

In year C, operations were conducted with a nominal net profit of $35,293. Dividends of $14,907, representing 6 per cent on the $248,450 of cumulative preferred stock, were paid, and the difference of $20,386 was retained to augment the surplus. In year B, the net sales increased 56.9 per cent, and the net profits expanded to the very substantial return of $470,460. Dividends of only $13,395 were declared, the balance of $456,975 being retained in the business. In year A, the net sales reached a high point in the history of the business, 155.8 per cent greater than the sales in year C, but the net profits at $476,677 were only slightly in excess of the net profits in year B. Dividends of 6 per cent, aggregating $11,880, were paid on the outstanding cumulative preferred stock and $75,000 on the outstanding common stock. Even after the payment of these dividends, $389,797 was transferred to surplus.

WOOLEN CLOTH MILLS, INC. [Schedule 52]
Comparative Figures for Years Ended June 30, 19—

	(C) Three Years Ago	(B) Two Years Ago	(A) One Year Ago
ASSETS			
Cash....................	$ 135,378	$ 172,305	$ 251,940
Accounts Receivable..........	1,001,813	1,298,942	996,445
Inventory...................	1,404,473	1,619,002	2,940,160
Current Assets..............	$2,541,664	$3,090,294	$ 4,188,545
Fixed Assets, Net............	1,662,705	1,811,022	2,388,570
Cash Value of Life Insurance...	135,763	154,919	174,000
Investments.................	84,630	82,697	78,955
Miscellaneous Receivables......	....	....	84,446
Deferred...................	4,706	4,855	4,658
TOTAL..................	$4,399,468	$5,143,742	$ 6,919,174
LIABILITIES			
Notes Payable to Banks.......	$1,375,000	$1,575,000	$ 2,650,000
Due Officers and Employees....	....	19,242	30,000
Accounts Payable............	49,067	92,838	111,867
Accruals....................	134,634	74,588	165,996
Reserve for Taxes............	13,560	123,002	337,692
Current Liabilities...........	$1,572,261	$1,884,670	$ 3,295,555
6% Cumulative Pref. Stock....	248,450	223,250	198,000
Common Stock..............	1,500,000	1,500,000	1,500,000
Surplus....................	1,078,757	1,535,822	1,925,619
TOTAL..................	$4,399,468	$5,143,742	$ 6,919,174
Net Working Capital..........	$ 969,403	$1,205,579	$ 892,990
Current Ratio................	1.62	1.64	1.27
Tangible Net Worth...........	$2,827,207	$3,259,072	$ 3,623,619
Net Sales...................	$4,862,922	$7,633,032	$12,439,656
Net Profit..................	35,293	470,460	476,677
Dividends..................	14,907	13,395	86,880

For many years insurance has been carried on the lives of two of the officers for the benefit of the corporation, $600,000 on the life of the president and $400,000 on the life of the vice-president. The cash surrender values of these insurance policies have grown steadily. In year C, the cash surrender value amounted to $135,763, in year B to $154,919, and in year A to $174,000. These items are carried as slow assets in the comparative figures, but the analyst should always remember that cash surrender value of life insurance is an extremely valuable asset and in emergencies has helped many business enterprises.

The item of investments decreased moderately from $84,630 in year C to $78,955 in year A. At no time over these 3 years did this item include more than a nominal stock interest in any business enterprise. In year A, the item comprised 22 separate investments, the smallest amounting to $620 and the largest to $4,680. Several of the items represented stock in corporations that had failed and had been reorganized, stock having been received in settlement of creditor obligations. In other cases, the stock interest represented investments in local enterprises which the management felt should have their support, such as the local electric company, the local gas company, and a local taxicab company. Few of the investments gave any return and all items were written down each year to reasonable values.

Very strangly, a substantial item of miscellaneous receivables of $84,446 appeared in year A. No such item had appeared in the balance sheets of either year C or year B. Upon investigation it was learned that miscellaneous receivables really consisted of two items, one for $4,446 representing a loan to one of the officers of the corporation to pay off the balance of a maturing mortgage on his residence, and the other a loan of $80,000 to a well-known manufacturer of men's clothing that was a large customer of Woolen Cloth Mills, Inc. An examination of the comparative balance sheets of this suit manufacturer clearly showed an overtrading condition; additional credit could not be obtained from a bank, and so the loan of $80,000 had been sought from the management of this mill. The loan was to run for 6 months, but whether it would be paid off or only partially reduced at maturity would be a mystery so long as the concern continued to overtrade. The loan had been granted as a business policy to protect the customer relationship.

Over the 3-year period the tangible net worth had increased each year as a result of the retained earnings. At the same time the net working capital had increased for the same reason from $969,403 to $1,205,579 in year B, and then decreased quite materially in year A to $892,990, a figure lower than the net working capital in year C. This decrease had been brought about by the very substantial increase in the net depreciated value of the fixed assets from $1,811,022 to $2,388,570, the introduction of the item of miscellaneous receivables of $84,446, and the usual expansion in the cash surrender value of life insurance.

While these changes were taking place, the current assets expanded from $2,541,664 to $4,188,545, the difference being made up almost entirely by the increase of $1,535,687 in the inventory. As the current assets increased, so did the current liabilities, but naturally by a somewhat different amount. The current liabilities amounted to $1,572,261 in year C, $1,884,670 in year B, and $3,295,555 in year A. But of all the changes that took place over these 3 years, the most unusual was the relationship between net sales and net working capital. Here is that comparison:

	Year C	Year B	Year A
Net Sales........................	$4,862,922	$7,633,032	$12,439,656
Net Working Capital................	969,403	1,205,579	892,990
Ratio of Net Sales to Net Working Capital.......................	5.02	6.33	13.93

With net sales of $4,862,922 and net working capital of $969,403 in year C, the ratio between these two items was 5.02 times. In year B, the net sales increased to $7,633,032 and the net working capital to $1,205,579, giving a ratio of 6.33 times. In year A, the net sales went to $12,439,656, and the net working capital dropped to $892,990. The relationship between these items now increased to 13.93 times.

No 5-year average of typical ratios has been computed for woolen cloth mills. A typical ratio of net sales to net working capital for this line of manufacturing would range, however, between 3.00 times and 3.50 times. If we use 3.25 as an average, it is easily seen to what extent Woolen Cloth Mills, Inc., was overtrading. In year C the turnover was 54.5 per cent greater than this average, in year B 94.7 per cent, and in year A 328.7 per cent. Each year the overtrading became more and more evident.

Condensed Analysis. The outstanding improvement over these years took place in the collection period. The average collection period was 75 days in year C, 62 days in year B, and 29 days in year A, a remarkable change during the last year. On the other hand, other management policies were not so soundly conceived or executed. The inventory expanded to an excessive figure, and in that process the current liabilities became heavy. The fixed assets, as a result of an expansion program undertaken in year A, became out of line.

The typical woolen cloth mill has an inventory on its statement date of raw wool, wool in process, and finished piece goods which approximates its net working capital. In contrast, the inventory at $1,404,473 in year C was 144.9 per cent of the net working capital, at $1,619,002 in year B was 134.1 per cent of the net working capital, and in year A at $2,940,160 was 392.2 per cent. The relationship of net sales to inventory was 3.46, 4.71, and 4.23 times respectively, ratios far better than the average. As we learned in Chap. XII, however, the inventory should never exceed the net working capital. That ratio was out of line for each year on the statement date and in year A, very excessively so.

As a result of carrying the heavy inventory, the current liabilities in year A, amounting to $3,295,555, were heavy. Where the average ratio of current liabilities to tangible net worth of a woolen mill on its statement date is around 30 per cent, here the figure was 91.2 per cent. A reduction in the inventory from $2,940,160 to $940,160 would release $2,000,000 cash and would reduce the current liabilities in year A to $1,295,555, which would represent 35.7 per cent of the tangible net worth, a very satisfactory relationship.

It would, however, be impossible to reduce the inventory by $2,000,000 and keep the inventory proportionately reduced throughout the year without reducing the annual volume of business below $6,000,000. It would take excellent management to handle that volume on the reduced inventory. So the problem here of overtrading, as in so many other cases, comes down in theory to whether the management, to put its house in order, would prefer consciously to cut its annual sales in half, or to invest in the business additional funds, which in this case would approximate $3,000,000. As a practical matter, probably neither policy would be followed. The management will continue to overtrade as long and as intensively as it is able to produce the maximum of immediate profits.

The situation here would have been somewhat less strained if $577,548 had not been used to expand the plant facilities in year A. The concern would have been in far sounder shape if these funds had been kept in current assets in year A to increase and to support the net working capital. The annual sales then could not have risen to $12,439,656, as the plants in existence in year B probably could not have produced the yardage of cloth to provide sales of this figure.

TYPICAL RATIOS OF NET SALES TO NET WORKING CAPITAL

The operating management of every business enterprise desires increased sales, as, above a certain point, sales bring into effect the law of increasing returns. Above that point, the cost per unit of producing a product drops, the cost of wholesaling or retailing a quantity of merchandise is lowered, and net profits increase at a more rapid rate. It might cost $50,000 to produce one automobile, but 500,000 of the same model can be produced at $1,600 each.

Ever-increasing sales will be the alpha and omega of the business world as long as the profit motive and the institution of the private ownership of property serve their broad fundamental purposes. But in the process of continued economic expansion, the business enterprise, to be successful, must be guided by policies that are based upon the clear understanding that increased sales must be constantly accompanied by a healthy collection period, moderate inventories, moderate fixed assets, adequate tangible net worth, and sufficient net working capital.

No greater mistake can be made than to attempt to do all the business that comes one's way. Frequently it is more desirable from the financial point of view to turn aside that portion of the business which promises to be only temporary, or which can be taken only by incurring risks of an unusual sort, the most important of which are heavy inventory and heavy liabilities. It is well to keep in mind that a profit forgone leaves a business enterprise more comfortable than a loss actually incurred. A concern is far better off if it fails to make a $45,000 profit than if it becomes subject to a $45,000 loss.

If net working capital is too small, there are three solutions: (1) increase the net working capital by retained earnings in current assets, (2) raise additional capital by the sale of stock or, in the case of proprietorships and firms, by the investment of additional cash funds, to be retained as current assets, and (3) reduce the volume of business. Which solution, or combination of solutions, should be followed depends upon the circumstances and upon the ability of the management to grasp the significance of a particular situation.

Maxim

The ratio of net sales to net working capital which should normally be maintained varies between manufacturers, wholesalers, and retailers, and also between the various lines of business activity in each of these three main types of operation. There is no broad standard. Among manufacturers, for example, the 5-year average of the median ratio of net sales to net working capital ranges from a high of 17.31 times for packers of meats and provisions, followed by 15.76 for bakeries, and 13.47 for manufacturers of dresses, to a low represented by manufacturers of agricultural implements and machinery with a 5-year average of 3.06 times, manufacturers of drugs with 3.15 times, and manufacturers of hardware and tools with 3.46 times.

Among wholesalers there is a natural tendency to have higher turnover relationships as the net sales per dollar of investment tend to be greater. The highest 5-year average of net sales to net working capital is disclosed by wholesalers of meat and poultry with 22.51 times, followed by wholesalers of cigars, cigarettes, and tobacco with 19.31 times, and wholesalers of baked goods with 15.88 times. For wholesalers, the lowest turnover is shown by wholesalers of men's furnishings with a 5-year average of 3.34 times, wholesalers of hardware with 3.75 times, and wholesalers of paints, lacquer, and varnishes with 3.86 times. Among retailers, this ratio ranges from a 5-year average of 21.16 times for independent grocery and meat markets to a low of 2.17 times for furniture stores, making at least half of their sales on installment.

Lines of Business Activity	Number of Times					
	Median					Five-year Average
	1955	1956	1957	1958	1959	
MANUFACTURERS						
Agricultural Implements and Machinery	2.94	2.64	2.70	3.49	3.52	3.06
Airplane Parts and Accessories	5.78	6.66	6.67	7.09	4.98	6.24
Automobile Parts and Accessories	4.60	4.65	3.69	3.85	4.65	4.29
Bakers	15.85	18.49	14.06	15.75	14.67	15.76
Bedsprings and Mattresses	5.45	5.30	4.51	4.36	6.29	5.18
Bodies, Auto, Bus, and Truck	5.39	5.26	5.57	4.17	5.21	5.12
Bolts, Screws, Nuts, and Nails	4.78	4.71	4.38	3.55	4.62	4.41
Breweries	9.99	8.27	8.26	9.14	8.62	8.86
Chemicals, Industrial	3.87	4.37	4.35	4.69	4.26	4.31
Coats and Suits, Men's and Boys'	4.96	5.48	5.24	4.88	5.13	5.14
Coats and Suits, Women's	5.72	7.33	8.70	7.32	9.23	7.66
Confectionery	6.27	5.56	6.70	6.36	6.45	6.27
Contractors, Building Construction	10.37	10.83	9.00	8.84	8.49	9.51
Contractors, Electrical	6.08	5.36	7.48	5.43	5.61	5.99
Cotton Cloth Mills	4.66	3.33	3.58	3.90	3.91	3.88
Cotton Goods, Converters, Non-factored	4.16	3.19	3.11	3.70	6.55	4.14
Dresses, Rayon, Silk, and Acetate	13.12	13.45	14.67	14.60	11.50	13.47
Drugs	3.13	3.03	3.35	3.15	3.11	3.15
Electrical Parts and Supplies	4.65	4.70	4.58	3.76	4.44	4.43
Foundries	4.98	5.23	4.50	4.05	4.33	4.62
Fruits and Vegetables, Canners	4.62	4.87	4.69	7.50	4.69	5.27
Furniture	5.29	4.78	4.90	4.27	5.34	4.92
Hardware and Tools	2.95	3.52	3.36	3.42	4.05	3.46
Hosiery	4.85	4.95	4.49	4.08	4.09	4.49
Lumber	4.32	4.02	3.72	3.67	3.14	3.77
Machine Shops	3.82	4.24	4.50	3.28	4.71	4.11
Machinery, Industrial	3.72	3.89	3.69	3.07	3.11	3.50
Meats and Provisions, Packers	16.61	15.20	16.88	20.32	17.52	17.31
Metal Stampings	5.83	5.59	5.01	3.78	4.16	4.87
Outerwear, Knitted	7.32	8.25	7.61	8.87	7.88	7.99
Overalls and Work Clothing	4.09	4.28	4.30	3.95	4.26	4.18
Paints, Varnishes, and Lacquers	4.54	4.53	4.78	4.42	4.95	4.64
Paper	4.98	4.77	4.86	4.17	4.96	4.75
Paper Boxes	6.17	6.45	6.15	5.35	6.40	6.10
Petroleum, Integrated Corporations	6.02	5.26	5.40	4.95	5.50	5.43
Printers, Job	6.51	7.64	6.58	7.05	7.91	7.14
Radio Parts and Supplies	4.29	4.99	4.68	4.20	4.56	4.54
Shirts, Underwear, and Pajamas, Men's	5.91	6.05	5.78	5.91	7.12	6.15
Shoes, Men's, Women's, and Children's	3.99	4.46	4.13	3.97	3.93	4.10
Soft Drinks and Carbonated Water, Bottlers	6.50	8.29	8.46	6.60	11.67	8.30
Steel, Structural Fabricators (Sell on Short Terms)	5.15	5.36	4.73	4.89	5.02	5.03
Stoves, Ranges, and Ovens	4.15	4.38	4.64	4.27	4.64	4.42

Ratios of Net Sales to Net Working Capital (*Continued*)

[**Schedule 53** (*Cont.*)]

Lines of Business Activity	Number of Times					
	Median					Five-year Average
	1955	1956	1957	1958	1959	
Wholesalers						
Automobile Parts and Accessories....	4.73	4.87	4.63	4.07	4.23	4.51
Baked Goods......................	15.78	17.02	18.57	14.06	13.98	15.88
Cigars, Cigarettes, and Tobacco......	23.75	17.53	17.55	18.52	19.20	19.31
Drugs and Drug Sundries...........	6.91	6.98	6.83	6.62	6.33	6.73
Dry Goods.......................	4.55	4.90	4.71	5.29	5.33	4.96
Electrical Parts and Supplies........	6.40	6.60	5.86	6.06	5.92	6.17
Fruits and Produce, Fresh...........	18.21	16.14	15.80	14.00	13.90	15.61
Furnishings, Men's.................	3.66	3.21	3.38	3.16	3.28	3.34
Gasoline, Fuel Oil, and Lubricating Oil	14.23	14.36	14.07	12.29	13.51	13.69
Groceries........................	10.09	10.57	10.71	10.07	10.85	10.46
Hardware........................	3.81	4.09	3.62	3.38	3.87	3.75
Hosiery and Underwear.............	5.32	5.15	4.90	4.27	5.83	5.09
Household Appliances, Electrical.....	8.29	7.87	6.32	7.35	7.23	7.41
Lumber..........................	9.67	7.61	7.25	5.89	5.96	7.28
Lumber and Building Materials......	6.06	4.56	4.92	5.72	5.45	5.34
Meat and Poultry..................	16.80	20.41	19.77	26.84	28.73	22.51
Paints, Varnishes, and Lacquers......	4.47	3.48	3.69	3.57	4.08	3.86
Paper............................	7.15	6.36	6.37	6.54	6.36	6.56
Plumbing and Heating Supplies......	4.74	4.83	4.38	4.02	4.42	4.48
Shoes, Men's, Women's, and Children's.........................	5.83	5.51	4.61	4.82	5.28	5.21
Wines and Liquors.................	9.07	8.95	8.51	9.46	10.35	9.27
Retailers						
Clothing, Men's and Boys'..........	3.11	3.20	3.14	2.96	3.08	3.10
Department Stores.................	4.03	4.02	3.95	3.82	3.91	3.95
Furniture, 50 Per Cent or More Installment......................	1.96	1.98	2.38	2.30	2.21	2.17
Groceries and Meats, Independent...	22.45	17.83	18.73	25.28	21.49	21.16
Lumber and Building Materials......	4.24	3.87	3.35	3.07	3.20	3.55
Shoes............................	4.12	4.72	5.01	4.83	5.26	4.79
Women's Specialty Shops...........	4.95	4.97	4.92	4.57	4.90	4.86

This ratio tends to be high in those lines which handle a large volume of sales per investment on account of short terms of sale, such as packers of meat and vegetables, wholesalers of cigars, cigarettes, and tobacco, and wholesalers of fresh fruits and vegetables. The ratio also tends to be high among those divisions of trade where the investment in fixed assets is the highest, as in these cases the net working capital is generally moderate or even low.

THEORY AND PROBLEMS

1. What does the ratio of net sales to net working capital indicate?

2. Why is the ratio of net sales to net working capital complementary to the ratio of net sales to tangible net worth?

3. Determine the ratio of net sales to net working capital for the following 2 years. Then explain whether, in your opinion, the increase in this ratio indicates improvement.

	Two Years Ago	One Year Ago
Net Sales	$860,100	$920,730
Current Assets	320,960	310,726
Current Liabilities	120,428	285,740

4. The figures of the Wholesale Grocery Corporation have been set up in comparative columns for the last three fiscal years as shown below. These figures are not audited.

WHOLESALE GROCERY CORPORATION
Comparative Figures for Years Ended December 31, 19—

	(C) Three Years Ago	(B) Two Years Ago	(A) One Year Ago
ASSETS			
Cash	$ 7,629	$ 12,904	$ 11,232
Notes Receivable	1,300	1,206	16
Accounts Receivable	65,149	73,777	58,075
Merchandise	149,370	214,929	205,306
Current Assets	$ 223,448	$ 302,816	$ 274,629
Fixed Assets, Net	1,709	6,094	7,446
Investments	143,137	146,860	149,766
Advances	211,390	215,338	217,222
Miscellaneous Receivables	....	....	1,408
TOTAL	$ 579,684	$ 671,108	$ 650,471
LIABILITIES			
Notes Payable to Bank	$ 80,000	$ 130,000	$ 120,000
Accounts Payable	34,045	60,193	39,235
Accruals	....	1,657	994
Current Liabilities	$ 114,045	$ 191,850	$ 160,229
Common Stock	50,000	50,000	50,000
Retained Earnings	415,639	429,258	440,242
TOTAL	$ 579,684	$ 671,108	$ 650,471
Net Working Capital	$ 109,403	$ 110,966	$ 114,400
Current Ratio	1.96	1.59	1.71
Tangible Net Worth	$ 465,639	$ 479,258	$ 490,242
Net Sales	$1,001,716	$1,272,244	$1,673,080
Net Profits	1,946	13,619	10,984
Dividends	None	None	None

NOTES: (1) The item of *Investments*, carried at $149,766 in the balance sheet for year *A*, contains a minority interest of $143,120 in a vegetable canning corporation. No balance sheets or income statements are available on this canning company. The balance of the item of Investments, amounting to $6,646, represents miscellaneous stocks and bonds, none of which is listed on a security exchange.

(2) The item of *Advances*, carried at $217,222 in the balance sheet for year *A*, represents $168,160 loaned to the Western Sheep Co., Inc., $49,062 to 10 customer hotels and restaurants. These loans have been outstanding for several years.

Sales are made on terms of 2 per cent discount in 10 days, net 30 days. Make the following computations for each of these 3 years, and then give your interpretation of each ratio.

a. Current assets to current liabilities
b. Current liabilities to tangible net worth
c. Fixed assets to tangible net worth
d. Net sales to inventory
e. Inventory to net working capital
f. Average collection period
g. Net sales to tangible net worth
h. Net sales to net working capital

5. The consolidated balance sheet and the consolidated income statement of the Industrial Machinery Manufacturing Co., Inc., and its six subsidiaries are given below. Post the balance sheet, net sales, and net profits on a columnar sheet of paper, and then compute the net working capital and the tangible net worth. Determine the following relationships and interpret each ratio, giving a particularly thorough interpretation of the first one:

a. Net sales to net working capital
b. Current assets to current liabilities
c. Current liabilities to tangible net worth
d. Fixed assets to tangible net worth
e. Net sales to inventory
f. Average collection period
g. Net sales to tangible net worth

INDUSTRIAL MACHINERY MANUFACTURING CO., INC.
Consolidated Balance Sheet, December 31, 19—

ASSETS

Current Assets
Cash in banks and on hand.......................... $1,454,658
Accounts and notes receivable (trade), less
 reserves amounting to $173,000.................... 1,701,480
Accounts receivable—miscellaneous................. 13,700
Marketable securities, at cost (quoted market price
 $24,659)... 22,765
Inventories at average cost, less reserves, as
 certified by responsible officials
Raw materials and supplies............ $ 348,571
Work in process...................... 942,779
Finished goods....................... 6,160,423 7,451,773 $01,644,376
Long-term Receivables
Trade accounts..................................... 183,881

INDUSTRIAL MACHINERY MANUFACTURING CO., INC. *(Continued)*

Miscellaneous Investments, Advances, Etc.

U.S. Government bonds ($25,000 face amount) deposited as collateral, at cost	$ 24,672		
Other	24,394		49,066
Amounts Due by Officers and Employees (partially secured)			29,715
Net Assets of Foreign Subsidiary Companies held in countries having exchange restrictions (excluding balances on intercompany accounts)			
Current assets, net	$ 860,378		
Fixed and other assets, less reserves for depreciation	346,525		1,206,903
Fixed Assets			
Land	$ 444,692		
Buildings	$3,048,752		
Plant machinery and equipment, etc	5,007,309		
	$8,056,061		
Less: Reserves for depreciation	4,673,874	3,382,187	$ 3,826,879
Good Will			61,035
Deferred Charges			
Expenditures developing patented product not placed on a commercial basis	$ 262,488		
Prepaid insurance, taxes, etc	42,837		305,325
			$16,307,180

LIABILITIES

Current Liabilities			
Notes payable			
Banks	$ 139,608		
Others	8,858	$ 148,466	
Accounts payable		385,347	
Accrued liabilities			
Salaries, wages, and royalties	$ 387,443		
Taxes	620,268		
Dividends declared	178,732	1,186,443	$ 1,720,250
Contingent Reserve, including parent company's interest in undistributed earnings of certain foreign subsidiary companies operating in countries having exchange restrictions			502,885
Minority Interest in Foreign Subsidiary Company operating in countries having exchange restrictions			31,665
Capital Stocks			
Prior preferred stock without par value ($2.50 cumulative dividends)—stated value $48.25 per share			
Authorized 100,000 shs.			
Issued (less 1,300 shares purchased for retirement) 68,700 "		$3,314,775	
$3 Convertible preference stock without par value (dividends cumulative)— stated value $133.33⅓			
Authorized and issued 181,135 "		2,415,133	
Common stock without par value—stated value $10			
Authorized 750,000 "			
Issued 335,320¼ "		3,353,203	9,083,111

INDUSTRIAL MACHINERY MANUFACTURING CO., INC. (*Continued*)

Surplus at Dec. 31, 19—, the date as of which the Plan of Recapitalization is deemed, for purposes of the surplus account, to have been consummated.................		4,065,364
Capital Surplus arising from purchase of prior preferred stock for retirement............................		12,285
Earned Surplus		
Appropriated for purchase of 1,300 shares of prior preferred stock..................................... $	50,440	
Unappropriated..................................	841,174	891,614
Contingent Liabilities		
Notes discounted, guaranties, etc......... $ 23,148		
		$16,307,180

CONSOLIDATED INCOME STATEMENT

Gross sales, less discounts, returns, and allowances (including sales of certain foreign subsidiary companies operating in countries having exchange restrictions, the profits from which are eliminated below)....................		$11,217,696
Deduct:		
Cost of goods sold, exclusive of taxes and depreciation..		6,514,953
Manufacturing profit before taxes and provision for depreciation..................................		$ 4,702,743
Deduct:		
Administrative, selling, and general expenses..........	$2,733,555	
Taxes (excluding provision for Federal income taxes amounting to $93,000 shown below)...............	648,645	
Interest on borrowed money.......................	9,221	
Depreciation......................................	358,422	3,749,843
		$ 952,900
Add: Cash discounts on purchases, interest, etc.........		77,487
		$ 1,030,387
Deduct: Provision for Federal income taxes.............		93,000
		$ 937,387
Deduct:		
Unrealized loss on foreign exchange (including $82,174 applicable to certain foreign subsidiary companies operating in countries having exchange restrictions)..		143,584
Consolidated net income for the year, before deductions shown below..........................		$ 793,803
Less:		
Profits earned by certain foreign subsidiary companies operating in countries having exchange restrictions, after deducting $82,174 for unrealized loss on foreign exchange:		
Minority interest's share....................... $	6,218	
Parent company's share transferred to contingent reserve...................................	18,031	24,249
Balance carried to earned surplus.............		$ 769.554

6. If you had just acquired control of the Industrial Machinery Manufacturing Co., Inc., what financial and operating policies would you follow to improve the financial condition and net profits in the years immediately ahead?

7. What types of commercial and industrial business enterprises tend to have a high ratio of net sales to net working capital?

PART IV

Comparative Analysis of Balance Sheets

PART IV *consists of two chapters that describe, in theory and in practice, the method of comparative analysis that has been used extensively but somewhat less thoroughly in Chaps. VI to XV, along with internal balance sheet analysis. Comparative balance sheet analysis is the study of the trend of the same items or computed items in two or more balance sheets of the same business enterprise on different dates; it is also the study of the trend of the proportions, that is, internal ratios computed from these figures, as of the different dates. Comparative balance sheet analysis is most conclusive and comprehensive only when based on a thorough knowledge of internal ratios. In this process the dates of successive balance sheets and a knowledge of the place of such dates in the natural business year of a particular line of business activity are significant. It is highly desirable that successive yearly balance sheets be drawn off on the same date each year and so represent the financial condition of a business enterprise at the same point in the natural business-year cycle. Where a series of two or more balance sheets are drawn off on different dates in successive years, it is often extremely difficult to make a sound comparative analysis. The analyst must realize that such figures are not strictly comparable and he must know why they are not comparable. Comparative analysis includes a description of the method of computing a statement of sources and applications of funds and the advantages to be obtained from this statement. Such a statement high-lights the changes in financial condition between two balance sheet dates, where funds have come from, and how those funds have been used.*

CHAPTER XVI

Comparative Analysis of Balance Sheets

The technique of comparative balance sheet analysis has already been used extensively in a practical way in Chaps. VI to XV. In each of these chapters three groups of three comparative balance sheets were set up and analyzed on a wide variety of manufacturers, wholesalers, and retailers. It might, however, be expedient to explain the theory of the technique that has been used and to accompany the explanation with applicable examples.

Internal balance sheet analysis is concerned with the study of proportions between items or groups of items in a balance sheet, and between items, groups of items, and computed items (net working capital and tangible net worth) with net sales. Comparative balance sheet analysis is the study of the trend of the same items, groups of items, and computed items in two or more balance sheets of the same business enterprise on different dates, and the study of the trend of the proportions (internal ratios) computed from these figures as of the different dates. Comparative balance sheet analysis is most conclusive and comprehensive only when based on a thorough knowledge of internal as well as comparative analysis. Without the knowledge of internal analysis, it may be extremely misleading. The great advantage in comparative analysis is that it portrays the trends of particular features of a business enterprise and of the enterprise as a whole.

If a train is moving forward at a known rate of speed, it is reasonable to assume that it will continue to move at approximately the same rate unless some obstacle interrupts its progress abruptly, or the motive power is increased or decreased. Similarly, it is reasonable to assume that unless some drastic change takes place in a business, it will continue to move in the same general direction as indicated by its comparative trends. It was on this assumption that the American Institute of Accountants wrote in a letter to the New York Stock Exchange, " . . . The changes in the balance sheets from year to year are usually more significant than the balance sheets themselves."[1] While this assertion may well be somewhat exaggerated, there is no doubt that in particular cases these changes from one year to another may be of greater importance than the internal relationship of selected items.

In the extensive number of cases that have been studied in the preceding chapters, comparative balance sheets with net working capital, current ratio, tangible net worth, net sales, net profits after all Federal income taxes, and dividends have been set up in comparative columns following the technique described in Chap. IV. By this method the amounts at which the different asset and liability items, current assets, current liabilities, net working capital, current ratio, tangible net worth, net sales, net profits, and dividends appear on successive dates are on the same horizontal line. As the result of this method of posting comparative figures, a comparison of each item from one year to another may easily be made.

About 1900, James G. Cannon took the progressive step of posting successive balance sheets in parallel vertical columns. He became the first analyst to make this simple mechanical arrangement a consistent policy in studying comparative financial statements. His study probably consisted more in noticing changes in important items in successive financial statements than in analyzing the trends of selected internal ratios.

By 1906, banking institutions had made little progress in following Cannon's lead and in setting up figures in comparative form. In that year, Charles W. Reihl in an article entitled "Credit Department of a Bank" published a very brief comparative statement form and advocated its wider adoption and use.[2] This form, unlike those now in wide use, did not provide for the comparison of all balance sheet items. There was space on the form for figures from nine comparative balance sheets, but the only items specifically listed were active (or current) assets, liabilities, surplus, active (net working capital) assets, other assets, net worth, outside resources for proprietorships or partnerships, date of statement, annual sales, and losses by bad debts. Progress in the development of the comparative setup of financial statements from that time to about 1923 was quite steady and consistent. Full comparative forms calling for all items in balance sheets and income statements are now in use by all progressive banking institutions, the mercantile agencies, and the publishers of industrial manuals.

---

[1] Letter dated Sept. 22, 1932, signed by George O. May as chairman of the Special Committee on Cooperation with Stock Exchanges. Published in *Audits of Corporate Accounts, Correspondence between the Special Committee on Co-operation with Stock Exchanges of the American Institute of Accountants and the Committee on Stock List of the New York Stock Exchange*, 1932–1934, p. 10.

[2] *Bankers Magazine*, Vol. 72, pp. 408–417, March, 1906.

IMPORTANCE OF BALANCE SHEET DATE

In comparative analysis, two sets of figures which are 1 month apart, 1 year apart, or 10 years apart may be set up in comparative columns for study. In the vast majority of cases that an analyst will study, the sets of figures will be separated by yearly intervals. Three, ten, or twenty sets of figures also may be posted in comparative columns, depending upon the length of time the analysis is to cover.

Occasionally, two sets of figures, which are separated by one or by a very few months, will be studied. In such a study one needs to be familiar with the seasonal nature of the particular line of business. Suppose, for example, a June 30 balance sheet of a manufacturer of candy is being compared with a September 30 balance sheet of the same year. Liabilities will normally be at a low point in June and at a high point in September. Receivables, inventory, and current liabilities will be low in June and much higher and generally increasing in September. An analyst must understand this situation. In contrast, the comparison of two or more fiscal balance sheets dated June 30 in consecutive years would normally be taken off at the same point of the season in the business year. Receivables, inventory, and current liabilities would be at the low point for each year, unless, because of some unusual influences, the natural business year was somewhat off balance.

A still more difficult set of balance sheets to analyze, without similar intimate background information, is a series of figures for consecutive years but with a different balance sheet date for each year. A balance sheet for year D might be dated June 30; a balance sheet for year C, September 30; a balance sheet for year B, April 22; and a balance sheet for year A, October 16. Each balance sheet would portray a condition at a different point in the natural business year of the particular line of business.

Every business enterprise has a fiscal date; and whenever possible, figures should be obtained for analysis as of that fiscal date for consecutive years. Moreover, it is most unusual for a balance sheet for representative concerns to be prepared on any date except the first or the last day of the month. Small businesses sometimes issue unaudited balance sheets on irregular dates. Under this circumstance, the analyst would normally wonder why the balance sheet for year B was dated April 22 and the balance sheet for year A was dated October 16. Often such a date is a day or two following the liquidation of some heavy liability. In this situation, every effort should be made to obtain balance sheets as of the fiscal date for year D, year C, year B, and, if the fiscal date was prior to October 16, also in year A. If it is necessary to analyze figures at odd dates, every effort should be made to discover why the odd date was used, and whether any unusual change occurred in the financial condition during the month preceding the statement date. In comparative statement analysis, balance sheets should be as comparable as it is reasonably possible to obtain them; that means drawn off on the same day each year and according to the same accounting principles.

Desirability of Consecutive Yearly Figures

Two balance sheets of the same business enterprise separated by a period of 10 years may be used for comparative analysis just as if they were 3 months or 12 months apart. Two balance sheets separated by a period of 10 years, but both financial statements drawn off on the same fiscal date, would certainly indicate the quantity changes in every asset and liability item and also the difference in important ratios between the two dates. This information, however, would be relatively moderate compared with the data that would be obtained from a series of 10 consecutive balance sheets, one on each fiscal date for the entire 10-year period. During that period many items may have increased substantially and then decreased. Other items may have been reduced and then increased.

A new plant, for example, may have been erected 9 years ago at a cost of $500,000. The net depreciated value of the fixed assets after the erection of the plant may have been $700,000. Over the intervening years the improvements which had been capitalized, less the accumulated depreciation, may have brought the depreciated value of the fixed assets at the end of the 10 years down to $400,000. The beginning and the ending balance sheets, if they were the only ones available, would show an increase in the depreciated value of the fixed assets from $200,000 to $400,000. With 10 consecutive yearly balance sheets available, the entire story, with the sudden increase from $200,000 to $700,000 in the fixed assets 9 years ago and then a steady decrease in the meantime, would be clear from even a casual study of the figures.

When the new plant was erected, it may have been largely financed by an issue of $400,000 four per cent 10-year debentures. Over the years, the debentures may have been reduced gradually from year to year and the balance of $150,000 called for payment 2 years ago. The beginning and ending balance sheets would disclose no debentures. The 10 consecutive yearly fiscal balance sheets would show the sudden rise of this funded debt item 9 years ago and the gradual reduction to extinction 2 years ago.

If the important internal ratios are determined for each year so that the internal analysis of each set of figures may be correlated with the comparative analysis, the deductions of the analyst become even more enlightening. To the knowledge of the fluctuations in each item is now added the qualitative interpretations of the important items. If the value of the fixed assets carried 9 years ago at $700,000 represented 80 per cent of the tangible net worth, that fact becomes available. Successive balance sheets would then disclose a gradual reduction in this heavy percentage as depreciation is earned and kept in the current assets and as a portion of the yearly net profits is retained in the business as current assets. The value of the fixed assets at $400,000 in year A may now be in splendid proportion, representing only 31 per cent of the tangible net worth.

When the $400,000 of debentures were issued, the funded debt may have represented 128 per cent of the net working capital, a very high percentage. A computation of this ratio for yearly internal analysis would have shown some fluctuation over the years, but with a downward tendency and final extinction when the $150,000 balance was paid off 2 years ago. A computation of selected ratios for each balance sheet would give the basis for analyzing the fluctuations in the internal make-up of the figures; some ratios would show healthy stability throughout the 10-year period, others would show fluctuations up and down, but explanations from the management, or from someone close to the management, would shed light upon the policies and the decisions that brought about the changes in the ratios.

The beginning and the ending balance sheets would also show an increase or decrease in net working capital and an increase or decrease in tangible net worth. The comparative yearly balance sheets would show the exact story in both items from year to year, probably fluctuations up and down, possibly a steady increase in the tangible net worth. Similar information would be readily available regarding every other item in the balance sheets, in income statements, and in all the important ratios. It is clearly evident why consecutive yearly balance sheets over the years are of the greatest value to the analyst in comparative analysis.

DIFFERENCES IN DOLLAR AMOUNTS

To the young analyst it is often expedient when studying two or more sets of comparative figures to add one more column, that column to contain the differences in dollar amounts in each item between the first and last set of figures. The experienced analyst follows this procedure in particularly complicated cases, not because it adds information that is not readily available at a glance, but because it crystallizes and high-lights the differences over the period. If an item has increased, a plus sign appears before the amount of the increase in this column; if an item has decreased, a minus sign appears before the amount of the decrease.

Manufacturer of Controlled Mechanism

The Controlled Mechanism Corporation was incorporated under the laws of the state of Connecticut 8 years ago with a nominal capitalization. The paid-in capital was increased from time to time and at the end of year *A* consisted of common stock carried at $60,000, capital surplus of $89,372, and retained earnings of $49,114. During the first 2 years of its existence, activities were concentrated on basic experimental and research work. Gradually the business became established and by the end of year *B* operations were being conducted on a tangible net worth of $124,685, with a healthy financial condition.

This concern operates in the highly specialized business of designing, developing, and manufacturing various types of engineering, computing, and controlled mechanisms and devices that are used primarily in aerial navigation. These products include position computers, lunar computers, automatic Mercator chart boards, and dead-reckoning tracers. All manufacturing is carried on in one plant.

The comparative figures for year *B* and year *A* are given in Schedule 54. The third column in this schedule gives the dollar changes upward and downward for each item between these two sets of fiscal figures. Most of the items show increases, the most important being the increase in the totals on both sides of the balance sheet of $202,186, in the total liabilities of $173,396, in the fixed assets of $85,570, in the serial notes payable of $67,375, in the development expense of $61,325, and in the net sales of $60,322. Seven items show decreases, cash of $1,097, due from officers of $1,445, prepaid items of $63, deferred royalty income of $12,000, a quite substantial shrinkage in net working capital of $64,116, current ratio of 1.24, and tangible net worth of $20,535.

The change in any one or in several of the items between year *B* and year *A* may readily be determined without the use of this increase-decrease column. There is no doubt, however, that, where used, this column does throw the important changes, either upward or downward, into bold relief. To the analyst, the significance of these changes should become immediately apparent. Instead of studying these figures by discussing only the outstanding features, the practice which has been generally followed in this volume, let us take up each figure, item by item, and analyze the significance of its trend, whether that significance is of minor or considerable importance. This is the manner in which an analyst would study the figures mentally.

Cash. Cash decreased $1,097 between the 2 years. The cash of $58,938 in year *B* was entirely unrestricted. Of the cash of $57,841 in the balance sheet for year *A*, $26,763 was restricted and in a separate bank account. This cash was advanced by one customer and could be used only to pay for merchandise and services needed to fulfill a specific contract. Moreover, cash could be withdrawn from this special account only by the signature of a cosigner who was a representative of this particular customer.

Receivables. Notes receivable increased $820 and accounts receivable increased $14,129, a total increase in receivables of $14,949. On the basis

CONTROLLED MECHANISM CORPORATION [Schedule 54]
Comparative Figures for Years Ended December 31, 19—

	(B) Two Years Ago	(A) One Year Ago	Increase or Decrease
ASSETS			
Cash..........................	$ 58,938	$ 57,841	−$ 1,097
Notes Receivable..................	502	1,322	+ 820
Accounts Receivable...............	22,204	36,333	+ 14,129
Inventory.......................	72,853	100,906	+ 28,053
Current Assets....................	$154,497	$196,402	+$ 41,905
Fixed Assets, Net.................	71,481	157,051	+ 85,570
Leasehold Improvements...........	15,727	27,966	+ 12,239
Due from Officers.................	2,567	1,122	− 1,445
Prepaid Items....................	2,252	2,189	− 63
Miscellaneous Receivables..........	7,000	9,655	+ 2,655
Development Expenses.............	33,010	94,335	+ 61,325
Patents..........................	1	1	....
TOTAL.......................	$286,535	$488,721	+$202,186
LIABILITIES			
Due to Banks.....................	$.......	$ 30,000	+$ 30,000
Accounts Payable.................	9,117	31,935	+ 22,818
Accruals........................	12,544	35,526	+ 22,982
Advances from Customer...........	43,178	71,738	+ 28,560
Due to Officers...................	....	1,661	+ 1,661
Current Liabilities.................	$ 64,839	$170,860	+$106,021
Serial Notes Payable..............	45,000	112,375	+ 67,375
Total Liabilities..................	$109,839	$283,235	+$173,396
Deferred Royalty Income..........	19,000	7,000	− 12,000
Common Stock....................	60,000	60,000	....
Capital Surplus..................	89,372	89,372	....
Retained Earnings................	8,324	49,114	+ 40,790
TOTAL.......................	$286,535	$488,721	+$202,186
Net Working Capital...............	$ 89,658	$ 25,542	−$ 64,116
Current Ratio.....................	2.39	1.15	− 1.24
Tangible Net Worth...............	$124,685	$104,150	−$ 20,535
Net Sales.......................	$208,794	$269,116	+$ 60,322
Net Profit.......................	10,319	40,790	+ 30,471
Dividends.......................	None	None	....

of the net sales for the respective years, the receivables give an average collection period of 40 days for year B, and of 51 days for year A. The collection periods in this case have little significance, as all manufacturing is carried on under specific contracts and the manner of payment is carefully stipulated in each contract. What is significant is the fact that $32,702 of the receivables was assigned to a depository as security for the bank loan of $30,000 outstanding at the end of year A.

Inventory. Inventory increased $28,053. The ratio of net sales to inventory was 2.9 for year B, and 2.6 for year A. The relationship in year B was satisfactory for a manufacturer producing highly technical apparatus under contracts. The relationship for year A was a little low, due to the fact that the inventory increased too much during the year and not because net sales were low. Moreover, the inventory was 395.1 per cent of the net working capital, a very unbalanced condition; this was due both to a slightly heavy inventory and to inadequate net working capital at the end of year A.

Current Assets. Current assets increased $41,095 during the year. This increase is the sum of the net differences in the four items going to make up the current assets.

Fixed Assets. The net depreciated value of the fixed assets, that is, the land, plant, and equipment, went up from $71,481 to $157,051, or a very substantial difference of $85,570. The fixed assets in year B represented 57.4 per cent of the tangible net worth, which was a reasonable proportion. The fixed assets in year A represented 151.1 per cent of the tangible net worth, a very excessive proportion. These additions to the plant assets were largely financed by increased borrowings in the form of serial notes payable in 3 to 6 years. If arrangements had not been made well in advance of this expansion program to obtain funds in this manner, the program could not have been carried out; the financial condition of this business could not have carried the burden. There is a real question as to whether the program was sound.

Leasehold Improvements. Leasehold improvements expanded $12,239. If leasehold improvements were grouped with the fixed assets, the two items in year B would become $87,208, and in year A $185,017. These two items would then represent 70.0 per cent of the tangible net worth in year B, which would be heavy, and 177.8 per cent in year A, which would be clearly and unquestionably excessive.

Due from Officers. Due from officers decreased $1,445, representing payments on account. This item was a nominal one in both years—$2,567 in year B and only $1,122 in year A.

Prepaid Items. Prepaid items decreased $63. This item likewise was moderate in both years—$2,252 in year B and $2,189 in year A.

Miscellaneous Receivables. Miscellaneous receivables increased $2,655. In year B, this item was $7,000 and represented a loan made in year E to a neighboring concern from which Controlled Mechanism Corporation purchased specialized equipment. The loan was a demand loan but the financial condition of this debtor was very extended and indicated no immediate likelihood of repayment. The $7,000 was also owing in year A. The increase of $2,655 in year A represented notes due in 12 months taken for the sale of secondhand machinery which could no longer be used efficiently. The concern that purchased the machinery was located in a nearby town. Its affairs were in fairly well-balanced condition and these notes would undoubtedly be met promptly at maturity.

Development Expenses. Development expenses increased $61,325. Here was a very spectacular increase in the expenditures for experimentation, expenditures that had been capitalized instead of being charged to expense. A more conservative financial management would have made this charge to expense.[3] The results of this accounting policy will be examined in the consideration of a later item. Development expenses, like good will, patents, and trade marks, is an intangible asset.

Patents. Patents were carried in both balance sheets at the same amount, $1. Like development expenses, patents is an intangible item. Unlike the item of development expenses, which was increased by the capitalization of expenditures during the year, the value at which a constantly increasing number of patents was being carried on the books had remained unchanged.

Total. The total of all the asset items increased $202,186. This figure is the sum of the net changes in the four items comprising the current assets and the six items showing changes among the fixed, miscellaneous, and intangible assets.

Due to Banks. Due to banks increased $30,000. No bank borrowings were disclosed in the balance sheet at the end of year B. During year A, bank borrowings had reached a peak of $75,000 but had been paid down to $30,000 at the end of the year. These borrowings were not on the unsecured straight note of the corporation; they were secured on the date of the balance sheet by the assignment on a nonnotification basis, as mentioned above, of $32,702 of the accounts receivable.

Accounts Payable. Accounts payable increased $22,818. Both the amounts due to banks and the accounts payable would normally expand along with any increase in the receivables and the inventory in the current assets. This increase in accounts payable, however, was moderate, because of the rather substantial increase in other current liability items.

Accruals. Accruals expanded $22,982. In addition to the typical accrual items of rent, wages, and taxes, this item in year B included a small amount of royalties payable, and in year A a substantial amount of roy-

---

[3] A skilled analyst has considered such situations very clearly in the following words: "To the writer profits from operation mean little or nothing as a strength indicator if more than offset by delayed but essential and necessary direct deductions from net worth. The real and important matter from the standpoint of any operation for any year or series of years is as to whether or not the subject has increased or been compelled to decrease its net worth."—WALL, ALEXANDER, *How to Evaluate Financial Statements*, p. 125 (Harper & Brothers, New York, 1936).

alties payable. These royalties were due for the use of six basic patents utilized by Controlled Mechanism Corporation in its operations, which were owned by others.

Advances from Customers. Advances from customers expanded $28,560. Because of the light working capital position and the extended financial condition disclosed by the low ratio of the current assets to current liabilities at the end of year *A*, the high percentage of current liabilities to the tangible net worth, and the high percentage of fixed assets to tangible net worth, customers had to advance sufficient cash funds so that this concern could fulfill its contracts. As the bank loan was paid down, the bank was reluctant to increase its extension of credit even on a secured basis. The officers had no additional funds which they could invest in capital stock, so the last resort to obtain necessary funds was the customers. The high quality of the research work and the experimentation of this enterprise had provided several products which were far superior to anything on the market, and in order to obtain these particular key products, the customers were perfectly willing to make cash advances to assist in financing operations. To protect themselves against any unwarranted use of these particular funds, the larger customers stipulated that the advances be set up in special checking accounts and that a cosigner be necessary to withdraw any funds. This arrangement, while cumbersome and complicated, was effective.

Due to Officers. Due to officers increased $1,661. No amounts were due at the end of year *B*. This amount at the end of year *A* represented a bonus to be paid in January.

Current Liabilities. Current liabilities increased $106,021, representing the sum of the net increases in the five individual current liability items. This increase is a very large one, the current liabilities increasing from $64,839 in year *B* to $170,860 in year *A*. As a general rule, the total of current liabilities fluctuates in close relationship to the changes in the total current assets. Here the fluctuation was far greater. While the current assets had increased $41,905, the current liabilities had increased $106,-021. The far greater increase was due to the fact that liquid assets to the approximate extent of the increase in fixed assets of $85,570 and of the increase in leasehold improvements of $12,239 had been withdrawn from current assets and put into slow assets.

Serial Notes Payable. Serial notes payable increased $67,375, rising from $45,000 at the end of year *B* to $112,375 at the end of year *A*. These notes were due serially in various amounts from 3 to 6 years after year *A*. They were secured by a first mortgage on the land, plant, and equipment and carried interest at the rate of 4 per cent per annum. The notes were held by a prominent life insurance company. The outstanding notes of $45,000 at the end of year *B* were rather moderate. The outstanding notes of $112,375 at the end of year A were heavy and excessive from every angle. Whereas the funded debt of a business enterprise should not exceed the net working capital, at the end of A the serial notes were 439.9 per cent as large as the net working capital. It might well be that difficulty will be experienced in meeting these maturities out of earnings or in refinancing these obligations as they mature. The situation is not healthy.

Total Liabilities. Total liabilities went up $173,396. This increase represented the combined increases of the current liabilities and of the serial notes payable. At the end of year B, the total liabilities amounted to $109,839 and, while substantial, were not out of line with the tangible net worth. At the end of year A, the total liabilities amounted to $283,235 and were 272.1 per cent of the tangible net worth, a very unbalanced relationship. This relationship became heavy not only because of the large increase in the total liabilities but also because of the shrinkage in the tangible net worth.

Deferred Royalty Income. Deferred royalty income decreased $12,000. This item arose in year C when one of the representative business corporations of the country made a cash payment to Controlled Mechanism Corporation for the use of certain of its patents over a 4-year period. Part of this cash payment became income in year C, and the balance was set up as this deferred royalty income account to be prorated as income over the period. The decrease of $12,000 represented the amount taken into income in year A.

Common Stock. Common stock remained unchanged at $60,000 during both years.

Capital Surplus. Capital surplus likewise remained unchanged at $89,372. This item arose in year D when common stock was sold for cash. The excess above $10 per share was set up on the books as capital surplus.

Retained Earnings. Retained earnings increased $40,790. This sum represented the book net earnings shown by the income statement for year A.

Total. The total of the liability items, deferred royalty income, and capital items increased $202,186. This increase balances the increase in the total of the asset items. There is no significance in this item, the significance being in the changes in the items which make up this figure.

Net Working Capital. Net working capital decreased $64,116. Here is a decrease of fundamental importance. Net working capital of $89,658 at the end of year B was turned over 2.33 times in net sales and was adequate to support the volume of business. The ratio between the net sales of $269,116 and the net working capital of $25,542 at the end of year A was 10.53. At this rate, the net working capital was inadequate and was turning over as fast as a counterfeit nickel. To operate a business on inadequate net working capital, as has already been stated, calls for heavy liabilities. This accompanying characteristic is clearly portrayed in these figures. The great shrinkage in net working capital was brought about by investing relatively large sums of liquid assets in fixed assets, leasehold improvements, and development expenses, with minor increases in other slow assets. The shrinkage would have been even greater if increases had not been recorded in the amount of the outstanding serial notes payable and the retained earnings.

Current Ratio. The current ratio decreased 51.9 per cent. At 2.39 in year *B*, the current ratio indicated a generally satisfactory relationship between the current assets and the current liabilities. At 1.15 in year *A*, it indicated a proportionately unsatisfactory and top-heavy condition. The margin between the current assets and the current liabilities for year *A* provided very slim security to any creditor and should certainly have indicated a fevered condition to the active management.

Tangible Net Worth. Tangible net worth decreased $20,535. This decrease is the difference between the increase in development expenses of $61,325 and the increase in the retained earnings of $40,790. The two items of development expenses and patents, as already mentioned, are intangible items, and so were deducted from the total of the common stock, capital surplus, and retained earnings of the respective years to arrive at the tangible net worth. The increase in development expenses in excess of the retained *book* net profits (which is also the increase in retained earnings) would bring a corresponding reduction in the tangible net worth. So, we have the unusual situation of an increase in retained earnings and at the same time a decrease in tangible net worth brought about by the capitalization of a certain type of expense. It is interesting to note at the end of year *A* that the capitalized development expenses carried at $94,335 was greatly in excess of the retained earnings of $49,114. If there were no item of development expenses, the retained earnings of $49,114 would be turned into a deficit figure of the difference, or of $45,221.

Net Sales. Net sales increased $60,322, representing favorable progress for the year from the viewpoint of increased business. Notwithstanding this progress, as has been indicated by the discussion of several of the items above, the internal financial condition of this enterprise had changed radically from an attractive, sound condition at the end of year *B* to a weak condition unbalanced by excessive fixed assets, top-heavy liabilities, and undernourished net working capital at the end of year *A*. The financial condition had become more than unsound; it represented a condition where oxygen was needed to keep the patient alive.

Net Profit. The net profit, or, as it has been termed during the past few pages in the discussion of the affairs of this concern, the *book* net profit, increased $30,471. The book net profit of $10,319 for year *B* was 4.94 per cent on net sales and 8.28 per cent on the tangible net worth. The book net profit of $40,790 for year *A* was 15.16 per cent on net sales and 39.18 per cent on the tangible net worth. Figures for both years were satisfactory and for year *A* apparently quite attractive. At this point, however, we must recall our discussion on net profits and realize that a final profit figure is, at times, arrived at by accounting conventions. In this case development expenses to the extent of $61,325 were capitalized during the year and it was on the basis of this practice that the net profit of $40,790 was recorded. On the other hand, if no part of these expenditures aggregating $61,325 had been capitalized but all had been charged to expense, the income statement instead of showing a net profit of $40,790 would have recorded a net loss for the year of $20,535, and the per cent profit on net sales and on the tangible net worth would have been turned into percentage losses. More conservative management would have followed this latter practice, and it is the one that would normally be followed by the analyst. So, whereas at first glance a very substantial net profit seemed to have been earned, actually a net loss was incurred for the year, on top of the decidedly unbalanced internal condition.

Dividends. No dividends were paid for either year.

EXPLANATION OF CHANGES

In comparative analysis the analyst, along with understanding the significance of the upward and downward changes in dollar amounts, should endeavor to search out and understand the policies, conscious or unconscious, which brought about those changes. Too often the analyst is given only the bare figures for study, with no supplementary facts or explanations. Trends may be obtained in comparative analysis, but the lack of supplemental information hinders at times the most precise deductions.

In Chap. XI, for example, the comparative balance sheets of the Men's Suit Co., Inc., were analyzed. Those figures disclosed steadily increasing year-end inventories on fluctuating annual net sales, giving a slower and slower relationship between these two important items. At the same time, the current liabilities increased from $196,353 in year *C* to $361,471 in year *A*. The current liabilities at the end of year *A* were 253.5 per cent of the tangible net worth.

There is no doubt that the condition of this business, at the end of year *A*, was extended with excessive current liabilities. When the inventory, which was the primary cause of this heavy debt, was analyzed, there were two possibilities: if the inventory on June 30 of year *A* included a substantial carry-over of spring suits, the business was in a weak condition; if the inventory contained a nominal carry-over of spring suits or none at all but contained instead fall and winter fabrics, suits, and topcoats, the heavy condition was materially mitigated. Which of these two extremes, or what condition between the two, existed could not possibly be determined from the bare figures. The necessary explanation had to come from the active management, or from someone close to the active management such as the accountant, the banker, or a principal creditor.

The technique of obtaining essential supplementary information for a complete understanding of comparative figures has been used many times in this volume. Although the practice is one that is widely used and is highly desirable, in many situations the analyst has only the figures for analysis; he must make the best use of them that he can. The following case will high-light the desirability of obtaining additional information where practical and reasonable.

Manufacturer and Retailer of Candy

The Pure Candy Corporation was organized 28 year ago. Operations were carried on profitably until 12 years ago when the owner sold control to a new group. The management of the new group proved incompetent and after 2 years of dwindling profits, there was ushered in an extended period of losses which ran for 8 consecutive years. In year C an experienced candy group purchased control. In year B the corner was turned with a net profit of $5,804, and in year A a very substantial net profit of $391,664, or 22.23 per cent on the tangible net worth, was recorded. This showing was most unusual.

In addition to manufacturing candy, this concern conducts a chain of 112 retail candy stores located in the states of Connecticut, Delaware, Maryland, New Jersey, New York, and Pennsylvania. In 52 of the stores, in addition to the distribution of candy, soda fountains are also operated. A small portion of the annual output of candy is sold at. wholesale.

The comparative figures of this corporation for year B and for year A, with the upward and downward dollar changes in each item in the third column, appear in Schedule 55. This comparative schedule is an unusual one as it discloses several radical changes. Along with an internal and comparative analysis of the figures, these changes will be discussed in the light of supplementary explanatory information, to illustrate the enlightenment thrown on figures by an intimate knowledge of managerial policies. It is management that makes an enterprise tick.

The most important changes between the figures for year B and year A are the spectacular increase in the fixed assets from $108,996 to $1,870,034, the expansion in the total liabilities from $359,207 to $1,892,386, represented largely by the item of real estate mortgages, the shrink-

Pure Candy Corporation [Schedule 55]
Comparative Figures for Years Ended December 31, 19—

	(B) Two Years Ago	(A) One Year Ago	Increase or Decrease
ASSETS			
Cash........................	$ 983,827	$ 646,718	−$ 337,109
Accounts Receivable..........	49,879	110,148	+ 60,269
Inventory...................	634,613	790,338	+ 155,725
Current Assets..............	$1,668,319	$1,547,204	−$ 121,115
Fixed Assets, Net............	108,996	1,870,034	+ 1,761,038
Investments............. ..	76,148	76,148	....
Miscellaneous Receivables.....	502	2,544	+ 2,042
Deferred Charges............	57,233	158,144	+ 100,911
Good Will...................	1	1	....
TOTAL.................	$1,911,199	$3,654,075	+$1,742,876
LIABILITIES			
Accounts Payable............	$ 268,223	$ 338,699	+$ 70,476
Accruals....................	20,716	77,633	+ 56,917
Reserve for Taxes............	70,268	162,800	+ 92,532
Dividends Payable...........	....	121,254	+ 121,254
Mortgage Maturities.........	....	8,000	+ 8,000
Current Liabilities...........	$ 359,207	$ 708,386	+$ 349,179
Real Estate Mortgages........	....	1,184,000	+ 1,184,000
Total Liabilities..............	$ 359,207	$1,892,386	+$1,533,179
Common Stock..............	1,273,259	1,212,546	− 60,713
Paid-in Surplus..............	227,741	227,741	....
Retained Earnings,..........	50,992	321,402	+ 270,410
TOTAL.................	$1,911,199	$3,654,075	+$1,742,876
Net Working Capital..........	$1,309,112	$ 838,818	−$ 470,294
Current Ratio................	4.64	2.18	− 2.46
Tangible Net Worth..........	$1,551,991	$1,761,688	+$ 209,697
Net Sales....................	$7,451,724	$9,569,238	+$2,117,514
Net Profit...................	5,804	391,664	+ 385,860
Dividends...................	None	121,254	+ 121,254

age in the net working capital from $1,309,112 to $838,818, the increase in net sales, and the very great increase in the net profits. Instead of analyzing these changes in the light of their importance, the technique used in the preceding example of treating the items in consecutive order will be followed.

Cash. During the interval reflected by the two comparative balance sheets, the cash was reduced from $983,827 to $646,718, or a decrease of $337,109. In year *B* the cash of $983,827 was an exceptionally strong feature of the balance sheet, especially as no part had been created by bank borrowings. The cash of $646,718 on hand at the end of year *A* was also sufficient for any normal needs. The decrease was brought about by rather substantial expenditures during the year in renovating many of the retail stores. All such costs involved cash expenditures. The reason for undertaking this improvement program will be outlined a little later.

Accounts Receivable. The accounts receivable amounted to $110,148 at the end of year *A*, having increased $60,269. The management declined to give any information regarding the amount of the net sales which represented wholesale volume on credit terms for both year *B* and year *A*, so there was no basis for analyzing these two figures. It would seem evident, however, that the wholesale business had increased during the year unless the accounts receivable at the end of year *A* included a considerable number of delinquent accounts. The increase during the year was relatively large.

Confectionery is generally sold by manufacturers on terms of 2 per cent discount in 10 days, net 30 days. The Pure Candy Corporation used these standard selling terms. Wholesale candy sales probably increased in November and December over the average monthly sales. If the average receivables on the books during the year amounted to $80,000 and the average collection period was 40 days, then the wholesale sales for year *A* would have ranged in the neighborhood of $750,000. This figure would have represented only 7.8 per cent of the net sales for year *A*.

Inventory. The inventory increased $155,725, or 24.5 per cent. For year *B* the ratio of net sales to the inventory was 11.7 times, and for year *A*, notwithstanding the increase, 12.1 times. As the net sales increased, the ratio with the closing inventory increased. That was certainly a favorable omen. Moreover, for both years, the ratio was the same or somewhat higher than the 5-year average of 8.2 times.

For year *B* the ratio of inventory to net working capital was 48.5 per cent, and for year *A*, 94.3 per cent. Here was quite a radical change, from a most favorable proportion to one which at best might be considered fair. The change was brought about, not by any great expansion in inventory because the management believed in speculating in inventory, but by the decrease in net working capital. As will be shown later, this decrease was due to the management policy of utilizing a considerable proportion of the net working capital for the rehabilitation of rundown retail stores, the purchase of a factory, and the purchase of two buildings where strategic retail stores were located. The conversion of some portion of the current assets into fixed assets brought about the decrease in net working capital and consequently gave this higher ratio with the inventory.

During year A, the method of pricing inventory was changed from first-in first-out to last-in first-out. The effect of this change was a reduction in the value of the inventory by $122,624. As a result, the valuation of the inventory carried in the balance sheet at the end of year A was somewhat more conservative than at the end of year B.

Current Assets. The current assets decreased moderately from $1,668,-319 to $1,547,204. The shrinkage in the cash of $337,109 was greater than the increases in the accounts receivable and the inventory by this difference in the current assets of $121,115.

Fixed Assets. Here was a most spectacular change, from $108,996 at the end of year B to $1,870,034 at the end of year A, or an increase of $1,761,038. The $108,996 at the end of year B represented machinery, equipment, and leasehold improvements at cost, less reserve for depreciation of $6,871. No more detailed breakdown was available. The following interesting segregation of the item was available as of the end of year A:

Factory land, building, machinery, and equipment, less depreciation....	$ 428,348
Other land and buildings, less depreciation..........................	856,758
Store equipment and leasehold improvements, less depreciation........	584,928
	$1,870,034

Throughout year B, the machinery and equipment had been located in a leased building. During the latter part of year B, the management decided to purchase a plant ideally located on a railroad siding in a near-by city. Early in year A, title to this plant was acquired and the machinery and equipment were moved into it. The purchase price was $404,000 of which $10,000 was cash and the remainder a first mortgage containing terms which will be described later.

Of the 112 retail stores, 2 had been located without change, 16 and 18 years respectively, in buildings which the management had decided were ideal locations. The rental charges, however, in relation to the volume of business at these locations were heavy. After a careful study, it was decided that the corporation would be better off if the two buildings and the underlying land could be acquired at certain prices. Both structures were office buildings and, at this particular time, were earning profits after taxes, interest, depreciation, and full upkeep. After considerable negotiations, titles to both locations and buildings were acquired, one for $200,000 and the other for $656,756. A cash payment of $18,000 was made in the purchase of the first building with a first mortgage of $182,000; and a cash payment of $40,756 in the purchase of the second structure with a first mortgage of $616,000.

When the present management acquired control of the business in year B, the retail stores were antiquated and neglected. Almost without exception, every store had to be modernized and streamlined to present an inviting appearance to draw customers. A program of renovation and remodeling was carried on throughout year A. Simultaneously, where leases were high they were renegotiated. If rentals could not be brought to a satisfactory basis, the stores were operated until the expiration of leases. Where leases expired during the year and could not be renegotiated satisfactorily the stores were closed. Extensive cash was used to carry out this program. Store equipment and leasehold improvements at the end of year A were carried on the books at the substantial sum of $584,928.

At the end of year B, the fixed assets represented only 7.0 per cent of the tangible net worth. At the end of year A, the fixed assets represented 106.1 per cent of tangible net worth. That was quite a change, not entirely in the right direction. There was absolutely no doubt that at the end of year A the concern was overloaded with fixed assets; in fact the concern was now in the real estate and office building business as well as in the candy manufacturing and distributing business. Here was a condition that might well be the cause of headaches in the future.

It is a very practical policy, as a general rule, for the operating management of a business enterprise to concentrate on the object for which the business is launched. There is too great temptation to take on side lines, which may or may not be profitable, and thus divert capital and energy into channels to which sufficient attention and knowledge cannot be given so that losses occur.

Investments. No change occurred in the item of investments during the year. Even though there was no change, an understanding of how the item arose would have some bearing upon the analysis. The prior management acquired 5 years ago a 48 per cent common stock interest in a manufacturer of hard candy located on the Pacific coast. At no time has this concern had outstanding any preferred stock; its capitalization consisted solely of common stock. This investment was made on the basis of the book value of the stock, an up-to-date appraisal of the fixed assets having been made for this purpose. The investment cost $76,148 and it has remained unchanged on the books of the Pure Candy Corporation over the years since that time.

A study of the comparative figures of this Pacific coast hard candy manufacturer showed that losses had been assumed every year for the past 5 years. At the end of year B, the concern had a tangible net worth of $12,622; at the end of year A it was only $8,460 and the current liabilities amounted to $21,692. The business was in a very unhealthy condition with every possibility that it would become bankrupt in the immediate future. The 48 per cent interest of the Pure Candy Corporation in the tangible net worth of $12,622 and $8,460, respectively, would represent $6,058 and $4,060. So here was an investment that at the end of year A was still being carried on the books at a cost of $76,148 when the asset had an economic value of only $4,060 and in the near future would probably be absolutely worthless. These facts could only be ascertained by studying the figures of the hard candy company and learning when the investment was made, the per cent of interest it represented, and the policy followed by the management in valuing the investment.

This situation, as explained in Chap. IV, may occur because of the so-called "conventions" of the accounting profession. One management may carry investments over the years at cost, even though the current value may be appreciably more or less. Another management may adjust such values yearly to agree with the books of the corporations or with the market values of the securities, if they are listed on a national security exchange or traded actively over the counter.

This item would have been more complicated if the Pure Candy Corporation had lent funds to the hard candy manufacturer over the years as working capital and had carried those loans, as some managements do, in the current assets. As it was, there had been no inter-company relations of any kind over the intervening years.

Miscellaneous Receivables. Miscellaneous receivables were moderate in both years, only $502 in year B and $2,544 in year A. In year B, the item represented loans to two employees. In year B, it represented loans to four employees, and $1,050 due from the sale of secondhand equipment.

Deferred Charges. The deferred charges increased $100,911 during the year. A comparative breakdown of this item for both years gave the following comparison:

	Year B	Year A
Prepaid Insurance	$31,562	$ 52,801
Prepaid Rent	15,986	35,994
Prepaid Store Rehabilitation	1,841	16,558
Prepaid Lease Commissions	4,406	20,904
Prepaid Expenses	1,903	14,889
Prepaid Taxes	1,535	16,998
	$57,233	$158,144

The individual items going to make up the total of the deferred charges in both years were quite substantial. Prepaid insurance was the largest individual item in both years, $31,562 and $52,801, respectively. Prepaid rent on retail stores was the second largest item. Then came prepaid lease commissions on rental negotiations, prepaid taxes, prepaid store rehabilitation, and a miscellaneous item of general prepaid expenses.

Good Will. Good will was carried unchanged in both balance sheets at $1.

Total. Total assets increased $1,742,876 during the year. The increase in this total was exceeded by the increase in the single item of fixed assets. Every item in the assets except two expanded during the year; those two were cash and good will.

Accounts Payable. Accounts payable increased $70,476. This item consisted entirely of unpaid invoices for merchandise. The amount was quite moderate in both year B and year A, as the corporation was in sound current condition and took advantage of all discounts when terms of purchase allowed discounts. This fact was verified by an outside trade investigation which indicated a splendid paying record with all suppliers of raw materials.

Accruals. In this particular case, accruals represented unpaid salaries and wages and nothing else. The item increased from $20,716 to $77,633 during the year because wages were higher, there were more employees, and the end of the fiscal year broke so that salaries and wages were accrued for 2 days longer in year A than in year B.

Reserve for Taxes. This item expanded from $70,268 in year B to $162,800 in year A, an increase of $92,532. Some portion of the increase represented income taxes, some portion real estate taxes on the properties acquired during the year, and some portion sales taxes on the larger volume of business.

Dividends Payable. No dividends had been paid by this corporation for years and years. In view of the profitable operations in year A, however, a dividend of 10 per cent was declared on the par value of the common stock in December, payable in January of the following year. The obligation accordingly became a current liability and was set up on the books of the corporation at $121,254.

Mortgage Maturities. When the factory and the two office buildings were purchased during year A, the mortgage terms were quite unusual, calling for the payment of only $4,000 yearly on the mortgage on the factory, and only $2,000 each on the two buildings, or a very moderate total of $8,000. As a result only $8,000 of the total mortgage obligations became a current liability in year A. Often the current maturity is not carried as a current liability in the balance sheet as issued by the corporation or the public accountant, and the analyst must then adjust the figures to obtain a basis for a sound analysis.

Current Liabilities. Every item in the current liabilities increased during the year, bringing about a total increase for the current liabilities of $349,179, or 97.2 per cent. The current liabilities were quite moderate in relation to the current assets and the tangible net worth in both years, amounting to only 22.5 per cent of the tangible net worth at the end of year B, and 40.2 per cent at the end of year A.

Real Estate Mortgages. No real estate mortgages appeared in the balance sheet at the end of year B. The factory was purchased subject to a mortgage of $394,000, payable $4,000 annually and the balance at the end of 15 years, and carried interest at the rate of 3 per cent per annum. The two office buildings were purchased subject to first mortgages of $182,000 and $616,000 respectively; both mortgages were to be amortized at the rate of $2,000 annually; both bore interest of 4 per cent per annum, and the unpaid balance in both cases fell due at the end of 10 years. The deferred portion of these three mortgages totaled $1,184,000, which was certainly heavy, being 41.3 per cent in excess of the net working capital. In addition to the fixed assets being top-heavy, now we have run across a second accompanying disturbing factor, excessive mortgage obligations.

Total Liabilities. Total liabilities expanded from $359,207 to $1,892,386, a very rapid growth for 1 year. The expansion was brought about by the increased current liabilities and the heavy real estate mortgages. Total liabilities at the end of year B were nominal, reaching only 22.5 per cent of the tangible net worth. At the end of year A, the total liabilities were 7.4 per cent in excess of the tangible net worth, an unbalancing proportion. Here was a third disturbing factor.

Common Stock. The common stock decreased $60,713 during the year. The decrease was brought about by the redemption of that amount of common stock at par value.

Paid-in Surplus. The paid-in surplus, amounting to $227,741, has remained unchanged over the years. The item arose from the original sale of common stock at a price in excess of the par value.

Retained Earnings. Retained earnings increased $270,410, representing net profits retained in the business in excess of the declared dividends of $121,254. This increase is quite a substantial one to have taken place in any one year.

Total. The increase in the total of all liability and capital items amounted to $1,742,876 and balanced the increase in all of the asset items. All the asset items except cash and good will increased during the year. All the liability and capital items except common stock and paid-in surplus increased. The principal increase in the assets was in the fixed properties, and the principal increase in the liabilities was in real estate mortgages. Both items arose out of the same business transactions.

Net Working Capital. The net working capital decreased $470,294. This decrease was brought about by the heavy expenditure of cash to renovate, modernize, and improve the retail stores. This program was essential for the revamping of the operating policies and such expenses had to be met out of the current assets. Although the net working capital was decreased considerably, the item amounted to $838,818 at the end of year A and was adequate for the current needs of this business. The decrease would have been greater if most of the net profits for the year had not been retained in the business.

Current Ratio. During the year the current ratio dropped from 4.64 to 2.18. Ratios for both years and the component items making up the current assets and the current liabilities for both years were healthy. The Pure Candy Corporation had available substantial lines of credit at banking institutions; the fact that no part of these credit facilities was being used on either of the two statement dates substantiated the sound current condition reflected in the current ratios.

Tangible Net Worth. The tangible net worth for both year B and year A comprised the sum of the common stock at par value, the paid-in surplus, and the retained earnings less the one intangible item in the assets, namely, the good will carried at $1. The increase in the tangible net worth of $209,697 represented the difference between the net profits in excess of the dividends (of $270,410) less the decrease in the outstanding common stock. The increase for the year was attractive progress.

Net Sales. The net sales increased $2,117,514, or 28.3 per cent. An increase of 28.3 per cent in net sales in 1 year is very unusual. The relationships between the net sales and the tangible net worth and between the net sales and the net working capital were very attractive for both years. The new management showed its colors with aggressiveness by producing better candy than had ever been produced by this corporation, and by raising its prices to cover the increased cost and produce a profit. This policy worked out to perfection.

Net Profits. For year B the *book* net profits amounted to $5,804, representing a nominal return of 0.08 per cent on the net sales and 0.37 per cent on the tangible net worth. A remarkable change took place in year A. *Book* net profits amounted to $391,664, representing 4.09 per cent on the net sales and 22.23 per cent, an almost impossible percentage, on the tangible net worth.

This improvement in *book* net profit showing was most remarkable. These figures, however, like the reported net profits of the Controlled Mechanism Corporation, needed some adjustment. The adjustment here was not due to the fact that certain expenses had been capitalized but to the fact that the investment item had been carried over the years at cost. Between year B and year A the actual value of the investment, as already explained, dropped from $6,058 to $4,060, or a decrease of $1,998. This relatively nominal amount had not been taken into the income statement. Between year C and year B, the book value of the investment had decreased from $18,060 to $6,058, or the sum of $12,002. If this loss had been taken into account for year *B*, instead of a *book* net profit of $5,804, there would have been a net loss of $6,198.

At this point, one mental calculation should be kept in mind. If the inventory had been taken on the first-in first-out basis as in previous years, and not on last-in first-out, the net profit before taxes would have been $122,624 greater, less corporate income taxes. The application of this hidden profit, and the hidden loss on the investment of $1,998, would give an actual net profit for year *A*, subject to additional Federal taxes, of $512,290.

Dividends. No dividends had been paid in year *B*. As a matter of fact none were actually paid in year *A*, but a dividend of $121,254, or 10 per cent on the outstanding common stock, was declared out of the year *A* earnings to be paid in January of the following year and the appropriation was set up on the books. The dividend was a liberal one, although it took only 30.9 per cent of the *book* net profits for the year.

THEORY AND PROBLEMS

1. Explain the difference between *internal* and *comparative* analysis of financial statements. Is one technique better than the other?

2. Does the fact that comparative financial statements have different dates make any material difference in a comparative analysis of figures for successive years? What background information must the analyst have to analyze a series of such financial statements properly?

3. The following comparative financial statements have been turned over to you for your analysis and comment. As you set up these figures on columnar paper, according to your standards, you will find that it will be necessary for you to condense them and then to determine the net working capital and the tangible net worth for both years. To the right add an increase-decrease column. Then make your analysis, bringing out carefully the most important points for the consideration of the management. Suggest any pertinent changes in policies which seem desirable to you in the light of your analysis. If additional information of any kind is needed for a more thorough analysis, make a list of these points at the end of your report. (NOTE: Keep in mind that it is no more difficult to analyze a large business than a small one. The same principles apply. However, a large business is somewhat less wieldy than a small one.)

WHOLESALE DRY GOODS CORPORATION
Comparative Consolidated Balance Sheets for Years Ended December 31, 19—

	(A) One Year Ago	(B) Two Years Ago
ASSETS		
Current Assets		
Cash on hand and in banks..................	$ 2,944,909	$ 2,959,101
Accounts receivable, customers'..............	10,073,488	9,125,490
Accounts receivable, other...................	218,546	157,950
Reserve for doubtful accounts and cash discounts..	*300,000*	*300,000*
Merchandise inventories at the lower of cost or market...............................	14,485,269	12,198,198
Total Current Assets..................	$27,422,212	$24,140,739
Other Assets		
Security investments held in connection with Employees' stock sales fund		
9,622 shares common stock, at par........ $	96,220	$ 96,220
Reserve for pensions......................		
5,680 shares common stock, at par........	56,800	56,800
5% gold debentures, at cost.............	—	9,767
Other stocks and bonds valued on the basis of market quotations..................	83,366	90,000
Miscellaneous investments...................	47,937	59,296
Reserves thereagainst........................	*22,085*	*21,313*
Due on sale of equipment under contract, etc....	22,206	30,678
Loans to employees.........................	22,281	28,843
Reserve thereagainst........................	*9,500*	*9,500*
Funds in closed banks.....................	60,402	99,279
Reserves thereagainst........................	*42,022*	*65,007*
Total Other Assets..................... $	316,145	$ 375,063
Land, Buildings, Equipment, etc.		
Land, at cost.............................. $	2,561,288	$ 2,559,410
Buildings and building equipment, at cost......	6,522,657	6,524,516
Furniture, fixtures, and equipment, at cost.....	3,123,969	3,105,978
Reserve for revaluation......................	*482,400*	*544,179*
Reserve for depreciation......................	*4,000,253*	*3,800,232*
Improvements to leased premises.............	76,947	92,454
Reserve for revaluation.....................	*27,901*	*38,943*
	$ 7,774,307	$ 7,899,004
Deferred Charges		
Prepaid expenses and other deferred items .... $	390,489	$ 361,555
Reserve thereagainst........................	*3,230*	*5,336*
Debt discount and expense..................	1,720	326,013
Reserve thereagainst........................	—	*323,561*
Store improvements, etc., amortized to date....	584,161	663,108
Reserve thereagainst........................	*498,660*	*613,837*
	$474,480	$407,942
	$35,987,144	$32,822,748

WHOLESALE DRY GOODS CORPORATION (*Continued*)

	(A) One Year Ago	(B) Two Years Ago
LIABILITIES		
Current Liabilities		
Notes payable, banks..........................	$ 1,000,000	$ 2,350,000
Accounts payable, net........................	2,872,069	2,622,777
Customers' credit balances...................	94,178	73,415
Installments of funded indebtedness due within 1		
year (subsequent maturities shown below)...	80,000	605,000
Accrued interest on funded indebtedness.......	1,666	119,187
Due to employees for commissions............	255,925	140,615
Accrued bonuses pay, to officers and employees.	205,825	—
Accrued real estate, personal property, and other		
taxes.....................................	527,682	359,586
Federal taxes on income.....................	663,865	360,000
Total Current Liabilities.................	$ 5,701,210	$ 6,630,580
Funded Indebtedness		
5% debentures.............................	$ —	$ 5,100,000
5% mortgage maturing in semiannual install-		
ments of $40,000 each, less amounts maturing		
within 1 year shown above.................	320,000	400,000
	$ 320,000	$ 5,500,000
Reserves		
Reserve for pensions........................	$ 468,827	$ 515,316
Other reserves.............................	6,673	32,357
	$ 475,500	$ 547,673
Capital Stock and Surplus		
Capital stock		
5% cumulative convertible preferred stock		
Authorized, 350,000 shares of $30 par value		
each		
Issued, 283,570 shares...................	$ 8,507,100	$ —
Common stock............................		
Authorized, 2,000,000 shares of $10 par		
value each		
Issued, 1,140,970 shares, 1936 (1935, 1,138,-		
110 shares)...........................	11,409,700	11,381,100
Treasury common stock, 28,681 shares......	*286,810*	*286,810*
	$19,629,990	$11,094,290
Paid-in surplus..............................	4,624,665	4,974,723
Retained earnings...........................	5,235,779	4,075,482
	$29,490,434	$20,114,495
	$35,987,144	$32,822,748

Notes in Connection with Consolidated Balance Sheet as of December 31, Year *A*

a. Physical inventories were taken by employees and valued by the management at the lower of cost or market, first-in first-out. In accordance with established policies of the management, merchandise in transit on statement date, costing approximately $1,350,000, is not included in the inventory and/or accounts payable.

b. Particular items of land, buildings, and building equipment carried, in the aggregate, at $1,934,560 before depreciation, are security for real estate mortgage payable in the amount of $400,000.

WHOLESALE DRY GOODS CORPORATION (*Continued*)
Comparative Consolidated Income Statements

	(A) One Year Ago	(B) Two Years Ago
Gross sales, less discounts, returns, and allowances	$81,302,409	$73,085,490
Miscellaneous operating income	64,707	64,773
Total	$81,367,116	$73,150,263
Cost of goods sold (including rent, merchandise and buying, and publicity costs)	68,017,681	61,906,187
	$13,349,435	$11,244,076
Operating expenses (including selling, general and administrative, and maintenance, etc.)	$ 9,264,563	$ 8,283,603
Customers' accounts written off, less recoveries	157,620	224,459
Depreciation and amortization	358,392	370,582
Taxes (other than Federal income taxes)	664,025	515,722
	$10,444,600	$ 9,394,366
	$ 2,904,835	$ 1,849,710
Other income	143,865	109,828
	$ 3,048,700	$ 1,959,538
Other Deductions		
Interest on 5% gold debentures	$ 257,187	$ 283,438
Interest on 5% mortgage payable	22,666	26,666
Other interest	93,284	146,966
Provision for loss on funds in closed bank	10,000	10,000
Other	35,152	22,561
	$ 418,289	$ 489,631
	$ 2,630,411	$ 1,469,907
Provision for Bonuses		
Executives' incentive bonus	$ 163,825	$ —
Special wage bonuses	166,486	—
	$ 330,311	$ —
	$ 2,300,100	$ 1,469,907
Provision for Federal Taxes on Income	$ 392,000	$ 185,000
Net Profit	$ 1,908,100	$ 1,284,907

4. We have found that the following relationships are important in analyzing the balance sheets of commercial and industrial business enterprises:

1. Current assets to current liabilities
2. Current liabilities to tangible net worth
3. Total liabilities to tangible net worth
4. Funded debt to net working capital
5. Fixed assets to tangible net worth
6. Net sales to inventory
7. Inventory to net working capital
8. Average collection period
9. Net sales to tangible net worth
10. Net sales to net working capital

Write down the letters which precede each of the following questions, and to the right of each letter, place the number or numbers of the relationships listed above which would help materially in answering that particular question.

a. Is the inventory top-heavy?
b. Is there any indication that the inventory contains an unusual amount of secondhand or shoddy merchandise?
c. Are collections of receivables satisfactory?
d. Are current obligations likely to be met at maturity?
e. Is the investment in fixed assets excessive?
f. Is the concern overtrading?
g. Are current liabilities heavy?
h. Is the funded debt likely to prove a heavy burden?
i. Is the concern transacting a normal volume of business for its tangible net worth?
j. Is the total debt moderate or heavy?

5. You are president and principal owner of a corporation that has been operating a large foundry very successfully. The owners of the Southern Foundry Company, Inc., have been anxious to sell their business to you. They have submitted balance sheets for the past 3 years and certain other information to you for your preliminary study. You turned the figures over to your comptroller, asking him to condense them and post them in comparative columns for you. He has returned the comparative figures to you in the form shown on page 472. You have decided to make your own analysis of these figures. The item of *Investments*, which has represented a substantial sum over these years, puzzles you, so you telephone the president of the Southern Foundry Company, Inc. He informs you that the investments as of year *A* represent no securities listed on an exchange, that they consist of 11 items ranging from $1,100 to $195,000, all in going companies, that each item is carried at cost and not book value, and that he believes most of the items have a greater book value then cost. No dividends were received on any of these investments during the year.

Add an increase-decrease column to the comparative figures and then make as thorough an internal and comparative analysis as you can. If you believe you could increase the profits and improve the financial condition, provided you were able to acquire the business at the right price, outline the policies you would follow, based on available information.

SOUTHERN FOUNDRY COMPANY, INC.
Comparative Figures for Years Ended December 31, 19—

	(C) Three Years Ago	(B) Two Years Ago	(A) One Year Ago
ASSETS			
Cash........................	$ 7,269	$ 6,263	$ 4,073
Notes Receivable...............	20,440	16,311	3,840
Accounts Receivable...........	103,695	57,160	82,251
Merchandise..................	207,703	217,136	270,867
Dividends Receivable..........	46,020	21,510	....
Current Assets................	$ 385,127	$ 318,380	$ 361,031
Fixed Assets, Net..............	506,194	503,028	517,397
Investments...................	278,622	278,622	278,625
Miscellaneous Receivables.......	19,853	52,188	94,656
Deferred Charges.............	1,170	1,657	3,165
TOTAL...................	$1,190,966	$1,153,875	$1,254,874
LIABILITIES			
Notes Payable to Bank.........	$ 170,000	$ 157,000	$ 153,750
Notes Payable, Other...........	25,050	17,490	12,056
Accounts Payable..............	53,830	14,542	88,919
Accruals.....................	12,846	14,907	13,019
Current Liabilities..............	$ 261,726	$ 203,939	$ 267,744
Mortgage Loan.................	....	....	3,743
Deferred Bank Loan...........	....	32,500	66,250
Preferred Stock...............	95,975	95,975	95,975
Common Stock...............	200,000	200,000	200,000
Retained Earnings............	633,265	621,461	621,162
TOTAL...................	$1,190,966	$1,153,875	$1,254,874
Net Working Capital...........	$ 123,401	$ 114,441	$ 93,297
Current Ratio.................	1.47	1.51	1.35
Tangible Net Worth............	$ 929,249	$ 917,436	$ 917,137
Net Sales.....................	$ 589,937	$ 687,507	$ 882,440
Net Profits...................	4,005	(L)11,804	(L)299
Dividends....................	None	None	None

CHAPTER XVII

Statement of Sources and Applications of Funds

A statement of the sources and applications of funds, also known as a *funds statement*, is a technical device designed to high-light the changes in the financial condition of a business enterprise between two dates. A statement of this nature is somewhat related to but very different from a statement of cash receipts and disbursements. In most of the items only the net changes that take place during the period are brought into the fund statement. If the accounts receivable, for example, were $22,000 at the beginning of the year and $20,000 at the end of the year, $2,000 of funds is shown to have come from accounts receivable. As a matter of fact, the concern may have collected $100,000, more or less, on accounts receivable, and, in turn, extended credit of $98,000, more or less, but the net result during the period would have been that it converted $2,000 into funds through the accounts receivable transactions. In a statement of cash receipts and disbursements the total received and the total disbursed are shown. In a statement of sources and applications of funds only the net changes are shown, so that the outcome of a transaction or of a series of transactions upon the financial condition of a business enterprise is reflected in a more striking manner.

Funds, in this particular type of statement, are what might be termed *working capital funds* as distinguished from actual *cash funds.* When any asset is acquired, money is invested in that asset. Cash may not be paid for it, but some fund of value is given in exchange when the asset is purchased. If fixtures are purchased *on account*, the business receives a *fund* or a *fund of money*, or money value, even though no cash enters into the transaction. An increase in liabilities provides the channel, the source, from which this fund is secured. In other words, the increase in accounts payable is the source of funds in this situation, and the increase in the value of fixtures is the application of the funds.

It sometimes happens that the results of operation disclose attractive net profits in the income statement for an accounting period, but sufficient cash is not available to declare and to pay a dividend. Strange as it may

473

seem, a business concern may operate profitably, year after year, and still its financial condition may become more and more unbalanced and unsound. The statement of sources and applications of funds gives a clear answer to the question of what has become of the net profits in such a situation, and also what has become of the funds obtained from all other sources.

Such a schedule is particularly enlightening to the businessman who has no knowledge of bookkeeping and accounting and who ponders the question, "Here, my income account shows I've made profits, but I'm having more and more difficulty in paying my bills and my cash is getting smaller and smaller. Have I actually made a profit, and if I have, what has become of it?" Moreover, a financial statement of this character covering a period of many years is an illuminating document, particularly in those cases where the balance sheet has become ambiguous because of write-ups and write-downs of fixed assets, inasmuch as the effects of all book entries not involving receipts and outlays of funds are omitted from this schedule.

A statement of sources and applications of funds also offers a means of analyzing in more detail the comparison of balance sheets by a recasting of the increase and decrease column. If the statement is set up in the more thorough and currently approved manner, it also brings into analysis certain operating figures not shown in the comparative balance sheets. Such a statement emphasizes the close relation between the income statement and the beginning and the ending balance sheets. It assists in highlighting the changes that take place during a particular accounting period in the financial status of the business.

Some banks request borrowers to furnish a funds statement along with their annual balance sheet and income statement. Accounting firms frequently include this schedule as a regular feature in their audit reports, and quite a few corporations include one in their reports to stockholders.[1]

SOURCES OF FUNDS

In any business enterprise, funds come from four sources: (1) the earnings of the business, that is, the net profits; (2) an increase in the liabilities; (3) a decrease in assets such as a liquidation in current assets, the sale of fixed, miscellaneous, or intangible assets, and earned depreciation on such assets; and (4) the contribution of additional funds. Let us consider each of these four sources.

[1] In recent years the following representative corporations have included a statement of sources and applications of funds in their annual reports to stockholders; Riegel Textile Corporation, New York; Buffalo-Eclipse Corporation, Buffalo; Leslie Salt Co., San Francisco; the Champion Paper and Fibre Company, Hamilton, Ohio; and the Minnesota and Ontario Paper Company, Minneapolis.

"The Statement of Source and Application of Funds" was the subject of Bulletin No. 3, Opinions of the Accounting Principles Board of the American Institute of Certified Public Accountants dated Oct. 1963. This Bulletin contained the following statement, "The Board [Accounting Principles Board] believes that a statement of source and application of funds should be presented as supplementary information in financial reports. The inclusion of such information is not

Net Profits

The sale of merchandise, for more than cost plus the everyday operating expenses of a business, usually provides an increase in assets or a decrease in liabilities by the amount of the net profit. In other words, the net profits are reflected in an increase of the earned surplus (retained earnings) account; a corresponding expansion must take place in the assets, a corresponding reduction must take place in the liabilities, or a partial change must take place in both the assets and the liabilities. Earnings from investments and from other so-called "miscellaneous" sources likewise find their way into the income statement, as will be outlined in Chap. XIX.

The net sales shown in the income statement may be considered, in the initial state, to represent a source of funds. If all sales are cash sales, then one may visualize a picture in which the sales provide the source of the funds, and the increase in the cash is the application of the funds. The greater portion of the cash so received during the accounting period, if not all of it, is spent for operating expenses, so that by the end of the period the funds applied are in places other than in the cash account. Because of this fact, all expenses incurred are deducted from the net sales, and only the net profit remaining, if any, is shown as a net source of funds for the accounting period as a whole. Net profit, and not net sales, accordingly, is treated as the source of funds. If the expenses of the business for the period exceed the net sales, no net funds are received for the simple reason that a larger sum of money was spent for expenses than came from the sales. If there is a net loss, the amount of the loss accordingly is shown as an application of funds. *becomes*

Increase in Liabilities

An expansion in liabilities indicates an increased use of borrowed funds, or, as in the case of merchandise purchased on credit and accrued expenses, a temporary withholding of cash until the liability is met. Short or long-term borrowings, either bank borrowings, a funded debt, or loans from affiliated concerns, directors, officers, and friends increase the cash funds.

Suppose, for example, that cash of $25,000 is borrowed from a banking institution. The increase in the notes payable is the source of the fund and the increase in the cash is the application. If the cash is used immediately to acquire a fleet of auto delivery trucks, the decrease in cash will be the source, and the increase in fixed assets will be the application of the $25,000 of funds. In the balance sheet for that period, only the net changes that took place will be shown, so that the increase in the notes payable

mandatory, and it is optional as to whether it should be covered in the report of the independent accountant."

becomes the source of the funds of $25,000, and the increase in fixed assets now becomes the application. In other words, the cash account is by-passed. If the management had given the notes payable directly to the concern from which the fleet of auto trucks had been purchased, instead of borrowing the cash from the bank and paying cash for the equipment, the analysis of the movement of funds would be identical.

Decrease in Assets

The decrease in some assets may be reflected by the increase in other assets. Thus, a decrease in inventory through cash sales brings about an increase in the cash. A decrease in fixed assets through the sale of a piece of real estate for a cash down payment and a mortgage increases the cash and creates an item of mortgage receivable in the assets. A decrease in fixed assets through earned depreciation brings about an indirect increase in cash.

A flat-bed printing press, for example, is sold by a job printer in a large city to a country printer on open account terms. Funds, from the viewpoint of our statement, are exchanged but no cash is actually exchanged. Such a transaction, however, may be viewed as one in which the country printer paid cash for the printing press, and the city job printer, in turn, immediately reloaned that cash to the purchaser on open account. The effect upon the financial condition of the seller is the same in either case. In this transaction, funds are withdrawn from machinery account of the seller and are invested in accounts receivable. Before the end of the fiscal period, unless the transaction took place in the last month or two of the fiscal year, the buyer will have paid his account in cash so that the final result in a statement of the sources and applications of funds would be the same if the transaction had been a cash one in the first place. If the country printer should pay his account before the end of the period, then in the statement of sources and applications of funds, the increase and decrease in accounts receivable for this particular transaction would wash out, and the source of funds would be the reduction in the machinery account, and the application of funds would be the increase in cash.

Earned depreciation on fixed assets, earned depletion charges, earned amortization of intangible assets such as patents and bond discount, earned amortization of deferred charges, and provisions for bad debt losses, not payable in cash, are deductions from gross profit before arriving at a final net profit figure. Hence, the amount of the increase in working capital funds brought about by the earnings of net profits is adjusted upward by adding to the net profits the amount of expenses which have not required cash outlay. These items are termed *non-cash* expenses.

Contribution of Funds

The contribution of funds is not an everyday occurrence in business. When it does occur, it usually takes place in the form of a direct investment of additional capital, generally in cash, but occasionally in some other asset or assets. In the case of a corporation, this increase is shown as an increase in capital stock or capital surplus, in a rare instance as a gift. In the case of a proprietorship or a partnership, the increase is shown as an increase in the net worth.

APPLICATIONS OF FUNDS

Funds obtained from the four sources described above may be employed for or applied to four different uses: (1) a net loss of the business for the accounting period; (2) a decrease in liabilities; (3) an increase in assets, current, fixed, or miscellaneous, and intangible assets where they are obtained by acquisition in contrast to a write-up; and (4) a decrease in capital funds.

Net Losses

If the net profit for a particular accounting period is a source of funds, a net loss as shown by an income statement is an application of funds. Where a loss has been assumed, funds have gone out of the business. A net loss must be offset by either a decrease in assets or an increase in liabilities, either or both of which would be the source of funds to provide for this particular application.

Decrease in Liabilities

A decrease in liabilities, either in one or more items in the current liabilities or in a funded debt, indicates that funds are being taken out of a business. If a note of $50,000 payable to a banking institution is paid off, the result is a shrinkage in cash as the payment is made in cash. The cash might or might not show this decrease between two statement dates. If cash does not reflect the decrease, the funds probably were obtained by collecting receivables or decreasing the inventory, either or both of which would provide the cash. In the second place, the cash might be provided, not out of an asset or assets, but by allowing the accounts payable to be built up by this amount, and the cash funds normally used to pay the accounts payable then being used to pay off the bank. In the third place, the net profits might be sufficiently large to provide the cash, or a combination of these various sources might be used.

Increase in Assets

When a plant (except in the case of a write-up), inventory stocks, receivables, investments, or other assets are increased, funds are being used or applied. These funds must come from any one or any combination of the various sources of funds. If a plant is purchased for $100,000 cash, the cash is the source and the increase in fixed assets is the application. However, of the $100,000 cash, $90,000 might have been provided by a mortgage taken by an insurance company, so that as far as the balance sheet of the buyer is concerned, the source of the funds would be $10,000 from its own cash, and the other $90,000 from the mortgage obligation in the liabilities.

Decrease in Capital Funds

A decrease in capital funds generally comes about in the form of withdrawals in the case of proprietorships and partnerships, and dividend disbursements in the use of corporations. A decrease, however, may also come about by the retirement of stock.

CHANGE IN NET WORKING CAPITAL

While financial statements of this character are not standardized as to form and content, attempts to display the ebb and flow of funds through working capital rarely seem to improve their analytical value. The decrease in current assets and the increase in current liabilities as sources of funds and the reduction in current liabilities and the increase of current assets as application of funds are best handled net, by means of computing simply the change in net working capital. An increase in net working capital in this manner represents a net application of funds, and a decrease represents a net source of funds. These changes in net working capital are available from the comparative balance sheets. The net changes in the various items in the current assets and in the current liabilities during the period often are assembled in a separate supplementary schedule, and the increase or decrease in net working capital is taken into the statement as a single source or application of funds.

ILLUSTRATIONS OF FUNDS STATEMENTS

The form and content of a statement of sources and of applications of funds have been suggested by the explanations in the preceding pages of the sources of funds and the uses to which such funds are put in carrying on a business enterprise. The body of the statement generally is divided into two parts,[2] one part showing the sources and the other the applications of the funds. The two sections of the statement are always in balance, that is, their totals must always be the same amount.

Information from Comparative Balance Sheets

A statement of sources and applications of funds may be prepared from two comparative balance sheets with an accompanying increase-decrease column. From the standpoint of the balance sheet, funds may come from three sources, an increase in liabilities, a decrease in assets, and an increase in net worth. In this arrangement, the increase in net worth is used to represent two sources of funds, namely, net profits and contributions of funds. Likewise, applications represent three uses of funds, decrease in liabilities, increase in assets, and decrease in net worth. Here again, the decrease in net worth represents two uses in the more complete statement, namely, net losses and decreases in capital funds.

When the only available information from which to create a financial statement of this nature is the comparative balance sheets, the increase or decrease in the valuation reserves, such as depreciation, amortization of intangible items, and bad debts, if included in the balance sheets, must be used as the amounts of non-cash expenses. Similarly, the funds applied to the purchase of fixed assets or to the increase of outstanding accounts receivable are the net amounts shown in the increase-decrease column after applying the changes in the valuation reserves. If there has been any sale or retirement of fixed assets, or any write-off of bad or doubtful accounts, the difference between the reserves for the 2 years as shown in the increase-decrease column of the comparative balance sheet is not the true amount of those items. Any error, however, is exactly offset by a contra or compensating error occasioned by the use of the difference between the corresponding reserves to indicate the amounts of non-cash expenses. If a bad account, for example, has been written off by cross entry between accounts receivable and reserve for doubtful accounts, the accounts receivable are affected in the same amounts as the reserve for doubtful accounts. The use of the net changes in these two accounts between any 2 years is a true reflection of the net source or application of funds relating to these two items.

[2] M. B. Daniels, in *Financial Statements*, pp. 71–73 (American Accounting Association, Chicago, 1939), gives a different side to this picture. "Funds Statements," he writes, "are often presented in two equated sections, 'sources' and 'applications,' respectively, but a running form, following the style of the income statement, in which certain related sources and applications are considered together, is preferable. . . . If the final figure of the statement . . . is a negative amount, it may be referred to as an excess of applications, supplied by a reduction of working capital. A comparative statement of current assets and current liabilities should be appended in support of the closing figure of the statement."

Retail Furniture Store. The figures in Schedule 56 give the comparative balance sheets for year *B* and year *A* of the Retail Furniture Company, Inc., with an increase-decrease column to the right. These balance sheets are dated November 30 of each year.

As explained in the footnote to this schedule, these balance sheets are set up in a slightly different manner than other balance sheets used in this volume. The accounts receivable are posted gross at $134,138 and $148,-093 for year *B* and year *A*, respectively. Normally, the reserves for bad debts carried at $2,872 and $3,069 in the liability sections of the two balance sheets would be deducted from the gross amount of the respective accounts receivable, and the accounts receivable then would be carried net. To the extent of these reserves for the 2 years, the total current assets and the net working capital are inflated. Similarly, the fixed assets are carried gross at $773,249 and $783,599 in year *B* and year *A*, respectively. To obtain the net value of these assets, the reserves for depreciation carried at $140,621 and $158,572, respectively, must be deducted. These two balance sheets are posted in this manner because the respective reserves for each year are helpful in the compilation of a somewhat more complete statement of sources and applications of funds.

No detailed income statement is available, in this example, to supplement either or both of these balance sheets. From the figures, a statement of sources and applications of funds for year *A* has been compiled in three successive steps. These steps are illustrated in Schedules 57 to 59. Similar statements could be prepared covering intervals of 2, 3, 4, or more years, just as this one covers a period of 1 year, provided the beginning and ending balance sheets are available.

Schedule 57 is a detailed preliminary statement of sources and applications of funds covering the year ending November 30, year *A*. In this first step, every item in the increase-decrease column of Schedule 56, the comparative balance sheets of the Retail Furniture Company, Inc., is set up under its applicable heading, *Increases in Liabilities, Decreases in Assets,* and *Increases in Net Worth* as sources of funds; and *Decreases in Liabilities, Increases in Assets,* and *Decrease in Net Worth* as applications of funds as already explained.

Under the three broad headings of sources of funds there are 11 individual items in Schedule 57. Seven items appear under *Increases in Liabilities,* two under *Decreases in Assets,* and two under *Increases in Net Worth.* The seven items under increases in liabilities range from bank loans of $156,508 and accounts payable of $46,314 down to due to stockholders of $1,079 and reserves for bad debts of $197, or a total of $251,074. The two items representing decreases in assets are notes receivable of $2,579 and miscellaneous receivables of $441, or a total of $3,020. The two items representing increases in net worth are common stock $25,000 and retained

RETAIL FURNITURE COMPANY, INC.   [Schedule 56]
Comparative Figures for Years Ended November 30, 19—

	(B) Two Years Ago	(A) One Year Ago	Increase or Decrease
ASSETS			
Cash..........................	$ 2,764	$ 4,244	+$ 1,480
Notes Receivable..............	12,603	10,024	− 2,579
Accounts Receivable...........	134,138	148,093	+ 13,955
Inventory.....................	263,610	512,215	+ 248,605
Current Assets...............	$ 413,115	$ 674,576	+$261,461
Fixed Assets..................	773,249	783,599	+ 10,350
Investments...................	....	6,266	+ 6,266
Prepayments..................	2,759	7,766	+ 5,007
Miscellaneous Receivables......	3,746	3,305	− 441
TOTAL....................	$1,192,869	$1,475,512	+$282,643
LIABILITIES			
Due to Banks..................	$..........	$ 156,508	+$156,508
Due to Stockholders...........	13,231	14,310	+ 1,079
Accounts Payable..............	105,307	151,621	+ 46,314
Accruals......................	20,472	18,926	− 1,546
Customers' Deposits...........	10,107	8,089	− 2,018
Current Maturity of Mortgage..	28,086	35,461	+ 7,375
Accrued Taxes.................	....	21,650	+ 21,650
Current Liabilities...........	$ 177,203	$ 406,565	+$229,362
First Mortgage................	371,915	324,636	− 47,279
Total Liabilities...............	$ 549,118	$ 731,201	+$182,083
Reserves for Depreciation......	140,621	158,572	+ 17,951
Reserve for Bad Debts.........	2,872	3,069	+ 197
Common Stock................	500,000	525,000	+ 25,000
Retained Earnings............	258	57,670	+ 57,412
TOTAL....................	$1,192,869	$1,475,512	+$282,643
Net Working Capital..........	$ 235,912	$ 268,011	+$ 32,099
Tangible Net Worth............	$ 500,258	$ 582,670	+$ 82,412
Net Sales.....................	750,393	$1,242,426	+$492,033

* This caption is not in strict conformity with the terminology used in the rest of this volume, as the *reserve for bad debts*, amounting to $2,872 in year *B* and $3,069 in year *A*, carried in the liability section of these balance sheets would normally be deducted from the respective items of accounts receivable to provide a net figure of accounts receivable. The total *current assets* and the *net working capital* are inflated each year to the extent of the respective reserve for bad debts. These two balance sheets have been set up in this particular manner to provide information from which to prepare the accompanying statement of sources and applications of funds.

earnings of $57,412, or a total of $82,412. Total sources of funds in this preliminary table aggregate $336,506.

[Schedule 57]   RETAIL FURNITURE COMPANY, INC.
Step I—Detailed Preliminary Statement of Sources and Applications of Funds for
Year Ended November 30, 19—(year *A*)

SOURCES

Increases in Liabilities
Bank Loans	$156,508	
Due to Stockholders	1,079	
Accounts Payable	46,314	
Current Maturity of Mortgage	7,375	
Accrued Taxes	21,650	
Reserves for Depreciation	17,951	
Reserves for Bad Debts	197	
		$251,074

Decreases in Assets
Notes Receivable	$ 2,579	
Miscellaneous Receivables	441	
		3,020

Increases in Net Worth
Common Stock	$ 25,000	
Retained Earnings	57,412	
		82,412
Total Sources of Funds		$336,506

APPLICATIONS

Decreases in Liabilities
Accruals	$ 1,546	
Customers' Deposits	2,018	
First Mortgage	47,279	
		$ 50,843

Increases in Assets
Cash	$ 1,480	
Accounts Receivable	13,955	
Inventory	248,605	
Fixed Assets	10,350	
Investments	6,266	
Prepayments	5,007	
		285,663
Decrease in Net Worth		None
Total Funds Applied		$336,506

Under the three broad headings of applications of funds there are nine individual items. Three appear under *Decreases in Liabilities* and six under *Increases in Assets*. There are no items in this case under the heading of *Decrease in Net Worth*. The three items under decreases in liabilities are accruals of $1,546, customers' deposits of $2,018, and first mortgage of $47,279, for a total of $50,843. The six items under increases in assets range from inventory of $248,605 down to prepayments of $5,007 and cash of $1,480 for a total of $285,663. Total applications aggregate $336,506 and balance total sources of funds.

Schedule 58, the second step, is an intermediate statement. Here the various items in Schedule 57 are rearranged in accordance with the more typical grouping of items in a balance sheet. Under sources of funds there are five broad divisions, *Current Assets, Current Liabilities, Non-cash Ex-*

RETAIL FURNITURE COMPANY, INC. [Schedule **58**]

Step II—Intermediate Statement of Sources and Applications of Funds for Year Ended November 30, 19—(year *A*)

SOURCES

Current Assets		
Decreases in Notes Receivable...........................		$ 2,579
Current Liabilities		
Increased Loans from Banks.............................	$156,508	
Increased Amounts due Stockholders.....................	1,079	
Increase in Accounts Payable............................	46,314	
Increase in Current Maturity of Mortgage................	7,375	
Increase in Accrued Taxes...............................	21,650	
		232,926
Non-cash Expenses		
Reserves for Depreciation..............................	$ 17,951	
Reserves for Bad Debts.................................	197	
		18,148
Decrease in Miscellaneous Receivables......................		441
Net Worth		
Sale of Common Stock..................................	$ 25,000	
Increase in Retained Earnings..........................	57,412	
		82,412
Total Sources of Funds..................................		$336,506

APPLICATIONS

Current Assets		
Increase in Cash.......................................	$ 1,480	
Increase in Accounts Receivable........................	13,955	
Increase in Inventory..................................	248,605	
		$264,040
Increase in Other Assets		
Fixed Assets..	$ 10,350	
Investments...	6,266	
Prepayments..	5,007	
		21,623
Current Liabilities		
Decrease in Accruals...................................	$ 1,546	
Decrease in Customers' Deposits........................	2,018	
		3,564
Deferred Liability		
Decrease in First Mortgage.............................		47,279
Total Funds Applied....................................		$336,506

penses, Decrease in Miscellaneous Receivables, and *Net Worth*. Under applications there are four broad divisions, *Current Assets, Increase in Other Assets, Current Liabilities*, and *Deferred Liability*.

Only one current asset item decreased, namely, notes receivable to the extent of $2,579. Five current liability items, however, increased as sources of funds. These items ranged from increased loans from banks of $156,508 down to increased amounts due stockholders of $1,079 for a total of $232,926. Two non-cash items increased, reserves for depreciation of $17,951 and reserve for bad debts of $197, totaling $18,148. Miscellaneous receivables decreased $441. Two items under net worth increased, sale of common stock $25,000 and increase in retained earnings $57,412, for a total of $82,412. Total sources of funds aggregate $336,506, the same figure as in Schedule 57.

As applications of funds, three current asset items increased a total of $246,040, the largest representing the expansion in inventory of $248,605

[Schedule 59]   RETAIL FURNITURE COMPANY, INC.

Step III—Final Statement of Sources and Applications of Funds for Year Ended November 30, 19—(year *A*)

SOURCES

Increase in Retained Earnings...........................		$ 57,412
Sale of Common Stock..................................		25,000
Non-cash Expenses		
Reserves for Depreciation............................	$ 17,951	
Reserves for Bad Debts..............................	197	
		18,148
Decrease in Miscellaneous Receivables.....................		441
Total Sources of Funds...		$101,001

APPLICATIONS

Payment on First Mortgage....		$ 47,279
Increase in Net Working Capital		
Increase in Current Assets............................	$261,461	
Increase in Current Liabilities........................	229,362	
		32,099
Increase in Fixed Assets................................		10,350
Increase in Other Assets		
Investments..	$ 6,266	
Prepayments.......................................	5,007	
		11,273
Total Funds Applied....................................		$101,001

and the smallest the increase in cash of $1,480. Three other asset items, fixed assets of $10,350, investments of $6,266, and prepayments of $5,007, increased for a total of $21,623. Two current liability items, the decrease in accruals of $1,546 and the decrease in customers' deposits of $2,018, amounted to the moderate sum of $3,564. A decrease in the first mortgage of $47,279 represented the balance of the application. Total applications of funds aggregate $336,506.

Schedule 59 is the third step and represents the final statement of the sources and applications of funds, arranged in the more generally accepted manner. In this schedule, the items are regrouped somewhat, but the most striking difference is the elimination of all increases and decreases in current asset items and current liability items and the substitution of a single item of increase in net working capital of $32,099. This figure is the difference in the increase in the current assets and the increase in the current liabilities for the year and, in this case, represents a net application of funds.

This final statement shows a total of $101,001 of funds utilized during year A. Of these funds $57,412 came from the increase in the retained earnings for the year, $25,000 from the sale of common stock for cash, $17,951 from the increase in the reserve for depreciation, and $197 from the increase in the reserve for bad debts, or a total of $18,148 as non-cash expenses, and $441 from a decrease in miscellaneous receivables.

Of these total funds, $47,279 was used to reduce the first mortgage debt, $32,099 was applied as a net increase in net working capital, $10,350 was used to increase the fixed assets, $6,266 in additional investments, and $5,007 in larger prepayments. The total funds applied aggregated $101,001 and balanced the total sources of funds.

A financial statement of this nature may be used as a supplementary schedule in studying the changes in the condition of any business enterprise, large or small, whether the concern is in sound current shape and operating profitably, or in an extended financial condition, near bankruptcy, and operating unprofitably. As pointed out previously, it is particularly helpful in those situations where operations have been profitable but the profits have been reinvested continuously in assets to such an extent that the concern, most of the time, seems to be short of cash. The applications side of the statement shows where the funds, in the broad sense of the term, have gone.

Information from Balance Sheets and Income Statements

To formulate a complete statement of the sources and applications of funds not only comparative balance sheets but also one or more income statements are essential. If the two balance sheets represent the condition of a concern on consecutive fiscal dates, then the income statement for the last fiscal year, ending on the same date as the last balance sheet, is necessary. If the comparative balance sheets cover a period of several years, it is necessary to have all the intervening fiscal income statements to obtain the exact amount of net profits and non-cash expenses for the full period.

Where the statement of sources and applications of funds covers only one fiscal period, the income statement furnishes net profits, dividends, and the non-cash expenses such as reserve for depreciation for the year, all of which are needed to compile a really complete statement of funds. The reserve for depreciation added during the year is sometimes shown in a balance sheet, depending upon the degree of condensation with which the balance sheet is prepared. The net profits and dividends occasionally

[Schedule 60]   COLD STORAGE WAREHOUSE CORPORATION
Comparative Figures for Years Ended December 31, 19—

	(B) Two Years Ago	(A) One Year Ago	Increase or Decrease
ASSETS			
Cash......................	$ 95,417	$ 142,588	+$ 47,171
Accounts Receivable.........	617,301	531,905	− 85,396
Customers' Loans Secured by Warehouse Receipts........	1,770,539	820,478	− 950,061
Current Assets..............	$2,483,257	$1,494,971	−$ 988,286
Plant and Property, Net.......	6,143,674	6,041,246	− 102,428
Investments.................	26,500	6,500	− 20,000
Prepaid Expenses...........	50,711	64,562	+ 13,851
Miscellaneous Assets.........	783	1,195	+ 412
TOTAL.................	$8,704,925	$7,608,474	−$1,096,451
LIABILITIES			
Customers' Loans Discounted.	$1,542,612	$ 146,737	−$1,395,875
Due on Term Loan...........	75,000	75,000	....
Accounts Payable...........	39,794	53,856	+ 14,062
Accruals...................	140,321	328,287	+ 187,966
Current Liabilities...........	$1,797,727	$ 603,880	−$1,193,847
Serial Term Loan............	300,000	225,000	− 75,000
30-Year 5% Income Deb......	....	2,690,000	+ 2,690,000
Total Liabilities..............	$2,097,727	$3,518,880	+$1,421,153
6% Cumulative Pref. Stock...	2,659,800	....	− 2,659,800
Common Stock..............	2,000,000	2,000,000	....
Retained Earnings...........	1,363,678	1,508,315	+ 144,637
Capital Surplus.............	583,720	581,279	− 2,441
TOTAL.................	$8,704,925	$7,608,474	−$1,096,451
Net Working Capital..........	$ 685,530	$ 891,091	+$ 205,561
Current Ratio...............	1.38	2.49	+ 1.11
Tangible Net Worth..........	$6,607,198	$4,089,594	−$2,517,604
Gross Income...............	$1,981,966	$2,695,880	+$ 713,914
Net Profit..................	242,280	397,318	+ 155,038
Dividends..................	186,186	252,681	+ 66,495

may also be found in a balance sheet, as some contain a condensed reconciliation of surplus.

Cold Storage Warehouse. Schedule 60 contains the comparative balance sheet figures as of the last two fiscal dates and the changes in each item between the 2 years in the increase-decrease column for the Cold Storage Warehouse Corporation. As there are no sales in the cold storage warehouse business, the figure of gross income is included below the balance sheet in place of net sales. Net profits and dividends for each of the 2 years are also included.

Several unusual changes took place between year B and year A in the financial condition of this corporation. In the first place the $2,659,800 of 6 per cent cumulative preferred stock outstanding at the end of year B was retired in year A, bringing about a very material reduction in the tangible net worth. In the second place, an issue of 30-year 5 per cent income

COLD STORAGE WAREHOUSE CORPORATION [Schedule 61]
Income Statement for Year Ended December 31, 19—(Year A)

Gross Income..		$2,695,880
Operating Expenses		
Plant and Warehouse, including Real Estate and Sundry		
Taxes...	$1,389,731	
General Administrative.............................	403,480	
Plant Depreciation.................................	147,129	
Total Operating Expenses..........................		1,940,340
		$ 755,540
Deductions from Income		
Interest on Term Loan..............................	$ 8,543	
Interest on Income Debentures......................	21,982	
Provision for Bad Debts............................	37,621	
Total Deductions from Income......................		68,146
Net Income before Federal Taxes......................		$ 687,394
Less: Provision for Federal Income and Excess Profits Taxes		290,076
Net Profit...		$ 397,318
Less: Dividends......................................		$ 252,681
Net Profits after Dividends..........................		$ 144,637

debentures amounting to $2,690,000 was sold to provide the necessary funds to retire the preferred stock. As a result of the issuance of these debentures, the funded debt, which amounted to only $300,000 at the end of year B, now amounted to $2,915,000 at the end of year A. In the third place, *Customers' Loans Secured by Warehouse Receipts* in the assets decreased from $1,770,539 to $820,478, and because of this reduction, *Customers' Loans Discounted* in the liabilities was reduced from $1,542,612 to $146,737. The current assets accordingly were reduced $988,286, and the current liabilities were reduced $1,193,847, bringing about an increase in the net working capital of $205,561. The income statement for the fiscal period of year A appears in Schedule 61.

This income statement begins with a gross income for the year of $2,695,880. From this figure is deducted operating expenses aggregating $1,940,340, including depreciation of $147,129, which leaves a balance of $755,540. From this balance there are deducted two items of interest amounting to $30,525 and provisions for bad debts of $37,621, leaving a net income before Federal taxes of $687,394. After deducting provisions for Federal taxes of $290,076, the final net profit amounts to $397,318. Out of this sum dividends of $252,681 were paid, leaving $144,637 to increase the retained earnings account.

The preparation of the final statement of sources and applications of funds for year *A* of the Cold Storage Warehouse Corporation is taken in three steps, just as the preparation of the statement of the Retail Furniture Company, Inc., was taken. The first step is shown in Schedule 62.

[Schedule 62]   COLD STORAGE WAREHOUSE CORPORATION
Step I—Detailed Preliminary Statement of Sources and Applications of Funds for
Year Ended December 31, 19—(year *A*)

SOURCES

Increases in Liabilities

Accounts Payable	$ 14,062	
Accruals	187,966	
30-year 5% Income Debentures	2,690,000	
		$2,892,028
Decrease in Assets		
Accounts Receivable	$ 85,396	
Customers' Loans Secured by Warehouse Receipts	950,061	
Plant and Property, Net after Depreciation	102,428	
Investments	20,000	
		1,157,885
Increase in Net Worth		
Retained Earnings		144,637
Total Sources of Funds		$4,194,550

APPLICATIONS

Decrease in Liabilities

Customers' Loans Discounted	$1,395,875	
Serial Term Loan	75,000	
		$1,470,875
Increases in Assets		
Cash	$ 47,171	
Prepaid Expenses	13,851	
Miscellaneous Assets	412	
		61,434
Decreases in Net Worth		
6% Cumulative Preferred Stock	$2,659,800	
Capital Surplus	2,441	
		2,662,241
Total Funds Applied		$4,194,550

In this schedule, the preliminary statement of funds was prepared directly from the comparative balance sheets with the increase-decrease column shown in Schedule 60. Each item in the balance sheet with an increase or decrease for the period was classified under its proper heading as a source or an application of funds.

The largest source of funds was the new issue of 30-year 5 per cent debentures amounting to $2,690,000. The second largest source was the decrease in *Customers' Loans Secured by Warehouse Receipts* of $950,061. Six other items, ranging down to $14,062 from an increase in accounts payable, brought the total sources of funds to $4,194,550. The largest application was $2,659,800 used to redeem the outstanding 6 per cent cumulative preferred stock. The second largest application was $1,395,-875 used to pay down *Customers' Loans Discounted*. Five other items,

COLD STORAGE WAREHOUSE CORPORATION   [Schedule 63]
Step II—Intermediate Statement of Sources and Applications of Funds for Year
Ended December 31, 19—(year *A*)

SOURCES

Current Assets		
Accounts Receivable......................................	$ 85,396	
Decrease in Customers' Loans Secured by Warehouse Receipts...	950,061	
		$1,035,457
Investments Sold..		20,000
Current Liabilities		
Accounts Payable....................................	$ 14,062	
Accruals...	187,966	
		202,028
Deferred Liability		
New Issue of 30-year 5% Income Debentures...........		2,690,000
Reserve for Depreciation..............................		147,129
Net Worth		
Net Profits for Year.................................		397,318
Total Sources of Funds...............................		$4,491,932

APPLICATIONS

Current Assets		
Cash..		$ 47,171
Increase in Other Assets		
Property and Plant.................................	$ 44,701	
Prepaid Expenses...................................	13,851	
Miscellaneous Assets................................	412	
		58,964
Current Liabilities		
Decrease in Customers' Loans Discounted..............		1,395,875
Deferred Liability		
Payment on Serial Term Loan.......................		75,000
Net Worth		
6% Cumulative Preferred Stock Retired...............	$2,659,800	
Decrease in Capital Surplus.........................	2,441	
Dividends Paid....................................	252,681	
		2,914,922
Total Funds Applied................................		$4,491,932

ranging down to $412, representing an increase in miscellaneous receivables, brought the total funds applied to $4,194,550.

The second or intermediate statement appears in Schedule 63. In this table the items in Schedule 62 are rearranged in the order that they appear in a typical balance sheet. At the same time the net profit figure of $397,318 and the reserve for depreciation of $147,129, both taken from the income statement, are inserted in the source of funds, and the dividends paid of $252,681 and the increase in the gross value of the property and plant of $44,701 were inserted in the applications. At the same time, the item representing the increase in retained earnings of $144,637 is eliminated as a source, as this sum is now represented by the difference in the net profits for the year of $397,318 as a source of funds and dividends paid of $252,681 as an application of funds. With these changes, the sources, and also the applications of funds, now aggregated $4,491,932.

[Schedule 64]   COLD STORAGE WAREHOUSE CORPORATION

Step III—Final Statement of Sources and Applications of Funds for Year Ended December 31, 19—(year *A*)

SOURCES

Net Profits...	$ 397,318
30-year 5% Income Debentures.......................	2,690,000
Non-cash Expenses	
Reserve for Depreciation............................	147,129
Sale of Investments..................................	20,000
Total Sources of Funds..............................	$3,245,447

APPLICATIONS

Payment of Dividends................................		$ 252,681
Retirement of 6% Cumulative Preferred Stock...........		2,659,800
Decrease in Capital Surplus...........................		2,441
Payment on Serial Term Loan..........................		75,000
Increase in Net Working Capital		
Decrease in Current Liabilities......................	$1,193,847	
Decrease in Current Assets..........................	988,286	
		205,561
Increase in Plant and Property........................		44,701
Increase in Other Assets		
Prepaid Expense....................................	$ 13,851	
Miscellaneous Assets...............................	412	
		14,263
Total Funds Applied.................................		$3,254,447

In the third and final statement, which appears in Schedule 64, somewhat more radical changes have been made. At this time, the increases and decreases in each current asset item and in each current liability item are weeded out. In their place appears, in this particular case, the one item in the application side of the statement of the increase in net working capital of $205,561 with two supporting items, decrease in current liabilities of $1,193,847 less decrease in current assets of $988,286. The various items again have been rearranged.

Here we have the final condensed statement with four sources of funds, net profits of $397,318, 30-year 5 per cent income debentures of $2,690,-000, non-cash expenses represented by the reserve for depreciation of $147,129, and the sale of investments of $20,000, a total of $3,254,447. The applications are more extensive. Here we have seven main items: Payment of dividends of $252,681, retirement of the 6 per cent cumulative preferred stock of $2,659,800, decrease in capital surplus of $2,441, payment on serial term loan of $75,000, increase in net working capital of $205,561, increase in plant and property of $44,701, and increases in other assets of $14,263. The total applications equal the total sources of funds of $3,254,447.

Three steps were used to obtain the final statement in both examples. With a little experience, it is a simple matter to construct the final statement of funds direct from cumulative balance sheets and the income statement. Where the statement of sources and applications of funds is to cover several years, the computations are the same but somewhat more lengthy.

THEORY AND PROBLEMS

1. What does the word *funds* in the term *Statement of Sources and Applications of Funds* mean?

2. What is the basic purpose in compiling a statement of sources and applications of funds?

3. State (*a*) four sources of funds and (*b*) four applications of funds. Describe two of the sources and two of the applications.

4. From the following comparative summary and additional information, prepare a statement of sources and applications of funds.

AMES MANUFACTURING COMPANY
Comparative Summary of Balance Sheets

ASSETS	Dec. 31 Year B	Year A	Increase Decrease*
Current Assets			
Cash.....................	$ 85,000	$ 35,000	$ 50,000*
Receivables (net)................	106,000	103,000	3,000*
Inventories.....................	158,000	146,000	12,000*
	$ 349,000	$ 284,000	$ 65,000*
Prepaid insurance, taxes, etc...........	$ 8,000	$ 7,000	$ 1,000*
Bond discount and expenses in process of amortization...................	40,000	65,000	25,000
Sinking fund deposit account..........	3,000	5,000	2,000
Property, plant, and equipment........	$1,860,000	$2,810,000	$950,000
Less: Reserve for depreciation........	852,000	879,000	27,000
	$1,008,000	$1,931,000	$923,000
	$1,408,000	$2,292,000	$884,000
LIABILITIES			
Current Liabilities			
Bank loans.....................	$ —	$ 100,000	$100,000
Current maturities of equipment obligations...................	—	25,000	25,000
Accounts payable................	63,000	42,000	21,000*
Accrued expenses...............	105,000	82,000	23,000*
	$ 168,000	$ 249,000	$ 81,000

AMES MANUFACTURING COMPANY (*Continued*)

Long-term Debt

4% first mortgage sinking fund bonds, due in 10 years	$ 650,000	$ 975,000	$325,000
Deferred equipment obligations	....	150,000	150,000
	$ 650,000	$1,125,000	$475,000

Capital Stock and Surplus

Capital stock	$ 250,000	$ 350,000	$100,000
Paid-in surplus	250,000	350,000	100,000
Retained earnings	90,000	218,000	128,000
	$ 590,000	$ 918,000	$328,000
	$1,408,000	$2,292,000	$884,000

Supplementary Information:

a. Property retirements recorded for the year aggregated $100,000. The excess of such cost over $10,000 salvage realized was charged to depreciation reserves.

b. Additional securities were sold during the year as follows:
2,000 shares of capital stock of $50 par value, sold at $100 per share
$350,000 par value of first mortgage bonds at 90
$175,000 deferred equipment notes at par

c. Bonds are subject to retirement through a sinking fund created by annual deposits of $25,000 on March 15. Bonds retired through the sinking fund in year *A* aggregating $25,000 were acquired for $22,000 plus accrued interest of $1,000.

d. Provision made by the company in year *A* for depreciation and for the amortization of bond discount and expenses were correctly computed.

e. The following analysis was made of earned surplus:

Balance at end of year *B*	$ 90,000
Net profit for year *A* after depreciation of $92,000	175,000
Discount on bonds retired	3,000
	$268,000

Deduct:

Dividends paid	$25,000	
Adjustment of depreciation reserves at end of year *B*, to basis of Treasury Department report	25,000	50,000
Retained earnings at end of year *A*		$218,000

[A.I.A. Examination]

5. Should the management of a business be interested in knowing why the net working capital increased or decreased during its immediately previous fiscal period? Would a statement of the sources and applications of funds throw any light on such changes? Explain your answer.

6. Some corporations become short of cash even though they are operating profitably. How does a statement of the sources and applications of funds explain such situations?

7. From the following verified data prepare in appropriate form a statement of sources and applications of funds for year *A* to be included in the annual report to the stockholders of State Stove Corporation.

STATE STOVE CORPORATION
Comparative Balance Sheets

ASSETS	Dec. 31 Year B	Year A	Increase or Decrease
Current and Working Assets			
Cash.........................	$ 390,000	$ 280,000	
Marketable securities............	527,000	220,000	
Accounts and notes receivable.......	$1,100,000	$1,137,000	
Less: Reserve for bad debts........	33,000	45,000	
	$1,077,000	$1,092,000	
Inventory.....................	1,240,000	1,512,000	
	$3,234,000	$3,104,000	
Current Liabilities			
Accounts payable................	$ 234,000	$ 306,000	
Preferred dividends payable.......	45,000	40,500	
Accrued liabilities...............	101,000	112,000	
Reserves for Federal income.......	150,000	225,000	
	$ 530,000	$ 683,500	
Net working capital.............	$2,704,000	$2,420,500	−$ 283,500
Investments			
Capital stock—State Credit Corp..	$ 100,000	$ 150,000	
Advances—State Credit Corp......	—	55,500	
	$ 100,000	$ 205,500	+$ 105,500
5-year mortgage notes...........	....	300,000	+ 300,000
	$ 100,000	$ 505,500	+$ 405,500
Fixed Assets			
Real estate.....................	$ 556,000	$ 373,000	−$ 183,000
Building and equipment..........	$2,935,000	$2,650,000	−$ 285,000
Less: Depreciation...............	1,260,000	1,105,000	155,000
	$1,675,000	$1,545,000	−$ 130,000
	$2,231,000	$1,918,000	−$ 313,000
Organization and development expenses........................	$ 304,000	$ 280,000	−$ 24,000
Good will.......................	3,212,000	....	− 3,212,000
Net book worth.................	$8,551,000	$5,124,000	−$3,427,000
Net book worth represented by			
4½% preferred stock.............	$3,000,000	$2,700,000	−$ 300,000
Common stock..................	3,750,000	1,013,000	− 2,737,000
	$6,750,000	$3,713,000	−$3,037,000
Retained earnings...............	$1,801,000	$1,411,000	−$ 390,000
	$8,551,000	$5,124,000	−$3,427,000

STATE STORE CORPORATION (*Continued*)

Condensed Income Statement, Year *A*

Net sales..	$6,365,000
Deduct:	
Operating charges..	5,300,000
Net operating revenue.....................................	$1,065,000
Add:	
Interest and dividend income..................................	33,000
Profit on sale of plant..	31,000
	$1,129,000
Deduct:	
Loss of sale of securities.....................................	86,000
Net income...	$1,043,000
Deduct:	
Provision for Federal income taxes............................	225,000
Net to stockholders...	$ 818,000

Other Data:

On Jan. 1, year *A*, the company sold its Norwalk properties for $519,000, receiving $219,000 cash and $300,000 five-year mortgage notes. The cost of the property was $585,000 with accrued depreciation to date of sale of $280,000.

During the first half of year *A*, a new plant was built on the company's land at a cost of $300,000 for buildings and equipment. It went into service on July 1. There were no other additions or retirements in year *A*.

Depreciation was provided at the rate of 5 per cent per annum on buildings and equipment in use, amounting to $125,000.

On Feb. 28, 3,000 shares preferred stock were retired at $110 per share plus accrued dividends of $3,000. Preferred dividends were declared for each quarter and amounted to $162,000.

On July 1, year *A*, a 10 per cent stock dividend was paid to the common stockholders, and 1,000 common shares were issued for cash at par. Cash dividends of $8 per share were paid on June 30 and Dec. 31 in the total amount of $638,000.

On Dec. 31, year *A*, the common stock was changed from $100 par to no-par-value shares, with a stated value of $1,013,000, and against the capital surplus so created there was charged good will of $3,212,000.

[A.I.A. Examination]

PART V

Income Statements

PART V *consists of five chapters which explain and analyze the income statement. The arrangement of the typical items in an income statement is discussed, and then that arrangement divided into three main divisions. These main divisions are the gross profit section, the operating profit section, and the final net profit or loss section. The final net profit or loss should be determined both before and after extraordinary and nonrecurring credits and debits. In the analysis of income statements, respective items of expense are set up as a proportion of net sales, which represent 100 per cent. If one is familiar with what might be called the normal proportions that particular items of expense should bear to net sales in a specific line of business activity, like the normal relations between balance sheet items, it becomes evident when a particular expense is excessive. If successive income statements are set up with each item as a percentage of net sales, trends are observable for comparative analysis. A basic understanding of the break-even point and the relationships between net sales, variable expenses, and total expenses is of great aid to the analyst. Six charts are used in the exposition and in the practical application of determining the break-even point. The percentage net profits, after all charges including Federal income taxes, on tangible net worth and on net sales are studied; typical percentage net profit figures for the years 1955 through 1959, inclusive, with a simple 5-year arithmetical average are presented for particular lines of manufacturing, wholesaling, and retailing.*

CHAPTER XVIII

Explanation of Income Statements

The balance sheet is supplemented by two complementary financial statements, the income statement and the retained earnings [surplus] account. The income statement is the schedule that shows the income and expenses of a business enterprise over a period of time and then gives a final figure representing the amount of profit or loss for the accounting period. In this chapter the income statement will be described, and in the following chapter the technique involved in interpreting these figures will be outlined.

The division of income between the different elements of our economy—labor, management, taxgatherers representing various governmental units, and stockholders—has made more and more necessary the objectivity of income statements. Accounting has met this growing challenge by trying to sharpen the concept and measurement of income.[1] In many

---

[1] "At one time the stockholders of general business corporations were permitted within wide limits to define profits or income for corporate purposes to suit themselves; but the corporation is a creation of the law, and the law has always the right to define the sense in which the word 'income' shall be used by those who take advantage of its creation. Ultimately, therefore, the definition of income may become a political question, and be determined by the attitude of legislators toward savings, industrial growth, and so forth."—*Changing Concepts of Business Income*, p. 19 (The Macmillan Company, New York, 1952). From the standpoint of classical economics, accounting profits (assuming "net profit" and "net income" are synonymous terms) are not economic profits. This is due to the fact that net profits of corporations which own land on which some or all of their plants, warehouses, premises, or stores are located include a return which is really economic rent in their accounting profits (see footnote 12, p. 512). As a result there is no idea as to what part of accounting profit represents economic rent earned on the site value of land, and what part represents the return on capital invested in a business including improvements to and on land. Here is confusion which accountancy has brought to business operations and to the present-day reasoning of labor leaders and pseudo economists; such mathematics as has been developed for and by accountancy is radically different from the mathematics which might have been developed in keeping with "classical" economics with its distribution of all income in the three well-defined streams, wages to employees, rent to landowners, and profits to the suppliers of capital. Some day an economic mathematician of a high order—possibly a second Paciolo, Leibnitz, or Descartes—who will understand the underlying necessity for keeping clearly separated the economic rent of land and the return on capital, will solve this problem which com-

important respects this has been done at the expense of the balance sheet. The amount of any expenditures properly chargeable against the income of the current or past years is determined, and the remainder is then carried forward in the balance sheet as an asset applicable to future periods. This is the basis on which unamortized bond discount is treated as an asset; it is the basis for the calculations of depreciation and amortization of property, plant, and equipment; and it is the justification for carrying forward inventories determined by ~~base stock, average cost, and~~ last-in first-out methods. As a result, the balance sheet, as we have discovered in earlier chapters, often does not reflect the current values of assets, a departure which becomes magnified during periods of rapidly rising or falling values.

In the case of a business enterprise with a tangible net worth of $35,000 or more, it is generally necessary to take two steps preparatory to analyzing the balance sheet. The first step is to condense the balance sheet into fewer items by grouping together captions of similar significance. This technique is absolutely essential with those business enterprises that have 20 or more items in the assets and liabilities, as it is impossible to grasp at one time the effective relationship between so many different captions. If, for example, a balance sheet contains an item *Due from Officers* of $4,521.93 and another item *Due from Employees* of $1,262.32, the combined item of $5,784.25 may effectively be made to read *Due from Officers and Employees*, since both items, in nine cases out of ten, carry similar significance from the analyst's point of view.

The second step is to obtain supplemental information about particular items that are not self-explanatory. Both these steps have been explained in considerable detail in earlier chapters. They are generally unnecessary in going over the affairs of a business enterprise with a tangible net worth of less than $35,000, since the balance sheet of such a concern invariably is simpler and more easily interpreted.

In a sense, the analysis of income statements is in direct contrast to the analysis of balance sheets. Whereas the balance sheet of a large corporation must be condensed into a smaller number of related items, the income account often must be expanded, since it frequently is so condensed as to be of little value. This is particularly true of large corporations whose securities are listed on an exchange or traded over the counter.

---

bines economics and mathematics. Not until this solution is found will the layman, management, and the legislator who makes our tax laws appreciate the relative importance of the ground rent value of land and of capital in obtaining the return which we insist, at this stage, in lumping together in one mathematical series as "accounting profit." See also "Economics and Accounting" by Ridgeway Hoegstedt in *Economics and the Public Interest*, pp. 111–119, edited by Robert A. Solo (Rutgers University Press, New Brunswick, N.J., 1955).

Under the Securities Exchange Act of 1934, managements of corporations with securities listed on a national security exchange may make written objection to the public disclosure of certain information submitted in confidence to the Securities and Exchange Commission. The Commission then determines whether, in its judgment, public knowledge of this information would be harmful to the continued successful operation of the corporation. In the majority of cases, the Commission has ruled against this managerial policy and has proceeded to make the information available to the public. Even when the Commission consents to the concealment of the data, the commercial banker can and invariably does insist, in his dealings with these same corporations, upon receiving a complete record in the form of the annual detailed audit. Rarely are other outside analysts in a position to obtain such close and helpful information.

This volume deals with the financial statements of industrial and commercial business enterprises. In the regulation of railroads, electric light, gas, and other public utilities, banking, insurance, and building and loan associations, Federal and state authorities have prescribed uniform accounts which must be followed in preparing the annual reports, including income statements, made to the various governmental agencies. Industrial and commercial corporations that come under the active scrutiny of the Securities and Exchange Commission likewise must file income statements in accordance with a specially prepared outline.[2] In the reports to their own stockholders, the managements of many of these corporations depart somewhat from the officially prescribed accounting procedure and submit their financial statements in different and often very condensed forms.

PRINCIPAL ITEMS IN INCOME STATEMENTS

The income statements of industrial and commercial corporations that must file with the Securities and Exchange Commission have reached a high degree of uniformity and completeness. But there are hundreds of thousands of other commercial and industrial concerns that are not required to file figures prepared with the same care and exactness. The earning figures of these concerns range from similar thoroughness to utter

---

[2] As explained on pp. 62 and 63, there were 2,307 issuers with securities listed and registered on national security exchanges as of June 30, 1960, which came under the supervision of the Securities and Exchange Commission. There were also 1,543 issuers (not including investment companies) filing information with the Securities and Exchange Commission under Sec. 15d of the Securities Exchange Act of 1934. In all, 3,840 issuers (not including investment companies) are currently filing information on specially prepared forms of the Securities and Exchange Commission. These are the larger, nationally known industrial and commercial business corporations in the country.

uselessness, because of varying degrees of condensation and unique arrangements and classifications of expense items. This condition becomes more acute with smaller business enterprises that make little or no use of trained accountants. However, this usually results from lack of knowledge and not from any deliberate policy of subtle concealment.

Many business concerns whose affairs come under no outside scrutiny report only *gross profits*, or *net earnings*, or some other single item or limited piece of operating information, with no supporting information indicating how the figures were obtained. In such cases, it is impossible to determine how effectively the business is being operated. Where no final profit and loss figure is made available, it is necessary to work backward through the yearly changes in the surplus account and the dividend or withdrawal payments, if available, to obtain at least some general idea regarding net profits or losses for respective years.

Most financial statement blanks used by banking institutions, credit departments of business enterprises, and mercantile agencies, except those for farmers, for stockmen, and for small business concerns, carry requests for an income statement.[3] A condensed income schedule is generally included in the statement blanks to be filled in by smaller business enterprises, while a more elaborate schedule is included in the long form for corporations and firms used by the Federal Reserve Bank of New York. In these long financial statement blanks, the full income statement takes up approximately three-quarters of an entire page and is in considerable detail.

A condensed and highly inadequate income statement may consist of three, four, or five items; an elaborate statement may consist of one hundred or more items. No matter how many items are included, they may be readily grouped and classified for the purposes of analysis into three broad sections: (1) the gross profit section, (2) the operating profit section, and (3) the final net profit or loss section, including all extraordinary debits and credits. Income statements have been divided into 16 primary items; these items, in turn, are classified under the three sections just mentioned. The important items included in each of these sections are described in succeeding paragraphs. These 16 items of primary importance are:

Gross Profit Section

1. Gross Sales
2. Returns and Allowances
3. Net Sales
4. Cost of Sales *Goods Sold*
5. Gross Profits *Margin*

[3] Such as Forms 6, 7, 8, 9, and 10 in Chap. IV.

Operating Profit Section

   6. Administrative and General Expenses
   7. Selling Expenses
   8. Provision for ~~Doubtful Accounts~~ Bad Debts
   9. Operating Profit

Final Net Profit or Loss Section

  10. Cash Discounts Earned and Given
  11. Interest Paid
  12. Net Profit or Loss before Extraordinary Charges
  13. Extraordinary Charges
  14. Federal Income Taxes _and State_
  15. Net Profit or Loss
  16. Net Profit or Loss after Adjustment by Carry-back or Carry-forward Tax Privilege

Gross Profit Section

The gross profit section begins with gross sales for the accounting period under review, from which are deducted returns and allowances to give net sales. From the net sales the cost of goods sold is then deducted to arrive at the gross profit. The percentage of gross profit on net sales indicates to the analyst whether the average markup on merchandise sold is sufficient normally to cover all expenses and to show a profit. If a particular retail drugstore with annual sales of $88,000 operates on a gross margin of 23.5 per cent and suffers a net loss, the reason for the loss may easily be traced. The typical gross margin of profit in this line is around 33.8 per cent on net sales, and the concern under the fluoroscope would be operating on an inadequate markup, or with an inadequate volume of business. A certain margin of gross profit is essential for every line of commercial and industrial activity. This margin varies moderately with the volume of net sales, the size and scope of the business, the size of the city or town in which the enterprise is located, the intensity of competition, and the terms of sale, but normally it should be sufficient to cover expenses and ensure a reasonable profit.

   1. *Gross Sales.* Every complete income statement of a commercial or industrial business enterprise starts with the amount of gross sales. This term refers to the aggregate selling price of all merchandise and services that have been sold during a given accounting period, the selling of which is the primary object of the business enterprise whose figures are under examination.

   The financial statement blanks for larger corporations used by some sources request a separation of sales into cash and credit sales, without *requirements*

which the average collection period cannot be determined. The income
statements in the long forms of the Federal Reserve Bank of New York
and the income statements of the Securities and Exchange Commission
require a separation of gross sales into sales to subsidiaries and affiliates
and sales to regular customers, data which in the case of complicated
corporate structures add very material enlightenment. The regulations
of the Securities and Exchange Commission also provide that "if income
is derived from both gross sales and operating revenues, the two classes
may be combined in one amount if the lesser amount is not more than ten
per cent of the sum of the two items."[4]

2. *Returns and Allowances.* Gross sales exceed net sales by the amount
of returns and allowances and are of significance for revealing these
charges. The extent of returns and allowances is an indication as to
whether the merchandise produced or handled is meeting the reasonable
requirements of customers. If merchandise is being misrepresented, if
paper cover stock is sold green instead of having been dried out properly,
if extensive defects are found in a line of coats produced by a manufacturer of ladies' wear, the high returns and allowances may indicate
wide dissatisfaction on the part of customers. Similarly, if a particular
line of fountain pens is defective, returns will be out of all reasonable
proportions and will involve unexpected expenses in replacements or
repairs, or both. Excessive returns and allowances thus greatly reduce
the receipts from gross sales and may also curtail the future volume of
sales as customers' confidence decreases. Improper control over returns
and allowances may quickly convert profitable operations into unprofitable ones.

requirements The income statement ~~form~~ of the Securities and Exchange Commission
provides at this point for the deduction of discounts allowed, along with
returns and allowances.[5] The Federal Reserve Bank of New York, however, makes discounts allowed a deduction from the last section of the
income statement. Whether from an analysis standpoint the item should
be included at this point or later in the schedule depends upon whether the
discount is a cash discount, or a trade or quantity discount. If it is a trade

Oct. 14, 1964.

[4] Regulation S-X, Rule 5-03(c), p. 11, ~~Aug. 30, 1958.~~

[5] W. A. Paton and A. C. Littleton in *An Introduction to Corporate Accounting
Standards*, p. 29 (American Accounting Association, Chicago, 1940), also lay emphasis
on this practice because of the effect on costs. "Costs are overstated unless discounts
and other allowances are deducted. It need not be considered improper, as a matter
of recording procedure, to charge cost accounts, provisionally, with gross invoice
prices, but if this is done an adjustment is later necessary to reduce the recorded figure
to the cash cost basis. Discounts taken are often interpreted as earned income, but
this view does not square with fundamental concepts; income is not realized through
the process of buying, for that is only the first step in the program of effort designed
to lead to revenue. In general, cash discounts are clearly cost adjustments. . . . The
real price is the net cash price (the least amount, if there are alternative terms), and
the matter is so understood by both parties."

or quantity discount, it might well be deducted here along with returns and allowances, as such discounts are really adjustments in selling prices.

3. *Net Sales.* The deduction of returns and allowances (also trade and quantity discounts) from gross sales gives the volume of net sales. The amount of net sales is the effective volume of business on which a profit is earned or a loss is assumed. It is the key figure in the income statement. It must be known for the computation of the turnover of inventory, the turnover of the net working capital, the turnover of the tangible net worth, and the average collection period, relationships that have been found essential in determining the inherent soundness of the balance sheet. The net sales figure is also essential in the so-called "sales analysis" as described in Chap. V, the process by which an analyst estimates, on the basis of the average monthly volume of business, the time required by smaller business enterprises to liquidate their accounts payable, and whether payments may reasonably be expected to be prompt or slow in the immediate future.

4. *Cost of Sales.* For retailers and wholesalers, the inventory at the beginning of an accounting period, plus purchases and less the inventory at the end of the period, gives the cost of sales. Regulations of the Securities and Exchange Commission provide that "occupancy and buying costs" for wholesalers and retailers may be included in cost of goods sold.[6] In the case of manufacturing enterprises, direct labor and all manufacturing expenses, including local real estate taxes on manufacturing properties, social security and unemployment taxes on factory employees, and that portion of depreciation which enters into the cost of production, must also be included.

The value of the inventory at the end of the year is the most important single figure in the final computation of net profit or loss. If this inventory figure happens to become understated purposely or accidentally, the results from operations will show smaller profits by the amount of the understatement. As the closing inventory figure is also the opening inventory figure for the following period, the profits for the following period will be increased by the same amount, provided there are no further errors. Conversely, when an inventory figure is overstated, the income statement for the closing period will show profits that are larger than the actual profits by the amount of the overstatement; and the following period, assuming that there are no other errors, will show profits that are decreased from the actual by the amount of overstatement at the close of the previous period.[7]

[6] Regulation S-X, Rule 5-03, 2A(b), p. 11, Aug. 30, 1958.

[7] "A major objective of accounting for inventories is the proper determination of income through the process of matching appropriate costs against revenues. An inventory has financial significance because revenues may be obtained from its sale, or from the sale of the goods or services in whose production it is used. Normally such revenues

The closing inventory is of much greater importance relatively in determining the net profit for an accounting period than it is in determining the balance sheet position. An error of 5 per cent in the total of the closing inventory, for example, may not be of major importance in reference to the current assets in the balance sheet, the relationship of net sales to inventory, or the relationship of inventory to net working capital, but such an error in the income statement may easily cut the profits in half or double them.

No management of a large manufacturing corporation can be in a position to plan its finances and operate with any degree of fairly consistent success unless definite means of knowing exact production costs of its various products are readily available, in other words, an adequate and practical cost system. The costs of a manufacturer are far more complicated than the costs of a wholesaler or a retailer. An adequate cost system enables the management to determine what articles should be produced with existing machinery and equipment; what quantities may be made profitably; how selling prices may be determined; and, by comparing with standard costs of other concerns, where additional savings may be made.

5. *Gross profit*. The gross profit is derived by deducting the cost of goods sold from the amount of net sales. The gross profit percentage of net sales is a most valuable figure in comparative analyses of concerns in the same line of business. This ratio answers the question, "Is the markup on cost to selling price sufficient to show a profit in a highly competitive business world?" The average or typical percentages of gross profits and expense items in terms of net sales are made available, from time to time, by certain of the more progressive trade associations, by certain universities, and by other organizations that have made financial studies for particular industries.[8]

---

arise in a continuous repetitive process or cycle of operations by which goods are acquired or sold, and further goods are acquired for additional sales. In accounting for the goods in the inventory at any point of time, the major objective is the matching of appropriate costs against revenues in order that there may be a proper determination of the realized income. Thus, the inventory at any given date is the balance of costs applicable to goods on hand remaining after the matching of absorbed costs with concurrent revenues. This balance is appropriately carried to future periods, provided it does not exceed an amount properly chargeable against the revenues expected to be obtained from ultimate disposition of the goods carried forward. In practice, this balance is determined by the process of pricing the articles comprised in the inventory."—*Restatement and Revision of Accounting Research Bulletins, Accounting Research Bulletin* No. 43, p. 28 (American Institute of Certified Public Accountants, New York, 1953).

[8] Studies of this nature have been made for many years by the National Retail Hardware Association, Indianapolis; the National Wholesale Druggists' Association, New York; the National Paper Trade Association, New York; the National Associ-

Within certain limits there is a natural gross profit in every line of merchandising and manufacturing. By natural gross profit it is meant that under ordinary business conditions staple materials and merchandise in any given standard line can be acquired and sold at about the same cost and price by those in that line who possess about the same amount of ability. In some lines the resulting gross profit is large, in others small; but in each line the ordinary market conditions are available to all engaged in that line. If there are 100 manufacturers in a certain type of business, some will be found with greater ability than others; also some may have insufficient capital, so that the gross profit may be greater or less in certain plants than in others, and the average gross profit of the hundred will not be as large as the "natural profit" of those possessing reasonable ability and capital. The importance of an accurate calculation of the gross profits rests upon the fact that if any given business concern cannot earn the natural gross profit, or at least exceed the average of all engaged in its line, it will not become a success. The concerns with the higher percentage gross profits are well on the way to the higher percentage net profits.

Operating Profit Section

In the operating profit section of the income statement, the various actual expenses in running a business are deducted from the gross profit, after the product is purchased or produced, to obtain an operating profit for the accounting period. These expenses in a detailed statement would be broken down, with many subdivisions, under administrative and general expenses and selling expenses. This section would also include a provision for doubtful accounts. In a condensed income statement, all these items may be combined together into the one item of operating expenses.

Certain expenses of the business are omitted from this section of the financial statement. These items are cash discounts earned, cash discounts given, interest on borrowed money, income taxes, and charges which are generally termed of an *extraordinary nature*. These particular items are omitted at this point, so that the operating profit will have been determined on a comparable basis for different concerns whose figures the

---

ation of Furniture Manufacturers, Chicago; the Graduate School of Business Administration, Harvard University, Cambridge, Mass.; the School of Retailing, New York University, New York; Eli Lilly & Co., Inc., Indianapolis; National Automobile Dealers Association, Washington, D.C.; National Stationery and Office Equipment Association, Washington, D.C.; National Appliance and Radio-TV Dealers Association, Chicago; National Retail Furniture Association, Chicago; and Robert Morris Associates, Philadelphia.

analyst might be studying. One corporation, for example, might have sufficient capital of its own to operate through a particular year without borrowed funds; a competitor might be utilizing funds furnished by a substantial funded debt and so have a representative charge for interest. By omitting the interest charge at this point, the operating profit, provided the earlier items in the income statement had been set up in the same manner, would be comparable in both businesses. The same situation exists with respect to cash discounts earned, cash discounts given, income taxes, and charges of an extraordinary nature.

Sometimes condensed into one all-inclusive item, operating expenses at other times are presented in great detail and may run to 50 or 60 items. An excessive amount in any one or several of these items might be the simple explanation of yearly operations in the red.

An analyst has a deep interest in learning that expenses are kept within proper bounds. Poor management that has become involved in paying excessive rent, burdensome interest charges, heavy traveling expenses, and exorbitant entertainment costs has brought many businesses to their untimely demise. In many lines of business, percentage standards for these particular expenses have been determined and are available as a basis for study and comparison. In general, these expenses rise and fall more slowly than the prime expenses which enter directly into the production of a particular commodity, that is, mill costs of production and the direct outlay for labor and material. The administrative, selling, and overhead expenses are very stubborn items to deal with when reducing selling prices.

6. *Administrative and General Expenses.* Administrative and general expenses cover officers' salaries, other salaries that are not factory or selling expenses, depreciation not specifically applicable elsewhere, telephone and telegraph, postage, legal expenses, local real estate taxes applicable to administration, social security and unemployment taxes applicable to administration, capital-stock taxes, franchise taxes, and occupancy expenses such as rent, light, heat.

7. *Selling Expenses.* Selling expenses include all salaries of those engaged in the distributing end of the business, salaries of salesmen, and wages of employees in the sales department. They also include commissions for selling, traveling expenses of salesmen, entertainment expense incidental to distributing operations, social security and unemployment taxes applicable to personnel in the selling end of the business, and advertising.

8. *Provision for Doubtful Accounts.* Before closing the books for an accounting period, the open accounts receivable must be scrutinized carefully for losses that should be charged off. Many accounts may be perfectly good though slow of collection, and many now thought to be

good may prove to be worthless. Losses assumed on receivables during the period, together with reserves set up for possible losses not yet recognized, are deducted at this point. Except in the case of concerns selling on an installment basis, the annual provisions for doubtful accounts should rarely exceed ¼ of 1 per cent on the net sales.

```
┌──────────────────────────────────────────────────────────────┐
│              FORM OF PROFIT-AND-LOSS STATEMENT                 │
│  Gross sales_____           │
│  Less outward freight, allowances and returns_____         │
│      Net sales_____           │
│  Inventory beginning of year_____            │
│  Purchases, net (or cost of goods produced)_____         │
│  Less inventory end of year_____            │
│      Cost of sales_____            │
│      Gross profit on sales_____            │
│  Selling expenses (itemized to correspond with ledger accounts kept)___ │
│      Total selling expenses_____            │
│  General expenses (itemized to correspond with ledger accounts kept)__ │
│      Total general expenses_____            │
│  Administrative expenses (itemized to correspond with ledger accounts │
│      kept)_____            │
│      Total administrative expenses_____            │
│      Total expenses_____            │
│      Net profit on sales_____            │
│  Other income:                                                 │
│      Income from investments_____            │
│      Interest on notes receivable, etc._____           │
│      Gross income_____            │
│  Deductions from income:                                       │
│      Interest on bonded debt_____            │
│      Interest on notes payable_____            │
│      Taxes, depreciation, etc. (separately shown)_____          │
│      Total deductions_____            │
│  Net income for the period_____            │
│  Add special credits to profit and loss (separately shown)_____ │
│  Deduct special charges to profit and loss (separately shown)____ │
│      Profit and loss for period_____            │
│  Surplus beginning of period_____             │
│  Add or deduct items in the surplus account attributable to prior periods_ │
│  Dividends paid_____            │
│      Earned surplus at end of period_____            │
└──────────────────────────────────────────────────────────────┘
```

FORM 18. Early income statement suggested in *Verification of Financial Statements* by the Federal Reserve Board, 1929.

9. *Operating Profit.* Gross profit, less administrative and general expenses, selling expenses, and provisions for doubtful accounts, gives the operating profit, or, as it is also termed, *net operating profit,* for the accounting period. This figure is the measure of the ability, skill, aggressiveness, and ingenuity of the management to operate a business successfully for its main purpose. Into this one final mathematical figure are translated the operating policies of the executive staff in connection with the primary purpose of the concern.

The operating profit is the sum available after all normal operating charges, but before cash discounts earned and given, before payment of interest and income taxes, before income from investments or miscellaneous extraordinary credits, before extraordinary charges of an unusual nature and charges not actually incurred in operations during the accounting period. Some managements are able to show an adequate profit up to this point, but seem to fail in supplementary policies, thus changing the operating profit into a materially smaller net profit or even into a final net loss. Both the operating profit and the final net profit or loss are necessary in determining the financial results from different phases of management operations.

Final Net Profit or Loss Section

In smaller business units the operating profit is generally synonymous with the final net profit or loss, In larger business units, other debits and credits are often made before arriving at the final figure representing net profit or net loss. These debits and credits are described in the following paragraphs.

10. *Cash Discounts Earned and Given.* Cash discount earned is an addition to and cash discount given a deduction from the operating profit. Both items are nominal in the case of small concerns; retailers, of course, have no discounts given and often few or no discounts earned. Large corporations selling on discount terms may have very substantial items as both debits and credits.

11. *Interest.* By having a separate item of interest paid at this point, the number of times the interest is earned "from operations" may be determined, a comparison of considerable importance to security analysts. This is particularly true of corporations that have one or several issues of funded debts outstanding. Where the item represents only interest on short-term bank loans, it is of somewhat less relative importance.

12. *Net Profit or Loss before Extraordinary Charges.* After the deduction of cash discounts earned and given and interest charges, a figure of net profit or loss from the normal operations of a business enterprise is obtained. This figure is a highly desirable one for yearly comparison and in the study of the operations of concerns in the same line of business. In many large concerns and most small ones, this figure is also the final net profit or loss for the accounting period, In the case of large representative corporations, other charges and credits, usually termed *nonoperating, nonrecurring,* or *extraordinary,* are now made to arrive at the final figure of net profit or loss for the period. The separate treatment of these items at this point facilitates the disclosure of unusual sources of income and charges in the income statement.

13. *Extraordinary Charges.* To the net profit or loss from normal operations there are now added such credits or deducted such debits as might have arisen outside the normal operations of the business, to arrive at the final figure of net profit or net income for the accounting period. These items are generally grouped under two captions, *Income Credits* and *Income Charges.* Income credits are of wide varieties, including, among other items, dividends and interest received on investments, profits on securities sold, royalties, income from rented properties, and tax adjustments. Regulations of the Securities and Exchange Commission regarding extraordinary credits cover four situations:

Dividends. State separately, if practicable, the amount of dividends from (*a*) securities of affiliates, (*b*) marketable securities, and (*c*) other security investments.

Interest on Securities. State separately, if practicable, the amount of interest from (*a*) securities of affiliates, (*b*) marketable securities, and (*c*) other security investments.

Profits on Securities. Profits shall be stated net of losses. No profits on the person's [concern's] own securities, or those of its affiliates, shall be included under this caption. State here or in a note herein referred to the method followed in determining the cost of securities sold, *e.g.,* "average cost," "first-in first-out," or "identified certificate."

Miscellaneous Other Income. State separately any material amounts, indicating clearly the nature of the transactions out of which the items arose.[9]

Income charges are of three broad types. The first type represents items not connected with the ordinary or normal operations of a business such as losses from floods and hurricanes, losses on securities sold, losses on the disposal of fixed assets, provisions for contingencies, expenses in carrying idle plants, and losses incurred in cancellation of leases. The second type represents operating expenses of prior years which came to light during the current accounting period, such as an inventory shortage, additional taxes, and payment for legal services in prior years. In theory these items should have been absorbed in the operating expenses of earlier years. The third type represents extraordinary items of operating expenses during the current accounting period such as expenses for guards and the transportation of nonstriking employees in case of a strike. Regulations of the Securities and Exchange Commission cover this wide variety of situations in a very general manner in two classes of income deductions:

Losses on Securities. Losses shall be stated net of profits. No losses on the person's [concern's] own securities, or those of its affiliates, shall be included under this caption. State here or in a note herein referred to the method followed in deter-

[9] Regulation S-X, Rule 5-03-2B, 7–10, p. 12, Aug. 20, 1958.

material

mining cost of securities sold, *e.g.*, "average cost," "first-in first-out," or "identified certificate."

Miscellaneous Income Deductions. State separately any significant amounts, indicating clearly the nature of the transactions out of which the items arose.[10]

INCOME STATEMENT, YEAR ENDED DECEMBER 31, 19—

Operating Division

Revenues:
- Gross . . . .　. . . . .
- Less adjustments for returns and discounts, allowances and other price adjustments . . . .　. . . . .
- Net . . . . ,　. . . . .

Operating Expenses:
- Merchandise or production cost of product or service sold . . . .　. . . . .
- Administrative expense . . . .　. . . . .
- Distribution expense . . . .　. . . . .
  - Total operating expense . . . .　. . . . .
- Operating income (net operating revenue) . . . .　. . . . .

Income Division

- Other net income (or loss) . . . .　. . . . .
  - Total net income . . . .　. . . . .
- Interest charges . . . .
- Accumulation of bond discount . . . .　. . . . .　. . . . .
- Balance of income before income taxes . . . .　. . . . .
- Provision for income taxes . . . .　. . . . .
- Net current income for stockholders . . . .　. . . . .
- Current dividends on preferred stock . . . .　. . . . .
- Net income for common stockholders . . . . ,　. . . . .
- Regular dividends (if any) on common stock . . . . .　. . . . .
- Excess of current net income over regular dividends (or excess of dividends over current net income) . . . .　. . . . .
- Adjustments of net income—profit and loss items[2] . . .　. . . . .
- Net addition to (or deduction from) surplus . . .　. . . . .

Surplus Division

- Unappropriated surplus, beginning of period . . . .　. . . . .
  - Total (or balance) . . . .　. . . . .
- Transfers to and releases from appropriated surplus　. . . . .
  - Total (or balance of) unappropriated surplus　. . . . .
- Reduction due to acquisition of treasury stock . . . . . .　. . . . .
- Special or irregular dividends . . . .　. . . . .
- Stock dividends . . . .　. . . . .
- Unappropriated surplus, close of period . . . .　. . . . .

---

[1] Depreciation and depletion charges and amortization of intangible assets should be separately listed or the total shown in a footnote.

[2] There is something to be said for including these adjustments prior to the charging of dividends. Adjustments of this character, of course, may affect the amount of taxable income.

FORM 19. Yearly income statement suggested in *Financial Statements* by M. B. Daniels, 1939.

In recent years, considerable question has been raised regarding the familiar accounting practice of making charges, the origin of which dates back to prior accounting periods, not as extraordinary charges to

---

[10] *Ibid,.* Rule 5-03-2B, 12–13, p. 12.

the current income statement but directly to the retained earnings [surplus] account. The earlier theory was that accumulated earnings in the retained earnings [surplus] account was the proper place to charge such items, because they were in effect adjustments of a retained earnings balance originally assumed to be correct but which in the light of subsequent events turned out to have been incorrect. It is the author's considered view that all such extraordinary charges should go through the current income statement,[11] as outlined above. This subject is discussed in considerably more detail in Chaps. XIX and XXIII.

14. *Income Taxes.* Federal, state, and local taxes are of many varieties. Property taxes, social security and unemployment taxes, capital stock taxes, and franchise taxes are all included in other appropriate parts of the income statement. The most important tax, imposed by Federal law and by some state laws, is the income tax on the net income of a corporation. If a business concern has a taxable net income in the accounting period covered by the income statement, there exists a liability for income taxes that must be set up at this point. Where net profits are reported before the Federal income tax, it is frequently impossible for the analyst to compute, even in a general way, the liability for taxes, because income as determined by generally accepted accounting procedure is often at wide variance with taxable income determined under statutes and regulations of the Federal government.

[11] A modified contrary opinion appears in *A Statement of Accounting Principles* by Sanders, Hatfield, and Moore, p. 39 (American Institute of Certified Public Accountants, New York, 1938). These authors explain: "There is some opinion in favor of passing all capital losses and gains through the income statement, on the ground that resort to surplus [retained earnings] account may be misused to relieve the income statement of proper charges, and to the end that the income statements may cumulatively show all changes, in net worth. Some capital gains and losses are, however, sufficiently abnormal to have no direct relation to current income, and sufficiently large to distort current income, even when clearly shown as separate items. In such cases charges or credits to surplus [retained earnings] are justifiable. In cases of doubt the tendency should be to include such items in the income statement."

A definite viewpoint on the other side appears in *Financial Statements* by M. B. Daniels, pp. 54–55 (American Accounting Association, Chicago, 1939): "Certain items of income or expense, profit or loss, while definitely affecting income of the current period expressed in terms of distributable funds, may be of an extraordinary or non-recurring nature, for example, proceeds of life insurance, collections (or payments) of judgments, moving expense, special litigation, research, and experiment costs. Such items may be legitimately excluded from operating income, but are definitely part of the entire income picture. . . . Some extraordinary and prior years' items may have been previously 'provided for' through appropriations of surplus [retained earnings], and in such a case the loss or expenditure when it occurs is often charged against the 'reserve.' Similarly, profit and loss items are often 'charged to surplus' [retained earnings] in accordance with a directors' resolution. Neither circumstance precludes showing the particular item in the income statement as an adjustment of net income, as otherwise it is never listed for any fiscal year. In the former instance an amount corresponding to the charge to the 'reserve' must of course be shown as a release therefrom in the surplus division of the statement."

15. *Net Profit*[12] *or Loss.* After the application of extraordinary income credits and income charges, and income taxes, the final net profit or net loss for the accounting period is obtained.[13] In a steadily increasing percentage of income statements, particularly those which appear over the signature of independent public accountants, the "net" when applied to profits or losses correctly indicates that every expense in the operation of a business enterprise has been deducted, and that all income from all

[12] Adam Smith in *The Wealth of Nations*, first published in 1776, pointed out, over and over again, that the production of all wealth is divided into three streams, one in the form of wages to employees, one in the form of rent to landowners, and one in the form of profits to the suppliers of capital. Three of the words, "wages," "rent," and "profits," as used by Adam Smith, carried connotations which are very different from their meanings in our present-day industrial life. We are particularly concerned with one of them at this point, namely, profits. According to Adam Smith, profit is the sum remaining after the payment of all wages ("wages" in economics includes payments to officers of corporations, to proprietors, to partners, and to farmers, as well as to what we today term "labor"), and rent on the unimproved value of land, as the return to capital. Then, Adam Smith carefully observed, "When those three different sorts of revenue belong to different persons, they are readily distinguished; but when they belong to the same they are sometimes confounded with one another, at least in common language." This sage observation is even more true today than in the early days of the industrial revolution. Many business corporations own title to land which is improved with factories, warehouses, office buildings, lofts, or stores. Under the mathematics of accountancy as practiced in 1961, the final "accounting" profit of such corporations, as the term is used in present-day income statements, includes two elements, a return representing economic rent on the value of land and a return to capital. However, we lack even a faint idea as to what part of "accounting" profit is represented by each of these two economic elements. Thus what we encounter today is the confusing reality that "accounting" or the "businessman's" profit is not "economic" profit. "Accounting" profit is a mathematical residue which results from the successive subtraction of many and varied items of expense from gross income. As a matter of fact over the years there has been quite an evolution as to what particular items should be deducted from gross income to arrive at an "accounting" profit. In one era, we find that depreciation is not an expense to be deducted before arriving at an "accounting" profit; at a later era, it is. Today, many charges are made to gross income which independent accountants often, if not generally, omitted prior to the Great Depression. These were what were termed "extraordinary and nonrecurring charges" and by some accountants were, and in some cases still are, made to surplus in which case they fail to appear as an expense in computing the "accounting" profit. "Accounting" profit is a concept of man-made legislation, of the courts, of the Securities and Exchange Commission, of accounting organizations, a concept which has always been in evolution but more particularly so since the passage of the sixteenth amendment to the Federal Constitution in 1913 allowing the Federal taxation of income. "Economic" profit, on the other hand, is a concept of a natural law of economics, and like the law of gravitation has remained and will remain unchanged over the ages. For an interesting analysis of the meanings of "profit" from the contrasting viewpoints of accountants, economists, lawyers, and businessmen see "Profits, a Semantic Problem Child" by Sidney I. Simon in *Economics and the Public Interest*, pp. 81–92, edited by Robert A. Solo (Rutgers University Press, New Brunswick, N.J., 1955).

[13] "The final gain or loss of any undertaking can be determined correctly only when it [a concern] has been completed or its affairs otherwise wound up. In this sense the only true income statement of an enterprise is one showing revenues, expenses, and income or loss for the entire period of its existence. Likewise, all balance sheets prepared during the operating life, and including unamortized costs of production factors such as materials and plant, are subject to inherent limitations. For obvious reasons

sources has been included. Such income statements have increased in number in recent years as a result of the policy fostered by the American Institute of Certified Public Accountants, the American Accounting Association, the Securities and Exchange Commission, and an increasing number of practicing accountants of suggesting that all credits and all debits go through the income statement. Occasionally qualifying terms are used such as *net profit before depreciation* or *before taxes*. In such cases the analyst must adjust the figures to obtain the real net profit or loss, often a difficult task that can be done only to an approximate degree.[14]

Many business concerns that have shown high or satisfactory net profits during a period of stable or rapidly advancing prices have been hard hit during a succeeding period of a general business recession. This change from apparent profits to losses is largely explained by the unwarranted expansion in fixed assets, often on long-term borrowed funds, the overbuying of inventories, and the multiplication of managerial expenses. Fixed charges often increase greatly when a business enterprise is on the up and up, and it becomes extremely difficult to reduce these charges appreciably when sales begin to shrink. Many business enterprises have appeared to be enjoying high profits until they failed. On the other hand, there are numerous examples of concerns where conservative, knowing managements have been quite content to restrict sales during a period of inflated prices and overexpanding business activity, to conserve their net working capital, to avoid any appreciable increase in their fixed assets, and to allow competitors to have their full share of abnormal trade. Business enterprises under such capable, farseeing managements have made little more than average profits when prices were rising but as a rule have suffered relatively less and often have had no losses during any succeeding period of declining prices and smaller volume of sales.

16. *Net Profit or Loss after Adjustments by Carry-back or Carry-forward Tax Privilege*. The final figure described under the item *Net Profit or Loss* will generally be the last item in the income statement. As a result of Federal tax legislation in 1942 and subsequent years, carry-back and carry-forward privileges will follow in occasional instances as a supplementary item. The theory behind the treatment of this supplementary

---

it is desirable, even necessary, to have an accounting at various stages in the history of an enterprise. Financial statements are thus for the most part interim reports and reflect a division of the life of an enterprise into more or less arbitrary accounting periods. The period of a year has been generally adopted for the presentation of complete financial statements."—Daniels, *op. cit.*, pp. 5–6.

[14] A successful wholesale distributor of wines and liquors recently set up a reserve for Federal income tax for the first 11 months of a fiscal year of $45,000. After this deduction the net profits for the 11 months amounted to $262,790. The audited figures for the entire fiscal year subsequently issued disclosed a reserve for Federal income tax of $196,313, leaving a net profit for the 12 months of $73,699, which was 72 per cent smaller than earlier reported net profit for the first 11 months of the fiscal year.

item has been carefully considered by the Committee on Accounting Procedure of the American Institute of Certified Public Accountants, as follows:[15]

While claims for refund of income taxes ordinarily should not be included in the accounts prior to approval by the taxing authorities, a claim based on the carry-back provisions of the Internal Revenue Code presumably has as definite a basis as has the computation of income taxes for the year. Therefore, amounts of income taxes paid in prior years which are refundable to the taxpayer as the result of the carry-back of losses or unused excess-profits credits ordinarily should be included in the income statement of the year in which the loss occurs or the unused excess-profits credit arises. Either of two treatments is acceptable: (a) the amount of taxes estimated to be actually payable for such year may be shown in the income statement, with the amount of the tax-reduction attributable to the amounts carried back indicated either in a footnote or parenthetically in the body of the income statement; or (b) the income statement may indicate the results of operations without inclusion of such reduction, which reduction should be shown as a final item before the amount of net income for the period.

Where taxpayers are permitted to carry forward losses or unused excess-profits credits, the committee believes that, as a practical matter, in the preparation of annual income statements the resulting tax reduction should be reflected in the year to which such losses or unused credits are carried. Either of two treatments is acceptable: (a) the amount of taxes estimated to be actually payable for such year may be shown in the income statement, with the amount of the tax reduction attributable to the amounts carried forward indicated either in a footnote or parenthetically in the body of the income statement; or (b) the income statement may indicate the results of operations without inclusion of such reduction, which reduction should be shown as a final item before the amount of net income for the period. However, where it is believed that misleading inferences would be drawn from such inclusion, the tax reduction should be credited to surplus [retained earnings].

The author agrees with the above statement of policy, with the exception of the last sentence to the effect that claims may be credited to surplus [retained earnings]. It is his considered opinion that in all instances the item should be run through the income statement. If such an item does appear in the surplus [retained earnings] account of a corporation under analysis, the analyst should adjust the income statement to include the item. The theory behind this practice is discussed in Chap. XXIII.

THEORY AND PROBLEMS

1. Name the three broad sections of the income statement and describe each section.

2. Why should depreciation be deducted as an item of cost before rather than after showing net operating profit?

[15] *Restatement and Revision of Accounting Research Bulletins, Accounting Research Bulletin* No. 43, pp. 91–92 (American Institute of Certified Public Accountants, New York, 1953).

3. State the arguments for and against including cash discounts earned and given in the *Final Net Profit or Loss* section of the income statement.

4. Give the meaning of the following terms used in the compilation of an income statement:

a. Gross sales
b. Net sales
c. Cost of sales
d. Gross profit
e. Selling expenses
f. Operating profit
g. Extraordinary charges
h. Net profit or loss

5. Describe four typical extraordinary charges. They may be either credits or debits, or both.

6. In your opinion, is the balance sheet or the income statement the most important financial statement? In other words, if you could obtain only one financial statement, would you prefer to have the balance sheet or the income statement? Give the reasons for your answer.

7. The income statement shown below was submitted in an annual report to stockholders. Study this financial statement and then answer the following questions:

a. If this income statement had been complete, what would have been the first item in it?
b. What would represent the difference between this first item and net sales?
c. Is it sound accountancy to group together in one item *cost of merchandise sold* and *buying, advertising, and occupancy expenses?* Explain your answer.
d. Is it possible to determine the gross profit from this schedule?
e. If possible, determine the operating profit from this schedule.
f. The surplus account included charges for adjustment of Federal income taxes for prior years of $2,711, and premium on preferred stock purchased of $26,426. Should either or both these charges have been included in the income statement? Explain your answer.

Income Statement

Net Sales		$24,405,072
Deduct:		
Cost of merchandise sold and buying, advertising, and occupancy expenses	$17,564,474	
Selling, general, and administrative expenses	4,176,862	
Depreciation of buildings	173,437	
Taxes (other than Federal and state income taxes)	473,650	22,388,423
		$ 2,016,649
Deduction net (including flood expense)		89,594
		$ 1,927,055
Deduct: Interest		40,183
		$ 1,886,872
Deduct:		
Federal income taxes	$ 244,774	
State income taxes	128,435	373,209
Profit for year carried to surplus		$ 1,513,663

CHAPTER XIX

Analyses of Income Statements

The income statement is the mathematical interpretation of the policies, experience, knowledge, foresight, and aggressiveness of the management of a business enterprise from the point of view of income, expenses, gross profit, operating profit, and net profit or loss. The final net profit or loss is the ultimate measure of the skill of the active management. A time always comes when the concern which is taking continuous losses must lock both the front and the rear doors and disappear from the field of active economic competition. Under these circumstances it would be most unusual if an analyst were not more favorably disposed toward the enterprise with the better operating record, although the financial condition of an occasional apparently successful concern will become progressively more unbalanced as a result of investing year after year greater funds in fixed assets than are retained in the business after dividend disbursements.

Moreover, the income statement is of special importance to the analyst who is interested in obtaining a long-range view of a business enterprise. It is essentially an interim report. Profits or losses are not fundamentally the result of operations during any short period of time. Allocations as between years of both charges and credits affecting the determination of profits are, in part, estimated and conventional and are based on assumptions as to future events, which may be validated or invalidated by experience.[1] While the items of which this is true are usually few in relation to the total number of transactions, they are sometimes large in relation to the other amounts in the income statement.

Short-term creditors, such as suppliers of raw material and merchandise, and commercial banking institutions that extend 3 to 6 months' unsecured loans, generally pay more attention to the condition of the balance sheet to support the extension of credit. Owners of long-term securities such as a funded debt, preferred stock, or common stock are inclined to pay more attention to the income statement.

The longer a claim is likely to continue, the more sustained will the

---

[1] See discussion in Chap. XXIV, "Synthesis."

516

interest be in the earning figures. The operating management and the stockholders will generally have the longest interest. Investors purchase securities in a corporation not merely to maintain their principal but also to obtain an income over the years, with possible appreciation. Any real diminution in that income generally affects the market value of their securities.

Where neither an income statement nor a reconciliation of surplus has been furnished an analyst, both progress and decline are, at times, easily concealed. An increase in surplus in the balance sheet might be due, not to earnings, but to the sale of additional stock or to the write-up of certain assets. Conversely, a reduction in surplus might result not from an operating loss, but from dividends or withdrawals in excess of earnings, a downward revaluation of assets, or miscellaneous charges made through the surplus account.

MANIPULATION OF PROFIT FIGURES

In a fascinating and comprehensive volume entitled *Security Analysis*, two authors devote eight chapters to the "Analysis of the Income Account."[2] Their "analysis," however, is only nominally concerned with variations in the expense items and their relations to net sales. Their primary objective is to acquaint the reader with those "artifices" and "window dressing" devices designed to misrepresent earnings and to conceal losses, devices that every analyst hopes and anticipates will gradually disappear in the evolution toward more uniform accountancy that is taking place.

Because of the lack of standard practice in handling the intricate problems involved in corporate accounting, "there are unbounded opportunities for shrewd detective work, for critical comparisons, for discovering and pointing out a state of affairs quite different from that indicated" by audited figures. Every stockholder, investor, speculator, and analyst should realize that net profits have been and still are subject "in extraordinary degree to arbitrary determination and manipulation." The two devices that are most commonly used for this purpose and that are of the utmost importance to the analyst are:

1. Making charges to the surplus [retained earnings] account, instead of to the income statement, or vice versa.

2. Overstating or understating depreciation, depletion, amortization, and other reserve charges.

---

[2] GRAHAM, BENJAMIN, and DAVID L. DODD, *Security Analysis*, 3d ed., Chaps. 9–15, 21 (McGraw-Hill Book Company, Inc., New York, 1951).

Charges to Surplus [Retained Earnings]

The apparent leeway allowed operating managements to decide whether certain extraordinary charges should be made to current operations through the income statement or should be made as adjustments to the surplus [retained earnings] account will be discussed in Chap. XXIII. Suffice it to state at this point that any charge to surplus [retained earnings] from the point of view of our analysis, should be made to the income account. Charges for reserve for inventory depreciation, expenses of carrying unused plant facilities, extraordinary write-downs on fixed assets, and reserves for contingencies, one and all, as explained in the preceding chapter, should be deductions in the income statement to arrive at a final net profit figure. If a study of net profits is being made over a period of years, and it is possible to prorate or to make these charges to the appropriate year or period, more accurate figures for net profits will, of course, be obtained. We are basically concerned with four figures, gross profits, operating profits, net profits after Federal income taxes but before extraordinary charges, and net profits after all charges. The manipulative device of making charges to surplus greatly affects the amount of the "reported" net profits.

Charging Reserves to Surplus [Retained Earnings]. Suppose that a corporation opened year *A* with an inventory of $1,000,000 and also closed year *A* with an inventory of $1,000,000. On the basis of these inventory figures, a final net profit of $100,000 is recorded from operations for the year.

Suppose, however, the management had opened year *A* with an inventory of $850,000 instead of $1,000,000, the difference of $150,000 representing a reserve for a possible drop in inventory values which was charged to the surplus [retained earnings] account at the end of year *B*, when no such reserve had been needed, and immediately absorbed as an offset to the inventory of $1,000,000 to bring the book figure down to the $850,000 level. On this beginning inventory of $850,000 in year *A* and the same inventory of $1,000,000 at the close of year *A* as outlined in the preceding paragraph, the final net profit for the year would now be $250,000, or $2\frac{1}{2}$ times as large as the actual net profit. This manipulation, which is not exactly unusual in accountancy, constitutes a practice of taking funds from surplus [retained earnings] and reporting these sums at a later date as net profit. The charge to the surplus [retained earnings] account goes unnoticed by all but the skilled analyst.

The reserve of $150,000 could be set up to hide current profits, or it could be set up by the management in the sincere belief that prices were high and that a drop would probably take place within the following 12 months or so. In other words, the reserve was set up before the actual loss was realized. In either case, if the charge is made to the surplus [retained earnings] account, the results are identical. If the shrinkage in inventory valuation takes place, it is charged to the reserve which was created for this contingency, with the result that the loss in inventory is not reflected in the income account for any year; it is charged indirectly to surplus [retained earnings]. Where this practice has been used, earning figures based solely on the income statement are not strictly comparable from year to year.[3] Similarly, for this same reason, income statements of concerns in the same industry are not always comparable.

By setting up an income statement in the manner explained in the preceding chapter, that is, by putting all charges through the income account and no charges through surplus [retained earnings], this situation cannot arise. Net profits determined by this technique will vary somewhat from the actual net profits earned in respective years, but they will be more in accord with actual facts than figures determined by other existing accounting theories.

Subtle Effect of Downward Appraisals. A similar subtle situation arises where fixed assets are reappraised, revalued, and written down for "conservative practices." Such a write-down results in an increase in net profits in the immediately future years to the extent of the decrease in yearly depreciation taken into the income statement, and to the extent of the permanent disappearance of the depreciation on the amount of the property written off. The dangers inherent in accounting methods of this sort are the more serious because they are so little realized by the public, so difficult to detect even by the expert analyst, and so impervious to legislation or stock-exchange corrections. In other words, the management of a

---

[3] From the standpoint of the effect upon net profit figures, a similar situation is obtained by undervaluing inventory at the end of an accounting period without the use of a reserve. Such a situation was clearly apprehended by Max Rolnik during an interesting round-table discussion on the subject "Inventory—What Is the Lower, Cost or Market?" held by the American Institute of Accountants on Oct. 20, 1937. "I don't think," said Mr. Rolnik, "we ought to let this meeting go by without some comment on the point that, while we accountants are concerned with seeing that the balance sheet and the income statement do not overstate the net worth and income, we must be careful not to get into a situation where we overstate the income for the subsequent periods. If we reduce the inventory below the market so as to show a conservative balance sheet for our bankers and a conservative income account for our stockholders, there is a likelihood that the following income statement will be overstated. In other words, we will have started the following year with an unduly low inventory, and as a result, realization of that inventory will give us profits in the subsequent year which are not true profits. They are due to what I may say is a bookkeeping adjustment. . . . Many companies are getting into the same situation because they have written down their plant values so low, in some cases down to a nominal figure, that they will not have any depreciation for the next five, ten, or fifteen years. They are going to overstate their income in the subsequent years and lead the unaware into believing that the concern is stronger and healthier, and the management abler, than they really are."—*American Institute of Accountants, Fiftieth Anniversary Celebration Volume, 1937,* p. 355 (American Institute of Certified Public Accountants, New York, 1938).

business enterprise may spend several hundred thousand dollars for real estate and plants and then decide that these prices were excessive, that their judgment was poor or warped by the conditions and the times. They may then proceed to write off the excess value by a charge to surplus [retained earnings], and by so doing, decrease future yearly depreciation charges and increase the net profits correspondingly. Financial statements submitted by registrants to the Securities and Exchange Commission under these circumstances must include information as to how much smaller the net profits would have been if the former values had been retained.

Effect of Writing Off and Writing Up Depreciable Assets. Under this same heading comes the practice of making one charge to surplus [retained earnings], to wipe off such items as leaseholds, leasehold improvements, organization expenses, development expenses, underwriting expenses, and other intangible items that have been acquired by purchase. Under sound accounting theory, the cost of these items should be charged to profit and loss over an appropriate number of years. By making one charge to surplus [retained earnings], the income statement is relieved of the future charges over the appropriate number of years and earnings for these years are correspondingly inflated.

A variation of this classic theme occurs when a certain type of expense that has been charged consistently, year after year, to the income statement is now partly or entirely capitalized and carried in the balance sheet, to be written off gradually over a period of years. For many years it was the general policy of oil-producing companies to charge drilling costs to expense. In more recent years many companies have begun to capitalize these costs and to amortize them by annual charges. Net profits for the two years, one when the costs were expense and one when the costs were capitalized, are hardly comparable. Likewise, before the net profits of two oil producers can be compared one must be sure that both producers have handled this item in a similar manner, including the number of years being used to amortize these costs.

Overstatements and Understatements

Overstatements and understatements of depreciation, obsolescence, depletion, and reserves for other purposes, such as for future losses and contingencies, are easily understood as a manipulative device, but not so easily noticed except by a most comprehensive study. To decide whether a particular charge for depreciation or depletion is adequate is often a matter of technical knowledge after the information has finally been obtained. This knowledge is more likely to be part and parcel of the equipment of the industrial engineer than of the financial analyst. What the analyst must and can at least do is to observe any deviations from past policies. Both the New York Stock Exchange and the Securities and Exchange Commission have insisted that any changes in accounting practices or charges from one year to another, of which these are the more important items, must be made known to stockholders of corporations which come under their circumspection. Obviously, whenever depreciation charges are overstated, or understated, reported net earnings are correspondingly distorted.

Rates of depreciation vary from product to product and from industry to industry. Within very general limits the average factory building depreciates at an annual rate of from 3 to 5 per cent; furniture, standard machinery, and equipment depreciate at the annual rate of 8 to 12 per cent; and patterns and tools generally depreciate at the annual rate of 20 to 30 per cent, although 100 per cent is not unknown or unusual.

There are various well-known engineering methods for computing depreciation. The commonest method is to divide the original value of the unit by the number of years of its theoretical life, and to allow an equal annual amount of depreciation for each year. In another case, the annual depreciation may increase by a graded amount each year, on the assumption that the rate of depreciation is greater the longer the property is in use. In still another case, the depreciation may be graded in the opposite direction, that is, the highest depreciation may be taken during the first year, and steadily decreasing percentages in each succeeding year. Finally, with small business concerns, depreciation often is taken intermittently, depending upon earnings from year to year; this method, which is obviously unsound, has no scientific basis and today no representative corporation would use it.[4]

At times, an amount representing a reserve for contingencies is charged to net income when no such reserve is appropriate or required. When such a provision is not properly chargeable to current revenues, the net income for the period is obviously understated by the amount of the provision. If such a reserve is set up and certain charges are made against it in subsequent years, it is evident that profits for such periods may be significantly increased by mere whim.[5]

[4] The principal methods by which yearly depreciation is determined are known as straight-line, declining balance, sum of the years digit, unit of production and hours of service, and gross operating revenue. For a brief description of these methods and the situations under which most of them are applicable, see Norman J. Lenhart and Philip L. Defliese, *Montgomery's Auditing*, 8th ed., pp. 273–277 (The Ronald Press Company, New York, 1957).

[5] The Committee on Accounting Procedure of the American Institute of Certified Public Accountants reviewed this problem of accounting. They expressed the opinon that general contingency "reserves such as those created: (a) for general undetermined contingencies, or (b) for any indefinite possible future losses, such as, for example, losses on inventories not on hand or contracted for, or (c) for the purpose of reducing inven-

Before their useful span of life is taken up by depreciation many machines must be retired because of the development of other machines that can produce the same product at a lower unit cost. Many machines, moreover, must be retired early because of a decrease in demand for the product that the machines produce. Obsolescence due to either or both of these causes cannot be forecast except in a general way. It is not customary to measure and to provide for obsolescence separately. Depreciation generally includes an allowance for obsolescence. Because of the nature of this charge, it can easily be overlooked, purposely or accidentally, and the result is an inflated net profit figure over a period of years, until obsolescence becomes so great that adjustments must then be made. Then that charge is often made by managements direct to surplus.

Net Profits after All Charges

In many business enterprises, part of the operating income arises from what may be termed *outside operations*, that is, from operations outside the principal activity of the concern. Income from outside operations may refer to the operation of an office building owned by a manufacturer of chemicals, to the operation of a radio broadcasting station by a manufacturer of furniture, to investments, and to rent. While the amount of net profits from all sources is the measure of managerial capacity, earnings from the main operations of a business are usually more stable than income from other sources in analyzing the earning power of an enterprise. A satisfactory margin of operating profit, as the income from regular operations is called, does not, however, always signify satisfactory earnings.

The profit or the loss assumed on the sale of a factory or a piece of unnecessary real estate, or the loss assumed on a charge-off on bad debts that occurred 2 years ago is just as much a credit or a charge against the judgment and the efficiency of the management as the sale of unit products on a high gross margin of profit. When a concern has an operating profit

---

tories other than to a basis which is in accordance with generally accepted accounting principles, or (d) without regard to any specific loss reasonably related to the operations of the current period, or (e) in amounts not determined on the basis of any reasonable estimates of costs or losses, are of such a nature that charges or credits relating to such reserves should not enter into the determination of net income. Accordingly, it is the opinion of the committee that if a reserve of the type described [above] is set up: (a) it should be created by a segregation or appropriation of earned surplus, (b) no costs or losses should be charged to it and no part of it should be transferred to income or in any way used to affect the determination of net income for any year; (c) it should be restored to earned surplus directly when such a reserve or any part thereof is no longer considered necessary, and (d) it should preferably be classified in the balance sheet as a part of shareholders' equity."—*Restatement and Revision of Accounting Research Bulletin, Accounting Research Bulletin* No. 43, pp. 42–43 (American Institute of Certified Public Accountants, New York, 1953).

of $55,000 and suffers a loss of $85,000 on an investment in a bankrupt subsidiary, there is a net loss of $30,000 for the year from the point of view of the complete operations of the business enterprise. A business may conceivably show operating profits each year for a number of consecutive years and retain all the operating profits in the business, but subsequently become bankrupt through unfortunate extracurricular activity which involves losses that are greater than operating profits.

Consolidated Income Account

In Chap. III, it was shown that if a corporation has 103 subsidiaries, the consolidated balance sheet might represent the condition of the parent company and all subsidiaries, or the parent company and only part—in a particular case, say, 50 of the 103 subsidiaries. In this case, the interest in the other 53 subsidiaries would be carried in the assets of the balance sheet as an item of investments. The complementary income statement would represent the incomes and expenses of the parent company and the 50 consolidated subsidiaries with all intercompany sales and income eliminated. Income derived from any of the other 53 subsidiaries would find its way into this partly consolidated income statement only in the form of such dividends as were declared and paid by these nonconsolidated subsidiaries and received by the parent corporation. This is the normal accounting procedure.

Actually, however, the complete picture of income, expenses, and profits is never available unless the analyst has a consolidated income statement of all subsidiaries, and, even more desirable, a consolidating statement that shows the individual items for each corporation as well as the consolidated figures of all. By this process all income and expenses of the entire group of related corporations appear in consecutive financial statements.

Where the income and expenses of the parent corporation and only certain of the subsidiaries are consolidated, it is always possible to omit the operating figures of profitable or unprofitable subsidiaries. This is an omission that may easily give a misleading picture to the partly consolidated income statement. For example, if the income statements of 10 of the subsidiaries are not consolidated and these 10 subsidiaries earned $1,000,000 during the accounting period and paid no dividends, generally no part of this $1,000,000 would find its way into the partly consolidated income account. A partially consolidated income statement may be quite misleading.

Even more questionable is the practice, which is occasionally followed, of issuing a consolidated income statement of the parent corporation and certain subsidiaries for one accounting period, and of the parent corporation and certain other subsidiaries for the following accounting period. Such a policy makes it impossible to compare the financial statements in successive years. In this situation it is imperative to have individual income statements of every subsidiary and a completely consolidated income statement of the entire group of related corporations for the successive years.

If, however, the income and expenses of all subsidiaries are consolidated with the figures of the parent company every year, the figures are absolutely comparable from year to year, even though new subsidiaries might be organized or acquired and old ones sold or dissolved during different periods. At the same time, as a supplemental schedule, an individual income statement of the parent corporation is always desirable in order to learn the exact income and expense items of the parent legal entity and the amount of dividends legally received, if any, from each subsidiary.

INTERNAL ANALYSIS

It has been said that in each industry, only one business enterprise is the most efficient and has the lowest cost. All others have higher costs; some are in serious need of experienced control. Furthermore, all too frequently, the producers with high costs are those that complain about low prices in the industry, although their complaints and their problems could be solved by an adequate control of their operating costs. This situation is realized and brought to the front by the qualified internal analysis of the income statement.

In the comparative analysis of income statements, important upward or downward changes in dollars and in percentages are investigated and studied to ascertain their causes. In an internal analysis of an income statement, all items are expressed as percentages of net sales. Each percentage is then compared with some predetermined base to ascertain whether particular items of expense are heavy, about normal, or low. Such an analysis is predicated upon the assumption that if any particular item of expense is abnormally large and some other item or items of expense are not smaller by the same approximate amount, the net profit will be proportionately smaller.

In this chapter we shall review three different sets of income statements, each illustrative of different features of analysis. The first case, a small retail men's furnishing shop, will illustrate the technique of internal analysis. The second case, a department store, will illustrate the technique of comparative analysis. The third case, a magazine publishing company, will illustrate the necessity of adjusting the reported income statement by the charges made to the surplus account, in order to obtain basic figures for analysis.

Retail Men's Furnishing Shop

The income statement in Schedule 65 contains the principal items of income and expenses of the Men's Furnishing Shop, Inc., for 1 year. This concern closed its fiscal year with a tangible net worth of $28,723. The first item in the income statement is gross sales for the year amounting to $80,752. From these gross sales, returns of $2,246 are deducted to give the net sales of $78,506. Cost of sales amounting to $55,033 is now deducted from the net sales to give the figure of gross profit of $23,473.

From the gross profit two items are deducted, an all-inclusive item of operating expenses of $25,522 and provisions for doubtful accounts of $251. The result is an operating loss of $2,300. Income credits for cash discounts earned amounting to $561 bring this figure down to $1,739, and

MEN'S FURNISHING SHOP, INC. [Schedule 65]
Income Statement for Year Ended December 31, 19—

	Amount	Per Cent
Gross Sales..	$80,752	102.86
Returns..	2,246	2.86
Net Sales..	78,506	100.00
Cost of Sales..	55,033	70.10
Gross Profit..	23,473	29.90
Operating Expenses..	25,522	32.51
Provision for Doubtful Accounts..	251	0.32
Operating Profit..	(L)2,300	(L)2.93
Income Credit: Cash Discounts Earned..	561	0.71
Total..	(L)1,739	(L)2.22
Interest Paid..	302	0.38
Net Loss..	(L)2,041	(L)2.60

interest paid of $302 increases the figure to $2,041, which is the net loss for the accounting period. There are no Federal income taxes, as operations resulted in a net loss for the year.

To make an internal analysis of these figures, every item in this schedule must be set up as a percentage of net sales. This has been done in the column to the right of the actual dollar figures. Gross sales of $80,752 become 102.86 per cent, returns of $2,246 become 2.86 per cent, and net sales of $78,506 become 100 per cent. Each successive item in the financial statement also becomes a per cent; cost of sales 70.10 per cent, gross profit 29.90 per cent, operating expenses 32.51 per cent, provisions for doubtful accounts 0.32 per cent, and so on down to the net loss of $2,041, which becomes a percentage loss for the accounting period of 2.60 per cent.

Every business enterprise is operated for the purpose of earning a net profit. Where a net loss is assumed, an analysis of the figures should indi-

[Schedule 66]   TYPICAL OPERATING EXPENSES FOR 38 LINES OF RETAIL TRADE
(Based on Percentage of Net Sales)
Most Recent Surveys of Respective Lines from 1953 to 1959

Line of Business	Year of Survey	Cost of Goods Sold[a]	Gross Margin	Components of Gross Margin				
				Total Salaries and Wages	Occupancy Cost	Advertising	All Other Expenses	Net Profit before Taxes[b]
		Per Cent	Per Cent	Per Cent	Per Cent	Per Cent	Per Cent	Per Cent
Appliance-Radio-Television Dealers[c]	1959	64.6	35.4	d	2.5	2.8	d	1.0
Auto Accessory and Parts Stores[e]	1955	65.6	34.4	20.3	4.7	1.2	5.5	2.7
Auto Dealers[f]	1959	85.0	15.0	d	1.0	0.8	d	1.4
Bakeries[e]	1955	58.1	41.9	21.9	6.1	0.6	9.7	3.6
Bars and Taverns[e]	1953	54.2	45.8	26.4	6.8	0.7	9.5	2.4
Book Stores[g]	1954	61.9	38.1	16.1	6.7	1.7	10.6	3.0
Camera and Photographic Supply Stores[e]	1954	69.1	30.9	16.5	4.8	1.9	5.3	2.4
Candy, Nut, and Confectionery Stores[e]	1955	64.2	35.8	20.2	8.5	0.3	6.4	0.4
Children's and Infants' Wear Stores	1957	67.5	32.5	16.6	6.9	1.3	6.0	1.7
Department Stores[h]	1959	65.9	34.1	18.4	2.6	2.2	9.6	1.3
Drugstores[i]	1959	64.4	35.6	19.3	2.3	1.5	7.8	5.7
Dry Goods and General Merchandise Stores[e]	1957	70.5	29.5	17.2	4.5	1.3	4.6	1.9
Family Clothing Stores[e]	1956	69.4	30.6	17.1	4.2	1.5	5.1	2.7
Farm Equipment Dealers[j]	1959	82.5	17.5	6.5	d	0.6	d	3.3
Farm Supply Stores[e]	1956	84.1	15.9	9.0	1.6	0.3	3.5	1.5
Floor Coverings Stores[e]	1954	64.3	35.7	21.4	4.5	1.8	6.3	1.7
Florists[k]	1953	52.6	47.4	24.3	7.0	1.8	11.0	3.3
Furniture Stores[k]	1959	61.6	38.4	21.1	5.7	5.1	5.0	1.5
Gasoline Service Stations[e]	1956	76.8	23.2	14.1	4.0	0.5	3.5	1.1
Gift, Novelty, and Souvenir Stores[e]	1957	60.0	40.0	20.8	8.7	1.2	7.4	1.9
Hardware Stores[l]	1959	69.5	30.5	18.5	3.7	1.6	5.4	1.3
Jewelry Stores (Primarily Cash and Open Credit)[e]	1953	55.6	44.4	24.2	7.4	2.2	6.9	3.7
Jewelry Stores (Primarily Installment Credit)[e]	1953	52.5	47.5	22.4	6.9	3.4	9.0	5.8
Juvenile Furniture Stores[e]	1954	66.6	33.4	16.1	6.8	2.6	4.7	3.2
Liquor Stores (Package)[e]	1955	80.3	19.7	10.5	2.9	0.3	3.4	2.6
Lumber Dealers[e]	1955	75.5	24.5	14.2	1.8	0.7	4.4	3.4
Meat Markets[e]	1954	79.3	20.7	13.2	2.3	0.2	3.6	1.4
Men's Wear Stores[m]	1959	64.6	35.5	16.2	3.1	2.9	d	3.4
Music Stores[e]	1956	64.2	35.8	18.8	5.2	2.1	7.2	2.5
Office Supply and Equipment Dealers[n]	1959	64.8	35.2	22.4	4.0	1.3	4.6	2.9
Paint and Wallpaper Stores[e]	1956	66.9	33.1	18.3	4.9	1.4	5.5	3.0
Shoe Stores (Family)[o]	1959	63.0	37.0	18.7	3.9	2.9	d	4.2
Sporting Goods Stores[e]	1953	71.4	28.6	14.7	5.1	1.7	5.1	2.0
Supermarkets[p]	1959	81.9	18.1	d	1.2	0.9	d	2.2
Toy Stores[q]	1959	65.9	34.1	d	5.1	1.7	d	d
Variety Chain Stores[h]	1955	62.7	37.3	19.4	4.4	0.4	7.6	5.5
Women's Ready to Wear Stores[e]	1953	67.7	32.3	17.0	5.4	1.3	5.7	2.9
Women's Specialty Stores[h]	1959	62.8	37.2	18.6	3.6	2.9	11.0	1.1

[a] The percentage figures under "Cost of Goods Sold" are identical with the corresponding figures under "Cost of Materials" in Schedule 6, p. 159. These two terms are synonomous.

cate the reasons for the loss so that corrective measures may be taken. In this case, either the net sales were too low for the tangible net worth, or some one or several of the items of expense were excessive. A study of the balance sheet as of the same date as the income statement indicated no unusual situation; the receivables were in healthy shape and bad debt losses of $251 or 0.32 per cent were clearly moderate; the value of the fixed assets was low, so yearly depreciation was relatively small; and the merchandise was being turned over a satisfactory number of times.

When no explanation is evident in an unsound balance sheet, the analyst must concentrate on the income statement. All items of expense shown in this concentrated schedule seem to show a normal relationship to the net sales with one exception, and that exception is the cost of sales at 70.10 per cent. Cost of sales in a well-operated retail men's furnishing shop ranges from 64 to 66 per cent. In other words, this one item of expense was approximately 5 per cent excessive. If the cost of sales had been 5 per cent lower, the result of operations would have been a net profit of 2.40 per cent instead of the net loss of 2.60 per cent. Operating expenses at 32.51 per cent, provision for doubtful accounts at 0.32 per cent, and interest at 0.38 per cent were all in satisfactory proportion to net sales for a men's furnishing store.

The reason why the cost of sales was excessive could be ascertained only by a detailed study of cost and selling prices of the individual items handled by the store, but it is clear that this one figure was heavy. On the one hand, the markup might have been too low, and on the other hand, the buying policy might have been unsound and high prices might have been paid for the merchandise.

---

[b] Net profit before taxes is shown here, rather than net profit after taxes, for purposes of comparison. The various sources from which these figures have been compiled use both unincorporated businesses (partnerships and proprietorships) and corporations in their studies. Since income taxes paid by owners of unincorporated enterprises are not based on business profits alone, the figures of both unincorporated businesses and corporations can be utilized on a comparable basis only before income taxes.

[c] National Appliance and Radio-TV Dealers Association, Chicago.

[d] Not available.

[e] Dun & Bradstreet, Inc., New York.

[f] National Automobile Dealers Association, Washington, D.C.

[g] American Booksellers Association, Inc., New York.

[h] Bureau of Business Research Bulletin, Graduate School of Business Administration, Harvard University, Boston. Ratios for department stores are based on companies with annual sales under $1,000,000.

[i] Eli Lilly and Company, Indianapolis.

[j] National Retail Farm Equipment Association, St. Louis.

[k] National Retail Furniture Association, Chicago. Ratios are for stores with annual sales from $250,000 to $500,000.

[l] National Retail Hardware Association, Indianapolis.

[m] New York University on Grant from Men's Wear Magazine, New York.

[n] National Stationery and Office Equipment Association, Washington, D.C.

[o] Washington University, St. Louis, on Grant from Footwear News, New York.

[p] Supermarket Institute Report in Progressive Grocer, June, 1960.

[q] Playthings Magazine, New York.

To the analyst who is familiar with income statements of retail men's furnishing stores, this conclusion would have been clear at a glance. In many manufacturing and wholesaling enterprises selling a large number of concerns in any one line of business activity, there are credit men who are intimately familiar with expense items in that particular line. The credit manager of a candy manufacturer should have expense items of retail and wholesale candy dealers at his finger tips; the credit manager of a wholesale grocer should be familiar with the expenses of retail grocers; and the credit manager of a men's clothing manufacturer should recognize normal expenses for retail men's clothing stores.

Standard Operating Ratios

Standard or average percentage costs for different-sized sales groups for particular divisions of industry and commerce have been made available by trade associations and by universities interested in studying the operating records of particular lines of business activity.[6] Similar studies have been made by Dun & Bradstreet, Inc., for many lines of retail trade.

Schedule 66 on page 526 gives a summary of the typical percentages of operating costs for 38 lines of retail and service trades for the latest years that studies of respective lines have been made available from 1953 through 1959. An increasing number of institutions and interested business organizations have been making studies of this nature in recent years. The income statements of concerns which operated both profitably and unprofitably for the year were used to determine these typical percentages. In this summary the salaries of owners and officers and the salaries and wages of employees were grouped into one percentage, whereas in the detailed study these items were generally separated. Likewise, under "All Other Expenses" have been grouped light and heat, taxes, bad debts, and other expenses, many of which were separate in most of the detailed studies. This schedule will, however, give an appreciation of the difference in typical costs of goods sold, typical gross margins, and general overhead expenses for different divisions of the retail and service trades, and an appreciation of the effect which a slight variance in expense percentages may have upon the final net profits of an individual business enterprise.

The percentage of gross margin from one year to another might increase only 1.20 per cent. Such a figure may be small in itself, but it may represent quite a substantial amount for a concern doing a large volume of business. A gain in gross margin may be brought about by a higher markup, by more careful buying on the part of management or the purchasing de-

---

[6] See footnote 8, pp. 504–505.

partment in larger businesses, and by reduction in manufacturing expenses in case of manufacturing concerns.

COMPARATIVE ANALYSIS

Income statements, like balance sheets, are of the greatest value when obtained over successive periods of time and so present comparative data at periodic intervals. Many corporations that publish annual reports to stockholders have in recent years presented their current income statement in comparison with that of one or more preceding years. The comparative analysis of balance sheets consists in comparing the fluctuations in the amounts represented by individual items in successive financial statements. In the same way, successive income statements are set up in parallel vertical columns and explanations of important changes in individual items are carefully obtained. The changes may be set down in other columns in absolute numbers, as horizontal percentages of the corresponding items in selected base years, or, as more generally used, as vertical percentages of the particular year's net sales.

It is not unusual for changes in accounting procedure to result in material differences in individual items from one year to another. If the figures are audited, it is the duty of the auditor to state in his report where different accounting practices have been used, together with the effect of the change on the current income statement. The Securities and Exchange Commission has prescribed:

Any change in accounting principle or practice, or in the method of applying any accounting principle or practice, made during any period for which financial statements are filed which affects comparability of such financial statements with those of prior or future periods, and the effect thereof upon the net income for each period for which financial statements are filed, shall be disclosed in a note to the appropriate financial statement.[7]

Department Store

The State Department Store, Inc., is located in an important city in one of the South Atlantic states. Operations are conducted on a tangible net worth slightly in excess of $700,000. For a period of 3 years ending year D operations were conducted with indifferent success, losses being assumed each year on steadily shrinking net sales. In year C, control of the store was sold to the owners of a chain of moderate-sized department stores, and operations were radically revamped. Several departments were eliminated, others added, a generally lower priced line of merchandise was

[7] Regulation S-X, Rule 3–07(a), p. 4, Aug. 20, 1958.

Oct. 15, 1964.

substituted, and more emphasis was placed on daily ~~modern~~ advertisements in local newspapers.

Notwithstanding these changes in merchandising policies, a considerable loss was assumed in year C and the volume of gross sales continued downward. A change took hold in year B. The gross sales increased slightly to $1,439,675 and the net loss for the year was reduced to the rather nominal amount of $6,609. In year A, a remarkable change took

[**Schedule 67**]   STATE DEPARTMENT STORE, INC.
Comparative Income Statements for Years Ended January 31, 19—

	(B) Two Years Ago		(A) One Year Ago		Change	
	Amount	Per Cent	Amount	Per Cent	Amount	Per Cent
Gross Sales..........	$1,439,675	108.74	$1,680,006	106.73	+$240,331	−2.01
Returns and Allow- ances..........	115,989	8.74	105,935	6.73	− 10,054	−2.01
Net Sales............	1,323,686	100.00	1,574,071	100.00	+ 250,385	......
Cost of Sales.......	859,047	64.90	1,007,872	64.03	+ 148,825	−0.87
Gross Profit........	464,639	35.10	566,199	35.97	+ 101,560	+0.87
Operating Expenses	543,447	41.05	533,369	33.88	− 10,078	−7.17
Operating Profit......	(L)78,808	(L)5.95	32,830	2.09	+ 111,638	+8.04
Income Credits:						
Discount Earned...	39,331	2.97	32,669	2.08	+ 6,662	−0.89
Income from Leased Departments....	31,963	2.42	46,669	2.96	+ 14,706	+0.54
Other Income......	10,010	0.75	5,891	0.37	− 4,119	−0.38
Profit after Income Credits..........	2,496	0.19	118,059	7.50	+ 115,563	+7.31
Other Charges.....	9,105	0.69	7,709	0.49	− 1,396	−0.20
Net Profit*..........	(L)6,609	(L)0.50	110,350	7.01	+ 116,959	7.51

*NOTE: No Federal income taxes in year B because of the loss and none in year A because of the carry-over of losses for previous years.

place. Gross sales increased to $1,680,006 and the final results from operations were the very substantial net profits of $110,350. Let us see how these changes took place.

The income statement for year B and for year A are set up in comparative form in dollars in Schedule 67. Following each of these dollar columns appear the respective amounts of each item converted into a percentage of the net sales as explained under the procedure for internal analysis. An understanding of the significance of internal analysis is just as essential for a comparative analysis of income statements as for balance sheets. The last two columns in Schedule 67 give the changes in dollars and in percentages of respective items between year B and year A.

Internal Analysis for Year B. An internal analysis of the figures covering operations for year *B* would have pointed out to the skilled analyst that two items were abnormally heavy, the returns and allowances of $115,989, representing 8.74 per cent of net sales, and operating expenses of $543,447, representing 41.05 per cent of net sales. Excessive returns and allowances are a vulnerable spot in any line of business activity. They indicate wide dissatisfaction on the part of customers; that dissatisfaction is registered in terms of excessive handling costs, often in the sale of part of the returns as spoiled, handled, or poor merchandise.

The deduction of returns and allowances of $115,989 from the gross sales of $1,439,675 left net sales of $1,323,686, or 100 per cent. From the net sales there was deducted cost of sales of $859,047. Cost of sales representing 64.90 per cent of net sales was in most satisfactory proportion, leaving gross profit of $464,639, or 35.10 per cent of net sales. Now came practically all other expenses—occupancy, advertising and publicity, salaries, delivery expenses—lumped into one sum of $543,477, or 41.05 per cent of net sales. If gross profit of 35.10 per cent was above normal then operating expenses of 41.05 were obviously wide of the mark. They were. Operating expenses for a department store of this size should range between 32 and 34 per cent. Because of these excessive expenses, operating profit became a red figure; even after substantial credits for discounts earned of $39,331, income from leased departments of $31,963, and other income of $10,010, a net loss of $6,609 was assumed on all operations for the year.

These figures were analyzed in this very manner by the new management of the store. An objective was now set of increased sales in year *A* which would give a wider base for all expense items; at the same time, it was decided that operating expenses would have to be reduced. Purchases were to be more carefully supervised to obtain better merchandise and so reduce the volume of returns and allowances and expenses in handling. By a comparison of the items in dollars and percentage, now let us see what progress was made toward these objectives in year *A*.

Comparative Analysis for Year B and Year A. Gross sales for year *A* totaled $1,680,006, an increase of 16.7 per cent over the gross sales for year *B*. For a management to set an objective of increased sales and then to go out and meet that objective is no simple task. Almost every concern in business is after increased sales on a higher margin of profit. To make and to meet such an objective is a real feat involving a high degree of initiative, ingenuity, aggressiveness, and skilled management. On the increased gross sales, the returns and allowances dropped from 8.74 per cent of net sales in year *B* to 6.73 per cent in year *A*. Here was progress.

As a result of greater gross sales and smaller returns and allowances, the net sales amounted to $1,574,071 in year *A*, compared with $1,323,686 in year *B*. Cost of sales was 64.03 per cent of net sales, and gross profits

35.97 per cent, both percentages reflecting only nominal changes as compared with year B.

When we come to operating expenses, the result was spectacular. The plan of cutting expenses on an increasing volume of business had been handled by the management in an exceptionally efficient manner. Operating expenses were reduced from $543,447 in year B to $533,369 in year A, and on the increased net sales the percentage of operating expenses to net sales dropped from 41.05 to 33.88 per cent. Progress of this type is rarely encountered within the period of 1 year. At 33.88 per cent, operating expenses were in line.

The immediate effect was a change from an operating loss of $78,808 in year B to an operating profit of $32,830 in year A. To this operating profit were added discounts earned of $32,669, income from leased departments of $46,669, and other income of $5,891. From this total of $118,059 were deducted other charges of $7,709, giving a final net profit of $110,350, or the most satisfactory return of 7.01 per cent on the net sales in year A, compared with the net loss of $6,609, or 0.50 per cent, on net sales in year B.

Here in six columns, two in dollar figures for successive years, two in percentage figures for successive years, and two columns representing the changes in dollars and in percentages, is the information arranged for a comparative analysis. The process involves the technique of arranging the figures in an income statement in the same sequence for the successive periods, and then having the dollar and percentage amounts of the same item in the same horizontal line. The process also involves the knowledge of internal analysis, so that the analyst would realize which items are excessive or out of balance for sound operations.

These computations in the last two columns in Schedule 67 are often helpful for ready reference, as they show the changes at a glance. The gross sales, for example, show an increase of $240,331 in year A over year B, but at the same time show a decrease of 2.01 per cent on the basis of net sales. Each item in the income account is treated similarly, down to the net profit which shows a change in the form of an increase of $116,959, or 7.51 per cent, on the net sales.

Percentage of Net Sales

Taken by itself, an income statement in which each item has been computed as a percentage of net sales for internal analysis does not always convey very enlightening information unless the analyst is skilled in the line of business under scrutiny. When this method is pursued month after month, or year after year, the variations in the percentages, however, act as indications of a changing financial condition even to the analyst with limited experience and knowledge. The longer the period of time which is covered by these comparative dollar and percentage figures, the more enlightening does comparative analysis become.

ADJUSTMENT OF AN INCOME STATEMENT

The two cases that have just been discussed, the retail men's furnishing shop and the department store, were both distributors of merchandise. Our third case is a manufacturing corporation. Before an analysis may be made, the income statement must be adjusted as a result of direct charges to the surplus account.

MAGAZINE PUBLISHING CO., INC.   [Schedule 68]
            Adjusted Income Statement for Year Ended December 31, 19—
                                       Year A

Gross Sales	$8,792,670	
Returns and Allowances	191,940	
Net Sales	8,600,730	
Cost of Sales	5,085,934	
Gross Profit	3,514,796	
Administrative and General Expense	2,055,316	Part I—From Income
Selling Expense	1,122,212	Statement
Provision for Doubtful Accounts	44,870	
Operating Profit	292;398	
Discounts Earned	18,636	
Total	310,034	
Interest Paid	35,197	
Net Profit before Extraordinary Charges	274,837	

Extraordinary Charges:		
Loss on Foreign Exchange	19,315	Part II—From Surplus
Additional Federal Taxes for Prior Years	21,138	[Retained Earnings]
Write-off on Foreign Subsidiaries	84,530	Account
Federal Income Tax	48,938	Part III—From Income Statement
Final Net Profit	$ 100,916	Part IV—Adjusted Net Profit

This particular corporation is engaged in publishing and distributing three magazines of its own, and also in printing six magazines as a jobber of printing for others. The business has been operated successfully for a long period of years, although profits have fluctuated widely from $320,-000 eight years ago to $23,000 three years ago. The headquarters and the printing plant are located in New Jersey, less than 30 miles from New York City. At the end of the year A, operations were being conducted on a tangible net worth of $2,501,038. The balance sheet reflected only a fair financial condition, the outstanding unfavorable feature being the fact that the real estate, machinery, and equipment, after depreciation, represented 98.6 per cent of the tangible net worth. Net working capital amounted to $1,362,162 and was created almost entirely by a funded debt of $678,000 and unearned subscription revenue of $622,662.

The figures in the income statement have been rearranged in Part I of Schedule 68. In the lower part of this schedule Federal income taxes are carried at $48,938. The net profit shown in the reported income statement is the last figure in Part I, which we have termed *Net Profit before Extraordinary Charges* of $274,837. The deduction of the Federal income tax at this point would have given a figure of $225,899.

In the report to stockholders and creditors, this sum was then credited to the surplus [retained earnings] account, which at the beginning of the year amounted to $2,100,125, to give a total surplus [retained earnings] of $2,326,024. At this point the surplus [retained earnings] account contained three charges, (1) loss on foreign exchange of $19,315, (2) additional Federal taxes for prior years of $21,138, and (3) write-off on foreign subsidiaries of $84,530. The deduction of these three items from the surplus [retained earnings] account left a final figure of $2,201,041. As no dividends were paid during the year, this final figure of $2,201,041 appeared as the surplus [retained earnings] in the balance sheet at the end of year *A*.

According to this accounting practice, as explained early in this chapter, charging these three items of expense, totaling $124,983, to the surplus [retained earnings] account prevented their appearing in the income account in the determination of net profits. The item of loss on foreign exchange of $19,315 was assumed during the year and without question was an expense for the year. The item of additional Federal taxes for prior years of $21,138 should have been charged in prior years. Errors in computing or in the determination of taxes for these particular years were made, and earnings in certain prior years were inflated to the extent of this sum. To some degree the errors for these prior years are offset by accepting the charge in year *A*. The final charge of $84,530 to write down investments in foreign subsidiaries is a loss chargeable to the lack of foresight of the management or to their lack of skill in the operations of these subsidiaries. Here was a definite loss. The loss might have been accumulating over a period of years and only now was being charged off; or it might be one that was entirely applicable to year *A* as a result of sudden internal changes in the political condition of the particular foreign countries in that year. In the author's opinion, the charge, as a loss, should go through the income statement and not, as handled by the accountants, by-pass the income statement and appear directly in the surplus [retained earnings] account.

These three charges appear in Part II of Schedule 68 and decrease the net profit, before Federal income taxes for year *A*, from $274,837 to $149,854. These are the adjustments which, according to our theory, must

and State

often be made to income statements in the determination of real over-all net profits or losses. The Federal income taxes—Part III of Schedule 68—are the same as appear in the orginal income statement. The final net profit, amounting to $100,916 in Part IV, differs from the reported net profit by the amount of these three specific charges.

By setting up income statements in this manner, the analyst is never under any illusions regarding final net profits. In fact, four so-called "profit figures" are obtained, all of which are essential for internal and comparative analysis, namely, gross profit, operating profit, net profit *margin* before extraordinary credits and charges, and a final net profit. The first three of these profit figures are always based upon the results of operations for the particular year and so are strictly comparable for internal analysis from year to year. The final net profit figure takes into consideration the over-all results of the management by including all extraordinary or so-called "nonrecurrent" credits and charges for the business enterprise.

THEORY AND PROBLEMS

1. Explain the effect of an understatement of inventory upon the financial statements of a commercial or industrial business enterprise, for the current and for subsequent fiscal years.

2. What effect does a write-down on the value of fixed assets have upon the net profits of future years?

3. What information is necessary for the development of a sound depreciation policy by a going industrial business concern?

4. The treasurer of a corporation submitted an unaudited balance sheet and supplementary income statement to a bank as a basis for a loan. The income statement disclosed a final net profit of $148,000 for the year. The bank sent one of its accountants to the office of the corporation to verify the figures. The accountant uncovered the following transactions that had not been taken into consideration in preparing the income statement which had disclosed the net profits for the year. Explain how each of these items should have been treated and what figure the final net profit should have been.

    a. Of the net profit reported for the year $30,000 represented profit on the sale of real estate not being used in the business.

    b. Depreciation for the year, estimated at $32,000 by the accountant, had not been taken into consideration.

    c. Dividends of $20,000 were paid on the common stock 3 days after the date of the financial statements.

    d. A write-down on inventory values amounting to $18,000 had been charged directly to the surplus account.

    e. Fixed assets had been written up $112,000, and that amount had been included in the earned surplus.

5. Give a convincing reason why dividends received on treasury stock should not be shown as income.

6. The following comparative income statements appeared in the last annual report to stockholders of the Biscuit Baking Company, Inc. Rearrange the figures, in the order that will show the most complete information, compute the percentage that each item bears to net sales as 100 per cent, and then analyze the figures.

BISCUIT BAKING COMPANY, INC.
Comparative Income Statements

	Year B	Year A
Net Sales..	$8,494,919	$7,143,647
Cost of Goods Sold...............................	6,556,366	5,539,960
Gross Profit on Sales.............................	$1,938,553	$1,603,687
Selling, Delivery, General, and Administrative Expenses Exclusive of Depreciation.........................	735,880	696,172
Net Profit on Sales before Depreciation..............	$1,202,673	$ 907,515
Other Income		
Reduction of depreciation for prior years to conform to revised income-tax basis........................	$ 96,813	—
Sundry..	10,881	$ 9,141
Total.....................................	$ 107,694	$ 9,141
Gross Income before Depreciation...................	$1,310,367	$ 916,656
Income Charges		
Cash discount on sales, interest on loans, etc.........	$ 89,760	$ 73,412
Loss on abandonment of fixed assets...............	—	11,002
Premium and expenses paid upon redemption of bonds	8,450	—
Price adjustment upon renegotiation of contracts with United States governmental agencies.............	2,485	—
Additional Federal income taxes for prior years and interest thereon..............................	71,162	—
Total.....................................	$ 171,857	$ 83,414
Net Income before Depreciation, Interest on First Mortgage Bonds, and Federal Taxes on Income..........	$1,138,510	$ 832,242
Provision for Depreciation.........................	70,468	96,255
Net Income before Interest on First Mortgage Bonds and Federal Taxes on Income.........................	$1,068,042	$ 735,987
Interest on First Mortgage Bonds or Notes		
Interest..	$ 6,401	$ 20,243
Amortization of debt discount and expense, including unamortized balance at date of redemption........	15,295	5,253
Total.....................................	$ 21,697	$ 28,496
Net Income before Federal Taxes on Income..........	$1,046,345	$ 707,491
Federal Taxes on Income...........................	$ 710,186	$ 305,300
Net Income for the Year before Provision for Reserve..	$ 336,159	$ 402,191
Provision for Possible Future Decline in Inventory Values	40,000	60,000
Balance of Net Income Transferred to Surplus.........	$ 296,159	$ 342,191

7. The following schedule gives the comparative income accounts of a manufacturer of electrical parts and supplies. If the items in this schedule need to be rearranged, change them so that you can obtain the maximum amount of information. Then determine the percentage between each item and the net sales for that year and make a thorough analysis of the figures.

Comparative Income Statements

	Year C	Year B	Year A
Gross Sales	$2,778,149	$3,599,017	$2,694,566
Returns and Allowances	92,704	101,622	99,723
Net Sales	$2,685,445	$3,497,395	$2,594,843
Materials, Labor, and Factory Expenses	$1,761,643	$2,254,695	$1,989,981
Maintenance and Repairs	82,428	121,359	70,419
Depreciation	114,225	112,870	110,391
Cost of Goods	$1,958,296	$2,488,924	$2,170,791
Gross Profit	$ 727,149	$1,008,471	$ 424,052
Administrative and General Expenses	249,945	289,321	263,082
Selling Expenses	103,401	120,222	104,106
Provision for Doubtful Accounts	9,868	7,774	7,652
Operating Profit	$ 364,935	$ 591,154	$ 49,212
Other Income Credits:			
Dividends	$ 122,158	$ 126,630	$ 61,121
Interest on Investments	19,205	23,915	17,425
Royalties	11,424	9,021	6,287
Gross Income	$ 517,722	$ 750,720	$ 134,045
Interest Paid	2,451	2,653	3,152
Net Profit before Federal Income Tax	$ 515,271	$ 748,067	$ 130,893
Federal Income Tax	72,800	106,900	53,600
Net Profit	$ 442,471	$ 641,167	$ 77,293

CHAPTER XX

Break-even Point

The capable top executive in soundly managed corporations wants to know both profitwise and costwise "where he is against where he ought to be" at any given time. "He wants to make planning and policy decisions knowing what the results must be in order to stay within certain profit and cost standards. . . . How can the executive do these things? One of the most helpful means is the break-even point control. Now, this is not a new concept. Early this century C. E. Knoeppel, often called the 'father' of break-even point control, developed the fundamental distinction between *fixed* expenses and *variable* costs contingent on volume.[1] But thinking about the concepts has not been static in the intervening years."[2] Much has been written on the subject in recent years.[3]

A "break-even point" may be defined as the level of operations at which there is neither a net profit nor a loss. With annual net sales in the neighborhood of $750,000, a particular manufacturer of manila and sisal rope would realize sufficient operating profit to cover all variable expenses, such as the cost of raw material, labor, and selling expenses, and all fixed expenses, such as administrative salaries, depreciation, real estate taxes, insurance, light, heat, and maintenance of buildings and machinery. Net sales in excess of approximately $750,000 would give increasing operating profits, as no part of the operating profit earned on sales above this point would be needed, in theory, to cover the fixed expenses.

The existence of a break-even point in every commercial and industrial

[1] C. E. KNOEPPEL, a series of articles appearing in *The Engineering Magazine*, Vol. XXXVI, October, 1908–March, 1909; subsequently published in book form under the title *Graphic Production Control* (Engineering Magazine Co., New York, 1918).

[2] RUCKER, ALLEN W., "'Clocks' for Management Control," *Harvard Business Review*, Vol. 33, No. 5, September–October, 1955.

[3] HECKERT, J. BROOKS, AND JAMES D. WILLSON, *Business Budgeting and Control*, 2d ed., pp. 359–401 (The Ronald Press, New York, 1955); KELLER, I. WAYNE, *Management Accounting for Profit Control*, pp. 372–386 (McGraw-Hill Book Company, Inc., New York, 1957); HEISER, HERMAN C., *Budgeting Principles and Practice*, pp. 25–33 (The Ronald Press Company, New York, 1959); MAY, P. A., "Profit Polygraph for Product Mix Valuation," *N.A.C.A. Bulletin*, Vol. XXXVII, No. 3, November, 1955; WEHN, WILBERT, "Break-even Points That Mean More in Profit Control," *The Controller*, Vol. XXVII, No. 7, July, 1959.

business enterprise is not a matter of theory; it is a very practical factor in the analysis of operations not only by the active management but by others who may be outside the business. This information may be visualized in a chart showing the relationship between net sales and operating profit before Federal income taxes.

Such a chart is of considerable value in analyzing past experiences and in projecting facts to disclose the effect on immediately future operations. More specifically, it may be used to compare net sales, expenses, and operating profits with a budget, to determine the probable unit cost at varying levels of production, to determine the effect of a reorganization or a change in operating policy, to compare the probable operating profits of different enterprises at various levels of operations, to determine the increase in net sales required to justify a given plant expansion, or to balance a given reduction in selling price, and to determine the effect upon operating profits of a change in wages or in materials cost.[4]

A graph of this nature is generally known as a break-even chart. The real value of such a chart "lies in its capacity to visualize the relationship between fixed expense, variable expense, and income. However arranged and plotted, it shows the point or zone where income balances outgo. This is the point where losses cease and beyond which profits are realized."[5] It becomes the mechanical means of measuring the effect of varying levels of sales secured at varying levels of selling and manufacturing costs. Such a chart may be plotted in several different forms, depending upon what information is desired; some are quite simple, consisting of a line or two, and others are quite complex with many lines and legends. Six examples will be described.

Conventional break-even analysis is predicated on the assumption that costs and expenses which are recognized for accounting purposes can be classified into two categories. The two categories are: (1) those whose amounts are not materially influenced by the level of activity in the short run, termed fixed expenses, and (2) those whose amounts are a function of activity, increasing in the same direction and in the same general proportion as activity, termed variable expenses. This classification admittedly is somewhat imperfect, but at the same time, practical and useful.

EXAMPLES OF BREAK-EVEN CHARTS

In every business enterprise there are certain fixed expenses, namely, administrative expenses, depreciation on fixed assets, repairs and main-

---

[4] KNOEPPEL, C. E., and EDGAR G. SEYBOLD, *Managing for Profit*, pp. 29–36 (McGraw-Hill Book Company, Inc., New York, 1937); SINCLAIR, PRIOR, *Budgeting*, pp. 382–394 (The Ronald Press Company, New York, 1934).

[5] SINCLAIR, *op. cit.*, p. 370.

tenance of fixed assets, insurance, real estate taxes when property is owned, rent when property is leased, interest on outstanding funded debt, if any, local taxes, light and heat. These items are termed fixed expenses[6] because they remain unchanged, or relatively unchanged, whether a business enterprise is operating at 25 or at 100 per cent of capacity. A certain volume of net sales must be obtained to produce the gross profit to cover these expenses before an operating profit is reached. Net sales below this point will result in operating losses, and above this point in increased operating profits.

[6] Walter Rautenstrauch and Raymond Villers find three sources of fixed expenses: (1) those occasioned by the possession of a business, (2) those assessed for purposes of capital recovery of investment in fixed assets, and (3) those which arise in the operation of a business. These three sources are then described as follows: "The *costs to possess* are interest on mortgages, local taxes, insurance and rent. These items of expense are based on the values of the assets possessed, and the rates of interest, insurance, and taxes applied to these values. The *costs of capital recovery* are determined by accounting for depreciation. . . . . Another group of total constant expenses arises from the operations of the business at any particular time. These expenses are determined in part by the organic features of the business and also in part by executive policy concerning appropriations for such operations. For instance, the annual expenses of heating, lighting, part of power (connected load charge in the case of purchased power) and a portion of maintenance and repair of buildings and machinery are, for any particular year, in the life of a business fairly constant, and specific amounts of money may be budgeted annually for meeting such expenses. These expenses, moreover, are within limits controllable by management, since the amount of such expenses depends in part on how such services are organized and managed. These expenses are, to a degree, regulated from time to time by the executives of the business but for any year are budgeted as specific amounts, and are therefore considered as constant over a wide range of sales. Another group of expenses, which is set up on an annual basis as a company anticipates its expenses for an approaching year or accounting period, consists of executive salaries and appropriations for advertising and other operating expenses which experience has shown are fairly constant, as sales vary over an appreciable range. A going concern at any particular time maintains a number of employees who are on annual salaries. The officers of the company, the department heads, and minor officials are in this class. The salaries of these employees are determined and regulated from time to time by executive action. But for any particular year, the total of such annual salaries is a determinable amount. If, later, the volume of business expands and the company prospers, salaries of officers may be raised and new salaried employees may be engaged. With a serious decline in sales, the number of salaried employees may be materially reduced. But, at any time, the company's books will show a list of salaried employees together with their monthly or annual salaries and the total of such salaries does constitute an anticipated constant cost of the present condition of the business. The executives of a business, in anticipation of a certain income from sales and from other sources, determine the annual appropriations for advertising and other promotional activities. Expenses so budgeted for a given year may be reduced in the following year if anticipated revenues are less, or may be increased if the prospects of increased sales seem to warrant. Accordingly, such expenses are constant at either higher or lower levels for an appreciable range of sales. Thus, expenses of the above kinds are regulated by executive action and are constant in time over a range of output. At any particular time, therefore, they are regulated constant expenses."—RAUTENSTRAUCH, WALTER, and RAYMOND VILLERS, *The Economics of Industrial Management*, pp. 87–89 (Funk & Wagnalls Company, New York, 1949).

An example will illustrate the typical unsound decision which may be made when one is unfamiliar with the practical aspect of what affects the break-even point, that is, the breakdown of costs into fixed expense and variable expense. A manufacturer had discontinued selling three important accounts because, as he said, he "couldn't afford to keep them." A competitor had quoted prices which were lower than the manufacturer's own cost of production. In arriving at the decision that he would be better off without these three accounts, the manufacturer had made the common error of assuming that if the sales of a product to a particular customer showed a conventional accounting loss, that business was unprofitable to the extent of that loss.

Sometime later when the manufacturer became acquainted with fixed and variable expenses, he was able to get those accounts back. Over an accounting period they showed a loss of $36,000 by conventional accounting methods. If, however, the three accounts had not been sold during this period, the operating profit would have been $82,000 less than was actually earned. This was due to the fact that the costs of the goods sold to these three customers included fixed manufacturing expenses of $118,000, and the accounts, therefore, contributed to the operating profit by absorbing $82,000 of these fixed charges which otherwise would have been added to the costs of the goods sold to the other customers.[7] To the uninitiated this example might seem a trifle farfetched. The remainder of this chapter, however, will show the significance of fixed expenses and variable expenses in making many decisions.

Simple Break-even Chart

The relationship between net sales and operating profit or loss is plotted in the simplest way in Form 20. This chart is based on the quarterly figures of the Knitted Underwear Corporation, located in North Carolina. Charts of this nature may be made from a series of monthly figures just as readily as from a series of quarterly figures, as used in this example. Occasionally they are plotted from a series of successive yearly figures, although changes in expense items such as salaries, wages, and selling prices may make it difficult to obtain yearly income statements that are fairly comparable. In a study of this nature it must be kept in mind that we are interested, not in net profit or loss after extraordinary and nonrecurring charges and after setting up proper reserves for income taxes, but solely in operating profit or loss as it reflects the result of the operation of the main activity of the business enterprise under consideration, and after the payment of interest on any borrowed funds.

[7] HARRISON, G. CHARTER, *The Gold Mine Is in Volume!* pp. 30–31 (G. Charter Harrison, Madison, Wis., 1950).

The figures in Schedule 69 give the comparative quarterly operations of the Knitted Underwear Corporation for each quarter of the year. In the first step to construct Form 20, it is necessary to ascertain the fixed expenses. These expenses generally cannot be obtained from typical condensed income statements. They are there, but in many cases they are hidden or grouped with other items. There is no ~~more~~ uniformity among

[Schedule 69]   KNITTED UNDERWEAR CORPORATION

Comparative Quarterly Income Statements

	1st Quarter	2d Quarter	3d Quarter	4th Quarter
Gross Sales..........................	$ 376,029	$696,004	$563,198	$675,313
Less: Returns and Allowances........	11,246	14,575	6,320	8,481
Net Sales...........................	$ 364,783	$681,429	$556,878	$666,832
Less: Cost of Sales				
Raw Material....................	$ 167,951	$312,724	$252,798	$303,049
Labor...........................	84,536	164,699	136,212	173,710
Variable Manufacturing Expenses...	40,128	70,572	57,588	69,146
Depreciation....................	10,800	10,963	10,764	10,884
Real Estate Taxes...............	2,286	2,002	2,186	2,104
Insurance.......................	2,404	2,388	2,210	2,296
Gross Profit........................	$ 56,678	$118,081	$ 95,120	$105,643
Less:				
Administrative Expenses..........	$ 29,748	$ 30,883	$ 32,520	$ 31,727
Selling Expenses.................	23,261	41,769	32,764	33,005
Doubtful Accounts...............	1,980	2,746	2,170	1,874
Operating Profit....................	$ 1,689	$ 42,683	$ 27,666	$ 39,037
Less: Discount Given...............	5,622	9,943	6,977	7,056
Net Profit or Loss before Extraordinary				
Charges.........................	$(L)3,933	$ 32,740	$ 20,689	$ 31,981
Add: Other Income..................	8,517	16,507	12,725	1,347
Net Profit before Income Taxes.......	$ 4,584	$ 49,247	$ 33,414	$ 33,328

accountants in the classification of expense items ~~than in the classification of balance sheet items~~. An item that is a semifixed expense may be considered as variable by one accountant or accounting firm and as fixed by another.[8] For the Knitted Underwear Corporation, the fixed expenses,

[8] In 1932, Walter Rautenstrauch wrote as follows: "As a general rule it is not possible to take the published statements of a company and without any experience with its details of operation arrive at a satisfactory segregation into constant [fixed] and variable total costs [expenses]. Any attempt to base an analysis of the economic characteristics of a business on a published statement only, must necessarily result in very rough approximations, and these are sometimes worse than useless because they are misleading."—A study entitled "The Economic Characteristics of the Manufacturing Industries" in *Mechanical Engineering*, Vol. 54, No. 11, p. 760, November, 1932. Five years later G. Charter Harrison emphasized this same viewpoint: " . . . To make any intelligible analysis of profit variations requires a fundamental change in the accounting set-up, namely the analysis of all costs and expenses as between fixed and variable. . . . While it is true that the revamping of accounting procedure so that costs and expenses are divided as between fixed and variable introduces technical

consisting of the following four items for each quarter, are available from the respective quarterly statements:

Table of Fixed Expenses

	1st Quarter	2d Quarter	3d Quarter	4th Quarter	Total for Year
Administrative Expense...........	$29,748	$30,883	$32,520	$31,727	$124,878
Depreciation.....................	10,800	10,963	10,764	10,884	43,411
Real Estate Taxes...............	2,286	2,002	2,186	2,104	8,578
Fire, Tornado, and Liability Insurance.........................	2,404	2,388	2,210	2,296	9,298
	$45,238	$46,236	$47,680	$47,011	$186,165

Average Fixed Expenses per Quarter................................$ 46,541

The principal item of fixed expenses in the above table is administrative expense, ranging from $29,748 in the first quarter to $32,520 in the third quarter, or total administrative expenses for the year of $124,878. Depreciation charges are the next largest, ranging from $10,764 to $10,963 for a yearly total of $43,411. Insurance covering fire, tornado, and liability aggregated $9,298 for the year, and real estate taxes amounted to $8,578. The total fixed charges for the year aggregated $186,165 and amounted to an average of $46,541 per quarter. Here are the charges that must be met every 3 months whether the plant is closed or operations are being conducted at 25 per cent capacity or at 100 per cent. This point is plotted on the vertical axis at A, the place where a loss of this amount is taken when the plant is shut down and no sales whatsoever are being made.

Successive points are then plotted at B, C, D, and E, representing the net sales and the operating profit for each respective quarter. If the profit income and loss statements from which these figures were taken had been prepared in a uniform manner and there had been no appreciable external influence, these points would tend to be in a straight line. The line may be drawn by the simple but practical method of inspection or by the more scientific algebraic method of least squares.[9] The area where this line crosses the

problems which will doubtless give accountants many headaches when this change is demanded by executives, generally I have no hesitation in predicting that that time must soon come."—*Swamped in a Sea of Figures*, pp. 11, 19 (G. Charter Harrison, Madison, Wis., 1937). See also the pamphlet, *The Profit Pattern, Road Map of the Manufacturer*, by G. Charter Harrison (Madison, Wis., 1947).

[9] The method of least squares is the mathematical process of taking a series of points whose trends can best be represented on a chart by a smooth line and fitting the line to these points. In our case the line is a straight line and not a curve. Frederick C. Mills, in *Statistical Methods*, rev. ed., pp. 246–250 (Henry Holt and Company, Inc., New York, 1940), technically explains this statistical process as follows: ". . . The

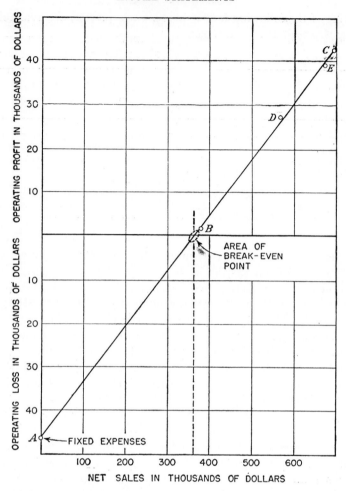

FORM 20. Simple break-even chart showing straight-line relationship between operating profit or loss and net sales.

heavy horizontal line representing the division between an operating profit and an operating loss will include the break-even point. In this case the quarterly sales volume at the break-even point is in the neighborhood of $355,000.

task of fitting is merely the determination of the constants in an equation of the form $y = a + bx$. The values of a and b which will give a line following most closely the trend of the data are to be obtained. A simple illustration may serve to demonstrate the various methods which may be employed. Nine points (1, 3; 2, 4; 3, 6; 4, 5; 5, 10; 6, 9; 7, 10; 8, 12; 9, 11) are plotted. Our problem is the fitting of a straight line to these points. [When plotted on a chart, these points will be somewhat scattered but will have a straight-line tendency.] By inspection approximate values of a and b may

The break-even point may also be arrived at by a simple mathematical computation. The first step in this computation is to estimate the dollar amount of net sales, fixed expenses, and variable expenses to be expected in an accounting period. Then, by dividing the dollar amount of fixed expenses by the difference between 100 per cent and the percentage of variable expenses to net sales, the break-even point will be obtained.

---

be determined. A thread may be stretched through the points in such a direction that it seems to follow the trend as closely as possible. The slope of the line thus laid out may be measured, the $y -$ intercept determined, and the desired equation thus approximated. Obviously this is a loose and uncertain method, and the results obtained by different individuals may be expected to vary rather widely. . . . The constants for this line of best fit may be determined by the method of least squares. . . . Assuming that each pair of measurements give an approximation to the true relationship between the variables, we wish to find the most probable relationship, and this is given by the line for which the sum of squared deviations is a minimum. We have, in the present example, nine pairs of values of x and y. Substituting these values in the generalized form of the linear equation $y = a + bx$, we secure the following observation equations: $3 = a + 1b$; $4 = a + 2b$; $6 = a + 3b$; $5 = a + 4b$; $10 = a + 5b$; $9 = a + 6b$; $10 = a + 7b$; $12 = a + 8b$; $11 = a + 9b$. Any two of these equations could be solved as simultaneous equations, and values of a and b secured. But these values would not satisfy the remaining equations. Our problem is to combine the nine observation equations so as to secure two *normal equations*, which, when solved simultaneously, will give the most probable values of a and b. The first of these normal equations is secured by multiplying each of the observation equations by the coefficient of the first unknown (a) in that equation, and adding the equations obtained in this way. Since the coefficient of a in the present case is 1 throughout, the nine observation equations are unchanged by the process of multiplication. The second of the normal equations is secured by multiplying each of the observation equations by the coefficient of the second unknown (b) in that equation, and adding the equations obtained. Thus the first equation is multiplied throughout by 1, and the second by 2, and so on. The process of securing the two normal equations is as follows:

Derivation of Normal Equations for Observation Equations

$3 = a + 1b$	$3 = 1a + 1b$
$4 = a + 2b$	$8 = 2a + 4b$
$6 = a + 3b$	$18 = 3a + 9b$
$5 = a + 4b$	$20 = 4a + 16b$
$10 = a + 5b$	$50 = 5a + 25b$
$9 = a + 6b$	$54 = 6a + 36b$
$10 = a + 7b$	$70 = 7a + 49b$
$12 = a + 8b$	$96 = 8a + 64b$
$11 = a + 9b$	$99 = 9a + 81b$
$70 = 9a + 45b$	$418 = 45a + 285b$

The two normal equations are: $70 = 9a + 45b$; $418 = 45a + 285b$. It remains to solve these equations for a and b. By multiplying the first equation by 5 and subtracting it from the second, a may be eliminated; a value of $68/60$, or 1.133, is found for b. Substituting this value in either of the equations a value of 2.111 is secured for a. The equation to the best fitting straight line is, therefore, $y = 2.111 + 1.133x$. In the actual application of the method it is not necessary to write out and total the equations, as is done above. We need only insert the proper values in the two equations:

$$\Sigma(y) = na + b\Sigma(x)$$
$$\Sigma(xy) = a\Sigma(x) + b\Sigma(x^2)$$

In the case of the Knitted Underwear Corporation, for example, the annual net sales for the year under review amounted to $2,269,922, or an average of $567,480 per quarter. Annual fixed expenses amounted to $186,165, or an average of $46,541 per quarter, and annual variable expenses to $1,972,682, or an average of $493,170 per quarter. By dividing the average quarterly variable expense by the average quarterly net sales, we obtain a figure of 86.9 per cent. By deducting this figure from 100 per

---

The symbols employed have the following meaning: $\Sigma(y)$: the sum of the values of y; $\Sigma(x)$: the sum of the values of x; $\Sigma(xy)$: the sum of the products of the x's and the y's; $\Sigma(x^2)$: the sum of the squares of the values of x; n: the number of pairs of values, the number of points plotted."

E. Dillon Smith, in *Mechanical Engineering*, Vol. 55, No. 8, pp. 516–517, August, 1933, has explained that according to this method of least squares "there are three different procedures possible: (1) the condition that makes the sum of the residuals least for X on Y; (2) the one that makes the normal form the (X,Y)'s the least; and (3) the one that makes the residuals least for Y on X."

Dr. Theodore H. Brown, professor of statistics at the Harvard Graduate School of Business Administration, has provided the author with the following explanation of the fact that not only three but actually an infinite number of different solutions are possible under the method of least squares: "The equations usually given in textbook tacitly make the assumption that the deviation should be drawn parallel to the Y or vertical axis. For this purpose the equation of the straight line is $y = a + bx$, where a and b are the constants determined from the data. If it is desired to measure the deviation parallel with the X-axis, one starts with the equation $X = A - BY$ where A and B are the constants determined by the data and where these values are not necessarily the same as those for a and b. These two methods of drawing the deviation are the extremes for a given problem. In fact the deviation can be drawn at any other constant angle which the investigator may desire to use. For each of the ways of drawing the deviation there is usually found a different line. The result is that the two lines used to determine a break-even point may not always intersect at precisely the same point. The decision made regarding the way in which the deviations are drawn has a simple meaning. When the deviations are drawn parallel to the Y-axis the assumption is that the X-values are absolutely accurate relative to the Y-values. The converse is true when the deviations are drawn parallel to the X-axis. Drawing the deviations at an angle of 45 degrees is equivalent to the assumption that X and Y-values are equally likely to error. There is still another possibility which will cause the intersection representing the break-even point to vary within an appreciable area. This arises from the fact that the data to which a line is fitted are experimental in character. They contain commonly the effect of many factors which cause the fitted line to depart from a position which it would occupy if such additional factors were not operating. The consequence of this principle is that the line finally fitted to a set of data should be considered as a center of an experimental band of possibilities within which the true position of the line would be located if all figures could be evaluated. The result of this principle for two lines is that there is a parallelogram formed by the boundaries of the two intersecting bands. Within this area the true intersection would be definitely known if all unwanted influences were precisely accounted for." Discussions and descriptions of the methods of least squares may be found in most current volumes on statistical methods, such as Alva M. Tuttle, *Elementary Business and Economic Statistics*, pp. 422–438 (McGraw-Hill Book Company, Inc., New York, 1957); John R. Riggleman and Ira N. Frisbee, *Business Statistics*, 3d ed., pp. 302–304, 349–353 (McGraw-Hill Book Company, Inc., New York, 1951); George R. Davies and Dale Yoder, *Business Statistics*, 2d ed., pp. 236–243 (John Wiley & Sons, Inc., New York, 1941).

cent, we obtain 13.1 per cent. Dividing the average quarterly fixed expenses of $46,451 by this figure of 13.1 per cent, we obtain $355,000 as the break-even point.

If the plotted points are not in a fairly straight line, an analysis should be made of the income statements and operating policies to obtain the explanation before the line is drawn by the method of inspection or by the method of least squares. That explanation would bring out the fact that the comparative income statements from which the operating profit figures have been taken were not on a comparable basis because of such factors as raising or lowering selling prices, raising or lowering rates of salaries or wages or particular items of manufacturing costs, shifting the percentage to total sales of the sales of the more profitable lines, or including among certain items extraordinary or nonrecurring charges that would throw operating expenses out of strict comparison.

If materially different selling prices or rates of salaries and wages were used in the various income statements, separate charts based on each rate should be made, if possible, from the income statements. If extraordinary or nonrecurring charges are grouped with other items, for the purpose of obtaining data to plot the chart, the income statements should be adjusted by the elimination of these charges.

In Form 20, a single line indicates the operating loss or the operating profit at any sales volume level. This is the simplest form of a break-even chart. A more typical and conventional chart has three plotted lines showing the relationship between variable operating expenses, total operating expenses, and net sales. In the construction of this chart the horizontal scale represents the percentage of plant capacity and/or the number of units produced, and the vertical scale represents dollars.

Conventional Break-even Chart

In any accounting period, net sales of a manufacturing concern, disregarding fluctuations due to sales made out of inventory, may fluctuate from zero to a high point theoretically represented by maximum plant capacity. In other words, the plant of a particular manufacturer may have a maximum monthly capacity of 200 identical pieces of machinery, representing total net sales of $40,000, or $200 per machine. In any single month, the net sales may thus fluctuate between zero and $40,000.

At capacity operations these machines may be manufactured at $150 each, or a total of $30,000. However, if the plant is operating at somewhat less than maximum capacity, the manufacturing cost per machine will be somewhat higher because of the fact that the fixed expenses amount to approximately $10,000 per month. Certain other expenses such as direct labor and raw materials will fluctuate in relation to the percentage of capacity operation. If the variable costs amount to $100 per machine, these costs must be added to the fixed expenses to obtain the amount of total expenses.

A line representing total expenses plotted from these figures, with the horizontal axis representing percentage of plant capacity and the vertical axis representing dollars, will give the total expenses for any rate of plant activity by direct reading. If on this chart there is now superimposed another line representing net sales, we have the more conventional break-even chart; the area where these two lines intersect will include the break-even point.

From such a chart it would be clear that when production is at capacity of 200 machines per month, the total sales would be $40,000 and the total expenses $30,000, leaving an operating profit of $10,000. If operations were at 75 per cent of capacity, or 150 machines, the net sales would be $30,000, and the total expenses $25,000, leaving an operating profit of $5,000. If operations were at 50 per cent of capacity, or 100 machines for the month, the net sales would be $20,000; the total expenses would also be $20,000, with the result that there would be no profit. Operations at less than 50 per cent capacity, or less than 100 machines, would result in an operating loss at the existing level of fixed expenses.

The first actual step in the preparation of the conventional break-even chart of this nature is to obtain and to plot the points representing quarterly net sales of the Knitted Underwear Corporation in percentage of plant capacity or on the basis of the number of units produced. These points are obtained from the following table:

Table of Quarterly Net Sales in Relation to Plant Capacity

	Net Sales	Dozen	Per Cent of Capacity
First Quarter...............	$364,783	97,000	32.3
Second Quarter............	681,429	186,000	62.0
Third Quarter.............	556,878	165,000	55.0
Fourth Quarter............	666,832	179,000	59.7

This particular plant has a normal quarterly capacity of 300,000 dozen knitted products. On this basis, when 97,000 dozen were produced in the first quarter, operations were at 32.3 per cent capacity. Net sales and the number of dozens produced increased during the second quarter. Operations were conducted at 62.0 per cent of capacity in the second quarter, 55.0 per cent in the third quarter, and 59.7 per cent in the fourth quarter. On the basis of the quarterly dollar net sales and the percentage of operations for each quarter, the points A, B, C, and D were plotted in Form 21, and the *net sales* line drawn from zero to fit, as close as possible, to these four points.

The next step is the determination of the quarterly *variable operating expenses*. These particular figures are sometimes grouped with fixed expenses in income statements, and breakdowns of individual items must be obtained to secure the necessary information. In this case, the figures are available from the comparative income figures in Schedule 69. Segregating these expense items we have the following table.

Table of Variable Expenses

	1st Quarter	2d Quarter	3d Quarter	4th Quarter	Total for Year
Raw Materials................	$167,951	$312,724	$252,798	$303,049	$1,036,522
Labor.......................	84,536	164,699	136,212	173,710	559,157
Variable Manufacturing Expenses	40,128	70,572	57,588	69,146	237,434
Selling Expenses..............	23,261	41,769	32,764	33,005	130,799
Doubtful Accounts.............	1,980	2,746	2,170	1,874	8,770
Total....................	$317,856	$592,510	$481,532	$580,784	$1,972,682

From this table the quarterly variable expenses, totaling $317,856 for the first quarter, $592,510 for the second quarter, $481,532 for the third quarter, and $580,784 for the fourth quarter, were plotted at E, F, G, and H at the same percentage of plant capacity represented by the respective net sales for these quarters. The line representing variable operating expenses is now drawn from zero to fit, as close as possible, to points E, F, G, and H.

The third step is the plotting of the line representing *total operating expenses*. We have already seen that the average quarterly fixed expenses amounted to $46,541. The point J is plotted on the vertical axis $46,541 above zero. The line representing total operating expenses is then drawn from J through the break-even point. If all figures are comparable and no adjustments need to be made, the line of total operating expenses will be parallel to the line representing variable operating costs, but above it to the extent of the fixed charges.

In this chart the area under the variable operating expense line represents the amount of variable cost at the various percentages of plant activity. The area between the variable operating expense line and the total operating expense line represents fixed expense and is constant at the different degrees of plant activity. The area between the net sales line and the total operating expense line is an operating loss to the left of the break-even point, and an operating profit to the right of that point. It will be noted that the profit realization point is at a plant activity of approximately 32 per cent. This indicates that when plant activity is below 32 per cent of capacity an operating loss will be incurred; when above, an operating profit will be earned. The conventional break-even chart of this nature graphically registers three different movements in relation to operating profit and loss at the same time, variable expense,

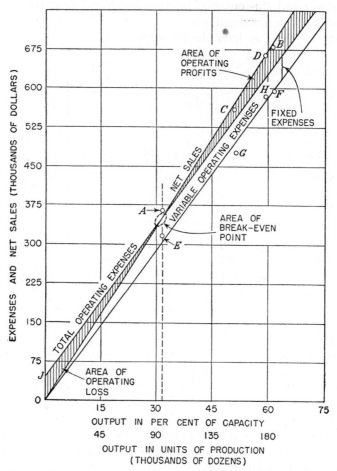

FORM 21. Typical break-even chart showing straight-line relationships of variable expenses, fixed expenses, total expenses, and net sales.

fixed expense, and net sales, just as the second hand, the minute hand, and the hour hand are related to give the correct time, at any moment, in terms of a progressive time scale of 12 hours.

Actually the lines used in Form 20 and Form 21 may be established at slightly different areas depending upon the method used. After the points are plotted, if the lines are drawn by the simple but practical method of inspection, the position may be slightly different than if they are drawn by one of the various formulas used in the methods of least squares, described in the footnote on pages 543–546. The break-even point actually falls within a restricted area. "The region within which the most probable

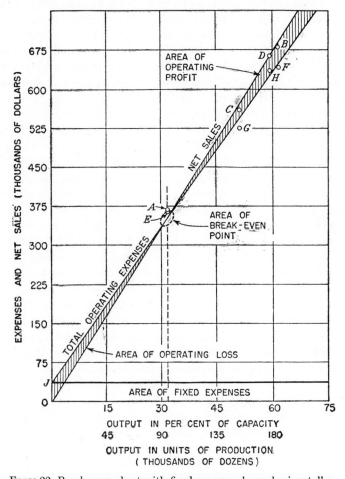

FORM 22. Break-even chart with fixed expense shown horizontally.

value of the break-even point may be expected to be found," explains E. Dillon Smith, "can be shown statistically to be a flattened oval. This outline of the area is due to the non-normal distribution of the deviation."[10] Such an oval will be found encompassing the break-even points in Forms 20 and 21, 22, 23, and 24.

The conventional break-even chart is often presented in a form where

[10] *Mechanical Engineering*, Vol. 55, No. 8, pp. 516–517, August, 1933.

the fixed expense represents a horizontal bar across the lower part of the chart instead of a line parallel to and above the line of variable expense. Such a chart is illustrated in Form 22. Here the area below the fixed expense line represents the same costs at every percentage of operation. The total operating expense line is made as in Form 21. The vertical distance between the line of fixed expense and the line of total operating expense represents the amount of variable expense at every percentage of capacity. The line of net sales is plotted identically in both charts. Where the line of net sales and the line of total operating expenses intersect in Form 22 is the area including the break-even point. A chart of this nature is somewhat simpler to construct than the chart in Form 21.

Both Form 21 and Form 22 represent charts that give highly simplified keys to the complex problem of variable operating profits. Not only do these charts illustrate graphically why operating profits tend to increase at a greater rate than net sales, but they also show the limits within which net sales must be maintained if satisfactory results are to be obtained. Certain of the important operating problems of business such as price reduction, pay-roll cuts, plant expansions, and the introduction of new products can be decided intelligently only in the light of the variable interrelationships of vital facts reflected by such charts.[11] Break-even charts are also used effectively in the study of these forces affecting the operations of individual plants, of branches, of departments, and of the manufacture of various products, all within one corporation.

Practical Modifications to Conventional Break-even Charts. The conventional break-even chart is plotted on straight-line relationships which assume that variable operating expenses and total operating expenses are directly proportional to plant activity. It is also assumed that the items classified as fixed expense remain constant throughout the entire range of activity from zero to 100 per cent. These assumptions are sufficiently accurate for all ordinary purposes.

As an everyday practical matter, however, the variable indirect expenses cannot be controlled to make them exactly proportional to plant activity at all levels, as a positive relationship does not actually exist. It is possible to determine an extra allowance for such items and to add that allowance to the theoretical variable expense.[12] When such an extra allowance is made, the variable expense line may be found to be a slight curve instead of a straight line. Similarly, certain fixed expenses are in reality semifixed, that is, they may be reduced moderately as sales income and activity decrease, although not proportionately. Property taxes, for example, have been known to be lowered in bad times, insurance coverage

---

[11] For mathematical computations involved in the detailed study of these features, see Sinclair, *op. cit.*, pp. 382–394.

[12] For a practical explanation as to how an extra allowance of this nature may be worked out, see H. R. Mallory, "The Break-even Chart," *Mechanical Engineering*, Vol. 55, No. 8, pp. 493–496, 515, August, 1933.

reduced as hazards become less, and overhead departments telescoped. If the semifixed expenses included in the fixed expense group are analyzed for their variations at given activites, there may be secured a more accurate estimate of total cost, differing somewhat from the theoretical total cost based on the definitely fixed and proportional relationship. The total

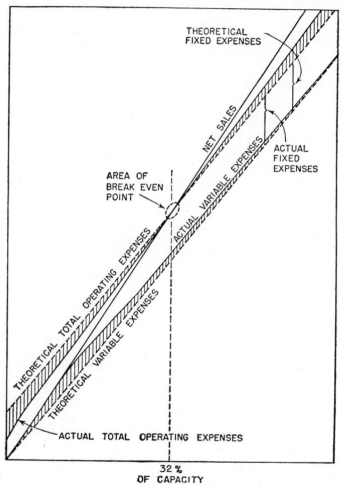

FORM 23. Typical break-even chart showing practical modifications to straight-line relationships.

expense line on this basis will also be a slight curve with a somewhat lower fixed expense at a low level of activity than at a high level.

Form 23 illustrates this situation. This chart is a slight enlargement of a section of Form 22. A dash line represents theoretical variable expense on a straight-line relationship; a continuous curve line, which meets both ends of this dash line, represents the actual variable expense. On this basis the actual variable expense is considerably greater than the straight-line relationship when operating at the low percentages of plant capacity. This excess gradually decreases as the actual and the theoretical expenses meet at 100 per cent of activity. Fixed expense, on the other hand, is somewhat lower than the straight-line relationship at the low levels of activity.

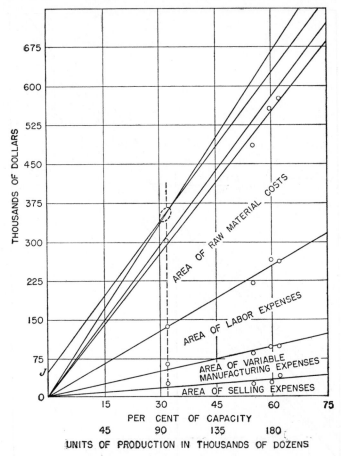

FORM 24. Break-even chart showing principal divisions of variable expenses.

As a result, the total actual expense is somewhat lower than the theoretical total expense to the left of the break-even point, and slightly higher to the right of the break-even point.

Detailed Conventional Break-even Chart

Form 24, a style of break-even chart which is widely used by managements, and particularly by those in charge of budget operations, is similar to Form 21, but with more lines. It has the same fixed expense, but in addition a breakdown of variable expenses is also shown. The major items of variable expense are plotted at the various percentages of capacity operations to give a straight-line relationship of the respective items of expense with increasing net sales.

In this particular example, the major variable expense items plotted are raw materials, labor, variable manufacturing expenses, and selling expenses. The vertical distance from the base of the chart to the first slanting line represents selling expenses at respective percentages of capacity operation. The vertical distance between the first and the second slanting lines represents variable manufacturing expense at respective percentages of capacity operations. Likewise, the vertical distance between the second and third slanting lines represents labor expense, and the distance between the third and fourth slanting lines, the cost of raw materials. Such a chart may be made as detailed as seems desirable and expedient, as items of variable expense may be grouped into any practical subdivisions in which the analyst is interested. Such charts are very practical and are more effective in bringing out important relationships than figures alone would be.

The Profitgraph

The name *profitgraph* has been applied to the break-even chart designed by C. E. Knoeppel, who was one of the first industrial engineers to develop and to apply this form of analysis. Knoeppel explained the reason for its development as follows. "So far the financial statement has been a financial tool rather than a management tool. It is a historical document and not in the least prophetic. It is static rather than dynamic. It performs only a part of the function of which it is capable. Few accountants have crossed the line between accounting and engineering, while many engineers have jumped the fence between the two."[13]

A rather elaborate specimen of a break-even chart showing the extent to which this type of analysis can be put was developed by E. S. La Rose. It is shown in Form 25. The two main lines in this chart are marked *A-A*1 and *B-B*1. The first is the line of total income from net sales. The area between these two lines at the left of the *crisis point*, a term that is used in place of the break-even point, represents a loss, and the area to the right a profit. Other critical points in this chart are styled the *danger point, unhealthy point, deadline,* and *budget.* The various costs and expenses are broken down into considerable detail in the legend at the right side of the chart. La Rose offers the following explanation of selected items plotted on this interesting chart:

[13] *Managing for Profit,* pp. 53–54.

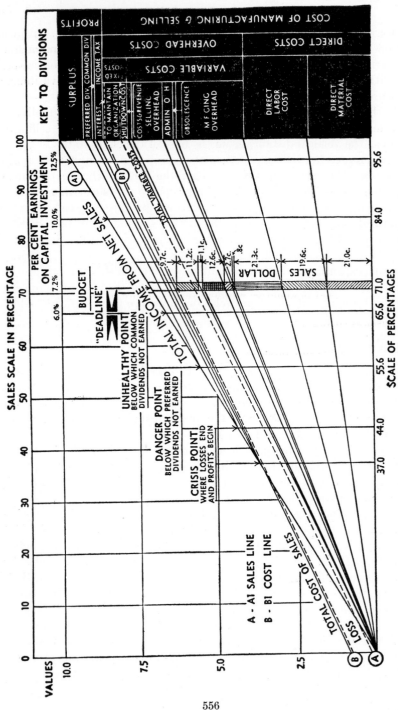

FORM. 25 Break-even chart with manifold legends and information.

556

First, there are shut down costs, such as insurance, taxes, and depreciation, less rental credit, received from the rental [in this particular case] of the excess building. Secondly, there are the salaries of the executive staff, superintendents, department heads and the remaining people who would be required to maintain the organization and who could not very well be eliminated. Thirdly, there is the interest on funded indebtedness, which is a fixed item in our case.

When the amount of fixed costs is determined, the requirements for preferred and common dividends are then included, making provision for Federal and State taxes. The per cent earnings required to make an adequate return on invested capital is known which might, as shown in this mythical profitgraph, be considerably greater than the return required for preferred and common dividends.

Upon making a provision for the fixed cost and earning requirements and knowing the ratio of direct labor, material and variable overhead costs to the sales dollar, the volume necessary to create the profit desired can then be determined on a ratio basis. Naturally, profits come first and variable allowances must be made accordingly.

It is believed that it would be well for every company to provide a reserve and budget for obsolescence as shown in the chart. This is true, especially in a period of business conditions . . . when new products or changes in style are vitally essential for the purpose of interesting buying power, the adoption of which is thereby liable to cause obsolescence.

It is believed that the chart readily pictures the direct cost, variable cost, total overhead cost, cost of manufacturing and selling and the break-down in profits. Management can then tell, at any point of volume, the allowance for direct material, direct labor, other costs, and the profit involved at the point of volume.[14]

The use of break-even charts with the various degrees of detail has received increasingly wide application during recent years by industrial engineers and by active managements in search of every possible aid to efficient operations. Charts of this nature, even the more simple charts, have received less attention by those outside active managements or those associated in a consulting capacity with active management, because of the difficulty of obtaining the necessary information. With the tendency toward more uniformity in accounting, which might well include a more exact breakdown of operating costs into fixed and variable, this effective form of analysis might well expand.

THEORY AND PROBLEMS

1. What is the break-even point?

2. Name five so-called "fixed expenses." Why are these items termed fixed expenses?

[14] National Association of Cost Accountants, *Year Book*, 1931, pp. 206–208 (National Association of Cost Accountants, New York, 1931).

3. What figures are related in plotting the points for a simple break-even chart? What is the principal advantage of a chart of this nature?

4. Describe the principal differences between a simple break-even chart and the conventional break-even chart.

5. What are the practical modifications that must often be made in the conventional break-even chart if very accurate information is desired?

6. Why is the so-called "break-even point" really an oval area and not a point?

7. How can the conventional break-even chart give a considerable amount of detailed information regarding the variable expense items at different percentages of operations?

8. A manufacturer of furniture operates with a fixed monthly expense of $13,000. Net sales and operating profit or losses before Federal income taxes for each 2-month period throughout year *A* are as follows:

	Net Sales	Operating Profit or Loss
Jan.—Feb.	$190,000	$ 4,600
Mar.—Apr.	93,000	(L) 10,000
May—June	140,000	(L) 4,000
July—Aug.	235,000	9,600
Sept.—Oct.	301,000	17,600
Nov.—Dec.	285,000	16,300

From these figures prepare a simple break-even chart and determine the approximate net sales for a 2-month period necessary to cross the line from an operating loss to an operating profit.

9. The following schedule gives the quarterly income statements of the Radio Parts Manufacturing Corporation. From these figures determine the average quarterly

RADIO PARTS MANUFACTURING CORPORATION
Comparative Quarterly Income Statements

	1st Quarter	2d Quarter	3d Quarter	4th Quarter
Gross Sales	$429,940	$564,236	$268,338	$104,890
Less:				
Returns and Allowances	28,160	42,614	18,712	4,180
Net Sales	$401,780	$521,622	$249,626	$100,710
Less:				
Cost of Raw Material	253,700	324,571	156,901	60,043
Factory Labor	50,062	62,160	30,764	12,725
Factory Burden	29,101	44,852	21,020	11,958
Rent	4,760	4,760	4,760	4,760
Insurance	3,622	3,742	3,546	3,484
Depreciation	2,380	2,122	2,467	2,002
Advertising	3,006	3,288	3,278	3,162
Administrative Salaries	8,802	8,724	8,636	8,569
Salaries, Sales Department	3,287	3,412	3,410	3,469
Operating Profit	$ 43,060	$ 63,991	$ 14,844	$(L)9,462

fixed expenses. Prepare a simple break-even chart as illustrated on page 544, and estimate from inspection the location of the break-even point in terms of quarterly sales. During the first quarter, operations were conducted at 71.6 per cent of capacity, in the second quarter at 94.1 per cent, in the third quarter at 44.7 per cent, and in the fourth quarter at 17.4 per cent. From available information prepare a break-even chart showing the principal divisions of variable expenses as illustrated on page 554 and the break-even point in terms of per cent of capacity operations.

10. A client recently leased manufacturing facilities for the production of a new product. Based on studies made by his staff, the following data have been made available to you:

Estimated annual sales.................. 24,000 units

Estimated costs:	*Amount*	*Per Unit*
Material.....................	$ 96,000	$4.00
Direct labor..................	14,400	0.60
Overhead.....................	24,000	1.00
Administrative expense.........	28,800	1.20
TOTAL.....................	$163,200	$6.80

Selling expenses are expected to be 15 per cent of sales, and net profit is to amount to $1.02 per unit. Compute a break-even point expressed in dollars and in units assuming that overhead and administrative expenses are fixed but that other costs are fully variable.

CHAPTER XXI

Net Profit to Tangible Net Worth

Underlying any thoughtful consideration of profits or losses are the conceptions of two fundamental economic realities, private property and the elusive profit motive. The institution of private property is descriptive of our way of economic life in the sphere of ownership; almost everything is owned by some person, some business enterprise, or some governmental unit, that is, almost everything except air and the animals of the air and the sea. If you are a deep-sea diver or a stratosphere-explorer you must buy oxygen; if you do not live near the ocean or the backwoods, you must pay cash directly to the dealer for your aquatic food or indirectly to the state through the agency of a fishing license. *or hunting*

People did not always live thus. In primitive societies, such as the Indians' way of life prior to their conflict with civilization, land was not privately owned; most tribes moved from place to place as the seasons changed and as the wild animals migrated. Water was free, and so were the bounteous gifts of nature. But the institution of private property existed even with the Indians; the warrior owned his own bows and arrows, tents, and simple clothing, and wampum made from periwinkle shells was the accepted medium of exchange.

The institution of the profit motive is merely another way of saying that business enterprises are organized to earn a profit. The will to profit often is not strong enough or intelligent enough to overcome natural economic or highly competitive factors, and if a business concern operates at a loss, year after year, the ultimate end is complete and total extinction. The quest for wealth, rather than for a happy, contented life, has always existed. With the gradual development of a higher and higher technique in manufacturing processes during the past 150 years and the growing emphasis upon the freedom of the market, the profit motive has increased in world-wide intensity.

If Soviet Russia and her satellites solve the problem of substituting a social consciousness for the profit motive of the individual, a miracle of the ages will have appeared on the pages of history. Even Henry George in his *Progress and Poverty* went no further than to advocate the total payment of ground rent as a tax, predicating his full program for creating a more just, logical background for a happier, fuller life on the institution of private property in all wealth, and on the profit motive which gives varying degrees of wealth, for, he wrote, with his ever-careful discernment, "there are differences among men as to energy, skill, prudence, foresight and industry."

PROFITS ATTRACT FUNDS

Money and the fields of activity that bring the greatest monetary return or profit seem to have a close affinity for each other. That affinity is an economic truism as old as orthodox English economic theories. The entrepreneur who offers the highest return commensurate with a recognized degree of security obtains the use of funds in the money market. If those cases are excepted where mistakes were made in judgment, the ability of the entrepreneur to offer a high return is based on the greater profits being earned by his enterprise at the time. The Mississippi Bubble of 1720, the Ponzi episode in Boston 200 years later in 1929, the equally disastrous if less widely known Clarke Bros. affair in New York in 1929, and the Stavisky scandal in France were all logical, if somewhat extreme, examples of this fateful affinity.

For this perfect reason, funds were drawn into the construction of canals, toll bridges, and toll roads in the latter years of the eighteenth century and in the early years of the nineteenth century. Similarly, because of the apparent high profits, funds were drawn successively into banking, insurance, the construction of railroads, the production of iron and steel, petroleum, automobiles, public utilities, motion pictures, chemicals, investment trusts, and, more recently, the manufacture of airplanes and the development of air transportation. As additional funds were invested in respective fields of transportation, public utility operations, and industrial and commercial endeavors, the net profits in those fields gradually decreased toward the average of the older, more established lines of business activity. Funds find their way into industries where profit possibilities are bright at the moment, while industries and divisions of industries with excess capital or where the capital is not efficiently or wisely administered are eaten into by operating losses, top-heavy executive salaries, unwise dividend disbursements, voluntary liquidation, and bankruptcies.

This early theory is even more fundamental than might be exemplified by isolated cases of forced credulity or general statements of economic history. Investors naturally prefer to place their funds where prospects of gain and return are brightest. Prior to the First World War, London was the money center of the world, as English investors for more than 100 years had recognized the possibility of greater returns by investing funds in the Argentine, on the continent, in Canada, in Africa, in India, and in the United States, rather than at home. At the opening of the First World War, approximately \$5,000,000,000 of our securities were held abroad, and a substantial portion of this immense sum was owned by investors in Great Britain.

In the years which followed that war, New York financiers began to compete with London for foreign loans. They were quite successful in obtaining their full measure of loans—too successful, in fact! Our financial circles recognized the possibility of greater profits in lending funds not only to the less developed portions of the world but also to Germany, Austria, Italy, and Japan. Subsequently, the foreign bond column of the daily financial press gave silent testimony to our youthful urge for experience, for easy profits. The long list of defaulted foreign bonds or bonds on which adjustments had been made was silent witness for many years to the part we so innocently played in international finance and in financing the rearming of our enemies for the Second World War.

MEASURES OF NET PROFIT

There are two widely used natural measures of net profit for commercial and industrial businesses, a comparison with the tangible net worth and a comparison with net sales. Both measures are complementary; the net profit on tangible net worth has become a guide to the use of funds invested in a business enterprise, the ability of the management to earn a return; while the net profit on net sales serves as a guide to particular operations and is more often utilized by active managements. Those enterprises that show the highest percentage net profit on tangible net worth and on net sales, not for a single year but over a sustained period of time, are naturally the most highly regarded. Those managements have done a better job, or the concerns are operating in industries which are favorably situated.

Sound business policies will generally dictate that some portion of net profits be retained in the business for expansion and development purposes. This does not mean that occasionally the surplus account should not be utilized to sustain a reasonably steady rate of dividends. Of two concerns, however, in the same line of business that have earned approximately the same dollar net profits year by year over a period of time, if one disbursed approximately one-half the net profits in dividends annually and the other paid out three-quarters the first one would be the more highly regarded by creditors, and the second by investors.

The *net profit*, as the term is used at this point, refers not necessarily to the reported net profit that appears as the final figure in the income statement. As explained in Chap. XIX, the reported net profit must, at times, be adjusted to take into full consideration unusual charges, factors, and situations. This profit figure, as it is used here, is after all charges, including Federal income taxes; it is the residue after all possible adjustments and charges, the *real* net profit.[1] Standards of net profit on tangible net worth on this basis have been computed in recent years for selected lines of business activity and appear in Schedule 70 on pages 566 and 567.

Other profit percentages on tangible net worth are sometimes worthy of exacting study in the comparison of the operations of competing business enterprises. Such profit percentages on tangible net worth are (1) the operating profit, (2) the net profit before extraordinary and nonrecurring charges but after all taxes, and (3), in the light of more recent tax laws, net profit after all adjustments but before income taxes. Fundamentally, however, it is the final net profit, after all possible charges, that indicates, year after year, how well the funds invested in a business enterprise may have been utilized. All other profit figures, while interesting, are of secondary importance.

Incentive of Profit to New Management

During 1960, there were 423,000 new business enterprises and, it is estimated, around 350,000 successions, an average of 2,380 per day, including those where ownership changed hands (*i.e.*, successions), so that the venture was a new one from the viewpoint of the new owner or owners. A large part of business births are small-scale enterprises with invested funds of $20,000 or less.

The underlying basis and the urge for this continual change, for the tremendous number of new business enterprises which come into existence, for the current all-time record number of active commercial and industrial business concerns, is the desire to make a profit in our system of free enterprise and private property. Many concerns—undoubtedly a very reasonable percentage of all new business concerns—are organized by men who want to be their own boss. But even where that urge might seem to be the underlying basic motive for the action, those concerns cannot remain in business without making a profit, even though that profit might be represented by the salary or salaries taken out weekly, semimonthly, or monthly by the owner or owners.

[1] In 1948 considerable discussion developed in Congressional hearings, labor circles, and the press as to whether or not aggregate "profits" of all corporations were too high! This subject is discussed in a pamphlet *A Study of the Theory of Corporate Net Profits* by Roy A. Foulke (Dun & Bradstreet, Inc., New York, 1949). The pamphlet outlines the assumptions of accountancy on which a profit figure is based and then discusses the relativity of the figure of net profit and the economic function of net profit in an incentive economy.

The profits of many neighborhood grocery stores, drugstores, and general stores are represented by the living which the owners make for their families in operating those stores. As business concerns grow in size and become more and more important in their neighborhood and in their industry, profits gradually change from a "living" for the owners to a combination of increased salaries plus an accounting profit after all salaries, and finally to corporate accounting profits, before and after taxes. It is this urge for profit in some one of these senses which is the reason why we have more active business concerns in existence in the United States today than ever before, and more in proportion to our population than anywhere on the face of the globe.

It is natural that when profits are relatively high, more new concerns are organized than go out of existence, either by bankruptcy or by voluntary liquidation. And the opposite trend takes place when accounting profits become smaller and smaller as a result of keener competition, and losses are assumed by an increasing proportion of the business population.

Possibly it is easy to earn a business profit. If it is, one would be inclined to feel that many of the millions of employed civilian labor force would organize and operate their own businesses. The great turnover each year in business concerns and the constantly high percentage of discontinuances for one cause or another might hold the answer. Possibly it is not quite so easy to operate a business profitably, a small one or a large one, year after year, during periods of inflation, deflation, good times, and bad times. Managements of relatively few business enterprises are able to do so.

It was the urge for profit which sent the New England traders in the colonial days in their ketches loaded with dried and salt fish, flour, bread, and barrel staves to the West Indies islands. It was the urge for profit which brought Samuel Slater to the United States from England in 1790 to build, equip, and operate the first textile mill in this country on the east bank of the Blackstone River in Pawtucket, R.I. It is this urge for profit which induces one man to open a small retail grocery store and another a gasoline service station.

Incentive of Profit to Managements

For managements of large representative established corporations, profitable operations involve a much broader horizon than the immediate result. Profits are the essential means for reaching wider economic and social objectives.[2] But profit means more than some relative mathematical

---

[2] This subject receives interesting consideration in an article entitled "To Whom and for What Ends is Corporate Management Responsible?" by Eugene V. Rostov in *The Corporation in Modern Society*, edited by Edward S. Mason (Harvard University Press, Cambridge, Mass., 1959).

black figure in the income statement at the end of an accounting period. Only profitable businesses over a period of years can provide jobs and opportunity for employees; only profitable businesses can earn a satisfactory return for investors on their earnings; only profitable concerns can spend money on improved tools and methods that make possible better products for customers; only profitable concerns can help others progress, including dealers who handle their products, and raw-material suppliers; and only profitable businesses can pay their share of the heavy costs of present-day government by participating in the payment of Federal income taxes.

It takes more than high profits to provide the environment under which funds of investors flow into business activity. During periods when investors fail to provide additional funds for management to expand the means of production, those funds must be obtained from reinvested earnings, earned depreciation, and borrowings from banks, insurance companies, and other creditors. So we come back by another route to the size of profits, profits of individual corporations and profits of all corporations. It is out of reinvested earnings that corporations must grow during those periods when investors are reluctant to provide the funds for expansion.

TYPICAL NET PROFIT ON TANGIBLE NET WORTH

Schedule 70 gives the median percentages of net profit to tangible net worth for 42 lines of manufacturing, 21 of wholesaling, and 7 of retailing for each of the 5 years from 1955 to 1959 inclusive and a 5-year arithmetical average for each of these 70 divisions of business activity.

Among manufacturers the highest 5-year average is shown by manufacturers of drugs with 15.89 per cent, followed by bottlers of soft drinks and carbonated water with 12.46 per cent, and manufacturers of industrial chemicals with 10.93 per cent. Typical percentage net profits, as can readily be seen by a glance at Schedule 70, are materially lower than these figures for the respective individual years, as well as for the 5-year averages.

The highest 5-year average among wholesalers is produced by wholesalers of baked goods with 11.56 per cent, followed by wholesalers of drugs and drug sundries with 9.23 per cent, and wholesalers of fresh fruits and produce with 8.43 per cent. At the lower extreme are wholesalers of hosiery and underwear with a 5-year average net profit on tangible net worth of 3.34 per cent, and wholesalers of shoes with 3.48 per cent.

For retailers the highest 5-year average is disclosed by independent meat and grocery stores with 10.66 per cent, followed by retail shoe stores with 6.23 per cent, and women's specialty shops with 6.05 per cent.

[Schedule 70] RATIOS OF NET PROFITS ON TANGIBLE NET WORTH

Lines of Business Activity	Percentage					
	Median					Five-year Average
	1955	1956	1957	1958	1959	
MANUFACTURERS						
Agricultural Implements and Machinery	7.85	6.72	6.68	10.76	6.36	7.67
Airplane Parts and Accessories	4.34	14.73	12.05	12.10	7.60	10.16
Automobile Parts and Accessories	12.40	8.35	10.24	6.18	8.50	9.13
Bakers	7.60	7.09	9.36	4.88	5.80	6.95
Bedsprings and Mattresses	7.49	7.06	6.27	4.66	5.39	6.17
Bodies, Auto, Bus, and Truck	9.89	7.29	6.72	3.45	4.72	6.41
Bolts, Screws, Nuts, and Nails	10.71	9.35	10.11	4.04	10.91	9.02
Breweries	3.19	3.14	5.58	4.27	7.78	4.79
Chemicals, Industrial	12.49	12.19	10.04	8.88	11.07	10.93
Coats and Suits, Men's and Boys'	4.50	6.77	2.64	2.81	5.06	4.36
Coats and Suits, Women's	7.55	4.89	4.70	8.95	6.65	6.55
Confectionery	4.82	6.88	6.93	7.95	6.54	6.62
Contractors, Building Construction	8.80	11.10	10.68	9.48	7.66	9.54
Contractors, Electrical	9.37	9.63	17.70	9.28	5.88	10.37
Cotton Cloth Mills	5.47	4.88	2.17	2.59	4.79	3.98
Cotton Goods, Converters, Non-factored	4.98	4.69	2.62	3.89	5.88	4.41
Dresses, Rayon, Silk, and Acetate	4.22	6.66	7.17	2.92	4.26	5.05
Drugs	15.25	15.33	18.87	17.09	12.93	15.89
Electrical Parts and Supplies	11.43	12.50	11.35	8.11	10.96	10.87
Foundries	9.34	12.54	9.72	3.69	6.97	8.45
Fruits and Vegetables, Canners	4.88	5.39	3.55	6.42	4.39	4.93
Furniture	10.38	10.54	7.70	5.63	8.94	8.64
Hardware and Tools	12.12	10.40	10.25	6.98	7.84	9.52
Hosiery	3.97	3.07	3.89	3.95	5.93	4.16
Lumber	11.53	7.17	5.32	7.67	8.87	8.11
Machine Shops	7.05	12.77	10.90	3.91	3.82	7.69
Machinery, Industrial	8.66	11.17	10.16	6.16	7.49	8.73
Meats and Provisions, Packers	7.80	8.31	6.04	5.57	8.10	7.16
Metal Stampings	10.18	12.59	10.09	4.44	7.78	9.02
Outerwear, Knitted	6.46	6.65	4.02	5.27	4.52	5.38
Overalls and Work Clothing	5.59	4.78	4.67	5.88	5.79	5.34
Paints, Varnishes, and Lacquers	6.58	6.83	6.14	7.67	9.91	7.43
Paper	10.76	11.46	8.48	7.75	8.45	9.38
Paper Boxes	12.17	11.99	9.49	7.17	8.09	9.78
Petroleum, Integrated Corporations	12.17	11.41	11.32	8.22	8.96	10.42
Printers, Job	9.26	8.32	7.44	5.12	7.67	7.56
Radio Parts and Supplies	10.56	14.32	10.22	9.19	10.12	10.88
Shirts, Underwear, and Pajamas, Men's	4.47	3.93	3.18	6.00	7.70	5.06
Shoes, Men's, Women's, and Children's	8.56	7.64	7.44	7.48	8.40	7.90
Soft Drinks and Carbonated Water, Bottlers	10.75	13.04	10.46	13.37	14.68	12.46
Steel, Structural Fabricators (Sell on Short Terms)	11.83	12.54	14.93	8.92	4.82	10.61
Stoves, Ranges, and Ovens	7.88	5.46	5.25	5.52	7.67	6.36

[Schedule 70 *(Cont.)*]

RATIOS OF NET PROFITS ON TANGIBLE NET WORTH *(Continued)*

Lines of Business Activity	Percentage					
	Median					Five-year Average
	1955	1956	1957	1958	1959	
WHOLESALERS						
Automobile Parts and Accessories....	6.65	8.07	6.35	6.26	6.78	6.82
Baked Goods.....................	12.23	11.95	9.49	11.71	12.40	11.56
Cigars, Cigarettes, and Tobacco......	4.45	5.59	4.81	6.25	5.70	5.36
Drugs and Drug Sundries...........	7.97	8.73	10.65	9.49	9.30	9.23
Dry Goods......................	3.78	4.04	3.96	3.14	3.61	3.71
Electrical Parts and Supplies.........	8.20	8.56	4.85	3.60	4.96	6.03
Fruits and Produce, Fresh...........	9.56	9.27	6.67	8.59	8.08	8.43
Furnishings, Men's................	5.54	3.96	6.70	7.31	6.41	5.98
Gasoline, Fuel Oil, and Lubricating Oil	9.23	7.09	8.62	7.33	8.94	8.24
Groceries........................	6.03	5.57	6.79	5.19	5.17	5.75
Hardware........................	5.76	6.32	4.39	5.44	4.90	5.36
Hosiery and Underwear.............	5.00	2.88	2.64	2.74	3.43	3.34
Household Appliances, Electrical.....	7.58	6.38	5.02	5.53	7.25	6.35
Lumber.........................	6.30	5.24	6.93	4.57	5.48	5.70
Lumber and Building Materials......	7.34	8.22	3.46	5.10	5.10	5.84
Meat and Poultry.................	9.86	10.22	7.36	5.00	9.17	8.32
Paints, Varnishes, and Lacquers......	6.08	6.39	6.72	1.86	4.07	5.02
Paper..........................	6.52	7.99	6.21	4.88	6.52	6.42
Plumbing and Heating Supplies......	8.55	9.85	3.86	4.02	6.97	6.65
Shoes, Men's, Women's, and Children's.........................	3.90	4.95	1.94	2.25	4.34	3.48
Wines and Liquors.................	5.23	6.29	7.02	5.93	6.68	6.23
RETAILERS						
Clothing, Men's and Boys'..........	8.13	5.75	3.78	4.11	4.38	5.23
Department Stores................	5.80	5.67	5.05	5.27	5.84	5.53
Furniture, 50 Per Cent or More Installment.......................	5.52	5.16	4.37	2.06	3.03	4.03
Groceries and Meats, Independent...	11.31	12.45	12.66	9.44	7.45	10.66
Lumber and Building Materials......	5.50	6.01	4.80	4.01	4.54	4.97
Shoes...........................	5.96	5.84	7.75	5.17	6.41	6.23
Women's Specialty Shops...........	7.17	4.94	6.12	4.81	7.23	6.05

THEORY AND PROBLEMS

1. Explain why the percentage figure of net profit on tangible net worth is significant.

2. Why are other percentage profit figures on tangible net worth, such as (*a*) operating profit, (*b*) net profit before extraordinary charges but after all taxes, and (*c*) net profit after all adjustments but before income taxes, at times of considerable significance?

3. According to classical economic theory, funds are drawn into those industries where the current rates of profit, commensurate with reasonable safety, are the highest. Briefly explain what is meant by this theory.

4. Figures of Wholesale Gasoline and Lubricating Oil, Inc., have been set up below in comparative columns ready for immediate analysis. Make a complete internal and comparative analysis of these figures based on your study of this volume up to this point.

WHOLESALE GASOLINE AND LUBRICATING OIL, INC.
Comparative Figures for Years Ended December 31, 19—

	(C) Three Years Ago	(B) Two Years Ago	(A) One Year Ago
ASSETS			
Cash..........................	$ 16,078	$ 17,993	$ 6,385
Accounts Receivable...........	69,190	63,529	89,939
Merchandise...................	....	2,128	50,853
Current Assets................	$ 85,268	$ 83,650	$ 147,177
Fixed Assets, Net..............	1,482	1,310	1,031
Investments...................	2,273	2,273	2,273
Prepaid or Deferred...........	1,706	2,082	1,782
Cash Value Life Insurance.......	145	1,116	1,832
TOTAL...................	$ 90,874	$ 90,431	$ 154,095
LIABILITIES			
Notes Payable to Bank.........	$ 6,000	$ 6,000	$ 26,500
Accounts Payable.............	53,745	53,149	93,115
Reserves...................	....	....	600
Current Liabilities..............	$ 59,745	$ 59,149	$ 120,215
Preferred Stock...............	....	20,000	20,000
Common Stock...............	20,000	100	100
Retained Earnings.............	11,129	11,182	13,780
TOTAL...................	$ 90,874	$ 90,431	$ 154,095
Net Working Capital...........	$ 25,523	$ 24,501	$ 26,962
Current Ratio.................	1.44	1.41	1.22
Tangible Net Worth.............	$ 31,129	$ 31,282	$ 33,880
Sales........................	$1,453,324	$2,189,739	$2,714,118
Net Profits...................	2,623	1,053	2,598
Dividends....................	None	1,000	1,000

5. As a stockholder, you have received a circular letter from a corporation which states that income from operations for the past year was materially greater than for the year before. The only information given is as follows:

For year A the gross income of the corporation was $4,700,000; after deducting $4,000,000 for cost of goods sold, general, selling, and administrative expenses, and $250,000 for depreciation, interest, and Federal income taxes, the net profit was stated to be $450,000, which was equivalent to 24 cents per share on the outstanding common stock, after paying 6% dividend on preferred stock.

The net income for year B had been $196,000, which had been equal to 2 cents per share on the outstanding stock after paying the preferred dividend.

You recall that the only stock changes during the two years were issues on Jan. 1, year A, of 200,000 shares of common stock and $500,000 preferred stock. In view of the large difference in the stated profit per share between year A and year B, you wonder if the reported result appears reasonable.

Prepare a financial statement explaining and reconciling the figures for the 2 years, showing the number of shares of common stock and the amount of preferred stock outstanding.

[Adapted from A.I.A. Examination]

6. The audited balance sheet and the income statement of the Paper Mill Corporation are given below. Post these figures on a columnar sheet, compute the net

PAPER MILL CORPORATION
Balance Sheet for Year Ended December 31, 19—
ASSETS

Current Assets
Cash in banks and on hand........................		$ 143,699
Customers' accounts receivable.....................	$ 564,263	
Customers' notes receivable.......................	11,262	
Miscellaneous accounts receivable..................	16,634	
	$ 592,159	
Less: Reserve for bad debts and cash discounts.........	21,525	570,634
Raw materials and supplies, and stocks finished and in process—at the lower of cost or market prices.......		1,406,842
Total Current Assets..........................		$2,121,175
Sundry Accounts and Notes Receivable................		5,979
Cash Value of Life Insurance (policy pledged for First Mortgage Bonds)................................		⌀ 17,395
Investments..		11,145
Land, Buildings, Machinery, and Equipment—at reproductive values as appraised, plus additions at cost.........	$10,397,619	
Less: Reserve for depreciation.......................	5,865,912	4,531,707
Prepaid Expenses...................................		42,356
		$6,729,757

LIABILITIES

Current Liabilities
Accounts payable—trade...........................		$ 355,963
Accounts payable—sundry..........................		7,017
Accrued expenses and interest......................		139,644
Purchase money notes..............................		15,000
Provision for income and profits taxes...............		112,230
Total Current Liabilities......................		$ 629,854
First Mortgage 4% Serial Gold Bonds payable in 5 years.		63,500
Purchase Money Notes, maturing monthly in 3 to 6 years		41,250
Reserve for Workmen's Compensation Insurance.........		8,843
Capital Stock		
Authorized and issued, 178,000 shares of no par value..	$ 4,073,500	
Less: In treasury, 100 shares........................	2,288	
	$ 4,071,212	
Paid-in Surplus....................................	1,311,222	
Retained Earnings.................................	603,876	5,986,310
		$6,729,757

PAPER MILL CORPORATION (*Continued*)
Income Statement for Year Ended December 31, 19—

Net Sales...	$7,917,978
Cost of Sales (exclusive of Depreciation)............................	6,430,932
Gross Profit, before Depreciation....................................	$1,487,046
General Expenses (exclusive of Depreciation).........................	604,889
Net Profit from Operations, before Depreciation..................	$ 882,357
Other Expenses—Net..	32,890
Net Income, before Depreciation and Federal Income Taxes........	$ 849,467
Provision for Depreciation of Plant and Equipment.................	312,711
Net Income, before Federal Income Taxes.......................	$ 536,756
Provision for Federal Income Taxes.............................	108,500
Net Income..	$ 428,256

working capital, the tangible net worth, and the percentage of net profit on the tangible net worth. Then make such other computations as seem expedient to you and write a thorough over-all internal analysis of this corporation.

7. Below are percentage net profits on the tangible net worth of corporations in ten different lines of business. After each figure place the capital letter which describes that ratio: *G*, good; *F*, fair; *P*, poor.

a. Manufacturer of bedsprings and mattresses............	12.62
b. Manufacturer of industrial chemicals.................	2.71
c. Manufacturer of electrical parts and supplies..........	1.22
d. Manufacturer of furniture.........................	5.59
e. Machine shop..	11.24
f. Manufacturer of knitted outerwear..................	10.17
g. Wholesaler of men's furnishings....................	9.30
h. Wholesaler of meat and poultry....................	8.70
i. Wholesaler of paper................................	1.88
j. Department store...................................	9.72

CHAPTER XXII

Net Profit to Net Sales

In certain industries, particularly those that specialize in the production of durable goods or of goods that are utilized in erecting, furnishing, and equipping homes, office buildings, apartments, lofts, and plants, it is exceedingly difficult to expand the sales volume greatly by reducing prices. The substantial investment in fixed assets in these lines of business activity provides a relatively low turnover of tangible net worth, that is, a relatively low volume of annual sales compared with the investment in a business enterprise. In recession years, net sales, every so often, may even fall below the tangible net worth in these lines of manufacturing activity. On the other hand, industries which have a low investment in fixed assets such as converters of cloth and manufacturers of women's, men's, boys' and children's apparel of all kinds tend to handle a large volume of sales in relation to tangible net worth.

An enterprise that is managed solely on the volume and the price theory generally needs particularly close watching by the active management of the business, by its stockholders if they differ from the active management, by its bankers, and by its trade creditors. There is always the possibility of a breakdown in demand brought about by some unforeseen event, such as the unexpected effect of a new policy, a change in style, or newly developed competition from other products. If liabilities are heavy, trouble invariably is in the offing. A business enterprise, like a human body, must have reserve strength available for every possible emergency.

So, although net profits are the economic end of the business enterprise, a business cannot be operated solely for the maximum of immediate profits. The proportions of its balance sheet, the size of its liabilities, the condition of its receivables, and the amount of merchandise must simultaneously be kept in healthy relationships to the net working capital and the tangible net worth. If net profits are unusually large, the basis of these profits should be carefully analyzed to ascertain if the result came from economic factors of a particularly favorable character which might be all too temporary, or from efficient operations and unusually capable, conscientious direction.

571

It is significant to find that for the accounting period ending June, 1958, the latest years for which these figures have been made available by the Internal Revenue Service of the U.S. Treasury Department, the average net income after taxes of all incorporated manufacturing enterprises in the United States was 6.9 per cent of their "total compiled receipts"[1] of $332,621,264,000 and 3.3 per cent of their total compiled receipts of $281,121,862,000 in 1953. For wholesale corporations, the ratio was much lower, 1.9 per cent on total compiled receipts of $115,445,818,000 in 1958 and 1.0 per cent on $81,500,014,000 in 1953. For retail corporations, the ratio was 2.1 per cent of total compiled receipts of $106,673,226,000 in 1958 and 1.2 per cent of $79,769,207,000 in 1953.[2] In other words, to realize $1 of net profit, the average manufacturing corporation in the year 1958 had to sell approximately $15 of goods, the average wholesaling corporation slightly over $50 of goods, and the average retailing corporation slightly under $50. To put it another way, the typical wholesaling corporation in 1958 had to sell a little over 3 times as much merchandise as the typical manufacturer, and approximately 1⅛ times as much as the typical retailer, to realize the same dollar net profit.

INCREASED NET SALES

There is a widespread point of view in business that the volume of net sales is the most important element in obtaining net profits. This point of view has been aptly condensed by G. Charter Harrison in the following words. "The primary factor in profits is sales volume, and the value of increased sales volume per dollar of sales, due to these increased sales not adding to the fixed charges, is far greater than any additional selling expense which would be required, in the majority of cases and under normal conditions."[3]

In other words, every business enterprise, as we have seen in Chap. XX, has what is known as a *break-even point*. Net sales above this point result in increasing net profits because very little additional expense is involved, all fixed expenses having been covered by the net sales up to the break-even point. Above this point, sales expense may be greatly increased to

---

[1] Unfortunately, the figure of net sales is not available in this study. The difference between "total compiled receipts" and net sales in a national study of this nature would, however, be relatively moderate.

[2] The 1958 figures are from *Statistics of Income, 1957-58, Corporation Income Tax Returns*, pp. 20, 23 (Internal Revenue Service, U.S. Treasury Department, Washington, D.C., 1960). The 1953 figures are compiled from *Preliminary Report, Statistics of Income for 1953*, Part 2, pp. 7, 9 (Internal Revenue Service, U.S. Treasury Department, Washington, D.C., 1956).

[3] HARRISON, G. CHARTER, *What! No Reports at All, Mr. Knudsen?* p. 9 (G. Charter Harrison, Madison, Wis., 1941).

obtain additional volume which is then more profitable up to the point of diminishing returns.

A manufacturer of nuts and bolts needs net sales of $100,000 per month, for example, to break even. Sales below that point will not cover all fixed expenses and a loss will be assumed. Above that point, however, net profits expand. On monthly sales of $150,000 a net profit of 2 per cent on sales might be recorded, while on monthly sales of $200,000 a net profit of 3 per cent might be earned. On the first $100,000 of net sales per month, all administrative salaries, office expense, plant maintenance and depreciation, real estate taxes, insurance, interest on funded debt, if any, are covered. These fixed expenses now being covered, additional sales bring an increasing rate of net profits. This rate continues until the plant is being operated at top capacity and top efficiency. Additional volume above this point would involve the erection of an addition to the plant or a new plant, all of which would then bring a sudden increase in fixed charges, or a rate of diminishing return. It is this specific knowledge applied to each business enterprise that is essential for the most effective sales operation. The measure is the rate of net profit on net sales.

It was because of this very substantial volume of net sales above the break-even point that the net profits of so many prime contractors and subcontractors were so large during the Second World War prior to renegotiations. Sales from five to ten times the normal peacetime volume of a "contractor" were not unusual, all with one or a very limited number of customers so that little or no sales expense was entailed, and with the operation of plant facilities at top capacity. In fact, these large net profits were a fundamental reason for the enactment of the initial law on renegotiations on the profits of contractors handling annual sales of war equipment, materials, and supplies in excess of $100,000.

TYPICAL NET PROFIT ON NET SALES

Schedule 71, on the following two pages, gives the typical median percentages of net profit to annual net sales for 42 lines of manufacturing, 21 of wholesaling, and 7 of retailing for each year for 1955 to 1959 inclusive, and a 5-year arithmetical average for each of these 70 divisions of industry and commerce. Business enterprises that show percentages above these figures would naturally be more highly regarded; those that show percentages below these figures would generally be less favorably regarded.

In 1955, 1957, and 1958 the highest median percentage profit on net sales among manufacturing lines was disclosed by manufacturers of drugs with 8.72, 9.45, and 10.53 per cent respectively, and in 1956 and 1959 by integrated petroleum corporations with 7.88 and 7.14 per cent respectively. The median percentage of net profit on net sales for wholesale and retail

[Schedule 71]   RATIOS OF NET PROFITS ON NET SALES

Lines of Business Activity	Percentage					
	Median					Five-year Average
	1955	1956	1957	1958	1959	
MANUFACTURERS						
Agricultural Implements and Machinery	4.10	3.97	3.14	3.97	3.15	3.67
Airplane Parts and Accessories	1.54	2.61	3.14	2.60	2.65	2.51
Automobile Parts and Accessories	3.80	3.08	3.75	2.53	3.23	3.28
Bakers	1.53	1.26	1.96	1.43	1.22	1.48
Bedsprings and Mattresses	2.61	2.19	2.61	1.37	1.74	2.10
Bodies, Auto, Bus, and Truck	3.09	2.83	1.59	1.50	1.03	2.01
Bolts, Screws, Nuts, and Nails	3.43	3.61	5.10	2.12	3.48	3.55
Breweries	1.52	1.32	2.52	2.13	3.63	2.22
Chemicals, Industrial	6.04	5.10	5.27	3.75	4.54	4.94
Coats and Suits, Men's and Boys'	1.14	1.28	0.59	0.70	1.05	0.95
Coats and Suits, Women's	1.12	0.90	0.54	1.07	0.69	0.86
Confectionery	1.66	2.05	1.74	2.40	1.93	1.96
Contractors, Building Construction	1.52	1.61	1.56	1.46	1.33	1.50
Contractors, Electrical	1.73	2.07	3.69	1.94	1.17	2.12
Cotton Cloth Mills	2.71	2.89	1.21	1.69	2.72	2.24
Cotton Goods, Converters, Non-factored	1.06	1.59	1.02	1.20	0.94	1.16
Dresses, Rayon, Silk, and Acetate	0.43	0.61	0.63	0.26	0.36	0.46
Drugs	8.72	7.30	9.45	10.53	6.62	8.52
Electrical Parts and Supplies	4.13	4.49	4.13	3.09	3.64	3.90
Foundries	4.17	4.77	3.70	2.33	3.15	3.62
Fruits and Vegetables, Canners	1.71	2.92	1.46	1.70	1.60	1.88
Furniture	2.88	3.30	2.22	1.79	3.12	2.66
Hardware and Tools	5.88	4.95	3.69	3.23	3.71	4.29
Hosiery	1.68	1.41	1.67	1.11	2.83	1.74
Lumber	6.53	4.80	3.54	3.30	4.00	4.43
Machine Shops	3.25	4.94	3.99	2.38	2.07	3.33
Machinery, Industrial	3.38	4.06	3.76	2.98	3.43	3.52
Meats and Provisions, Packers	1.04	0.85	0.78	0.58	1.18	0.89
Metal Stampings	3.37	3.96	4.14	1.54	3.15	3.23
Outerwear, Knitted	1.58	1.25	1.15	0.96	0.96	1.18
Overalls and Work Clothing	1.56	1.47	1.49	2.01	1.78	1.66
Paints, Varnishes, and Lacquers	2.46	2.53	2.03	2.43	3.59	2.61
Paper	6.81	6.87	5.30	5.75	6.36	6.22
Paper Boxes	5.04	4.18	3.51	3.45	3.54	3.94
Petroleum, Integrated Corporations	8.59	7.88	7.61	6.16	7.14	7.48
Printers, Job	2.84	2.28	2.13	1.70	2.53	2.30
Radio Parts and Supplies	2.56	3.59	3.27	3.67	4.05	3.43
Shirts, Underwear, and Pajamas, Men's	1.29	0.80	0.77	1.42	1.48	1.15
Shoes, Men's, Women's, and Children's	2.36	2.50	1.82	2.24	2.14	2.21
Soft Drinks and Carbonated Water, Bottlers	4.40	5.06	5.60	6.87	5.34	5.45
Steel, Structural Fabricators (Sell on Short Terms)	3.39	3.99	3.84	3.72	1.63	3.31
Stoves, Ranges, and Ovens	3.03	2.00	1.81	2.06	2.68	2.32

RATIOS OF NET PROFITS ON NET SALES (*Continued*)   [Schedule 71 (*Cont.*)]

Lines of Business Activity	Percentage					
	Median					Five-year Average
	1955	1956	1957	1958	1959	
WHOLESALERS						
Automobile Parts and Accessories....	1.71	1.93	2.05	1.93	1.78	1.88
Baked Goods....................	2.60	2.18	2.01	2.50	2.35	2.33
Cigars, Cigarettes, and Tobacco......	0.36	0.39	0.33	0.44	0.33	0.37
Drugs and Drug Sundries..........	1.70	1.59	2.36	1.78	1.63	1.81
Dry Goods.......................	1.00	0.93	1.07	0.67	0.78	0.89
Electrical Parts and Supplies........	1.50	1.55	1.29	1.05	1.23	1.32
Fruits and Produce, Fresh...........	0.94	1.49	0.60	0.86	1.18	1.01
Furnishings, Men's.................	2.70	1.38	2.18	1.65	1.59	1.90
Gasoline, Fuel Oil, and Lubricating Oil	1.29	0.94	1.03	0.77	1.66	1.14
Groceries..........................	0.69	0.63	0.72	0.62	0.58	0.65
Hardware..........................	1.81	1.70	1.47	1.71	1.42	1.62
Hosiery and Underwear.............	1.59	1.09	0.64	0.75	0.71	0.96
Household Appliances, Electrical.....	1.01	0.92	0.82	0.86	0.88	0.90
Lumber............................	1.07	1.18	1.39	1.04	1.28	1.19
Lumber and Building Materials......	1.54	2.15	1.30	1.24	1.35	1.52
Meat and Poultry..................	0.94	1.12	0.77	0.44	0.61	0.78
Paints, Varnishes, and Lacquers......	1.70	2.49	2.32	0.71	1.54	1.75
Paper.............................	1.12	1.43	1.19	0.78	1.17	1.14
Plumbing and Heating Supplies......	1.88	2.08	1.09	1.06	1.72	1.57
Shoes, Men's, Women's, and Children's..........................	1.01	1.06	0.64	0.56	0.97	0.85
Wines and Liquors.................	0.86	0.97	1.05	0.94	1.45	1.05
RETAILERS						
Clothing, Men's and Boys'..........	3.91	2.51	2.07	1.94	1.96	2.48
Department Stores.................	2.06	2.15	1.83	1.91	2.03	2.00
Furniture, 50 Per Cent or More Installment.......................	3.09	2.56	1.49	0.95	1.54	1.93
Groceries and Meats, Independent...	1.25	0.91	1.01	1.02	0.67	0.97
Lumber and Building Materials......	1.65	1.88	1.66	1.65	1.92	1.75
Shoes.............................	1.83	1.40	2.44	1.54	1.92	1.83
Women's Specialty Shops...........	2.34	1.49	1.90	1.53	2.42	1.94

trades was lower and varied less from year to year than in the manufacturing lines. For wholesalers, the highest median rate of return on net sales was shown in 1955 by wholesalers of men's furnishings with 2.70 per cent, in 1956 by wholesalers of paints, lacquers, and varnishes with 2.49 per cent, in 1957 by wholesalers of drugs and drug sundries with 2.36, and in 1958 and 1959 by wholesalers of baked goods with 2.50 and 2.35 per cent respectively. For retailers, the highest rate of return on net sales in 1955 and 1956 was shown by furniture stores with more than half of their sales on installment with 3.09 and 2.56 per cent respectively, in 1957 by retail shoe stores with 2.44 per cent, in 1958 by men's and boys' clothing stores with 1.94 per cent, and in 1959 by department stores with 2.03 per cent.

For the entire 5-year period, the highest average percentage net profit on net sales for manufacturers was disclosed by manufacturers of drugs with 8.52 per cent, followed by integrated petroleum corporations with 7.48 per cent, and paper mills with 6.22 per cent. The 5-year average net profits on net sales for wholesalers and retailers were materially lower. The highest 5-year average among the wholesalers was disclosed by wholesalers of baked goods with 2.33 per cent, followed by wholesalers of men's furnishings with 1.90 per cent, and wholesalers of automobile parts and accessories with 1.88 per cent. The highest 5-year average among the retail distributors was shown by men's and boys' clothing stores with 2.48 per cent, followed by department stores with 2.00 per cent, and women's specialty shops with 1.94 per cent.

Of the 70 divisions of industry and commerce comprising this 5-year running study, 32 disclosed net profits on net sales in excess of 2 per cent in 1955; 38 in 1956; 32 in 1957; 25 in 1958; and 29 in 1959. For the 5-year spread of years, 29 of the 42 manufacturing lines showed average net profits on annual sales in excess of 2 per cent, only 1 out of 21 wholesaling lines, and 2 out of 7 of the retailing lines.

THEORY AND PROBLEMS

1. What are the comparative advantages of or reasons for computing the percentage of net profit on both tangible net worth and net sales?

2. Every commercial and industrial business enterprise is in existence to earn net profits. Even though this statement is an economic truism, why should a business concern not be operated solely for the maximum of immediate profits?

3. A wholesale or retail business enterprise generally must sell approximately three times as much merchandise as a manufacturing concern, on the average, to realize the same dollar profit. Can you explain why this is so?

4. Company X and Company Y are competitors. They have both transacted approximately the same net sales each year for the past 4 years. Over these 4 years they have had the same aggregate operating profits, as the following table indicates:

	Company X	Company Y
Year A....................	$12,500	$17,500
Year B....................	14,000	15,200
Year C....................	14,200	13,600
Year D....................	18,600	13,000
Total Operating Profits...	$59,300	$59,300

Which of these two concerns is operating the more effectively? Give your reasons.

5. Comparative figures for a period of 3 years of the Department Store Corporation are given below. Approximately 30 per cent of the annual net sales are made on cash terms; the remainder on net terms due on the tenth of the month following the sale. Compute the percentage net profit on the net sales for each year and interpret the 3-year results. Then prepare an increase-decrease column and make a comprehensive internal and comparative analysis of these figures.

DEPARTMENT STORE CORPORATION
Comparative Figures for Years Ended January 31, 19—

	(C) Three Years Ago	(B) Two Years Ago	(A) One Year Ago
ASSETS			
Cash..............................	$ 53,064	$121,344	$ 89,642
Accounts Receivable.................	68,793	95,483	82,290
Merchandise........................	106,708	113,407	134,515
Current Assets......................	$228,565	$330,234	$306,447
Fixed Assets, Net...................	27,149	27,314	29,290
Miscellaneous Receivables.............	1,918	2,945	804
Prepaid............................	44,457	42,154	45,812
TOTAL.......................	$302,089	$402,647	$382,353
LIABILITIES			
Accounts Payable...................	$ 69,702	$110,152	$ 64,489
Accruals...........................	....	12,373	....
Reserves for Taxes..................	5,097	....	16,657
Other Liabilities.....................	....	....	3,066
Current Liabilities...................	$ 74,799	$122,885	$ 84,212
Deferred Income....................	740	850	1,623
Preferred Stock.....................	191,400	191,400	191,400
Common Stock......................	3,828	3,828	3,828
Retained Earnings..................	31,322	83,684	101,290
TOTAL.......................	$302,089	$402,647	$382,353
Net Working Capital.................	$153,766	$207,349	$222,235
Current Ratio.......................	3.04	2.68	3.64
Tangible Net Worth.................	$226,550	$278,912	$296,518
Net Sales..........................	$673,745	$780,766	$877,175
Net Profits.........................	27,258	52,362	36,746
Dividends..........................	None	None	19,140

6. The balance sheet, statement of surplus, and income statement of the Fruit & Vegetable Canning Company, Inc., are given on pages 578 and 579. Post these figures on a columnar sheet of paper and compute the net working capital, the tangible net worth, the percentage profit on tangible net worth, and the percentage profit on net sales. Compare and interpret these two percentage profit figures. Then make a comprehensive, over-all internal analysis of the accompanying figures, using such ratios as apply to this situation.

FRUIT & VEGETABLE CANNING COMPANY, INC.
Balance Sheet for Year Ended December 31, 19—
ASSETS

Cash and Demand Deposits..........................			$ 3,192,282
Accounts Receivable			
Trade (less allowance for cash discounts)..............	$	818,399	
Employees.......................................		477	
Other...		230,398	
		$1,049,274	
Less: Allowance for doubtful accounts..............		56,551	
			992,723
Inventories, at average cost			
Finished merchandise.............................	$9,447,297		
Work in process..................................	629,233		
Wrapping materials, manufacturing supplies, etc.......	821,941		
		10,898,471	
Merchandise and/or cash with salesmen..............		64,999	
Total Current Assets........................		$15,148,475	
Property, Plant, and Equipment, at cost			
Land...	$	80,715	
Buildings and improvements..............	$ 839,270		
Machinery and equipment................	1,329,329		
Furniture and fixtures..................	60,214		
Automobiles and trucks.................	147,222		
	2,376,035		
Less: Allowance for depreciation........	1,211,030		
		1,165,005	
			1,245,720
Prepaid Expenses and Deferred Charges			
Insurance.......................................	$	88,677	
Advertising supplies..............................		22,809	
Repaid and renewal supplies, etc....................		118,246	
Interest...		29,596	
Other items.....................................		17,119	
		276,447	
Brands and Trademarks, at cost......................		344,997	
		$17,015,639	

LIABILITIES

Notes Payable			
To banks..	$6,915,000		
To others.......................................	1,182,992		
		$ 8,097,992	
Accounts Payable			
Trade...	$	95,532	
Employees.......................................		6,971	
Other...		17,767	
		120,270	
Dividends Payable.................................		20,397	
Accrued Liabilities			
Salaries and wages................................	$	35,831	
Taxes, other than taxes on income...................		25,966	
		61,797	
Provision for Contingencies.........................		10,019	
Provision for Federal and State Taxes on income, estimated		188,332	
Total Current Liabilities (Forward).............		$ 8,598,807	

FRUIT & VEGETABLE CANNING COMPANY, INC. (*Continued*)
CAPITAL

Total Current Liabilities (Brought Forward)....		$ 8,598,807

Preferred capital stock, 6% cumulative; par $100, redeemable at $105 per share plus accrued dividends. Authorized 20,000 shares, retired and not reissuable 6,356 shares, outstanding 13,598 shares...................... $1,359,800
Class B common capital stock, par $10, authorized 200,000 shares, outstanding 142,080 shares.................... 1,420,800

	$2,780,600
Earned Surplus, as annexed..........................	5,636,232
	8,416,832
	$17,015,639

Statement of Surplus
For the Year Ended December 31, 19—

	Earned
Balance, Jan. 1, 19—..	$ 6,896,674
Add: Profit for the year, as annexed..............................	144,896
	$ 7,041,570

Deduct:
Cash dividends

Preferred stock $29.25 per share..............................		$ 397,742
Class A common stock $20.80 per share.......................		320,257
Excess of redemption value ($60 per share) over par value ($10 per share) of class A common stock (15,397 shares called for redemption)..		687,339
		$ 1,405,338
Balance, Dec. 31, 19—..		$ 5,636,232

Income Statement
For the Year Ended December 31, 19—

Sales, Less Returns...		$21,683,635
Cost of Sales...		18,051,366
Gross Operating Profit..		$ 3,632,269
Selling, Administrative, and General Expenses......................		3,512,573
Profit from Operations..		$ 119,696
Other Income, less Other Expenses...............................		47,187
		$ 166,883

Extraordinary Items

Net Proceeds on Termination of Lease..................	$ 19,673	
Special Profit on Sale of Apricots......................	477,278	
	$466,951	

Expenses

Abandonment of Advertising and Wrapping Materials..	$165,872	
Provision for and Settlement of Claims, Suits, Losses, etc.	100,325	
Deferred Advertising Written Off...................	56,042	
	$322,239	
		144,712
		$ 311,595
Provision for Federal and State Taxes on Income..................		166,701
Net Profit..		$ 144,896

PART VI

Surplus Accounts

PART VI *consists of one chapter on the analyses of retained earnings [surplus accounts]. Often there are two related accounts, capital surplus and retained earnings. It is important, from the viewpoint of both accounting and analysis, that these two accounts be kept separate. Capital surplus may be created in several ways, such as by a write-up of fixed assets or by the segregation of capital funds in excess of the stated value of no-par stock. Retained earnings, however, are created in only one way, by the retention of net profits in a business. The computation of the net profit of smaller business enterprises over an accounting period has never been difficult or complicated by accounting rationalization. During the first quarter of this century, however, a theoretical justification arose for omitting certain charges, or certain items of expense, from the income statements of larger corporations. The accounting theory under which these charges were made directly to retained earnings instead of to the income statement is analyzed and discussed. The evolution in accountancy theory and practice in recent years, notwithstanding some difference of opinion, has been toward the practice of making all charges to the income statement. The effect upon net profit is pointed out, with the final admonition that no net profit figure from an income statement should be taken at its face value until the reconciliation of retained earnings has been examined and the net profit figure adjusted by the amount of debits or credits made directly to that account.*

CHAPTER XXIII

Analyses of Retained Earnings [Surplus Accounts]

The last item in the balance sheet of a commercial or industrial corporation, before the total of aggregate liabilities and capital funds, is generally *retained earnings*[1] [earned surplus]. This account is the direct connecting link between the income statement and the balance sheet. Occasionally there are two accounts, *capital surplus*[2] and *retained earnings.* The *capital surplus*, at times, is also termed *paid-in surplus.* In these cases *retained earnings* invariably is the last item in the balance sheet.

It is evident from a glance at any balance sheet that retained earnings may be affected by a change in any other item on either side of the finan-

[1] The Committee on Terminology of the American Institute of Certified Public Accountants recommends the discontinuance of the use of the term *surplus*, because of its ambiguity, in *Accounting Terminology Bulletin No. 1, Review and Résumé*, pp. 30–31 (American Institute of Certified Public Accountants, New York, 1953). To the layman, this term as used in accounting is misleading. The specific recommendations of the Committee were as follows: "1. The use of the term *surplus* (whether standing alone or in such combination as *capital surplus, paid-in surplus, earned surplus, appraisal surplus*, etc.) be discontinued. 2. The contributed portion of proprietory capital be shown as (*a*) Capital contributed for, or assigned to, shares, to the extent of the par or stated value of each class of shares presently outstanding. (*b*) Capital contributed for, or assigned to, shares in excess of such par or stated value (whether as a result of original issue of shares at amounts in excess of their then par or stated value, or of a reduction in par or stated value of shares after issuance, or of transactions by the corporation in its own shares), and capital received other than for shares, whether from shareholders or others. 3. The term *earned surplus* be replaced by terms which will indicate source, such as *retained income, retained earnings, accumulated earnings*, or *earnings retained for use in the business.* In the case of a deficit, the amount should be shown as a deduction from contributed capital with appropriate description. . . . 6. Any appreciation included in the stockholders' equity other than as a result of a quasi-reorganization should be designated by such terms as *excess of appraised or fair value of fixed assets over cost* or *appreciation of fixed assets.*"

[2] Progress in substituting other captions for *capital surplus* is reviewed in the four-teenth edition of *Accounting Trends and Techniques.* Table 10 shows that in 1948, 375 out of 445 corporations whose annual reports to stockholders were reviewed carried the word "surplus" in the capital surplus caption while 70 used various terms replacing "surplus." By 1959 the annual reports of 244 out of 495 corporations whose reports were reviewed carried the word "surplus" while 251 used various terms replacing "surplus." Among the new terms in use were *additional paid-in capital, capital in excess of par or stated values, additional capital,* and *other capital.*—p. 11 (American Institute of Certified Public Accountants, New York, 1960).

cial statement in which it appears. An increase or a decrease in any item in the assets, if accompanied by a corresponding increase or decrease in the liabilities, will not disturb the retained earnings account. On the other hand, an increase or decrease in any item on either side of the balance sheet, without a corresponding change on the same or the other side, inevitably affects retained earnings, not only because retained earnings is the balancing account, but because a change in an asset or a liability without a corresponding change in an offsetting balance sheet item must relate to the income or outgo of the business, represented by this account. Whether or not the amount by which an asset or a liability is changed is actually entered in the income statement, retained earnings must reflect that change, up or down, as this account must balance the balance sheet.

EXPLANATION OF CAPITAL SURPLUS

The retained earnings account should represent actual earnings retained by a corporation since its organization or reorganization, over and above dividend disbursements. As a result of losses, this account at times may represent a deficit or an impairment of capital. The distinction between retained earnings and capital surplus is important, since ordinarily only the former is available for dividend payments. Moreover, retained earnings alone represents the excess of net profits over all dividends.

How Capital Surplus Arises

When a corporation is distributing securities to the public, the management often has the fixed assets, which, for example, previously might have been carried at $200,000, reappraised, and carried on the books at a new figure, say, $350,000. This increase, known as a *write-up*, is represented by a new item now called capital surplus, rather than by an increase in the retained earnings, since the difference represents no real earnings. Often these reappraisals are made during periods of high prices; years later when prices have fallen, the reappraised values represent inflated figures.

An item of capital surplus may also be created by the sale of capital stock in excess of its par value or, if no-par stock is issued, at a price in excess of that at which the stock is carried on the books of the corporation. That is, if a corporation sells 100,000 shares of no-par stock at $10 per share, and carries the stock on its books at $5 per share, the difference, amounting to $500,000, would be treated as capital surplus.

Capital surplus generally arises from the following seven sources:

1. Sales of par value capital stock for consideration in excess of par, which excess is known as premium on capital stock.

2. Sales of no par stock in which part of the proceeds is designated as the stated value of capital stock and the remainder is allocated to paid-in surplus.

3. The reduction of the par or stated value of previously issued capital stock. This credit may be best described as "paid-in surplus arising from reduction in par (or stated) value of capital stock."

4. Conversion of securities with higher stated values than those into which converted.

5. Capitalization of earnings in the form of stock dividends to the extent of amounts in excess of par or stated value of the stock issued.

6. Sale of stock donated by stockholders or the donation of property to the corporation by stockholders (donated surplus).

7. Assessments, levied against stockholders, of amounts in excess of par or stated value.[3]

The analyst should always ascertain whether an item of capital surplus *, or one of its synonyms,* was created from some arbitrary bookkeeping or accounting procedure or from the investment of additional cash in the business.

Reappraisals may write down as well as write up the value of fixed assets. In a depression, fixed assets valued at $350,000 may be written down to $200,000 in recognition of values forever lost and gone. The $150,000 book loss will then be charged against capital surplus already available or created by recapitalization. The recapitalization may take the form of a reduction in par value of par-value stock, change from par to no-par stock, reduction in the stated value of no-par stock, or piecing together of shares. By any of these means, there is made available a capital surplus against which to write off such a charge. Finally, such devaluations may be charged against current income, if the income is sufficiently large or in the event that no capital surplus is available.

Capital Surplus *(or a synonym),* Should Be a Separate Item

When inquiring for an explanation of a sudden substantial increase in retained earnings, the analyst may occasionally learn that the fixed assets have been written up by a reappraisal and the increase added, without any earmark, to the retained earnings account. This practice is grossly misleading. It is rarely countenanced by reliable accountants and under no consideration would be allowed by the Securities and Exchange Commission. A reconciliation of the retained earnings account would reveal the source of the credit as being a markup of fixed assets rather than actual

[3] For a list of transactions or conditions that result in capital (paid-in) surplus, see Norman J. Lenhart and Philip L. Defliese, *Montgomery's Auditing*, 8th ed., p. 393 (The Ronald Press Company, New York, 1957).

(or, any synonym)

earnings. The sources of capital surplus and retained earnings should be carefully investigated by the analyst, if he hopes to estimate the asset value of a business with any degree of accuracy and to detect attempts at both over- and understatement of invested capital and earning power.

RECONCILIATION OF SURPLUS ACCOUNTS

The retained earnings account in any two successive balance sheets of the same corporation is represented by two different figures. During the interval covered by the dates of the two balance sheets, the retained earnings will have increased or decreased. The schedule of credits and debits between these two dates is termed the *Reconciliation of Retained Earnings*. In the case of proprietorships or partnerships, the schedule is known as the *Reconciliation of Net Worth*. The first figure in the schedule is the amount of retained earnings in the initial balance sheet. The net profits during the period and, under certain accounting theory and practice, miscellaneous credit adjustments serve to increase the opening balance. Withdrawals, dividends, and charges are deducted; the balance is the amount of the retained earnings as shown in the more recent balance sheet. The credits or charges that are made to retained earnings are generally determined by the management of the business concern in consultation with its accountants.

Net Profits of Small Concerns

It is not particularly difficult, nor is any unusual wizardry necessary, to determine the net profits of a small retail business enterprise. With some semblance of book records and a physical inventory at the beginning and the close of an accounting period, the net profit before dividends or withdrawals is represented by the difference in the excess of the value of all the assets over the liabilities between the two dates. If exact bookkeeping records are maintained, the net profit may also be determined by deducting successively from gross sales all items of expense of the business as outlined in Chap. XVIII. The formula is simple, widely used, readily understood, universally and almost intuitively known. No matter what the items of expense are or how they occurred, they are deducted one and all before arriving at a residue to represent the final net profit.

The same process is used by small or moderate-sized manufacturing enterprises. The only change, in the case of manufacturers, is the addition of direct labor, depreciation on buildings, machinery, and equipment, and other factory charges to the list of expenses already mentioned. This formula for computing net profit is probably used by the great majority of the smaller and medium-sized business enterprises of the country.

Net Profits of Large Corporations

In considering the operating records of corporations with distributed stock interest, that is, corporations with capital securities listed or traded in on some national stock exchange or over-the-counter, there is occasionally found a vital modification of this simple, everyday, practical accounting convention. This modification consists in quarantining certain items of expense, carefully keeping them away from the income statement, but turning the charges over to what, at times, is a ubiquitous retained earnings account.

Sometime during the first quarter of this century the theoretical justification for this practice was created on the basis that an income statement should be concerned fundamentally not with including all items of expense, but in showing the net profit from operations for the year, unaffected by losses and adjustments applicable to earlier years. The emphasis was on sustained earning power without undue minimizing by irregular charges or credits. In other words, two arbitrary tests were created to determine whether an item of expense constituted a charge against current operations.

1. Was the expenditure for normal operations?
2. Was it incurred or accrued during the year under review?

Under this theory, charges and credits of an extraordinary nature are made by some managements and accountants to retained earnings. The application of this theory to the accounting practices of nationally known industrial and commercial corporations has naturally resulted in many unusual situations. Thus a profit or loss incurred by the sale of fixed assets, charges for carrying a manufacturing plant not in actual use, profits or losses incurred in the sale of securities, charges to wipe out underwriting costs, tax refunds or additional taxes, so-called "extraordinary" write-downs of inventory and receivables—one and all might be made to the income statement or to retained earnings, depending upon the point of view of the operating management or the compromise between the views of the management and the accountants, if outside independent accountants are making the audit.

In view of the complexities introduced by adjustments to the retained earnings account and the fact that the classification of income and retained earnings charges is often based on the whims of the management, the analyst must be on his guard against manipulations designed either to over- or to understate earnings. Probably the least justification exists for charging to retained earnings such items as write-downs on inventories and on receivables when the design is to have the charge omitted from year to year and never applied to the income statement.

Credits to retained earnings are rarer than debits, but for consistency must sometimes be made. When, for example, a corporation has been putting charges for additional taxes through the retained earnings account, any unusual tax rebate must logically be credited to retained earnings. If a loss on the sale of a capital asset were charged to retained earnings, it would be only logical to credit a profit on the sale of some capital asset. One exception to the general practice of adjusting profit and loss figures occurs when an asset that was once written up arbitrarily is now written down. Where both the write-up and the write-down are book entries, they should not appear in the income statement.

Tendency toward Making All Charges to Profit and Loss. In the years preceding 1937 this policy of making extraneous charges to the surplus account to lighten the income statement became so widespread that a reaction set in among accountants themselves. Since that time the discussion has been continuous on this subject, and although the trend is to make fewer and fewer charges to retained earnings, the practice of making all charges to the income statement has not reached the point where it is uniform accounting procedure. At a round-table discussion held at the annual convention of the American Institute of Certified Public Accountants as far back as 1937, several well-known accountants brought this subject out in the open and expressed their views rather definitely.

William H. Bell [Haskins & Sells]: . . . Accountants as a rule countenance too much crediting and charging off of items directly to surplus [retained earnings] which ought to go to income. We ought to make as good an effort as we can to determine a net income for every year, having regard to the various contingencies—set up reserves for them if you like—and not go wild with respect to the equalization of profits over a number of years or anything of that sort. If, however, we are faced with patent litigation, so that there is even a reasonable possibility that we are going to have to pay additional taxes for prior years, soak them into the income for this year, unless the thing is so enormous that it is definitely going to distort the income results—and that is seldom going to happen. I like to see a surplus [retained earnings] account that is clean and that has but one credit, net income, and charges for dividends.

Edgerton Hazard [Patterson, Telle & Dennis]: The new utilities commission rules have followed out Mr. Bell's idea. The new classified accounts of public utilities just issued for next year have followed Mr. Bell's theory, and they require that current year's adjustments of prior years' expense items are to be thrown into the current year's expenses and revenues if they don't materially distort the picture from year to year, which will probably have a clarifying effect upon some of the surplus [retained earnings] accounts of utilities in this state.

David Himmelblau [David Himmelblau & Company]: . . . I never did believe in surplus [retained earnings] adjustments; I still don't. I think they are the convenient device of many managements to prevent showing the full facts.[4]

---

[4] Round-table discussion on "Practice Problems of Accountants in Connection with Registration Statements," *The American Institute of Accountants, Fiftieth Anniversary Celebration Volume,* 1937, pp. 320–323 (American Institute of Certified Public Accountants, New York, 1938).

Under this theory of putting all charges through the income account, the effective reporting of the results of administering all of the assets of a business enterprise is fundamental; the basic interest is the over-all effectiveness of management.

For example, if current recurring earnings reported in the income statement are satisfactory, the reader may miss completely the significance of a large write-off of long-accruing obsolescence against present surplus [retained earnings]. He may not see the question: Were past statements of income reported as correctly as could have been expected from a discerning management? In this connection it must be evident that the perspective to be gained from an examination of a series of past income statements which are complete in their presentation of material facts may be very useful. . . . A definite position is taken here to the effect that all determinants of income in the broadest senses—including unusual and irregular factors—should be reported in the income statement before the net results are passed to the stock equity of the balance sheet.[5]

This point of view is further reinforced by bulletins issued by the Committee on Accounting Procedure of the American Institute of Certified Public Accountants and by the Executive Committee of the American Accounting Association, containing considered discussions regarding this question. The conclusions of the Committee on Accounting Procedure of the American Institute of Certified Public Accountants were carefully expressed as follows.

Over the years it is plainly desirable that all costs, expenses, and losses, and all profits of a business, other than decreases or increases arising directly from its capital-stock transactions, be included in the determination of income. If this principle could in practice be carried out perfectly, there would be no charges or credits to earned surplus [retained earnings] except those relating to distributions and appropriations of final net income. This is an ideal upon which all may agree, but because of conditions impossible to foresee it often fails of attainment. From time to time charges and credits are made to surplus [retained earnings] which clearly affect the cumulative total of income for a series of years, although their exclusion from the income statement of a single year is justifiable. There is danger that unless the two statements are closely connected such items will be overlooked, or at any rate not given full weight, in any attempt on the part of the reader to compute a company's long-run income or its income-earning capacity.[6]

Within the general terms of this statement is a recognition of the fundamental importance of an accounting policy by which all costs, expenses, and losses, except those arising from capital-stock transactions, are run

[5] Paton, W. A., and A. C. Littleton, *An Introduction to Corporate Accounting Standards*, pp. 99–100, 102 (American Accounting Association, Chicago, 1940).
[6] *Restatement and Revision of Accounting Research Bulletins, Accounting Research Bulletin No. 43*, p. 17 (American Institute of Certified Public Accountants, New York, 1953).

through the income statement. The opinion of the Executive Committee of the American Accounting Association on this question, issued as far back as 1941, is considerably stronger ~~and more definite~~.

For any one year the income statement should reflect all realized revenues, and all costs and losses written off during that year, whether or not they have resulted from ordinary operations.

1. The income statement for any given period should be divided into such sections as may be required to show not only particulars of revenues from and the expenses of the operations of the current period, measured as accurately as may be at the time, but also profits and losses from revenue realization and cost amortization not ordinarily associated with the operations of the current period.

2. The current-operations sections of the income statement should disclose revenues realized and operating costs, including applicable depreciation and other amortization of assets. This section should be subdivided or departmentalized to show the sources and results of each major income-producing activity and to furnish information helpful in the determination of trends in revenues and expenses.

3. Other sections of the income statement should list in reasonable detail interest on borrowed money, adjusted for debt discount and premium; so-called capital gains and losses; extraordinary charges and credits to income, including substantial adjustments which may not be attributable to the ordinary operations of the current year; gain or loss from the discharge of liabilities at less or more than their recorded amount; and income and profits taxes.

4. Income should not be distorted or artificially stabilized by creating arbitrary reserves either by appropriating income or surplus or by overstating expenses in certain periods and subsequently charging to such reserves expenses and losses pertaining to succeeding periods. Earned surplus [retained earnings] reserved for contingencies or for similar purposes does not lose its character as earned surplus [retained earnings]; expenses or losses arising from contingencies thus anticipated should be reflected not as reductions of the reserve but in the income statement of the period in which they are recognized.

5. Corporate income is not affected by the issuance, purchase, or retirement of the corporation's own stock, adjustments of capital-stock accounts, or dividend distributions by the corporation.

The objective of the income principle is to develop a series of income statements which, for the life history of the corporation, will include *all gains and losses*. To this end the income statement for each fiscal period should show not only the items affecting current results, but also any adjustments for gains or losses which may not be regarded as strictly applicable to the operations of the current period but which have nevertheless been first recognized in the accounts during the period. If net income is to have any meaning the factors influencing it must be isolated and given a distinct and unified expression. This is possible if all gains and losses are carried through a single medium to earned surplus [retained earnings]. It is impossible if expense charges, losses, or income credits may be carried directly to surplus [retained earnings] or to surplus reserve. This comment does not apply to operating reserves created by means of carefully determined charges to current operating expenses.

In view of the emphasis given to computations of earnings per share, and to other measures of corporate performance, a common yardstick is needed. The fact that it may not be possible to measure precisely at the end of any year all costs which have been acquired or dissipated during that year makes it essential to encompass within a single statement not only the best possible measure of income from ordinary operations, but also gains and losses from events not always associated with the transactions of a single year.[7]

This subject received further attention from the Committee on Accounting Procedure of the American Institute of Certified Public Accountants. It was pointed out that there is some difference of opinion as to what constitutes the most practically useful concept of profit or loss. On one hand, net profit is defined according to a strict proprietory concept by which it is presumed to be determined by the inclusion of all items affecting the net increase in "proprietorship" during the period except dividend distributions and capital transactions. The form of presentation which gives effect to this broad concept of net profit has sometimes been designated the "all-inclusive" income statement. On the other hand, a different concept places its principal emphasis upon the relationship of items to the operations, and to the year, excluding from the determination of net profit any material extraordinary items which are not so related or which, if included, would impair the significance of net profit so that "misleading" inferences might be drawn from the figures. This concept would require the income statement to be designated on what might be called a "current performance" basis, because its chief purpose is to aid those primarily interested in what a business concern was able to *earn* under the operating conditions of the period covered by the statement. The discussion of this subject then continues.

Proponents of the *all-inclusive* type of income statement insist that annual income statements taken for the life of an enterprise should, when added together, represent total net income. They emphasize the dangers of possible manipulation of the annual earning figures if material extraordinary items may be omitted in the determination of income. They also assert that, over a period of years, charges resulting from extraordinary events tend to exceed the credits, and the omission of such items has the effect of indicating a greater earning performance than the corporation actually has exhibited.

They insist that an income statement which includes all income charges or credits arising during the year is simple to prepare, is easy to understand, and is not subject to variations resulting from the different judgments that may be applied

[7] Bulletin entitled *Accounting Principles Underlying Corporate Financial Statements*, June, 1941, pp. 5–7 (American Accounting Association, Chicago).

in the treatment of individual items. They argue that when judgment is allowed to enter the picture with respect to the inclusion or exclusion of special items, material differences in the treatment of borderline cases develop and that there is danger that the use of *distortion* as a criterion may be a means of accomplishing the equalization of income. With full disclosure of the nature of any special or extraordinary items, this group believes the user of the financial statements can make his own additions or deductions more effectively than can the management or the independent accountant.

Those who favor the *all-inclusive* income statement largely assume that those supporting the *current operating performance* concept are mainly concerned with establishing a figure of net income for the year which will carry an implication as to future earning capacity. Having made this presumption, they contend that income statements should not be prepared on the *current operating performance* basis because income statements of the past are of only limited help in the forecasting of the earning power of an enterprise. This group also argues that items reflecting the results of unusual or extraordinary events are part of the earnings history of the corporation and, accordingly, should be given weight in any effort to make financial judgments with respect to the company. Since a judgment with respect to the financial affairs of the corporation should involve a study of the results of a period of prior years, rather than of a single year, this group believes that the omission of material extraordinary items from annual income statements is undesirable since there would be a greater tendency for those items to be overlooked in such a study.

On the other hand, those who advocate the *current operating performance* type of income statement generally do so because they are mindful of the particular business significance which a substantial number of the users of financial reports attach to the income statement. They point out that, while some users of financial reports are able to analyze a statement and eliminate from it those unusual and extraordinary items that tend to distort it for their purposes, many users are not trained to do so. Furthermore, they contend it is difficult at best to report in any financial statement sufficient data to afford a sound basis upon which the reader who does not have an intimate knowledge of the facts can make a well considered classification. They consider it self-evident that management and the independent auditors are in a stronger position than outsiders to determine whether there are unusual and extraordinary items which, if included in the determination of net income, may give rise to misleading inferences as to current operating performance. Relying on the proper exercise of professional judgment, they discount the contention that neither managements nor the independent auditors, because of the absence of objective standards to guide them, have been able to decide consistently which extraordinary charges and credits should be excluded in determining earning performance. They agree it is hazardous to place too great a reliance on the net income as shown in a single annual statement and insist that a realistic presentation of current performance must be taken for what it is and should not be construed as conveying an implication as to future accomplishments. The net income of a single year is only one of scores of factors involved in analyzing the future earnings prospects or potentialities of a business. It is well recognized that future earnings are dependent to a large extent upon such factors as market trends, product developments, political events, labor relationships, and numerous other factors not ascertainable from the financial statements. However, this group insists that the net income for the year should show as clearly as possible what happened in that year under that year's conditions, in order that sound comparisons can be made with prior years and with the performance of other companies.

The advocates of this *current operating performance* type of statement join fully with the so-called *all-inclusive* group in asserting that there should be full disclosure of all material charges or credits of an unusual character, including those attributable to a prior year, but they insist that such disclosure should be made in such a manner as not to distort the figure which represents what the company was able to earn from its usual or typical business operations under the conditions existing during the year. They point out that many companies, in order to give more useful information concerning their earning performance, make a practice of restating the earnings of a number of prior years after adjusting them to reflect the proper allocation of items not related to the years in which they were first reported. They believe that material extraordinary charges or credits may often best be disclosed as direct adjustments of surplus [retained earnings]. They point out that a charge or credit in a material amount representing an unusual item not likely to recur, if included in the computation of annual net income, may be so distorting in its results as to lead to unsound judgments with respect to the current earning performance of the company.[8]

Adjustments to Reported Net Profits

The accounting policies of the managements of corporations are sometimes designed to minimize reported profits in good years and to enhance reported profits in poor years. This policy may be motivated by a desire to avoid public criticism and a clamor for dividends when earnings are high, as well as to conceal an impaired position in poor years. In recent years, corporations have made fewer adjustments through the retained earnings account and more adjustments directly against current operations.

The analyst is primarily and fundamentally interested in ascertaining (1) the amount of net profit from normal operations of a business enterprise, and (2) the amount of net profit after all charges, whether the charges are made to the income account or to retained earnings, as well as gross profit and operating profit. Net profit is the one final measure of the ability of the management to operate a business enterprise successfully in our economic system; it must take into consideration all the policies of the management. If the president of a company is able to show a net

[8] *Restatement and Revision of Accounting Research Bulletins, Accounting Research Bulletin No. 43*, pp. 60–63 (American Institute of Certified Public Accountants, New York, 1953).

profit of $150,000 from operations and then loses $150,000 by poor investment policies, those facts should be clearly known. Such a management would not be so highly regarded as the management that earned the same profit and was able to keep a firm grasp on those profits. A similar situation would be created if a management showed an operating profit of $100,000, but that sum was offset by a write-down in inventory of the same amount. Such a management would need more careful watching than one that earned the same profit and had no write-down in inventory.

The last figure in the income statement, therefore, should never be accepted unequivocally as the absolute net profit or loss, or *book* net profit or loss, until the retained earnings account has been carefully scrutinized and all debits or credits to that account are used to obtain an adjusted net profit figure. Such adjustments were made in the study of the earnings, after all charges, of the Magazine Publishing Co., Inc., in Chap. XIX.

ANALYSIS OF MISCELLANEOUS CHARGES

After all charges to the retained earnings account (except write-downs of assets to the extent they had previously been written up) are transferred to the income statement, those charges should be carefully studied. In the case of borderline and poor credit risks, the amount, the extent, and the nature of individual expenses often solve crucial operating policies by bringing to light those places where the management has unnecessarily lost or spent too much money through poor judgment. If substantial write-downs are taken on inventory or on receivables, something must be wrong with the purchasing or credit policy. Often, detection of the ailment becomes clear by the study of the adjusted income statement; the ailment may be overlooked when so-called *extraordinary and nonrecurring charges* are allowed to remain in the retained earnings account. Detection will often suggest the explanation and, at times, the remedy.

Extraordinary charges invariably should be segregated and analyzed individually. Frequently the analyst will find that the manufacturing and distributing operations have been carried on intelligently and profitably, but the final results have been unsatisfactory because of unprofitable outside operations, such as losses assumed in financing a subsidiary, or extraordinary sums spent fruitlessly on research. The goal of maximum net profit will be more nearly approached by ascertaining and then correcting in the adjusted income statement the causes for losses that are out of line with sound management policies.

DIVIDEND DISBURSEMENTS

The amounts of net profits and dividend disbursements or withdrawals are of interest to the analyst as tests of managerial capacity and conservatism toward dividend policy. Since assets depreciate, operating expenses mount, and contingencies arise, inadequate earnings or excessive dividend payments may eventually destroy a sound asset structure as shown by the balance sheet.

As a general rule, dividends should be paid from earnings only,[9] but this does not mean that these earnings must be current earnings. If the current earnings are insufficient, dividends may be paid from the accumulated earnings of prior years, that is to say, from earned retained earnings. But the facts to be taken into consideration before dividends may be safely paid from the net earnings vary according to the circumstances in each case. If the directors declare dividends which prove to have been illegal, they may be faced with suits to recover the money thus unlawfully distributed. Where a business is prosperous and collections are normal, cash is allowed to accumulate in the bank to meet the expected declaration of dividends by the directors, with very much the same definiteness in planning as attends the preparation to pay current bills before they fall due.

As a rule, the operating management of a corporation should not declare a dividend unless sufficient funds are on hand or at least in sight to pay the dividend, in addition to its requirement of cash working capital. In many cases, while the earnings according to the books may warrant dividend payments, a dividend may be passed when the actual cash is not available. There are other cases in which the cash on hand at the moment may not be sufficient, but the business may be well established and the inflow of cash may be counted upon in advance of the actual receipts. Sometimes specific restrictions are imposed upon the declaration of dividends under certain circumstances, either through special charter provisions or through indentures accompanying senior security issues.

An examination of the dividend distributions of many corporations reveals marked differences regarding the accumulation of earnings and what is done with them. Among the several varieties of management policies in this respect are four general classes: dividends are paid to the last dollar after providing for moderate reserves; the smallest possible dividend is paid in order to accumulate large retained earnings; between these two extremes, liberal reserves may be set up for every reasonable purpose, a substantial amount added to retained earnings, and all that is left distributed to the stockholders; and lastly, regular dividends of a

---

[9] There have been notable exceptions. "In January, 1669, Colbert decided that it would be wise to arouse new interest in the company [French West India Company founded in 1664] by having it pay a dividend. He ordered it to pay those investors who had voluntarily put in at least 3,000 *livres* before December 1, 1665, 4 per cent on their investment for the period from December 1, 1665, to December 1, 1668. Those who had put in additional sums during the period were to receive 5 per cent. To pay the dividend Colbert secured for the company 404,545 *livres* from the royal treasury. Thus the dividend was a governmental manipulation, rather than a commercial transaction."—COLE, CHARLES W., *Colbert and a Century of French Mercantilism*, Vol. II, p. 17 (Columbia University Press, New York, 1939).

certain amount, say, 5 or 6 per cent, are paid, the remaining profits, if any, being carried to retained earnings, and dividends paid from retained earnings when the current earnings are insufficient.

THEORY AND PROBLEMS

1. How would you describe the capital of a corporation that has an issue of 100,000 shares of common stock of no-par value, but a stated value fixed by the board of directors of $5 per share and an excess over liabilities of $1,500,000?

[A.I.A. Examination]

2. State your opinion of each of the following two conditions of a corporation, suggesting any changes, with your reasons, that you believe necessary.

   a. A competent appraisal of the property accounts was made in year A and the current values thus reported were set up on the books and carried at these higher values in its published statement as of the end of the fiscal year;

   b. In setting up the appreciated values on the books, a charge was made increasing the property account values, and a credit in like amount entered to *Surplus*, the only account of this nature used by the corporation in its record keeping.

3. State five ways in which capital surplus may arise.

4. During the first quarter of this century, the theory was widespread that the net profit finally shown in the income statement should represent net profit from operations. Discuss the pros and cons of this theory.

5. At the present time, the theory seems to prevail that the net profit finally shown in the income statement should be after all charges. Discuss this theory, pointing out the effect upon the reconciliation of retained earnings account.

6. If extraordinary and nonrecurring credits and debits appear in the retained earnings statement, why should adjustments be made in the income statement by including these particular items, before determining the net profit figures?

7. Below is an Income Statement and Retained Earnings of a manufacturer of paints and varnishes. The income statement discloses *Net Profit for Year* of $1,362,740. In your opinion, is this amount the correct net profit for the year? If not, adjust the income statement so that the final figure will be the correct net profit for the year.

Income Statement
For Year Ended December 31, 19—

Gross Profit from Sales, before Deducting Depreciation....		$2,673,068
Selling, Administrative, and General Expenses, excluding Depreciation..		453,629
Operating Profit before Deducting Depreciation.........		$2,219,439
Other Deductions, less Other Income....................		6,887
Profit before Depreciation and Federal Taxes...........		$2,212,552
Provision for Depreciation......................		548,814
Profit before Provision for Federal Taxes...............		$1,663,738
Provision for Federal Income and Profits Taxes		
Normal Income Taxes...........................	$ 284,590	
Other Taxes.......................................	7,979	
Surtax on Undistributed Profits.....................	8,429	
		300,998
Net Profit for Year...............................		$1,362,740

Retained Earnings

Balance—Jan. 1, 19—................................ $3,174,028

Add:

Net Profit for the Year............................ $1,362,740
Reduction of Reserve for Loss on Bank Claims.........   2,950
Capitalization of Items Disallowed as Repairs by Revenue
  Agent, less Provision for Depreciation in prior years...   7,325

    1,373,015

    $4,547,043

Deduct:

Creation of Reserve for Revaluation of Plant not used in
  business... $ 27,815
Net Adjustment of Taxes for prior years...............   4,664
Net Adjustment of Expenses pertaining to prior years...   7,572
Dividends Paid in Cash on Common Stock............. 1,500,000

    1,540,051

Balance—Dec. 31, 19—............................. $3,006,992

8. Some accountants have argued for an "all-inclusive" income statement, while others have insisted that at times certain items should be charged to retained earnings or otherwise kept out of the net income figure. Explain the position of these two groups and give the principal arguments offered by each group.

PART VII

Synthesis

PART VII *consists of one chapter. Here the author has given what might be termed the philosophy behind the financial statement, and a summary of more recent evolution in accounting principles and practices. The financial statement is not an absolute reality; it is based on recorded facts, so-called "accounting conventions," and personal judgment. How these factors affect the values at which items are recorded in balance sheets is explained. A method, a technique of understanding and interpreting financial statements is necessary because of the inadequacy of accountancy; balance sheets often contain values which have no relation whatsoever with actual current economic values. Here is the reason, within the very practice of accountancy itself, why the basis of the valuation of many items such as inventory, investments, and miscellaneous receivables must be known before it is possible to make a sound analysis. Influences exerted toward creation* ~~the~~ *of accounting standards and* ~~increased uniformity~~ *in accounting practices by such well-known institutions as the New York Stock Exchange, the Board of Governors of the Federal Reserve System, the American Institute of Certified Public Accountants, the American Accounting Association, and the Securities and Exchange Commission are outlined. The authoritative publications of these organizations over the years have had great influence on the practice of accountancy and the evolution of accounting standards.*

narrowing the areas
of differences

CHAPTER XXIV

Recent Evolution in Accountancy Theory and Practice

"It has been asserted . . . that an ideal condition for the practice of accountancy would be one under which the economic value of any asset was easily ascertainable at any time. It has also been asserted that, under this condition, the ideal aim of accountancy should be to exhibit *all* profits and losses in a profit and loss statement. But the circumstance remains that the ideal condition . . . does not in fact prevail."[1] In other words, under these ideal conditions, every asset—cash, receivables, merchandise, investments, land, buildings, machinery, furniture, fixtures, miscellaneous receivables—would be carried in the balance sheet at its actual current economic value.

The fact that many assets are not so valued is one of the basic reasons for the need of analyzing financial statements. The first step in that practice, as has been pointed out, is to ascertain as nearly as possible the current, going, economic value of items that might have values higher or lower than the figures at which they are carried in the balance sheet. The analyst must ascertain many factors behind the scenes if he is to learn the real value of such items as *investments, investments in and advances to subsidiaries and affiliates, miscellaneous receivables, due from officers and directors,* and at times the *accounts* and *notes receivable.* Assets do not represent current economic values because "balance sheets and income accounts are largely the reflection of individual judgments," explained George O. May, and "their value is therefore to a large extent dependent on the competence and honesty of the persons exercising the necessary judgment."[2]

RELATIVITY OF FINANCIAL STATEMENTS

In a subsequent study, George O. May elaborated on these intangible features which play such a great part in present-day accountancy.

[1] MacNeal, Kenneth, *Truth in Accounting*, p. 182 (University of Pennsylvania Press, Philadelphia, 1939).
[2] May, George O., *Audits of Corporate Accounts*, p. 8, Correspondence between the Special Committee on Cooperation with the Stock Exchanges of the American Institute of Accountants and the Committee on Stock List of the New York Stock Exchange, 1932–1934.

He wrote:

. . . It seems to me fundamentally important to recognize that the accounts of a modern business are not entirely statements of fact, but are, to a large extent, expressions of opinion based partly on accounting conventions, partly on assumptions, explicit or implicit, and partly on judgment. As an English judge said many years ago when business was far less complex than it is today, "The ascertainment of profit is in every case necessarily a matter of estimate and opinion."[3]

The relativities of values expressed in balance sheets and in income statements are rarely realized by the typical layman and stockholder, or by many bankers, credit men, and analysts, most of whom assume that these values are definite and absolute. This illusion of absoluteness has been encouraged by the very appearance of balance sheets and income statements distributed by the millions each year to stockholders and to creditors, financial statements in which all items have generally been carried out to the cent, giving an appearance of great exactness.[4] As explained in earlier pages of this volume, the nature of these financial statements was admirably summarized on traditional ground a number of years ago by the American Institute of Certified Public Accountants:

Financial statements are prepared for the purpose of presenting a periodical review or report by the management and deal with the status of the investment in the business and the results achieved during the period under review. They reflect a combination of recorded facts, accounting conventions, and personal judgments; and the judgments and conventions applied affect them materially. The soundness of the judgments necessarily depends on the competence and integrity of those who make them and on their adherence to generally accepted accounting principles and conventions.[5]

In this carefully worded summarization of the nature of financial statements, figures used in balance sheets and in income statements are qualified as to their absolute exactness by three premises. These figures are based upon a "combination of recorded facts"; they are valued in accordance with "accounting conventions"; and their monetary size is determined by "personal judgments." Let us see in specific terms exactly how these premises apply to particular items.

[3] MAY, GEORGE O., *Twenty-five Years of Accounting Responsibility, 1911–1936,* Vol. II, p. 52 (American Institute Publishing Co., Inc., New York, 1936).
[4] Since 1927 the Bethlehem Steel Corporation has omitted cents from the audited financial statements contained in its annual corporate reports to stockholders. This policy has since been followed by a steadily increasing number of nationally known corporations: Gulf Oil Corporation (1936), Standard Oil Co. of New Jersey (1938), Consolidated Edison Corporation (1939), General Foods Corporation (1939), Ingersoll Rand Company (1939), and United States Steel Corporation (1939).
[5] *Examination of Financial Statements by Independent Public Accountants,* p. 1, (American Institute of Certified Public Accountants, New York, 1936).

Recorded Facts

Among the items whose values are carried in financial statements *substantially* ~~largely~~ on the basis of recorded facts are cash on hand, cash in bank, the face value of notes receivable, accounts receivable, inventory, amount of notes payable, accounts payable, interest payable, the volume of gross sales, returns of merchandise, net sales, cost of merchandise sold, rent, wages, salaries, and the cost of fixed assets. The amount at which each one of these specific items is carried in a financial statement is based upon recorded historical events, upon transactions which have actually taken place and which have been carefully recorded in the books of account in the exact dollar-and-cent values of a certain time, or over a certain period of time. This very practice creates fundamental problems in handling values in accounting. These problems are discussed in the immediately succeeding pages.

Of the items listed in the preceding paragraph, fixed assets, that is, land, buildings, machinery, equipment, tools, furniture, and fixtures, are of outstanding importance because the components of fixed assets, where acquired at different times in the past, are carried in dollars of different values. All the other items, with the exception of the inventory or that part of the inventory which might be valued by base stock, average cost, or last-in first-out methods, are carried at values measured in current, or approximately current, dollars The components comprising fixed assets, if purchased over a period of years, might consist, for example, of the dollars paid for land 20 years ago, the unamortized portion of dollars paid to erect certain buildings 19 years ago, and the unamortized portion of dollars expended for machinery, equipment, and tools over each of the past 10 years and of furniture and fixtures over the past 5 years.

During periods of fluctuating price levels, either up or down, the value of the dollar varies considerably. As a result the depreciated economic (current) values of the various components of fixed assets often vary materially from the respective depreciated accounting values on the statement date, and the depreciation charged into the income statement will consist of dollars of different values depending upon the dates on which the particular assets were acquired. As Samuel J. Broad has pointed out, oranges and grapefruits are being added and subtracted in the same schedule. "It is like having 100 oranges of revenues and deducting 80 oranges of cost and 10 grapefruits of cost and saying that the profit left is 10 oranges."[6] It's really adding and subtracting oranges, grapefruits, apples, pears, peaches, and grapes in the same schedules! Solomon Fabricant

[6] BROAD, SAMUEL J., "The Impact of Rising Prices upon Accounting Procedures," *The Journal of Accountancy*, Vol. 86, No. 1, p. 14, July, 1948.

called such combination of dollar figures arising in different price levels "heterotemporal" prices.[7]

Accounting is an art which has to do with the systematic record-ation, compilation, and presentation of monetary values over a period of time or in time. Such an art may be inaccurate even though the records are maintained in the most exacting of all sciences. In fact, the only peri-ods of time in which accounting, as currently practiced, could possibly be accurate would be during those days or weeks when the dollar values of all assets carried on the books of a particular business enterprise were stable, and simultaneously, the book values and the current economic values of all such assets were identical. Such a situation could hardly exist.

Accounting Problems Created by Fluctuating Price Levels. Since April 18, 1775, when 800 British soldiers marched out of Boston and at dawn on the following morning encountered 60 minutemen drawn up on the common at Lexington, Mass., we have had five periods of important price inflation. Each period occurred during or following a major war, the Revolutionary War, the War of 1812, the Civil War, the First World War, and the Second World War. Between 1774 and 1779, wholesale prices, it has been carefully estimated, rose almost threefold, that is, from an index of 23 to an index of 69, when the studies of Warren and Pearson are changed to a 1947–1949 base as an index of 100.[8] Between 1811 and 1814, wholesale prices rose from an index of 38.4 to 55.5, or 45 per cent. Between 1861 and 1865, wholesale prices rose from an index of 27.2 to 56.4, or slightly more than doubled. Between 1915 and 1920, wholesale prices increased from an index of 30.8 to 68.9, and between 1940 and 1959, from 51.1 to 119.5, more than doubling in both periods. In other words, a 1947–1949 dollar was worth $4.31 in 1774 and $1.45 in 1779, $2.60 in 1811 and $1.80 in 1814, $3.68 in 1861 and $1.77 in 1865, $3.25 in 1915 and $1.45 in 1920, $1.96 in 1940 and 83 cents in 1960. While these fluctuations were moder-ate compared with the fluctuations in the value of German and French currency after the First World War and of Greek and Chinese money after the Second World War, they were of sufficient magnitude to present vital business problems and vital accounting problems from the viewpoint of "recorded facts."

It has by no means been an unusual occurrence for labor leaders to decry the size of profits, after taxes, reported by the U.S. Department of Com-merce for all corporations which have ranged from $17,200,000,000 in 1952 to $23,800,000,000 in 1959. These profits might be characterized as

[7] FABRICANT, SOLOMON, "Business Costs and Business Income under Changing Price Levels: the Economist Point of View," *Income Movement in a Dynamic Econ-omy,* p. 146 (American Institute of Certified Public Accountants, New York, 1950).
[8] WARREN, GEORGE F., FRANK A. PEARSON, and HERMAN M. STOKER, *Wholesale Prices for 213 Years, 1720 to 1932,* Table I, pp. 6–11 (Cornell University, Ithaca, N.Y., 1932).

"accounting" profits, as in the first place they included realized inventory profits, and in the second place, the deduction for depreciation, in accordance with recognized accounting practice, was estimated on the basis of cost as a recorded fact. The depreciated economic value of the fixed assets of all corporations at this time, however, was materially greater than the depreciated accounting value. As a result, depreciation based on cost was materially smaller than it would have been if based on current economic values, and "accounting" profits were greater than they should have been—according to this school of thought—to the extent of this difference. Moreover, accumulated depreciation on the basis of cost was insufficient to replace worn-out fixed assets acquired at lower price levels in earlier years.[9] This problem became a practical one for many corporations, which in recent years have charged into expenses an increased amount for depreciation, over and above normal depreciation, to make up

[9] "The final test of the soundness of any accounting principle is, in my opinion," wrote Willard J. Graham, "simply this: Will the application of the principle produce accounting information that is most likely to lead to correct decisions, to the formulation of sound judgments? It is primarily from this standpoint . . . that the cost of goods sold, and the annual charge for depreciation, should be based on current costs rather than on original costs. . . . I have frequently challenged the members of my classes . . . to state one business problem the solution of which depended upon information about past costs, assuming information about current costs and probable future costs to be available. The challenge has never been accepted. Certainly management requires knowledge of current inventory costs, not past cost, and insofar as the depreciation factor enters into a management decision, only current and future costs can have any possible bearing."—GRAHAM, WILLARD J., "The Effect of Changing Price Levels upon the Determination, Reporting, and Interpretation of Income," The Accounting Review, Vol. XXIV, No. 1, p. 18, January, 1949.
In the annual report to stockholders covering the year 1953 for Aktiebolaget Volvo of Göteborg, Sweden, well-known manufacturers of automobiles, trucks, and tractors, the accountants based depreciation of fixed assets on prevailing prices. The explanation in the "Comments on the Account" section of the report read as follows: "Depreciation has hitherto been on cost prices but the Board has decided that in the future depreciation will be dependent on the prices prevailing at the time. Retroactive depreciation in accordance with this has been made for the year 1952." The "added" charge to the income statement for 1953 representing the difference with depreciation based on "prevailing price-values" over "cost-price values" amounted to 1,917,000 kroner. The annual report to stockholders for the year 1959 contained the following statement in the "Balance Sheet" section of the report: "The depreciation for machinery and equipment includes kr. 3,000,000 for extra depreciation over and above the Company's normal depreciation."
In 1959 Simca Société Anonyme, Paris, also manufacturers of automobiles, trucks, and tractors, listed 2,000,000 "American" shares on the American Stock Exchange. The prospectus issued at the time the shares were offered to the American public contained a footnote to the balance sheet as of Dec. 31, 1958, explaining the application of index numbers to the valuation of properties as outlined in footnote 17, page 611: "The Company has valued its properties on three separate occasions, at the end of 1945, 1949, and 1951, on the basis of co-efficients of revaluation authorized by the French Government on those dates." The explanation then continued, "Thereafter, the Company has charged against earnings depreciation on the higher amounts, as permitted by the French tax law."

this approximate difference, even though the charge is not recognized by the Internal Revenue Service as a deduction in computing Federal income taxes.

Cost Represents Initial Value. From this discussion, it would seem that cost, as one of the recorded facts of accountancy and as the basis for determining subsequent "book" values and periodic depreciation, would appear to have certain limitations. When any commodity or service is acquired in the market, cost is the best available evidence of the economic value prevailing at that moment. In other words, cost at the point of acquisition expresses price, what the contracting parties consider the goods or services to be worth. There is, however, a concept more basic than cost. In this sense, cost expresses initial value, and as such is a datum of very considerable importance. From this reasoning it would be a short step to consider financial accounting in terms of values rather than costs.[10] In other words, what seems to be needed at this stage in the evolution of accounting is a new significant definition of cost for fixed assets comparable with the definitions of cost which have been evolved for inventories, a definition which would be just as effective in keeping accounting economically sound as well as mathematically sound during periods of widely fluctuating prices, as well as during periods of relatively stable prices. This problem is presented by William A. Paton in the following manner:

Cost is not merely a figure on a piece of paper, an empty datum. Cost expresses economic power contributed or economic sacrifice incurred. Cost is a substantive economic measure. With this conception in view it becomes necessary to restate or convert recorded data when there has been a marked and persistent change in the value of the dollar. Without such restatement or qualification the recorded

---

[10] "This point has the more force when it is remembered that many assets are acquired by the particular accounting entity by other processes than purchase and sale. The most important example is the acquisition of property through the act of investment, as when a party invests land, patents, or some other noncash resource in becoming a stockholder. Other examples are acquisition by inheritance or gift, discovery, or accretion. The rancher doesn't leave the new lambs out in the cold, or fail to take them into his financial reckoning, because he can't find purchase invoices for them. The orthodox basis for recording assets acquired by other processes than purchase, of course, is fair market value at date of acquisition. I would also like to suggest, that the basic data of all economic analyses are values. We are all valuers, appraisers, in the sense that we are continuously endeavoring to evaluate, size up, the phenomena of the market. And the more intelligently we carry on this process the more effectively we react to the changes in the economic fabric—the more able we are to 'roll with the punches.' Moreover, it must be recognized that accounting is a primary source of valuation data. Without accounts the process of appraising, valuing, the complex flow of activity in any enterprise is almost impossible. Let's, then, modify our conception of the 'cost basis' and interpret such basis as a means of recording and bringing periodically to our attention the significant economic data of the business enterprise."—PATON, WILLIAM A., "Accounting Problems Relating to the Reporting of Profits," an address given at a Business Conference, Youngstown, Ohio, Mar. 30, 1949, sponsored by the Economic and Business Foundation.

data no longer represents true cost. That is, so-called "actual cost," paradoxically, may not be "actual cost." If, for example, I own a piece of land that cost me 5,000 1938 dollars and someone asks me today what the land cost me, I am not responding accurately if I say that the cost is $5,000, providing my questioner is thinking in terms of a very different measuring unit, the 1948 dollar, and I know that he is using the 1948 dollar in his thinking. I should say: "I paid 5,000 1938 dollars, but if I express my actual cost in terms of current 1948 dollars the answer to your question is approximately $10,000."[11]

Suggested Modifications in Accounting to Overcome Effects of Changing Price Levels. The effect upon accounting of constantly changing price levels—or values—received the careful attention of two authors from two somewhat different viewpoints quite a number of years ago and was the subject of a survey conducted by the American Institute of Certified Public Accountants in 1948. These two authors were Henry W. Sweeney, who produced a pioneering study entitled *Stabilized Accounting*[12] in 1936, and Kenneth MacNeal, who wrote *Truth in Accounting*[13] in 1939, an original study, from which an excerpt was quoted to open this chapter.

The problem of how recorded facts were affected by fluctuating price levels was a practical one with which accountants had to grapple in Germany, France, and Italy during the inflation following the First World War. As a result, the literature on this study is extensive in German, French, and Italian. Sweeney made a study of the accounting methods used to maintain real values in those countries during that period of inflation and also of the literature on this subject in those languages and then wrote *Stabilized Accounting*. In the introduction he explained that "the success of the whole system of business depends upon the truthfulness of accounting. The truthfulness of accounting depends largely upon the truthfulness of the dollar—and the dollar is a liar! For it says one thing and means another." That was clearly evident from 1950 to 1960.

Stabilized accounting is a method of converting values by means of an index number from cost or depreciated cost to current economic values. It is not unlike the process of converting the foreign-money figures on the preclosing trial balance of a foreign branch into domestic-money equivalents. Sweeney, however, suggests this technique only when the general price level has varied at least 5 per cent within the accounting period under examination, and provided that most of the assets, liabilities, and net worth items that are on the books at the end of the accounting period first appeared on the books when the general price level was at least 5 per cent above or below its position at the end of the accounting period. In an extensive discussion, the author gives a variety of examples showing how

[11] *Ibid.*
[12] Harper & Brothers, New York, 1936.
[13] University of Pennsylvania Press, Philadelphia, 1939.
14 American Institute of Certified Public Accountants, New York, 1963.

the technique would work in practice and how the income statement would integrate with the balance sheet. One quotation concerning a simple balance sheet with only two asset items, cash of $750 and fixed assets of $1,000, explains the technique:

The cash of $750 is already stabilized in the general price level of December 31, 19—. For a money-value item is always stabilized in the current price level. The fixed asset cost $1,000 when the general index was 100. At the end of the year, when this index was 150, $1,500 must have been needed to buy as many goods and services in general as $1,000 could buy when the asset was bought. Hence, as at the end of 19— the actual original outlay of $1,000 must be expressed as $1,500. The depreciation of 50% on this asset must, likewise, be expressed in the general price level as at the end of the year. This is accomplished simply by taking depreciation of 50% on $1,500, the original cost adjusted for the change in the general price level. Consequently, the stabilized debit for depreciation against profit-and-loss and the stabilized credit to the depreciation reserve both become $750. Similarly the real-value item, capital stock, becomes stabilized in the general price level of December 31, 19— as follows: $1,000 × 150/100 = $1,500.[14]

In the process of using index numbers to stabilize values, the procedure described above is applied first to the assets, next to the liabilities, and then to the investment in the business. When this procedure has been completed, the residue of profit and loss remaining from the activities of all accounting periods up to the date of stabilization is available. All that needs to be done to ascertain this residue is to subtract the total of the "stabilized" liabilities from the total of the "stabilized" assets. In this process there are two kinds of surplus and deficit just as there are two kinds of profit and loss, realized and unrealized. The net amount of surplus or deficit that appears on a balance sheet may be zero, but there may be both a realized surplus and an unrealized deficit of the same amount, or a realized deficit and an unrealized surplus of the same amount.

The main differences between Sweeney's suggestion and the typical balance sheet stabilization utilized in European accounting practices during the inflation following the First World War were four in number. First, the foreign method was usually quite content to stabilize the paper-money figures on the basis of gold money (usually the national gold money), despite the fact that the general purchasing power of gold money itself kept fluctuating. Second, the foreign method usually did not attempt to separate surplus into its realized and unrealized sections and then show the changes in each section. Third, the foreign method usually made no attempt to construct a stabilized income statement. Fourth, the foreign method apparently paid no attention to devising a thorough and systematic method of treating money-value profit and loss.[15]

[14] Sweeney, op. cit., pp. 24–25.
[15] Ibid., pp. 38–40.

In *Truth in Accounting*, Kenneth MacNeal tackled this fundamental problem of values without the use of index numbers. "The great majority of contemporary certified financial statements," he wrote, "must necessarily be untrue and misleading due to the unsound principles upon which modern accounting methods are based." These principles have been discussed at various points in this volume where we have learned that the actual current values of many items in balance sheets are different, at times greatly different, from their book or "accounting" values.

Because balance sheets do not generally reflect current economic values, MacNeal developed the theory that marketable assets in balance sheets should be valued at market price, nonmarketable reproducible assets should be valued at replacement cost less depreciation, and occasional nonmarketable, nonreproducible assets at original cost. The practical effect of this theory is materially different from the orthodox accounting theory of unamortized costs. "With the exception of occasional nonmarketable and nonreproducible assets," wrote MacNeal, "this procedure would produce a balance sheet whose fluctuations of net worth, between the beginning and the end of any period, would describe accurately the net total of all profits and losses during that period from whatever sources." General builders, contractors, architects, and mechanical engineers with tools and machinery do this as a routine part of their work.

Moreover, depreciation based on current economic values in contrast to historical costs, that is, recorded facts, tends to "recover" from current operations sufficient funds to replace the physical capital consumed.

The oft-repeated objection that future replacement costs are unknown and may be greater or less than total accumulated depreciation is entirely irrelevant. The capital "recovered" by way of depreciation charges is generally reinvested in physical assets immediately at the current price level. By what may be called the process of "equivalent replacement," most fixed assets consumed during an accounting period are, in effect, replaced during that same period.[16]

These innovations are suggested because balance sheets as currently prepared "are composed of a bewildering mixture of accounting conventions, historical data, and present facts wherein even accountants are often unable to distinguish truth and fiction." Creditors, stockholders, and analysts "have a right to believe that the figures given to them state values, not private prophesies, and the only values that any one knows how to state are economic values." This is the practice followed by investment bankers when merging two or more companies, and when an experienced businessman sells his business. "Booms and depressions probably

[16] GRAHAM, WILLARD J., "The Effect of Changing Price Levels upon the Determination, Reporting, and Interpretation of Income," *The Accounting Review*, Vol. XXIV, No. I, p. 22, January, 1949.

engender more financial catastrophes than all other causes put together, and yet their influence on assets and on the financial standings of companies is largely concealed in the financial statements now published. Values may decline to a point where a mortgage cannot be refunded, or they may rise to a point where it is obviously common sense to convert them into cash. Yet in each of these cases stockholders and creditors are kept in ignorance of the true situation."

In July, 1948, the American Institute of Certified Public Accountants distributed a questionnaire, asking answers to or opinions on seven specific questions (in two cases the questions were divided into two parts), to 410 selected key business excutives, bankers, economists, labor representatives, accounting teachers, controllers, and others who, it was felt, would have sufficient economic and accounting background to give carefully considered replies. Usable replies were received from 188 individuals by September 30, 1948. In the letter accompanying the summary of the survey, it was pointed out that the most frequent criticism of accounting methods in general use centered around the basic problem we have been considering, the fact that "an income figure derived on the basis of actual cost of inventories and plant facilities may be substantially larger than 'economic income' when current values are materially different from historic costs."

One of the questions in this survey specifically concerned the over-all problem of economic income. It read: "Would you favor reporting a figure for net income which approximated 'economic income' if that were accepted for tax purpose?" Of the usable replies to this question 61, or 51.2 per cent, answered "Yes," and 58, or 48.8 per cent, "No." A second question tied the concept of economic income to tax acceptability. This question read: "Would you favor reporting a figure for net income which approximated 'economic income' even if it were not accepted for tax purpose?" Of the usable replies to this question 44, or 36.5 per cent, replied in the affirmative and 77, or 63.5 per cent, in the negative. The following question threw additional light on this problem. It read: "Do you believe that a change in the direction of 'economic income,' if accepted [for tax purposes], should be followed year in and year out—in years of low profits as well as high profits?" The replies to this question showed a high degree of acceptability. Of the usable replies to this question 108, or 94.7 per cent, answered in the affirmative, and only 6, or 5.2 per cent, in the negative.

The final question in this interesting survey was concerned with the use of price indexes as a means of determining economic values. This is the process which was widely used during the inflation in the European countries following the First World War and which Sweeney outlined so clearly in *Stabilized Accounting*. This question read: "To avoid the difficulties of estimating future replacement costs or requiring appraisals, it has been suggested that price index numbers could be used to measure the approximate difference between historical cost and current cost.[17] Do you believe that such index numbers would be satisfactory for such measurement?" Of the usable answers 56, or 54.3 per cent, replied "Yes" and 47, or 45.7 per cent, "No."[18]

Accounting Conventions

Although fixed assets are generally carried on the books at cost, plus improvements and less depreciation, that is, on the basis of recorded facts, that basis often provides a figure that is higher or lower than the current economic value. A plot of land and a building might have been purchased for $50,000 five years ago and that figure presumably represented a fair economic value at the time. Today, that plot of land and building might be carried on the books at $46,000; the fair market value of the property

---

[17] The French Government legislated for a solution to this problem after the Second World War by a series of laws, decrees, and orders published from August, 1945, to May, 1948. Under this legislation, fixed assets were allowed—it was not compulsory —to be revalued at their economic worth in current francs, with a proviso that the maximum value at which any asset could be taken up in the accounts should not exceed its cost multiplied by a legal coefficient of increase for the particular year of acquisition. Depreciation reserves could be adjusted in a similar manner. The legal coefficient for 1947 was one, for 1945 two, for 1942 six, for 1939 nine, and so on gradually until for 1914 and prior years it was sixty. The "legal coefficient" as used here is a kind of arbitrary index number fixed by law. The schedule of legal coefficients and a brief explanation of their use in French accounting may be found in an article, "Revaluation of Fixed Assets in France," by John Kennerly, A.C.A., *The Accountant*, Vol. CXIX (New Series), No. 3860, pp. 469–470, Dec. 11, 1948 (London). For studies regarding the desirability of restating conventional accounting figures by the use of a general price-level index, applied to American business, see *Price-level Changes and Financial Statements—Case Studies of Four Companies* by Ralph C. Jones (1955), and *Price-level Changes and Financial Statements—Basic Concepts and Methods* by Perry Mason (1956), both published by the American Accounting Association.

[18] Because the interest in this subject continued high, George O. May suggested that a Study Group be formed to give comprehensive consideration to all phases of the subject of "business income" and that such a Study Group include economists and representatives of labor as well as accountants. This Group was organized and then spent between three and four years on their project. In 1952 the Study Group published *Changing Concepts of Business Income* (The Macmillan Company, New York), a volume of 160 pages of highly condensed material. While collateral problems received careful attention, the effect of inflation on balance sheets and income accounts was probably the underlying consideration in the study. Views on this subject were quite divergent, as would be expected from a group representing diverse interests. Minority opinions, comments, and dissents from fifteen individuals and one comment signed by two individuals were included in the study.

The use of index numbers, for Federal income tax purposes, in determining depreciation charges on fixed assets acquired in different years, was suggested by several qualified individuals who testified before the Committee on Ways and Means of the House of Representatives in July, 1953.—*General Revenue Revision, Hearings before the Committee on Ways and Means, House of Representatives*, Part 2, pp. 703, 724, 732, 733, 740, and 749 (83d Cong., 1st Sess., Washington, D.C., 1953).

might be $56,000, or $36,000. The value of a building and the site on which it stands is assumed to be the aggregate of the value of the land and the cost of reproduction, less depreciation, of the building. The land, as Henry George has so strikingly explained, might increase, however, in economic value because it happens to be located at the intersection of two increasingly busy thoroughfares. In such a situation, the true aggregate value of the property might come to be the value of the land, less the probable cost of removing the building.

This practice by which items are carried on the books at figures different from the actual economic values at the date of a financial statement is the result of what is known as an *accounting convention*[19] and represents one of the limitations to existing accountancy. It is also an accounting convention in most lines of industry and commerce, outside the cutting-up textile trade, for the accountant to rely upon his client's certificate for the value of the inventory on the statement data, or to verify the correctness of quantities and prices, but not of grades or conditions. Many accountants who specialize in the cutting-up textile trades in New York have an intimate knowledge of the value of piece goods of various constructions and of dresses, coats, and suits; they actually verify grades and conditions, as well as quantities and prices.

In small business enterprises the valuation of assets based on accounting conventions or premises is of relatively little significance. As businesses grow in size and invest substantial sums in plants or in retail stores, this premise grows in importance. If a plant is closed, its valuation on the books remains unchanged except for added depreciation. The properties

[19] Since 1947 there has been a rather strong movement for a departure from the cost basis of accounting. The United States Steel Corporation in its annual report for 1947 included an item in its consolidated statement of income of "Added Wear and Exhaustion of Facilities to Cover Replacement Cost" of $26,300,000, an amount which was over and above its normal depreciation based on original cost. As explained in the annual report for the following year, 1948, "This added amount, which represented 30 per cent of the normal depreciation, was determined partly through experienced cost increases and partly through study of construction cost index numbers. Although this was materially less than the experienced cost increase in replacing worn-out facilities, it was a step toward stating total wear and exhaustion in an amount which would recover in current dollars of diminishing buying power the same purchasing power as the original expenditure." As a result of the strong insistence of the Securities and Exchange Commission and the position of the Committee on Accounting Procedure of the American Institute of Certified Public Accountants expressed in *Accounting Research Bulletin* No. 33, December, 1947, and reiterated in a general letter to members of the American Institute of Certified Public Accountants on Oct. 14, 1948 (both reprinted in *Restatement and Revision of Accounting Bulletins, Accounting Research Bulletin* No. 43, pp. 67–71, published by American Institute of Certified Public Accountants, New York, 1953), the United States Steel Corporation abandoned this technique of depreciation accounting. In its place there was then adopted a new method described as "accelerated depreciation," a principle that the determination of depreciation to be recognized in the accounts may be based directly on use as measured by actual production

of some retail enterprises increase in value as the neighborhood becomes more important; in other cases the values drop. In both situations the properties are invariably carried at cost plus improvements less depreciation. In the first situation, the property is undervalued in the balance sheet; and in the second situation, overvalued.

As corporations grow in size and sell securities to the public, determining what portions of the values of certain so-called "fixed" assets are used up as expense in each fiscal period and what portions are carried forward to the next accounting period in the balance sheet becomes a fundamental problem. This is no simple matter when applied to vast amounts of fixed assets, and, according to our existing accounting principles, it is based on conventions. In other words, each individual item of fixed assets, land, building, each piece of machinery, equipment, tools, furniture, and fixtures, is not appraised separately each year. Instead, depreciation is taken on each class of fixed assets, except land, on a different schedule and charged to expense for each accounting period. This depreciation is now deducted from the recorded value of the asset to which it applies, to determine the "conventional" value for the balance sheet.

In 1876 the Supreme Court stated that the public "rarely ever took into account the depreciation of the buildings in which the business is carried on,"[20] and in 1878 it supported the government in a claim that a railroad company should not be allowed to include a depreciation charge in operating expenses, claiming that "only such expenditures as are actually made can, with any propriety, be claimed as a deduction from earnings."[21] In 1909 the Court reversed its earlier opinion: "Before coming to the question of profit at all, the company is entitled to earn a sufficient sum annually to provide not only for current repairs but for making good the depreciation and replacing the parts of the property when they come to the end of their life."[22] It is easy to see that an accounting convention based on a Supreme Court decision would greatly influence the practice of accountancy.

Personal Judgments

Financial statements prepared by someone within a business organization may conceivably present a far different result from that which would be

[20] *Eyster v. Centennial Board of Finance*, 94 U.S. (1876). For an interesting "early" study pointing out how legislatures "enact revenue measures in utter disregard" of accounting principles see "The Federal Corporation Tax and Modern Accounting Practice" by A. M. Sokolski in the *Yale Review*, Vol. 18, Feb., 1910, pp. 372–389.

[21] *United States v. Kansas Pacific Railway Co.*, 99 U.S. 459 (1878).

[22] *Mayor and Alderman of City of Knoxville v. Knoxville Water Co.*, 212 U.S. 13 (1909); MAY, GEORGE O., *Twenty-five Years of Accounting Responsibility, 1911–1936*, Vol. II, p. 307. For an exhaustive treatment of court decisions relating to accounting, see *The Law of Accounting and Financial Statements* by George S. Hill (Little, Brown & Company, Boston, 1957).

found by an independent, experienced, certified public accountant.[23] Accountants, themselves, depending upon their policy, training, experience, and practice, may differ in how they would report the condition[24] of a particular business concern as of a given date. At times, accounting

[23] According to regulations of the Securities and Exchange Commission, "An accountant will be considered not independent with respect to any person [business enterprise], or any of its parents or subsidiaries, in whom he has, or had during the period of the report, any direct financial interest, or any material indirect financial interest; with whom he is, or was during such period, connected as a promoter, underwriter, voting trustee, director, officer, or employee."—Regulation S-X, Rule 2-01(b), p. 2, Aug. 20, 1958. The subject of the "independent accountant" has received careful attention by the Securities and Exchange Commission several times. Further elaboration and refinements of what comprises "independence" will be found in accounting series *Releases* of the Securities and Exchange Commission, No. 2, May 6, 1937, No. 22, Mar. 14, 1941, No. 47, Jan. 25, 1944, and in an address "The Conflict of Independence in Accounting" delivered by Donald C. Cook, Vice-chairman of the Securities and Exchange Commission, before the annual meeting of the American Institute of Certified Public Accountants, held at Boston, Oct. 3, 1950.

[24] In an examiner's report prepared for the Securities and Exchange Commission in June, 1938, a nationally known firm of accountants was charged with "casuistry" in its defense of its alleged failure to "present fairly the financial position of the Missouri Pacific Railway Company." Testimony of several accountants and the hearings supported the views of the examiner's report.—Securities and Exchange Commission, *Release* No. 2325, Dec. 6, 1939.

In August, 1938, the Securities and Exchange Commission brought charges that the Alleghany Corporation had made "false and misleading statements as to its assets, liabilities, profit and loss and surplus accounts" in its financial statements for the years 1934 to 1937, inclusive. These charges were substantiated in the final report of the Commission.—Securities and Exchange Commission, *Release* No. 2423, Mar. 1, 1940.

On Aug. 5, 1942, the Commission issued a voluminous report of 110 pages containing its detailed findings and opinions concerning the figures of the Associated Gas & Electric Company, as audited over the years by a well-known firm of public accountants. In this most extensive report, the accountants were bitterly condemned for certifying "obviously manipulated" financial statements. These financial statements were "marked by the paucity of the information disclosed and by failure to reveal significant circumstances necessary so that the information might be properly evaluated. . . We are left with the feeling that the principal purpose of the company was not to disclose frankly, but to mystify, baffle, mislead, and conceal, and that the audits and certificates of the accountants did nothing to prevent the accomplishment of that purpose."—Securities and Exchange Commission, *Release* No. 3285A, Aug. 5, 1942. For an interesting interpretation of this release of the Securities and Exchange Commission, which marked a milestone in thoroughness and significance, see *Your Investments*, Vol. 3, No. 9, September, 1942.

On July 9, 1947, Thomascolor Incorporated filed a registration statement with the Securities and Exchange Commission. A *Findings and Opinion* report of the Commission stated that "the financial statements included in the original registration statement overstated registrant's assets and minimized, if not deliberately concealed, information that would have fairly disclosed the true nature of the assets with which it was represented the registrant's business would be conducted." The financial statements included in the original registration, for example, contained an item, Patents and Patent Applications of $2,014,941.03. This item "failed to distinguish between amounts which should have been identified with patents and those arising from promotion. The record discloses that a substantial portion of the entire sum originally identified as patents and patent applications was actually promotion cost arising from

firms have had an employee who has performed his work in an unfortunately inefficient and ineffective manner.[25] There have also been cases where accountants have seemed to miss or to overlook vital information in the preparation of their audit or in their examination of financial statements.[26]

---

the issuance of registrant's stock at par value. . . . "—Securities and Exchange Commission, *Release* No. 3267, Nov. 26, 1947.

Well-known cases illustrating the accountant's responsibility in law to third parties are the following: *Ultramares Corporation v. Touche et al.*, 278 N.Y. 104, 15 N.E. (2d) 416 (1938); *Smith v. London Assurance Corporation*, 109 App. Div. 882, 96, N.Y.S. 820; and *Craig v. Anyou*, 208 N.Y.S. 259 (1925). How accounting treatment of items has differed among accounting firms, and how the same accounting firm has used different treatment on what seemed to be similar items under similar circumstances are illustrated in the summary of an extensive survey by William W. Werntz and Earle C. King, "An Analysis of Charges and Credits to Earned Surplus," *The New York Certified Public Accountant*, Vol. XVI, No. 9, September, 1946.

[25] In February, 1938, it was disclosed that the tangible net worth of the Interstate Hosiery Mills, Inc., had been arbitrarily and whimsically inflated over a period of years to somewhat over $1,000,000 by a senior supervising accountant of a firm of accountants, who had been in charge of auditing the books of the corporation for many years.—Securities and Exchange Commission, *Release* No. 2048, Mar. 22, 1939.

[26] In December, 1938, the fantastic situation came to light where the assets of the well-known wholesale distributor of drugs, druggists' supplies, and liquor, McKesson & Robbins, Inc., had been inflated progressively over a period of years to reach the rather substantial figure of approximately $21,000,000. For full details see the 501-page *Report on Investigation in the Matter of McKesson & Robbins, Inc.*, published in December, 1940, by the Securities and Exchange Commission pursuant to Sec. 21a of the Securities Exchange Act of 1934. The ensuing spontaneous reaction to this unusual situation burst forth in criticism of the methods of accountancy and the relationship of accountants to operating managements.

In April, 1946, Drayer-Hanson Incorporated filed a registration statement with the Securities and Exchange Commission covering a proposed public offering of 80,529 shares of its Class A stock, of which 59,030 shares were sold in the following year at $10 per share. It was subsequently learned that the balance sheets included in the registration statement were materially misleading for the reason that the work in process inventory as of Apr. 30, 1946, was overstated approximately $87,000 and that the income statement for the 10 months ended Apr. 30, 1946, which showed net earnings of approximately $181,000, was misleading for the same reason. No physical inventory had been taken and the auditors "without justification implied in their certificate that the system of internal check and control and the cost accounting system . . . furnished reliable costs with respect to cost of sales and raw materials, work in process, and finished foods inventories."—Securities and Exchange Commission, *Release* No. 67, Apr. 18, 1949.

In December, 1946, Health Institute, Inc., filed a registration statement covering 50,000 shares of preferred stock and 40,000 shares of common stock to be sold to the public for $907,500. The statement contained a balance sheet as of Nov. 20, 1946. A subsequent amendment contained a balance sheet as of Jan. 1, 1947. At a hearing the accountant "admitted that the certificates affixed [to both balance sheets] falsely stated that such balance sheets fairly presented the financial position of Health Institute, Inc., at the respective dates."—Securities and Exchange Commission, *Release* No. 68, July 5, 1949.

The financial affairs of each of the corporations mentioned in the footnotes immediately preceding had been audited by well-known accounting firms in many cases for several years. It is evident that standards of accounting practice are based

Even though the intentions of operating managements and of accountants are of the best, the human quality of judgment plays an unconscious part. Very different conclusions are frequently reached by perfectly honest and capable individuals on the same basis of physical facts. Let us see how judgment enters into the estimation of three items—the valuation of inventory, the determination of a reserve for bad debts, and the determination of the rate of depreciation to be used on the various divisions of the fixed assets.

Valuation of Inventory. On page 303, Chap. XI, is a schedule of five items that make up a hypothetical inventory. It was shown in that chapter that the inventory could be valued at several different figures and still be carried at "cost or market whichever is lower" depending, first of all, upon whether individual items or the inventory in the aggregate were valued at the lower of cost or market. Some person's judgment decides which technique and, consequently, which value should be used.

In the continued discussion in that chapter, it was learned that the inventory could be carried at cost or market, whichever is lower, and still have widely different valuations depending upon the method of computation—first-in first-out, base stock, retail method, standard cost, or last-in first-out. In every case, someone must decide which method of valuation will be used; that particular method will affect the valuation of the inventory in the balance sheet, the cost of goods sold, and hence the net profit in the income statement.

Reserve for Bad Debts. The amount of reserves to be set up for bad debts is likewise an exercise of judgment alone. Someone familiar with the receivables must examine every item that is past due, study the credit file on each account, and on the basis of that information decide whether a reserve should be set up against all or part of each account. If six different men independently should make the same study, each would suggest a different amount as a reserve for bad debts.

Depreciation. When it comes to depreciation, judgment enters into two necessary decisions: first, the rates of depreciation to be used on the various types of fixed assets subject to depreciation, and second, the method of depreciation to be used. The rate of depreciation, which is based upon the useful life expectancy of an asset, is an engineering rather than an accounting problem. Useful life expectancy in itself is a generality. A toggle press might wear out within 3 years at one plant and last 20 years in another.

The method of depreciation selected will give different values to assets over the years and different charges to the income statement, even though

upon the training, experience, and individual judgment of respective accountants and that the effective influence of business management upon so-called "independent" public accountants has varied widely.

the same life expectancy is used. These methods might vary from straight-line depreciation, which is most commonly employed by industrial concerns, to the sinking fund method, the fixed percentage of diminishing value method, or depreciation based upon output or the number of hours a machine is in operation.

EVOLUTION IN ACCOUNTING PRINCIPLES

As has been stated, accountancy in the United States is a profession of relatively recent origin, the first important accounting firm having been organized in 1883, and the first provision for the certification of accountants having become a law in New York State in 1896. Progress toward more uniform accounting, with a steadily increasing degree of reliability, has been made over the years as a result of campaigns of education and enlightenment carried on by bankers, trade associations, credit men's associations, professional accounting organizations, the Board of Governors of the Federal Reserve System, and the Securities and Exchange Commission.

While many sources have been interested in and have exerted their influence toward the progressive improvement in the practice of accountancy, probably the renaissance in this vital broad subject was due more to William Z. Ripley than to any one other individual. With his wide practical interest in economics, he had no hesitancy in pointing out in unmistakable terms the unsound misleading accounting practices followed by the managements of many railroads.[27] Gradually his interest broadened into the field of accountancy as reflected in the annual reports of managements of industrial corporations to their stockholders, culminating in the critical citation of extracts from the figures of representative corporations whose securities were listed on the New York Stock Exchange.[28] There seems little doubt that the violent exposures of misleading practices that received such wide publicity from Ripley's pen, together with his suggestion that an agency of the Federal government "address itself vigorously to the matter of adequate and intelligent corporate publicity," provided the basis, along with the stock-market crash of 1929, for the eventual legislation creating the Securities and Exchange Commission.

Sources of Influence on Accountancy

There is a widespread feeling in the profession that an accountant, like a doctor, should be allowed to perform his work in his own way. Account-

[27] RIPLEY, WILLIAM Z., *Railroad Finance & Organization* (Longmans, Green & Co., Inc., New York, 1915).

[28] RIPLEY, WILLIAM Z., "Stop, Look, Listen!" *Atlantic Monthly*, September, 1926. This and other supplementary essays were subsequently published in *Main Street and Wall Street* (Little, Brown & Company, Boston, 1927).

ants have strongly supported their right to place their individual interpretation upon accounting problems, and to treat their relations with clients on a confidential basis. At times, individual accountants and firms have failed to realize that their very actions were of wide interest to others, such as creditors, stockholders, investors, speculators, employees, and the public. In a very broad way accountants are trustees of business knowledge and information. They should be, and many accountants are, in fact, very practical everyday philosophers of business activity. Specific progress away from this individualistic interpretation of the treatment of problems toward more uniform accountancy standards and principles has been made over the years by five institutions, the New York Stock Exchange, the Board of Governors of the Federal Reserve System, the American Institute of Certified Public Accountants, the American Accounting Association, and the Securities and Exchange Commission.

New York Stock Exchange. The recognized bulwark of American conservatism, the New York Stock Exchange, particularly prior to the organization of the Securities and Exchange Commission, had made basic contributions toward uniformity in accountancy practice. The New York Stock Exchange was in a unique position to insist upon cooperation from the managements of corporations whose securities were listed on the Big Board. The establishment of certain standard accounting policies under such sponsorship had widespread effect.

In 1900, for example, the National Tube Company, in its application to list both its 7 per cent cumulative preferred stock and its common stock, agreed to publish at least once in each year "proper detailed statements of its income and expenditures, also a balance sheet giving a detailed and accurate statement of the condition of the company at the close of its last fiscal year." Here was the creation of a basic precedent. It showed the awakening interest of the management of the New York Stock Exchange in accountancy; "proper detailed statements of its income and expenditures," and a "balance sheet giving a detailed and accurate statement," implied the recognition that accounting principles of some kind were coming into existence. A consciousness of method was being created. The layman did not realize that far-reaching principles were being created by these decisions, by these agreements between the New York Stock Exchange and representative corporations. The stockholder was to be entitled to at least a minimum of essential information; if that minimum tended toward some standard, the road of the analyst would become less rocky.

This agreement applied only to the National Tube Company. It did not apply to corporations whose securities were already listed or traded on the New York Stock Exchange. It was the practice, however, to incorporate such new requirements in the succeeding agreements with all

See 30/ Storey, Reed K., *The Search for Accounting Principles,* (American Institute of Certified Public Accountants, New York, 1964) for a condensed essay on the evolution and development of accounting principles in the United States. This essay is the result of a study financed by a research grant to the University of Washington. (B)

corporations that made application to list additional securities, so that the influence of innovations of this character became cumulative. By 1900, when this agreement was made with the National Tube Company, the New York Stock Exchange had been in existence 108 years, but only in the years immediately preceding 1900 had the need of some degree of standards in accountancy become recognized.

The Niagara Falls Power Company in 1910 agreed to publish quarterly income statements,[29] and in 1926 the Exchange announced that corporations whose stocks were listed in the future must agree to publish quarterly statements of earnings. In 1916, the General Motors Corporation agreed "to publish semiannually beginning June 30, 1917, a consolidated income account and balance sheet," the first agreement of this kind to call for extensive interim financial information from any listed industrial corporation. In the following year, the American Smelting and Refining Company signed a similar agreement.[30]

In 1930, after several public utility holding companies, under the tacit approval of accounting firms, had taken into earnings stock dividends of subsidiaries at market value, the New York Stock Exchange made its first specific ruling on accountancy practice, that a corporation should not itself take up or permit any subsidiary, directly or indirectly controlled, to take up as income stock dividends received at an amount greater than that charged against earnings, earned surplus, or both of them. Here was a fundamental accounting pronouncement that would have to be followed by accounting firms auditing the figures of corporations where securities were listed on the New York Stock Exchange. It was followed.

When it was discovered in 1933 that the Allied Chemical and Dye Corporation was taking into earnings, over the certificate of a certified public accountant, dividends on its own treasury stock, the Exchange declared through its president that it was improper for a corporation to increase its income by including therein dividends on its own stock, and this, of course, would be particularly true where the dividends paid were not fully earned. An individual can hardly give himself something! Neither can a corporation!

Since July 1, 1933, independent audits have been required from all corporations that have applied to the New York Stock Exchange for the listing of their securities. At this date the Securities and Exchange Commission was just around the corner.

Board of Governors of the Federal Reserve System. Under the authority of the Federal Reserve Act of 1913, the 12 Federal Reserve banks were

---

[29] SCHULTZ, BIRL E., *Stock Exchange Procedure,* p. 19 (New York Stock Exchange Institution, 1936).

[30] *Ibid.,* p. 20.

organized. Among the powers accorded to the Federal Reserve banks was the privilege of rediscounting commercial paper as defined by law for member banks, and under such supplementary rules and regulations as might be drawn up by the Federal Reserve Board. When offering commercial paper for discount, the member bank sent along with the promissory note the balance sheet, and also, if readily available, the income statement of the maker of the note, so that the Federal Reserve bank receiving the application would have information upon which to analyze the financial strength of the original borrower.

The Federal Reserve System was organized several years after James G. Cannon had stressed in his speeches, over and over again, the importance to banking institutions of developing and using financial statement blanks to obtain more accurate financial information. The Federal Reserve Board had an immediate natural interest in the development of a practical comprehensive balance sheet form as described in Chap. I for its own use, as well as for the extensive use of member banks. From its strategic position in our economy, it also had a deep interest in the development of somewhat more uniform methods to be used in the preparation of balance sheets, so that the analyst would have more uniformly reliable information on which to base his interpretation of figures of business concerns.

The April, 1917, number of the *Federal Reserve Bulletin* published by the Federal Reserve Board contained an article, *Uniform Accounts*, which represented a significant milestone toward more uniform accounting practice. This article listed the minimum tentative requirements to be followed by an accountant in the verification of financial statements. It also contained a condensed statement of accounting principles and rules applicable to certain specific items in financial statements and gave suggested forms for the presentation of balance sheets and income statements. These proposals had been developed by the American Institute of Certified Public Accountants and had been approved by the Federal Reserve Board after several conferences. Representatives of the Federal Trade Commission also attended these conferences.

In the following year, this article was republished by the Federal Reserve Board in the form of a pamphlet bearing the more explanatory title, *Approved Methods for the Preparation of Balance Sheet Statements.* The preface to this enlightening and forward-looking condensed study of 21 pages explained: " . . . It is recognized that banks and bankers have a very real interest in the subject, because they are constantly passing upon credit based upon statements made by manufacturers or merchants. It is quite as much of vital interest to merchants and manufacturers, because they realize that credit sometimes suffers by reason of losses incurred by bankers through credits given to merchants and manufacturers whose statements do not correctly reflect true conditions. Lastly, it is of immense importance to auditors and accountants, because they have a professional as well as a practical interest in having the character of their professional work formulated and standardized."

The pamphlet was submitted by the Federal Reserve Board for the consideration of banks, bankers, and banking associations, merchants, manufacturers, and associations of accountants. The suggestions which this pamphlet contained received wide circulation, attention, and acclaim, as it was the first authoritative guide to the minimum procedure to be followed by public accountants in the United States in the verification of figures in financial statements. It was, however, only a beginning. In May, 1929, the study was completely revised and republished by the Federal Reserve Board, this time under the title of *Verification of Financial Statements*. It is evident that the contribution of the Federal Reserve Board by sponsoring these studies was considerable.

American Institute of Certified Public Accountants. In a round-table discussion on the subject of more uniform accounting held as far back as 1937 by the American Institute of Certified Public Accountants, one accountant summarized the possibilities succinctly. "It seems to me that while it is desirable to have standardization, we must standardize on one basis—telling a story clearly and telling it truly. As far as expressing the affairs of a corporation is concerned, standardization can be along just four lines, it seems to me: First, the general form of a statement; second, the arrangement of statements; third, the terms in which statements are expressed; and fourth, the method of arriving at the values shown thereon."[31]

Accountancy, after all, is not an absolute science with immutable laws but a relative one in constant evolution to serve the changing needs of business. Moreover, accounting has inherent limitations. Every balance sheet "is, as judicial authorities have recognized, necessarily a matter of estimate and opinion, and in some cases the limits of a reasonable difference of opinion may be fairly wide."[32] It is the width of this difference of opinion that is being steadily reduced.

The revised pamphlet published in May, 1929, by the Federal Reserve Board under the title of *Verification of Financial Statements* was now re-

[31] CRANSTOUN, WILLIAM D., Round-table discussion on the subject "To What Extent Can the Practice of Accounting Be Reduced to Rules and Standards?" held Oct. 19, 1937, included in *The American Institute of Accountants, Fiftieth Anniversary Celebration Volume*, 1937, p. 260 (American Institute of Certified Public Accountants, New York, 1938).

[32] MAY, GEORGE O., A lecture given at Northwestern University, Chicago, Ill., on Jan. 11, 1932, entitled "The Accountant and the Investor," *Twenty-five Years of Accounting Responsibility*, Vol. 1, p. 6 (American Institute Publishing Co., Inc., New York, 1936).

studied and revised by the American Institute of Certified Public Accountants, to conform to improving accounting practices. In January, 1936, this enlarged pamphlet was published under the title of *Examination of Financial Statements by Independent Public Accountants*. This pamphlet prescribed the minimum procedure to be followed in the verification of figures and in the form of presentation of the results, both, however, being sufficiently flexible to require the exercise of individual judgment as to procedure in verification of financial data and as to the most appropriate form of presentation. A more elaborate *Statement of Accounting Principles*, the work of three men, Thomas H. Sanders, Henry R. Hatfield, and Underhill Moore, was published by the American Institute of Certified Public Accountants in 1938. The statement represented a material contribution in the formulation and study of accounting principles. These studies are discussed briefly a little later in this chapter.

In May, 1939, a special committee of the American Institute of Certified Public Accountants on auditing procedure issued a report that has become known as *Extensions of Auditing Procedure*. This report was modified somewhat and then approved by the membership in September, 1939. It dealt with four significant aspects of auditing procedures: (1) examination of inventories, (2) examination of receivables, (3) appointment of independent certified public accountants, and (4) the form of independent certified public accountants' report.

Although many accounting firms for years prior to 1939 had made observations or tests of physical inventories and had obtained independent confirmation of receivables in the examinations of financial statements, this report in effect made such procedures mandatory where "practicable and reasonable." These procedures have been extended since October, 1942, to require disclosure of their omission in the independent accountant's report "regardless of whether they are practicable and reasonable."

In *Extensions of Auditing Procedure* the desirability of having the independent public accountant appointed by the board of directors or by the stockholders of a corporation, instead of by the active management, was stressed. It was suggested that the accountant be appointed early in the fiscal year. The study also contained a suggested short form of accountant's report representing a revision of the form set forth in the *Examination of Financial Statements*. In recognition of new requirements of the Securities and Exchange Commission, this form of report was further amended in February, 1941, by the insertion of a sentence indicating that the examination was "made in accordance with generally accepted auditing standards applicable in the circumstances. . . ."

In the latter part of 1939, a Committee on Auditing Procedure was created by the American Institute of Certified Public Accountants to publish the results of studies from time to time on particular phases of

and a Committee on Terminology a series of 4 Accounting Terminology Bulletins

auditing procedures. The first pronouncement was in the form of a bulletin published in October, 1939. By October, 1948, this committee had issued 24 such bulletins. They covered such matters as *Clients' Written Representations Regarding Liabilities and Other Matters, Auditing under Wartime Conditions,* and *Physical Inventories in Wartime.* These bulletins tended to provide a basis for more uniform thorough auditing procedures.

In 1938 the Committee on Accounting Procedure was reconstituted and enlarged. With this new organizational setup, this committee has published a series of 51 *Accounting Research Bulletins* from September, 1939, to August, 1959, dealing with general accounting principles, specific accounting procedures, and terminology. These bulletins, like those on auditing procedure, have tended toward a degree of uniformity in accountancy, although from the footnotes on pages 71–72 regarding that part of *Bulletin No. 43* which defines current assets "for accounting purposes" and on pages 77–78 regarding that part of *Bulletin No. 43* which concerns the treatment of tax-anticipation notes, it is clear that certain "principles" may be subject to some difference of opinion.

Since 1947 annual surveys of *Accounting Trends and Techniques in Published Corporate Annual Reports* have been published by the American Institute of Certified Public Accountants. The primary aim of these studies has been to give a broad perspective on the latest accounting practices and trends as disclosed in the published annual reports of representative corporations, with particular emphasis on the topics dealt with in the more recent *Accounting Research Bulletins.* Where possible comparable statistics from the reports of the same corporations have been provided for earlier years. These surveys have been unusually enlightening. They represent real contributions to the knowledge of actual accounting practices. The most recent survey published in 1960 covered the current practices of 600 representative corporations for the calendar year of 1959, compared with practices used in many cases during ~~the preceding six~~ *selected earlier* years.

American Accounting Association. Difficulties that have stood in the way of developing the recognition of more uniform accounting principles and the practice of more uniform accountancy were accepted as challenges by the American Association of University Instructors in Accounting; at their twentieth annual meeting in 1934, the members voted to broaden the purposes and the activities of the organization. The executive committee, the governing body of the association, formulated a statement of objectives which was one of the most significant declarations to have been published in that era regarding far-reaching objectives and possibilities of evolution in accounting. It was very much in contrast to other statements issued during these "formative" years, which tended to emphasize the difficulties in developing trends toward uniformity in accounting

35 *In 1935 the name of this organization was changed to American Accounting Association and the membership, previously restricted to professors of accounting, opened to anyone interested in accounting*

principles and the desirability of continuing the practice by which each accountant, like a doctor, would solve his own problems in his own individual way.[38]

In 1936 the executive committee issued a tentative statement of accounting principles relating to the financial reports of business corporations. This was followed in 1941 by a revision entitled *Accounting Principles Underlying Corporate Financial Statements.* In 1948, this statement was reissued with changes under the title *Accounting Concepts and Standards Underlying Corporate Financial Statements.* The prefatory notes in this statement contained the following considerations:

The basic objective has been to stimulate the continued study and discussion of accounting standards and their periodic restatement, thereby assisting in the orderly development of accounting concepts and their wider acceptance both among accountants and among others in any way influenced by or interested in the findings of accounts.

So many decisions are dependent on interpretations of corporate reports that uniform, objective, and well-defined standards have become a requisite for the use of the reports by persons having an interest in an individual enterprise or in the broader problems relating to the national economy. Because basic accounting concepts and standards remain relatively undisturbed even during periods of economic change, restatements will involve primarily changes in emphasis.

Although a comprehensive understanding of the financial position and operating activities of a corporation is derived only in part from financial statements, it should nevertheless be possible for a person moderately experienced in business and finance to obtain from such statements basic information on which he may rely with confidence.

In the application of standards individual differences in industries or in enterprises within an industry may require that allowance be made for well-established practices, but the standards here recommended are believed to be capable of general application. Any deviation therefrom should be carefully weighed and, if made, disclosed both qualitatively and quantitatively in the financial statements. The acceptance by any business organization of the concepts and standards presented here should be viewed not as a submission to arbitrary rules and restraints but as providing an opportunity for interpretation and comparison by means of the common language of accounting.

The above paragraphs were followed by statements of principles regarding assets, revenues, and expenses in the income statement, liabilities and stockholders' interests, and fourteen standards to be followed in the preparation of financial statements. Then followed the "concluding comment":

If accounting standards are to merit acceptance, financial statements in which

---

[33] This statement of objective was published in full in the 1945 and 1950 editions of *Practical Financial Statement Analysis.*

they are incorporated must supply dependable information for the formulation of judgments. These judgments made in an economic setting subject to important changes can be relied upon only if such standards are adhered to consistently. Changes in accounting policy should be limited to those that will lead to improved standards.

Accounting for the business activities of modern corporations will continue to offer many problems. As business structure becomes increasingly complex, the special and often diverse interests of investors, management, labor, and government will place increasing demands upon accounting and accountants. The application of accounting concepts and standards in the solution of these problems requires on the part of accountants a high degree of integrity, competence, and social responsibility.

The growing bibliography on accounting standards and principles in 1940 received its most elaborate and fascinating addition up to that time from the American Accounting Association. *An Introduction to Corporate Accounting Standards,* the work of two men long interested in this field of endeavor, W. A. Paton and A. C. Littleton, has since received the sustained consideration by those interested in the evolution of accountancy. Moreover, the growing series of *Accounting Research Bulletins* issued by the Committee on Accounting Procedure of the American Institute of Certified Public Accountants on important timely accounting problems and the steady increase in the accounting series *Releases* of the Securities and Exchange Commission have done much to bring increased uniformity and higher standards of practice to accountancy. These studies have gone a long way on the road to provide the basic principles discussed in the statement of objectives prepared by the executive committee of the American Accounting Association.

Securities and Exchange Commission. Today the most potent influence tending to iron out practical, everyday accounting problems is the Securities and Exchange Commission, which, according to the Securities Act of 1933, was given the authority to define "accounting, technical, and trade terms" and which has become increasingly interested in this all-important problem since that date. The problem is designated "all-important" for, as outlined in Chap. I, every policy of the active management finds its way somewhere into the figures of a business enterprise.

The Securities and Exchange Commission, up to the present time, has compiled no summary of questionable accounting practices which have arisen in connection with the financial statements filed with it. The initial public records of any such questionable practices, or the desirability of new practices based upon the evolution of accounting standards which would provide for the ever-widening disclosure of sound and understandable information, are located in deficiency memoranda or similar documents issued after the examination of particular financial statements by the accounting staff of the Commission. No complete compilation of deficiency memoranda has been made.[34]

On April 1, 1937, however, the Securities and Exchange Commission announced a program for the publication, from time to time, of opinions regarding specific accounting principles for the purpose of contributing to the development of uniform standards and practices in major accounting questions.[35] As the first of these interpretations, the Commission published a letter written by Carman G. Blough, who at that time was the chief accountant of the Securities and Exchange Commission,[36] to a registrant, discussing the impropriety of charging losses resulting from the revaluation of assets to capital surplus rather than to earned surplus.

Releases in the Accounting Series of the Securities and Exchange Commission on important accounting questions affecting registrants have continued to be written from time to time as important matters have needed explicit and detailed clarification. Up to April 12, 1960, there were 86 such studies released. These studies have been contributions in the development of accounting standards. Releases are issued as a result of specific inquiries from registrants or from their accountants on problems which have a wide application, to amend rules in Regulations S-X, and whenever the chief accountant issues a ruling that has wide application.

No attempt has been made to build up a synthesis of universal accounting rules and standards. Individual problems are handled as they arise. Behind all releases in this series is the theory of full disclosure, which played a basic part in the creation of the Securities and Exchange Commission and its subsequent development.

Authoritative Studies

Although accounting standards and accounting principles have been evolving slowly, over the years, there is no doubt that progressive tendencies have been at work. Older methods become less effective under altered conditions; earlier ideas become irrelevant in the face of new problems. Thus surrounding conditions generate fresh ideas and stimulate the

[34] Securities and Exchange Commission, *Release* No. 7, May 16, 1938, did, however, contain an analysis of the deficiencies commonly cited up to that time by the Securities and Exchange Commission in connection with financial statements filed under the Securities Act of 1933 and the Securities Exchange Act of 1934. The list is interesting and most comprehensive. That part of the analysis which had to do with balance sheets, income statements, and surplus accounts, showing how skilled accountants, in the early years of the SEC, had failed to follow specific instructions and how differently, at times, they prepared figures which the analyst must study, was included in Chap. XXIV of the 1945 and 1950 editions of *Practical Financial Statement Analysis*.

[35] Securities and Exchange Commission, *Release* No. 1, Apr. 1, 1937.

[36] In November, 1944, Carman G. Blough became Director of Research of the American Institute of Certified Public Accountants.

ingenious to devise new methods. And as such ideas and methods prove successful they, in turn, begin to modify the surrounding conditions. Moreover, it must be kept in mind that new accounting and auditing procedures are not final but evolutionary, both in themselves and in their adaptation to a constantly evolving business world.

Beginning in 1917, and continuing for several years, the influences of the Board of Governors of the Federal Reserve System and the American Institute of Certified Public Accountants were jointly exerted to create more exacting minimum standards for the verification of financial statements. The influences of the New York Stock Exchange, the American Institute of Certified Public Accountants, the American Accounting Association, and the Securities and Exchange Commission, as we have seen, have been exerted, from time to time, in changing or modifying standards which have had to do with particular accounting practices. The Securities and Exchange Commission, as an agency of the Federal Government—a "disinterested" third party—has been in a peculiarly strategic position to create, to modify, and to see that such standards as it might announce, after careful analysis and study, were carried out by accounting firms which prepared financial statements in behalf of registrants.

In the years following 1895, when the executive council of the New York State Bankers' Association had recommended the use of such financial statements as the Committee on Uniform Statements might suggest, until 1917, commercial bankers had made considerable progress in the development and use of more uniform and complete financial statement blanks. Much had also been accomplished in the improvement in quality and in the verification of financial statements by independent scrutiny and audit. At the same time, there had been developed no uniform minimum requirements for the essential verification of financial statements which were said to have been audited, or standards as to the extent of minimum details to be shown in financial statements, in contrast to the grouping of different items. An accountant would be employed by one concern to make a particularly thorough audit, and by another concern to make a relatively superficial one. Good will would be grouped into one figure with fixed assets in one balance sheet, and would be shown separately, as it should, in another balance sheet. The differences in the extent and in the quality of two such audits would be unknown to a banker, to a credit man, or to an analyst, who obtained both balance sheets over the certificate of a public accountant. The lack of exact information, as a result of the groupings of extraneous items, would vary considerably. In this situation, the initial problem by 1917 subdivided itself into two parts:

1. The improvement in standardization of the forms of balance sheets and income statements.

2. The adoption of methods which would ensure greater care in compiling the balance sheet and the income statement, and their proper verification.

Verification of Financial Statements. Out of the consideration of both these points came the article, already mentioned in this chapter, *Uniform Accounts* published in the April, 1917, number of the *Federal Reserve Bulletin,* and the subsequent publication of this study in pamphlet form with the title *Approved Methods for the Preparation of Balance Sheet Statements* during the following year. Here were the first specific instructions for the verification of assets and liabilities by accountants which, in a broad way, would tend to meet the requirements of industry, commerce, and banking. In approximately 15 pages, these detailed instructions gave the minimum requirements to be followed by an accountant in confirming the amount of all important items in a balance sheet, cash, notes receivable, securities, inventories, cost of fixed property, deferred charges to operations, notes and bills payable, accounts payable, contingent liabilities, accrued liabilities, bonded and mortgage debts, capital stock, and surplus.

The income statement received less detailed consideration. The minimum procedure for verifying the important items, such as sales, cost of sales, gross profit on sales, selling, general, and administrative expenses, net profit on sales, other income, deductions from income, net income, surplus additions and deductions, was described. Then followed a suggested brief form of certificate which is now long out of date, a suggested form for an income statement, and a suggested form for a balance sheet.

This publication was the first of its kind; it served as the most authoritative guide for the minimum requirements in this field for a period of 12 years. Over these years, criticisms and suggestions for minor changes, improvements, and elaboration were made. Some accountants regarded the original program as more comprehensive than their conceptions of a so-called "balance sheet audit," but not more than was required in the preparation of financial statements to be submitted as a basis for credit or for loans of cash. Some accountants felt that the instructions were not as clear as they might have been. The suggested form of certificate did not make clear that the examination was not a complete audit of the accounts, and to that extent, it was somewhat misleading.

In May, 1929, this pamphlet, as already mentioned, was revised by the American Institute of Certified Public Accountants and published by the Federal Reserve Board in an enlarged brochure of 28 pages under the title, *Verification of Financial Statements.* This revision was prepared along the same general lines as the earlier publication, but with refinements and minor changes to bring the ideas somewhat more into line with the changing philosophy of accountancy.

Examination of Financial Statements by Independent Public Accountants. The pamphlet *Verification of Financial Statements* remained the standard description of the procedure in verifying individual items in financial statements for 7 years. In June, 1936, another step was taken. This pamphlet was now revised under the somewhat more elaborate title of *Examination of Financial Statements by Independent Public Accountants* and was published, not by the Federal Reserve Board but by the American Institute of Certified Public Accountants. The pamphlet consisted of 41 pages and emphasized the importance of the recognition of accounting principles and the consistency of their application in the preparation of financial statements. In addition to expanding the accounting and auditing principles and rules set forth in the earlier bulletins, it outlined a modified program for larger and smaller concerns, and introduced additional accounting principles relating to surplus, unrealized profits, and comparative financial statements.

A Statement of Accounting Principles. The next noteworthy contribution toward the development of more uniformity in accounting standards was a 2-year study undertaken by a committee composed of Thomas H. Sanders of the Graduate School of Business Administration, Harvard University, Henry R. Hatfield of the University of California, and Underhill Moore of the School of Law, Yale University, and published in 1938 as *A Statement of Accounting Principles.*[37] This study was divided into six parts: (1) general considerations, (2) the income (profit and loss) statement, (3) the balance sheet, (4) consolidated statements, (5) comments and footnotes in financial reports, and (6) a summary of accounting principles, which gives a 4-page "very general summary" of the high lights of the first five parts of the study.

This study marked a real step, and one that had long been needed, toward the objective of a written exposition of accounting principles. Like the initial *Approved Methods for the Preparation of Balance Sheet*

---

[37] This study was undertaken at the suggestion of the Haskins & Sells Foundation, as the letter of invitation to the committee explained: "Accounting practices at present are based, in a large measure, upon the ethics and opinions of reputable accountants, and to some extent upon the accounting provisions of the various laws, but wide variations of opinion often exist among equally reputable practitioners. There is no unified body of opinion, nor is there any official tribunal for the final determination of technical differences of opinion." By a process of slow building, based upon its regulations and rendering of successive decisions on accounting problems coming under its sphere of influence, as explained on p. 626, the Securities and Exchange Commission might well, at some time, become the entity that will fill this niche in our economic life. "Therefore, it would seem appropriate and opportune that a committee composed of eminent accountants and lawyers should be appointed to formulate a code of accounting principles that would be useful in the clarification and improvement of corporate accounting and of financial reports issued to the public." This contribution to accounting theory and practice was published by the American Institute of Certified Public Accountants, New York, in 1938.

Statements, published by the Federal Reserve Board, it is clearly a preliminary study, open to the consideration of those interested in this vital and long-needed movement. The authors, instead of giving dogmatic opinions of principles which are in evolution, went somewhat to the other extreme in the diplomatic interpretation of how accounting problems may be handled. "The existence of a body of generally accepted accounting principles," they explained "does not mean that there is only one proper accounting treatment for every situation with which the accountant must deal. For many such situations, there are available a number of treatments which are in accord with the generally accepted principles. But the affirmation of the general acceptance of accounting principles does mean that many, and indeed, most of the possible treatments are inappropriate." This is a diplomatic statement of the case. The use of the word "inappropriate" is a lenient characterization of many situations.

The amount of detailed information to be given in a financial statement, wrote the authors, should be related to its purpose. In explanation of this assertion it was then pointed out that "it is necessarily left largely to the management to judge what information it is appropriate to give to the public." In actual practice, this is generally the case, but it is not unusual for accountants in particular situations to guide, advise, and insist that certain information be given to the public. The more widespread the agreements on accounting principles become, the more will accountants be able to insist on thoroughness. That the authors recognized this situation is implied in two suggested rules:

1. Any general impression clearly conveyed by the statements should be a true impression. The statement, though technically correct, should avoid creating a false impression in the mind of the reader.

2. No information should be omitted which, if disclosed, would materially alter the impressions given by the statements.

The two chapters on the income statement and the balance sheet explain the principles under which information appears under the various captions in both financial statements. Both chapters are largely explanatory. One controversial point comes to light where the authors would allow certain charges to surplus, a practice, as explained in Chaps. XIX and XXIII, which is largely disappearing in the current evolution of accountancy. They write: "As far as possible net income should be so determined that it will need no subsequent correction. When, however, such correction becomes necessary, it may be made through current income only if it is not so large as to distort the statement of that income. Otherwise it should be made through earned surplus." The present tendency, and a sound one from the point of view of analysts as well as many accountants, is to put even these charges through the income statement.

In contrast to this opinion, the authors in another part of the volume explained that it is objectionable to write off bond discount and expense in advance, when relatively small, against capital surplus, since that proceeding relieves later income accounts and earned surplus accounts of charges which properly should be made against them. It is still more objectionable, they continued, to amortize these balances against capital surplus by devices which fail to disclose the full character of the proceeding. The authors then point out that, among other methods, it is permissible when a debit balance remains in bond discount and expense account, after the related bonds have been retired by a refunding operation prior to their maturity, to write off the entire unamortized balance at once out of earned surplus.

Consideration is given to the question as to whether the book value of investments in subsidiaries should be permanently maintained at cost or be subject to adjustment for profits or losses of the subsidiary. When the subsidiary has made profits, subsequent to the purchase of the securities by the parent company, some authorities approve showing a proportionate increase in the book value of the held securities. "This procedure," the authors now explain, "while having some logical basis, is of questionable propriety." The practice, however, has become more and more common, as in no other way does an analyst know the value of many such investments when he is studying an individual balance sheet of the parent company without supporting or supplementary information to help him. The constant carrying of an investment of this nature at cost of $100,000 when the book value of the subsidiary has increased $500,000 creates a hidden reserve that has a decided bearing on a clear understanding of the financial picture.

While this volume represented one more progressive step on the road to the determination of accounting principles, the study was not quite as authoritative, as definite, or as clear as the title would lead one to expect. The volume was more in the nature of observations regarding auditing procedure than a statement of principles. Moreover, there was a tendency to follow the customary practice in accountancy; that is, instead of setting up standards, to surround many of the observations with hedges that tended to emphasize the continued lack of principles.[38]

An Introduction to Corporate Accounting Standards. A noteworthy contribution toward the development of a more exact theory of uniform accountancy is the monograph *An Introduction to Corporate Accounting*

---

[38] For a detailed and exacting critique of this volume see William A. Paton, "Comments on 'A Statement of Accounting Principles,'" *The Journal of Accountancy,* Vol. 65, No. 3, pp. 196–207, March, 1938.

Standards by W. A. Paton of the University of Michigan and A. C. Littleton of the University of Illinois, published in 1940.[39] This volume is an elaboration of the basic concepts believed to be essential to a sound fundamental structure of corporate accountancy which originally appeared in the relatively brief and tentative *Statement of Accounting Principles Underlying Corporate Financial Statements* in 1936.[40] The original statement was enlarged and an exposition was given of the compelling reasons for the adoption of standards and for the selection of the particular standards recommended.

A considerable portion of accounting literature up to this point has disclosed an attitude suggesting that the treatment of individual accounting situations presents so many possibilities that it is difficult to select any one treatment as acceptable to the exclusion of the others. This is the point of view presented in *A Statement of Accounting Principles.* If accountants cannot agree on the principles by which the amount of profit or the extent of any equity is to be measured, what purpose is served by certified statements?

An Introduction to Corporate Accounting Standards comes closer to furnishing the answers. It is divided into seven chapters: (1) Standards, (2) Concepts, (3) Cost, (4) Revenues, (5) Income, (6) Surplus, and (7) Interpretation. Through these chapters the authors have woven together the fundamental ideas of accounting instead of stating standards such as are being evolved by the Securities and Exchange Commission and the Committee on Accounting Procedure of the American Institute of Certified Public Accountants. "The intention," the authors write in describing the basis of their study, "has been to build a framework within which a subsequent statement of corporate accounting standards could be erected. Accounting theory is here conceived as a coherent, coordinated, consistent body of doctrine which may be compactly expressed in the form of standards, if desired." In this sense, standards become gauges by which to measure departures, when and if departures seem necessary.

In the delineation of the successive steps from standards to concepts to cost to revenue to income, the authors arrive at the basic conclusion that the fundamental problem of accounting is the division of the stream of costs between the present and the future in the process of measuring periodic income. Here is the present-day emphasis on the income statement. "The technical instruments used in reporting this division are the income statement and the balance sheet. Both are necessary. The income statement reports the assignment to the current period; the balance sheet exhibits the costs incurred which are reasonably applicable

[39] This study of 156 pages was published by the American Accounting Association.
[40] *The Accounting Review*, Vol. XI, No. 2, pp. 187–191, June, 1936.

to the years to come." The authors then continue: "The balance sheet thus serves as a means of carrying forward unamortized acquisition prices, the not-yet-deducted costs; it stands as a connecting link joining successive income statements into a composite picture of the income streams."

In the sound presentation of balance sheets and income statements, fundamental differences in basic theory and practice are evident from the ideas expressed by the authors of *A Statement of Accounting Principles*. A definite position is taken to the effect "that all determinants of income in the broadest sense—including unusual and irregular factors—should be reported in the income statement before the net results are passed to the stock-equity section of the balance sheet." In other words, all charges of every kind, as outlined in Chaps. XIX and XXIII, should go through the income statement, and not just the smaller items of irregular charges. When a variable policy is pursued, a reader of financial statements may miss the significance of a large write-off of long-accruing obsolescence against present surplus. He may also miss the significance of the fact that past income statements were not reported as correctly as could have been expected from a discerning management.

The Fund Theory of Accounting and Its Implications for Financial Reports. Seven years later there appeared the study *The Fund Theory of Accounting and Its Implications for Financial Reports* by William J. Vatter.[41] This study represents another interesting "attempt to set up a framework around which the ideas of accounting may have better and fuller expression and from which may develop a broader application of certain accounting techniques which now have but limited uses." As the author explains, there have been two different schools of thought which have been made to serve as the integrating framework of accounting theory, the "proprietary" theory which dates at least from the beginning of the nineteenth century and the "entity" theory which is of comparatively recent origin. Vatter outlines a third, the "fund" theory. The essence of the proprietary theory is that accounting records and statements are maintained and prepared from the standpoint of the owner or owners of a business, aimed at a measurement of and the analyses of changes in the net worth of a business.[42] In the entity theory,

---

[41] This study of 141 pages was originally published as a Supplement to the *Journal of Business of the University of Chicago*, Vol. XX, No. 3, Part 2, July, 1947. Subsequently it was republished as an independent study by the University of Chicago Press, Chicago.

[42] "In this scheme the assets are the proprietor's property; liabilities are the proprietor's debts and the emphasis of accounting is focused upon profit—in the sense of accretions to the proprietorship that arise from the operations of the enterprise. This system of ideas did fit the facts of the case fairly well when businesses and other enterprises were organized as individual 'proprietorships'; and the notion of profit thus involved was a useful and workable one."—VATTER, WILLIAM J., *The Fund*

the business undertaking is generally considered "as an entity or institution of its own right, separate and distinct from the parties who furnish the funds, and it has become almost axiomatic that the business accounts and statements are those of the entity rather than those of the proprietor, partner, investors, or other parties or groups concerned."[43]

Accounting, according to the fund theory, has grown far beyond the possibility of basing its operations upon any kind of single-valued or general purpose theory. The uses to which accounting data are put are too numerous to base a frame of reference upon a single "personality" to whom accounting reports are directed. The same financial statements and records today are used by management,[44] by social control agencies,[45] by present owners and creditors, and by prospective investors and creditors.[46] These three broad areas of use for accounting information are

---

Theory of Accounting and Its Implications for Financial Reports, pp. 2–3 (The University of Chicago Press, Chicago, 1947).

[43] PATON, W. A., and A. C. LITTLETON, *An Introduction to Corporate Accounting Standards*, p. 8 (American Accounting Association, Chicago, 1940).

[44] "The most direct demands upon accounting records and reports are made by management, for it is management that determines the scope of that procedural system which underlies the accounting process itself. In this sphere the accounting system is a device for facilitating the managerial process, quite apart from the production of over-all financial reports. . . . Still further, accounting data in special forms and combinations are employed by management to aid in the solution of problems of policy, strategy, or procedure."—Vatter, *op. cit.* p. 8.

[45] "Various governmental units rely upon special forms of accounting summaries to implement taxation, to regulate prices and production, to control the issuance and marketing of securities, to protect creditors and others from the effects of excessive or restrictive practices with respect to dividends, to deal with 'unfair' competitive or labor practices, or to arbitrate disputes that affect the public interest. Trade and other voluntary associations employ accounting data to study and interpret developments within sundry industries. Economists and statisticians employ accounting data for various analyses. . . ."—*Ibid.*, p. 8.

[46] "Not only present owners and creditors but also prospective lenders or investors rely upon accounting reports to furnish information which bears upon the questions they must face and the decisions that they must make. The kinds of data that are useful in establishing a line of credit over short time periods, moreover, are not the same as those needed for long-term investment decisions; and there are numerous special uses for information service provided by accounting records and reports."—*Ibid.*, pp. 8–9.

In 1950, R. K. Mautz published an original study entitled *An Accounting Technique for Reporting Financial Transactions* (Bureau of Economic and Business Research, University of Illinois, Urbana, Ill.). This monograph is not concerned with a basic underlying theory of accounting. It is interesting, however, because it is concerned with two new (or, if combined, one) financial statements to supplement the conventional financial statements in current use, namely a Statement of Financing and a Statement of Enterprise Growth. Financial transactions, explains the author, "arise out of the financing activities of an enterprise; financing is provided largely by those interests which we commonly think of as having an equity in the enterprise. . . . Any interest which advances assets to the enterprise for a period of time may be said to be a financing interest. Stockholders advance assets or funds to the enterprise for, usually, an indeterminate period; bondholders advance funds for a definite period,

sufficiently different to indicate that no single "personality" could possibly maintain the various points of view and attitudes that are involved.

In the fund theory of accounting there are involved a segregation of assets for a given purpose and a partial recognition of the set of separate operations which pertain to those assets. A given corporation may, for example, have several "funds," a cash and bank fund, a general operating fund, an investment fund, a sinking fund—current, a sinking fund—investments, a capital fund; maintenance of branch accounts and departmental accounts may be separate "funds." For each fund a separate balance sheet and a separate "statement of operations" would be prepared[47] as well as the usual over-all balance sheet and income statement. "The accounts of each fund," explains Vatter, "recognize not only all the asset items but also all the equities that pertain to that fund; in addition, there are also present complete classifications of revenue, expense, and income accounts. These, taken together, provide a general ledger trial balance complete in all respects as to the operations covered by the definition of the fund. . . . The notion of a fund has not been encumbered by personalistic thinking. . . . "

---

usually of considerable duration; banks advance funds on notes payable also for a definite period but generally one of short duration. These sources are generally thought to be the principal financing interests and are sometimes called equities in the balance sheet. . . . A supplier who advances material to the company on credit also becomes a financing interest. The amount advanced by any single supplier may not be significant and the length of time the purchase goes unpaid may be short, but when suppliers (accounts payable) are considered as a group, they frequently represent an important financial aid, and one which, if withdrawn, would imperil the very existence of the company." The ordinary ledger accounts contain a considerable amount of useful information about the financial activities of a business. "Not now made available in accounting statements, these data can be organized into simple reports aimed at (1) presenting a summary of the enterprise financing program, and (2) accounting for enterprise growth; or if desired these two reports may be combined into one which serves a dual purpose. With supporting textual comment, such reports constitute a report upon the financial activities of the enterprise and its management in the same way that an income statement constitutes a report upon the profit-seeking activities of an enterprise and its management." The Statement of Financing would contain (1) types of financing interests dealt with, (2) amount of financing provided by each interest (perhaps a dollar-day average), and (3) cost of financing obtained from each interest. In addition, the author suggests that the doctrine of full disclosure be extended to reporting on financial activities and, accordingly, that details of important financial transactions be included as descriptive material in the body of the report or in footnote fashion. The Statement of Enterprise Growth would contain (1) total dealings with each enterprise interest and (2) relationship of transactions effecting increases in the enterprise total of properties and equities to those effecting decreases.

[47] "The emphasis accorded in recent years to systems of budgetary control and the maintenance of departmental accounts for the purpose of administering the budget have tended to create a fund emphasis in the field of departmental accounting. The operations of administrative units are the basis for various kinds of accounting reports which, although based upon analyses that are perhaps more correctly to be described as statistical than accounting procedures, nevertheless are formulated and prepared within the accounting department and by the accounting staff. . . . Thus the notion

The central idea in the terminology of the fund theory is a service concept of assets. Basically, a fund is a collection of service potentials that have been brought together for some functional purpose—administrative, entrepreneurial, or social. In this sense assets are economic in nature; they are embodiments of future want satisfaction in the form of service potentials. This definition covers cash, bank deposits, and receivables, items which, it would seem, can be included only by stretching the imagination of the definition in terms of unamortized cost of the "entity" theory. Services are thus put into a fund for a specific purpose, not to remain there undisturbed for an indefinite period, but to be directed at the objectives specified in the purpose of the fund. The operations of a fund involve the conversion and ultimate release of the impounded services through certain channels; expense is simply the draining off or the release of converted services into those channels during a period of time.

The recognition that assets are service potentials provides both operational content and homogeneity of substance for accounting terminology. The concept of assets is related to the expense stream and the corresponding flow of revenue. Equities are not claims or obligations, nor are they mere legal liabilities; rather, they represent the restrictions that apply to the fund of assets. In this theory "the equality of assets and equities rests on the fact of residual equity, not on the idea that property 'belongs' to someone or that some fictitious person must account to owners for the assets intrusted to it."

Thus, under the fund theory, there are a few basic ideas with which to attack the problem of accounting theory: the notion of a fund, a service concept of assets, a restricted concept of equities, and a recognition that expense and revenue are basic flows, not specific effects of individual transactions. A balance sheet for credit purposes might be different from a balance sheet for some other purpose. The valuations in such a balance sheet would be based upon the credit aspects of the case and the classification and arrangement of data would be tailored for that purpose—the credit statement would be intended to exhibit or to test solvency. It would be revolutionary but the fund theory would countenance special purpose statements in terms of different arrangement of data and different bases of valuation. It would also remove the implication of exhaustiveness in the balance sheet, that is, it would serve to prevent the drawing of inferences that the balance sheet shows all the assets and all the equities, an inference too often drawn by accountants and laymen.

Accounting Research Bulletins of the American Institute of Certified Public Accountants and Accounting Series Releases of the Securities and

---

of a fund outruns the limits of formal accounting and shades off into the statistical tabulation."—Vatter, *op. cit.*, pp. 44–45.

and Opinions of the Accounting Principles Board

Exchange Commission. At the present time the greatest influence upon the theory and practice of accounting is being exerted by two organizations, both of which have been described earlier in this chapter, the American Institute of Certified Public Accountants and the Securities and Exchange Commission. As significant problems evolve or arise in the accounting field, they are considered individually by each of the twenty-one members of the Committee on Accounting Procedure of the American Institute of Certified Public Accountants. Often there are interesting dissenting opinions. A subcommittee of three members makes recommendations on terminology. The extent and breadth of the considerations of the over-all Committee and the care given to the preparation of "bulletins" on the subjects which come up for consideration have grown steadily so that the accumulated influence of its decisions and recommendations has expanded from year to year. Moreover, a pattern of accounting theory is beginning to appear as successive studies have supplemented earlier ones.

Accounting Research Bulletins represent the considered opinion of at least two-thirds of the members of the Committee on Accounting Procedure, reached on a formal vote after examination of the subject matter by the Committee and the Research Department of the Institute. Except in cases in which formal adoption by the membership of the American Institute of Certified Public Accountants has been asked and secured, the authority of each bulletin rests upon the general acceptability of the expressed opinions. It is recognized that any general rules may be subject to exception; it is felt, however, that the burden of justifying departure from accepted procedures must be assumed by those who adopt other treatment. Since 1963 bulletins have appeared under the

The *Accounting Series Releases* of the Securities and Exchange Commission, as previously explained, are issued in answer to specific inquiries from registrants or accountants, to amend rules in Regulation S-X, and whenever the chief accountant of the Commission issues a ruling on some specific subject which might have wide application. Whereas the authority of the recommendations in *Accounting Research Bulletins* rests in their general acceptability, the recommendations of the Securities and Exchange Commission have the force of law applied to financial statements which must be filed with the Securities and Exchange Commission. The current gradual evolution in accounting theory and practice is largely the result of the studies and recommendations of these two institutions.

The Immediate Future

There have been three well-recognized periods in the development of accountancy. The first period encompassed the early years when efforts were made by The Mercantile Agency in the 1870's and by James G. Cannon in the 1890's to obtain balance sheets, which at that time were better known as *property statements,* for the use of the mercantile and bank creditors. Rarely were these early financial statements audited. As banking institutions began to extend credit on unsecured promissory notes, as the use of the corporate form of business organization expanded, and as corporations sold securities to the public, more and more financial statements were made available. During these early years, the balance sheet added very materially to the knowledge of creditors.

The second period covered the years when accountants permitted themselves complete freedom of action in drawing up financial statements and consequently there gradually arose the recognition of the fact that some body of accounting standards had to be created. This complete freedom in the treatment of accounting situations became more evident in investment than in credit circles, not because there were greater variations in treatment but because accountancy became a means of manipulation by insiders at the expense of the great body of investors. The classification of current assets and current liabilities differed widely among recognized accounting firms. Irrelevant items were often grouped together in balance sheets; receivables and merchandise, good will and fixed assets; charges were made almost as much to surplus as to income, and depreciation charges often varied with income.

Out of this complete freedom of action of the accountant came the third period, which exists today, a period in which accountants as well as bankers, mercantile creditors, investors, and analysts have perceived the fact that evolving standards[48] are essential as accountancy fulfills its key role in our economic life. Action during this period was first taken by the New York Stock Exchange in isolated instances, more basically by the Federal Reserve Board, cautiously at first and then in a broad way by the American Institute of Certified Public Accountants, outspokenly by the American Accounting Association, and, under the mandate of Congress, by the Securities and Exchange Commission.

Today and tomorrow the greatest influence in carrying on the evolution of accountancy toward standards undoubtedly will continue to be made by the Committee on Accounting Procedure of the American Institute of Certified Public Accountants and the Securities and Exchange Commission. That there is room for continued development is axiomatic to anyone who must examine hundreds or thousands of financial statements yearly, financial statements, audited and unaudited, of large representative corporations and of small proprietorships, of business enterprises in large cities and in small country villages, for management, for

[48] WISE, T. A., "The Auditors Have Arrived," *Fortune,* Vol. LXII, No. 6, pp. 144–148, 239–244, December, 1960.

investors, for creditors, and, unfortunately, for what seems to be the needs of modern government. As one of the ancient philosophers taught: "Change is the only permanence."

THEORY AND PROBLEMS

1. It has been said that financial statements "reflect a combination of recorded facts, accounting conventions, and personal judgments." Explain what is meant by

   a. Recorded facts
   b. Accounting conventions
   c. Personal judgments

2. Are financial statements accurate to a cent as far as economic values are concerned? Explain your answer.

3. Name four important institutions that have been sources of influence in the recent evolution of accountancy and accountancy practice. Describe the influence of one of these sources on the evolution of accountancy.

4. Why did the Federal Reserve Board (now known as the Board of Governors of the Federal Reserve System) become interested in the quality of balance sheets and income statements in 1917?

5. What institution is probably exerting the greatest influence on the trend of accountancy today? How is this day-to-day influence exerted?

6. Name one authoritative study on accountancy that was sponsored by (a) Federal Reserve Board, (b) American Institute of Certified Public Accountants, and (c) American Accounting Association.

7. It has been said that accountancy conforms itself to the needs of business, not business to the needs of accountancy. Explain this statement.

*Interquartile Range of Ratios
for 72 Lines of Business Activity*

The median ratio of current assets to current debt of manufacturers of industrial chemicals is given as 2.66 on page 644. To obtain this figure the ratios of current assets to current debt for each of the 67 concerns were arranged in a graduated series, with the largest at the top and the smallest at the bottom. The median ratio of 2.66 was the ratio halfway between the top and the bottom. The ratio of 3.79 representing the upper quartile was one-quarter of the way down the series from the top (or halfway between the top and the median). The ratio of 1.86 representing the lower quartile was one-quarter of the way up from the bottom (or halfway between the median and the bottom).

Explanation of Terms Used in the Following Tables

Average Collection Period: The number of days that the total of trade accounts and notes receivable (including assigned accounts and discounted notes, if any), less reserves for bad debts, represents when compared with the annual net credit sales. Formula—divide the annual net credit sales by 365 days to obtain the average credit sales per day. Then divide the total of accounts and notes receivable (plus any discounted notes receivable) by the average credit sales per day to obtain the average collection period.

Current Assets: Total of cash, accounts, and notes receivable for the sale of merchandise in regular trade quarters less any reserves for bad debts, advances on merchandise, inventory less any reserves, listed securities not in excess of market, state and municipal bonds not in excess of market, and United States Government securities.

Current Debt: Total of all liabilities due within one year from statement date including current payments on serial notes, mortgages, debentures, or other funded debts. This item also includes current reserves such as gross reserves for Federal income taxes, and for contingencies set up for specific purposes, but does not include reserves for depreciation.

Fixed Assets: The sum of the cost or appraised value of land as the case may be, and the depreciated book values of buildings, leasehold improvements, fixtures, furniture, machinery, tools, and equipment.

Funded Debt: Mortgages, bonds, debentures, serial notes, or other obligations with a maturity of more than one year from the statement date.

Inventory: The sum of raw material, material in process, and finished merchandise. It does not include supplies.

Net Profits: Profit after full depreciation on buildings, machinery, equipment, furniture, fixtures, and other assets of a fixed nature; after reserves for Federal and state income taxes; after reduction in the value of inventory to cost or market, whichever lower; after charge-offs for bad debts; and after all miscellaneous reserves and adjustments; but before dividends.

Net Sales: The dollar volume of business transacted for 365 days net after deductions for returns, allowances, and discounts from gross sales.

Net Sales to Inventory: The quotient obtained by dividing the annual net sales by the statement inventory. This quotient does not represent the actual physical turnover which would be determined by reducing the annual net sales to the cost of goods sold, and then dividing the resulting figure by the statement inventory.

Net Working Capital: The excess of the current assets over the current debt.

Tangible Net Worth: The sum of all outstanding preferred or preference stocks (if any) and outstanding common stocks, retained earnings (surplus), and undivided profits, less any intangible item in the assets, such as good will, trademarks, patents, copyrights, lease-holds, mailing lists, treasury stock, organization expenses, and underwriting discounts and expenses.

643

1959 Table of Fourteen Important Ratios with Inter-
Table of

Line of Business	Number of Concerns	Inter-quartile Range	Current assets to current debt	Net profits on net sales	Net profits on tangible net worth	Net profits on net working capital	Net sales to tangible net worth
			Times	Per cent	Per cent	Per cent	Times
Airplane Parts and Accessories	42	Upper Quartile	3.49	4.59	12.24	24.28	4.30
		MEDIAN	2.14	2.65	7.60	12.73	3.23
		Lower Quartile	1.47	1.09	4.25	6.30	2.11
Automobile Parts and Accessories	74	Upper Quartile	3.62	5.88	15.21	25.89	3.66
		MEDIAN	2.69	3.23	8.50	14.14	2.59
		Lower Quartile	1.88	1.63	4.54	7.52	2.22
Bedsprings and Mattresses	62	Upper Quartile	6.32	3.24	8.87	13.36	5.53
		MEDIAN	3.50	1.74	5.39	8.37	2.76
		Lower Quartile	2.01	0.17	1.25	2.44	2.36
Bolts, Screws, Nuts, and Nails	56	Upper Quartile	4.04	6.19	16.69	27.13	4.42
		MEDIAN	2.96	3.48	10.91	18.22	2.52
		Lower Quartile	1.82	1.78	3.46	11.22	1.77
Breweries	34	Upper Quartile	3.22	4.89	14.52	42.93	3.00
		MEDIAN	2.34	3.63	7.78	28.00	2.35
		Lower Quartile	1.54	0.08†	0.05†	0.78	1.92
Chemicals, Industrial	67	Upper Quartile	3.79	6.91	15.96	40.04	3.25
		MEDIAN	2.66	4.54	11.07	22.10	2.29
		Lower Quartile	1.86	3.04	5.91	10.94	1.58
Coats and Suits, Men's and Boys'	190	Upper Quartile	3.49	1.91	9.20	11.15	6.80
		MEDIAN	2.15	1.05	5.06	6.07	4.86
		Lower Quartile	1.67	0.58	2.84	3.02	2.71
Coats and Suits, Women's	85	Upper Quartile	2.79	1.87	14.40	15.98	12.30
		MEDIAN	1.83	0.69	6.65	8.20	6.50
		Lower Quartile	1.47	0.22	3.00	3.68	5.04
Confectionery	41	Upper Quartile	3.83	3.60	10.81	22.60	4.61
		MEDIAN	2.97	1.93	6.54	11.45	2.83
		Lower Quartile	2.25	0.75	2.53	3.72	2.19
Contractors, Building Construction	159	Upper Quartile	2.77	3.24	13.42	21.36	8.64
		MEDIAN	1.81	1.33	7.66	12.45	5.85
		Lower Quartile	1.35	0.33	3.27	4.18	2.70
Contractors, Electrical	49	Upper Quartile	4.03	2.72	12.22	22.76	8.26
		MEDIAN	2.42	1.17	5.88	10.44	4.31
		Lower Quartile	1.67	0.32†	1.72†	1.32†	2.46
Cotton Cloth Mills	49	Upper Quartile	6.44	3.77	7.55	17.55	2.59
		MEDIAN	4.09	2.72	4.79	10.03	2.08
		Lower Quartile	2.90	1.56	3.84	7.48	1.55

† Loss. * Building construction contractors and electrical contractors have no
carry materials such as lumber, bricks, tile, cement, structural steel, and building
tractors carry electrical equipment and supplies to complete particular jobs on which
selling terms, each contract being a special

QUARTILE RANGE FOR 72 LINES OF BUSINESS ACTIVITY

Manufacturers

Net sales to net working capital	Collection period	Net sales to inventory	Fixed assets to tangible net worth	Current debt to tangible net worth	Total debt to tangible net worth	Inventory to net working capital	Current debt to inventory	Funded debts to net working capital
Times	Days	Times	Per cent	Per cent	Per cent	Per cent	Per cent	Per cent
7.72	34	7.4	30.3	22.6	47.2	55.3	68.2	12.7
4.98	56	4.9	40.6	59.7	68.0	84.8	88.3	23.2
3.57	61	3.3	55.7	118.9	138.0	157.5	137.0	47.4
7.40	33	7.8	24.6	22.8	31.7	55.1	58.2	8.6
4.65	42	6.4	36.8	32.8	56.3	82.7	94.7	35.0
3.35	49	4.1	56.4	69.2	105.6	127.8	127.2	59.7
7.75	26	10.0	15.1	14.6	33.3	46.2	45.4	8.8
6.29	35	8.1	22.8	23.3	62.2	68.4	63.0	23.9
4.73	48	6.0	40.9	54.4	89.5	90.9	108.3	39.1
8.86	25	9.7	37.5	19.7	33.2	61.8	48.0	13.6
4.62	31	6.3	56.4	29.2	52.2	83.4	76.8	35.7
3.28	37	5.0	73.1	51.8	85.5	110.2	130.2	64.0
9.77	12	21.7	61.1	13.6	35.5	38.6	97.8	34.5
8.62	18	16.7	77.0	23.3	48.1	53.2	128.6	65.6
6.49	24	11.4	104.7	38.5	92.6	80.6	207.2	190.8
7.36	32	9.7	32.2	19.6	49.8	44.2	72.0	31.9
4.26	40	7.1	58.0	29.3	65.2	61.5	91.9	54.4
2.72	46	4.9	76.3	54.2	109.7	93.3	135.9	98.2
7.53	27	6.5	2.5	35.2	68.2	55.9	65.1	6.3
5.13	48	5.2	6.6	71.9	134.4	84.2	93.0	16.3
3.04	77	4.3	15.8	73.1	206.1	128.1	133.4	48.0
13.53	31	16.4	3.6	49.8	84.1	57.9	91.2	10.8
9.23	45	9.5	7.4	93.7	141.2	88.3	132.3	29.9
6.22	52	5.0	15.3	158.0	196.7	123.1	220.5	56.9
10.61	12	18.1	28.8	19.7	36.2	48.6	52.6	13.5
6.45	19	8.5	43.2	30.2	42.8	77.0	74.8	35.7
4.71	38	6.5	56.2	37.6	61.6	98.9	124.1	58.3
14.40	*	*	8.8	34.8	53.0	*	*	9.9
8.49	*	*	20.4	75.7	120.0	*	*	21.8
6.03	*	*	35.1	165.4	220.2	*	*	49 5
11.88	*	*	7.0	25.8	85.9	*	*	2.5
5.61	*	*	15.0	48.0	114.1	*	*	20.1
3.14	*	*	30.4	95.5	157.2	*	*	70.8
5.69	14	7.3	34.7	9.7	20.1	47.9	28.2	15.5
3.91	35	5.5	48.1	17.0	45.6	60.6	42.9	27.8
2.41	47	4.4	61.6	31.3	92.6	77.0	78.0	51.9

inventories in the credit sense of the term. Building construction contractors only equipment to complete particular jobs on which they are working. Electrical con- they are working. Concerns operating in these lines generally have no customary job for which individual terms are arranged.

1959 TABLE OF FOURTEEN IMPORTANT RATIOS WITH INTER-
Manufacturers

Line of Business	Number of Concerns	Inter-quartile Range	Current assets to current debt	Net profits on net sales	Net profits on tangible net worth	Net profits on net working capital	Net sales to tangible net worth
			Times	Per cent	Per cent	Per cent	Times
Cotton Goods, Converters, Non-Factored	40	Upper Quartile	4.71	1.11	7.07	8.64	12.67
		MEDIAN	2.08	0.94	5.88	5.45	6.38
		Lower Quartile	1.70	0.46	2.96	3.05	0.78
Dresses, Rayon, Silk, and Acetate	84	Upper Quartile	2.32	1.81	14.49	21.36	14.54
		MEDIAN	1.81	0.36	4.26	7.01	8.48
		Lower Quartile	1.40	0.10	1.02	1.56	6.31
Drugs	42	Upper Quartile	4.67	12.51	20.57	37.59	2.60
		MEDIAN	3.52	6.62	12.93	17.43	1.99
		Lower Quartile	2.42	4.60	9.24	13.23	1.30
Electrical Parts and Supplies	94	Upper Quartile	3.74	6.60	18.06	29.45	3.85
		MEDIAN	2.76	3.64	10.96	16.03	2.89
		Lower Quartile	1.65	2.19	6.37	8.08	2.14
Foundries	105	Upper Quartile	4.39	4.03	11.04	19.95	3.25
		MEDIAN	3.19	3.15	6.97	13.88	2.28
		Lower Quartile	2.09	1.64	4.19	8.36	1.79
Furniture	139	Upper Quartile	4.59	5.23	17.45	28.24	4.20
		MEDIAN	2.82	3.12	8.94	15.34	3.05
		Lower Quartile	1.97	1.15	3.48	5.30	2.46
Hardware and Tools	98	Upper Quartile	5.00	5.66	14.57	23.06	3.49
		MEDIAN	3.35	3.71	7.84	12.90	2.53
		Lower Quartile	2.57	1.80	4.87	9.09	1.77
Hosiery	74	Upper Quartile	5.67	4.52	8.59	16.94	3.43
		MEDIAN	3.12	2.83	5.93	11.25	2.09
		Lower Quartile	2.00	0.61	1.63	4.65	1.47
Lumber	74	Upper Quartile	5.88	8.80	11.52	27.23	3.16
		MEDIAN	3.04	4.00	8.87	15.85	1.72
		Lower Quartile	1.91	2.20	5.14	7.56	0.92
Machine Shops	143	Upper Quartile	5.16	4.42	9.84	22.55	2.95
		MEDIAN	2.76	2.07	3.82	8.83	1.84
		Lower Quartile	1.75	0.23	0.37	0.73	1.40
Machinery, Industrial	439	Upper Quartile	4.65	5.79	11.74	17.95	3.08
		MEDIAN	3.34	3.43	7.49	11.39	2.06
		Lower Quartile	2.31	1.31	3.26	4.37	1.61
Meats and Provisions, Packers	69	Upper Quartile	3.28	2.54	13.21	39.74	9.65
		MEDIAN	2.34	1.18	8.10	22.24	6.76
		Lower Quartile	1.70	0.75	5.14	12.67	5.52

QUARTILE RANGE FOR 72 LINES OF BUSINESS ACTIVITY (*Continued*)
(*Continued*)

Net sales to net working capital	Collec- tion period	Net sales to inventory	Fixed assets to tangible net worth	Current debt to tangible net worth	Total debt to tangible net worth	Inventory to net worknig capital	Current debt to inventory	Funded debts to net working capital
Times	Days	Times	Per cent	Per cent	Per cent	Per cent	Per cent	Per cent
13.74	29	11.3	0.4	24.7	71.6	64.9	54.7	8.8
6.55	**37**	**7.1**	**1.3**	**78.0**	**108.3**	**86.8**	**108.9**	**24.5**
0.86	83	1.7	5.3	129.1	524.4	113.3	155.8	96.4
19.64	21	18.1	4.9	58.2	40.4	40.3	118.5	6.3
11.50	**28**	**14.0**	**9.2**	**92.3**	**97.3**	**86.7**	**167.9**	**23.6**
8.18	39	8.8	14.4	175.3	151.4	135.4	238.0	42.3
4.51	37	8.9	18.9	19.1	37.1	42.3	50.4	8.4
3.11	**44**	**6.0**	**34.1**	**26.8**	**55.9**	**55.6**	**78.1**	**19.5**
2.08	61	4.3	48.5	37.7	70.3	75.7	127.9	53.9
6.34	33	7.4	20.7	24.1	41.1	57.2	52.1	14.9
4.44	**46**	**4.8**	**40.0**	**38.2**	**68.3**	**83.4**	**73.9**	**31.6**
3.25	57	3.9	57.7	73.9	122.9	118.4	127.2	55.0
6.94	30	13.9	33.6	16.4	34.0	32.6	62.5	11.8
4.33	**38**	**8.6**	**47.2**	**25.1**	**56.5**	**50.4**	**100.3**	**29.6**
3.20	45	5.7	65.2	38.3	97.6	78.8	162.6	86.9
7.57	32	8.2	17.3	18.1	38.7	49.8	49.7	8.8
5.34	**41**	**6.3**	**33.8**	**33.6**	**66.8**	**79.3**	**67.9**	**22.7**
3.88	51	4.3	53.2	66.7	107.8	116.4	103.0	47.2
6.33	34	6.6	23.8	18.1	30.2	52.9	42.7	11.1
4.05	**40**	**4.7**	**33.6**	**28.2**	**44.6**	**77.4**	**55.4**	**26.8**
3.01	45	3.3	51.4	42.7	69.4	98.9	81.8	38.9
6.71	25	10.1	29.8	11.9	28.8	50.9	37.1	10.5
4.09	**38**	**5.4**	**42.5**	**23.0**	**53.4**	**76.5**	**56.9**	**52.3**
2.81	46	4.2	62.0	42.1	115.3	117.8	103.6	82.5
6.15	28	8.2	24.0	11.2	35.9	41.6	40.5	25.1
3.14	**36**	**5.2**	**44.7**	**20.6**	**59.7**	**75.8**	**70.0**	**62.8**
1.98	45	3.8	61.0	38.3	90.0	102.3	103.2	171.4
8.03	34	16.6	33.1	13.9	32.0	37.6	47.6	22.9
4.71	**43**	**7.1**	**51.8**	**31.4**	**60.4**	**66.2**	**89.0**	**42.1**
2.53	55	4.1	70.2	50.6	88.7	95.0	206.8	71.1
4.55	39	6.4	21.7	18.5	35.1	51.9	45.0	12.7
3.11	**52**	**4.3**	**32.3**	**29.5**	**54.9**	**71.4**	**68.8**	**26.2**
2.39	65	3.2	44.0	49.0	81.9	93.0	102.6	39.4
34.15	9	38.7	42.2	20.8	44.5	46.6	71.9	34.9
17.52	**12**	**28.2**	**60.4**	**34.2**	**73.7**	**68.0**	**126.9**	**60.5**
11.53	15	18.4	76.3	59.1	108.7	105.4	194.1	121.0

1959 TABLE OF FOURTEEN IMPORTANT RATIOS WITH INTER-
Manufacturers

Line of Business	Number of Concerns	Inter-quartile Range	Current assets to current debt	Net profits on net sales	Net profits on tangible net worth	Net profits on net working capital	Net sales to tangible net worth
			Times	Per cent	Per cent	Per cent	Times
Metal Stampings	107	Upper Quartile	4.38	5.20	11.17	24.04	3.82
		MEDIAN	2.97	3.15	7.78	15.72	2.40
		Lower Quartile	2.02	0.77	1.84	9.98	1.86
Outerwear, Knitted	72	Upper Quartile	3.64	2.10	10.61	30.06	6.97
		MEDIAN	2.24	0.97	4.52	5.02	5.16
		Lower Quartile	1.62	0.13	0.69	1.20	3.60
Overalls and Work Clothing	58	Upper Quartile	4.66	2.80	9.71	13.48	5.42
		MEDIAN	3.05	1.78	5.79	7.82	3.71
		Lower Quartile	1.99	0.60	2.51	3.27	2.71
Paints, Varnishes, and Lacquers	135	Upper Quartile	5.60	5.32	16.17	31.81	4.44
		MEDIAN	2.95	3.59	9.91	15.50	2.69
		Lower Quartile	2.14	1.11	3.95	7.28	2.20
Paper	63	Upper Quartile	3.55	8.30	12.15	34.98	1.88
		MEDIAN	2.66	6.36	8.45	26.21	1.56
		Lower Quartile	2.18	4.24	6.59	19.18	1.17
Paper Boxes	63	Upper Quartile	4.55	5.09	12.37	38.42	4.25
		MEDIAN	3.14	3.54	8.09	21.76	2.35
		Lower Quartile	2.07	1.59	5.95	12.67	1.89
Petroleum, Integrated Corporations	35	Upper Quartile	3.00	9.52	11.62	51.34	1.77
		MEDIAN	2.46	7.14	8.96	37.06	1.17
		Lower Quartile	1.75	4.53	6.86	19.73	1.04
Printers, Job	65	Upper Quartile	3.62	4.54	12.26	40.64	4.44
		MEDIAN	2.27	2.53	7.67	19.23	2.54
		Lower Quartile	1.70	0.85	3.77	10.31	2.19
Shirts, Underwear, and Pajamas, Men's	54	Upper Quartile	2.71	3.35	21.06	29.65	7.42
		MEDIAN	2.02	1.48	7.70	9.96	5.46
		Lower Quartile	1.54	0.47	3.36	3.90	3.41
Shoes, Men's, Women's, and Children's	111	Upper Quartile	3.28	3.71	12.60	16.09	4.57
		MEDIAN	2.36	2.14	8.40	9.93	3.60
		Lower Quartile	1.64	1.37	5.60	6.63	2.87
Steel, Structural Fabricators (Sell on Short Terms)	94	Upper Quartile	5.70	3.90	9.41	12.37	4.13
		MEDIAN	3.60	1.63	4.82	8.47	2.72
		Lower Quartile	2.11	0.37†	0.81†	2.12†	2.19
Stoves, Ranges, and Ovens	52	Upper Quartile	4.92	4.71	13.33	20.00	4.12
		MEDIAN	3.58	2.68	7.67	10.01	2.89
		Lower Quartile	2.27	1.28	2.10	2.90	2.07

† Loss. ** Job printers have no inventories in the credit sense of the term. They only

QUARTILE RANGE FOR 72 LINES OF BUSINESS ACTIVITY *(Continued)* *(Continued)*

Net sales to net working capital	Collection period	Net sales to inventory	Fixed assets to tangible net worth	Current debt to tangible net worth	Total debt to tangible net worth	Inventory to net working capital	Current debt to inventory	Funded debts to net working capital
Times	Days	Times	Per cent	Per cent	Per cent	Per cent	Per cent	Per cent
6.92	22	9.7	28.0	18.8	40.9	43.8	57.6	14.4
4.16	**33**	**6.2**	**40.3**	**27.7**	**66.5**	**67.3**	**87.5**	**31.4**
2.80	45	4.7	60.5	49.3	98.3	100.5	123.0	65.5
15.09	14	15.6	3.6	27.9	48.8	45.2	62.3	7.8
7.88	**20**	**8.5**	**17.7**	**56.8**	**76.4**	**80.2**	**96.4**	**20.4**
5.41	46	5.3	30.2	100.8	122.8	134.9	139.2	43.5
9.24	23	5.8	7.9	24.7	54.0	65.4	37.8	15.2
4.26	**30**	**4.7**	**14.8**	**39.0**	**92.6**	**87.6**	**56.3**	**23.6**
2.98	45	3.7	27.2	69.5	130.6	112.2	85.0	37.9
7.30	23	8.6	21.7	17.0	33.9	48.6	48.2	5.3
4.95	**36**	**6.1**	**31.8**	**29.6**	**43.9**	**67.1**	**80.3**	**17.6**
3.87	49	4.9	46.8	45.9	94.6	90.6	107.7	31.6
6.07	24	8.5	55.4	15.5	28.9	44.1	57.8	34.4
4.96	**30**	**6.8**	**72.2**	**18.4**	**41.1**	**68.9**	**80.9**	**65.7**
3.29	36	6.0	89.1	24.1	57.5	87.9	108.6	106.9
8.14	22	10.2	37.9	12.4	39.7	37.3	55.8	22.8
6.40	**28**	**9.3**	**50.6**	**21.7**	**60.7**	**65.6**	**83.1**	**56.2**
3.13	32	7.4	76.1	38.9	92.2	89.2	135.1	126.0
7.24	37	10.0	73.5	16.1	29.6	53.0	95.6	38.5
5.50	**41**	**9.0**	**89.6**	**19.9**	**50.2**	**63.9**	**123.6**	**78.7**
3.89	50	7.0	105.0	27.4	76.1	79.7	158.5	204.8
13.96	32	**	44.3	20.9	33.9	**	**	19.0
7.91	**39**	**	**59.5**	**29.4**	**62.8**	**	**	**57.4**
5.29	47	**	76.7	50.3	87.4	**	**	83.2
9.73	35	10.9	3.1	45.6	37.7	77.0	59.0	2.5
7.12	**47**	**5.4**	**5.2**	**84.2**	**113.5**	**111.1**	**88.3**	**11.4**
3.71	66	4.2	15.9	140.3	134.3	158.9	127.3	31.9
5.90	37	7.8	10.5	37.4	63.4	63.0	57.4	11.4
3.93	**54**	**5.1**	**18.5**	**59.1**	**84.9**	**91.1**	**83.8**	**21.6**
3.03	68	3.6	29.1	116.9	136.9	147.8	147.7	38.1
6.48	32	7.9	21.1	15.5	14.5	42.9	39.7	15.2
5.02	**48**	**5.7**	**33.7**	**24.7**	**25.9**	**64.5**	**68.6**	**33.0**
3.06	67	4.6	43.0	54.5	58.2	90.1	103.4	45.4
6.50	37	7.4	16.5	18.2	34.3	47.9	42.1	13.6
4.64	**50**	**5.7**	**31.6**	**30.0**	**67.7**	**68.4**	**65.0**	**22.9**
2.91	71	4.3	41.6	51.3	88.4	94.0	93.1	36.1

carry current supplies such as paper, ink, binding materials, and lead for type-casting.

1959 Table of Fourteen Important Ratios with Inter-

Table of

Line of Business	Number of Concerns	Inter-quartile Range	Current assets to current debt	Net profits on net sales	Net profits on tangible net worth	Net profits on net working capital	Net sales to tangible net worth
			Times	Per cent	Per cent	Per cent	Times
Automobile Parts and Accessories	213	Upper Quartile	4.39	3.32	10.49	13.41	4.90
		MEDIAN	2.84	1.78	6.78	9.13	3.21
		Lower Quartile	2.08	1.01	3.08	4.71	2.39
Baked Goods	48	Upper Quartile	2.59	3.88	16.55	99.37	5.51
		MEDIAN	1.95	2.35	12.40	51.25	4.09
		Lower Quartile	1.37	0.67	3.43	12.27	3.39
Cigars, Cigarettes, and Tobacco	79	Upper Quartile	2.92	0.78	10.34	12.95	24.43
		MEDIAN	2.05	0.33	5.70	8.59	16.59
		Lower Quartile	1.60	0.14	3.10	5.48	10.00
Confectionery	26	Upper Quartile	4.19	2.30	11.28	15.67	14.68
		MEDIAN	2.60	0.80	7.00	7.52	8.11
		Lower Quartile	1.79	0.28	2.97	3.78	4.76
Drugs and Drug Sundries	78	Upper Quartile	3.19	2.26	12.13	16.73	8.48
		MEDIAN	2.66	1.63	9.30	11.31	5.26
		Lower Quartile	2.02	0.69	5.19	6.05	4.10
Dry Goods	161	Upper Quartile	5.16	2.18	8.88	11.64	6.60
		MEDIAN	2.62	0.78	3.61	4.46	4.52
		Lower Quartile	1.90	0.34	1.71	1.75	3.28
Electrical Parts and Supplies	134	Upper Quartile	3.38	1.94	10.03	13.83	7.44
		MEDIAN	2.43	1.23	4.96	6.83	5.07
		Lower Quartile	1.90	0.59	2.44	2.93	2.74
Fruits and Produce, Fresh	49	Upper Quartile	5.17	4.37	27.11	60.41	14.89
		MEDIAN	2.84	1.18	8.08	24.28	9.40
		Lower Quartile	1.88	0.43	5.13	9.56	6.29
Furnishings, Men's	36	Upper Quartile	5.19	5.96	15.12	20.68	4.39
		MEDIAN	2.79	1.59	6.41	6.51	2.78
		Lower Quartile	2.09	0.70	1.91	2.10	1.43
Gasoline, Fuel Oil, and Lubricating Oil	47	Upper Quartile	2.62	2.85	13.75	24.73	11.29
		MEDIAN	1.95	1.66	8.94	8.97	4.51
		Lower Quartile	1.38	0.52	5.67	8.13	3.37
Groceries	250	Upper Quartile	4.50	1.13	9.89	13.74	13.83
		MEDIAN	2.65	0.58	5.17	7.36	8.67
		Lower Quartile	1.83	0.29	2.59	3.38	6.14
Hardware	196	Upper Quartile	6.48	2.57	8.81	9.68	4.79
		MEDIAN	3.42	1.42	4.90	5.63	2.87
		Lower Quartile	2.29	0.66	2.36	3.07	2.22

QUARTILE RANGE FOR 72 LINES OF BUSINESS ACTIVITY (*Continued*)
Wholesalers

Net sales to net working capital	Collection period	Net sales to inventory	Fixed assets to tangible net worth	Current debt to tangible net worth	Total debt to tangible net worth	Inventory to net working capital	Current debt to inventory	Funded debts to net working capital
Times	Days	Times	Per cent	Per cent	Per cent	Per cent	Per cent	Per cent
6.62	30	6.1	6.1	22.0	47.3	73.0	39.5	6.1
4.23	**38**	**4.5**	**12.9**	**42.1**	**76.3**	**93.4**	**56.2**	**17.7**
3.24	45	3.5	28.4	67.5	107.4	119.4	84.2	36.2
33.15	10	48.9	61.7	17.3	28.7	43.4	115.2	22.6
13.98	**14**	**31.2**	**80.0**	**27.8**	**48.0**	**68.6**	**206.6**	**58.4**
9.09	20	14.3	97.0	37.3	70.2	90.9	266.4	121.0
37.46	13	32.9	5.0	38.6	76.7	61.9	75.0	8.4
19.20	**18**	**22.6**	**11.7**	**75.0**	**103.1**	**82.1**	**118.3**	**24.8**
11.66	21	18.4	21.2	123.6	153.6	129.4	166.1	41.5
23.54	22	26.6	4.1	19.0	17.8	54.5	50.7	7.0
11.92	**28**	**13.5**	**10.2**	**54.9**	**128.7**	**78.7**	**83.5**	**24.4**
6.14	32	8.2	23.7	80.8	155.9	110.9	132.0	49.9
9.26	27	9.2	6.7	36.2	55.7	73.8	56.8	10.7
6.33	**35**	**7.2**	**17.4**	**51.6**	**70.7**	**89.6**	**70.6**	**20.9**
4.37	46	5.8	30.0	83.3	109.3	107.1	89.6	42.6
7.88	37	7.2	2.1	16.8	43.1	50.8	39.7	7.2
5.33	**49**	**6.1**	**4.9**	**51.7**	**59.8**	**76.6**	**73.2**	**17.0**
3.87	64	4.9	11.4	94.9	94.0	110.0	116.7	38.4
8.16	32	8.5	5.1	36.6	52.2	68.6	56.6	9.3
5.92	**44**	**5.9**	**11.9**	**58.8**	**82.5**	**82.9**	**82.8**	**17.4**
3.84	59	3.4	25.3	94.4	150.0	109.9	119.6	27.5
20.33	12	90.9	14.6	15.4	56.2	8.5	98.3	9.6
13.90	**20**	**52.3**	**26.5**	**34.0**	**119.3**	**30.7**	**215.1**	**67.9**
10.75	30	25.0	45.3	67.6	423.3	75.0	420.7	159.6
4.49	26	7.4	1.2	14.3	43.0	51.6	41.6	7.0
3.28	**42**	**4.0**	**3.7**	**50.9**	**65.1**	**70.3**	**66.9**	**16.8**
2.83	59	2.6	17.8	73.7	142.7	87.7	118.7	26.5
17.50	19	29.3	20.0	28.0	31.6	27.3	110.0	4.5
13.51	**33**	**14.2**	**44.1**	**48.0**	**74.9**	**62.9**	**168.7**	**18.7**
6.44	40	10.3	68.9	118.4	107.1	89.4	387.0	52.6
17.78	11	14.7	7.7	24.2	61.1	72.9	35.7	10.6
10.85	**15**	**11.2**	**14.8**	**48.7**	**96.0**	**100.8**	**60.1**	**29.3**
7.40	21	7.8	31.3	88.2	169.8	141.1	84.2	60.3
7.04	27	5.6	8.2	17.3	46.9	71.0	27.2	10.7
3.87	**36**	**3.8**	**16.3**	**34.4**	**74.0**	**85.6**	**48.9**	**20.7**
2.75	50	3.2	24.6	61.2	115.9	114.1	76.4	35.6

1959 Table of Fourteen Important Ratios with Inter-
Wholesalers

Line of Business	Number of Concerns	Inter-quartile Range	Current assets to current debt	Net profits on net sales	Net profits on tangible net worth	Net profits on net working capital	Net sales to tangible net worth
			Times	Per cent	Per cent	Per cent	Times
Hosiery and		Upper Quartile	5.53	5.21	11.12	11.21	6.38
Underwear	37	MEDIAN	2.90	0.71	3.43	4.66	3.77
		Lower Quartile	1.92	0.15	0.75	0.77	2.41
Household		Upper Quartile	2.87	1.60	12.05	13.99	9.22
Appliances,	103	MEDIAN	1.91	0.88	7.25	8.39	7.00
Electrical		Lower Quartile	1.51	0.59	3.98	3.87	4.71
Iron and Steel		Upper Quartile	4.41	4.21	13.02	17.57	4.68
Sheets, Strips,	72	MEDIAN	3.06	3.02	10.53	14.06	3.43
Bars, and Plates		Lower Quartile	2.19	2.13	8.39	9.24	2.80
		Upper Quartile	4.62	2.08	9.50	11.26	9.02
Lumber	91	MEDIAN	3.21	1.28	5.48	7.31	4.57
		Lower Quartile	1.76	0.08	1.65	1.95	2.41
Lumber and		Upper Quartile	4.32	3.11	9.61	15.40	5.83
Building	109	MEDIAN	2.90	1.35	5.10	6.15	4.16
Materials		Lower Quartile	2.02	0.62	2.80	3.61	3.13
		Upper Quartile	4.23	1.54	14.36	30.41	23.52
Meat and Poultry	43	MEDIAN	2.28	0.61	9.17	12.12	12.69
		Lower Quartile	1.68	0.30	4.59	7.94	7.54
Paints, Varnishes,		Upper Quartile	9.01	2.30	6.54	10.20	5.28
and Lacquers	36	MEDIAN	3.54	1.54	4.07	4.20	3.27
		Lower Quartile	2.11	0.57	0.30	2.18	1.80
		Upper Quartile	3.93	1.64	9.13	12.94	7.51
Paper	129	MEDIAN	2.71	1.17	6.52	7.55	5.01
		Lower Quartile	1.90	0.69	3.99	4.83	3.60
Plumbing and		Upper Quartile	5.00	3.02	11.03	14.47	4.85
Heating	179	MEDIAN	3.13	1.72	6.97	7.63	3.65
Supplies		Lower Quartile	2.18	0.74	2.43	2.82	2.60
Shoes, Men's,		Upper Quartile	3.60	1.57	7.94	8.20	7.96
Women's, and	62	MEDIAN	2.30	0.97	4.34	4.73	5.05
Children's		Lower Quartile	1.70	0.07†	0.35†	0.39†	3.42
		Upper Quartile	3.69	2.07	11.48	17.50	7.58
Wines and Liquors	52	MEDIAN	2.09	1.45	6.68	11.18	5.92
		Lower Quartile	1.57	0.66	3.89	6.20	3.55
Womenswear,		Upper Quartile	3.37	3.79	21.68	32.76	5.83
Coats, Suits,	36	MEDIAN	2.53	1.30	5.68	6.92	4.87
and Dresses		Lower Quartile	1.91	0.18	0.90	1.19	3.09

† Loss.

Index

A

A, B, AND C STOCK, analysis of, 113, 116–117

ABC COMPANY, balance sheet of, 150

ACCEPTANCES, TRADE:
Bank credit and, 8
For merchandise, machinery, or equipment, 96, 100–101
And sale of merchandise, 80–82
In small business, 155

ACCESSORY SHOPS (see Women's Specialty Shops)

ACCOMMODATION PAPER, 7–8

ACCOUNTANCY:
Early days of, 21–23, 189–190
Evolution in theory and practice of, 601–639
Future of, 637–639
Legal recognition of, 22
As a science, 621
Sources of influence on, 617–626
Studies on, 626–637
Uniform standards in, 618

ACCOUNTANTS:
Certification of, 617
Certified public (see American Institute of Certified Public Accountants; Certified Public Accountants)
Differing methods of, 614
Earliest firms of, 21
European, problems of, 607
Independent, 614, 616n., 629
Inventory valuation by, 335–336
Minimum requirements for, in verification of financial statements, 620
Responsibility of, 615n.
As trustees of business information, 618

ACCOUNTING (See also Accountancy):
Cost basis of, 612n.
Criticism of methods in, 610
Definition of, 604
Depreciation, 612n.

ACCOUNTING (continued):
French, 611n.
As language of finance, 29–30
Origin of, 65–66
Problems in, price levels and, 604–606
Stabilized, 607–608
Index numbers and, 608–609
Suggested modifications in, 607–611

ACCOUNTING CONVENTIONS, 302, 587, 611–613

ACCOUNTING FIRMS:
Asset classification used by, 189–190
First American, 189–190, 617

ACCOUNTING PRACTICE AND PRINCIPLES:
Authorized studies on, 626–637
Changes in, 521, 529
Evolution in, 617–639
Standards for, 615n.
Uniformity in, 617–626
Federal Reserve Board statement of, 620

ACCOUNTING PROFITS, 497n., 512n.

ACCOUNTING THEORIES:
Entity, 633–634
Fund, 633–636
Proprietary, 633

ACCOUNTS, annual closing of, 214–217

ACCOUNTS PAYABLE, 96, 101
Inventory and, 169
Net, 162
As source of funds, 473

ACCOUNTS RECEIVABLE:
Aging of, 358
Analysis of, 359
Assigned, 106n.
Charge-off and, 4
As current assets, 179–180
Heavy, 4
Income flow and, 156
Miscellaneous, 35–37
Decrease in, 36
From officers and directors, 37, 58, 88–89, 101
Past-due, 4

657

9/24/65 76 Check Wade Smith to check footnote 18 page 76, #19
fifth edition.

130-1 1st NIB Chicago comparative statement form

13—
136
301
533
604
604